COLLECTED WORKS OF ERASMUS

VOLUME 30

COLLECTED WORKS OF
ERASMUS

PROLEGOMENA TO THE ADAGES

ADAGIORUM COLLECTANEA

translated and annotated by John N. Grant

INDEXES TO ERASMUS' ADAGES

by William Barker

University of Toronto Press

Toronto / Buffalo / London

The research and publication costs of the
Collected Works of Erasmus are supported by
University of Toronto Press.

© University of Toronto Press 2017
Toronto / Buffalo / London
Printed in the U.S.A.

ISBN 978-1-4426-4877-7

Printed on acid-free paper

Library and Archives Canada Cataloguing in Publication

Erasmus, Desiderius, –1536
[Works. English]
Collected works of Erasmus.

Includes bibliographical references and indexes.
Contents: v. 30. Prolegomena to the adages. Adagiorum collectanea.
ISBN 978-1-4426-4877-7 (v. 30 : hardcover)

1. Title.

PA8500 1974   199'.492   C740-06326X

University of Toronto Press acknowledges the financial assistance
to its publishing program of the Canada Council for the Arts
and the Ontario Arts Council, an agency of the Government of Ontario

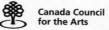
Canada Council Conseil des Arts
for the Arts du Canada

ONTARIO ARTS COUNCIL
CONSEIL DES ARTS DE L'ONTARIO
an Ontario government agency
un organisme du gouvernement de l'Ontario

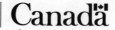
Funded by the   Financé par le
Government   gouvernement
of Canada   du Canada

Collected Works of Erasmus

The aim of the Collected Works of Erasmus
is to make available an accurate, readable English text
of Erasmus' correspondence and his
other principal writings. The edition is planned
and directed by an Editorial Board, an Executive Committee,
and an Advisory Committee.

This volume, the final one to be published in the series devoted to Erasmus' *Adages* (CWE 30–36), is dedicated in grateful memory to Sir Roger Mynors, an architect and originator of the Collected Works of Erasmus, who was also the major translator and annotator of volumes 31 to 34.

Contents

Preface

This is the last of the seven volumes of The Collected Works of Erasmus that are devoted to the *Adagia* – the final one with respect to its date of publication, though the first of the seven in its volume number. The content falls into two parts.

The first comprises an essay, 'Erasmus' Adages,' on the original publication of adages in the *Collectanea* (3), the development from this to the full *Adagia* (20), and Erasmus' sources for proverbs (38). This is followed by a translation and annotation of the *Collectanea* (85). The debt owed to the fine edition of the *Collectanea* which was begun by Felix Heinimann and completed by M.L. van Poll-van de Lisdonk and published in ASD II-9 in 2005 is considerable. The indexes to the whole of the *Adagia* that also appear in that volume were also valuable for the statistics provided in the sections 'From the *Collectanea* to the *Chiliades*' and 'Erasmus' sources.'

The second part contains seven indexes to the adages in volumes CWE 30 to 36. A modern index would normally try to cover all names, subjects, and even material in the commentary of the footnotes. We have instead followed the approach set forth in Erasmus' note of 1528, which begins the index section of this volume. Because of limited space, caused by indexing in three languages, we were not able to cover all the possible subjects or footnoted material. The modern user who has access to the electronic version of these volumes will, however, be able to access everything, though subjects will always remain elusive, as Erasmus himself acknowledged in his note. Included are: Erasmus' 1528 Note on Indexes (369), a Greek index to the adages (372), a Latin index (447), an Index of Early Modern English Proverbs (550), a translation of Erasmus' own Index of Topics followed by a listing of the topics in alphabetical order, English and Latin (568), the main English Index of Erasmus' Adages (635) with a Supplementary Index of Names (767), and an Index of Scriptural References (836).

Normally the volumes in this series do not acknowledge the exceptional editorial assistance provided by individuals at the University of
Toronto Press. Nevertheless, for her ingenious solutions and extraordinary
labour in compressing the indexes to fit within this volume, both editors
wish to express their profound thanks to Philippa Matheson.

JNG and WB

ERASMUS' ADAGES

JOHN N. GRANT

Erasmus' Adages

The *Collectanea*

In 1495 Erasmus took up residence in Paris as a student of theology, but in the following four years that he spent there, in addition to learning Greek, he also devoted much of his energy to two related activities – tutoring students and writing about pedagogical matters. One topic of the educational tracts that he worked on was the art of letter-writing, which, as *De conscribendis epistolis*, would not be published until 1522. During this period he also produced early drafts of *De copia* and *De ratione studii* (both first released for publication by Erasmus in a fuller form in 1512).[1] This interest in humanistic education was not sudden, since, as early perhaps as 1488, he had composed an epitome of the *Elegantiae* of Lorenzo Valla, to which he may have turned again during this stay in Paris.[2]

Related to these interests is Erasmus' first major publication. For in February of 1500, when he returned to Paris after spending several months

* * * * *

1 In March 1498 (the exact date is not certain) he had composed a preface to *De conscribendis epistolis* in the form of a letter addressed to one of his pupils, Robert Fisher (Ep 71). Erasmus returned to the tract in May of 1499 (Ep 95), when he tells us that he was about to dedicate it to Jacob Batt's pupil, Adolph of Burgundy. Then in November of 1499 he sent a copy of the work to another of his pupils, William Blount, Lord Mountjoy, accompanied by a letter (Ep 117). Ep 66, probably written in 1497, is a dedicatory letter to *De ratione studii*, addressed to Thomas Grey, one of Erasmus' pupils in Paris. Both of these tracts then were substantial enough for Erasmus to be thinking of having them published. The title of his early thoughts on the rich oratorical style (*copia*), in existence in 1499 if not before, was *Brevis de copia praeceptio* (see introduction to Ep 260 at CWE 2 225).
2 See ASD I-4 193–4.

in England, he set to work on compiling an anthology of classical proverbs. The collection, taking up only 76 leaves, made its appearance in mid-summer, probably in July,[3] being published by a German printer, Johann Philipp, and entitled *Adagiorum collectanea*. Although the work is not an instructional manual or educational tract, the printer seems to have been well aware that the book would be of practical value to students interested in improving their writing and speaking skills. The blurb on the title page of the book makes this clear.

> This book not only has originality but is also a work that will be marvellously helpful for adding charm and distinction to every genre of the written or spoken word. You will be aware of this, young men (*adulescentes*), if you are in the habit of dropping such delightful gems into your letters and everyday conversation. If you are sensible, then, you will buy this rare treasure that is on sale at such a bargain price (*tantillo nummulo*).

This echoes Erasmus' own sentiments as expressed in his dedicatory letter. The work, he writes, was 'likely to bring some profit and pleasure to its prospective readers: those ... who dislike the current jargon and are searching for greater elegance and a more refined style' (Ep 126:29–31). In a similar vein, in his letter to Erasmus that stands at the beginning of the *Collectanea* Fausto Andrelini praises the 'usefulness and charm' of Erasmus' collection of adages, 'destined as they are to provide a considerable amount of delight as well as edification' (Ep 127:4–5 and 11–12).

The compilation of material gleaned from one's reading was an important element in humanistic educational practice for both teacher and student. To the former Erasmus gives this recommendation in *De ratione studii*:

> There is nothing to prevent several apt literary devices such as the aphorism, the historical example, and the proverb ... occurring in the same speech. Accordingly, the teacher, who should be well versed in the best authorities, will compile a small, widely chosen anthology of this sort. (CWE 24 678)

* * * * *

3 The colophon gives no date of publication. The *terminus post quem* of June 15, 1500 is provided by the date of Fausto Andrelini's letter that begins the volume (Ep 127). At Ep 133:5–8, written at the end of September, Erasmus says that a youth whom he had sent to England with copies of the *Collectanea* in the hope of generating some money has been gone for eight weeks (see also Ep 128:1–2; Ep 129:60–1).

As for the student, in *De copia* Erasmus treats at length and in some detail the desirability of having students create a commonplace notebook of their own, organized by subject headings under which he should record maxims, similes, anecdotes, historical exempla, fables, proverbs and similar material that related to each heading.[4] For students, then, the collection of proverbs in *Adagiorum collectanea* provided them with material that could supplement their own records based on their own reading.

The work turned out to be a great success, and Johann Philipp did a reprint of the volume in 1505. A corrected and slightly enlarged second edition of the *Collectanea* appeared in Paris at the end of 1506 (according to the colophon, on Christmas Eve), this time published by the much more distinguished printer, Josse Bade (Badius Ascensius), himself a scholar of note, and a second run of this appeared two weeks later, dated by its colophon to 8 January 1507. Now the proverbs were numbered for the first time, twenty new proverbs were introduced at the end (nos 819 to 838), and Greek versions were added to a large number of proverbs. Three proverbs of the 1500 edition were dropped, one being replaced with a new entry.[5] There was also an index of the proverbs, arranged not alphabetically, but listed in the order of presentation. It is the text of this edition of 1506 that is the basis for the translation of the *Collectanea* in this volume.

The success of the publication could not have rested solely on the student market that Johann Philipp had in mind in his promotional material. The collection must have attracted a much wider readership both because of its novelty (it was the first anthology of classical proverbs to be printed in northern Europe) and the intrinsic appeal and interest of the proverbs

* * * * *

4 See CWE 24 635–48. The keeping of notebooks was initially promoted in Italy by Guarino Guarini, who was indebted to Manuel Chrysoloras, and then by Guarino's son Battista; see R.R. Bolgar *The Classical Heritage and its Beneficiaries* (Cambridge 1973) 268–75. Although the quotations from *De ratione studii* and *De copia*, given above, date to some twelve years after the *Collectanea* appeared, it is very likely that the views expressed there were held by Erasmus in the 1490s. He certainly had knowledge of humanistic educational methods from his own reading and from his personal acquaintance with those who had been educated in Italy; see J.K. Sowards in CWE 23 xxx–xxxiii; Ann Moss *Printed Commonplace-books and the Structuring of Renaissance Thought* (Oxford 1996) 101–15.

5 The three proverbs dropped were *Cato in Catonem*, *Festus dies*, and *Quae haec est fabula*. These are printed in an appendix at the end of the *Collectanea*. The additions were C 376 and, at the end, 819–38.

themselves. Men of education could enjoy this collection and the information that Erasmus provided in his comments upon them. Testament to its popularity is the fact that the 1506 edition was frequently reprinted by various presses during Erasmus' lifetime. There are thirty or so of these editions or reprints, the most significant being those done by the scholar-printer Matthias Schürer in Strasbourg, starting with one in 1509 and followed by another eight before Schürer's death in early 1520.

What prompted Erasmus to produce this anthology of proverbs? He returned from England to Paris on 2 February 1500 after a traumatic experience in Dover. There the English custom officials confiscated most of Erasmus' money, to the value of twenty pounds, much to his dismay. In a letter written to Jacob Batt, undated but probably written in March of 1500, Erasmus refers to the loss of his money ('the wound I suffered in England'), expressing the futility of his ever 'paying off the score' (that is, of ever recovering his money). It is of significance that he immediately proceeds to write of his intention 'to compile a thesaurus of ancient adages, working in great haste.' However, he continues, since he is penniless ('my own resources are less than nothing'), he has doubts whether he will find a printer.[6] These, however, as we have seen, were resolved by the readiness of Johann Philipp to take on the work. It is a fair inference that Erasmus saw the publication of his collection of adages as a means of acquiring money that would make up for the financial loss he had suffered in Dover and would allow him to live in Paris in a less uncomfortable style than his straitened financial situation imposed upon him.

An additional stimulus may have been his engagement during the two previous years with *De conscribendis epistolis*. While working on this pedagogical tract Erasmus must have become familiar with the published letters of distinguished humanists – most accessible in the twelve books of epistles that appeared in the *Omnia opera* of Angelo Poliziano, which included letters written by humanists other than Poliziano himself.[7] In the *Collectanea's* prefatory letter (Ep 126:149–68) Erasmus points out that Ermolao Barbaro, Pico della Mirandola, and Angelo Poliziano 'adorned their prose at all points

* * * * *

6 Ep 123:5–8, 13–14, 17–18. See also Ep 119 and c 325.
7 Erasmus refers only twice to a letter of a humanist as his source for a proverb: c 306 (for Ermolao Barbaro) and c 25 (for Agricola). On many other occasions, however, he is drawing, without acknowledgment from the printed correspondence of the humanists, much of it in Poliziano's *Omnia opera*; see notes on c 23, 24, 34, 79, 91, 92, 114, 387, 404, 405, 407, 453, 454, 466, 482, 587, 781. He was also familiar with the correspondence of Francesco Filelfo (see c 373, 374).

with adages and with those figurative expressions which exhibit a family resemblance to the adage.'[8] This was particularly true in their letters.[9]

Erasmus' ownership of a manuscript of a collection of Greek proverbs, attributed (wrongly) to Diogenianus, a grammarian of the Hadrianic period, may have also been a factor in his decision to compile his anthology. He describes this manuscript in unflattering terms, saying that it was the only anthology of Greek proverbs available to him. The contents, however, were 'so mutilated and so jejune ... that I gained little help from them' (Ep 126:110–12). The manuscript was almost certainly a copy of one of three manuscripts of Diogenianus owned by George Hermonymus, Erasmus' Greek instructor in Paris,[10] and it is not unlikely that Hermonymus made use of this anthology of proverbs when he was teaching ancient Greek at an introductory level.[11] Despite the manuscript's shortcomings Erasmus may well have thought that the presence of Greek proverbs in the projected collection would give his publication added appeal to students and other readers in northern Europe. It is worth noting in this regard that when Matthias Schürer printed the *Collectanea* in 1509 he compared Erasmus' anthology favourably with the *Proverbiorum libellus* of Polydore Vergil of Urbino (on which see the appendix below) because the latter contained very few Greek proverbs (*Graecanicas ... paroemias ... perpaucas*).[12]

* * * * *

8 Felix Heinimann, in his brilliant study of Erasmus' and Polydore Vergil's sources for their collection of proverbs (see Heinimann passim), identifies Erasmus' familiarity with the correspondence of the humanist as an important impetus for undertaking the *Collectanea* (Heinimann 181). See also Mietzke L. van Poll-van de Lisdonk, 'Humanists, Letters, and *proverbia*: Some Aspects of Erasmus' First Collection of Proverbs,' *Erasmus of Rotterdam Society Yearbook* 26 (2006): 2–7.

9 Although proverbs had been virtually ignored in the western manuals of letter-writing (the *artes dictandi*), the printing in 1470 of Cicero's correspondence with Atticus, with its abundance of proverbs, and new knowledge of Greek theory, which recommended the use of proverbs in letters, stimulated humanists such as Poliziano and Barbaro to insert many proverbs in their correspondence. See Heinimann 177–81.

10 These were Oxford, Bodley Grabe 30, of which Hermonymus had himself made at least two copies (Bodley Laud 7 and Vienna, Supplementa Graeca 83). See n23 below.

11 Heinimann (162) points out that Greek proverbs seems to have been used in the West first as an aid in language instruction at the elementary level, as they were by Guarino at his school in Verona.

12 In his address to the reader; see ASD II-9 9 for the complete text of the letter.

The conjunction of his financial loss, his engagement with the art of writing letters, and the possession of a manuscript of Greek proverbs probably gave him the idea of a project that could be done quickly and profitably.[13]

Erasmus' correspondence of the first half of 1500 reveals some fluidity in his early concept of the anthology. In one letter, addressed to Jacob Batt, he foresees publishing 'only two, or at most three hundred' ancient adages (Ep 123:14–16). In another, however, he expresses confidence that he will 'run up a total of more than three thousand' (Ep 125:49–51). Finally, in a letter to Jacob Batt, dated 12 April, he says:

> I am getting ready my work on adages, which is to be published, I hope, directly after Easter; and, I may tell you, it is a work of no small extent, costing endless pains, for my collection consists of about eight hundred proverbs, partly Greek and partly Latin. This I shall dedicate to your pupil Adolph, if it seems appropriate.[14] (Ep 124:49–54)

As this final number of 'about eight hundred' is closest to the number of adages that we actually find in the published version of the *Collectanea* in 1500, it looks as if the anthology was at that date in April not far removed in scope from that of its final shape. As for the dedication, when the anthology was actually published, it was addressed, not to Batt's pupil, but to William Blount (Lord Mountjoy), Erasmus' own pupil and patron, and Erasmus says in the dedicatory letter that he has undertaken the task of collecting the most ancient and famous adages partly through the wishes of both Blount and another Englishman, Richard Charnock (Ep 126:23–5). Whatever the truth of Erasmus' inspiration may be,[15] the English connection is emphasized by the inclusion in the 1500 volume of a letter to Prince Henry of England

* * * * *

13 R.J. Schoek (*Erasmus of Europe. The Prince of Humanists 1501–1536* [Edinburgh 1993] 76) suggests that what emerged as the *Collectanea* may have been in Erasmus' mind when he went to Paris in 1495 and perhaps even earlier. He notes the presence of proverbs in the earliest of Erasmus' letters, but this does not necessarily mean that he had formulated a plan to produce a printed collection of proverbs.

14 He also states his intention to dedicate the work to Batt's pupil, Adolph of Burgundy, at Ep 123:16.

15 Given Erasmus' earlier twice-stated intention of dedicating the work to Jacob Batt's pupil, his naming of Blunt and Charnock as his inspiration may be simply flattery and a convention of a dedicatory letter.

(the future Henry VIII), and a poem put in the mouth of England herself in which the country takes pride in her king and his children.[16]

In the anthology the actual proverbs are printed apart as headings, separated from the accompanying commentary. In a few cases this can consist of as many as twenty lines of printed text (as in *Collectanea* 1 and 784), though many of the adages have only one or two sentences of explanation. In its most useful form the commentary gives the source or origin of the proverb, its meaning and how it could be used, and this could be done quite concisely, as in C 152:

> *Hodie nullam lineam duxi,* I haven't done a stroke today. This can be said by an artisan or a scholar to mean that he has done absolutely no work on a particular day. Pliny tells us the source of the adage: 'It was the constant habit of the painter Apelles never to spend a day, however busy it was, without practising his art by drawing a line. The proverb originated with him.'

In the volume of 1500 there are, by my count, 821 headings, although none of these is numbered, numeration being added in the 1506 edition.[17] Seven of these headings are not themselves proverbs but are descriptions of proverbs referred to in the accompanying commentary, such as 'Proverbs indicating contempt' in what became *Collectanea* 397 in the 1506 edition.[18] Sometimes more than one proverb is given in the heading, and sometimes additional proverbs appear in the commentary on each item. When all these aspects are taken into account, the 1500 edition of the *Collectanea* offers 953 proverbs. Since the 1506 edition dropped three proverbs and added twenty-one,[19] Josse Bade's version contained 971 proverbs, although the actual number of the final proverb was DCCCXXXVIII (838).[20]

* * * * *

16 For the letter see Ep 104. For the poem (*Prosopopoeia Britanniae*) see CWE 85 31–41; ASD I-7 99–114. It was also printed in the 1506 edition of Erasmus' Latin translations of Euripides' *Hecuba* and *Iphigeneia in Aulis*.

17 Because the final heading in *1500* has the number 818 in *1506*, one sometimes reads that the 1500 edition had 818 adages. But one should not confuse headings with proverbs and one has to take into account the errors in the numeration in *1506* and the small number of adages that were dropped or added in *1506* (see n5 above and n20 below).

18 See also C 93, 98, 108, 238, 370, 408.

19 See n5 above.

20 There are some mistakes in the numbering: two proverbs are given the same number on three occasions (65 and 65A, 241 and 241A, 495 and 495A); two

The majority of the proverbs (over 60%) are purely Latin in form, being drawn directly from Latin authors. Erasmus' most popular Latin sources are, in descending order, Plautus, Horace, Terence, Cicero, Jerome, Gellius, Persius, and Pliny the Elder.[21] Of Greek authors Plato is decidedly Erasmus' favourite source; Erasmus quotes him (and Pseudo-Plato) just under seventy times, almost as often as Cicero, but always and only in Latin; his quotations come from Marsilio Ficino's translation of the Platonic corpus. This reliance on Latin translations of Greek authors is also evident in his quotations from Plutarch. Yet in the *Collectanea* of 1500 we do find 156 proverbs cited in their original Greek form[22] and there were others of Greek origin, even though they were given only in a Latin translation. Of the proverbs given in Greek just over a hundred were drawn from Erasmus' manuscript of the proverbs ascribed to Diogenianus.[23] None of the other proverbs given in their Greek form was taken from the original Greek source. Erasmus culled them from Latin writers such as Gellius, Cicero, Martial, and Donatus (28 in number) or from the writings of other humanists, especially Ermolao Barbaro, Angelo Poliziano, Filippo Beroaldo, and Niccolò Perotti (27).[24]

One of the purposes of the second edition was to supplement a large number of entries in the 1500 edition that lacked a Greek version, and

* * * * *

proverbs that share an accompanying commentary are given separate numbers (474 and 475); a proverb that is part of the commentary on c 634 is erroneously assigned the number 635.

21 A quick count of Erasmus' quotations from these authors produces the following numbers: Plautus: 158; Horace: 113; Terence: 103; Cicero: 70; Jerome: 52; Gellius 43; Persius: 40; Pliny the Elder 39. These numbers include quotations that Erasmus drew by way of intermediate sources such as Angelo Poliziano and Ermolao Barbaro.

22 Two of them occur twice ('Know thyself' and 'All things in common').

23 The close relationship between Erasmus' manuscript and those of George Hermonymus is shown by features in the *Collectanea* that are peculiar to the three manuscripts owned by Hermonymus (see n10 above). Three adages in the *Collectanea* occur only in this branch of the tradition of 'Diogenianus': c 358 ('Jupiter has no children'), 446 ('Resentment is the last thing to grow old'), 638 ('One swallow does not make a summer'). In addition there are some textual agreements between the form of some adages as they appear in the *Collectanea* and in this group of manuscripts; see, for example, c 301, 344, 356, 359, and 363.

24 In *1500*, in his commentary on c 480, he refers to Apostolius of Byzantium, whose collection of proverbs he was to use extensively in the *Chiliades*, but the reference is taken over from Poliziano. Erasmus first saw a manuscript of this collection in Venice in 1508.

such additions occurred in 182 cases.[25] Again, as in the 1500 edition, the major source by far for the Greek form of the proverbs was Diogenianus (140 occasions). However, between the appearance of the first and second editions of the *Collectanea* Erasmus had completed Latin translations of Euripides' *Hecuba* and *Iphigenia in Aulis* (published in September of 1506), and had cooperated with Thomas More in a translation of some of the dialogues of Lucian (published in November 1506). He must have acquired or had access to texts of Greek authors as his knowledge of the language increased, since in the 1506 edition he appears to have drawn the Greek versions of some proverbs directly from the authors themselves: Hesiod, Theocritus, Plutarch, Aristophanes, Lucian, Homer, and Aristotle.[26] He also seems now to have knowledge of another collection of proverbs from antiquity, ascribed to Zenobius, and to have drawn from it in a small number of instances.[27] There is a little evidence to suggest that he also used the *Suda* (or 'Suidas' as Erasmus, like his contemporaries, called this work, thinking that this was the name of the author).[28]

Just as Erasmus frequently fails to name his humanistic sources for some of the proverbs in the collection, so he often makes no mention of contemporary works on which he draws for the accompanying commentaries. Although he names Poliziano and Barbaro on several occasions,[29] these references appear in fewer than one-third of passages where these

* * * * *

25 Twelve of the twenty new adages at the end of the edition (nos 819–38) also had Greek versions attached to them.

26 Hesiod: c 221, 738; Theocritus: c 823, 824; Plutarch: c 825; Aristophanes: c 722, 835; Lucian: c 836, 837; Homer: c 82; Aristotle c 95

27 A version of this collection had been published in 1497. His dedicatory letter in the 1500 edition makes it clear that this was not known to Erasmus in 1500. For his use of the edition in *1506* see c 26n and c 248n.

28 The second sentence in the commentary on c 606 was added in the edition of 1506. and the source of the information given there, about the name given in antiquity to the heaviest anchor, may have been *Suda* K 1642. At c 394 the verb in the adage in *1500* is βιητιᾷ, taken from Giorgio Merula's commentary on Juvenal 2.15. In *1506* this is replaced by περαίνεται, taken probably from *Suda* O 821. Erasmus' sole reference to 'Suidas' (in c 20 and present in *1500*) is derived from Poliziano. The *editio princeps* of the *Suda* was published in 1499 in Milan.

29 About a dozen instances for Poliziano (c 12, 38, 145, 321, 387, 396, 404, 406, 477, 481, 496) and a somewhat fewer number for Barbaro (c 25, 92, 130, 303, 306, 367, 693, 710)

two scholars are Erasmus' source.[30] Other humanists referred to in the *Collectanea* are Domizio Calderini (C 171, 371, 661, 666), Francesco Filelfo (C 373, 374), Giorgio Merula (C 391, 392), Giovanni Campano (C 173), Rodolphus Agricola (C 25), Giorgio Valla (C 171), and Pico della Mirandola (C 466). He never names Filippo Beroaldo, though he draws from his *Annotationes centum* and his *Appendix annotamentorum* for more than a dozen adages.[31] The same is true for Giambattista Pio, whose *Annotationes priores* Erasmus uses on only a few occasions.[32] Niccolò Perotti's *Cornucopiae* is another of his sources, used for just under a score of the proverbs,[33] but there is only an oblique reference to him in C 778 as 'a man of no little learning.' More identifiable would have been Raffaele Regio from the description of him in C 395 as 'that man who purges the text of Quintilian of corruptions.'[34]

Most of these sources would have been readily available to Erasmus in Paris in early 1500. The reputation of Poliziano's *Miscellanea*, Barbaro's *Castigationes Plinianae*, and Perotti's *Cornucopiae* must have meant that these works were accessible to Erasmus in libraries if he did not have his own personal copy. The same goes for standard editions of Martial and Juvenal, which included the commentaries of Domizio Calderini, Giorgio Merula, and Giorgio Valla,[35] and which were frequently reprinted. We know too that he used an edition of Persius that included the commentaries of Iohannes Britannicus and Josse Bade,[36] one of the frequently printed editions of Horace that contained the ancient commentaries of Pseudo-Acron and Porphyrion as well as the two Renaissance ones by Cristoforo Landino and Antonio Mancinelli,[37] and an edition of Cicero's *Ad familiares* with the commentary of Hubertinus Crescentinas.[38] At first sight, however, it is surpris-

* * * * *

30 The other adages where Poliziano is or may be a source are C 14, 15, 17, 18, 20, 23, 24, 27, 34, 39, 43, 55, 94, 151, 453, 455, 463, 469, 470, 472, 473, 479, 480, 482, 483, 551, 706. As for Barbaro see C 27, 79, 91, 92, 115, 119, 307, 365, 366, 407, 576, 694, 698, 699, 781, 786.
31 C 6, 7, 8, 10, 15, 19, 109, 112, 113, 132, 322, 367, 464, 495, 495A. See Filippo Beroaldo the Elder *Annotationes centum* ed Lucia A. Cipponi (Binghamton, NY 1995).
32 C 11, 28, 29, 328, 461, 462; cf C 35.
33 C 117, 118, 128, 138, 139, 265, 330, 363, 471, 605, 701, 702, 703, 778, 780, 816
34 See C 395 n2.
35 See C 171 nn3 and 6; C 391 n1; C 392–4.
36 See C 235 n1 and C 241n, C 257 nn1–2. It is suggested in ASD II-9 123 (on C 238) that Erasmus probably used an edition published in Lyons in January of 1499 by Nicolas Wolf.
37 See C 275n, 491 n1, 492n, 600 n1. For Landino see CEBR 2:285–6.
38 See C 293 n2.

ing that Erasmus had access to works like Pio's *Annotationes*,[39] and especially the *Observationes* of Domizio Calderini,[40] only a part of which was ever published.[41] Erasmus' probable source for these was a volume (bearing neither title nor author) that was published in Brescia in 1496, and contained not only these last two works but others of a similar nature such as Beroaldo's *Annotationes* and *Appendix annotationum*, as well as Poliziano's *Miscellanea*.[42]

It may have been his use of these humanists that led Erasmus to introduce into his work some modern (or at least non-classical) proverbs. He cites Poliziano as a source for c 404 and 405 and Filelfo for c 373 and 374, but he includes other non-classical proverbs as title-adages without naming any source: c 197, 254, 500, 723, 724, 725. On over thirty occasions he includes in his discussion of the title-adage similar sayings of his own time. One example is at c 416 'You play the fox, but only against a fox,' where after explaining the sense of the classical adage, he adds, 'Even today there is a common saying "The monkey tries to trick the fox," both animals being extremely crafty.'[43] The reason for the presence of these modern proverbs is not difficult to see. As Margaret Mann Phillips wrote, 'one of the great aims of Erasmus' life' was to 'establish continuity between the classical world and his own' (Phillips 9). A similar concern to connect pagan and Christian thought can explain the presence of proverbs from the New and Old Testaments. Title adages from these sources can be found at c 4 (*bis*), 372, 438, 456, 750, and Erasmus includes another dozen or so biblical references in his commentaries.[44]

One of the most attractive features of the later *Adagia* is the critical and satirical eye that Erasmus casts on contemporary society: on the church and its officers, on opponents of the new humanism, on unscrupulous princes and the downtrodden poor, or on human deficiencies in general. There is little of this in the *Collectanea*, but there is enough to make us think that Erasmus had at least an inkling that the discussion of proverbs could provide a vehicle for social criticism. A rare and serious moralizing comment

* * * * *

39 See c 28, 29, 328, 461.
40 See c 120.
41 The part published consisted of only fifteen chapters from book 3 of his *Observationes*; see Campanelli passim.
42 *Gesamtkatalog der Wiegendrucke* (Leipzig 1925–   ) 4114, Hain-Copinger 2946
43 He adduces modern sayings at c 4, 6, 59, 61, 109, 110, 114, 115, 162, 167, 171, 210, 212, 311, 324, 331, 368, 372, 514, 524, 530, 533, 571, 648 (*bis*), 679, 717, 746, 773.
44 c 53 (*bis*), 151, 207, 255, 315, 316, 406, 655, 659, 750

is to be found at c 282 'Everyone wants things to go better for himself than for others,' where Erasmus concludes his brief discussion by saying that 'we must realize that this adage does not advocate what we ought to do but is critical of what is customarily and commonly done.' More satirical in tone are Erasmus' remarks on the rapacity of lawyers at c 14, the ignorance of those who criticize Cicero's writings as obscure at c 380, the lack of originality of some preachers whose sermons are limited in number and learned by rote (c 489) or the portentous rubbish in the sermons of others (c 269). He uses c 322 ('Many bear the wand, but few feel the god') to point to the shortcomings of those who seem to have only the formal qualifications of a theologian or scholar, as well as to the inadequacies of some monks in the service of the church.[45]

Despite the success of the 1500 publication, Erasmus had misgivings about it. In 1504 he wrote:

> I regret the first edition [of the *Adages*] both because it is so full of printer's errors through the fault of the printer, and because some people encouraged me to hurry the work, which now begins to seem to me thin and poor. (Ep 181:91–5)

This dissatisfaction was shared by others. Erasmus tells us in a letter of 1517 that the distinguished French humanist, Robert Gaguin (who died in 1501) had expressed some disappointment in the collection: Erasmus had been *ieiunus* in gathering the proverbs, having passed over many more from such a wide field (Ep 531:452). One would not be pushing this criticism too far if one were to suppose that Gaguin felt the meagreness to lie not just in the quantity of proverbs but in the nature of the commentaries on many of the items. The modest additions in the revised edition of 1506 did not allay Erasmus' dissatisfaction; when he went to Italy in the fall of 1506 he was intent on producing a vastly expanded collection of adages. The result of his efforts was to be the Aldine *Adagiorum Chiliades*, containing almost thirty-three hundred adages, accompanied by much richer commentaries than one finds in the *Collectanea*.

At first sight it may seem strange that the appearance of the *Adagiorum Chiliades* in 1508, published by the Aldine press, did not consign the *Collectanea* to oblivion. If anything, the *Chiliades* of 1508 and its later editions seem to have stimulated the market for the much slimmer volume.

* * * * *

45 Only occasionally does he touch on textual problems, a topic that is much more prominent in the later *Adagia*. See c 121, 405, 531.

The *Collectanea* was directed at students, but it also appealed to the general, educated layman. Such a readership could continue to profit from a reference work that was still useful and was considerably cheaper than the huge *Chiliades*. The *Collectanea* was in a sense the poor man's version of the *Adagiorum Chiliades*. The latter was a vast repository of classical learning in which the reader would find information on a vast array of topics: botany, geography, zoology, textual criticism, politics, the secular concerns of the church and its officers, to name only a few. All this was reinforced by a massive increase in the references drawn from the classical authors. And now, these references were less dependent on the publications of other humanists and much more on the work of Erasmus himself, who was not only more skilled in Greek but also had access to many more Greek texts. Erasmus was writing now, not so much for students, but more with fellow scholars and humanists in mind, for whom the *Collectanea* offered much less in substance.[46]

Appendix:
The Collectanea *and the* Proverbiorum libellus *of Polydore Vergil*

Erasmus produced the first collection of classical (that is, both Greek and Latin) proverbs to be printed in northern Europe, and in fact he thought he was the first humanist to publish such an anthology (Ep 126:112–13). However, he had actually been anticipated by another scholar, Polydore Vergil of Urbino, who published a similar, though smaller, collection in Venice in 1498, entitled *Proverbiorum libellus*, and containing 306 proverbs. The format was much the same as in Erasmus' *Collectanea*: headings for the proverbs, followed by a short commentary. Polydore himself raised the question of his priority, much later, in a letter of 1519 to Richard Pace, an English diplomat, a letter that appeared in the July 1521 edition of Polydore's proverbs. But this troubling problem, to see the question from Erasmus' point of view, had surfaced earlier. In February 1517, writing to Guillaume Budé, Erasmus dates his first awareness of the very existence of Polydore to some years after the appearance of the *Collectanea* (Ep 521:455–9). He brought up the topic with Polydore himself in a letter of 1520, claiming that Polydore's

* * * * *

46 Comparable, in the last two decades of the 15th century, is the movement of the leading humanists away from line-by-line commentaries of complete works of individual authors to collections of learned notes on difficult problems from a range of authors. The most outstanding example of the latter must be Poliziano's *Miscellanea*. See van Poll-van de Lisdonk (above n8) 9–11.

volume of proverbs had first appeared some months after the date of publication of his *Collectanea* (Ep 1175:55–64). In this Erasmus was erroneous,
but he may not have been deliberately practising deceit, as he was probably thinking of an edition of Polydore's that appeared in Venice in November 1500, and the first edition may not have been known to him. Clearly
Erasmus was quite sensitive about the issue. What is the resolution to this
question? Did Erasmus draw on Polydore's *Libellus* when compiling his
Collectanea?[47]

There are about 140 proverbs common to the two collections, but, despite this and despite verbal similarities in some of the commentaries that
accompany the title proverbs, it seems impossible to come up with incontro-
vertible evidence that settles, one way or another, the question of whether
or not Erasmus drew on Polydore's work. The first scholar to address the
problem in detail was Theodore C. Appelt, as part of a doctoral disserta-
tion for the University of Chicago.[48] His conclusion was that 'a compari-
son of the two booklets does not yield convincing evidence that Erasmus
was insincere when he denied Vergil's charge of plagiarism' (76). This finding won general acceptance, but there were still a number of examples
where similarities between the two works were left unexplained and had
to be imputed to coincidence to an implausible extent if Erasmus had not
used Polydore's collection. The weakness of Appelt's case lay in his failure to consider the possibility that both Erasmus and Polydore were drawing on the same sources and to identify them. This deficiency was recti-
fied by the work of Felix Heinimann (see n8 above), who was the first to
reveal the vast extent to which Polydore and Erasmus had drawn, often
without acknowledgment, on a common stock of humanistic works, such

* * * * *

47 It may be noted that Polydore Vergil was himself accused of plagiariz-
ing for his anthology, the plaintiff being a certain Lodovico Gorgerio who
delivered his accusations to Duke Guidobaldo in his *Invectiva in Polydo-
rum*; see Denys Hay, *Polydore Vergil. Renaissance Humanist and Man of Letters* (Oxford 1952) 22–3. Somewhat earlier, Lorenzo Lippi (c 1440–85), professor of rhetoric and poetry in Pisa and a poet in his own right, had put
together a collection of one hundred proverbs; see Sebastiano Timpanaro
'Appunti per un futuro editore del *Liber proverbiorum* di Lorenzo Lippi' in
Tradizione classica e letteratura umanistica. Per Alessandro Perosa (Rome 1985)
391–435. Again, however, like Gorgerio's work, this had not appeared in
print.
48 Theodore C. Appelt *Studies in the Contents and Sources of Erasmus' 'Adagia'*
(Chicago 1942). He deals with the question of the relationship between the
two works on pp 68–77.

as Angelo Poliziano's *Miscellanea*, Ermolao Barbaro's *Castigationes Plinianae*, Filippo Beroaldo's *Annotationes centum*, and Niccolò Perotti's *Cornucopiae*, to name only the most significant.[49] The most striking examples of verbal similarity could be explained by the fact that both Erasmus and Poydore were copying or closely paraphrasing a common source. Heinimann's diligence in tracking down Erasmus' and Polydore's sources strengthened the consensus view that Erasmus had compiled his *Collectanea* independently of Polydore, as may be demonstrated by just two examples.

Both Polydore (no 54) and Erasmus (c 265) include the proverb *Ede nasturtium* 'Eat cress' in their works, and both supply a Greek version of this: Ἔσθιε κάρδαμον. The problem posed by its presence in the two anthologies is that no such proverb is found in any of the Greek collections, and the Latin form is not attested in Classical Latin either. Heinimann (164) showed that the proverb, both in its Latin and Greek form, was an invention of Niccolò Perotti, based on a passage in Pliny which gave the etymology of *nasturtium* as *a narium tormento*, literally 'from the torturing of the nostrils,' and stated that this gave rise to a proverb (*Naturalis historia* 19.155). Pliny, however, did not give the proverb itself. It was Perotti in his *Cornucopiae* (202:44–8) who gave the expression the status of a proverb and fabricated the Greek form of it; he is the probable source for the presence of this adage in the collections of both Polydore and Erasmus.[50]

The second example and the most problematical piece of evidence that Appelt had difficulty in explaining was the close similarity between Erasmus' and Polydore's brief commentaries on what is c 119 ('Mastic-chewers') in Erasmus' work and no 205 in Polydore. Erasmus writes:

> *Graecum adagium adversus eos qui nimio comendi*[51] *studio superfluunt: quasi qui dentibus exterendis fricandisque omnem operam insumant.*[52]

In Polydore (no 205) we read:

* * * * *

49 These were works that any aspiring humanist must have read and studied repeatedly. Polydore actually edited the *Cornucopiae* and he may have studied under Filippo Beroaldo the Elder. For the extensive use Erasmus made of such sources see 11–12 above.

50 In his commentary on the proverb Polydore copies Perotti almost word for word. Erasmus' brief commentary is quite different.

51 Both *1500* and *1506* have the erroneous reading *comandi*.

52 'A Greek adage directed at those who are obsessed with their appearance, on the grounds that such persons spend all their time brushing and cleaning their teeth.'

Graecorum hoc vetus est adagium adversus eos qui nimio se comendi studio superfluunt: quasi dentibus exterendis et fricandis tantum incumbant prae desidia.

These two passages cannot be independent of each other. Appelt (72) hypothesized, somewhat unconvincingly, that the 'two writers, unknown to each other, translat[ed] the same Greek passage in the same words.' Heinimann (173 n75) solved the problem by identifying a common source: Ermolao Barbaro's *Glossemata* s.v. Ocnos (Pozzi 1416–17), which reads:

adversus eos qui nimio se comendi studio superfluunt, quasi dentibus exterendis et fricandis tantum incumbent prae desidia.

Since Erasmus drew on this same item in Barbaro's *Glossemata* for part of his commentary on C 27 ('Rope-gnawers'), which has no counterpart in Polydore, it is more likely that in C 119 Erasmus was drawing on Barbaro and not on Polydore.

More recently, however, in his hypertext edition of Polydore's collection the American scholar Dana Sutton has come to the conclusion that Erasmus did in fact use Polydore's *Libellus*. In his introduction he states '[Erasmus'] essential dependence on Polydore is visible: he provides similar explanations supported by the same key quotations. Clearly material taken from Polydore lies at the core of the work.'[53] Sutton bases this view, firstly, on the verbal similarities in some of the commentaries and, secondly, on the number (and to some extent the distinctive nature) of those proverbs that are common to the two collections. Given the use both Erasmus and Polydore made of Poliziano, Barbaro, Perotti in their search for proverbs it should not not seem surprising that a fairly substantial number are common to both collections.[54] With respect to the appearance in both collections of unusual proverbs, it should be noted that the three proverbs that Sutton cites as examples appear in the works of humanists that Erasmus draws on extensively elsewhere.[55] As for the verbal similarities, these can be ex-

* * * * *

53 Introduction §7 (accessible at http://www.philological.bham.ac.uk/polyadag/intro.html)
54 As far as the number is concerned, it is interesting to note that Appelt (76) drew exactly the opposite conclusion, thinking that Erasmus would have taken over even more of the proverbs in Polydore's work if that was one of his sources.
55 C 7 (= Polydore 2) comes from Beroaldo's *Annotationum Appendix*, C 366 (= Polydore 18), and C 695 (= Polydore 251) are drawn from Ermolao Barbaro's *Castigationes Plinianae*; see annotations on these adages below.

plained to be a result of Polydore's and Erasmus' use of the same humanist sources, as demonstrated by Felix Heinimann.

If Erasmus drew on Polydore, we should be able to find some instances of distinctive verbal similarities in the proverb commentaries that cannot be explained by the use of a common source. I have come across only one possible example. c 167 and Polydore 149 give the proverb *saepe etiam est holitor valde opportuna loquutus* ('Even a gardener oft speaks to the point'). It is taken from contemporary editions of Aulus Gellius and is a Latin translation of a Greek verse cited by Gellius (2.6.9) as having the status of a proverb: Πολλάκι καὶ κηπωρὸς ἀνὴρ μάλα καίριον εἶπεν. Polydore's commentary is quite brief. He paraphrases Gellius closely and then adds the following final sentence: *quod admonet non esse propter authoris humilitatem probam sententiam neglegendam* 'This advises us that we should not ignore a fine sentiment on account of its source being a man of low status.' Erasmus' commentary is longer (he quotes two other examples with similar meaning) but begins in much the same way. After giving the Greek form of the proverb he says that according to Gellius this verse was a familiar proverb among the Greeks. He then continues: *Paraenesis est non esse contemnendam salutarem et utilem sententiam propter humilitatem auctoris* 'This is an exhortation that we should not scorn a helpful and useful sentiment on account of its source being a man of low status.' The similarity in the interpretation of the proverb is not surprising since it is close to what Gellius writes. But what of the verbal similarities? My own view is that they are unlikely to be coincidental. Either Erasmus drew from Polydore, though giving a more forceful rendition, or both Polydore and Erasmus are culling the same source, as they did on many other occasions. However, no such source has yet been identified.[56] So the situation remains the same. On the charge of having plagiarized Polydore Vergil's *Proverbiorum libellus* in his *Collectanea* the

* * * * *

56 As is the case with a less significant (in my opinion) similarity in the interpretation of another proverb, *indulgere genio* 'To indulge one's genius' drawn from Persius 5.151. This is Polydore 160 and c 510. Erasmus writes *animo suomet obsequi ac voluptati operam dare* 'to give in to one's feelings and devote oneself to pleasure.' In Polydore we find *obsequi naturae et voluptati operam dare* 'to give in to one's nature and devote oneself to pleasure.' The verbal similarity may be purely coincidental. Josse Bade's explanation of the phrase in his commentary on Persius (see 12 above), *da operam et te totum tribue genio naturali, desiderio et voluptatibus* 'devote yourself to and give yourself wholly to your natural inclinations, to desire and to pleasure' is not that dissimilar, but this commentary could not have been a common source for Erasmus and Polydore since it appeared in January of 1499, after Polydore's *Libellus* was published.

verdict is still 'not proven.' Moreover, on a general consideration, if Erasmus did draw on Polydore, it would have been not only disingenuous for him to claim to have produced the first collection of classical proverbs, it would also have been foolhardy. If Erasmus had access to Polydore Vergil's *libellus*, then surely fellow humanists in Paris would have also known of this work.

As a final note, it must be added that, although Erasmus did not, as far as can be ascertained, draw on Polydore Vergil's collection for his *Collectanea*, his sensitivity over the issue of possible plagiarism did not prevent him from occasionally drawing on the Italian humanist's work for the *Adagia* at a later date (see 43–4 below).

From the *Collectanea* to the *Chiliades*

In the late summer of 1506 Erasmus left Paris for Italy, arriving there in September, the same month in which the Parisian humanist Josse Bade published his Latin translations of Euripides' *Hecuba* and *Iphigeneia in Aulis*. November of 1506 also marked the appearance in print of Erasmus' Latin translations of some of the dialogues of Lucian (see 11 above). Even though these publications indicate a great advance in Erasmus' proficiency in the Greek language (over the level of competence that he had acquired in Paris prior to the appearance of his *Collectanea* in 1500), his main aim in going to Italy was to perfect his skills in that area and to widen his acquaintance with Greek works of literature in their original language.

On arriving in Italy he almost immediately acquired a doctorate from the University of Turin, and then moved on to Bologna where he stayed for about a year (November 1506–November 1507) as a guest of Paolo Bombace, who held the chair of Greek in the university of that city. For most of the time we may assume that he was engaged in study and reading. Near the end of his stay in Bologna, Erasmus wrote to the famous printer-scholar Aldus Manutius in Venice on 28 October 1507 (Ep 207) to ask him if he would publish a corrected and revised edition of his Latin translation of the two plays of Euripides that Josse Bade had published the year before.[57] Aldus agreed and the translation appeared in December of 1507. From what happened later it seems that Erasmus and Aldus must have corresponded further and agreed to work together on a new collection of classical adages.[58] Erasmus arrived in Venice at the end of 1507 and lived as a guest

* * * * *

57 According to Erasmus Bade's edition was 'chock-full of errors' (Ep 207:33).
58 The correspondence between Aldus and Erasmus on this point has not survived.

of Aldus and his father-in-law, Andrea d'Asola, while the new project came to fruition.

In a section which Erasmus added in the 1526 edition of the *Adagia* he describes the process that led to the publication in September 1508 of the *Adagiorum Chiliades* in Venice: 'I was bringing nothing to Venice with me except the confused and unsorted materials for a book that was to be, and that material was confined to published authors.' He continues: 'With the greatest temerity on my part, we both set to work together, me to write and Aldus to print. The whole business was finished inside nine months more or less' (*Adagia* II i 1 *Festina lente* 'Make haste slowly' CWE 33 14). Erasmus' words strongly suggest that the *Chiliades* was very much in an inchoate form when he arrived in Venice, and that most of it had then been put together at a quite hectic pace, hectic because there was an enormous transformation of the 1506 edition of the *Collectanea*. The final heading of this edition was numbered 838; the new edition of 1508 had 3271 headings,[59] and a new title, *Thousands of Adages*, aptly reflecting the vast increase in the number of the proverbs. The expansion, however, related not just to the number of adages, impressive though that is, but also to the size of the accompanying commentaries, which far surpassed the norm in the *Collectanea*.

Because of their subject matter much of the two longest essays in the 1508 edition, *Adagia* II i 1 'Make haste slowly' and *Adagia* III i 1 'The labours of Hercules,' must have been composed by Erasmus while in Venice. For in the former much of the commentary is taken up with discussion of the anchor-and-dolphin emblem that was the trade mark of the Aldine press, while in the latter Erasmus focuses to a great extent on the production of the *Chiliades* itself as an example of Herculean effort, at the same time anticipating and defending himself against possible criticism that the work might prompt.[60]

* * * * *

59 This is the number given by Felix Heinimann (ASD II-4 7). The final proverb in the *Chiliades* of 1508 has the number 3260, but there were many errors in the numbering. For example, twenty-six proverbs in the first chiliad had the same numbers as another twenty-six, the numbers 837–62 occurring twice. As the title of the new volume suggests, the adages were grouped in thousands and were numbered consecutively within each thousand. What became the standard numbering, by thousands and by centuries, was introduced in the edition of 1515.

60 The importance of these two proverbs is marked not only by their length and content but also by their position as the first in a new chiliad. Accordingly, the choice of 'Between friends all is common' to begin not only the first chiliad but also the whole collection must have special significance (it was no 94 in

In *Adagia* II i 1, however, Erasmus may not be telling the whole truth with respect to the little amount of work that he had done on the new edition before coming to Venice. For in *Adagia* III i 1 he claims to have finished the work, that is the *Chiliades*, not in nine months, but 'in less than a year and a half with the assistance of only one library.'[61] Since this adage was probably composed in the late spring or early summer of 1508,[62] the 'year and a half' would stretch back almost to the beginning of his residence in Bologna at the end of 1506, giving a more plausible time frame for Erasmus' work on the new edition.

It is natural and not without interest to speculate about how much Erasmus had done prior to his arrival in Venice. One would expect him to have used his *Collectanea* as a starting point, and indeed we find that four hundred and fifty of the proverbs in the *Collectanea* appear in the *first* chiliad of the new *Chiliades*. Even more striking perhaps is that Erasmus draws on seventy-four proverbs from the *Collectanea* in the first hundred headings of the whole work.[63] Jacques Chomarat[64] has also pointed

* * * * *

the *Collectanea*). The blessings of friendship (*amicitia*) were dear to Erasmus' heart, and what *amicitia* entailed in the sharing of all things by friends is made explicit in the accompanying commentary. The adage, however, is also seen by Erasmus as an important example of how proverbial wisdom unites and is common to the pagan and Christian worlds. 'Nothing,' Erasmus observes (*Adagia* I i 1 CWE 31 30:27–8), 'was ever said by a pagan philosopher which comes closer to the mind of Christ.' For a detailed development of this notion see Kathy Eden, '"Between Friends All is Common": The Erasmian Adage and Tradition,' *Journal of the History of Ideas* 59 (1998): 405–19, and *Friends Hold All Things in Common: Tradition, Intellectual Property and the Adages of Erasmus* (New Haven and London 2001).

61 CWE 34 179. He refers to the same time-span of a year and a half just before the passage quoted (CWE 34 178, near foot of page).

62 The impression that Erasmus gives of how the work came into being is that Aldus was type-setting what Erasmus gave him as he received it, and that the actual production of the book stretched over several months. See Allen Ep 2682:31–2, written in 1532: *[in meis Adagiis], quae simul et a me scribebantur et ab Aldo excudebantur* 'in my *Adagia* which I was composing and Aldus was printing out at the same time.' If this is correct, *Adagia* III i 1 could hardly have been composed much later than early or mid summer of 1508.

63 It should be noted, however, that there is little that is systematic in his choice of these. For the ten adages at I i 68–73 and I i 75–8 he draws on C 144, 91, 63, 445, 256, 257, 236, 310, 496, and 817, in that order.

64 Jacques Chomarat, *Grammaire et rhétorique chez Erasme* (Paris 1981) 2.768 with n254. His figures for long essays in each of the five chiliads in the 1536 edition are (in numerical order) 51, 19, 5, 4, and 1. One must remember that several

out that the first chiliad contains a high proportion of the longer essays (on his criterion of their taking up at least one full column in LB). Given Erasmus' description of the way in which the 1508 edition was produced in less than nine months, once he had arrived in Venice, it seems unlikely that he had much time during this period for the composition of lengthy disquisitions in addition to II i 1 and III i 1. Fourteen of the fifty-one longer essays that Chomarat identifies for the first chiliad actually appear in the first hundred,[65] and, on the basis of their content, almost all of these could have been composed during his stay in Bologna or even earlier inasmuch as they contain references to authors and works that would have been accessible to him at this period. So in *Adagia* I i 40 *Sus Minervam* 'The sow teaches Minerva,' in a considerable expansion over the five-line commentary of *Collectanea* 783, there are quotations from Pliny, Varro, Suetonius, Cicero, and St Jerome, as well as a Latin paraphrase of a passage in Aristotle. Another possible example of what Erasmus might have done before his arrival in Venice is *Adagia* I ii 44 'A Corycean was listening.' This is an expansion of *Collectanea* 112, which was accompanied in the 1500 edition by nine lines of Latin text, with quotations from Strabo (in Latin) and Cicero. For the proverb and the brief accompanying commentary in the 1500 edition Erasmus had been completely dependent on Filippo Beroaldo.[66] The essay on the proverb in the 1508 edition of the *Adagia* expands to take up thirty-three somewhat longer lines of Latin in ASD, and, in addition to Strabo and Cicero, draws on the *Suda* and Stephanus of Byzantium, giving a Latin paraphrase of the last two.[67] The Greek version of this proverb, Κωρυκαῖος ἠκροάζετο, absent from the

* * * * *

of these are the result of expansion in later editions; so, for example, *Adagia* III iii 1 *Sileni Alcibiadis*, III vii 1 *Scarabaeus aquilam quaerit*, IV i 1 *Dulce bellum inexpertis*.

65 Chomarat (n64 above) includes three of 'The Precepts of Pythagoras' that are found in *Adagia* I i 2, but one of these (*Choenici ne insideas*) was not particularly long in 1508, considerable additions being made in 1517/18 and 1526, as well as a smaller addition in 1520. The proverb *A fabis abstineto* was also much shorter in 1508 than it was in 1536. Only *A piscibus abstineto* can be regarded as having one of the longer commentaries in the 1508 edition. So a more accurate figure for the first chiliad is 49, of which twelve appear in the first hundred.

66 *Annotationes* 59; see 12 above.

67 ASD II-1 258–60. Erasmus must have read the *Suda* and Stephanus in the original Greek (in Bologna?). The first printed edition of the *Suda* appeared in 1499 (Milan), while the geographical lexicon of Stephanus of Byzantium was first printed by Aldus Manutius in 1502.

Collectanea in *1500* and *1506*, Erasmus might have taken directly from Zenobius, either the 1497 edition, or the Aldine edition of Aesop's fables (printed
in 1505), which also contained a collection of the proverbs ascribed to
Zenobius.

Given the high incidence in the first chiliad of the longer essays and
of the proverbs that had appeared in the *Collectanea*, it seems likely that
some of the work that Erasmus did for his new edition before he came to
Venice served as a basis for what was to appear in the first chiliad. The same
may be said for the second half of the second chiliad (II vi 1–II x 100). For
the material in this half-chiliad draws to a great extent from his *Collectanea*,
from Latin authors (rather than Greek), from the proverb collections of Diogenianus and Zenobius, and from the *Suda* – works, as we have seen, that
were accessible to him before his arrival in Venice. This is the view of Felix Heinimann, who believed (ASD II-4 6) that much of this half-chiliad had
been done partly in Bologna, partly before he came to Italy. Erasmus' sole
primary source for the Greek proverbs in the 1500 edition, the collection of
proverbs ascribed to Diogenianus, is used on about 50 occasions in the first
chiliad, and 111 occasions in the second chiliad. Of the latter 67 appear in
II vi 1–II x 100.[68] Apart from the predominant use of these limited sources,
we find a long series of proverbs beginning with the same letter stretching
from *Adagia* II viii 71–II x 100, in a reverse alphabetical order (in the Latin
alphabet). This series, interrupted occasionally by proverbs not conforming
to the alphabetical principle, starts with proverbs beginning with *u / v* and
ends with proverbs beginning with *g*.[69] This clearly shows that Erasmus had
compiled some kind of file in which the proverbs had been entered by the
first letter of the Roman alphabet, one that he must have started long before
he travelled to Venice, and one that may also have contained references to
where the adage occurred.[70]

On his arrival in Venice, however, the new resources made available
to him astounded him, as his own account, written in 1526, informs us:

* * * * *

68 These figures differ from those given by Phillips (in Appendix III p 396),
   probably because she seems to have counted only those instances where Erasmus names Diogenianus as his source. While Erasmus usually does this, there
   are instances where Diogenianus is not named, yet almost certainly must be
   the source (for example, I viii 75, II vii 47).
69 This sequence continues into the third chiliad. See Chomarat (n64 above) 763–4.
70 A less pervasive use of such a file is manifest also in the first half of the second
   chiliad (see ASD II-3 3) and in the first two centuries of the third chiliad (III i
   62–III i 82, III ii 11–III ii 66).

When I, a Dutchman, was in Italy, preparing to publish my book of *Proverbs*, all the learned men there had offered me unsought authors not yet published in print who they thought might be of use to me and Aldus had nothing in his treasure-house that he did not share with me. Johannes Lascaris did the same, so did Battista Egnazio, Marco Musuro, Frate Urbano. I felt the benefit of kindness from some people I knew neither by sight nor name ... Just consider what advantages I should have lost, had not scholars supplied me with texts in manuscript. Among them were Plato's works in Greek, Plutarch's *Lives* and also his *Moralia* which began to be printed when my work was nearly finished, the *Doctors at Dinner* of Athenaeus, Aphthonius, Hermogenes with notes, Aristotle's *Rhetoric* with the scholia of Gregory of Nazianzus, the whole of Aristides with scholia, brief commentaries on Hesiod and Theocritus, Eustathius on the whole of Homer, Pausanias, Pindar with accurate commentary, a collection of proverbs under Plutarch's name and another ascribed to Apostolius to which I was given access by Girolamo Aleandro. (*Adagia* II i 1 CWE 33 14)

These new sources provided Erasmus with more examples of the occurrence of individual adages and in some cases they provided new adages. An example of the former is *Adagia* I i 93 'Adopt the outlook of the polyp.' This is an expansion of *Collectanea* 255, which had nine lines of Latin text, with brief references to St Paul, Pliny, and Plautus, the source of the Greek version of the proverb being Diogenianus 1.23. In the *Chiliades* of 1508 the proverb has expanded to seventy-five lines of text in ASD,[71] and has references to or quotations from Euripides, Homer, Plutarch (twice), Lucian, Athenaeus (twice), Aristophanes, the *Historia Augusta*, Horace, Aristotle, and the Old Testament, in addition to the references in the *Collectanea*, with quotations in Greek being drawn from Plutarch (the *Moralia*) and Athenaeus, even though no Greek editions of these last two authors had yet appeared in print.[72] Even if Erasmus had composed much of this new commentary before the end of 1507, he must have made additions from the new sources such as Athenaeus that became available to him in Venice. As for adages that were unknown to Erasmus before his arrival in Venice the proverb collection of Apostolius of Byzantium was a bountiful source. While he draws on this collection most copiously in the second half of the *Chiliades* (for example, III ii 91–III v 14), he includes a few in the first chiliad, where

* * * * *

71 ASD II-1 198–202
72 Plutarch *Opuscula* LXXXXII (the *Moralia*) was printed by Aldus in 1509, and Athenaeus did not appear until 1514.

Diogenianus and Zenobius were his major sources as far as proverb collections were concerned: so, for example, I i 13, I ii 99, I ii 100.[73]

If it is impossible to be precise about how much of the material in the *Collectanea* dates from Erasmus' pre-Venetian period, one can be certain, however, that the appearance of the *Adagiorum Chiliades* in September of 1508 must have given both Aldus and Erasmus deep satisfaction. Nor would an owner-reader of the *Collectanea* have been dissatisfied with having to purchase this new work. It was not just new; it was different both in scale and quality from the *Collectanea*, drawing on what must have seemed even to an educated reader an astonishing range of authors and topics, and treating the proverbs in a much more expansive way. And of course the number of entries had almost quadrupled. Moreover, Erasmus provided a lengthy and valuable introductory essay on the nature of the proverb and its different uses, as well as two indexes, one giving the proverbs in alphabetical order, the other grouping them under topics such as greed, friendship, generosity.[74]

In the dedicatory letter to Lord William Mountjoy that forms the preface to the *Chiliades* of 1508 Erasmus writes that he had planned to include in the book a collection of material similar to proverbs: 'remarkable metaphors, witty sayings, noteworthy epigrams, unusually delightful allusions, and poetic allegories.' However, he goes on to say: 'I was put off by the labour involved ... and, limiting myself to the course I have run, I now hand the torch to anyone else who may be willing to take over the race from me.'[75] He writes in a similar vein in 'The labours of Hercules':

> ... since the work knows no limits and aims at being generally useful, is there any reason why we should not share the labour and by our joint efforts finish it? I have completed my task, I am tired and hand on the torch; let me have a successor who is ready to take his turn ... I have finished the part which offered most work and least reputation; I should be content to watch others adding what will be both easiest and most rewarding. (*Adagia* III i 1 CWE 34 180)

* * * * *

73 A few that are now found in the first chiliad actually appeared much later in the collection as printed in 1508. For example, what is now I ii 93 (from Apostolius 12.76) and I ii 100 (from Apostolius 18.62) were nos 3245 and 3258 respectively in *1508*.

74 The topical index took up forty folio pages. Its organization followed that advocated for commonplace notebooks, topics being juxtaposed on the principle of similarities or opposites, as Erasmus recommends in *De copia* (see CWE 24 635–6). Erasmus continued to add to the index in subsequent editions. For the final version see 579–632 below.

75 Ep 211:25–6, 34–8

There is no reason to doubt Erasmus' sincerity when he wrote these words in 1508. The nine months of intense toil at the Aldine press seem to have exhausted him and at the same time precluded any desire on his part to undertake new editions of the *Chiliades*. Moreover, he had other more important interests that were more suited to an erudite Augustinian canon: biblical scholarship, theology, and the church Fathers. He planned to turn his talents to these, since 'I did not think it was right for me ... if I were to spend a great part of my life up to old age, in working at an occupation which was not mine.'[76] Erasmus' resolve to have nothing more to do with his *Adagia* was not to last, however sincere the feelings he expressed in the dedicatory letter may have been. He supervised eight more editions of the *Chiliades*, the final one appearing in 1536, the year of his death. So, in fact, he spent at least a fair part of life 'up to old age' engaged in this secular work.

On the completion of the *Chiliades* in September of 1508 Erasmus left Venice, and, accompanied by his pupil, Alexander Stewart, son of James IV of Scotland, travelled in Italy, before settling in Rome. In May of 1509, however, he was persuaded by his English friends to return to England after the accession of Henry VIII to the throne, in the hope of winning patronage. He was to reside there for five years, breaking his stay only for a brief visit to Paris in 1511 to oversee the production of *Praise of Folly*. It was probably during this visit that he agreed to undertake a second edition of the *Chiliades* that was to be printed by Josse Bade.[77] In 1513 he entrusted the material for this second edition to Franz Birckmann for delivery to Bade. Birckmann, however, gave the material, not to Josse Bade in Paris, but to Johan Froben in Basel. Froben had published an unauthorized reprint of the *Chiliades* in 1513, and Erasmus was fearful that Froben would postpone the new edition until the reprint had sold out. The delay, however, was minimal and the new edition appeared in 1515, Erasmus himself having arrived in Basel in August 1514. All the succeeding authorized editions came from the Froben press, appearing in 1517/1518, 1520, 1523, 1526, 1528, 1533, and 1536. It is beyond the scope of this essay to examine in detail the nature of the expansion in these editions, and what follows focuses only on its highlights. For more detail the reader must turn to other works, in particular to Phillips.

Of the eight editions that followed the 1508 Aldine those of 1515, 1533, and 1528 (in descending order of significance) show the greatest amount of

* * * * *

76 Ep 211:41–4
77 Ep 219:4–5, 263:22

expansion – and it was adding and expanding that were Erasmus' modes of procedure in all the later editions. The amount of material dropped from earlier editions was minuscule.[78] In the 1515 edition the number of adages increased to over 3400, while the 1533 edition contained 488 new proverbs, and the edition of 1528 had 123 new adages. The final edition of 1536 ended with *Adagia* v ii 51 (4151).

As far as the 1515 edition is concerned, more important than the increase in the number of proverbs were the additions that Erasmus made to those already present in the 1508 edition. In the prefatory letter of *1515* addressed to his readers Erasmus claims to have increased the material of the 1508 edition by twenty-five percent, mostly by expanding the commentary on existing adages rather than by adding new proverbs. Some of the expansion is of a modest nature: Erasmus frequently adds the name of a source or identifies more specifically the work from which he is drawing; he also provides Latin translations to follow the Greek that he quotes. These are items that we might describe as 'mere book-keeping.' Of more substance are the completely new examples he provides in his discussion of a particular proverb. He continues with this type of expansion in all the new editions of the work. We can see Erasmus himself at work in this process in two copies of different editions of the *Adagia*, those of 1523 and 1526. These contain annotations in Erasmus' hand, and most of these prefigure changes and expansions to be found in *1526* and *1528* respectively.[79] A manuscript, also in Erasmus' hand, containing material for the large expansion of the 1533 edition also survives.[80] One topic, that of textual corruption in the manuscripts and printed editions of the classical authors, was of abiding interest to Erasmus. And so, in addition to the minor expansions just mentioned, it is not surprising that successive editions present new, usually brief, discussions of textual matters.[81]

* * * * *

78 For example, *Adagia* iv v 44, prompted by Erasmus' engagement with Irenaeus, was introduced as a new adage in *1528*, and replaced one that was dropped from the collection. The lengthy 'Not even an ox would be lost' (*Adagia* iv v 1) was introduced in the edition of 1526. Again the adage that had hitherto occupied this position ('Hail, dear light') was dropped. René Hoven, 'Les éditions successives des *Adages*: Coup d'oeil sur les sources et les méthodes de travail d'Erasme,' in *Miscellanea Jean-Pierre Vanden Branden* (Brussels 1995) 257–81 at 270–1, counts seven adages in *1508* that were suppressed in *1515*, including three that were doublets.

79 See ASD ii-8 6–7 and Hoven (n78 above) 259–61.

80 See ASD ii-8 6–13.

81 For a sampling of this topic in different editions see Grant 165–81.

A more significant innovation of the 1515 edition is the insertion of material that has really little to do with a particular proverb or with how or where it was used. Instead, a proverb sometime serves simply as a starting point for Erasmus' commentary on the social mores of his time. *Adagia* I ix 12 'To exact tribute from the dead,' whose commentary amounted to only a few lines in *1508*, was expanded in *1515* first by a short paragraph on the meaning and etymology of φόρος 'tribute' but then, after this philological exposition, Erasmus embraces at considerable length a much wider topic, the cult of wealth among Christians, particularly among the nobility, who exact taxes from the poor at every opportunity. Even priests are guilty of this vice, says Erasmus; they demand cash for every service they provide – baptism, marriage, even for hearing confession. A briefer addition, again containing criticism of a characteristic of the times, occurs in II vi 12 'For sluggards it is always holiday.' This time Erasmus directs his aim at how too many Christians devote themselves to licentious behaviour on holy days. Yet, despite this, he adds, popes are actually increasing the number of such days.[82]

One of the innovations of the 1515 edition was to break down each chiliad into centuries. Just as he had placed a lengthy essay at the beginning of the second and third chiliads in *1508* ('Make haste slowly' and 'The labours of Hercules'), so he sometimes marked the beginning of a new century of proverbs in *1515* with an important essay. Such is II v 1 *Spartam nactus es, hanc orna* 'Sparta is your portion; do your best for her.' This actually appeared in *1508* between what is now numbered II i 30 and II i 31, but was moved, like some other adages, to the beginning of a century. Its expansion, from its one paragraph of commentary in *1508*, amounts to almost six pages of English translation in CWE 33 (pp 237–43). Here Erasmus' target is a favourite one – the calamitous effects of war. Erasmus criticizes several princes and kings of Europe for the wars they wage to increase the size and wealth of their realm.[83] As an example of an innocent victim of war, Erasmus praises the fine and admirable qualities of his pupil Alexander Stewart, who died, needlessly in Erasmus' view, at the age of eighteen, along with his father at the battle of Flodden in 1513.

Erasmus' most famous anti-war tract is *Dulce bellum inexpertis* 'War is a treat for those who have not tried it,' which had the important position of

* * * * *

82 Another essay that was expanded, comparatively briefly, was 'With unwashed hands' (*Adagia* I ix 55), where the additional material criticizes those who claim to be theologians but have little or no knowledge of Greek, Latin, or Hebrew.
83 These include Charles the Bold, Charles VIII of France, and Louis XII of France and James IV of Scotland.

opening a chiliad as well as a century (*Adagia* iv i 1). This saying has a short commentary of a few lines in *1508*, where it was no 1404; the English translation of the commentary that accompanies it in *1515* amounts to almost forty pages in CWE.[84] This powerful condemnation of war struck such a responsive chord that it was published separately as a pamphlet soon after the edition appeared.[85] The two other essays that were considerably expanded in 1515 were 'The Sileni of Alcibiades' (*Adagia* iii iii 1, no 1706 in *1508*) and 'A dung-beetle hunting an eagle' (*Adagia* iii vii 1, no 913 in *1508*). The former (taking up nearly twenty pages of English translation)[86] discusses how the external and physical nature of persons often belie the internal and spiritual. The second, more satirical in tone than most of the other long pieces, uses a fable primarily to condemn the abuse by rulers of their power.[87]

Because of the increased engagement with contemporary social, political, and religious questions Margaret Mann Phillips (106–19) describes the 1515 edition of the *Chiliades* as 'the Utopian edition,' emphasizing Erasmus' connection with the publication of Thomas More's *Utopia*. Erasmus knew More well and stayed with him on more than one occasion (including when he was writing *Praise of Folly*) during his prolonged visit to England. Both were sympathetic to the poor and their afflictions, both were condemnatory of the abuse of power. More's influence may well have encouraged Erasmus to widen the scope of the *Chiliades* to embrace these social issues in *1515*. The main focus, however, of the work, however, was still to provide information on many subjects from the classical world relating to the proverbs.[88]

In subsequent editions there were few new essays of any great length, the most prominent being *Adagia* iv v 1 'Not even an ox would be lost,' a completely new addition of *1526*. However, Erasmus continued to expand the commentary on adages that were present in *1515*. Substantive additions occur, for example, in 'As warts grow on the eye' (*Adagia* ii viii 65) in *1517/18*, and in 'Esernius versus Pacidianus' (*Adagia* ii v 98), also in *1517/18*.

The continuous expansion from one edition of the *Adagia* to the next allows us insight into Erasmus' reading and activities at particular points in

* * * * *

84 CWE 35 399–440 (including footnotes)
85 In Erasmus' lifetime it was printed separately in cities throughout Europe, including Basel, Louvain, Leipzig, Paris, and London.
86 CWE 34 262–82
87 By its nature as 'king of the birds,' the eagle naturally stands for a ruler. Its wily and resourceful opponent, however, is not free of flaws; see CWE 35 178n.
88 See W. Barker *The Adages of Erasmus* (Toronto 2001) xviii.

his life.[89] He wrote a preface to a new edition of Aristotle (edited by Simon Grynaeus) that appeared in 1531 in Basel, published by Johan Bebel, and it is no coincidence therefore that there are over thirty examples drawn from Aristotle's *Rhetoric* and *Nicomachean Ethics* in the expansion of the 1533 edition (*Adagia* IV vii 59–v ii 46).[90] Similarly, Erasmus supplied a prefatory letter (Ep 704) and notes for an edition of Quintus Curtius Rufus that appeared in Strasbourg in June 1518, published by Matthias Schürer. Again, it occasions no surprise, then, that most of the references to this author in the *Adagia* are to be found in the edition of 1517/18.[91] One of the Latin authors edited by Erasmus himself is Seneca the Younger. The first edition appeared in 1515 and Erasmus' work on it probably prompted the insertion of just under forty quotations from Seneca in the edition of the *Adagia* of the same year.[92] In subsequent editions of the *Adagia*, however, he used this author sparingly, until, that is, the edition of 1528, in which he quoted from Seneca two dozen or so times. Dissatisfaction with the 1515 edition of Seneca[93] had eventually led Erasmus to re-edit the author, and preparatory work on a new edition, which the Froben press published in early 1529, had begun as early as 1525.[94] The new Senecan additions to the *Adagia* of 1528, whose date of publication was September of that year, the same month in which printing began on the new edition of Seneca, were probably owed to

* * * * *

89 In compiling the statistics for this section the *index nominum* for the whole of the *Adagia* in ASD (II-9 447–90) was used. Although the index does not claim to be complete, it provides enough information to be extremely useful for tracing the occurrences of authors in particular editions.

90 See *Adagia* IV viii 4n (CWE 36 354).

91 Twelve of a total of twenty references to and quotations from Curtius in the *Adagia* appear in the edition of 1517/18, but the other eight do not make their appearance until the edition of 1533. (Phillips gives the total as 19, perhaps counting as one the two quotations in III vii 32.)

92 A quick count of the total number of quotations from Seneca amounts to 113. I count 29 examples in *1508*. Among all the editions that of 1515 contains the highest number.

93 Erasmus had left for England in May 1515 before the edition was ready and had entrusted the task of overseeing its production to 'the still inexperienced' Beatus Rhenanus and 'the enthusiastic but incompetent Wilhelm Nesed, who botched the job of correcting' (D.F.S. Thomson, 'Erasmus and textual scholarship in the light of sixteenth-century practice' in *Erasmus of Rotterdam: The Man and the Scholar: Proceedings of the Symposium held at the Erasmus University, Rotterdam, 9–11 November 1986* [Leiden and New York] 158).

94 See Ep 1656, written in 1525, a letter to Robert Aldridge in Cambridge asking him to collate a manuscript in King's College against his 1515 edition of Seneca. Erasmus continued to ask his correspondents to search out manuscripts, even when the printing of the new edition had begun.

the work he did on this new edition. It is striking that most of the new quotations in *1528* (17 out of 25) are taken from *De beneficiis*, the work that was printed first in the Senecan edition (pp 1–75), and Erasmus himself says that when printing began he was extremely well prepared for producing the text of *De beneficiis*.[95] To give but one more example of how his scholarly work carried over into the expansion of the *Adagia*, Erasmus produced in 1526 an edition of the Latin translation of Irenaeus' *Adversus haereses*; all four references to or quotations from this work in the *Adagia* appear in the edition of 1528.

Sometimes it is not so much Erasmus' own activities that account for his choice of authors at a particular time as the appearance in print of an author whose work had been available up till then only in manuscript form. In 1513 there appeared the first edition of the *Apocolocyntosis* or, as Erasmus usually termed it, the *Ludus de morte Claudii*, the humorous work attributed to Seneca that describes the fate of the emperor Claudius in heaven and in the underworld after his death; his young friend Beatus Rhenanus published another edition in 1515. Seven of the nine references or quotations to the *Apocolocyntosis* first appear in the 1515 edition of the *Adagia*.[96] Another work edited by Beatus Rhenanus, this time the *editio princeps* of the *Opera omnia* of Tertullian, was published in 1521. All but one of the fifteen quotations from Tertullian first appear in *1523* or later editions.[97]

An example of how the publication of a new printed text of a Greek author furnished Erasmus with more material for his next edition of the *Adagia* is the appearance, in 1526, of the Aldine edition (in five volumes) of the medical writer Galen, the *editio princeps* of the text in Greek. Erasmus received a complimentary copy of this edition from the press, for which he wrote a letter of thanks to Gianfrancesco Torresani on September 3,

* * * * *

95 Ep 2056:3–4. The *De beneficiis* was also a favourite work which Erasmus drew on in his letters. One reason for his particular interest in this work is that Erasmus seems to have had access to an excellent, early Carolingian MS for this work (and for *De clementia*). This has been identified as MS N (= Vatican, Palatinus latinus 1547), now recognized as the extant archetype of these two dialogues. See Allen VIII 25 (the introduction to Ep 2091, the prefatory letter to the Senecan edition of March 1529) and Thomson (n93 above) 159.

96 *Adagia* I ii 65, I iii 1 (*ter*), II vi 46, IV iv 25, IV iv 79. Elsewhere in the *Adagia* Erasmus draws on the work at I i 33 (in *1517/18*) and II iv 21 (in *1520*).

97 The exception is at *Adagia* II iv 17, where the quotation appeared in the 1508 edition, having been taken over, however, from *Collectanea* 31.

1526.[98] There are just over thirty quotations from Galen in the final edition of the *Adagia*, and of these the majority (twenty-two) made their first appearance in the 1528 edition.[99] A second example relates to an edition of the hymns of Callimachus produced by the Froben press in 1532 and prepared by Sigismund Gelenius, a talented and learned humanist, who arrived in Basel circa 1524 and stayed for a period in the household of Erasmus. Helped by a recommendation from Erasmus, Gelenius worked for the press and devoted his talents as editor, collaborator, and translator to it until his death in 1554.[100] In this volume of Callimachus part of the work of the fifth-century anthologist Stobaeus was included anonymously under the title *Gnomologium*. Erasmus drew on this section for the edition of 1533 for additions to several adages: *Adagia* II ii 53, III i 13 (Menander), III i 18 (Euripides, wrongly assigned, as in Stobaeus, to Menander), III i 63, III iii 15, III iii 60, III iii 75, and III ix 44.[101] Similarly, most of the quotations from Gregory Nazianzus appear in *1528* when Erasmus was drawing from an edition printed in the same year in Hagenau that contained letters of Gregory and Basil, as at *Adagia* II vi 14 and II ix 7.[102] In the 1532 Froben edition of Basil, produced under the guidance of Erasmus, new letters of Gregory were included. From these Erasmus added a few new references to Gregory in the edition of the *Adagia* that came out in the following year.[103]

Another Greek author whose printed works were a stimulus to a renewed engagement of Erasmus with the author was the orator Aeschines. Erasmus referred to his speech *In Ctesiphontem* four times in *1508*, without

* * * * *

98 Ep 1746. Erasmus' copy of the edition survives in the Provincial Library of Friesland at Leeuwarden (see van Gulik on no 137 of the mailing list).

99 Four more quotations were added in the edition of 1533: IV vii 33 (*bis*), 34, 35. The few earlier quotations contain no Greek or very little (see *Adagia* I iii 6 and II v 81). An exception is *Adagia* IV iv 56, added, according to ASD II-7 213, in the edition of 1515.

100 For Gelenius see CEBR 2:84–5. Erasmus thought highly of him (see Epp 1702, 1767, 2901).

101 See ASD II-5 549:695n, and notes to the individual adages. Erasmus owned this edition (no 314 in the mailing list, on which see van Gulik). Gelenius was also heavily involved in the 1533 edition of Suetonius and other historical works, including Ammianus Marcellinus (see 35 and n110 below).

102 The same is true for a quotation from Basil at *Adagia* I ix 34. The Hagenau edition is not present in the mailing list of Erasmus' library, but van Gulik (on no 96 of the mailing list) believes that Erasmus owned a copy of it.

103 As at *Adagia* I iv 98, IV ix 34. Erasmus owned two copies of this edition (nos 189 and 250 in the mailing list).

quoting any Greek.[104] He probably had at hand the Latin translation of the speech by Leonardo Bruni. The orations of Aeschines were first printed in Greek in an Aldine edition of 1513 that included the speeches of several other Greek orators. Erasmus, however, did not apparently own this edition until late 1525 at the earliest.[105] He added one quotation in Greek from the author in 1526 (*Adagia* III vii 22), then a further eighteen in 1528 and ten in 1533.[106]

Sometimes the use of an author in the expansions of the *Adagia* is not linked either to Erasmus' own publications or to a recently published edition of the author concerned, but to the preparation of a new edition by humanists living in his vicinity. This seems to be the case with Pindar and Ammianus Marcellinus. For the former Erasmus had relied on a manuscript in preparing the edition of 1508. However, the edition of the *Adagia* of 1526 has a large number of new quotations from the Greek lyric poet,[107] and it has been plausibly suggested that the preparation in Basel of a new edition of this poet prompted Erasmus' renewed interest in Pindar.[108] The edition, from the press of Andreas Cratander, appeared in February of 1526, a month after the publication of the new edition of the *Adagia* that came out that year, but Erasmus may have had access to proofs and other materials much earlier. As for Ammianus Marcellinus all references to and quotations from this author make their first appearance in 1528.[109] Perhaps the accessibility to Sigismund Gelenius (mentioned above in connection with Callimachus) of a valuable 9th/10th manuscript of Ammianus from Hersfeld had stimulated Erasmus' interest in this author at that time. It was Gelenius

* * * * *

104 *Adagia* I iii 26, I iv 15, I iv 73, I ix 62. At *Adagia* I ii 17, where he does quote Greek from Aeschines, his source is Pliny.

105 See Allen VII 547, for books ordered by Erasmus. This volume is Husner no 132 in the mailing list, on which see van Gulik.

106 I count 35 references to Aeschines in all. Phillips' number (38) may include mentions of Aeschines when Erasmus is actually quoting Demosthenes. The main point, however, is that 50% of them occur in 1528 and 80% in the two editions of 1528 and 1533 combined. An anomalous example occurs at *Adagia* I iii 26 where the Greek from Aeschines' speech against Ctesipho is added in the edition of 1523, two years before Erasmus apparently ordered it. Did he have access to someone else's copy of the printed work in 1523?

107 So, for example, almost half of the quotations from Pindar in the first 1500 adages were added in 1526.

108 Felix Heinimann and Emanuel Kienzle in ASD II-4 249

109 The quotation from Ammianus in *Adagia* III vii 13 was added in 1528, not in 1526 as stated in CWE 35 223 n3. Phillips (394) gives the number of references to Ammianus as eighteen.

who, in 1533, guided through the Froben press an edition containing several Roman historical works, being himself primarily responsible for the text of Ammianus.[110]

One author may serve as an example of how frequently Erasmus reread his authors and constantly added to his store of proverbs and their sources in the new editions of the *Adagia*. In II i 1 'Make haste slowly' Erasmus includes Athenaeus as one of the authors to whom he now had access, in manuscript form, on his arrival in Venice (CWE 33 14). The first printed edition, however, did not appear until 1514 (edited by Marcus Musurus), and this was too late for the *Adagia* of 1515. However, he used the edition of Athenaeus extensively[111] to add references to and quotations from Athenaeus in the edition of 1517/18, augmenting the sixteen that appeared in the edition of 1508. An examination of the first chiliad produces the following statistics for the citations from Athenaeus:[112]

1508	1515	1517/18	1520	1523	1526	1528	1533	1536
16[113]	0	50	4	6	0	33	1	1

* * * * *

110 This was an augmented and revised version of a Froben edition of 1518 that contained Suetonius, the *Historia Augusta*, Ammianus Marcellinus, and some other items of Roman imperial history. Although the title page of that edition had given the impression that Erasmus was the editor of the whole volume, he seems to have worked almost exclusively on the text of Suetonius. The text of Ammianus' *Res gestae* in this earlier edition had been simply purloined from a 1517 edition published in Bologna. I am indebted to van Gulik (on no 261 of the mailing list) for almost all of this information regarding the text of Ammianus.

111 Erasmus' own copy of the printed Aldine edition is now in the Bodleian library (Auct 1 R inf.1.1). It is item no 239 in Husner's mailing list.

112 Phillips (395) gives the number of references to Athenaeus in the first chiliad as 105. My number (111) is slightly larger, including a few where Erasmus gives several quotations from Athenaeus in the same adage. Phillips may have regarded such instances as one reference to Athenaeus.

113 On a few occasions in *1508* Erasmus does not actually quote any Greek when referring to Athenaeus (at *Adagia* I i 71, I v 69, I vi 2, I vii 23, I ix 49). For the others he must have drawn the Greek from the manuscript of Athenaeus at his disposal (see the reference to Athenaeus in *Adagia* II i 1 [25 above]). Erasmus also drew from the manuscript in *Adagia* II iii 82–8, 91 (probably) and 92. In 1423 Giovanni Aurispa had brought a tenth-century manuscript of Athenaeus to Venice. While preparing the 1508 edition Erasmus may have used this MS. See J.-C. Margolin, 'Erasme et Athenée,' in *From Wolfram and Petrarch to Goethe and Grass. Studies . . . in Honour of Leonard Forster* (Baden-Baden 1982) 213–47.

It is not surprising that Erasmus used Athenaeus most extensively for the 1517/18 edition, the first one for which he could use the printed edition. However, he obviously turned to this author again for the 1528 edition and even made sporadic use of him for other editions.[114] This same procedure can be seen with respect to other authors.[115]

The ninth and final edition of the *Adagia* came out in March of 1536, just four months before Erasmus' death in July of that year. It would be hard, however, to justify describing it as new, since only five fresh adages were added at the end (*Adagia* v ii 47–v ii 51), although a number of new references or quotations were inserted elsewhere.[116] To all intents, however, the edition of 1533 marks the culmination of Erasmus' work on the *Adagia*, and in it Erasmus returned, in one aspect, full circle to the *Collectanea* of 1500. Although his sources for the new proverbs include Greek authors that he had used extensively before, such as Aristophanes, Plato, and Aristotle, and others that he had drawn on more sparingly, such as the orator Aeschines and Sophocles,[117] most of the new adages are drawn from Latin

* * * * *

114 In the group drawn from Athenaeus at *Adagia* II iii 82–8, 92–3 (mentioned in the preceding note) Erasmus added a fragment of Greek tragedy taken from Athenaeus in *1526* in *Adagia* II iii 91, and in *Adagia* II iii 92 he added a quotation in *1517/18* and another sentence relating to Athenaeus in *1533*.

115 As is the case with Quintus Curtius Rufus, whom Erasmus uses comparatively infrequently. As mentioned above, most of the references to this author appear in 1517/18. In the first chiliad, however, two of the eight references were added in *1533*.

116 A dozen new quotations from Ovid were added in this edition, including six from the *Tristia* (I ii 34, I iii 96, I v 49, I ix 24, III iv 46, III v 18). Erasmus also drew on Cicero; for example, from *De finibus* at I v 7 and III i 1, and *Academica* at I v 6 and II x 90. Elsewhere Erasmus adds quotations or references to a range of authors, often by way of a short addition at the end of his discussion: Seneca at I iv 43, Strabo and Stephanus of Byzantium at IV iv 54, Catullus at II i 79, Origen at I iii 65 and III i 95, Macrobius at I x 71, Ausonius at II iv 48. Sometimes the addition is as brief as 'This is used by Synesius' (*Adagia* I ix 58 CWE 31 214).

117 Aristophanes: quoted on just under forty occasions, most of the quotations being drawn from the *Birds* and the *Knights*. Plato: over thirty quotations, drawn from several of the dialogues, including the *Republic* (7), *Laws* (5), *Theaetetus* (4), *Phaedrus* (3), and *Laches* (3). Aristotle: almost exclusively from the *Rhetoric* and the *Nicomachean Ethics* (see 31 above). Aeschines: he adds another ten quotations to what he had added in *1528* (see 34 n106 above). Sophocles: he draws directly from the *Antigone* in a series of adages beginning at v i 85 and continuing to v ii 7 (27 quotations in all), and from the *Electra* in a series running

literature, in particular Plautus and Cicero, two of the authors that had furnished him with a large number of examples in the *Collectanea*.[118] Of the new adages added in *1533* (and *1536*) Margaret Mann Phillips counts 293 references to or quotations from Cicero and 133 from Plautus.[119] Erasmus quotes from virtually all genres in the Ciceronian corpus, but primarily from the speeches (especially the *Verrines*) and to a lesser extent the correspondence and the rhetorical works.[120] He seems to have used a new edition of Cicero produced by Andreas Cratander in Basel in 1528, and the appearance of this edition may have stimulated him to make further use of a favourite author for a new edition of the *Adagia*.[121] As for Plautus, Erasmus draws from every comedy in the Plautine corpus except the fragmentary *Vidularia*.[122] Linked to his renewed interest in early Latin literature is his frequent use in *1533* of Pompeius Festus and Nonius Marcellus, valuable sources for early Latin.[123] His reading for the 1533 edition, however, was by no means confined to literary texts. Erasmus draws quite heavily (comparatively speaking) from legal texts such as the *Pandects*, and Gratian's *Decretum*.[124] This was prompted to a considerable extent by information given Erasmus by his friend Bonifacius Amerbach, referring him to Andrea Alciati's work *De verborum significatione*, published in 1530.[125] Erasmus used this work as well as other suggestions for proverbs taken from legal and other texts made by Amerbach himself.[126]

* * * * *

from v ii 25 to v ii 36. In addition he cites three fragments, one drawn from a scholion in Aristophanes (IV viii 84) and two from Stobaeus (IV x 38 and v i 38).

118 See 10 n21 above.

119 These numbers are for just under five hundred adages. Phillips' count for the whole of the first chiliad is about the same, 289 for Cicero and 134 for Plautus (Phillips 396 and 400).

120 For the rhetorical works see *Adagia* v ii 8n (CWE 36 601).

121 The use of the Basel edition of 1528 is suggested by Franz Heinimann and Emanuel Kienzle in ASD II-6 529:326n. Although the works of Cicero appear on several occasions in the mailing list, the Basel edition does not fit any of the entries.

122 The highest number of quotations comes from the *Pseudolus* (21), followed by *Trinummus* (15) and *Mostellaria* (14).

123 See 63–4 below.

124 See *Adagia* IV ix 1n (CWE 36 419).

125 For the letter see A. Hartmann and B.R. Jenny eds *Die Amerbachkorrespondenz* 4 (Basel 1953) no 1683.

126 See ASD II-8 41 nn48 and 50; IV vii 75n (CWE 36 332–3). Erasmus acknowledges Alciati's work as his source at IV ix 36, praising his learning and reputation as a

In sum, the edition of 1533 well illustrates how Erasmus drew on all aspects of his intellectual life – his correspondence with fellow humanists, his own and others' publications, his library acquisitions, and his own extensive reading (and re-reading) of the classical authors – to provide material for the new editions that followed his great achievement of the *Chiliades adagiorum* of 1508.

Erasmus' sources

Everything that Erasmus read provided him with material for his collection of proverbs from antiquity. His sources from the classical corpus range from Homer to Ammianus Marcellinus and hardly any subject area of the classical period was ignored. He also drew from patristic writers, among whom St Jerome was particularly favoured, and from scripture itself. Some of his sources, however, would have been unfamiliar even to the educated among his readers. This applies in particular to collections of proverbs that had been transmitted from antiquity and others that had been compiled in the Renaissance period.

Proverb Collections (Classical and Medieval)

DIOGENIANUS

In the prefatory letter to the *Collectanea* of 1500 Erasmus writes that although numerous Greek authors had put together collections of proverbs only the *Synagoge* 'Collection' ascribed to Diogenianus was available to him.[127] And indeed all the Greek that is to be found in the *Collectanea* of 1500 is derived either directly from Diogenianus or indirectly from Latin authors such as Aulus Gellius or from humanists such as Angelo Poliziano and Ermolao Barbaro.

There is general agreement that the author of the collection cannot be either the grammarian Diogenianus who is mentioned by the *Suda* (Δ 1140) as living in the time of the emperor Hadrian or the Diogenianus to whom Hesychius (see 46 below) refers in the preface of his work as the author of a lexicon that included proverbs but for the most part lacked any explanation of them. How or why his name was attached to the collection that Erasmus used is not known.

* * * * *

jurist. For Erasmus' use in 1533 of another scholar's work, Johannes Alexander Brassicanus, see 43 below.
127 Ep 126:108–12 CWE 1 259

Erasmus was familiar with this collection because his Greek tutor in Paris, George Hermonymus, owned a manuscript of the work (now Oxford, Bodley Grabe 30). Erasmus also possessed a copy of this manuscript, and used it for the *Collectanea* of 1500. He must also have had it at hand when he was in Venice, since he added material from Diogenianus that was not in the *Collectanea*, to the *Chiliades* of 1508.[128]

Modern readers must have recourse to the edition by E. Leutsch, which was published in 1839 in the first volume of *Corpus paroemiographorum Graecorum* (CPG). It is organized in centuries, the last item being 8.76.[129]

The similarities between this collection and the anthology ascribed to Zenobius (see below) show that the two collections go back to the same original source.

PLUTARCH

Erasmus refers to and draws on collections (*Collectiones* or *Collectanea*) of proverbs that he says are attributed to Plutarch, thereby implying some (justified) doubt about this ascription.[130] The proverbs in question run from *Adagia* II vii 83 to III vii 99 and then resume at *Adagia* III x 76, after the long sequence of quotations from Homer. This second series continues to III x 84, with the exception of II x 82. Erasmus' major source for these was almost certainly a manuscript in Florence (Laurentianus 80.13) that belonged to Janus Lascaris, who, Erasmus tells us, lent him a manuscript containing 'a collection of proverbs under Plutarch's name'[131] in Venice in 1508.[132] It contains five groups of proverbs of which one, originally the second collection in the series, is described as 'Proverbs of Plutarch used by the Alexandrians.'[133]

* * * * *

128 For example, II vii 15–19, 23, 24, 30, to cite only a few cases
129 Bühler (1.189 n1) states that the actual number of proverbs in the *Synagoge* is 787, when one takes into account some proverbs that ought to have been given separate status and also proverbs that the editors of CPG added without changing the overall numeration.
130 See in particular *Adagia* III vii 86: 'In the *Collected Proverbs* Plutarch, if the title is not wrong, informs us . . .' (CWE 35 272). He is referring here to the name of Plutarch in the title. See also, for example, III vii 83, 84, 86.
131 CWE 33 14 (in *Adagia* II i 1)
132 See Bühler 1.67–8.
133 This can be found in Otto Crusius' edition in CPG *Supplementum* (item IIIa). Crusius also shows ('Analecta ad Paroemiographos Graecos,' item II in CPG *Supplementum* p 15) that the description 'Proverbs of Plutarch used by the Alexandrians' was taken erroneously by earlier scholars to be a subscription to what was actually the first collection, which is printed and designated as such in CPG 1.321–42. The other three collections are most conveniently found

ZENOBIUS OR 'ZENODOTUS'

According to the *Suda* (Z 63A) Zenobius, who taught in Rome in the time of Hadrian, put together an epitome of the proverb collections of Didymus (comprising ten books) and Lucillus Tarrhaeus (comprising three). Erasmus almost always uses the name Zenodotus for this grammarian,[134] an error which is probably based on an arbitrary emendation of Marcus Musurus in a scholion on Aristophanes *Clouds* 133.[135]

The *editio princeps* appeared in 1497 in Florence from the printing house of Philip Junta, and Erasmus seems to have been able to make use of this for the second edition of his *Collectanea*.[136] The proverbs are organized alphabetically and represent what is termed *Zenobius vulgatus*. They are most readily accessible in CPG 1 (pp 1–75, amounting to 552 in number). A similar but different version of the proverbs of Zenobius, based on a manuscript from Mount Athos (now Paris, supplementa Graeca 1164) was published in 1868, being edited by Emmanuel Miller, who had discovered it.[137] This was made up of three distinct collections, giving a total of 372 proverbs, which were not organized alphabetically. This second version, the so-called Athoan Zenobius, was known, at least in part, to Erasmus since Laurentianus 80.13, the manuscript mentioned above under 'Plutarch' and lent to him by Janus Lascaris, is also a witness to the Athoan recension of Zenobius.

Here it is relevant to adduce an untitled miscellany volume published by the Aldine press in Venice in 1505, the best-known item in the volume being Aesop's fables.[138] Among other works, however, it contains a large number of proverbs, arranged alphabetically and including those that appear in Zenobius' collection, although there is no mention of Zenobius or indeed of anyone else as the person responsible for the anthology. The title of this section of the book is 'Collection of proverbs of Tarrhaeus and Didymus and of those in the *Suda* and others.' The scope of the collection is indicated by the fact that it contains just over 400 proverbs under the

* * * * *

in CPG *Supplementum*, item VI (H. Jungblut, 'Über die Spichwörtersammlungen des Laurentianus 80, 13'). See Bühler 1.67–8, with n57; ASD II-6 473; *Adagia* III v 30n.

134 An exception occurs at *Adagia* III i 1 (CWE 34 173).

135 See Bühler 1.102 n52.

136 See 11 above.

137 E. Miller *Mélanges de littérature grecque contenant un grand nombre de textes inédits* (Paris 1868) 349–84. The fundamental work on Zenobius is Bühler 1, 4, and 5.

138 See 60 below under 'Aesop and *Aesopica*.'

letter alpha against the 159 to be found in the Zenobius collection in CPG 1. There can be little doubt that Erasmus made use of this volume when he was preparing the 1508 edition of the *Chiliades*, even though it was not until 1525 that he acquired it for his library.[139]

Proverb Collections (Modern)

APOSTOLIUS OF BYZANTIUM

Michael Apostolius (or Apostolis), with the cognomen Byzantius, indicating his origin in Constantinople, spent much of his life after the fall of that city in 1453 in Crete, though he made some trips to Italy. Among other activities he worked for Cardinal Bessarion, copying manuscripts and searching out new ones for his patron. His dates are uncertain; he was born around 1421, while the date of his death lies probably between the years 1480 and 1486. On arriving in Crete he began to gather proverbs and, like Erasmus himself, continued to add to his collection until his death.[140] Then his son Arsenius, who was born in 1468 or 1469 and died in 1535,[141] took over possession of it, and he too added to the anthology. It was a manuscript copy of Arsenius' collection that Girolamo Aleandro lent to Erasmus in 1508 in Venice when he was working on the *Chiliades* with Aldus Manutius.[142] Only a small part of the work was ever printed in Arsenius' lifetime, a selection of *Apophthegmata*, which was published in Rome in 1519.

Apostolius' collection, most accessible to modern readers in CPG 2, edited by E. Leutsch, is organized by centuries, eighteen in number. In that edition entries that were added by Arsenius to his father's work are printed in a smaller font below the main text and given a number followed by a lower-case letter. However, the manuscript used by Erasmus seems to have contained more proverbs than the manuscripts used by Leutsch.[143]

* * * * *

139 See van Gulik on Husner no 198.
140 Three manuscripts of the collection, written by Apostolius himself, survive and all differ from each other. See Bühler 1.294–6.
141 His life span coincided closely then with that of Erasmus.
142 See *Adagia* II i 1 CWE 33 14. Erasmus actually met Arsenius in person at some time during his stay in Venice (in 1508), as a letter from Arsenius to Erasmus, written in 1521, makes clear: 'the learned Muses brought us together at Venice' (Ep 1232A:11–12, CWE 8 294).
143 Some that are found in Pierre Pantin's edition of Arsenius, published in 1619, do not appear in the Apostolius collection as given in CPG, but are to be found in *Mantissa proverbiorum* (also in CPG), having been drawn by Leutsch

Erasmus uses the collection extensively,[144] but only rarely names his source on these occasions.[145] When he does refer to Apostolius either by name or indirectly, it is only to criticize him. At *Adagia* I iii 99 he describes Apostolius as 'an author whom I would not quote except for the lack of anyone better' (CWE 31 317).[146] A similar remark ('he is not a very serious authority') is made in *Adagia* II iv 66. He describes some of Apostolius' proverbs as coming 'from the common dregs' (III v 6) or 'smacking of the common herd' (III v 5) and says that he has deliberately not used some of those that Apostolius took 'from common everyday speech' (*Adagia* III iii 89). Some of the proverbs were clearly of a non-literary nature, but no less proverbial because of that. In Ep 269:71–4 Erasmus admits that the collection surpasses all others in the number of items it contains, but adds that it also surpasses them in the flaws and ignorance it shows.

BRASSICANUS

Johannes Alexander Brassicanus, born in 1500 or 1501 in Tübingen, succeeded to the chair of philology held by Johann Reuchlin in Ingolstadt after Reuchlin's death in 1522.[147] Two years later he was given the chair of rhetoric at Vienna. His first encounter with Erasmus took place in Antwerp in 1520, when he received a letter of recommendation from the Dutchman (Ep 1146), after which he enjoyed a friendly relationship with him for some years. He was best known as a poet, but he also edited some patristic authors.[148] Perhaps as a break from his more serious studies, Brassicanus put together a small collection of proverbs (123 in number, accompanied by 18 *Symbola Pythagorae*), which was published in 1529 in Vienna as *Brassicani*

* * * * *

from non-Apostolian manuscripts. See ASD II-2 71:45n (on *Adagia* I vi 43); II-2 149:452n (on *Adagia* I vii 23); II-5 255 (on *Adagia* III iv 29).

144 Stretches where Erasmus draws on Apostolius occur at III ii 89–100; III iii 2–6, 8–51, 53, 59–80, 83, 85–99; III iv 1–4, 13–42, 49–52, 54–72, 74–100; III v 2–14.

145 According to Phillips' table on the frequency of Erasmus' sources Apostolius is referred to on only six occasions. She counts only the actual occurrences of his name.

146 See also *Adagia* III iii 42, 66 and *Adagia* III i 85, though in this last instance he mentions that Poliziano himself did not grudge to cite him as a witness in one passage. He is referring to *Miscellanea* 16; see *Collectanea* 480 and notes.

147 Brassicanus is one of the interlocutors in the colloquy *Apotheosis Capnionis*, the subject of which was the supposed deification of Reuchlin (see CWE 39 244–55). This was composed immediately after Reuchlin's death. See CEBR 1:191–2.

148 Erasmus owned a copy of Brassicanus' edition of Salvianus of Marseilles (Husner no 326), published by Froben in 1530, and inserted a quotation from this work in 1533 at the end of *Adagia* III v 1 (see ASD II-5 297 and van Gulik on Husner no 326).

proverbiorum symmicta. He sent a copy to Erasmus, whose congratulations, expressed in Ep 2305, written in April 1530, were not free of criticism, since Erasmus pointed out that some of the proverbs, all of which were claimed by Brassicanus to be new, had already appeared in the *Adagia.*[149] Despite this, for the expanded edition of the *Adagia* of March 1533 Erasmus in turn drew on Brassicanus' anthology to some degree for more than thirty proverbs,[150] and did so without acknowledgment of his source.[151] It was perhaps in an effort to forestall any possible accusation of plagiarism on his part that in a letter of May 1533, written to Viglius Zuichemus (Allen Ep 2810:49–54) Erasmus maintained that for his *Symmicta* Brassicanus had taken about thirty proverbs from the *Adagia,* and complained of Brassicanus' grumpiness in his letters.

POLYDORE VERGIL

Erasmus mistakenly believed he was the first humanist to publish a collection of classical proverbs. In this endeavour he had been anticipated by Polydore Vergil of Urbino (ca 1470–1555), whose *Proverbiorum libellus* appeared in Venice in 1498, two years before the publication of the *Collectanea.*[152] Although there are considerable number of similarities shared by the two works, Erasmus does not seem to have drawn on Polydore's *libellus* for his *Collectanea* of 1500, and denies on several occasions any dependence on Polydore at that time (see 15–20 above).

Erasmus' sensitivity to the issue of plagiarism in the *Collectanea* did not restrain him, however, from drawing, at a later date, on Polydore's *libellus* in a few entries in the *Adagia,* and, as is the case with Brassicanus' collection, Erasmus never gave any acknowledgment of his source. In the expansions of the edition of 1515 one of the new proverbs is *Isthmum perfodere* 'To dig through the Isthmus' (*Adagia* IV iv 26). Since the proverbial status of this phrase seems to be attested in only one other text, Polydore's

* * * * *

149 Ep 2305:41–7. Erasmus cites *Adagia* II i 33, II iv 82, III iii 97.
150 Most of these were new proverbs (see ASD II-8 14 n46, and *Adagia* IV iii 86 CWE 36 52 n2), but some of his additions to proverbs already in the *Adagia* were also inspired by Brassicanus (see ASD II-4 305:547n). An erroneous reference of Erasmus in *Adagia* I vi 40 (to Seneca book 2 instead of Seneca book 11) may be based on a misunderstanding of Brassicanus' reference; see ASD II-2 69:33n.
151 Erasmus did not simply copy what Brassicanus had written. He usually amplified the quotations and even went far beyond Brassicanus' comments as at *Adagia* IV vii 92 and IV viii 14. At *Adagia* IV vii 65 he emends the text of the proverb itself.
152 For Polydore Vergil see CEBR 3:397–9.

Proverbiorum libellus, it seems likely that the entry was prompted by Erasmus' knowledge of this collection, even if the accompanying essay is predominantly Erasmus' own composition. At the end of *Adagia* III iv 24 'Until the north wind stops' Erasmus evokes another proverb *Cum pluit, molendum esse* 'When it rains, get on with the grinding.' He says this appears elsewhere, but it is not to be found either in the *Collectanea* or anywhere else in the *Adagia.* The source again is Polydore (no 189).[153] At a much later date, in the edition of 1528, in an addition to *Adagia* III i 87 he cites two sayings, *ubi mel, ibi fel* ('where there's honey, there's gall') and *ubi uber, ibi tuber* ('where there's a breast, there a hard swelling'). Both of these sayings occur side by side in Polydore's *libellus* (no 47).[154]

Greek Authors
Grammarians, Lexicographers, Commentators, Encyclopedists

ATHENAEUS
The Greek writer Athenaeus (AD c 170 to c 230), who hailed from Naucratis in Egypt, but who lived in Rome, was the author of a lengthy account, in fifteen books, of a fictitious banquet, entitled *Deipnosophistae* (translated in CWE as 'Doctors at Dinner'). Athenaeus used the banquet to allow the learned guests to discuss many matters relating to food and music as well as other topics, and to quote extensively from Greek literature and drama. This encyclopedic work is a priceless source for fragments of lost works and for information relating to food and drink in the ancient world. Erasmus had access to a manuscript of the *Deipnosophistae* when he was preparing the 1508 edition of the *Chiliades* in Venice,[155] but made more extensive use of the work for the edition of 1517/18, when he had at his disposal his copy of the *editio princeps* of 1514. [156]

ETYMOLOGICUM MAGNUM
From the ninth century AD onwards several etymological lexicons were compiled. The only one that appeared in print in Erasmus' lifetime was the so-called *Etymologicum magnum,* which was probably put together in the early twelfth century. This was published in 1499 in Venice, under the editorship

* * * * *

153 See ASD II-5 253:253n.
154 See ASD II-5 91:749–50n.
155 As he tells us in *Adagia* II i 1 (CWE 33 14)
156 See van Gulik on this item in Erasmus' library, mailing list no 239. See also 35–6 above.

of Zacharias Kalliergis, with an introduction written by Marcus Musurus. Erasmus' copy has survived, and is in the Jagellonian Library in Cracow. Evidence from the front and rear boards suggests that Erasmus procured the volume in Paris, either between 1500 and 1506 or after his return from Italy in 1511.[157]

EUDEMUS OF RHODES

Eudemus was a pupil of Aristotle and compiled a collection of Greek rhetorical expressions (*Lexeis rhetoricae*). Only a small part of this has ever been published.[158] Eudemus is occasionally cited in the *Suda* and Apostolius of Byzantium, but Erasmus must have had access to a manuscript of the work for most of his citations.[159]

EUSTATHIUS

Eustathius, archbishop of Thessalonica, lived in the 12th century and compiled extensive commentaries in Greek on the *Iliad* and *Odyssey*. These included a large number of proverbs which Eustathius had drawn from many classical sources, including poetry as well as prose. Phillips (397) counts 48 references to him, none of which, however, appeared in the additions of the 1533 and 1536 editions.

Eustathius is one of the authors named by Erasmus in *Adagia* II i 1 among those whom he knew from manuscripts that were made available to him when he was preparing the 1508 edition of the *Adagia* in Venice.

HARPOCRATION

Valerius Harpocration of Alexandria was a Greek grammarian, who probably lived in the second century AD. He compiled a *Lexicon of Ten Orators*,[160] in which the entries were arranged alphabetically. Although he draws on this work, Erasmus mentions him only once by name, at *Adagia* II viii 94 (in an addition made in 1523). On most occasions he conceals his real source when giving examples from Greek orators (so, for example, Hyperides and Lysias in *Adagia* IV i 83, and Antiphon in *Adagia* IV ix 75).[161] Sometimes he describes his source inaccurately as a scholiast or commentator on Demosthenes (as

* * * * *

157 See van Gulik on this item, mailing list no 277.
158 K. Rupprecht, 'Apostolis, Eudem und Suidas,' *Philologus* Supplementband xv Heft 1 (1922)
159 See *Adagia* III i 61n (CWE 34 383).
160 Sometimes referred to as *Rhetorical Dictionary* in CWE
161 See also *Adagia* IV ix 60, 64, 96; IV x 4, 12, 17, 24, 27, 35.

at *Adagia* III iii 29 and III iv 50). The reason for this error is that Harpocration's lexicon was printed as an appendix to an Aldine edition of Ulpian's scholia on Demosthenes, published in 1503.

HESYCHIUS OF ALEXANDRIA

Hesychius, who lived in the fifth century AD, compiled a Greek lexicon of rare words, which also contained many proverbs. The *editio princeps*, done by Marcus Musurus for the Aldine press, appeared in 1514, and is no 297 in Husner's mailing list of Erasmus' library. Erasmus refers to him in his introduction to the *Adagia* (see CWE 31 11) but this reference was inserted in *1517/18*, and it is probable that Hesychius was not known to Erasmus when he was preparing the edition of 1508, or even the edition of 1515. Erasmus quoted the work on about 140 occasions, most of which first appeared in the editions of 1526, 1528, and 1533.[162]

POLLUX

Julius Pollux was a Greek writer from Naucratis in Egypt who lived in the second century AD. His encyclopedia that survives in ten books (entitled *Onomasticon*) is organized by topic rather than alphabetically, and is an abridgment of the original work. It includes many citations from ancient literature and conveys much information on a disparate range of topics, including, for example, theatre, ancient music, hunting, and physiology. The *editio princeps* was produced by the Aldine press in 1502 and was in Erasmus' library (Husner no 296). There are about sixty citations of or references to the work in the *Adagia*, and Erasmus seemed to turn to it for most of the editions, although the edition of 1528 has the most examples (22), followed by the editions of 1508 (12) and 1515 (12).

STEPHANUS OF BYZANTIUM

Stephanus, whose *floruit* was the 6th century AD, compiled a geographical lexicon, which survived in the form of an epitome. Apart from the geographical information the work included mythological and religious topics. The *editio princeps* was produced by the Aldine press in 1502, and Erasmus would have had access to it for the *Chiliades* of 1508, but he also refers to Stephanus in later editions, though the work does not appear in Husner's mailing list of Erasmus' library. Since a number of proverbs have a geographical connotation, it is not surprising that Erasmus often adduces

* * * * *

162 Van Gulik on mailing list no 277, following information given him by Sir Roger Mynors. According to Phillips (398) he is mentioned by Erasmus on 123 occasions.

Stephanus' work.[163] Just fewer than half of the references to Stephanus date from the 1508 edition, while about one-quarter of them were added in *1528*. They are most frequent in the second chiliad (just more than 40% of the total).

STOBAEUS

Stobaeus, who lived in the early 5th century AD, put together an anthology of quotations from classical Greek authors. The *editio princeps* was published in 1535, too late for Erasmus to use. The *Adagia* has more than thirty citations of him and most of these appeared in the 1508 edition, having been taken from a manuscript. However, without knowing fully what he was doing, for the edition of 1533 Erasmus drew on a part of Stobaeus' work that was printed under the title *Gnomologium*, without any author being identified, alongside Callimachus' hymns in an edition produced by Froben in 1532.[164] This is no 314 in Husner's mailing list of Erasmus' library.

SUDA OR 'SUIDAS'

This huge lexicon, virtually an encyclopedia, contains about 30,000 entries, organized alphabetically. It was put together in the 10th century AD. Up to the 1930s the author of the work was thought to be a certain Suidas, but this is simply a variant of the Greek *Souda* (= *Suda*), which means something like 'fortress' and does not denote the author of the work. It contains much useful information about all aspects of the classical world, as well as many fragments of lost works by important Greek authors, and includes a good number of proverbs. Phillips (402) counts 392 references to the work in the *Adagia*, thus making it one of Erasmus' most extensively used sources. The *editio princeps* appeared in Milan in 1499 and was not available to Erasmus for the *Collectanea* of 1500. He seems to have used it for the revised edition of 1506[165] and it is possible that he owned this edition before he left for Italy. The work is no 344 in Husner's mailing list. Erasmus may also have had access to a manuscript of the *Suda*, for in the edition of 1508, at *Adagia* III vii 61, Erasmus prefers to read ξαίνεις in place of ξένεις of the *editio princeps*.[166]

* * * * *

163 See for example *Adagia* III iv 39 (relating to Psyra), IV i 7 (Tenedos), IV iv 1 (Phocis), IV vi 28 (Abdera).
164 See *Adagia* II ii 53; III i 13, 18, 63; III iii 15, 60, 75; III ix 44; IV i 1 (CWE 35 400 n2); IV v 15.
165 See 11 n28 above.
166 See ASD II-6 456–7:580n. But Erasmus would have found ξαίνεις in Zenobius (Aldus) at column 110.

Technical / Scientific Works

DIOSCORIDES

Dioscorides, a Greek physician from Asia Minor, had particular interests in pharmacology and botany. He lived in Rome in the first century AD from the reign of Nero to that of Vespasian for the last fifty or so years of his life. His pharmacological work *De materia medica*, in five books, was still held in high repute in the 16th century. Erasmus owned three copies of the work: the *editio princeps* of the original Greek text, published by the Aldine press in 1499 (Husner no 203), probably the one he ordered in 1525;[167] one containing Latin commentaries and Latin translations composed by Giambattista Egnazio and Ermolao Barbaro (Husner no 201); another Latin translation with commentary by Marcello Virgilio (Husner no 202). Most of the thirty or so references to Dioscorides in the *Adagia* first appeared either in 1508 or 1528 (the number is about the same), and there is little or no Greek in any of the quotations.

GALEN

This renowned physician, whose life straddled the second and third centuries AD, was born in Pergamon, but spent most of the second half of his life in Rome at the imperial court. The *editio princeps* of his works in the Greek language was issued by the Aldine press in 1526, in five volumes, and Erasmus received a complimentary copy from the press,[168] probably the work that is no 137 in the mailing list of his library. Most of the thirty or so quotations from this author, usually in the original Greek, made their first appearance in *1528*.

NICANDER

Nicander (3rd or 2nd century BC) composed two didactic poems that survive, the *Theriaca*, on antidotes to poisonous bites from snakes or other animals, and the *Alexipharmaca*, which dealt with poisons from other sources. Erasmus quotes directly only from the former and only in *Adagia* III i 85, where he gives two lines of the poem in Greek, a new addition of *1515*. The other few citations of this author are drawn from secondary sources such as Athenaeus (I vi 3, wrongly ascribed by Erasmus to Numenius, and IV vii 11) or Pliny the Elder (I vii 56). At *Adagia* I iv 34 in *1508* Erasmus cites a fragment of Sophocles that he seems to have taken from a scholion on

* * * * *

167 See Allen VII 547 (Appendix xx).
168 See 32–3 above.

Nicander *Theriaca* 18. Since both of Nicander's poems had been printed by the Aldine press in 1499 alongside Dioscorides (see above), he would have had ready access to the book when in Venice.

OPPIAN

Oppian (2nd century AD) wrote a didactic poem on fish and fishing, entitled *Halieutica*. Erasmus cites this in only two adages, on both occasions in Greek. At *Adagia* II i 1 (CWE 33 8) two passages are given in Greek, and ten lines of the poem are quoted at *Adagia* III v 38. Since both of these instances occur in *1508* and the *editio princeps*, by the Junta press, was not produced until 1515, Erasmus must have had access to a manuscript while in Venice, perhaps one owned by Marcus Musurus, who was responsible for the *editio princeps*. Erasmus possessed a copy of the Aldine edition of 1517 (Husner no 89).

PAUSANIAS

Pausanias, a Greek geographer, was the author of Περιήγησις τῆς Ἑλλάδος 'Description of Greece' in ten books, each of which covered a particular area of the country. His *floruit* was in the second century AD. He is named among the authors to whose works Erasmus gained access by way of manuscripts made available to him by fellow humanists (*Adagia* II i 1 CWE 33 14). The *editio princeps* was issued by the Aldine press in 1516. There are twenty-nine citations, most of which are to be found in *1508*. Only five quotations are given in Greek, three in *1508* (and therefore drawn from a manuscript)[169] and two in *1526*.[170] Erasmus owned the Aldine edition of Pausanias, which he had bound with the Aldine edition of Herodotus (Husner no 272). This is now in the British Library.

STRABO

Strabo, a Greek geographer and historian, lived in the time of Augustus and spent some time in Rome. His historical writings (forty-seven books) have not survived. His *Geographica*, in seventeen books, is cited by Erasmus on more than seventy occasions. Most of these (just over fifty) make their first appearance in *1508*, but Erasmus turned to him for later editions, especially that of 1528 (eleven new citations) and 1526 (six). Most of the quotations are given in Latin, often based on Guarino of Verona's translation, which was printed on many occasions in the 15th century and a copy

* * * * *

169 I i 90, I iv 83, and IV ii 27
170 III vii 3 and IV iv 1

of which was owned by Erasmus (Husner no 274). The *editio princeps* of the Greek text, which was not published until 1516, was ordered by Erasmus in the following year (Ep 629:17). It too appears in the mailing list of Erasmus' library (Husner no 275). Erasmus must had access to a Greek manuscript for the edition of 1508 since he sometimes quotes from the author in Greek, as he does frequently in the sequence of entries drawn from Strabo at *Adagia* II iv 42–50, 52–7.

THEOPHRASTUS

Theophrastus succeeded Aristotle as the head of the Peripatetic school and had a wide range of interests. Most of his numerous works have not survived, but two important botanical works *Historia plantarum* and *De causis plantarum* have come down to us, and Erasmus refers to or quotes from these works especially, usually drawing on the Latin translation of Theodorus Gaza. Only rarely does Erasmus draw on another extant work of Theophrastus, his *De lapidibus* (see, for example, *Adagia* I v 87); for fragments of lost works of Theophrastus he uses authors such as Plutarch, Athenaeus, and Harpocration.

The Aldine press printed Theodorus' translations of both Aristotle and Theophrastus in 1504 and again in 1513, and one of these (probably the later one)[171] was in Erasmus' library.

Rhetoric

DEMOSTHENES, HYPERIDES, LYSIAS, ANTIPHON, ISOCRATES, AESCHINES

Erasmus does not seem to have read extensively in the works of the Greek orators. The most famous of these, Demosthenes (384–322 BC), is quoted on about thirty occasions but half of these are taken indirectly from other sources and not from Demosthenes himself. The major source of these is Harpocration's *Lexicon of Ten Orators*[172] but other sources include the *Suda* and Plutarch. Erasmus quotes most often from the *First Olynthiac* when he does draw directly from the orator. None of the few references to or quotations from Lysias (c 459–c 380) or Hyperides (389–322) is drawn directly from their works, the sources including Harpocration, the *Suda*, and

* * * * *

171 So van Gulik on Husner no 211, on account of numerous new references to Aristotle in the 1515 edition of the *Adagia*
172 As at *Adagia* IV ix 60, IV ix 96, IV x 12, IV x 17

Apostolius.[173] The sole reference to Antiphon (c 480–11) at *Adagia* IV ix 75 also comes from Harpocration. Of the other orators of the fifth and fourth centuries BC Isocrates (436–338) and Aeschines (c 397–c 322) are quoted directly from their speeches. Most of the eight references to or quotations from Isocrates occur in the later editions of the *Adagia*, those of *1526* (3) and *1533* (2). Froben published an edition of his *De pace* in 1522 in a bilingual version (which also included other works by different authors), and it is perhaps no coincidence that all five references to Isocrates in *1526* and *1533* relate to this speech. There are about three dozen references to Aeschines, most of which occur in the editions of 1528 (18) and 1533 (10). There are five references in *1508* but none of these contained any Greek drawn directly from Aeschines.[174] Erasmus possessed the three-volume Aldine edition of 1513 entitled *Oratores graeci*, described as 'Orationes rhetorum 16 graece' in the mailing list (Husner no 132). This must be the volume that he ordered from Italy in 1525 (see Allen VII 547, Appendix XX). Its late acquisition accounts for the occurrence of the majority of quotations from Aeschines in *1528* and *1533*.

ARISTIDES

The Greek orator from whom Erasmus quotes most often lived much later. Aelius Aristides, an orator and rhetorician, was prominent in the Second Sophistic movement in the second century AD. Erasmus had access to a manuscript (complete with scholia) when he was preparing the 1508 edition of the *Chiliades*.[175] All the more than fifty references to and quotations from this author appear in *1508*.[176] Erasmus says that he had access to the whole of Aristides, but if so he did not make full use of the manuscript since he draws primarily from two works: *De quattuor*, an essay on four prominent Athenians (Pericles, Cimon, Miltiades, and Themistocles), and *Panathenaicus*. The sole exception to this is at *Adagia* I v 27 where he refers to Aristides' *Symmachicus*. The 1513 Aldine edition of Greek orators, just mentioned, contained two speeches of Aristides, the *Panathenaicus* and a

* * * * *

173 For Lysias see, for example, *Adagia* III iii 29, III iv 16, IV iii 71, IV x 4; for Hyperides *Adagia* II viii 94, III iv 50, III v 2.
174 At *Adagia* I ii 17 Erasmus takes the Greek from Pliny; at I iii 26, the Greek was added in *1523*.
175 *Adagia* II i 1 (CWE 33 14)
176 Two apparently later insertions at *Adagia* I i 24 (*1515*) and I ii 31 (*1517/18*) consist of material that was already present in *1508* in other adages. See CWE 31 72 n14; 31 174 n10.

panegyric of Rome, but Erasmus does not seem to have made use of either of them for the later editions of the *Adagia*.[177]

Biography

DIOGENES LAERTIUS

Diogenes Laertius, of the first half of the third century AD, is the author of a work in ten books that describes the lives and doctrines of the ancient philosophers. He is cited on more than eighty occasions in the *Adagia*.[178] The *editio princeps* of the work in Greek appeared in 1533, though the Greek text of his lives of Aristotle and Theophrastus had been printed much earlier, in volume two of the Aldine edition of Aristotle (published in 1497). Fifty of the quotations taken from Diogenes made their first appearance in 1508. For this edition Erasmus must have made use for the most part of a printed Latin translation, but he also drew on a Greek manuscript on a few occasions where he gives a quotation in Greek, as at I vi 50, I vii 63, I vii 68.[179] Very few quotations were added in the succeeding editions until 1526, when seventeen new ones are to be found. For this Erasmus used a Latin edition of Diogenes that had been published in 1524, being a reworking by Valentinus Curio of the earlier Latin versions. Erasmus owned a copy of this volume (Husner no 305), which has survived.[180] The *editio princeps* of the original Greek text appeared in 1533 in Basel, and Erasmus possessed a copy of this as well (Husner no 304, on which see van Gulik), making use of it when he added another dozen citations to his edition of the *Adagia* of that year.[181]

PHILOSTRATUS

Flavius Philostratus, born c AD 170, was the author of *Life of Apollonius of Tyana* and *Lives of the Sophists*. The former was published in Greek in 1504 by the Aldine Press, and in the first two editions of the *Adagia* Erasmus

* * * * *

177 Van Gulik (on Husner no 132) suggests that it was not purchased until 1525. The *editio princeps* of Aristides was produced by Philip Junta in Florence in 1517.
178 Phillips (396) gives the number as 78.
179 On the Latin translations of Diogenes Laertius see ASD II-2 231:40–41n.
180 It is now in the library of Yale University; see van Gulik on Husner no 305.
181 As, for example, at II iii 79 and IV x 64

quotes a dozen examples in Greek from it, ten in *1508* and two in *1515*. Most of his quotations from the *Lives of the Sophists* occur first in *1533*, ten in number, there being only two in *1508*. Erasmus also quotes from the *Imagines* on a few occasions.[182]

Major Literary Authors

The three Greek literary authors on whom Erasmus draws most are Homer, Aristophanes, and Plutarch.[183]

HOMER

Homer provides one of the more surprising sections of the *Adagia*. For two full centuries (III viii and III ix) and most of a third (III x 2–75) Erasmus gives quotations from Homer's *Iliad* (III viii 1–III ix 35)[184] and *Odyssey* (III ix 36–III x 74) that were used, in his view, as proverbial expressions. This section and its content seem, for the most part, at odds with the nature of the adage as defined by Erasmus himself. What, for instance, is the evidence that many of these quotations satisfy the criterion of common, public usage?[185]

ARISTOPHANES

For Aristophanes Erasmus used the *editio princeps* that was edited by Marcus Musurus for the Aldine press and published in Venice in 1498. It is no 116 in Husner's mailing-list. It came equipped with scholia, of which Erasmus made good use. Since this edition lacked the *Lysistrata* and the *Thesmophoriazusae*, which were published for the first time in an appendix of the Junta edition of 1515/1516, Erasmus' references to these two plays were drawn

* * * * *

182 At *Adagia* I ii 16, II i 39 and 40, IV ii 25. It is possible that the *Imagines* is the work of a different member of the Philostrati family. See n196 below.

183 Phillips (Appendix III) gives the number of references to these three authors as 666, 596 and 618 respectively. However, the last number for Plutarch also includes references to the proverb collections that are erroneously ascribed to this author.

184 With the exceptions of III viii 2 and III viii 6, which are drawn from the *Odyssey*, though Erasmus' sources may have been Lucian and Aulus Gellius respectively.

185 There is no doubt that some literary quotations become so familiar that they pass into common usage and become proverbial, their literary provenance being forgotten or unknown, but that is rarely the case here.

from a manuscript[186] or from the Junta edition.[187] Throughout his life Erasmus turned frequently to this author. In the 1533 edition of the *Adagia*, for example, he included about forty quotations from Aristophanes in the new additional material, primarily from the *Knights* and the *Birds*.

PLUTARCH

The *editio princeps* of Plutarch's *Moralia* was published by the Aldine press in 1509, and Erasmus tells us that the printing of the work had begun just about when he was completing his material for the 1508 edition of the *Adagia*.[188] Erasmus' copy of the edition has survived, now being in the Provincial Library of Friesland at Leeuwarden.[189] This library also possesses Erasmus' Aldine edition of Plutarch's *Lives* that appeared in 1519 and was probably acquired by Erasmus around 1525.[190]

PLATO

After these three the next most popular Greek author favoured by Erasmus in the *Adagia* is Plato, the Greek author most frequently quoted and cited in the *Collectanea*, though never in the original Greek. For the *Collectanea* Erasmus used primarily the Latin translation of Marsilio Ficino.[191] For the *Adagia*, where he is cited on 428 occasions, according to Phillips (400), Erasmus usually quotes in Greek, drawing on a manuscript for the edition of 1508. The *editio princeps* was issued by the Aldine press in 1513 and is no 218 in Husner's mailing-list of Erasmus' library.[192] Erasmus repeatedly turns to

* * * * *

186 At *Adagia* II x 13 Erasmus writes (in *1508*): 'The adage is mentioned by Aristophanes in the *Lysistrata*. This is not to be found among the published plays, but I have read it in manuscript' (CWE 34 133). For the *Lysistrata* see ASD II-4 265:24n and II-4 287:148n.

187 He refers to the *Lysistrata* in *Adagia* II ix 82 and II x 52, in both cases in the edition of 1523. At *Adagia* III ii 22 Erasmus adds a quotation from the *Thesmophoriazusae* in *1526*. The Juntine edition does not seem to have been in Erasmus' library. If he did not actually possess it, he may have used Bonifacius Amerbach's copy of this edition, now in the library of the University of Basel: see ASD II-5 119:319n (on *Adagia* III ii 22).

188 *Adagia* II i 1 CWE 33 14

189 See van Gulik on Husner no 208.

190 See van Gulik on Husner no 267.

191 See Maria Cytowska, 'Erasme de Rotterdam et Marsile Ficin son maître,' *Eos* 63 (1975) 165–79.

192 Van Gulik (on no 218) thinks that this is a book he ordered in 1525 (see Allen VII 547 Appendix xx), though it seems extremely strange, given his fondness

this author in the successive editions of the *Adagia*; there are, for example, over thirty citations in the new material that was added in *1533*.

ARISTOTLE

Aristotle is adduced by Erasmus in the *Adagia* less frequently than Plato, but is still a considerable presence in the work, being cited on just over 300 occasions. Erasmus owned the *editio princeps*, published in five volumes by the Aldine Press over a period of four years (1495 to 1498),[193] but he does not seem to have acquired them until 1525 or 1526 when he ordered them to be sent from Venice (Husner no 214, on which see van Gulik).[194] He also owned the edition of Johan Bebel that appeared in 1531 (Husner no 215), for which he wrote a lengthy introduction. Erasmus draws from virtually the whole Aristotelian corpus, the scientific as well as the philosophical and rhetorical parts. He refers to a manuscript of Aristotle's *Rhetoric* with scholia in *Adagia* II i 1 (CWE 33 14).

LUCIAN

It is no surprise that Erasmus was attracted to the 2nd-century-AD satirist Lucian, whose prose dialogues were a strong influence on Erasmus for his *Colloquies*. Indeed, one of his earliest works, co-authored by Sir Thomas More, was a collection of Latin translations of a number of Lucian's dialogues, published by Josse Bade in Paris in late 1506.[195] For these translations Erasmus used the 1503 Aldine edition of Lucian's *Opera*,[196] as is demonstrated by M.H.H. Engels of the Provincial Library of Friesland at Leeuwarden,[197] which holds Erasmus' personal and annotated copy. Phillips (399) counts 335 references to or quotations from Lucian in the *Adagia*, most of them occurring in the first chiliad. The reason for this concentration may be that Erasmus drew on Lucian while he was preparing the new and expanded version of his *Collectanea*, either in Bologna in 1506–7 or even earlier.

* * * * *

for Plato, if Erasmus did not have this Aldine volume in his library before then. Van Gulik suggests that the book he ordered in 1525 is now in the Royal Library in the Hague.

193 Now in the Cathedral Library at Wells in England
194 Allen VII Appendix xx
195 See CWE 39 xxviii and xlvi n28.
196 This also contained some works by Philostratus, the sophist of the second or third century AD, including the *Lives of the Sophists* and the *Imagines*.
197 See van Gulik on Husner no 123.

EURIPIDES, SOPHOCLES, AESCHYLUS

Of the Greek tragedians Euripides is by far the most fruitful source for the *Adagia*.[198] As is the case with Lucian, there is a heavy concentration of Euripidean quotations in the first chiliad,[199] again probably indicative that much of what was to appear in that chiliad was based on what Erasmus worked on while residing in Bologna with Paulo Bombace. After Euripides, Erasmus favoured Sophocles, with somewhat more than half the number of Euripidean references.[200] The references to Aeschylus, an author who does not appear in the mailing list of Erasmus' books, amount to only one-sixth of the number for Euripides. The figures given by Phillips for Aeschylus are misleading, however. Almost two-thirds of the quotations from the dramatist in the first two chiliads are actually drawn at second hand from authors such as Stobaeus, Pollux, and Aristophanes (particularly the *Frogs*).

PINDAR

The only other two Greek literary figures of note that are used by Erasmus to a significant degree are Pindar and Theocritus.[201] Pindar, the famous lyric poet of the 5th century BC, is named among the authors whose works were made available to Erasmus in manuscript form while he was in Venice,[202] and some fifty or so quotations occur in the 1508 edition. However, most of the quotations, amounting to 176 in all according to Phillips (400), were added in the editions of 1526 and 1533. Erasmus possessed a copy of the splendid edition of Zacharias Kalliergis that was published, with scholia, in Rome in 1515 (Husner no 105), probably acquiring it in 1518.[203] Erasmus' renewed engagement with the author for the 1526 edition of the *Adagia* may have been prompted by the preparation of a new edition of Pindar under-

* * * * *

198 Erasmus published Latin translations of Euripides *Hecuba* and *Iphigeneia in Aulis*, first with Josse Bade in 1506, then with Aldus Manutius in December of 1507 (see 20 above).
199 Phillips (397) counts 200 references to Euripides, of which 112 are to be found in the first chiliad.
200 Phillips (401) counts 115 for Sophocles. Thirty-nine of these, taken directly from the *Antigone* and the *Electra*, appeared among the adages that first appeared in the 1533 edition. Another three were drawn from Stobaeus and a scholion of Aristophanes.
201 Phillips (400 and 402) counts 176 references to and quotations from Pindar, and 150 for Theocritus.
202 'Pindar, with accurate commentary': *Adagia* II i 1 CWE 33 14
203 Ep 642:5

taken in 1525 by the printer Andreas Cratander in Basel, where Erasmus was residing at this time.[204]

THEOCRITUS

There are four copies of Theocritus, the bucolic poet of the 3rd century BC, in the mailing list of Erasmus' library, testimony to a continuing interest of his in this author. The second edition of the *Collectanea* of 1506 included two new adages, in Greek, drawn from Theocritus (*Collectanea* 823 and 824), an author not mentioned in the 1500 edition, and Erasmus probably took them from the 1496 Aldine edition of Theocritus,[205] which also contained Hesiod, *sententiae* of Theognis (on whom see below under 'minor authors'), and a collection of *gnomai* taken from different authors, including Menander (see below).[206] As for the *Adagia*, I count 157 citations, all but three of which are confined to four editions: *1508* (74), *1515* (24, note especially the run of citations from IV iv 8 to IV iv 24), *1526* (36, only nine of which appear in the new adages of that edition), and *1533* (20). In 1518 Erasmus acquired the 1516 edition of Zacharias Kalliergis (Husner no 98), which included, for the first time, the accompanying scholia, and he refers to these on several occasions, especially in *1526*.[207]

HESIOD

The poet Hesiod, whose dates are uncertain but who is generally thought to have lived around 700 BC, is cited by Erasmus on about ninety occasions. Of the two best-known of his poems, the *Works and Days* and the *Theogony*, it is the former to which Erasmus primarily turns. Well over fifty quotations from the poet are to be found in *1508*, to which another two dozen were added in *1515*. The comparatively few quotations in later editions tend to be taken indirectly, from other authors such as Aristotle (IV viii 34) or from ancient scholia attached to authors such as Pindar

* * * * *

204 See 34 above.
205 This volume appears in the mailing list as no 294, but it is uncertain at what date Erasmus obtained it. The other three editions owned by Erasmus are Husner nos 98, 99, and 106.
206 Erasmus refers to these writers sometimes as *gnomologoi*, because of the gnomic content of much of their one-liners.
207 As at II ii 49, II iv 22, and II vi 11. Even in *1508* Erasmus refers to the scholia (as at II i 86 and IV i 27), where he must have drawn his information from a manuscript containing them. He refers to such a manuscript in II i i (CWE 33 14).

(II iii 56, IV viii 69) or Aeschines (V i 76). Even the verse of Hesiod that provided the heading for one of the latest of the large essays, 'Not even an ox would be lost' (IV v 1), added in *1526*, was taken from Columella. Hesiod, then, was one of Erasmus' early favourites, but the *Adagia* gives little evidence that he turned to this author for further study after the edition of 1515.[208]

CALLIMACHUS

The hymns of the Hellenistic scholar-poet Callimachus (born c 310 BC) were certainly well known to and studied by the fifteenth-century humanists, the most conspicuous indication of that being Angelo Poliziano's Latin translation of Hymn 5. Erasmus, who owned a copy of the 1532 Froben edition of the hymns, quoted or cited Callimachus on fifteen occasions in the *Adagia*, but with one possible exception he quotes the poet by way of secondary sources such as the *Suda*, the scholia on Theocritus and Aristophanes, or Athenaeus. His only direct access may have been with an epigram ascribed to Callimachus in the Greek Anthology (*Anthologia Palatina* 5.6), quoted in *Adagia* II iv 90, but it is more probable that he drew the quotation from the collection of *gnomai*, taken mostly from Stobaeus, that were printed in the just-mentioned 1532 edition of Callimachus.[209]

MENANDER

It may be apposite to adduce here another literary figure of the Hellenistic period, the New Comedy poet Menander (died circa 291 BC), of whose plays substantial parts did not come to light until the twentieth century. Erasmus cites Menander on more than sixty quotations and by far the majority of these are drawn from sources such as Stobaeus, Plutarch, and the *Suda*. Only a dozen or so are drawn directly from the collection of *gnomai* in the 1496 edition of Theocritus, and these are not identified by Erasmus as coming from Menander.[210]

* * * * *

208 The edition of 1515 shows signs that Erasmus mined this author for material. See the sequence of adages drawn from Hesiod at IV iii 85–9 and IV iv 4–6, added in this edition.

209 The citation occurs at Stobaeus 3.28.9. In fact it was the *Planudean Anthology*, not the *Anthologia Palatina*, that was available in print in the early 15th century. For other use Erasmus made of the *Gnomologium* in the edition of Callimachus see 33, 47 above.

210 See *Adagia* III i 83 nn2 and 5 (CWE 34 386), III i 100 n7 (CWE 34 389); IV ii 35 n2 (CWE 35 522), IV iv 63 n4 (CWE 36 104), and IV v 9 n1 (CWE 36 144).

Greek Historians

HERODOTUS

Herodotus, the earliest of the Greek historians whose work has survived, wrote a history in nine books that leads up to the great clash between Persians and Greeks in the early decades of the fifth century. His dates are uncertain, but his life span may have covered much of that century (480?– 420?). Erasmus cites him on just under sixty occasions (only nine times, according to my count, in *1508*), but usually not in Greek.[211] More often Erasmus paraphrases in Latin what Herodotus recounts about something relating to a proverb and the accompanying discussion. Erasmus owned the *editio princeps* of the original Greek text, published by the Aldine press in 1502.[212] He also owned the Latin translation of the history by Lorenzo Valla,[213] a mistake in whose translation Erasmus refers to in *Adagia* II i 43.

THUCYDIDES

The other great historian of the fifth century, Thucydides, is virtually ignored. His history of the Peloponnesian War is cited on just over half a dozen occasions, mostly in the later editions (*1528* and later). Sometimes Erasmus gives quotations in Greek or in Latin translation with Greek components (I x 27, II ix 72, IV v 40). Erasmus owned the *editio princeps*, published by the Aldine press in 1502 (Husner no 278), but it is not certain when he acquired it.[214] The same is true of a copy of Lorenzo Valla's translation of Thucydides.[215]

XENOPHON

Xenophon (c 428/7–c 354) was a prolific author, writing on a wide range of topics. These included a history entitled *Hellenica* covering events from

* * * * *

211 I count 17 instances where he gives at least some Greek. A dozen of these occur in the later editions (*1523* and later). But he quotes in Greek in *1508* at II i 55.
212 He gave away a copy of this publication to a friend in 1518 but then purchased another one which was bound with the Aldine edition of Pausanias (Husner no 272). Erasmus' copy of this two-author volume is now in the British Library.
213 Van Gulik, on Husner no 311, identifies the volume owned by Erasmus as the 1510 Paris edition published by Jean Petit.
214 See van Gulik on Husner no 278.
215 This is listed by Husner as no 406, seemingly bound with two other works, an edition of the *Adagia* and a copy of Martin Luther's *Enchiridion pro pueris instituendis*; see van Gulik on this item.

411 to 362 BC. Erasmus seems to quote only twice from this work, in *Adagia* I i 60 in *1523*, and III v 59 in *1526*. The rest of the dozen or so quotations are taken from non-historical works such as the *Symposium* or the quasi-historical *Cyropaedeia*. Erasmus possessed a copy of Xenophon in the original Greek (Husner no 204), probably the Aldine edition of 1525, which he ordered that same year.[216] Most of the quotations appear first in *1533*.

Minor Authors

AELIAN

Claudius Aelian (c AD 170–235) taught rhetoric at Rome but composed in Greek. He published collections of anecdotes of a striking nature, *De natura animalium*, concerned as the title suggests with the animal kingdom, and *Varia historia*, the subjects of which were humans rather than animals. There are at least sixteen references to Aelian in the *Adagia* but several of these were gleaned by way of other sources such as Apostolius or the *Suda*. *Adagia* II i 44 is exceptional, if not unique, in that the original Greek is quoted. The text was presumably taken from a manuscript that Erasmus had access to when in Venice preparing the *Chiliades*. The *editio princeps* of the Greek texts did not appear until 1556.

AESOP AND *AESOPICA*

Erasmus draws on fable-literature both as a source of proverbs and as a way of explaining a proverb's meaning. So in *Adagia* III ii 98 'Shadows instead of substance' he quotes the verses of 'a certain Gabrias' that describe how a dog barked at its own reflection in a stream and thereby lost the piece of meat it had in its mouth. The name Gabrias (an error for Babrius) is found in the Aldine edition of 1505 that included a collection of fables ascribed to the famous fabulist Aesop[217] and a life of Aesop, as well as the fables credited to Gabrias.[218] A handful of references or quotations relate to Gabrias, though he is not always cited as Erasmus' source.[219] Erasmus draws from Aesop on about three dozen occasions, not always, however,

* * * * *

216 See Allen VII 547 Appendix xx.
217 Little of what is known of Aesop is certain; his *floruit* may be dated to the first half of the sixth century BC.
218 A more important part of the volume, as far as the *Adagia* is concerned, was a vast collection of proverbs (see 40–1 above).
219 He is named at *Adagia* IV i 96 and IV ii 40, but not in *Adagia* III v 8 and III vi 91.

naming him. A third of these are actually drawn from secondary sources such as Gellius (as at II ii 40 and IV i 42) or the scholia of Aristophanes (as at II vi 27 and III iii 67).

Erasmus used the 1505 Aldine edition in Venice when he was preparing the expanded *Chiliades*, but does not seem to have acquired this particular volume (Husner no 198) until much later.[220]

ALCIPHRON

Alciphron, a writer of the 2nd or 3rd century AD, composed fictitious letters purporting to be by Athenians living in the 4th century BC. They are interesting in that they often reflect aspects of New Comedy, particularly Menander. There are only seven quotations in the *Adagia*, all in the original Greek, and taken from the second of two volumes of letters published by the Aldine press in 1499 under the supervision of Marcus Musurus.[221] All but two of these appear first in *1508*. The exceptions occur in *Adagia* IV viii 20 and IV x 6 (both added in *1533*).

LYCOPHRON

The dates of Lycophron, a Greek poet, have been a subject of great dispute, ranging from a birth date in the late 4th century BC to a *floruit* in the 2nd century of that era. The sole surviving work, *Alexandra*, is a long dramatic monologue, in which, at great length, a slave reports to Priam a speech of Cassandra. It was first printed in 1513 in a volume that also contained Pindar, the hymns of Callimachus and Dionysius Periegetes. The *editio princeps* of Tzetzes' scholia on the poem appeared in 1546. The half-dozen references to the work or its scholia appear in *1508* and must have been drawn from a manuscript to which Erasmus had access in Venice.[222]

THEOGNIS

The work of Theognis, an elegiac poet of the sixth century BC, has come down to us in a collection of nearly 1400 lines, some of which, however, are

* * * * *

220 See van Gulik on Husner no 198.
221 This was entitled *Epistolae diversorum philosophorum, oratorum, rhetorum sex et viginti*. This volume included letters by Synesius, Aelian, and Dionysius, as well as by Alciphron. See van Gulik on Husner no 320, which he believes may refer to the two volumes, bound as one.
222 A reference to Lycophron in an adage added in *1528* (IV vii 19) was taken from Stephanus of Byzantium.

not by Theognis. A selection of verses from the surviving work was printed in the Aldine edition of Theocritus, published in 1496, an edition owned by Erasmus.[223] Of the more than forty quotations in the *Adagia* almost all are to be found in the edition of 1508.

Christian Writers

IRENAEUS

The handful of quotations from Irenaeus, bishop of Lyons (c 130–200) all make their first appearance in the edition of *1528*. Although Irenaeus wrote in Greek, his works have survived only in translation. Just as Erasmus' use of Tertullian is linked to the *editio princeps* of the whole corpus of Tertullian done by Beatus Rhenanus in 1521, so the four citations of Irenaeus[224] must be linked to Erasmus' own *editio princeps* of the Latin version of Irenaeus' *Adversus haereses*, which appeared in 1526. In fact, one of these (*Adagia* IV v 44) provides the sole evidence for a new proverb 'Neither inside nor outside.'

JOHN CHRYSOSTOM

From 1525 to 1533 Erasmus was very much occupied with the works of John Chrysostom (347–407), archbishop of Constantinople, editing and translating several of them during that period. He edited the *Opera* (in Latin) in 1530. Most of the twenty or so quotations from this author make their first appearance in *1528* or *1533*, and the majority of these are in Greek.

PROCOPIUS OF GAZA

Letters of this rhetorician and theologian of the 5th / 6th century AD appeared in the two-volume collection of letters that was published by the Aldine press in 1499. This work was in Erasmus' library (see above on Alciphron). Erasmus quotes from these letters on four occasions.[225]

SYNESIUS

Synesius (c AD 370–413) was a Christian Neoplatonist and was elected bishop of Ptolemais (Libya) near the end of his life. He composed hymns and rhetorical discourses, but it was his letters with which Erasmus was most familiar.[226] There are a dozen or so references to them, mostly in

* * * * *

223 See 57 above.
224 *Adagia* I viii 58, I ix 37, II vi 51, IV v 44
225 *Adagia* I iii 52, I vii 29, I ix 92 (all in *1508*) and *Adagia* II iv 90 (in *1526*)
226 Some of these had been published in 1499 (see n221 above).

Greek and almost all in the edition of 1508.[227] The other work which Erasmus quotes from on a few occasions is *Encomium calvitii* 'Praise of Baldness.' This he knew from a Latin translation that was printed in Froben's 1515 edition of *Praise of Folly.*[228]

Latin Authors
Grammarians, Lexicographers, Encyclopedists, Commentators

FESTUS

Sextus Pompeius Festus, a grammarian living perhaps in the late 2nd century AD, made an epitome of a work of one of the greatest of Augustan scholars, Marcus Verrius Flaccus, *De verborum significatu*. This dictionary seems to have focused primarily on the works of early Latin writers. Festus' epitome was in turn epitomized by Paul the Deacon in the time of Charlemagne, and it is Paul the Deacon's version that constitutes most of what we now have of Festus' work. However, a damaged and fragmentary manuscript containing part of Festus' own epitome, rather than that of Paul the Deacon, survived into the fifteenth century, the codex Farnesianus (= Naples iv.a.3), and this manuscript or a close relative of it was known to Erasmus.[229] Erasmus owned two editions of Festus. One is Husner no 286 and the other, Husner no 384, is almost certainly the 1513 Aldine edition of Perotti's *Cornucopiae*. In addition to Festus' epitome both of these, like many other early editions of Festus, also contained the related works of Nonius Marcellus and Marcus Terentius Varro.[230] Of the just over eighty references to or quotations from Festus in the *Adagia* most (37) first appeared in 1515,[231] but a disproportionately large number (28) first appeared in 1533, most occurring in the 488 new entries that are to be found in this edition.[232]

NONIUS MARCELLUS

Nonius Marcellus compiled a kind of encyclopedia in twenty books, drawing his information and quotations from many sources, including ancient commentaries, grammatical treatises, and literary works, many of which did

* * * * *

227 A brief reference to Synesius is added to I ix 58 in the edition of 1536.
228 See CWE 34 413 n1 on *Adagia* III iii 29.
229 *Adagia* IV iv 52 (CWE 36 96 n3)
230 Erasmus refers to the Aldine edition at *Adagia* v i 59 and v i 78.
231 This suggests that Erasmus already owned the Aldine edition of 1513 of Perotti and the other works while preparing for the edition of 1515.
232 The rest occur in *1508* (11) *1526* (3) *1520* (1) and *1528* (1). Phillips' count of references to Festus (Appendix III p 397) is 79 for the whole work, of which she counts 20 in the 488 adages added in *1533*.

not survive into the medieval period. This work is therefore of consider-able value. It was entitled *De compendiosa doctrina* 'A compendium of learn-ing.' He lived probably at the beginning of the fourth century AD. Of the just under seventy quotations of or references to the work in the *Adagia*, 31 appear for the first time in *1533*, almost all in the new proverbs in that edi-tion. In *1508* the number of references or quotations is 15, in *1515* it is 17. On Erasmus' own copies of the work see on Festus (above).

VARRO

Marcus Terentius Varro was a polymath who lived at the end of the Roman republic (116–27 BC). Almost all of his many works have been lost,[233] and only about a quarter of his *De lingua latina* (books 5–10) has come down to us. Erasmus makes greatest use of this work of Varro in the first chiliad of the edition of *1508* (I count thirteen citations in the first two chiliads, ten in the first and three in the second, and all but one of these appears in *1508*). This suggests that Erasmus worked on Varro as a source for his expanded edition of the *Collectanea* either in Italy before his visit to Venice or even before he went to that country.[234] On the only virtually complete work to survive, his *De re rustica*, see 66 below.

AULUS GELLIUS

This writer of the 2nd century AD put together a large number of short es-says organized in twenty books, the work bearing the title *Noctes Atticae* ('Attic nights'). The topics of this encyclopedic work range widely, and include philology, philosophy, religion, history, literary and textual criti-cism, and ancient law. It is valuable in that it provides many fragments of works, both Greek and Latin, that have not survived, and this was an important source for the *Collectanea*, particularly with respect to Greek quotations. Erasmus continued to use Gellius for the *Adagia*, most fre-quently in the first chiliad, which contains 61 of the 112 occurrences as counted by Phillips (395), but not to the same extent as he had in the *Collectanea*.

Erasmus owned more than one edition of the work. It is the 1509 Venice edition of Johan de Tridino that appears in the mailing-list of his library,

* * * * *

233 The greatest loss is his encyclopedic work *Antiquitates rerum humanarum et div-inarum*, in 41 or 45 books, even though some of its content has trickled down to us through later writers. Erasmus cites this, by way of Aulus Gellius, at II viii 55.
234 See 23–4 above.

but he had previously bought a much older edition in Siena (probably in early 1509).[235]

MACROBIUS
Ambrosius Theodosius Macrobius, whose *floruit* is about AD 400, wrote a work, the *Saturnalia*, that has similarities with Athenaeus' *Deipnosophistae*. It is the account of a supposed discussion among several learned men on historical, literary, and philological topics. Virgilian criticism is an important theme of the work, in which many authors are cited by the participants. Like the *Deipnosophistae*, the *Saturnalia* provides fragments of works that have been lost, though they are less numerous than those given by Athenaeus. About two-thirds of the forty-five or so references to this author appeared in *1508*, but Erasmus continued to use Macrobius in most of the subsequent editions, even including one reference to him in *1536* (*Adagia* I x 71).

ANCIENT COMMENTATORS
Erasmus also drew on several ancient commentaries on important classical authors that have come down to us: Donatus on Terence, Servius on Virgil, Pseudo-Acron and Porphyrion on Horace, Asconius on Cicero. These will be referred to under the authors that are the subject of their commentary.

Technical / Scientific Works

PLINY THE ELDER
Pliny the Elder was a prolific writer of the 1st century AD, but only thirty-seven books of his *Naturalis historia* have come down to us. This is a valuable account of many aspects of the ancient world – astronomy, zoology, botany, geography, and mineralogy among others, and he is an author that Erasmus makes considerable use of in the *Adagia*. Among Latin writers he is surpassed only by Cicero, Plautus, and Horace in the number of times he is cited.

At least two of three Froben editions of the work, published in 1525, 1530, and 1535, were in Erasmus' library (Husner nos 205 and 207).[236] The

* * * * *

235 See van Gulik on Husner no 281.
236 A third copy of Pliny's work is mentioned as no 412 in the the mailing list. This may be a duplicate copy of one of the others, but it is possible that Erasmus owned all three of the Froben editions of 1525, 1530, and 1535 (see van Gulik on Husner no 205).

edition that he used before the Froben editions was that of de Zanis, published in Venice in 1496, now in the library of the University of Basel (Inc. 483). He gave this volume to his godson, Erasmius Froben. Erasmus also owned a copy of Ermolao Barbaro's famous *Castigationes Plinianae*, devoted primarily to rescuing the text from the pervasive corruption that bedevilled it (Husner no 279). Erasmus had already drawn from this work when working on the *Collectanea* of 1500, probably using a borrowed copy.

VARRO, CATO, COLUMELLA, PALLADIUS

Three works from antiquity on the topic of agriculture, Varro's *De re rustica*, in three books, the *De agri cultura* by Marcus Porcius Cato (234–149 BC), and the *De re rustica* (in twelve books) of Columella, a writer of the early imperial era, were often printed together in editions of the 15th and 16th centuries. Such a composite volume (*Scriptores rei rusticae* 'Writers on agriculture') was in Erasmus' library (Husner no 324); this also contained Pomponio Leto's commentary on Columella, the work on agriculture by the late-empire writer Palladius,[237] and notes by Filippo Beroaldo.[238]

Of these works Columella's is cited by Erasmus most often: twenty-four occasions, of which nine (all from book ten) appear first in *1528*.[239] Next comes Varro (thirteen in the first two chiliads, where Varro is adduced most often),[240] while Erasmus draws on Cato's work on only six occasions.[241]

POMPONIUS MELA, VEGETIUS, VITRUVIUS

In this category of technical / scientific writings there are a few other works which Erasmus uses, but only occasionally. Pomponius Mela, who was a contemporary of the emperor Claudius, wrote three books on geography

* * * * *

237 Erasmus seems to have quoted from Palladius on only one occasion, in *Adagia* II iii 41, where he quotes the proverb 'Necessity knows no holidays' from Palladius 1.6.7.
238 Van Gulik (on Husner no 304) thinks that Erasmus' volume is most probably the 1504 edition printed in Bologna, and not the Juntine edition of 1521, as suggested in ASD II-5 223:370n. Erasmus borrows a quotation from Leto's commentary and includes it in the 1533 edition of the *Adagia*.
239 Most of the others appear first in *1508* (5) and *1515* (4).
240 See Phillips 402. Of the total citations from Varro (64) forty-two are to be found in the first two chiliads. It should be noted that Erasmus also draws on the fragments of one of Varro's literary works, his Menippean satires, by way of authors such as Nonius Marcellus and Gellius.
241 Only one of these is to be found in *1508*. Two make their first appearance in *1526*, and three in *1533*. More often (on thirteen occasions) Erasmus cites fragments of Cato's lost works by way of authors such as Gellius and Festus.

entitled *De chorographia*. Erasmus cites him on four occasions.[242] Vegetius, of the 4th / 5th centuries, was the author of a handbook on military tactics, *De re militari*, and Erasmus cites him a few times, sometimes as Modestus, the name under which the work circulated in the 15th century. The work was sometimes printed in editions of Cicero, and this gave rise to the belief that Cicero was the author of the work.[243] Vitruvius, the writer on architecture from the Augustan period provides only one quotation (I ix 34, added in 1528).

Legal Texts

THE *DIGEST* AND GRATIAN

In the *Collectanea* Erasmus refers on some occasions to the *Digest* (see, for example, C 12 and 14), but he almost always draws them indirectly by way of other humanists, especially Angelo Poliziano. In the *Adagia* he cites not only the *Digest* but also, though much less frequently, the other works that were part of the consolidation by the emperor Justinian (AD 527–68), the *Codex Justinianus* and the *Institutiones*. By far the greatest number of legal citations occurs in 1533, in which Erasmus draws often from Alciati and makes use of suggestions offered by Boniface Amerbach.[244] Erasmus also quotes from Gratian's *Decretum* (*Corpus iuris canonici*), again drawing from Alciati's *De verborum significatione*.[245]

Rhetoric

QUINTILIAN

Because of Erasmus' interest in rhetoric and education it is no surprise that he knew well the work in twelve books of Quintilian (1st century AD) entitled *Institutio oratoria*, which dealt first of all with the education of the young and then in much greater detail the acquisition of oratorical skills.[246] In the *Adagia* the work is cited on more than eighty occasions. These appear predominantly in the first two chiliads, and most of them make their first

* * * * *

242 *Adagia* I ii 44, I vi 14, I ix 62, IV vi 28. The first three appeared in 1508, the last in 1526.

243 There are half a dozen quotations from Vegetius / Modestus, three in 1515 and three in 1526. A seventh example (*Adagia* V i 73, added in 1533) is wrongly attributed to Cicero; see CWE 36 583 (n1 on the adage).

244 See ASD II-8 14 nn48–50, *Adagia* IV ix 1n (CWE 36 419).

245 See *Adagia* IV viii 21 and 25.

246 Quintilian was an important source for several works of Erasmus, including *De copia* (see ASD I-6 8–9) and *De ratione studii* (see ASD I-2 102–4).

appearance in *1508*. This suggests that Erasmus had drawn extensively on Quintilian when he was planning the new edition of the *Collectanea* either on his arrival in Italy in the fall of 1506 or even before his trip to Italy. Erasmus often refers to this author by his *nomen* Fabius.

CICERO
The works on rhetoric by Marcus Tullius Cicero, the great orator of the Republic, were also widely used by Erasmus (see below).

VALERIUS MAXIMUS
Valerius Maximus composed his *Facta et dicta memorabilia* 'Memorable Doings and Sayings' in nine books, and this may be included in the category of rhetoric, since the author's purpose was to provide a kind of handbook of illustrative examples that orators could use. The collection was published in the reign of Tiberius, to whom the preface is addressed. Ten of the two dozen or so quotations drawn from the work make their first appearance in *1508*, but Erasmus reverts to it for the edition of 1533, in which we find six quotations. This quasi-historical and anecdotal work was extremely popular in the Renaissance and was frequently printed from c 1470 onwards. This makes it difficult to identify precisely the volume in Erasmus' library (no 298 in Husner's mailing list) described as 'Valerius Maximus cum commento.'

Major Literary Authors

CICERO
The classical author on whom Erasmus drew by far the most for the *Adagia* was the orator Cicero. Given the size of the Ciceronian corpus and the fact that much of it, particularly the speeches and the correspondence, lent itself to the use of proverbs, this is not altogether surprising. His rhetorical works, such as *Orator* and *De oratore,* were also frequently used. Phillips counts just under nine hundred references to and quotations from this author. Cicero was an important source for Erasmus in all the editions of his collection of proverbs, starting with the *Collectanea*[247] of 1500 and continuing to what may be regarded as virtually the final edition of the *Adagia,* the edition of 1533.[248] Erasmus made some use of the ancient fragmentary commentary of

* * * * *

247 See 10 n21 above.
248 For example, Cicero is the predominant source at *Adagia* IV ix 12–23, 29–32 and 39–53, a series in which individual adages often have several Ciceronian quotations. See also 37 above.

Asconius Pedianus (first century AD) on some of the speeches, particularly for the Verrines (as at IV ix 42), though this part of the commentary is not thought to be the work of Asconius.[249]

PLAUTUS

Of other Latin authors Plautus and Horace are the next two most frequently cited in the *Adagia*, being used to about the same extent. Plautus was by far Erasmus' main source in the *Collectanea*,[250] and his familiarity with this author may have been one of the factors that gave him the idea in the first place of producing a collection of proverbs from classical literature. As has been seen, Erasmus returned to him again for the additions to the new edition of the *Adagia* of 1533.[251] The particular edition which Erasmus owned (Husner no 213) and frequently used was that edited by Giambattista Pio (with commentary) and published in Milan in January of 1500.[252] Although he refers sometimes to the commentary, he never actually names Pio. While in Venice in 1508, Erasmus did some work on this author with Aldus Manutius[253] and there is mention of this in the introduction to the Aldine edition of Plautus of 1522. Erasmus' name, however, is absent from the title page of the edition.

HORACE

Horace (65–8 BC) was a favourite author of Erasmus in his youth and he had learned his poetry by heart according to Beatus Rhenanus.[254] Only one edition of Horace is found in the mailing list (Husner no 88), and this was almost certainly one of the Aldine octavo editions.[255] For both the *Collectanea* and the *Adagia*, however, Erasmus used *Horatius cum quattuor commentariis*, an edition of Horace that contained the ancient commentaries of Pseudo-Acron and Porphyrion as well as the humanist commentaries of Cristoforo Landino and of Antonio Mancinelli.[256] This volume first appeared in 1492 but was often reprinted. Erasmus frequently refers to Acron and Porphyrion

* * * * *

249 See *Adagia* I v 56 n12 (CWE 31 434). Five of the seven occurrences of Asconius appear in the additions of 1533; see Phillips 395.

250 See 10 n21 above.

251 See 37 and n122 above.

252 See *Adagia* IV iii 40 n2 (CWE 36 27).

253 Erasmus refers to his contribution on more than one occasion; see Epp 589:45n, 1341a:440–3, 1479:110–13, 1482:57–60.

254 Allen I 70

255 See van Gulik on no 88.

256 See ASD II-9 190:196n (C 489) for Pseudo-Acron. See also C 275n for Landino. For the *Adagia* Phillips (393, 401) counts thirteen examples from Pseudo-Acron and only four from Porphyrion.

in his discussion of particular adages, but, as is his wont with regard to other authors, he often draws from the humanist commentaries without acknowledgment. One exception occurs at *Adagia* I i 9 where Erasmus explicitly names and criticizes Landino for his mistaken interpretation of *umbrae* at Horace *Epistles* 1.5.26–30. Of the Horatian corpus the *Sermones* and *Epistles*, by their very nature, provided by far the greatest amount of material for the *Collectanea*[257] and the *Adagia*. Phillips (398) counts 475 quotations of and references to the poet.

TERENCE AND VIRGIL

Terence, who with Plautus is one of the two writers of Roman comedies whose work has survived, is the next most quoted Latin author after Horace (on more than two hundred and fifty occasions), followed closely by Virgil (just under two hundred and thirty).[258] Erasmus was the editor of an edition of Terence produced by the Froben press in Basel in 1532, identified by van Gulik as a possible candidate for item 117 ('Terentius cum commentariis') in the mailing list. The notes that accompany the text, quite numerous for the first two plays in the volume, the *Andria* and the *Eunuchus*, show Erasmus' conjectural flair, his metrical expertise in the prosody and metres of the plays, as well as his good use of the ancient commentary of Donatus (4th century AD) on five of the six plays of Terence for help in textual and other matters.[259] For the *Adagia* Erasmus adduces Donatus on some thirty occasions (Phillips 397), while he makes some use of the commentary of Servius (late 4th century AD) on Virgil, drawing on it on twenty-one occasions (Phillips 401).

OVID

Ovid (born in 43 BC) was a very popular poet in the Middle Ages and Renaissance, and was by no means overlooked by Erasmus, being quoted by

* * * * *

257 There are only a dozen or so quotations from the *Odes* in the *Collectanea*, compared with just over a hundred taken from the *Sermones* and the *Epistles* (including the *Ars Poetica*).

258 For the numbers see Phillips 402–3. Although Terence and Virgil are drawn on by Erasmus to about the same extent in the *Adagia*, Virgilian quotations are much less numerous than Terentian ones in the *Collectanea*, only a score, mostly from the *Eclogues*, as opposed to more than a hundred from Terence. Erasmus also adduces Servius on two occasions in the *Collectanea* (c 225 and c 831) and draws on him without naming him at c 678.

259 See Thomson (31 n93 above) 162–5. In contrast, van Gulik on no 117 minimizes Erasmus' contribution to the publication.

him on 125 occasions in the *Adagia*, the most popular poem being the *Ars Amatoria*. In fact, this work and the other amatory ones (*Heroides*, *Amores*, *Remedium Amoris*) contribute just more than half of the total number. The *Metamorphoses* (or *Transformationes*, as Erasmus sometimes calls the poem) makes up for just less than a quarter. Eighty or so of the total make their first appearance in the edition of 1508 and a few continued to be added in subsequent editions. Thirteen new quotations are found in *1533*, and twelve new ones are to be found in the final edition of 1536, somewhat surprisingly given the modest expansion in that edition over *1533*.

JUVENAL, MARTIAL, PERSIUS

The satirists of the so-called Silver Latin period (roughly from the middle of the first century AD into the first quarter of the second), Persius, Martial, and Juvenal, provided Erasmus with much material for the *Adagia*, being cited or quoted on more than three hundred occasions. Of the three Juvenal is most favoured, but the other two are not far behind.[260] For Juvenal Erasmus drew on the published commentaries of Domizio Calderini and Giorgio Merula.[261] These two humanists also wrote commentaries on Martial, both used by Erasmus,[262] but for Martial only Calderini is acknowledged as a source in the *Collectanea*.[263] Of the three poets Persius presents the greatest difficulty because of his style and the many allusions that his six poems (the whole corpus) contain, and it is surprising at first sight that Erasmus quotes him so often. Without a commentary most readers of Erasmus' time would have found much of the poetry impenetrable. In fact Erasmus seems to have used an edition containing the commentaries of Johannes Britannicus and Josse Bade.[264]

APULEIUS

Of later writers Apuleius, of the 2nd century AD, is quoted just under fifty times, the majority appearing first in *1508*. His novel, the *Metamorphoses*

* * * * *

260 The numbers given by Phillips (398–400) are: Juvenal 127; Persius 99; Martial 92.
261 Calderini is named at c 171, Merula at c 391 and c 392, and Erasmus continued to use their commentaries in the *Adagia*.
262 A copy of Martial ('Martialis cum duobus commentis') is no 113 in the mailing list. The two commentaries are those by Calderini and Merula.
263 At c 371 (cf *Adagia* II v 80), 661 (cf *Adagia* I v 63) and 666. At c 390, however, Erasmus draws on Merula's commentary on Martial 6.62.4 for the reference to Seneca.
264 See 12 above.

(also called *De asino aureo* 'The Golden Ass'), is the work most frequently cited (twenty-two times according to my count), followed by his *Apologia* (fourteen), a speech in which the author defended himself against the charge of practising magic. Erasmus owned Filippo Beroaldo the Elder's edition, with voluminous commentary, of the *Metamorphoses* that was first published in Bologna in 1505, and then frequently reprinted. It is no 197 in the mailing-list. Which edition this is and when Erasmus acquired it cannot be determined.[265]

AUSONIUS

The later author, the poet Ausonius, of the fourth century AD, was also well known to Erasmus, who quoted him on thirty occasions in the *Adagia*, almost all of which are to be found in the 1508 edition. The copy of Ausonius in his library is probably the 1511 edition produced in Paris by the press of Josse Bade.[266]

CATULLUS, PROPERTIUS, TIBULLUS, LUCRETIUS, LUCAN, STATIUS

Something needs to be said about the little use Erasmus made of what are considered to be major literary figures of Latin literature. Of the lyric and love poets of the late republic and early empire Catullus is most favoured (invoked almost twenty-five times, mostly in *1508*). Propertius gets half of that number and Tibullus gets half of the number for Propertius. Lucretius, the Epicurean author of *De rerum natura*, is cited on only three occasions, perhaps not surprisingly given the nature of the poem. One might have expected the Neronian poet Lucan, the author of the historical epic *De bello civili*, to have appealed to Erasmus and to have provided Erasmus with material from many of his gnomic verses, but he is quoted on only three occasions.[267] Slightly more numerous are the quotations from another poet of the 1st century AD, Publius Papinius Statius, who was very popular in the Renaissance.[268]

SILIUS ITALICUS, VALERIUS FLACCUS

It is not so surprising that less important authors of the 1st century AD are virtually ignored. Silius Italicus, the author of the epic *Punica* and 'the

* * * * *

265 See van Gulik on this entry.
266 See van Gulik on Husner no 156.
267 *Adagia* I iv 32, II v 28 and IV vi 35 (the last, perhaps, by way of a secondary source). Erasmus refers to the poet at *Adagia* II ii 38, but does not quote from him.
268 *Adagia* I iv 12, I vi 24, II iv 46, III iv 58; see also IV x 97.

most tedious writer of the whole Silver Age,'[269] is quoted by Erasmus on only two occasions, while Valerius Flaccus, another poet of the same century and the author of the epic poem *Argonautica*, is quoted but once (*Adagia* II i 38).

Roman Historians

LIVY

Of the leading Roman historians Livy (59 BC–AD 17), whose aim was to write a complete history or Rome from its beginnings to his own day, was by far the most fruitful source for Erasmus in the *Adagia*, there being more than seventy quotations drawn from the work, aptly entitled *Ab urbe condita* 'From the Foundation of the City.' This was a massive work comprising 142 books, of which less than a third has survived. The greatest number of quotations (33) first appeared in *1508*, but Erasmus seems to have devoted considerable time to this author while preparing the edition of 1528. For not only did he add a further twenty new quotations in that edition, including one that was his sole source for a new proverb,[270] he corrected or expanded some of the quotations in earlier editions.[271] The cause for Erasmus' renewed interest in Livy for the 1528 edition of the *Adagia* may have been the preparation of a new edition that Froben published in Basel in 1531, to which Erasmus contributed a foreword.[272] Froben published a revised and expanded version of the 1531 edition in 1535; this contained new notes by Beatus Rhenanus and Sigismund Gelenius[273] and was based on collation of new manuscripts. This revised edition may account for a dozen or so new quotations from Livy that were added in *1533*.[274] Erasmus possessed one of these editions in his library.[275]

* * * * *

269 H.J. Rose *A Handbook of Latin Literature* (London 1966) 391
270 *Adagia* IV vii 37, from Livy 10.24.5
271 See, for example, *Adagia* I i 20 and II i 23.
272 This was the first edition to contain books 41–5, but Erasmus does not seem to draw on any of these books.
273 For Gelenius see 33 above.
274 Erasmus had been actively involved in the preparations for the revised edition, specifically in the search for a manuscript containing the lost books of the third decade. This was supposed to be owned by Pietro Bembo, with whom Erasmus corresponded on the matter (Ep 2925; cf also Allen Ep 2435 introduction).
275 See van Gulik on Husner no 259. Erasmus may also have possessed the 1518 edition of Livy, which first made use of the Mainz manuscript that contained

Erasmus refers on a few occasions to the *periochae*, summaries of the contents of each book of Livy's work,[276] wrongly attributing them to Florus, a historian who composed an epitome of military history, quoted once by Erasmus, at *Adagia* I i 77.

TACITUS

In stark contrast with Livy stands Tacitus, the other leading Roman historian, who chronicled the Empire. His greatest works were the *Annales*, as they are now known, covering the period from the death of Augustus to the death of Nero, and the *Historiae*, which begins with what immediately followed Nero's demise. Much of both works has not survived. From this corpus Erasmus quotes directly only once at *Adagia* I x 61, the quotation appearing first in *1533*.[277] In the same edition Erasmus introduces quotations from (or paraphrases of) Tacitus' *Dialogus de oratoribus* on seven occasions[278] and that small number is the sum of Tacitean references in the *Adagia*. It is hard not to link the date of these additions with the appearance in 1533 of a new edition of Tacitus' *Opera* done by Erasmus' friend Beatus Rhenanus and published by the Froben press in Basel.[279]

JULIUS CAESAR AND SALLUST

Of republican historians whose work (at least in part) has survived Julius Caesar (100–44 BC) is quoted on only seven occasions[280] and Sallust (86–35 BC) on twelve.[281] No edition of Caesar is to be found in the mailing-list; Husner no 308 is listed as *Opera Salustij*, but the edition cannot be identified with any certainty.[282]

* * * * *

parts of books 33 and 40 unknown up to that time (possibly Husner no 411; see van Gulik on no 259 and ASD II-5 210:8n). In an addition in *1520* to *Adagia* IV v 26 he refers to the Mainz MS, while at the same time emending a corrupt passage in it.

276 *Adagia* II i 79, IV vi 48, IV viii 1

277 Two other references / quotations, one from the *Annales* (*Adagia* I iii 1, added in *1515*) and one from the *Historiae* (IV vi 35, appearing first in *1508*) were taken from intermediary sources, the first from Beatus Rhenanus, the second from a work by Raimondus Marlianus, a professor at Louvain (see ASD II-8 37:436–7n).

278 I iv 26, I v 52, I x 42, II ii 89, III vii 32, IV iv 95, IV vii 80

279 See I iv 26 14n (CWE 31 338). See also van Gulik on Husner no 269.

280 Five of these appear first in *1533*, the other two having been added in *1526*. All but one are taken from *De bello Gallico*.

281 Seven of these appeared in the edition of 1508. The others were added in *1523* (2) and *1533* (3).

282 See van Gulik on Husner no 308.

NEPOS AND SUETONIUS

Two authors writing in the biographical tradition were also sources drawn upon by Erasmus. Twenty-four of the *Lives* composed by Cornelius Nepos, who lived in the 1st century BC, have survived. In all the printed editions that appeared before 1566 all the *Lives* except *Atticus* and *Cato* were falsely ascribed to a certain Aemilius Probus. Erasmus quotes this Aemilius six times and Nepos twice (both quotations being from *Atticus*), four of these appearing first in 1526, three in 1523, and one in 1508. Erasmus found a more useful source in Suetonius, the biographer of the twelve Caesars from Julius Caesar to Domitian. There are about three dozen quotations from these *Lives of the Caesars*, with examples from *Augustus* and *Tiberius* accounting for about half. Most of the quotations appeared in the *Chiliades* of 1508, but some were added in later editions, especially that of 1517/18. Erasmus' renewed interest in Suetonius for this edition of the *Adagia* coincides with the appearance in 1518 of a Froben edition of that author edited by Erasmus himself.

CURTIUS RUFUS

Quintus Curtius Rufus, who probably lived in the 1st century AD, wrote on Alexander the Great (*De rebus gestis Alexandri Magni*), in ten books, of which the last eight survive. Erasmus read this author when travelling to England from Brabant in early 1517. Finding the text quite corrupt, he prepared a new edition of the work and sent his manuscript to Matthias Schürer of Strasbourg, who printed it in 1518.[283] This edition, bound with a history of the Wends of the German Baltic coast, is no 268 in Husner's mailing list of Erasmus' library. Of the nineteen references to and quotations from this author that are found in the *Adagia* most (12) appear in 1517/18, the edition of the *Adagia* that Erasmus must have been preparing at about the same time as he was working on Curtius Rufus.[284] The other seven instances make their appearance in 1533.

PLINY THE YOUNGER

We may include here the collection of letters of Pliny the Younger (born in AD 61 or 62), the nephew of Pliny the Elder. This is of strong historical interest, since the topics touched on by the letters include information about important contemporaries of the author, and one book contains Pliny's correspondence with the emperor Trajan. There are just over forty quotations

* * * * *

283 Ep 704 is the prefatory letter of this edition.
284 See 31 n91 above.

from this author, all but one being drawn from the letters.[285] The majority of these occur first in *1508*, although Erasmus adds half a dozen quotations in *1533*. In the *Chiliades* of 1508 Erasmus refers to the Aldine edition of Pliny that was to appear in November of 1508, just two months after the publication of the *Chiliades*, stating that it was greatly superior to previous printed editions. It is natural to suppose that Erasmus had taken the opportunity to appraise the new edition even before it was published. He gave his own copy of it as a present to Louis Carinus in 1519. The copy of Pliny's letters that is to be found in the mailing list (Husner no 67) may be the second Aldine edition of 1518.[286]

HISTORIA AUGUSTA

What is now known as the *Historia Augusta* is a collection of biographies of the Roman emperors that cover the period from AD 117 to 284, though there is a lacuna for the years 244 to 259.[287] The lives of the emperors are attributed to six authors and it is by their names that Erasmus quotes the work on about thirty occasions in the *Adagia*. The authors are Aelius Lampridius, Aelius Spartianus, Julius Capitolinus, Flavius Vopiscus, Trebellius Pollio, and Vulcacius Gallicanus. The last-named of these, however, is never quoted in the *Adagia*. More than half of the quotations first appeared in the 1508 edition of the *Adagia*, and after that the edition of 1517/18 contains the greatest number of new quotations, not surprisingly since Erasmus was working on an edition of Suetonius and the writers of the *Historia Augusta* that appeared in 1518.[288]

AMMIANUS MARCELLINUS

A more valued historian of which Erasmus made use was Ammianus Marcellinus, of the fourth century of the common era. His history started where Tacitus had finished and continued down to his own times. The first part of the work is unfortunately lost, and what has come down to us begins in the fourteenth book. Erasmus quotes him on eighteen occasions, all of which make their first appearance in *1528*.[289]

* * * * *

285 The exception is in *Adagia* I i 30, where Erasmus quotes from Pliny's *Panegyricus*.
286 See van Gulik on Husner no 67.
287 The date and authorship of the work has been the topic of much dissension.
288 Although Erasmus is named as editor of the whole volume, he does not seem to have engaged in any serious way with any part other than Suetonius (see 35 n110 above).
289 See 34–5 above.

Minor Authors

PUBLILIUS SYRUS

Publilius Syrus, whose name is sometimes given by Erasmus as Publius or Publianus, lived in the first century BC, and composed mimes, theatrical productions in which, contrary to what we might infer from the name of the genre, the actors spoke lines. There has come down to us a collection of apophthegms drawn from the plays, though this collection also contains lines from other authors. Erasmus cites him on sixteen occasions, all but three first appearing in 1508.[290] Erasmus edited the collection along with the *Disticha Catonis* in 1514.

The Bible

In the *Collectanea* we find five adage titles that Erasmus took from biblical sources.[291] Of these only two survived into the expanded *Chiliades*: what are now *Adagia* I viii 40 'The blind leading the blind' and II i 64 'Is Saul also among the prophets?' However, Erasmus culled a few others, from both the Old and the New Testament: *Adagia* I vii 100 'Iron sharpeneth iron' (from Proverbs 27:17), III v 13 'A dog goes back to his vomit' (from 2 Peter 2:22), III vi 23 'A whited wall' (from Acts 23:3), and IV v 47 'The blind and the lame will not enter the temple' (from 2 Samuel 5:6).[292]

More commonly Erasmus draws on the Bible to provide proverbs that are similar in meaning or relate in some way to the adage title, most frequently from St Paul (over three dozen examples) but also from the Old Testament as well as the Gospels. An extreme example of this occurs in *Adagia* IV i 1, in a section of which Erasmus invokes many biblical quotations (see CWE 35 416–18). Sometimes he relates the proverbs under discussion to some aspect of Christian living.[293]

* * * * *

290 Phillips (401) counts only nine examples.
291 c 4 (actually two proverbs), c 372, c 456, and c 750
292 Two other proverbs (*Adagia* I ix 39 and IV v 67) also appear in the Bible (Matt 12:33 and Matt 6:4), but since they are to be found also in other works drawn on by Erasmus (Diogenianus and Plato respectively) the Bible may not have been Erasmus' primary source. See Index of Scriptural References 836–9 below.
293 As, for example, at *Adagia* III v 62 and *Adagia* IV iii 96. For a helpful list of passages that refer to Christian thought or practices see Phillips 383–90 (Appendix 1).

Christian and Patristic Authors

JEROME

St Jerome (c 341–420) deserves pride of place, since he was far and away
the patristic author most often quoted by Erasmus in the *Adagia*, being
cited on about 120 occasions, most frequently in the 1508 edition (I count
74 instances there). As one would expect, of his works it is the correspondence that is the most fruitful source for proverbial use, though Erasmus
also draws quite frequently from the polemical works *Adversus Rufinum*
and *Adversus Iovinianum*. Erasmus was primarily responsible for the editing of the letters in the first four volumes of the *Omnia opera* produced
by the Froben press in 1516.[294] We know that he had begun work on
a commentary on Jerome in December of 1500, and that he was saving up to purchase the complete works.[295] In fact, Erasmus had quoted
Jerome frequently in the *Collectanea*, the number of quotations from him
being surpassed only by those taken from Plautus, Horace, Terence, and
Cicero.[296]

AUGUSTINE

After Jerome, Augustine (354–430) is the Church Father most quoted, though
barely so, being just in front of Gregory of Nazianzus. I count thirty-four
instances, drawn from a wide range of works in the corpus. Erasmus was
in charge of an edition of the *Opera* of Augustine, a collaborative effort that
was published in ten volumes in 1528–29 by the Froben press in Basel, and
it not surprising therefore that the largest number of citations (fifteen) occur
first in the 1528 edition of the *Adagia*.

BASIL

Almost half of the two dozen or so quotations from St Basil (c 330–79),
renowned as a theologian and monastic founder, are taken from his correspondence, much of which was printed, along with letters of Gregory of
Nazianzus, in editions published in 1528 in Hagenau and then in 1532 by

* * * * *

294 Husner no 243 lists six volumes of Jerome from the Froben press (see van
    Gulik on this item),
295 Ep 138. Erasmus also owned a two-volume edition of Jerome's works (without
    the letters) that was published in Venice in 1497, the copy now being in the
    library of the University of Munich. Much of this paragraph is indebted to
    van Gulik on Husner no 243.
296 See 10 n21.

Froben in Basel. There are only six quotations (with no Greek) in *1508*, all but one of which were taken from the tract written to his nephews entitled *Ad adulescentes*. All the other quotations, most of which are in Greek, make their first appearance in either *1528* or *1533*.

GREGORY OF NAZIANZUS

The printed work of Gregory of Nazianzus (329–89), also known as Gregory the Theologian, consists of his *Orationes* and his correspondence. Erasmus cites him on just over thirty occasions, slightly more often from the letters than from his speeches. Most of the citations appear first in *1528* or *1533*, prompted by the editions just mentioned.[297] Quotations from the *Orationes* are also more frequent in these two editions of the *Adagia* even though sixteen of them of them were printed much earlier in an Aldine edition of 1516 entitled *Orationes selectissimae XVI*.

LACTANTIUS

Lactantius Firmianus (c 250–325), who was born in Africa, taught in Bithynia at the instigation of Diocletian and then was brought to Gaul by Constantine. He seems to have converted to Christianity at an elderly age. Much of his work was regarded as heretical. There are only seven citations in the *Adagia*, including a reference to his poem *De ave Phoenice* (*Adagia* II vii 10). All but one of these appeared first in *1508*.

TERTULLIAN

The *editio princeps* of the complete works of Tertullian (c 160–c 240) was done by Erasmus' friend, Beatus Rhenanus, and appeared in July 1521. This must have acted as a spur to Erasmus, since of the fifteen citations from this author only one appears in an edition of the *Adagia* earlier than that of 1523,[298] in which eleven of the fifteen made their first appearance. This suggests that the copy of this edition in Erasmus' library was the 1521 edition and not the second edition of 1528.[299]

* * * * *

297 The primary content of the 1532 edition, produced under the guidance of Erasmus, was the *Opera* of St Basil, but it also contained some new letters of Gregory that were missing from the Hagenau edition of the letters of Gregory and Basil of 1528.
298 The exception occurs in *Adagia* II iv 17, where a quotation from the *Apologeticum*, occurs in the edition of 1508. The same quotation had already been used in c 31.
299 See van Gulik on Husner no 227.

Humanists of the 15th and 16th Centuries[300]

With the invention of printing the most common way in which humanists publicized their abilities was to commit to print more or less comprehensive commentaries on the works of individual authors, often based on their university lectures. Some humanists soon turned away from this kind of commentary and preferred instead (or as well) to publish in one volume numerous short notes or essays on particular problems in different texts and authors.[301] These notes, dealing as they did with difficult problems of interpretation in well-known texts, were much more learned in nature than most of the notes to be found in continuous commentaries. In the introduction to the *Collectanea* (11–13 above) it is shown that in this first collection of proverbs Erasmus drew extensively from both kinds of works, but that, more often than not, he did so without acknowledgment.

ANGELO POLIZIANO, FILIPPO BEROALDO, GIAMBATTISTA PIO

Of the more learned genre Angelo Poliziano's *Miscellaneorum prima centuria* was the greatest example and Erasmus names him as his source more often than he does anyone else.[302] By contrast he does not mention at all in the *Collectanea* Filippo Beroaldo or Giambattista Pio, on whose collection of learned notes he also drew: the former's *Annotationes centum* and *Appendix annotamentorum*,[303] and the latter's *Annotamenta*.[304] Nor did he mention them later in the *Adagia* although he continued to draw on their work. Pio's commentary on Plautus is extensively used in the edition of 1533, where many new examples of adages are taken from this author, and Beroaldo's commentary on Suetonius *Galba* 4.2 is one of Erasmus' sources for *Adagia* I v 83.[305]

* * * * *

300 On Erasmus' use of the collection of proverbs by Apostolius, Brassicanus, and Polydore Vergil see 41–4 above.

301 Domizio Calderini (1446–78) seems to have been the first to plan such a publication with three books of *Observationes*. See Campanelli passim; also C. Dionisotto, 'Calderini, Poliziano et altri,' *Italia medioevale e umanistica* 11 (1968) 151–85.

302 For Erasmus' use of Poliziano in the *Collectanea* see 11 n29, 12 n30 above.

303 The first of these had been first published separately in Bologna in 1488, the second first appeared as an appendix to Beroaldo's commentary on Suetonius of 1493.

304 Sometimes referred to as Pio's *Annotationes priores*

305 Beroaldo's *Oratio proverbiorum* may have provided Erasmus with material for his expansion of C 702 in *Adagia* II iii 48; see Maria Cytowska 'Erasme et Beroaldo' *Eos* 65 (1977): 265–71, at 267.

ERMOLAO BARBARO, NICCOLÒ PEROTTI, DOMIZIO CALDERINI

A somewhat different work was the *Castigationes Plinianae* of Ermolao Barbaro, which was published in Rome in 1492 / 1493, and which Erasmus also used for the *Collectanea*.[306] This was an opus, rather like a commentary, devoted exclusively to Pliny, and the whole of his *Naturalis historia*. But Barbaro confined himself almost exclusively to the numerous passages where he suspected textual corruption, and the result is a philological and scholarly *tour de force*, far above the level of the usual commentaries of the time. As is the case with Poliziano, Erasmus names him as his source much more often than he does in the case of other humanists.[307] Another distinguished scholar on whom Erasmus drew for the *Collectanea* was Niccolò Perotti, the author of a massive work entitled *Cornucopiae*.[308] Constructed as a commentary on Martial's *Liber spectaculorum* and book one of the epigrams, it ranged widely over the whole area of lexicology, with hundreds of examples from Latin and Greek literature, and served also as a store of knowledge for mythology and Roman history.[309]

As was to be expected, for the *Collectanea* Erasmus also made use of the published commentaries of the classical authors such as Plautus, Horace, Martial, Juvenal, and Persius,[310] but he names his source infrequently or not at all. It should occasion no surprise that for the new edition of the *Adagia* in 1508 and for subsequent editions Erasmus continued to use these sources and indeed to cast his net more widely to embrace the work of even more of his fellow humanists. So, to give only a few examples, Erasmus turns again to Barbaro's *Castigationes* at *Adagia* I v 31 and II iv 43 for the edition of 1528 and to the humanist's letters at *Adagia* I iv 71 and IV v 79 for the edition of 1523. Perotti too is used, being named or identified as the author of the *Cornucopiae* on a few occasions (*Adagia* I ix 1 and II i 44 in *1508*, *Adagia* I vii 33 in *1520*). Erasmus also refers to Domizio Calderini, whose commentaries on Martial and Juvenal he certainly knew well, on several occasions.[311]

* * * * *

306 See 11 n29 above.
307 See 11 n29 above.
308 See 12 n33 above.
309 Erasmus owned one of the Aldine editions of the work, which also contained Nonius Marcellus, Festus Pompeius and Varro (Husner no 384).
310 See 12–13 above
311 *Adagia* I v 63, II v 80, III v 76, and IV vi 35, and only the first of these is critical of Calderini.

GIAMBATTISTA EGNAZIO, PAOLO BOMBACE, CRISTOFORO LANDINO, CAELIUS RHODIGINUS

Some humanists Erasmus mentions out of gratitude or a wish to compliment them. The most obvious example occurs in *Adagia* II i 1 where he names the scholars who provided him with texts when he was preparing the expanded *Chiliades* in Venice in 1508.[312] Baptista Egnatius, named in *Adagia* II i 1 CWE 33 14, is thanked again for having lent Erasmus a commentary on Aristotle (*Adagia* II i 65 in *1517/18*), and in *Adagia* I vi 1 Erasmus expresses his considerable admiration for Paolo Bombace, whom he credits with the emendation of καὶ μῶρος κηπωρός in *Adagia* I vi 1, even though he himself later found confirmation of the conjecture in Stobaeus. More often, however, Erasmus names a humanist only to criticize him. It has already been mentioned that in *Adagia* I i 9 he takes the commentator Cristoforo Landino to task for his mistaken explanation of *umbrae* at Horace *Epistles* 1.5.28. Another target of Erasmus' disparagement is Caelius Rhodiginus (Lodovico Ricchieri), whose *Antiquarum lectionum libri XVI*, appearing in 1516, prompted critical remarks from Erasmus in *1517/18* (*Adagia* I i 2 CWE 31 34–5), *1520* (I viii 56 and II iv 42), and *1526* (I x 21 and II i 45).[313]

THEODORUS GAZA AND ANDREA ALCIATI

We may conclude this survey of humanists with two of whom Erasmus thought highly. Theodorus Gaza died when Erasmus was still a young boy, but his Latin translations of Greek works, particularly Aristotle's *Historia Animalium* and *Problemata* and of Theophrastus' *De causis plantarum* and *Historia plantarum* were standard editions widely used in the sixteenth century. Though Erasmus could well have read the original Greek, he often uses and refers to Gaza's translations even as late as the edition of 1528.[314] The second is Andrea Alciati, who was born in 1492 and was thus a young boy when Erasmus' *Collectanea* appeared in 1500. Alciati became one of the greatest jurisconsults of his age, though he was adept in many branches of learning. His anthology of illustrated verse (the *Emblemata*, first appearing in 1531 and later expanded) rivalled Erasmus' *Adagia* in its international circulation. However, it was his legal works with which Erasmus was most familiar. A composite volume of some of these, including the *Dispunctiones*,

* * * * *

312 See CWE 33 14.
313 Reference has been made to Erasmus' disparagement of Apostolius and his collection of proverbs (see 42 above).
314 See *Adagia* I viii 30, I viii 42, I ix 13, I ix 67, and III vii 76. Erasmus also translated parts of Gaza's Greek grammar into Latin. See CEBR 2:81.

the *Praetermissa* and the *Paradoxa*, was first published in 1518 and reprinted on several occasions. Erasmus owned a copy of this, probably the 1523 edition.[315] He thought very highly of Alciati, describing him as 'a luminary of our age not only in Roman law but in all kinds of learning' (*Adagia* I v 45 CWE 31 423). The first references to him in the *Adagia* appear in 1526.[316] In 1533 Erasmus drew and elaborated on a dozen or so proverbs mentioned in Alciati's *De verborum significatione*, which was published in 1530, having been informed of the work by his younger friend Bonifacius Amerbach.[317]

* * * * *

315 Husner no 135. See Heinimann and Kienzle ASD II-1 521:43–46n.
316 As at *Adagia* I iii 59, I v 45 and I vii 34
317 See A. Wesseling in ASD II-8 14 n49 and *Adagia* IV vii 75 (CWE 36 332–3). At the same time Amerbach sent Erasmus a list of proverbs in other works, some of which Erasmus used in the new edition of 1533. This led to Erasmus' use of the sixth-century historian Procopius of Caesarea at *Adagia* IV ix 5, IV ix 6, and IV ix 77. Erasmus, however, does not acknowledge Amerbach's help.

THE *ADAGIORUM COLLECTANEA*

translated and annotated by
JOHN N. GRANT

1 Similes habent labra lactucas / Like lips like lettuce

Cicero in his speeches writes that, according to Lucilius, Crassus Licinius laughed only once in his whole life.[1] Pliny the Elder says in book seven, chapter nineteen, 'It is a common belief that Crassus, the grandfather of the Crassus who was killed while fighting the Parthians, never laughed and because of this was called Agelastus "Laughless." Similarly it is commonly believed that many people have never wept.'[2] Jerome in *Against Rufinus*: 'Am I at least to succeed in making the sternest of men laugh, so that, in the end, you will imitate Crassus, who is said by Lucilius to have laughed only once in his whole life?'[3] According to many sources[4] this Crassus was certainly an eloquent and upright man, but he was dour and ill-natured, and he never gave up a grudge against his enemies. Some say that he never laughed, others that he did so but once. And what was it that was so funny that it could wring a laugh from such a stern man? The answer is a very well-known saying that is reported in many authors, 'Like lips like lettuce,' about an ass eating thistles.[5] Lettuce is a soft and tender plant, while a donkey's lips are extremely rough and hard. We can use this proverb to indicate that something bad has befallen a person who is bad in the same way, for example, if an intransigent pupil gets an equally stubborn teacher, dishonest citizens get dishonest leaders, an abusive prosecutor gets an abusive pleader for the defence, untutored minds get unsophisticated writings, or a nagging wife gets a captious husband. To sum up, we can use it whenever dreadful things befall dreadful persons and people get what they deserve, even though they think what they are getting is fine, just as to an ass thistles are like lettuce leaves.

* * * * *

1 *Adagia* I x 71. There does not appear to be a Greek version of the proverb. Otto 896

1 Cicero *De finibus* 5.30.92 and *Tusculan Disputations* 3.15.31 (not in his speeches). Macrobius 2.1.6 cites Cicero as the source of the story without naming the work. Mynors (CWE 32 383) suggests that Erasmus was thinking of the Pseudo-Ascanius commentary on the *Verrines*. The reference to the poet Lucilius is to 1299–1300 Marx (1315–16 Krenkel).

2 Pliny *Historia naturalis* 7.79

3 Jerome *Adversus Rufinum* 1.30 PL 422A, CCSL 79 30

4 See above n1.

5 Erasmus seems to exaggerate the popularity of the adage. His immediate, and perhaps only, source for it is Jerome *Letters* 7.5 (CSEL 54 30), whom he quotes at *Adagia* I x 71 and partly quotes here about an ass eating thistles. The provenance of the adage has been thought to be Roman comedy (CRF *Incerta* 102).

2 Risus Sardonius / A Sardonic laugh

In book seven of his *Letters to Friends* Cicero says to Fabius Gallus, 'You seem to me to be afraid that if we have him we may have to smile with a γέλως Σαρδώνιος[1] the Greek phrase meaning 'Sardonic laugh.' On this passage the commentators are certainly conscientious in adducing what they can.[2] They say that there is a certain Sardinian plant that brings death to those who are careless enough to eat it; as they die, they look as if they are smiling. In addition, they talk about a living creature, a *tarcotella*, whose bite they believe prompts a similar death.[3] I leave it to them, however, to consider how these theories are consistent with the rest of the letter. We have discovered that some very old proverbs relating to laughter were frequently on the lips of the Greeks. For example, there is 'An Ionian laugh,' directed at homosexuals,[4] 'A Megarian laugh,' directed at those who laugh at an inappropriate time,[5] and this one, which Cicero used, 'A Sardonic laugh,' which was said in antiquity of those who laughed excessively and uncontrollably.[6] Anyone who has read book one of Plato's *Republic* will cease to have any doubts about the meaning of the last one. There Socrates says of Thrasymachus, a proud and arrogant fellow, 'Then he, hearing this, gave a great guffaw and

* * * * *

2 *Adagia* III v 1 (with a greatly expanded discussion). The adage occurs at Diogenianus 8.5, but the Greek was probably drawn from the edition of Cicero (see n1) that Erasmus used. Polydore Vergil 302; Otto 1586

1 Cicero *Ad familiares* 7.25.1, addressed to Fadius, not Fabius. The text given by Erasmus is corrupt, and has been corrected in different ways. The person referred to is actually Tigellius, an associate of Julius Caesar, not, as Erasmus suggests at the end of the discussion, Caesar himself.

2 Erasmus gives explanations that can be found in contemporary printed editions of Cicero's *Letters*, as in those with the commentaries of Hubertinus Crescentinas and Martinus Phileticus. The information about a Sardinian plant can also be found in Zenobius 5.85, but Erasmus did not have access to Zenobius' collection of proverbs when he was preparing the *Collectanea* in 1500; see c 26n.

3 The spelling of this name, whatever the creature may be, seems to be unique. It may be a reference to the tarantula. Strabo (11.4.5–6) tells of a spider whose bite had the same effect as described here.

4 Diogenianus 3.87. See c 833 and *Adagia* I v 69.

5 Diogenianus 3.88 and *Adagia* I v 70. The interpretation given by Diogenianus is that the expression refers to those who smirk, inappropriately, in a self-satisfied manner – inappropriately because they will soon experience failure of some kind. He says that the adage is based on the short time in which Megarian comedy flourished.

6 A source for this particular interpretation of the phrase has not been identified.

COLLECTANEA C 2 / ASD II-9 48

laughed sardonically. He then said, "By Hercules! This is the well-known irony of Socrates."[7]

From all this I think it is clear what Cicero was hinting at, namely that when Caesar returned they would have to joke less freely and less openly. That whole letter is in agreement, to the most precise degree,[8] with this interpretation.

3 Nihil graculo cum fidibus, nihil cum amaracino sui / A jackdaw has no business with a lute, a pig has no business with marjoram

At the end of his work *Attic Nights* Aulus Gellius neatly and wittily directs these two adages at dim-witted, uncultured, and ignorant men who are able to laugh at polished writing and more refined scholarship, but are unable to understand what they are reading.[1] They take pleasure only in what they have learned – squalid, meaningless and naive stuff. Gellius uses these adages as a stick to drive away such men from his collection of notes, the most polished work one can come upon. He says, 'There is an old saying, "A jackdaw has nothing to do with the lyre, a pig has nothing to do with marjoram."' For the jackdaw is a chattering, raucous bird, and should therefore be kept far away from musicians. Perfume does not suit a pig's snout, for which the only good smell is the smell of dung.

4 Sanctum dare canibus, margaritas porcis / To give dogs what is holy, to throw pearls before swine

This is to be found in the Gospels and has the same meaning as the preceding proverb.[1] I am well aware that the ancients strongly believed in preventing

* * * * *

7 Plato *Republic* 1.337A. When Erasmus cites Plato in the *Collectanea*, he does so in Latin, using almost always the Latin translations of Marsilio Ficino. See Maria Cytowska 'Erasme de Rotterdame et Marsile Ficin son maître' *Eos* 63 (1975) 165–79.
8 Erasmus uses the expression *ad amussim* (c 773 and *Adagia* I v 90 By rule).

3 This proverb was later divided to make two separate adages, becoming *Adagia* I iv 37 (Otto 766) and I iv 38 (Otto 1720). It is also discussed by Filippo Beroaldo in chapter 14 of his *Appendix annotamentorum* (*Lampas* 1.321). This work of Beroaldo's first appeared in 1493, in his commentary on Suetonius. It was an appendix to his *Annotationes centum*, published in Bologna in 1488 (see 12 n31 above); see Heinimann 167 n49. Polydore Vergil 37
1 Gellius *Noctes Atticae* preface 19. In early editions of Gellius, the *praefatio* stood at the end of the work.

4 Not repeated in the *Adagia*. Erasmus draws from Pico della Mirandola *De hominis dignitate* (page 156 of the 1942 edition of E. Garin).
1 Matt 7:6, the source of the proverb

the mysteries of philosophy and theology from becoming common knowledge. This is proclaimed loudly and clearly by the hieroglyphic writings of
the Phoenicians and Egyptians, the riddles of Pythagoras,[2] the teachings of
the prophets, and the parables in the Gospels. Even Paul, who spoke 'words
of wisdom only to those who were ripe for it,'[3] was of the same mind, as
was his pupil Dionysius, who adjures Timotheus not to divulge the mysteries of the sacred rites.[4] When Dionysius had asked Plato questions about
some arcane philosophical topics, Plato responded in a riddling way.[5] Even
today there is a very common proverb 'Do not scatter roses before swine.'[6]
Jerome: 'For they themselves decided that pearls should not readily be cast
before swine or that what is holy should not readily be given to dogs.'[7] What
appears in Aesop's fable, 'The cock has found a jewel,' is similar.[8]

5 **Manus manum fricat / One hand rubs another**
In Plato in the *Axiochus* 'One hand rubs another; give something and you
get something' is cited from some poet.[1] The sense is that if you receive a
service, you should give one in return.

6 **Dimidium plus toto / The half is more than the whole**
Aulus Gellius in his *Nights* says one of the questions posed at dinner parties was what Hesiod means when he says in his Ἔργα καὶ Ἡμέραι, that is,
his *Works and Days*, Νήπιοι οὐδὲ ἴσασιν ὅσῳ πλέον ἥμισυ παντός 'Fools do not

* * * * *

2 See C 98–106.
3 1 Cor 2:6
4 Dionysius Areopagiticus *De ecclesiastica hierarchia* 1.1 PG 3 369
5 Plato *Letters* 2.312D. The Dionysius mentioned here is Dionysius II, the tyrant
   of Syracuse.
6 Suringar 198
7 Jerome *Letters* 84.3.6 CSEL 55 124
8 Phaedrus 3.12. Erasmus' source was probably an edition of *Aesopus latinus*.

5 *Adagia* I i 33. Otto 1036
1 Pseudo-Plato *Axiochus* 366C, citing Epicharmus, a comic poet from Sicily, fragment 273 Kaibel. Erasmus does not cite the proverb in Greek (given as ἁ δὲ
   χεὶρ τὰν χεῖρα νίζει in Plato), only in Latin (see C 2 n7). The usual form of the
   proverb in Latin is *Manus manum lavat* 'One hand *washes* another' (Seneca *Apocolocyntosis* 9; Petronius *Satyricon* 45), a more literal translation of the Greek.
   'Give something and you get something' later became *Adagia* II viii 8.

6 *Adagia* I ix 95, in a greatly expanded form. Erasmus draws much of this,
   including the error in the reference to Plato's *Republic* (see n2) from Filippo
   Beroaldo's *Appendix annotamentorum* 3 (*Lampas* 1.313); see C 3n and Heinimann
   169 n54. Otto 558

know how much the half is more than the whole.'[1] The reason for such discussion was that these words presented something of a puzzle. They are cited, with explanation, by Plato, both in his *Laws* book three and the *Republic* book four.[2] He points out that this wisest of poets has used a pleasing obscurity and ambiguity to commend moderation, beyond which or short of which no action can be virtuous.[3] For what is whole must have already passed the half-way point; the middle point is therefore better than the whole. This expression began as an oracular utterance and then acquired such proverbial status that every philosopher and poet used it frequently. Even nowadays it is on everyone's lips that there should be moderation in all things.[4]

7 Mutuum muli scabunt / One mule scratches another

Marcus Varro gave proverbial titles to many of his works and 'One Mule Scratches Another' is one of them.[1] This is also cited in Nonius Marcellus and can also be found in the letters of Ausonius and Symmachus.[2] It

* * * * *

1 Gellius *Noctes Atticae* 18.2.13, referring to *Works and Days* 40. Erasmus draws the Greek from Gellius. His Latin translation is cast in the form of a dactylic hexameter, *ignorant stolidi quam toto dimidium plus*. It is normal to find in 15th-century editions of Gellius a Latin translation following a Greek quotation, in verse if the original was in verse. These Latin additions (lacking any manuscript authority) were the work of Theodore Gaza. A variant version of the Latin translation given here is found in a 1493 edition of Gellius: *ignorant stolidi quam toto sit medium plus*.
2 Plato *Laws* 3.690E (with explanation); *Republic* 5.466C (not book 4), where there is no explanation. The point of Hesiod's paradox is that his brother Perses had won possession of all of that their father had left, but had frittered it away. And so it would have been better for him to have been satisfied with only half of the inheritance, sharing it with Hesiod.
3 A paraphrase of Horace *Satires* 1.1.107
4 Suringar 59

7 *Adagia* I vii 96. The adage is the subject of Filippo Beroaldo's *Appendix annotamentorum* 2 (*Lampas* 1.312), where there are references to Nonius (and to Varro), Ausonius and Symmachus, discussed in more detail than Erasmus gives; see C 3n. Polydore Vergil 2; Otto 1162
1 Varro *Menippean Satires* 322–5 Buecheler. Only fragments of the work survive. They can be found in *Petronii saturae* ed F. Buecheler, Berlin 1904. This proverb is cited on several occasions by Nonius Marcellus (see 66 n240 above) pp 165, 231, 339, 350 Lindsay.
2 Ausonius *Technopaegnion* 25.4 (p 177 Green); Symmachus *Epistolae* 10.1.3, where the MSS offer *aemulos* 'rivals' for *mulos* 'mules.' Beroaldo, however, quotes him with the correct text.

is taken from mules, which rub each other with their mouths, and suits those who admire and praise each other, answering like with like. These extravagant exchanges are very wittily mocked by Horace.[3] He says: 'An orator and lawyer in Rome were brothers. / They heard nothing but compliments from each other, / So that one was a Gracchus to the other, one was a Mucius.'

A little later he writes: 'I come off as Alcaeus by his vote. Who does he come off as, by my vote? / Who else but Callimachus?'

8 Senes mutuum fricant / Old men rub one another

No different in sense from the preceding adage is one that originated in the baths in the following way.[1] The emperor Hadrian once saw an ex-soldier rubbing himself down against the marble walls because he did not have a slave. He then gave him slaves and money. When other veterans saw how successfully this had turned out for him, some of them also began to rub themselves down against the walls in the presence of the emperor, hoping to entice him in this way to be generous to them. He, however, called the old men out and told them to rub each other down. In this way there was no need of slaves. This joking remark became part of everyday language.

9 Iumenta quoniam manibus carent, alterius frictione indigent / Since pack-animals have no hands, they need someone to rub them down

An apophthegm of Scipio Aemilianus, directed at those who cannot perform any noble deed and therefore need others to say great things about them.[1]

* * * * *

3 Horace *Epistles* 2.2.87–9 and 99–100. The transmitted text of the first of these passages is difficult to interpret and is certainly corrupt. Gracchus and Mucius are examples of a distinguished orator and jurist respectively (they were not brothers). In the second passage Alcaeus and Callimachus are renowned Greek poets.

8 *Adagia* I vii 98. Referred to in the commentary of Polydore Vergil 2
1 The story is told in the *Life of Hadrian* (17.6–7) in the *Historia Augusta* (see 76 above). However, Filippo Beroaldo recounts the story, without naming the source, in his *Appendix annotamentorum* 2 (*Lampas* 1.312), from which Erasmus probably drew some of the material in the immediately preceding adage. It is very likely that Erasmus is here dependent on Beroaldo; see c 3n. In *Adagia* I vii 98 he includes a retort of Scipio Aemilianus that Beroaldo also mentions in his chapter in his *Appendix*; see next adage.

9 Not repeated in the *Adagia* as a proverb in its own right. Mentioned in *Adagia* I vii 98. See previous adage.
1 Taken from Plutarch *Moralia* 201c *Apophthegmata Romanorum* by way of Filippo Beroaldo *Appendix annotamentorum* 2 (*Lampas* 1.312). Scipio Aemilianus

10 **Lampada cursus tibi trado / I hand on the torch in the race to you**

Taken from a very ancient ritual that was part of some festivals. Prometheus is said to have instituted games in which runners carried blazing torches. 'When one of the runners was tired out, he handed his torch over to someone else for the next part of the course. This runner also passed it on to someone else when he was exhausted, and this procedure continued to the end.'[1] This gave rise to the proverb 'to hand over the torch in the race,' referring to when one is tired and entrusts what one is doing to someone who is fresh; for example, if a person is exhausted from reading aloud and orders the rest to be read out by someone else. Marcus Varro in *On Agriculture*: 'I am not handing over the torch to you in the race.'[2] Cicero in *To Herennius*: 'For it is not the same in the army as in the stadium,[3] where the runner who takes up the blazing torch is swifter than the one who passes it on to him. The general who takes over an army is not better than the general he replaces. In a race a tired man gives the torch to one who is fresh. In the case of an army an experienced general hands it over to one who is not experienced.'[4] Persius: 'Why, when you are in front of me, do you ask me to hand over to you the torch at the finish of the race?'[5]

11 **In eo ipso stas lapide ubi praeco praedicat / You stand on the very block where the crier calls his wares**

It is clear from many sources that there was a raised stone in the Roman

* * * * *

(Scipio the Younger) was the conqueror of Carthage in 146 BC. The point of the apophthegm is that if one can do something for oneself, there is no point in getting someone else to do it for you. The interpretation given by Erasmus is his own. See *Apophthegmata* 5.413 CWE 38 578.

10 *Adagia* I ii 38. Polydore Vergil 300; Otto 909

1 Hyginus *Astronomica* 2.15. On this Hyginus, to be distinguished from an earlier namesake, who was appointed by Augustus to the librarianship of the Palatine library, see H.J. Rose *A Handbook of Latin Literature* (London 1966) 446–7. Erasmus reports on the passage of Hyginus by way of Beroaldo's *Appendix annotamentorum* 18 (*Lampas* 1.307–8); see C 3n. Beroaldo (while explaining Lucretius 2.79) also refers to Varro, the *Rhetorica ad Herennium*, and Persius.

2 Varro *Res rusticae* 3.16.9. A translation of the text in modern editions would have 'now' instead of 'not.'

3 The text reads *palaestra*, strictly denoting a gymnasium for wrestling.

4 *Rhetorica ad Herennium* 4.46.59 (traditionally, but erroneously, ascribed to Cicero)

5 Persius 6.61

11 *Adagia* II x 77. Otto 912n

forum from which auctioneers called out what was up for sale. Chrysalus, the slave in *The Bacchis Sisters* of Plautus, alludes to the stone when he says this of an old man whom he is cheating out of his money: 'You foolish man, you are unaware that you are now being sold, / And yet you are standing on the very stone where the crier calls his wares.'[1]

The expression means therefore that someone participates in his own undoing.[2]

12 Non eras in hoc albo / You were not on this roster

The meaning is 'you were not in this group.' Pliny in the preface of his *History of the World*: 'When I took this work on, you were not on this roster,' meaning that the addressee was not in the number of those who Pliny believed would read it.[1] Poliziano used the same adage in a very witty way: 'I have no objection to having whatever I write about, no matter how trifling, subjected to censure or exposed to risk, provided that ignorance and envy – two literary pestilences that I especially mistrust – are not in this roster.'[2] The expression is taken from the praetor's roster, on which Ulpian writes in the second volume of the *Digest*, book 4: 'Labeo says that the man who names his opponent in the roster and makes clear what he is going to say also performs the act of publication.'[3]

13 Herculei labores / The labours of Hercules

Used proverbially of actions from which others profit but which bring only ill will to the person who performs them.[1]

* * * * *

1 Plautus *Bacchides* 814–15, but probably taken from Giambattista Pio's *Annotationes priores* 10 (*Lampas* 1.381–2)
2 This final sentence is an addition of *1506*.

12 *Adagia* I vii 34. Cf Otto 49.
1 Pliny *Naturalis historia* praefatio 6. Pliny sometimes uses the title *History of the World*.
2 Angelo Poliziano, at *Miscellanea* 90 (1.301 Maier)
3 *Digest* 2.13.1.1, drawn from Poliziano (*Miscellanea* 82; 1.295 Maier), who points out that *album* 'roster' is the reading in the Florentine manuscript of the *Pandects*, against *alium* 'other' in the other manuscripts.

13 *Adagia* III i 1, with one of the longest and best-known essays in the collection. The expression is not found in the collections of Greek proverbs, but is quite common in Latin. Otto 801
1 For the interpretation that good services bring ill will Erasmus may have had in mind Horace *Epistles* 2.1.10–12.

14 Nec omnia nec passim nec ab omnibus / Not everything, nor everywhere, nor from everybody

An elegant adage about propriety and moderation in accepting gifts. It survives[1] in the original copies[2] of a letter of the deified Severus and the emperor Caracalla.[3] It is cited by Ulpian in book one of 'On the duty of the proconsul,' and under the same title in the first book of the *Digest*.[4] What the letter says is as follows: 'As far as gifts are concerned, listen to what our views are. There is a Greek proverb Οὔτε πάντα οὔτε πάντη οὔτε παρὰ πάντων[5] "Not everything, nor everywhere, nor from everybody." For it is very rude to take no gifts from anyone; to accept them from everyone, however, is the vilest and most rapacious of actions.'

That was the view of the Greeks. Our lawyers do quite the opposite, accepting all gifts everywhere and from everybody. And even this is not enough to describe their actions; add 'plundering everything, everywhere, from everybody.'

15 Lolio victitant / They live on darnel

This is a riddling proverb, applied to those who are myopic, that is, who do not see at all well. Plautus in *The Soldier*:

Is it surprising that you live on darnel, such a cheap type of grass?
Why do you say that?

* * * * *

14 *Adagia* II iv 16. The Latin version is Poliziano's own suggestion of how the Greek phrase might be translated (see n1). Polydore Vergil 73
  1 What follows (down to 'most rapacious of actions') is drawn, without acknowledgment, from Angelo Poliziano (*Miscellanea* 95; 1.306 Maier). Erasmus gives credit to Poliziano in *Adagia* II iv 16.
  2 The phrase in Erasmus' quotation is *in archetypis* (for the singular in Poliziano; see n3). The word *archetypon* has a range of meanings among the humanists; Poliziano regularly uses it when he refers to the Florentine manuscript of the *Pandects*. He means that, in his opinion, this manuscript is one of the original ones that Justinian ordered to be preserved in many cities; see Rizzo 313. Poliziano is not referring to original copies of the letter itself; see next note.
  3 Erasmus has misunderstood Poliziano, who says that the Greek proverb had been lost from most manuscripts of the *Digest* but 'it is *in Archetypo*, just as it appeared in a letter of the deified Severus and the emperor Antoninus.' In the *Digest* Ulpian refers to and quotes from the letter.
  4 *Digest* 1.16.6.3
  5 Poliziano reads πάντοτε 'always' for πάντη 'on every side.'

15 *Adagia* II i 29. Otto 967

Because you are short-sighted.
You scoundrel, you are blind, not just short-sighted.[1]

Ovid attests in book one of his *Fasti* that darnel harms the eyes: 'May the fields be free of darnel that damages the eyes.'[2]

16 Cornicum oculos configere / To pierce crows' eyes

This occurs in the speeches of Marcus Tullius, though the location escapes me for the moment.[1] Its sense is to find fault with and correct the achievements of the ancients, as if they had no insight at all. Jerome in his second apologetic against Rufinus: 'Now indeed because of the diversity of the regions different copies are in circulation and the true old translation has been spoiled and corrupted. Do you think it is in our power either to decide which copy of several has been perverted[2] or to write a new work on the basis of the old one and, when the Jews mock us, to pierce their crows' eyes, as the saying goes?'[3] I admit that I have not read any precise information in an appropriate authority about the meaning of the expression or about how it became a proverb. I conjecture, however, that it is the long life of crows and their harmonious cohabitation that gave rise to this adage. There is certainly general agreement that the crow is a bird that lives very long, and, in addition, that it is a symbol of concord. One might think, therefore, that a person who tries to condemn and overturn what antiquity accepted with great accord wishes 'To pierce crows' eyes.'

* * * * *

1 Plautus *Miles gloriosus* 321–3. The reading in the MSS of Plautus and in most printed editions of the time was *olio* or *oleo* 'olive oil' for *lolio* 'darnel.' Poliziano corrected the text in *Miscellanea* 66 (1.282 Maier), and also referred to the Ovidian passage. In addition he invoked the support of Fulgentius, a grammarian of the late 5th and early 6th centuries, who provides evidence for *lolio*. The emendation and the three pieces of evidence appear, however, in Filippo Beroaldo's *Annotationes centum* 81 (see C 3n), as well as in Poliziano's *Miscellanea*. Erasmus does not acknowledge his obvious debt to one or both of these humanists, either here or at *Adagia* II i 29.
2 Ovid *Fasti* 1.691

16 *Adagia* I iii 75. Erasmus' explanation of the proverb is not convincing, and he himself talks about his continued search for the proverb's meaning as late as 1524 (Ep 1479). See CWE 31 295, where the suggestion is made that the proverb means something like 'to give a man a taste of his own medicine' or 'to pay back someone in kind.' Otto 435
1 Cicero *Pro L. Murena* 11.25; *Pro L. Flacco* 20.46
2 The correct text has *verum sit* 'is authentic' for *versum sit* 'has been perverted.'
3 Jerome *Adversus Rufinum* 2.27 PL 23 450D, CCSL 79 64

17 Fuimus Troes / We Trojans have ceased to be

In his essay 'On Inoffensive Self-Praise' Plutarch writes that in Sparta there was a chorus made up of three groups of singers, old men, boys, and young men. The old men's song was ἄμμες ποτ᾽ ἦμεν ἄλκιμοι νεανίαι 'we too were young man in our time.' The song of the boys was ἄμμες δὲ γ᾽ ἐσόμεσθα πολλῷ κάρονες 'we shall be far better than many in the future.' The young men sang ἄμμες δ᾽ ἐσμέν, αἰ δὲ λῆς αὐγάζεο 'we are strong now; look if you will,' indicating that they were now what the old men had been and what the boys hoped to be, and that they were prepared to put this claim to the test.[1] After this the past tense was used proverbially to indicate something that had been lost, an example of which is the phrase, full of pathos, *fuimus Troes* 'we were Trojans,' meaning 'we are nothing now.'[2] Also from Cicero *nos quoque floruimus* 'we too once flourished,'[3] and what the same person said about the conspirators after they had been executed: *vixerunt* 'they have lived.'[4] Related to this is Menedemus in Terence who says that he *had* a son rather than he *has* one, and the pimp in Plautus who says, 'Those saddest of words: *I had!*'[5]

18 Quondam fuerunt fortes Milesii / The Milesians were brave in days of yore

Even a proverb added to the reputation of the Milesians for softness and a luxurious way of life. Aristophanes in the comedy entitled *Wealth*: Πάλαι ποτ᾽ ἦσαν ἄλκιμοι Μιλήσιοι 'The Milesians were strong in days of yore.'[1] By this we understand that they are now effeminate and unmanly.

* * * * *

17 *Adagia* i ix 50. Cf Diogenianus 2.30, but Erasmus' main source is Angelo Poliziano (*Miscellanea* 88; 1.299 Maier), who cites the passage from Plutarch and Cicero's use of *vixerunt* 'they have lived.' Polydore Vergil 92

1 Plutarch *Moralia* 544E *De se ipsum citra invidiam laudando*. Erasmus draws the Greek from Poliziano, but αὐγαξέω was printed in error for αὐγάζεο.

2 Virgil *Aeneid* 2.325

3 Cicero *Ad familiares* 4.13.2; 14.4.5

4 Reported in Plutarch *Cicero* 22.4. The reference is to the execution of associates of Catiline involved in the conspiracy to seize power in 63 BC when Cicero was consul.

5 Terence *Heautontimorumenos* 94; Plautus *Rudens* 1321, referring to the loss of riches. Neither of these references is in Poliziano.

18 *Adagia* i ix 49. This appears in Poliziano's discussion of the immediately preceding adage in *Miscellanea* 88 (1.299 Maier), from where Erasmus drew the Greek version. Polydore Vergil 91

1 Aristophanes *Plutus* 1002, 1075, from Poliziano

19 Sexagenarios de ponte deiicere / To throw the sexagenarians off the bridge

A proverb with a historical basis. In antiquity at the time of elections young men violently drove old men off the gangways in the Campus Martius, where voting customarily took place.[1] Ovid mentions this custom: 'Some think that the weak old men were hurled from the bridges / So that the young alone might vote.'[2]

After this the right to vote was taken away from sexagenarians. Macrobius in the *Saturnalia* book one: 'You want to disfranchise learned men when it is a question of voting on the use of words, and, as it were, toss the sexagenarian elders off the bridge?'[3]

20 Crambe bis posita mors / Twice-served cabbage is death

According to Pliny *crambe* is a type of cabbage.[1] Suidas says that *crambe* is served at banquets because it prevents drunkenness,[2] but that when re-cooked it produces dreadful nausea.[3] Because of this, cabbage became to be used proverbially by the Greeks to indicate something contemptible. For they have the following proverb Δὶς κράμβη θάνατος, 'Twice-served cabbage is death.' Juvenal is alluding to this when he indicates the boredom of having to listen to the same speech over and over again

* * * * *

19 *Adagia* I v 37. Erasmus draws from Filippo Beroaldo's *Annotationes centum* 6; see C 3 and Heinimann 177 n89. Polydore Vergil 112; Otto 1638
1 The gangways along which the voters walked at election time were called *pontes* 'bridges.'
2 Ovid *Fasti* 5.633–4 (in Beroaldo)
3 Macrobius *Saturnalia* 1.5.10 (in Beroaldo). The reference is to authors whom Cicero and Varro tried to emulate, the point in question being the use of a singular or plural verb with the word *mille* 'thousand.'

20 *Adagia* I v 38. For the Greek version and for much of his commentary Erasmus draws here, without acknowledgment, from Poliziano, who discusses the meaning of *crambe* at Juvenal 7.154 in *Miscellanea* 33 (1.253–4 Maier). Previous humanists had been puzzled by the word. For example, Domizio Calderini (see C 171 n3), whom Poliziano quotes at length, had suggested that the word was the title of a declamation. Poliziano gives the explanation that Erasmus offers here. Polydore Vergil 24; Otto 454
1 Pliny *Naturalis historia* 20.79
2 *Suda* K 2318. 'Suda' means 'palisade, fortress.' At the end of his discussion of Juvenal 7.154 in *Miscellanea* 33 Poliziano refers to 'Suidas' (up till well into the 20th century the work was thought to be the work of an individual named 'Suidas') and to the efficacy of *crambe* in preventing drunkenness.
3 There is nothing in the *Suda* about re-cooked cabbage causing nausea.

and says, 'Cabbage served up again and again is the death of unhappy teachers.'[4]

21 Ne Hercules quidem adversus duos / Not even Hercules can take on two

On one occasion Hercules learned that several persons were setting an ambush for him when he was on his own. He did not stay to fight but sought safety in flight. The Greeks were quick to seize upon this to create the proverb 'Not even Hercules can take on two.'[1] The meaning is that no one has so much strength that on his own he is a match for several others and that not even the bravest of men should be ashamed of yielding to superior numbers.

22 Aestimare leonem ab unguibus *et alia in eundem sensum* / To know a lion by its claws *and other adages with a similar meaning*

Ἐκ τῶν ὀνύχων τὸν λέοντα γινώσκειν, To know a lion by its claws. This means to form an opinion of an entire topic on the basis of a single, slight feature, to infer much from little, and to draw sweeping conclusions from small details; for example, if someone were to form a judgment on a man's complete talent and intellect on the basis of some word spoken by him. Those who have never seen an actual lion often conjecture what a great animal it is from the claws that they have been shown. This is not unlike Ἐκ γεύματος γινώσκειν 'To judge from the slightest taste,'[1] Ἐκ τοῦ κρασπέδου τὸ ὕφασμα 'To judge the fabric from its border,'[2] Τὸν Αἰθίοπα ἐκ τῆς ὄψεως 'To judge

* * * * *

4 Juvenal 7.154

21 *Adagia* 1 v 39. This version of the story is to be found only in the branch of the manuscript tradition of Diogenianus that descends from Oxford, Bodley Grabe 30; see 7 n10 above. Poliziano uses the proverb at *Epistolae* 4.7 (1.55 Maier). Otto 584

1 Diogenianus 7.2. The proverb is also in Zenobius 5.49. Erasmus does not give, however, in either *1500* or *1506*, the Greek version of the proverb (Μηδ᾽ Ἡρακλῆς πρὸς δύο or Οὐδ᾽ Ἡρακλῆς πρὸς δύο).

22 The source of this and the other adages that he cites here as being similar in meaning is probably Diogenianus 5.15, which contains all of them, in virtually the same form. Erasmus acknowledges his source, in a general way, in the final sentence. The titular adage here later becomes *Adagia* 1 ix 34, where Erasmus gives as his source Lucian (*Cataplus* 4). All the Greek versions were added in *1506*. The Latin translation of the titular adage is the same as in Poliziano *Epistolae* 9.2 (1.118 Maier).

1 C 361 and *Adagia* 1 ix 37

2 Most of the manuscripts of Diogenianus give the proverb in the version Ἐκ τοῦ

an Ethiopian from his face,'[3] Ἐκ τοῦ καρποῦ τὸ δένδρον 'To know the tree by its fruit,'[4] and Κέρκος τῷ ἀλώπεκι μαρτυρεῖ 'The fox is given away by his brush.'[5] All of these are given by the Greek writers of adages.

23 Amussis alba / An unmarked rule

We say that something is done with 'An unmarked rule' when we want to indicate that no choice or discrimination underlies a course of action. The *amussis* is a cord used by builders to make sure the walls are plumb. There is a reference to it in the lucubrations[1] of Gellius in the following passage: 'For all those writers, especially the Greek ones, after reading a great deal of varied material, transformed[2] whatever they came upon *alba linea* "with a white line," as the saying goes, interested only in quantity.'[3]

24 In albo lapide alba linea / A white line on white stone

The very common Greek adage Λευκῷ λίθῳ λευκὴ στάθμη 'A white line on a white stone,' has the same kind of origin.[1] In Plato's *Charmides* Socrates

* * * * *

κρασπέδου τὸ πᾶν ὕφασμα 'To judge the *whole* fabric from its border.' Erasmus' version here reflects an error in his own manuscript of Diogenianus (see 7 n10 above). The proverb becomes *Adagia* I ix 36 (Otto 663).
3 *Adagia* I ix 38
4 *Adagia* I ix 39
5 *Adagia* I ix 35

23 *Adagia* I v 88. Erasmus is drawing from Poliziano *Epistolae* 11.20 (1.161 Maier) for the use of *amussis* here as an alternative to *linea*, the expression used by Gellius in what is quoted at the end of his discussion. See Heinimann 177 n89. The Greek original appears in Diogenianus 6.8 (λευκὴ στάθμη) but Erasmus gives only the Latin version at this point (see next adage). Otto 51
1 Erasmus uses here the Latin word *lucubrationes* 'studies by lamplight,' referring to the title of Gellius' work, *Attic Nights*.
2 This translates *convertebant*, the (erroneous) manuscript reading in the Gellian tradition. In the *Adagia*, however, the reading is *converrebant* 'they swept together,' which is what is printed in modern editions. This is an emendation that is credited by editors of Gellius to Ludovicus Carrio, who edited Gellius for Stephanus (Henri Estienne), the edition appearing in 1585, but Erasmus has prior claim.
3 Gellius *Noctes Atticae* preface 11

24 This does not become a proverb in its own right in the *Adagia*, but it is mentioned in Erasmus' discussion of *Adagia* I v 88 and is described as an expanded version of 'An unmarked rule.' Erasmus has drawn much of the material in his explanation from Poliziano *Epistolae* 11.20 (1.161 Maier); see Heinimann 177.
1 This Greek form of the adage is cited by Poliziano in *Epistolae* 11.20, taking it from *Suda* Λ 325. A shorter form λευκὴ στάθμη is found at Diogenianus 6.8.

refers to it, saying that when he was among beautiful young men it was as
if he were using 'A white line on white stone,' since he could not distinguish clearly between different forms of beauty and loved them all equally.
We add his words: 'You know, dear friend, that I have no ability to eval-
uate and discriminate. In the presence of men renowned for their beauty
I am like a white cord on a white wall. Almost all such men give me great
pleasure.'[2]

It can also be used of those who explain what is obscure with obscurities, what is ambiguous with ambiguities.[3]

25 Canis in balneo / A dog in a bath

The Greek version of the adage is Τί κυνὶ καὶ βαλανείῳ 'What has a dog
to do with a bath?' This is cited in a letter by Rodolphus Agricola[1] as an
old Greek proverb.[2] I name this man as the most worthy of public honour in the whole of Germany. I do so all the more gladly because when I
was a boy his pupil was my teacher, Alexander the Westphalian.[3] To the

* * * * *

2 Erasmus gives a Latin version, based on Marsilio Ficino's translation, of the
passage from Plato *Charmides* 154B.
3 Erasmus is following Diogenianus here.

25 This appears as *Adagia* I iv 39 in the form *quid cani et balneo?* – which is how
Erasmus translates the Greek version of the proverb here. The proverb, in its
Greek form, does not appear in Diogenianus or in Rodolphus Agricola's letter
(see n2), and that may account for the absence of the Greek version in 1500
(what is given here as the first sentence of the commentary was actually added
in 1506 to the titular heading). The Greek proverb can be found in the *Suda*
(T 584) and Lucian (*Adversus indoctum* 5, *De parasito* 51). Lucian is the more
likely source (see C 836 n1, 837 n1).
1 Rodolphus Agricola (1444–85) was a leading humanist in northern Europe.
He was highly thought of by Erasmus who wrote a tribute of him (and his
pupil Hegius; see n3) in Ep 23. Erasmus' eulogy is more expansive in *Adagia*
I iv 39. Agricola's most famous work was *De inventione dialectica*, which was
not published until 1515. See CEBR 1:15–17.
2 The letter appeared in Agricola's translation of Pseudo-Plato *Axiochus*, and is
also to be found in Alardus Amstelredamus ed *Rodolphi Agricolae ... lucubrationes* (Cologne 1529) 205–13 (with a brief commentary). The proverb appears
near the end of the letter on page 210 of that edition. See Lisa Jardine 'Invent-
ing Rudolph Agricola' in Antony Grafton and Ann Blair eds *The Transmission
of Culture in Early Modern Europe* (Philadelphia 1990) 39–86. Alaard of Ams-
terdam (1491–1544) was responsible, at least in part, for the publication of *De
inventione dialectica*. For Alaard see CEBR 1:19–20.
3 Alexander Hegius, rector of Erasmus' school at Deventer, from 1483 to 1498.
Erasmus left the school in 1484. For Hegius see CEBR 2:173.

latter I owe the dutifulness of a son, to Agricola the love of a grandson. Lest, however, Agricola's glorious accomplishments may be questioned because it is a fellow German who is vaunting his qualities, I shall give the epitaph written for him by Ermolao Barbaro.[4] And all agree, I believe, that of all Italians Barbaro had impeccable integrity and unquestioned scholarly achievements.

> Under this stone, the jealous Fates decreed
> The Frisian hope, his country's light, should come,
> Rodolphus Agricola; in life indeed,
> He brought such praise to Germany his home
> As ever Greece could have, or ever Rome.[5]

In the letter that I have mentioned this Rodolphus uses eloquence and sincerity to try to persuade the town council of Antwerp to place in charge of their school someone who has studied languages and literature and not to entrust this task to an inarticulate scientist or theologian. These latter persons may have the confidence that they can speak on any topic, but they have no idea on how to speak. Rodolphus says, 'What good will a theologian or a scientist do in a school? As much good as a dog in a bath, as the Greeks say!' A dog has no place in the baths. Very similar to this proverb is 'music in time of mourning,' about joking at an inappropriate time.[6]

26 Intus canere / To play privately to oneself

The Greek version is Ἀσπένδιος κιθαριστής 'A lyre-player from Aspendus.'

* * * * *

4 Ermolao Barbaro (1453–93) was an outstanding humanist of his generation. See CEBR 1:91–2. Erasmus refers to him and draws from his work on numerous occasions in the *Collectanea*; see 11 n29, 12 n30 above.

5 The translation is that to be found in CWE 31 349. See 2.124 Branca (*Carmina* 5).

6 Ecclus 22:6

26 *Adagia* II i 30. As is the case with the preceding adage, the Greek proverb and its translation are additions to the heading in *1506*. The Greek form of the adage is not to be found in Diogenianus, and Erasmus probably took it from Zenobius 2.30, an edition of Zenobius having appeared in 1497. Erasmus did not have access to it for his 1500 edition of the *Collectanea*, but he seems to draw on it for *1506* (see c 188, 248, 373, 504, 746, 793, 819, 820, 838). Proverbs of Zenobius were also printed in the Aldine edition of Aesop's fables in 1505, in which the Greek version here occurs in column 46, but it is doubtful whether Erasmus had a copy of this Aldine edition when he was preparing the revised edition of 1506. Otto 196

It means to do something for one's own advantage. Many public officials nowadays are lyre-players of this kind. The proverb is taken from a statue of a lyre-player who was depicted holding the lyre to his left, with the strings turned towards him. He seemed to be playing privately for himself, not for others to hear, since those who sing publicly display the strings so that the audience can see them; they do not have them facing inwards. Cicero mentions both the statue and the proverb in the third speech against Verres: 'And as for the lyre-player from Aspendus, whom you have often heard of and who is proverbial among the Greeks and who was said to sing everything privately to himself, Verres removed even him and set him up in his own private quarters, thereby beating the lyre-player at his own game.'[1] Cicero is humorously attacking Verres' greed in putting the lyre-player in his own private rooms. The result of this was that while the lyre-player sang privately to himself, Verres privately sang his own tune to an even greater degree.[2] Cicero used the same proverb just as suitably against Rullus in his speech about the agrarian law. He said, 'And this tribune of the plebs sings this song, not for you, but privately for himself.'[3] For Cicero shows in this speech that although this law seemed to be for the common weal it had been concocted for the benefit of the decemvirs, not the general population.

27 Spartum rodentes / Rope-gnawers

Σχοινοτρῶγες, Rope-gnawers. This was a proverbial expression, according to Varro, directed at idlers.[1] Taken from a picture of Socrates, the painter. While listing this artist's works, Pliny says in book three, chapter five, 'And the sluggard, called Ocnus, twisting the rope that the ass gnaws at.'[2]

* * * * *

1 Cicero *Verrines* 2.1.20.53
2 In other words, Verres was a master at looking after his own interests.
3 Cicero *De lege agraria* 2.26.68

27 This was dropped after the *Collectanea* but compare *Adagia* I iv 83 The sluggard twists the rope. The form Σχοινοτρῶγες is a coinage taken, with the rest of the first sentence, from Ermolao Barbaro (*Glossemata*, Pozzi 1416–17; see Heinimann 173 n75). It is based on the form σχινοτρῶγες 'chewers of mastic' (cf C 119), which is attested only in the *Suda* (Σ 1793). For the rest of his commentary on the proverb Erasmus draws to some extent on Poliziano (*Miscellanea* 81; 1.295 Maier), who replaces *orno* in contemporary editions of Propertius at 4.3.21 with *Orco* and also refers to the passage in Pliny (see n2).
1 The reference to Varro, taken over from Barbaro, has not been identified; see Heinimann (1992) 78 n18.
2 Pliny *Naturalis historia* 35.137, not book 3

Propertius also had views about the same person: 'Worthier to twist the rope for Ocnus sideways sitting, / And feed for aye the ass that's always eating.'[3] The same kind of picture is said to have been in Delphi, dedicated by Polygnotus of Thasos.[4] People deny that an idle and lazy man is meant; they think rather that it refers to a conscientious and hard-working man, but one who has a spendthrift for a wife. Because of this Pausanias says that the ass in the picture was not male, but female. Ermolao attests that the same topic on a marble carving can be seen in two places in Rome, on the Capitol and in the gardens of the Vatican.[5] It will be right to give the name 'Ocnus the ass,'[6] meaning 'lazy ass,' to those who not only do not make a large contribution to anything, but even spoil what others have toiled to achieve. To give an example, Jerome made the rope, while those who have distorted his works should all have the name of Ocnus. A large number of those who teach literature deserve this appellation. But all the same it is surprising that Pliny said it was the man twisting the rope who was called lazy and not the ass that gnawed at it. Pausanias writes that there was a common proverb about this same Ocnus in his *Ionia*: Συνάγει Ὄκνου τὴν θώμμιγα 'He twists the rope of Ocnus.'[7]

28 Inter sacrum et saxum / Between the shrine and the stone
This adage is applied to those who are confused and exposed to the gravest danger. It may have originated with the fetial priests[1] since they struck

* * * * *

3 Propertius 4.3.21–2, also cited by Poliziano (see introductory note). The translation is taken from CWE 31 374. Propertius' words really mean 'worthier than Ocnus to twist a rope,' but it is clear from the fuller commentary at *Adagia* I iv 83 that Erasmus understood the passage in the way that the translation here suggests ('for Ocnus').

4 This and the two following sentences are based on Pausanias 10.29, but Erasmus closely follows Ermolao Barbaro's version of the passage in Pausanias in his *Castigationes Plinianae*; see next note.

5 Ermolao Barbaro in his *Castigationes Plinianae* on 35.11 (Pozzi 1138)

6 Erasmus mistakenly connects Ocnus with the ass instead of with the rope-twister. In this error he follows Giambattista Pio in his dedicatory letter to his *Annotationes priores*; see *Lampas* 1.385.

7 Pausanias 10.29. In *Adagia* I iv 83 Erasmus gives the proverb as Συνάγει Ὄκνος τὴν θώμιγγα 'Ocnus [the sluggard] twists the rope.' Also taken from Ermolao Barbaro

28 *Adagia* I i 15. Erasmus drew from Giambattista Pio's *Annotationes priores* 10 (in *Lampas* 1.382–3), as did Polydore Vergil in his *Proverbiorum libellus* (no 13); see Heinimann 177 n89. Otto 1564

1 In ancient Rome these priests (*fetiales, patres patrati*) were involved in the formal declaration of war against enemies and in the making of treaties.

their sacrificial victim with a rock. The treaty they made in this way was regarded as the most sacred and most inviolable. In Plautus Tyndarus, one of the two prisoners in the play, says on the discovery of their deceit, 'Now I am completely done for. Now I stand between the shrine and the stone, and I do not know what to do.'[2]

29 Asinus stramina mavult quam aurum / An ass prefers straw to gold

A saying of Heraclitus became proverbial: Ὄνον σύρματα ἀνελέσθαι μᾶλλον ἢ χρυσόν 'An ass preferred straw to gold.'[1] Said of blockheads who prefer what is bad to what is good.

30 Asinus inter simias / A donkey among apes

Ὄνος ἐν πιθήκοις, A donkey among apes. In his comedy entitled The Necklace Menander brings on a husband complaining in the following way about what he suffers at the hands of his wife: 'Then my mistress wife would make me a common topic of gossip. My face would be branded. I would become a donkey among apes, as they say. In other words, all would make fun of me.'[1] There is general agreement that the ape is the cheekiest of all animals. It even dares to sit on a lion's haunches and harass it with insulting noises. Today there is a proverb with a similar metaphor, 'An owl among crows.'[2]

* * * * *

2 Plautus *Captivi* 616–17

29 This does not appear in the *Adagia* until the edition of 1533 (*Adagia* IV viii 38). There Erasmus gives a different and more convincing interpretation of the proverb, namely that the usefulness of things varies from person to person. At the end of his discussion there, however, he gives one use of the proverb that is similar to what he says here in the *Collectanea*. Polydore Vergil 244

1 Heraclitus fragment 9 Diels-Kranz, cited in Aristotle *Nicomachean Ethics* 10.5 (1176a6–8). The correct reading is ἂν ἑλέσθαι 'would prefer' for ἀνελέσθαι. Erasmus' source for this Greek adage is Giambattista Pio's *Annotationes priores*, in the epilogue of the dedication (*Lampas* 1.385), complete with the error in the Greek; see Heinimann 177 n 89.

30 *Adagia* I v 41. The Greek version of the proverb was added in 1506.

1 Erasmus is drawing from Gellius *Noctes Atticae* 2.23.9, where Gellius quotes a passage from Menander's *Plocium* (fragment 333 Körte-Thierfelder) and then gives the very free Latin adaptation by Caecilius, the Roman writer of comedies. Erasmus does not quote the passage in Greek here, apart from the proverb. In the Menandrian passage the expression refers to the physical appearance of the wife, not to the husband, as Erasmus says. The source of his error is a mistake in the Latin translation, by Theodore Gaza, that followed the Greek text of Menander in early editions of Gellius (see C 6 n1). Caecilius actually drops the proverb in his Latin version.

2 Suringar 20. Cf *Adagia* III ii 74 The owl has one cry and the crow another.

31 Dies omnia revelat / Time reveals all things

Tertullian in his *Apologetic against the Gentiles* says, 'It is good that time reveals all things, as even your proverbs and sayings attest.'[1] From these words of Tertullian one can infer that the verses of Sophocles quoted by Aulus Gellius in his *Nights* became proverbial: 'See that you conceal nothing, since time, which sees all and hears all, will bring all things to light.'[2] Gellius adds that a very ancient poet, whose name escaped him at that moment, wrote 'truth is the daughter of time,' since the truth never lies hidden for ever.[3] At some point it bursts forth, even if it is only time itself that brings it to light.

32 Quam quisque norit artem, in hac se exerceat / Each man had best employ what skill he has

Even Cicero himself testifies, in book one of the *Tusculan Disputations*, that this saying was a Greek proverb. These are his words: 'But as for this man,[1] however learned he may be, as indeed he is, he should leave these topics to Aristotle, and devote himself to teaching music. For this Greek proverb gives good advice: "Each man had best employ what skill he has."'[2] It is very similar to the proverb we have placed elsewhere: 'Let the cobbler stick to his last.'[3]

* * * * *

31 *Adagia* II iv 17. Otto 1756
1 Tertullian *Apologeticum* 7.13
2 Gellius *Noctes Atticae* 12.11.6, quoting TGF 4 Sophocles fragment 301 (280 Nauck). The Greek original of the proverb is πάντ' ἀναπτύσσει χρόνος 'time unfolds all things.' Erasmus gives the Greek here, but with ἀνακαλύψει 'will bring to light' for ἀναπτύσσει 'unfolds.' Theodore Gaza's Latin translation of the Greek passage here (with ἀνακαλύψει) was *omnia revelabit dies*, which Erasmus clearly follows; see c 6 n1.
3 Gellius ibid. The source of the quotation has not yet been identified. Holford-Strevens 24 suggests that there is a lapse of memory on the part of Gellius here and that the quotation is perhaps a conflation of Plutarch *Moralia* 266E *Quaestiones Romanae* 12 (on whether Saturn / Kronos [= Chronos 'Time'] is the father of Truth) and Pindar *Oympians* 2.17 'Time is the father of all things.' See Tosi no 297 and F. Saxl 'Veritas filia temporis' in *Philosophy and History. Essays Presented to E. Cassirer* (Oxford 1936) 197–222 on its popularity as a motto from the Renaissance onwards.

32 *Adagia* II ii 82. Otto 167
1 The reference is to Aristoxenus, a musical theorist.
2 Cicero *Tusculan Disputations* 1.1.41, citing Aristophanes *Wasps* 1431 ἔρδοι τις ἦν ἕκαστος εἰδείη τέχνην. Erasmus does not give the Greek.
3 c 153, which later became *Adagia* I vi 16

33 Aurum lapide, auro mens hominum exploratur / Gold is tested by the touchstone, the mind of men by gold

Of the many aphorisms of Chilon of Sparta this one especially pleased learned men: 'Gold is tested by whetstone and *indice* "by touchstone" (for *index* is the word for touchstone in Latin), to see whether it is pure or adulterated. But in the case of humans, it is gold that determines whether they are good or bad.'[1] The proverb can also be expressed in this way: 'Humans test gold by whetstone, but humans are themselves tested by gold.'

34 Ne Momus quidem haec carpat / Not even Momus would carp at this

Said of something perfect and irreproachable. Plato in the *Republic* says that even Momus could not criticize the study of philosophy.[1] Momus was a god of reproach who found fault with Venus' sandal when he could not find any aspect of the goddess herself to criticize.[2]

35 Diomedaea necessitas / The compulsion of Diomede

Plato in his *Republic* book six: 'He will be compelled by the compulsion of Diomede, as they say, to do whatever these people approve.'[1] The expression signifies unalterable necessity.

36 Sutorium atramentum / Cobbler's blacking

Cicero to Paetus in book nine of his *Letters*: 'Now his father has been accused by Mark Antony. It is thought that he has been acquitted with the use of cobbler's blacking.'[1] There seems to be a proverb underlying this

* * * * *

33 Cf *Adagia* II iv 51 What the touchstone is to gold, gold is to men.
  1 Diogenes Laertius 1.71. Chilon of Sparta (6th century BC) was one of the Seven Sages of ancient Greece; see *Apophthegmata* 2.164 CWE 37 209. The original Greek form of the expression can be found in E. Diehl *Anthologia lyrica Graeca* 2 (1925) 191. Erasmus does not give the Greek in the *Collectanea*, but does so in the *Adagia*. It is thought to be part of a drinking song (*Scolia anonyma* 33 in Diehl).

34 Cf *Adagia* I v 74. Otto 1129
  1 Plato *Republic* 6.487A (see C 2 n7)
  2 This sentence is taken from Poliziano *Epistolae* 1.4 (1.4 Maier).

35 *Adagia* I ix 4, translated loosely at CWE 32 181 as 'To have Diomede on your track.' The expression is also discussed by Giambattista Pio in his *Annotationes posteriores* 1, who also gives the same Latin translation of the passage in Plato (*Lampas* 1.388). The Greek equivalent is Διομήδειος ἀνάγκη; see Zenobius 3.9; Zenobius (Aldus) column 70.
  1 Plato *Republic* 6.493D (see C 2 n7)

36 *Adagia* III v 74
  1 Cicero *Ad familiares* 9.21.3

expression, but a rather obscure one. He means that the defendant has been acquitted by bribing the jurymen, not without scandal, however. For because of its nature cobbler's blacking leaves some stain, even if it does not give a very black coating.

37 Fucum facere / To play a trick

The proverb means to deceive by cunning pretence. Terence: 'A trick was played on the woman.'[1] Cicero to his brother Quintus: 'If you realize that a man who has made a promise to you wants to play a trick on you, as the saying goes, you should conceal the fact that you have heard and are aware of this.'[2] We take the word *fuci* 'dyes' to have the sense 'deceitfulness' and *offuciae* 'paints' to mean 'obfuscation.'[3]

38 Calculum reducere, apponere calculum / To take back a move (or counter), to add a counter

A metaphor that according to Nonius is used by Cicero in the *Hortensius* must surely be proverbial: 'And so I allow you, as is the case in the twelve stones of old, to take back your move if you are dissatisfied with any given proposition.'[1] It seems to be taken from some kind of calculator or, if not that, certainly from the game of draughts. 'To take back a move' has the sense of revoking a concession that was given somewhat unwisely and to change something you regret. This is very much Poliziano's explanation when he says, 'Since he regretted the move he had made, he asked that he be allowed to take back his counter.'[2] *Apponere calculum* 'To add a counter' is also a very similar proverb,[3] meaning 'to make an addition,' taken from methods of calculating: 'Although you have loved him most

* * * * *

37 *Adagia* I v 52. Otto 723
1 Terence *Eunuchus* 589
2 Quintus Cicero *Commentariolum petitionis* 9.35. Erasmus frequently ascribes this work to the famous orator rather than to his brother (see for example c 40 and 400). The error is corrected in *Adagia* I v 52.
3 The word *offuciae* is quite rare. For its figurative sense 'tricks, delusions' see Plautus *Captivi* 656 and Gellius *Noctes Atticae* 14.1.2. Erasmus gives its meaning here as *obscuratio*.

38 *Adagia* I v 55
1 Cicero *Hortensius* fragment 60 Müller, cited by Nonius Marcellus pp 250–1 Lindsay. The text as given in Nonius is corrupt and *scriptis* 'lines' should probably be read for *scrupis* 'stones.' See CWE 31 432 on *Adagia* I v 55 (line 5).
2 *Miscellanea* 90 (1.302 Maier). The reference to Poliziano was dropped in the *Adagia*.
3 This additional proverb is perhaps based on Poliziano in *Epistolae* 8.12 (1.110 Maier).

dearly for some time now, I would like all the same this counter of mine to be added as a commendation.'[4] In Pliny the Younger we find *albus calculus* 'a white counter' in the sense of devoted support.[5]

39 Qui digito scalpunt uno caput / A man who scratches his head with one finger

A verse that was first written by the poet Calvus about Pompey but then extended to all those whose manliness was questionable.[1] It is found in Juvenal.[2]

40 Manibus pedibusque niti. Omnibus nervis. Noctesque diesque / To strive with hands and feet. With every sinew. By night and day

This is a proverb from comedy that expresses the utmost effort. Hands indicate industriousness in finishing something; feet indicate swiftness in getting it done. Davus in *The Woman of Andros* of Terence: 'As your slave I must strive with hands and feet.'[1] 'To use every sinew' has the same sense. What Cicero says to his brother Quintus has much the same sense: 'Strive in this way with every sinew and with all your faculties.'[2] Also when we wish to indicate never-ending exertion we say that we are doing something 'By night and day.'[3]

41 Remis ac velis / With oars and sails

The following adages signify unbelievable speed. Plautus in his *Comedy of Asses*: 'As fast as you can "With oars and sail," hasten and flee,' meaning 'as

* * * * *

4 It is suggested in ASD II-1 531, on *Adagia* I v 55, that this quotation (in which the verb is *accedere*, not *apponere*) may be Erasmus' own invention.
5 Pliny *Letters* 1.2.5. The *calculus* 'pebble' was used in voting.

39 *Adagia* I viii 34, with somewhat different wording. The lemma and text are drawn from Poliziano *Miscellanea* 7 (1.231 Maier). Polydore Vergil 286; Otto 553
1 Licinius Calvus fragment 18 in FPL Buechner. Calvus was a contemporary of Catullus in the first century BC. He uses these words in a scurrilous couplet, the gesture referring to picking up a man for sexual purposes. The fragment (with its author) is cited at Seneca *Controversiae* 7.4.7 and in the scholia to Lucan 7.726.
2 Juvenal 9.133

40 *Adagia* I iv 15 (Otto 1034), 16 (the same as III ix 68), and 24 (Otto *Nachträge* p 255)
1 Terence *Andria* 675–6
2 Quintus Cicero *Commentariolum petitionis* 14.56 (see C 37 n2)
3 For example, Horace *Ars poetica* 269

41 *Adagia* I iv 18. Otto 1521

quickly as possible.'[1] Common expressions in everyday speech are to flee *alatis pedibus* 'on winged feet'[2] and *volare* 'to fly' in the sense of 'to rush.'[3] One also finds *velis equisque* 'with sail and horses,' meaning 'as quickly as possible.'[4]

42 Vertere vela / To turn one's sails about

This means to abandon one's opinion or way of life for the complete opposite, the metaphor being taken from sailing. Plautus in *Epidicus*: 'Whenever a wind arises in the open sea the sail is completely turned about.'[1] Terence expressed the same idea in *The Mother-in-Law* in the following way, without the metaphor, however, and Donatus tells us that the idea is universal: 'To be sure, this is how things are, in my opinion: we are important or insignificant, depending on what life gives us.'[2]

43 Terrae filius. Caeli filius / A son of earth. A son of heaven

In antiquity men of obscure and low birth were proverbially called 'sons of earth,' since the earth is the common parent of all things.[1] If they acquired nobility by their own accomplishments, they were called 'new men.' Persius:

> Manius is ready to hand as my heir. A son of earth, you say?
> Ask me, who is my great-great-grandfather?
> I'll tell you, just give me a moment. Go one further back,
> And yet another? These are all sons of earth.[2]

* * * * *

1 Plautus *Asinaria* 157
2 Ovid *Fasti* 5.666; also Jerome *Letters* 4.1.2 CSEL 54 19
3 Cf Plautus *Persa* 199.
4 The expression *velis equisque*, which became *Adagia* I iv 17, is an imaginary proverb. Erasmus may have taken it from Poliziano's *Praefatio in Suetonium* (1.503 Maier). It is an emended form of *viris equisque* at Cicero *De officiis* 3.33.116 and Cicero *Ad Quintum fratrem* 2.14.2.

42 *Adagia* I ix 60. Otto 1855
1 Plautus *Epidicus* 49
2 Terence *Hecyra* 379–80 and Donatus on 380

43 *Adagia* I viii 86. Erasmus draws for the most part from Poliziano *Miscellanea* 18 (1.241–2 Maier), the starting point of which is the meaning of *fraterculus gigantis* at Juvenal 4.98. Polydore Vergil 261; Otto 1763 and Otto *Nachträge* p 218
1 Cf Tertullian *Apologeticum* 10.9.
2 Persius 6.56–9

Cicero to Atticus: 'And to this son of earth, whoever he may be, I would not dare to entrust a letter on such important matters.'[3] Also to Trebatius: 'Cornelius, your friend, of high birth, a son of earth.'[4] And Juvenal: 'Hence, I'd prefer to be the Giants' little brother.'[5] This is a reference to the proverb since the Giants were sprung from the earth according to the myths of the poets.[6] In a similar fashion men who were unknown and then suddenly gained prominence were called 'sons of heaven,' as if they had descended from the sky.[7] In the books of Moses Melchizedek is introduced as 'without father, without mother.'[8]

44 In luto haerent. Haerent in salebra / They are stuck in the mud. They are stuck on a barrier
Terence in *Phormio*: 'You are sticking in the same mud.'[1] Taken from travellers. Those who cannot extricate themselves from a difficult and complicated situation are said to be stuck in the mud or 'stuck on a barrier.'[2] If those who are stuck in mud pull out one foot, the other foot sinks down more deeply. Then in order to pull this one out, they have to push down on the other one.

45 In aqua haeret / He is stuck in the water
Something quite similar to the previous adage appears in Cicero in book three of *Moral Obligations*: 'He has much to say in many passages, but he

* * * * *

3 Cicero *Ad Atticum* 1.13.4
4 Cicero *Ad familiares* 7.9.3. The name Cornelius was corrected to Gnaeus Octavius in the 1523 edition of the *Adagia*. When Poliziano cites the passage in *Miscellanea* 18, he reads *Cn Octavius, an Cn Cornelius quidem* 'Gnaeus Octavius, or Cnaeus Cornelius.'
5 Juvenal 4.98
6 As at Hesiod *Theogony* 184–5
7 More usually the idea is expressed by phrases such as *delabi caelo* 'to drop down from heaven' or *caelo missus* 'sent from heaven.'
8 Melchizedek, king of Salem, is mentioned at Genesis 14:18, but the phrase 'without father, without mother' is taken from Hebrews 7:3.

44 Cf *Adagia* I iv 99 You are sticking in the same mud, and IV iii 70 He is stuck in shallow water, where the second proverb given here is mentioned. Otto 994 (for the first adage given) and 1572 (for the second)
1 Terence *Phormio* 780
2 Cicero *De finibus* 5.28.84. This is used by Poliziano *Miscellanea* 18 (1.241 Maier), who is probably Erasmus' source for the expression, as he was for much of C 43.

45 *Adagia* I iv 100. Polydore Vergil 171; Otto 142

is stuck in the water, as the saying goes.'[1] He means that Epicurus is by no means consistent in his argumentation. He gets himself mixed up when what he says in one place conflicts with what he said elsewhere. Because of this he is all at sea and cannot stand on solid ground.

46 Semper aliquid novi adfert Africa / Africa always produces something novel

'Αεὶ φέρει τι Λιβύη κακόν / Semper fert Africa mali quippiam / Africa always brings some evil

This can be said of those who either try themselves to create or proclaim strange things. Pliny in his *Natural History* book eight chapter sixteen explains in this way the origin of the adage, when he discusses lions. He says:[1] 'These have a great desire to mate and for this reason the males get angry. This is especially apparent in Africa since, because of the shortage of water sources, all the wild beasts gather together at just a few rivers.[2] For this reason hybrid monstrous animals were produced, since in their couplings, whether by force or mutual pleasure, the males variously mated with the females of each species.[3] This gave rise to a common saying in Greek[4] that Africa is always bringing forth some novelty.'

47 Quot servos habemus, totidem habemus hostes / We have as many enemies as we have slaves

Macrobius put this adage in book one of his *Saturnalian Feast* in the following words: 'What do you think was the origin of that very presumptuous proverb that is in common use, "We have as many enemies as slaves"? It is not a case of our having enemies but of making enemies.'[1] The point of this saying is that we should not trust people and think them friends if they serve us out of fear and not out of love. Let us not embrace those words of a despot: 'Let them hate, so long as they fear.'[2]

* * * * *

1 Cicero *De officiis* 3.33.117

46 First title: *Adagia* III vii 10. Polydore Vergil 254; Otto 35. For the second title, added here in 1506, see C 526.
1 Pliny *Naturalis historia* 8.42
2 See Aristotle *Historia animalium* 8.28 (606b20).
3 The Latin here is ungrammatical and untranslatable. The translation reflects the text in modern editions of Pliny.
4 Cf Zenobius 2.51.

47 *Adagia* II iii 31. Polydore Vergil 19; Otto 1637
1 Macrobius *Saturnalia* 1.11.13, citing Seneca *Letters* 47.5
2 A favourite saying of the Emperor Caligula (see Suetonius *Caligula* 30), but in

48 Sophocles. Laudiceni / Sophocleses. Laudiceans

So that we may better understand this proverb, I would like to quote at some length the words of the younger Pliny with which he wittily describes the absurd pretentiousness of some young men:[1]

> But, in heavens' name, before my time (as old men are wont to say) there was no place even for the noblest of young men unless a man of consular rank introduced them. Such was the reverence for this very honourable profession. Nowadays all the barriers of modesty and reverence are down, and anyone can pass through. Instead of being introduced, they burst in. An audience no better than the speakers[2] accompanies them, a hired claque. There is an agreement with this claque, and gifts of money are handed out in court as openly as if they were at the dinner table. These fellows move from one court to the next, earning the same fee. Then some wit called them 'Sophocleses' from σοφῶς 'wisely' and καλεῖσθαι 'to be called.' In Latin such persons were called Laudiceans.[3]

Both terms are used to insult those who foolishly aspire to win praise for their oratory. For in Greek Sophocles means a man who is called wise, while Laudiceans means those who speak to win fame. In the former there is an allusion to the poet's name, in the latter to the name of a city. Both terms can be applied to those hired admirers referred to by Pliny.

49 Dedi malum et accepi / I got as bad as I gave

The younger Pliny also says in his *Letters*,[1] 'Caecilius Classicus, a dreadful fellow and a self-professed scoundrel, had served as proconsul in that region (that is, Baetica) and had been both brutal and extortionate. This was the same year that Marius Priscus served in Africa.[2] Now, Priscus came

* * * * *

origin it is a fragment of the early Roman tragedian Accius (TRF Accius 203). It became *Adagia* II ix 62.

48 *Adagia* II iii 30
1 Pliny *Letters* 2.14.3–5
2 Reading *actoribus* 'speakers' for *auctoribus* 'authors' in *1500* (*authoribus* in *1506*). The reading of the early editions is *auctoribus*.
3 The point of the joke in Latin is a supposed pun, based on false Latin etymology and the name of the city of Laodicea. The term 'Laudicean' can be thought to derive from *laus* 'praise' and *dicere* 'to say.'

49 *Adagia* II ii 83. Otto 500
1 Pliny *Letters* 3.9.2
2 Marcus Priscus too was charged with extortion during his proconsulship in Africa (AD 97–8). See Pliny *Letters* 2.11.2.

from Baetica, and Classicus came from Africa. Because of this a quite witty
saying arose among the Baeticans, "I got as bad as I gave" (for distress often
actually prompts witticisms).'

One can use the adage whenever such an exchange has taken place,
one bad thing being countered by another; for example, if a father marries
off his ne'er-do-well son and gets a ne'er-do-well daughter-in-law in return.

50 Clavum clavo trudere / To drive out one nail by another
This means to rebuff one fault with another fault, one evil with another
evil; to meet force with force, malice with malice, depravity with depravity.
A new love drives out an old one, like a nail driving out a nail. We should
answer slander with slander, brazenness with brazenness, just as one nail
drives out another one. St Jerome uses this adage.[1] The Greek form of the
expression is Πάτταλον ἐξέκρουσας παττάλῳ 'You have driven out a nail with
a nail.'[2]

**51 Malo nodo malus quaerendus est cuneus / A hard wedge must be sought
for a hard knot**
This adage is similar in meaning to the immediately preceding one: we
must act shamefully with those who have no shame, craftily with those
who are crafty, slanderously with those who slander us, ungratefully with
those who are ungrateful to us. This one too is in Jerome.[1]

**52 Si tibi machaera est, et nobis urbina est domi / You may have a sword,
but I too have a spit of my own**
This is very like the proverb in Jerome we have just mentioned. It is spoken
by Chrysalus in *The Bacchis Sisters* of Plautus, when he answers threats with
threats and responds to the soldier's ferocity with equally fierce words.
For both a sword and a spit are kinds of weapons.[1] 'You may have a

* * * * *

50 *Adagia* I ii 4. Cited in the commentary of Polydore Vergil 284 (= *Adagia* II ii
   63). Otto 396
1 Jerome *Letters* 125.14.1 CSEL 56.1 132
2 The Greek means literally 'you have driven out one *peg* with another one.'
   This mistake arose because the correct Greek form of the proverb was missing
   from Erasmus' manuscript of Diogenianus (see 7 above) at this point (5.16).
   The proper Greek original of *clavum clavo trudere* is ἥλῳ τὸν ἧλον ἐκκρούειν.

51 *Adagia* I ii 5. Otto 480
1 Jerome *Letters* 69.5.1 CSEL 54 686

52 *Adagia* II ix 13
1 Plautus *Bacchides* 887. The correct reading, *vervina*, is attested by Fulgentius, a grammarian of the late fifth century. It is the diminutive of *veru(m)*

sword, but I too have a spit of my own.' In other words, if you deal
with us in a warlike and ferocious way, we have the means to crush your
ferocity.

53 **Suo sibi hunc iugulo gladio, suo telo. Incidit in foveam quam fecit / I
am cutting his throat with his own sword, with his own weapon. He fell
into the pit that he had made**
In *The Brothers* of Terence the old man Micio finds fault with his brother's
harshness in these words: 'Old age brings this particular vice; we are more
preoccupied with money than we should be.'[1] His brother Demea turns
these words back against him at the end of the play when the circumstances
suit him:

> It's not my words I am following but yours, Micio.
> A little while ago you wisely said, 'It is a fault common to all
> That in old age we are too preoccupied with money.' This flaw
> We should avoid.[2]

After he had put his brother in a tight spot with these words, so that
he could not refuse the land he was asking for, he added, 'I am cutting
his throat with his own sword.'[3] This adage is also found elsewhere in this
poet.[4] We shall use it quite wittily if we ever discomfit a man by taking
advantage of an opportunity he himself has given us, or if we refute someone with his own words, or if we show someone that we are doing to him
what he said in his own interests – in short, whenever we turn anything
at all against the man who initiated it. The same metaphor is to be found
in Plautus in his *Amphitryo*: 'And this man is to be driven out of his house
with his own weapon, his wicked cunning.'[5] And in a Hebraic proverb a
man who is caught by the thing that he had used to try and catch someone else is said to have fallen into the pit that he had constructed as a

* * * * *

which means 'spit.' The corrupt form *urbina* survives in all the editions of the
Adagia.

53 *Adagia* i i 51 (Otto 759) and i i 52 (Otto 1750). Cf also Otto 713. The second
   part of the heading (*Incidit ... fecit*) was added in *1506*.
1 Terence *Adelphoe* 833–4
2 Terence *Adelphoe* 952–5
3 Terence *Adelphoe* 958
4 Perhaps Erasmus is thinking of *Eunuchus* 417, where *iugulare* is used metaphorically.
5 Plautus *Amphitryo* 269 (with *telo suo* 'his own weapon')

trap for others[6] and to have been caught by the noose that he had spread out.[7]

54 Irritare cabrones *et item alia paroemia similia*[1] / To stir up hornets *and other similar proverbs*

There can be no doubts in anyone's mind that every saying in Plautus ought to be regarded as a proverb. The charm and antiquity of this poet is so great that scholars can use each of his *clausulae* as if they were proverbs.[2] Why should what the ancients did in the case of Homer not apply to Plautus, the writer of comedies, who is so rich in sayings, who is so witty, and who is so ancient?[3] According to Macrobius 'all of Homer's apophthegms were regarded as proverbs and were on everyone's lips everywhere.'[4] I have not thought it a nuisance or unprofitable, therefore, to review all the most ancient sayings from Plautus' plays.[5] This one from *Amphitryo* especially occurs to me: 'You will stir up hornets.'[6] This relates to women's natural disposition; if you stand up to them when they are angry, you provoke them all the more. They do not tolerate anyone who argues against what they believe. Jerome used this adage in his *Letters*.[7] The hornet is an insect with a very deadly sting. In book eleven chapter twenty-one of his *Natural History* Pliny says that 'their stings hardly ever fail to cause fever' and adds that 'according to some sources a man dies if he is stung twenty-seven times.'[8] Plautus expresses the same idea using a different metaphor, and there is

* * * * *

6 Ps 7:16 (Vulgate); Prov 26:27

7 Ps 9:16 (Vulgate). This appears later as *Adagia* I i 53 *Suo ipsius laqueo captus est* 'He was caught in his own noose.'

54 *Adagia* I i 60. Ermolao Barbaro uses this proverb in *Epistolae* 10 (1.13 Branca). Otto 453

1 The editions erroneously read *similis* for *similia*.

2 By *clausulae* Erasmus may be thinking of ἐπιφωνήματα, a rhetorical term referring to phrases, sometimes gnomic in nature, that rounded off a section or argument. He is of course guilty of gross exaggeration.

3 Later editions of the *Collectanea*, published by Matthias Schürer, offer *venusto* 'charming' for *vetusto* 'ancient,' the reading in 1500 and 1506.

4 Macrobius *Saturnalia* 5.16.6 (not quoted exactly)

5 Plautus is Erasmus' source for almost all of the following adage titles, down to c 90.

6 Plautus *Amphitryo* 707

7 Erasmus is confusing this adage with *cornutam bestiam petere* 'to assail a horned beast,' which occurs in Jerome *Adversus Rufinum* 1.31 PL 23 443A, CCSL 79 32 and is quoted in C 241A, where it is ascribed to Plautus.

8 Pliny *Naturalis historia* 11.73

no doubt that it is proverbial: 'If you wish to oppose a Bacchant in her bacchic frenzy, / You'll make one who is mad even madder. She'll strike you the more. / If you give in, you will get away with only one blow.'[9] The Bacchants used to strike with their wands those who got in their way.

55 Vitam humanam plus aloes habere quam mellis / There are more aloes than honey in human life

In the same play such a sentiment is expressed by the character Alcumena: 'This is the lot of every human in life, / So the gods decreed, that sorrow is joy's companion, / That more misfortune and pain be present immediately . . .'[1] Apuleius shows that we should have no doubts about the expression being proverbial. This is what he writes in his *Florida*: 'But it is indeed a true saying that the gods have never given mortals good fortune without some trouble joined to it.'[2]

56 In aere piscari, venari in mari / To fish in the air, to hunt in the sea

Both proverbs were spoken by Libanus in *The Comedy of Asses* when he had been told by his master Demaenetus to cheat his wife of money.[1] He meant that it was impossible to get anything from a tight-fisted woman. He says, 'You might as well order me to fish in the air, and to hunt with a javelin in the open sea.' We shall use the saying correctly when we want to indicate that nothing should be sought where it could in no way be found; for example, if anyone were to seek a life of contentment in the midst of wealth or pleasures. Boethius also uses these metaphors in his poetry.[2]

57 Nudo vestimenta detrahere / To tear the clothes off a naked man

The same Libanus was advised by his master to get money from him by a trick so that his son might buy his girl-friend. Libanus says, 'That's a

* * * * *

9 Plautus *Amphitryo* 703–5

55 *Adagia* I viii 66. Erasmus probably drew the saying directly from Poliziano's *Praefatio in Suetonium* (1.502 Maier), since he does not give the actual source of the saying, Juvenal 6.181, which refers to a wife, not to human life in general. Otto 1083
 1 Plautus *Amphitryo* 634–6. Erasmus cuts short the quotation, the result being that 'immediately' makes no sense. The next part says 'something good befalls us.'
 2 Apuleius *Florida* 18 (pages 34–5 in Helm's 1910 edition)

56 *Adagia* I iv 74. Otto 27
 1 Plautus *Asinaria* 99–100
 2 Boethius *Consolatio philosophiae* Metrum 8.5–8

57 *Adagia* I iv 76. Otto 1249

great joke! You are telling me to tear the clothes off a naked man.'[1] In the previous example he obviously meant that his master's wife was too clever and attentive to be cheated of anything; in this case he means that his master has nothing to be deprived of.

58 Hostimentum est opera pro pecunia / Service for money is a fair exchange

These are the words of the bawd Clareta in the same play, when a young man casts up all the kindnesses he has bestowed on the courtesans. The sense is: 'You wanted the girl and she was given to you. I wanted money and you gave it to me. Neither of us has anything to complain about.' This saying will suit those boastful persons who think they have done a great kindness if they give some gift to a poor person; they brag about it and think they should get great credit for it. However, they do not remember how much the poor man has served and obliged them. According to Plautus 'Service for money is fair exchange.' For Festus Pompeius *hostimentum* means 'recompense for a kindness.'[1] It is worth noting that *par pari referre* 'to render like for like' also has the appearance of a proverb.[2]

59 Quasi piscis, itidem est amator lenae: nequam est nisi recens / To a bawd a lover is like a fish, only good for anything if he is fresh

Words that are worthy of a procuress. Even today there is a proverb, 'A house-guest is like a fish – he smells bad after three days.'[1]

60 Ad suum quemque hominem quaestum aequum est esse callidum / Each for his own advantage is rightly hard-headed

Also spoken by the same bawd.[1]

* * * * *

1 Plautus *Asinaria* 91–2

58 *Adagia* II iv 14. The source is Plautus *Asinaria* 172. The correct name of the character is Cleareta.
1 Pompeius Festus 91.11 Lindsay
2 This proverb becomes *Adagia* I i 35. The remark is prompted by the appearance of *par pari datum* at the beginning of Plautus *Asinaria* 172. The sense of c 561 is similar.

59 *Adagia* IV i 74. Otto 1429. The source is Plautus *Asinaria* 178.
1 Suringar 171

60 *Adagia* III vii 19. Otto 1500
1 Plautus *Asinaria* 186, with a slight difference in word order. Plautus *Truculentus* 416 agrees exactly with Erasmus' wording, but Erasmus must have had the verse in *Asinaria* in mind.

61 Necesse est facere sumptum qui quaerit lucrum / You must spend money to make money

The man who wants to make a profit must first incur expense, as the common proverb says: 'It is not easy to call back falcons if your hands have nothing in them' and 'a fish cannot be caught without bait.'[1]

62 Fortiter malum qui patitur, idem post potitur bonum / Take the rough like a man and the smooth is yours hereafter

A very well-known saying.[1]

63 Lupus est homo homini, non homo, qui qualis sit non novit / A man is a wolf, not a man, to the one who knows nothing of his character

This warns us not to trust persons we do not know even if they seem honest.

64 Festo die si quid prodegeris, profesto egere liceat nisi peperceris / Wasteful in holiday time, want in ordinary time unless you live thriftily

This is spoken by the miserly old man Euclio.[1] It instructs us not to be so lavish in our spending on special occasions that we lack money for ordinary daily expenses. Festivals were celebrated by the offering of sacrifices or by day-time feasts or by games honouring the gods or by public holidays. Ordinary days were for personal and civic business.

65 Ferre iugum / To bear the yoke

In *Curculio* Palinurus says, 'Does she yet bear the yoke?'[1] He is asking whether a girl is old enough to have a man. For what follows shows clearly that this is the sense. The young man immediately replies, 'She has been

* * * * *

61 Not in *Adagia*. Otto 972. The source is Plautus *Asinaria* 217.
1 Suringar 130A and 130B

62 The source is Plautus *Asinaria* 324. Like the preceding adage, this did not make its way into the *Adagia* as a separate entry, but is cited in *Adagia* I vi 62 No bees, no honey. The translation of the saying here adopts the one given at CWE 32 44.
1 Cf Suringar 191.

63 *Adagia* I i 70. Otto 990. The source is Plautus *Asinaria* 495.

64 *Adagia* I ii 69
1 Plautus *Aulularia* 380–1

65 *Adagia* I ii 71
1 Plautus *Curculio* 50–1

untouched by me as if she were my sister.' Horace in his *Odes*: 'Not yet can she bow her neck and bear the yoke.'[2]

65A Nemo ire quemquam prohibet publica via / No one forbids anyone to travel by the public road
Everyone has the right to make use of what is open to all and is in the public domain.

66 Flamma fumo est proxima / Fire follows smoke
Whoever wants to avoid misfortune should avoid circumstances where it may arise; for example, a man who does not want to be corrupted should shun dissolute company, a man who does not want to have sex should not give a kiss. The speaker immediately adds, 'Smoke can burn nothing, but fire can.'[1]

67 Qui e nuce nucleum esse vult, frangit nucem / He who wants to eat the kernel of a nut breaks the shell
Whoever wants success must not shirk hard work.

68 Verberare lapidem / To beat a stone
Planesium the courtesan warns her lover not to strike his slave, who was inured to beatings, to avoid hurting his hand. She says, 'Please, do not hit a stone, lest you damage your hand.'[1] This will be suitable to apply to anyone who competes in abuse and slander with those who relish such things and are not offended by them.

69 Vorare humum / To swallow the hook
This means to be greedy to get those things that will ruin us if we succumb to them. It was used by the parasite Curculio to describe a pimp when he begins to read a letter that is meant to deceive him.[1] Chrysalus in *The Bacchis*

* * * * *

2 Horace *Odes* 2.5.1–2

65A This was erroneously numbered LXV instead of LXVI in *1506*. *Adagia* III v 27. Plautus *Curculio* 35

66 *Adagia* I v 20. The source is Plautus *Curculio* 53. The speaker is a slave giving advice to his young master on the perils of a love affair. Otto 666
1 Plautus *Curculio* 54, the implication being that if there is smoke, there is the danger of fire.

67 *Adagia* II ix 35. Plautus *Curculio* 55. Otto 1255

68 *Adagia* II v 72. See Otto 916n (not recognized there as a proverb).
1 Plautus *Curculio* 197

69 *Adagia* II v 74. Otto 781
1 Plautus *Curculio* 431

Sisters uses the same metaphor to express the same idea: 'Now this thrush is going for the worm in the trap.'[2]

70 Intra praesepis suas / Safe in his own fold

This means 'safe and sound.' Plautus in *Casina*: 'He knows that if gets his way in this, the woman he loves will be safe in his own fold,' meaning 'secure and at hand.'[1] For what is shut up within our walls cannot escape. These words refer to an old man who was scheming to have the servant-girl he loved married off to his bailiff. His plan was to enjoy the girl in the country whenever he wished, without the knowledge of his wife. Also in *The Ropes*: 'He summons me before my master who will arbitrate – safe in my own field.'[2]

71 Aliquam reperitis rimam / You find a chink

It seems to have been taken from fish or birds that have been caught and then applied metaphorically to tricksters, who always find some way of escaping justice no matter how bad their cause is. Horace: 'That cursed Proteus will slip through these chains.'[1]

72 Necessum est vorsis gladiis depugnarier / We must exchange our swords for new weapons and fight to the end

In other words, to succeed we need a different method.[1]

73 Nunc nos collatis signis depugnabimus / Now we shall join battle and fight to the end

This means to fight at close quarters. It was taken from Homer[1] and is used

* * * * *

2 Plautus *Bacchides* 792. This verse is the source for *Adagia* IV v 71 To go after food from a snare.

70 *Adagia* I vii 50
1 Plautus *Casina* 56–7
2 Plautus *Rudens* 1038. The title *Rudentes* 'The Ropes' is found (incorrectly) in early editions.

71 *Adagia* III ii 75. The source of the phrase is Plautus *Curculio* 510. Otto 1542
1 Horace *Satires* 2.3.71

72 Not in *Adagia* as an independent entry, but cited in *Adagia* III v 88. Plautus *Casina* 344. See Otto 760.
1 The Plautine context and Erasmus' explanation of the expression support the (unusual?) meaning of *vorsis gladiis* given here.

73 Not in *Adagia* as an independent entry, but cited in *Adagia* III v 88. Plautus *Casina* 352
1 The reference to Homer (dropped in *Adagia* III v 88) is odd, given the distinctive Roman flavour of the expression (literally, 'standards having been

proverbially by scholars. We are said to fight at close quarters whenever we are debating and use arguments that are particularly relevant to the issue.

74 **In saltu uno duos apros capere / To catch two boars in one copse**
This means to catch two men red-handed in one swoop. Chalinus in *Casina*: 'Now I shall catch two boars in one copse.'[1]

75 **Frigidam aquam suffundere / To pour cold water**
This means using disparaging remarks to damage the good will between persons who are fond of each other, thereby making the relationship a cooler and less committed one. And yet to pour cold water also means to help and urge on, as can be inferred from the *Pandects*.[1] The procuress in *The Little Chest* accuses married women of secretly bearing ill will against courtesans although openly they are very pleasant to them; they try to the best of their ability to prevent their husbands having affairs with them. Since the procuress thought this behaviour was quite shameful, she said, 'They are civil enough to women of our class in public. In private, however, at the slightest chance they treacherously pour cold water on us.'[2]

76 **Confringere tesseram / To break one's token**
In the same play the young lover says that he has bound himself by oath to marrying the bawd's daughter. He therefore begs the bawd not to allow him to become a perjurer by his failure to do so. To this the bawd replies in these words: 'Away with you, find a place where you can back up your oath.

* * * * *

joined'). Cf Homer *Iliad* 13.126–35 and in particular 131: 'shield pressed on shield, helmet on helmet, and man on man.'

74 *Adagia* III vi 63. Otto 124
1 Plautus *Casina* 476. Chalinus says this when he hears an old man and his bailiff planning how the former will get access to a slave-girl who is supposed to marry the bailiff.

75 *Adagia* I x 51. See I x 51n (CWE 32 379–80) for the different interpretations of the proverb offered at greater length than in the *Collectanea*; Otto 137n
1 *Digest* 3.2.4, where there is a reference to grooms who threw water over their horses to make them run faster. See *Adagia* I x 51. This sentence is an addition of 1506.
2 Plautus *Cistellaria* 33–5

76 *Adagia* I x 50. Otto 1769

Here with us, you have now broken your token.'[1] This metaphor seems to be drawn from a grain-allotment[2] or from a token that is a symbol of friendship.[3]

77 Quod dedi, non datum vellem / I'm sorry I gave what I did

An expression showing that someone regrets an action that has been done and cannot be undone;[1] it also indicates that he will beware in the future of doing something again that he will regret. In case anyone doubts that this is proverbial, I shall add the words of the same procuress: 'In this new business I shall make use of that old saying, "I'm sorry I gave what I did; what is left I shall not give." '[2]

78 Mihi istic nec seritur nec metitur / I have naught to do with the sowing and reaping there

This is in Plautus in *Epidicus*.[1] The meaning is: 'That business you speak of there brings no profit or loss to me.'

79 Nihil homini amico est opportuno amicius / There is no greater friend for a man than a timely one

This one is in the same play.[1] However, this saying is expressed in the following way in a Greek proverb 'Goodwill untimely differs not from hate.'[2] For help that is given at the wrong time usually generates hate rather than gratitude.

* * * * *

1 Plautus *Cistellaria* 502–3
2 One function of a *tessera* 'token, ticket' in Rome was to give the bearer access to free corn.
3 The last part of the sentence ('or from a token ... friendship') was added in 1506.

77 *Adagia* II iv 59. Polydore Vergil 282; Otto 499
1 Cf *Adagia* II iii 72.
2 Plautus *Cistellaria* 505–6

78 *Adagia* I vi 82. Otto 1106
1 Plautus *Epidicus* 265

79 *Adagia* IV i 75
1 Plautus *Epidicus* 425
2 Erasmus does not give the Greek here. The Latin form is probably drawn from Ermolao Barbaro *Epistolae* 81 (= Poliziano *Epistolae* 9.5) 1.102–3 Branca. It reappears, with a slight change of wording, as *Adagia* I vii 69 Goodwill untimely differs not from hate, where the Greek form of the proverb, Ἄκαιρος εὔνοι᾽ οὐδὲν ἐχθρᾶς διαφέρει (Diogenianus 1.48, Zenobius 1.50), is given.

80 Farcire centones / To stuff a patchwork quilt

This means to deafen a listener's ears with boastful stories. For in *Epidicus*, when a soldier is preparing to tell of his military exploits in the usual manner of a soldier, Periphanes says, 'Why don't you look for someone else in whom to stuff a patchwork quilt?'[1] He means 'someone to whom you may tell your boastful lies.'

81 Aliter catuli longe olent, aliter sues / Dogs and hogs smell very different

The sense of this proverb is that it is not just clothing that distinguishes one man from another; in each person there is some inborn quality, peculiar to each individual, that shines out on his face and in his eyes. This allows us to distinguish easily between free man and slave, well-born man and peasant, good man and bad. This is why Quintilian says, 'He does not have even the face of a free man.'[1]

82 Ab unguiculo ad summum capillum (*Homerus:* Ἐς πόδας ἐκ κεφαλῆς) / From toenail to the topmost hair (*Homer: From head to foot*)

This is what the ancients said when they wished to indicate the whole person. Plautus in *Epidicus*: 'Look, Epidicus, right from the toenail to the topmost hair.'[1] If we wish, therefore, to imply that a man's natural talents and his character can be clearly seen, we could say, in a quite pleasing way, that he shows what kind of man he is 'From toenail right to the topmost hair.' Horace: 'Handsome from head to heel.'[2]

83 Tragulam iniicere. Fabricam facere / To cast a spear. To do some dirty work

Both of these sayings mean to engage in tricks for the purpose of deceit. Similarly, the verb *machinari* has the metaphorical sense of 'to engage in a

* * * * *

80 *Adagia* II iv 58. Otto 371
1 Plautus *Epidicus* 455

81 *Adagia* I viii 77. The source is Plautus *Epidicus* 579. Otto 361
1 Quintilian 6.3.32

82 *Adagia* I ii 37. The second part of the title, the reference to and quotation from Homer (see *Iliad* 18.353 and 23.169), was an addition of 1506. Otto 1822
1 Plautus *Epidicus* 622–3
2 Horace *Epistles* 2.2.4

83 *Adagia* II viii 88 (in the commentary on which Erasmus mentions *fabricam facere*). Otto 1796

cunning plot.'[1] Apocides in Plautus' *Epidicus*: 'They are preparing to cast a spear at you.'[2] Again, elsewhere: 'He has done some dirty work.'[3]

84 Malam messem facere / To reap a harvest of calamity

Epidicus in the same play: 'It's a bitter pill to reap a harvest of calamity in return for kindnesses given.'[1] In other words, it is intolerable to suffer an injury as a result of a favour given. Cicero: 'As you have sown, so also shall you reap.'[2]

85 Ego quoque pol metuo, ne lusciniolae defuerit cantus / I too have fears, that the nightingale may stop singing

This occurs in Plautus in *The Bacchis Sisters*.[1] It means that someone has such an abundant supply of something that he can never be without it; for example, a woman without words, Cicero without rhetorical skills, a sophist without quibbles.

86 Ad vivam cutem / Down to the quick

Meaning 'down to the bare skin,' so that there is nothing left apart from the bare body. Chrysalus in the same play: 'I shall shear him of gold, down to the quick.'[1]

87 Aspergere aquam / To sprinkle with water

To restore consciousness to someone who has fainted because of sudden anguish. This generally happens when a person suddenly gets bad news. Such a person usually recovers when water has been sprinkled in his face

* * * * *

1 The verb *machinari* is based on *machina* which in its literal sense means 'war machine.' The metaphor is therefore similar to the metaphorical use of *tragula* in the proverb here.
2 Plautus *Epidicus* 690. The name of the character is Apoecides, and the correct text has the third person singular ('he is preparing').
3 In the second half of Plautus *Epidicus* 690, where the correct text has the present tense ('he is doing')

84 *Adagia* III vii 55 (with *miseram* 'wretched' for *malam* 'bad'). Also mentioned in *Adagia* I viii 78 As you have sown, so also shall you reap. Cf Otto 1104.
1 Plautus *Epidicus* 718
2 Cicero *De oratore* 2.65.261

85 *Adagia* III vi 77. Polydore Vergil 163; Otto 991
1 Plautus *Bacchides* 38

86 *Adagia* II iv 13. Cf c 335.
1 Plautus *Bacchides* 242

87 *Adagia* III ii 60. Otto 137

and the blood has been drawn from the heart. Plautus: 'You have sprinkled me with water.'[1]

88 Aspergo. Olfacio. Devoro / I sprinkle. I smell. I swallow
Sometimes even a simple verb is used metaphorically in a proverbial way, as is the case with *aspergo*, in the example just given; Cicero often uses it in the sense of 'to spoil slightly.' *Against Vatinius*: 'On whom you sprinkle some stain.'[1] And in the same work: 'Lest his reputation may seem to be sprinkled with some blemish from your shameful behaviour.' And often elsewhere 'to sprinkle with abuse,'[2] 'to sprinkle with mirth,' 'to sprinkle with witticisms.' In the same way *olfacere* 'to sniff' can mean 'to suspect,' *subolere* 'to smell' can mean 'to be suspected,' *olfacere* 'to sniff' can mean 'to pursue curiously and carefully.' The verb *devorare* 'to swallow' can mean 'to endure a painful experience as if free of feeling,' the metaphor being taken from those those who drink down bitter potions or medicines, even though they shudder at the thought of the taste. And so in Cicero and Quintilian we find 'to swallow disgust,' 'to drink down vexation.'[3]

89 Valere pancratice, athletice, pugilice, basilice / To be as fit as a pancratiast, as an athlete, as a boxer, as a king
These expressions are used in Plautus in the sense 'to be healthy and have all one's strength.'[1] In the same author *musice valere* 'a life of pure music' refers to living in a luxurious and comfortable style,[2] *basilice valere* 'to flourish like a king'[3] to living in a fine and magnificent way.

90 Acetum habere in pectore / He has vinegar in his bosom
This is said of someone who has wit and a sharp tongue. It also appears several times in Plautus. In *The Bacchis Sisters*: 'Now I shall find out whether

* * * * *

1 Plautus *Bacchides* 247; *Truculentus* 366

88 These verbs are metaphorical rather than proverbial; cf *Adagia* I vi 81.
1 Cicero *In Vatinium* 17.41, then 6.15
2 As at Apuleius *Metamorphoses* 8.2
3 For example, Cicero *Philippics* 6.17 and Quintilian 11.2.41

89 *Adagia* II viii 86. Otto 198
1 Plautus *Bacchides* 248, *Epidicus* 20, *Persa* 30
2 Plautus *Mostellaria* 728; cf *Adagia* II iii 34.
3 The phrase *basilice valere* does not appear to be attested in classical Latin.

90 *Adagia* II iii 52; cf C 270. Otto 9

there is vinegar and a sour heart in your bosom.'[1] And in Terence *habere salem* 'to have wit': 'The man who has wit, as you have.'[2]

91 Homo homini daemonium / Man is a god to man

Ἄνθρωπος ἀνθρώπου δαιμόνιον, Man is a spirit (or god) to man. It suits someone who suddenly and unexpectedly saves or helps another person. For the ancients thought that being a god consisted simply and solely of assisting mortals. So Virgil: 'A god gave us this respite.'[1] And Pliny in his *History of the World* book two: 'Being a god is helping a mortal.'[2]

92 Tangere ulcus. Tangere vivum. Hanc anagyrim ne moveas / To touch on a sore spot. To touch to the quick. Don't disturb this anagyris.

When we say something that especially hurts another person we are said to touch on a sore spot. Terence: 'Was there anything less necessary than to touch on this sore spot?' Donatus points out that there is a proverb underlying these words.[1] 'To touch to the quick' has very much the same sense, meaning to say something so abusive that it is truly hurtful. Ermolao: 'Don't disturb this anagyris, to use a medical proverb.'[2] The anagyris is a kind of plant.[3]

93 Pythagorica adagia / The adages of Pythagoras

No one doubts that most of the sayings of Pythagoras became proverbial.

* * * * *

1 Plautus *Bacchides* 405; cf Plautus *Pseudolus* 739.
2 Terence *Eunuchus* 400–1

91 *Adagia* I i 69. Diogenianus 1.80. Also in Zenobius 1.91 and *Suda* A 2536. The source of the Greek, however, may be Ermolao Barbaro, either *Epistolae* 81 (= Poliziano *Epistolae* 9.5) 1.108–9 Branca, since Erasmus draws on this same letter for the immediately following adage (see C 92 n2), or *Castigationes Plinianae* on *Naturalis historia* 2.18 (Pozzi 39). Polydore Vergil 1; Otto 517
1 Virgil *Eclogues* 1.6
2 Pliny *Naturalis historia* 2.18. The correct text is 'being a god is for one mortal to help another.' Erasmus omits a word (*mortali*), restored in the *Adagia*.

92 *Adagia* I vi 79 (for the first). For the third see *Adagia* I i 65. Otto 1810
1 Terence *Phormio* 690 and Donatus in his commentary on 690
2 Drawn from Ermolao Barbaro's *Epistolae* 81 (1.108 Branca), published in the Aldine edition of Angelo Poliziano's *Omnia opera* (1498) as *Epistolae* 9.5. See CWE 31 108 for the different interpretations of the third of the proverbs given under this entry. See also Diogenianus 1.25 and C 727.
3 This sentence was added in 1506. Erasmus may have found the information about the anagyris at Pliny *Naturalis historia* 27.30.

93 In the *Adagia* Erasmus includes 'The precepts of Pythagoras' in I i 2 (see CWE 31 31–50). They are more usually known as *Symbola Pythagorae*. The title is here a

The ancients venerated him to such an extent that through the whole region of Italy that was once called Magna Graecia his precepts were preserved by being engraved on bronze tablets. Jerome mentions some of these in his work *Against Rufinus*.[1]

94 Κοινὰ φίλων πάντα / Between friends all is common
Between friends all is common.[1] This became such a popular proverb that it is referred to as a proverb even by a comic character in Terence. He says, 'For this is an old saying, "Between friends all is common." '[2] This adage is cited in Plato and credited to Euripides.[3]

95 Est amicus alter ipse / Ἕτερος αὐτός / A friend is another self
This advises us to think of our friends' affairs as our own. The Greeks say that two bodies have one soul, μία ψυχή.

96 Duorum temporum maxime habenda est ratio, mane et vesperi / We must pay closest attention to two times, morning and evening
In other words, we must attend to what we are going to do and to what we will have done.

* * * * *

descriptive tag for the adages that he then gives as C 94–106, for which Jerome is his major source (see n1). For other examples of such generic headings, see C 98, C 108, C 238, C 370, C 397, C 408 below.
 1 Jerome *Adversus Rufinum* 3.39 PL 23 507–8, CCSL 79 109. Erasmus follows Jerome closely in the order in which he gives the precepts and often draws directly from him for the interpretation. Jerome does not give the Greek versions.

 94 *Adagia* I i 1 (00 n4). The usual form of the proverb in Greek is Κοινὰ τὰ φίλων 'The [possessions] of friends are held in common' (Diogenianus 5.76, Zenobius 4.79). Erasmus may have added πάντα 'all' either on the basis of Terence *Adelphoe* 804 (see n2), or from Martial 2.43.1 (see C 369 n2). See also Bühler 5.488–99 on Zenobius Athous 5.93. Polydore Vergil 132; Otto 87
 1 Erasmus gives no Latin translation in the heading, but the first line of the commentary (*amicorum communia omnia*, a paraphrase of Terence *Adelphoe* 804) serves this purpose.
 2 Terence *Adelphoe* 804 with *omnia* 'all things'
 3 As at Plato *Laws* 5.739c and elsewhere, but no reference is made to Euripides on any of these occasions. Poliziano mentions Euripides when using this proverb (in Latin) in the epilogue of his *Miscellanea* (1.311 Maier), and this may be Erasmus' source. The saying comes from Euripides *Orestes* 735.

 95 *Adagia* I i 2, in which most of the following proverbs (C 99–107) are mentioned. The Greek in the heading and at the end of the brief discussion was added in 1506. The Greek was probably taken directly from a Greek source, such as Aristotle *Nicomachean Ethics* 9.9 (1170b6–7). It is not in Diogenianus. Otto 111

 96 Omitted from the *Adagia*

97 **Post deum veritatem colendam / After God truth must be worshipped**
Truth alone makes mortals closest to God.

98 **Aenigmata Pythagorica / The riddles of Pythagoras**
Closer to proverbs are those riddles with which, as Jerome also attests, Aristotle concerns himself most diligently.[1]

99 **Stateram ne transilias / Exceed not the balance**
This means 'do not deviate in any way from what is just.'

100 **Ignem gladio ne fodias / Stir not the fire with a sword**
This means 'do not hurl curses at a man who is already in a swollen rage.'

101 **Coronam ne carpseris / Pluck not a garland for yourself**
This means 'keep the laws of your cities.'

102 **Cor ne comederis / Do not eat your heart out**
This means 'cast out sorrow.'

103 **Quum profectus fueris, ne redeas / When you have left, do not return**
This means 'after death, do not long for this life.'

104 **Hirundinem in domum ne recipias / Do not allow a swallow into your home**
This means 'do not have garrulous people under the same roof as yourself.'

* * * * *

97 Omitted from the *Adagia*

98 Despite having a separate number, this heading is obviously not a proverb, but introduces a series of more enigmatic sayings. Erasmus is also following Jerome in making a distinction between the preceding sayings and those that follow from this point.
  1 For example, Jerome *Adversus Rufinum* 3.39 PL 23 508, CCSL 79 104

99 In *Adagia* I i 2 (CWE 31 33)

100 In *Adagia* I i 2 (CWE 31 36)

101 Referred to in *Adagia* I i 2 (CWE 31 46)

102 Given with a different form of the verb (the future imperative *edito*) at *Adagia* I i 2 (CWE 31 37).

103 Given as 'Do not turn back when you have come to the final stage' at *Adagia* I i 2 (CWE 31 40)

104 Given as 'Do not have swallows under the same roof' at *Adagia* I i 2 (CWE 31 44); Polydore Vergil 99

105 Per publicam viam ne ambules / Walk not in the public highway

This means 'do not follow the errors of many.'

106 Oneratis superimponendum onus, deponentibus non committendum / Give an extra burden to those already laden, not to those who are laying their burden down

This means that additional precepts must be given to those who strive for virtue, while those who surrender themselves to idle leisure must be abandoned.

107 Super choenice non sedendum / One must not sit on a choenix

This means 'do not trouble yourself about tomorrow's food.' A choenix is the amount of food given for a day.

108 Tria Apollinis oracula / Three oracles of Apollo

Although the following oracles and others like them were probably thought of as proverbs in antiquity, it is not part of my present purpose to go through them all. For there would be no end to it. I shall give only those that are regarded as proverbs by authors who would have known this. One that is particularly well known, from three oracles of Apollo, is *Nihil nimis* 'Nothing to excess,' which Socrates quotes in Plato as an old saying.[1] Moreover, there is also the comic poet in whose works there is no saying that is not proverbial, this being particularly true of one put in the mouth of Sosia, who is both freedman and cook: 'I think this is especially good advice in life – nothing to excess.'[2] In the *Charmides* of Plato Socrates attests that these three precepts were on an inscription on the doors of the temple of Apollo: Γνῶθι σεαυτόν 'Know thyself,' Μηδὲν ἄγαν 'Nothing too much' and, thirdly, Ἐγγύα πάρα δ' ἄτη 'Stand surety and ruin is at hand.'[3] Socrates thinks that

* * * * *

105 In *Adagia* I i 2 (CWE 31 41)

106 A variant of this occurs at *Adagia* I i 2 (CWE 31 41). This adage ends the series drawn from Jerome (see C 93n).

107 This occurs in a slightly different version in *Adagia* I i 2 (CWE 31 33), where Erasmus prefers a different interpretation. It may be drawn from Diogenes Laertius 8.17.

108 The heading is not itself an adage, but introduces three sayings: 'Nothing to excess,' 'Know thyself,' and 'Stand surety and you will lose' (cf *Adagia* I vi 95–7). Erasmus does this elsewhere (see C 93n). Otto 1236 and 1229

  1 Plato *Menexenus* 247E. It is also cited at *Philebus* 45E, but there the speaker is Protarchus, not Socrates.

  2 Terence *Andria* 60–1

  3 Plato *Charmides* 165A, where the speaker is Critias, not Socrates. The Latin versions of the Greek proverbs are given by Erasmus here as *nosce te ipsum, nihil*

the first of these came from Apollo, the others from mortals, and that all three of them ('know thyself,' meaning that one should recognize one's limitations, 'nothing to excess,' and 'stand surety and ruin is at hand') mean much the same, namely, that we should not attempt anything beyond our abilities. 'Know thyself' means that you should know your own capabilities. The last saying means that we should not give surety for someone since the companions of surety are disputes and debt, as Pliny writes.[4]

109 Optimum condimentum fames / Hunger is the best sauce

This is a saying of Socrates[1] that even today is in common use.[2] The meaning is that everything you eat (or do) when you are hungry and greedy for it tastes (or seems) good. Another saying of Socrates, 'The things that are above us are nothing to us,' is similar.[3] This saying is referred to by Lactantius, specifically as a proverb.[4]

110 Iniquum petendum ut aequum feras / Ask an unfair share to get a fair share

Quintilian says in book five, 'The common saying "Ask an unfair share to get a fair one" has much to be said for it.'[1] This was well perceived by Syrus, a character of Terence, who asked a pimp to hand over a girl to Aeschinus, his young master, for half of what he had paid for her.[2] The result was that the pimp was even eager to give up the girl for no more than what he had laid out. Even nowadays there is a common saying that 'the man who strives to buy a golden chariot will certainly get one wheel.'[3] We must aim for the highest so that we can attain moderate success.

* * * * *

nimis, and sponsioni non deest iactura, in which he uses the Latin translation of Plato by Marsilio Ficino. The Greek versions of the first two sayings appeared in 1500, the third (see n4 below) was added in 1506. Erasmus did not need to draw on any specific source for the Greek versions of the first two since they were extremely well known. See for example Juvenal 11.27, adduced in C 369.
4 Pliny Naturalis historia 7.119. The source for the Greek version of this proverb was Ermolao Barbaro's commentary on this passage (see Pozzi 550).

109 Adagia II vii 69. Drawn from Beroaldo's Annotationes centum 19 (see C 3n). Otto 639
1 Xenophon Memorabilia 1.3.5; Cicero De finibus 2.28.90
2 Suringar 165
3 Adagia I vi 69. Polydore Vergil 6; Otto 1714
4 Lactantius Divinae institutiones 3.20.10

110 Adagia II iii 26. Polydore Vergil 176; Otto 865
1 Quintilian 4.5.16 (not book 5). The erroneous reference is corrected in the Adagia.
2 Terence Adelphoe 240–4
3 Suringar 93

111 Mendacem memorem esse oportet / A liar should have a good memory
In the same book we find also 'A liar should have a good memory.'[1] For
nothing is more difficult than for a liar to be consistent in everything he
says. Therefore the man who wants to be a good liar should learn by heart
the techniques for sharpening one's memory.

112 Coriceus auscultavit / A Corycaean has eavesdropped
In book fourteen Strabo[1] mentions the following story: 'The whole area of
the sea that flanked Corycus, a mountain in Asia,[2] was once packed with
pirates, who were called Corycaeans from the name of the mountain. They
dispersed themselves among the different harbours of the area and watched
out for traders. By eavesdropping they learned about the merchants' car-
goes and destinations. Then, after gathering together, they attacked and
robbed the traders at the appropriate place.' This became such a talking
point that it gave rise to the proverb 'A Corycaean has eavesdropped.' By
this we mean that our private plans are being observed by the curious. Cicero uses this adage in his *Letters to Atticus*. He says, 'For all the Corycaeans
seem to be eavesdropping on what I say.'[3]

113 Σκυτάλη Λακωνική / Scytala Laconica / A Spartan despatch
Perhaps some will think that what Cicero wrote to Atticus, 'There's a Spartan despatch for you,' has the force of a proverb. The expression refers to
a confidential letter that is written in Spartan fashion – no one can read it

* * * * *

111 *Adagia* II iii 74. Polydore Vergil 68; Otto 1093
   1 Quintilian 4.2.91

112 *Adagia* I ii 44 (where the discussion is greatly expanded). Here Erasmus draws
    heavily on Filippo Beroaldo *Annotationes centum* 59 (see Heinimann 168 n51
    and c 3n) for the content of the passage in Strabo (see n1 below). Polydore
    Vergil 126 and 127; Otto 449
   1 Strabo 14.1.32, cited in Latin. The first edition of Strabo in the original Greek
    did not appear until 1516.
   2 This phrase, 'a mountain in Asia,' is not in Strabo but occurs in Beroaldo's
    account of the story.
   3 Cicero *Ad Atticum* 10.18.1

113 See *Adagia* II ii 1 and cf c 136. Here Erasmus draws on Filippo Beroaldo *Anno-*
    tationes centum 62 (see c 3n), though Erasmus gives details from Gellius that
    Beroaldo does not provide. In *1500* no Latin equivalent for the Greek version
    is given. It is added in *1506*, for consistency rather than for help in under-
    standing the Greek. Erasmus' source of the Greek version may have been Ci-
    cero's text (Beroaldo gives only a transliterated version of the Greek). Polydore
    Vergil 75

except the sender and the recipient.[1] Anyone who wishes to find out more about this way of sending letters should read Plutarch in his *Lysander*.[2] Gellius also refers to the *scytale* in his *Nights* book seventeen chapter nine and explains it as a *surculus loratus* 'a rod covered with thong,' though in the text there we read *loricatus* 'cuirassed.'[3]

114 **Duos parietes de una dealbare fidelia / To whitewash two walls out of the same bucket**
This means to try to get double thanks for the same deed and to put two persons under an obligation to you by a single action. Marcus Curius to Cicero: 'But, my great friend, do not show this letter to Atticus. Allow him to misunderstand the situation and to think me a loyal man, not one who is accustomed to whitewash two walls out of the same bucket.'[1] Curius wanted both Atticus and Cicero to think most highly of him; he would be a good investment for Atticus, while at the same time he would provide Cicero with interest, so to speak. It is taken from those who undertake the task of whitewashing walls. In our own times we commonly hear a similar, quite witty saying: 'Do you want to get two sons-in-law from the same daughter?'[2]

115 **Aut bibat aut abeat / Ἢ πινέτω ἢ ἀπελθέτω / Let him drink or leave**
Cicero in *Tusculan Questions* book five: 'It is my opinion that in life we should follow the law that holds good at Greek drinking parties. The law

* * * * *

1 Cicero *Ad Atticum* 10.10. 3, taken from Beroaldo
2 Plutarch *Lysander* 19, taken from Beroaldo
3 Gellius *Noctes Atticae* 17.9.6–15. In 1500 the source is erroneously given as book 16. The phrase in question, *surculum loricatum* (in the accusative case), instead of *surculum loratum* 'covered with thong,' is actually an intrusive gloss to be found in 15th-century printed editions of Gellius. The phrase does not appear in modern editions and had already been dropped in the Aldine edition of 1515. See Grant 168.

114 *Adagia* I vii 3, where a more persuasive interpretation of the adage is given. The sense is close to 'running with the hare and hunting with the hound' (CWE 32 308), that is, pretending to support each of two opposing positions. In a letter to Pico della Mirandola (*Epistolae* 81 = Poliziano *Epistolae* 9.5; see 1.102 Branca) Ermolao Barbaro uses a similar expression, *duos parietes linere* 'to plaster two walls,' which is based on the Greek proverb δύο τοίχους ἀλείφειν mentioned in *Adagia* I vii 3. Polydore Vergil 281; Otto 1342
1 Cicero *Ad familiares* 7.29.2
2 Suringar 62.4

115 *Adagia* I x 47. The Greek in the title, probably Erasmus' own effort, was added in 1506. Polydore Vergil 299; Otto 253

says, "Let him drink or leave." And quite right too. For a man should enjoy equally with others the pleasure of drinking or should leave before
encountering the violence of drunkards when he himself is still sober. In
the same way you can flee and leave behind you the assaults of fortune
that you cannot endure.'[1] So much for Cicero. In Greece the young men
used to pick βασιλεῖς 'masters of ceremonies'[2] for their drinking parties
by the throw of the dice.[3] This is the reason for Horace's words, 'nor
will you chose the master of the wine by casting dice.'[4] They prescribed
how much they wished each person to drink. They also had banquet-rules,
which they called νόμοι 'laws.'[5] This includes the one that Cicero refers
to, 'Let him drink or leave,' which also became proverbial. It has certainly some moral force and is suited to many situations, but especially
when we want to indicate that we should act in conformity with the behaviour of those with whom we live or, if we do not like to do so, that
we should leave their company altogether. Even nowadays there is a common saying 'you must bark along with the dogs you have chosen to live
with.'[6]

116 Andabatarum more pugnare / To fight like the Andabatans

This means to dispute with someone in a thoughtless and irrational way,
as if your eyes are closed. For the Andabatans rushed against their opponent with their eyes covered, not able to see where they should strike
or how they should parry blows. And so those who do not understand
their own principles or the principles of the person with whom they
are in dispute are said to fight like the Andabatans. Jerome in *Against
Helvidius*: 'To prove this he piles up countless examples from Scripture,
brandishing his sword in the darkness like the Andabatans.'[1] Again in
Against Jovinian:[2] 'My reluctance to reply puts me at risk. It is as if I am

* * * * *

1 Cicero *Tusculan Disputations* 5.41.118
2 Literally the Greek word means 'kings.'
3 This sentence is drawn from Ermolao Barbaro's commentary on Pliny *Naturalis
historia* 14.88 (Pozzi 733–4).
4 Horace *Odes* 1.4.18
5 Also from Ermolao Barbaro (see n3 above)
6 Suringar 24. This saying becomes *Adagia* I vii 4, also described as a contemporary proverb.

116 *Adagia* II iv 33. Polydore Vergil 107; Otto 105 and 1270
1 Jerome *Adversus Helvidium* 5 PL 23 188C
2 Jerome *Adversus Iovinianum* 1.36 PL 23 260A

between two precipices and, so to speak, between the Symplegades[3] of necessity and prudence; I destroy my modesty on the one hand or the strength of my case on the other. If I reply to these charges, I blush with shame. If my modesty makes me say nothing, I shall seem to be retreating and giving my opponent the opportunity to strike me down. It is better, however, to fight with closed eyes, as the saying goes, like the Andabatans, than not to repel with the shield of truth the darts aimed at me.' Cicero to Trebatius: 'A man whom previously we could not deprive of watching even an Andabatan,'[4] meaning a blindfolded gladiator.

117 Tute lepus es et pulpamentum quaeris / A hare thyself, and goest in quest of game?

This means that you are seeking elsewhere what you already have at your disposal. It was said in *The Eunuch* of Terence by a soldier about a young man who was making a play for a prostitute although he himself could take on that very role.[1] In Greek the expression is Λαγὼς κρεῶν ἐπιθυμεῖ 'A hare is hungry for meat.'[2]

118 Prius leporem testudo praeverterit / Sooner will the tortoise outrun the hare

Πρότερον χελώνη παραδραμεῖται δασύποδα,[1] Sooner will the tortoise run faster than the hare. Said of an extremely difficult task.

* * * * *

3 In Greek mythology the Symplegades were rocks that separated and then closed again, trapping anything that tried to pass between them. Jason and the Argonauts encountered them in their quest for the Golden Fleece.

4 Cicero *Ad familiares* 7.10.2. Trebatius loved to watch gladiatorial spectacles, even those including a blindfolded participant.

117 *Adagia* I vi 7. This adage and the following one are drawn from Niccolò Perotti's *Cornucopiae* (801:11–19); see Heinimann 164–5 and n35. Polydore Vergil 28; Otto 941

1 Terence *Eunuchus* 426

2 One would expect δασύπους 'hare,' as in Perotti (and also Diogenianus 4.12), and not λαγώς. However, the former word was mangled by the printer in *1500*, and Erasmus must have corrected it in *1506* to λαγώς, the common word for 'hare,' without checking his sources. Cf *Adagia* I vi 7.

118 *Adagia* I viii 84. See note on preceding adage for Erasmus' source. Polydore Vergil 27

1 Diogenianus 7.57. Erasmus may have used both Perotti and Diogenianus for the Greek version of the proverb, which appears in *1500*.

119 Lentiscum mandentes / Mastic-chewers

Σχινοτρώκται,[1] Munchers of mastic. A Greek adage directed at those who are obsessed with their appearance,[2] on the grounds that such persons spend all their time brushing and cleaning their teeth. For a dentifrice was customarily made from this resin.[3]

120 Callipedes / Callipedes

In antiquity this was a proverbial name for someone who was very dilatory in doing things and was extremely slow. Suetonius in *Tiberius*: 'Finally he permitted prayers to be offered for his journey and return, the result being that he was commonly called Callipedes as a joke.'[1] The person of this name was the butt of a Greek proverb because he was always running and yet he never advanced by as much as a foot. Cicero to Atticus, when finding fault with the tardiness of Varro, says, 'Two years have passed, but that Καλλιπίδης hasn't moved a foot, although he has never stopped running.'[2]

* * * * *

119 *Adagia* I viii 33. Erasmus has closely followed Ermolao Barbaro for his commentary on this adage. See his *Glossemata* (Pozzi 1416–17) on 'Ocnus' and Heinimann 173. For the Greek version of the adage Erasmus has chosen the form of the agent noun to be found in Diogenianus (8.13) rather than the form used by Barbaro (σχινοτρώξ). Also in Zenobius 5.96 and *Suda* Σ 1793. Polydore Vergil 205, which closely follows Barbaro's commentary (see 17–18 above).
   1 Cf Diogenianus 8.13 Σχῖνον διατρώγειν 'To chew on mastic.'
   2 There is an error in the Latin text here in both *1500* and *1506*. The translation reflects the verb *comendi* for the erroneous *comandi*.
   3 The information is drawn from Ermolao Barbaro, who refers to Martial 14.22. Cf also Martial 3.82.9, 6.74.3.

120 *Adagia* I vi 43. Erasmus is drawing from Domizio Calderini's *Ex tertio libro observationum* (see Campanelli 115, 139–41), in which both passages quoted here appear. The correct form of the name is 'Callippides,' the form as it appears in modern texts of Cicero (see n2), the etymological connection being with horses rather than with feet. Calderini gives the name as Καλλιπίδης and Callipides, while Perotti (*Cornucopiae* 802:59–62), who also cites the two passages, gives it as *gallipes*. For Calderini see C 171 n3. Polydore Vergil 98. Otto 305
   1 Suetonius *Tiberius* 38, where the MSS offer the spelling 'Gallipides' for the name.
   2 Cicero *Ad Atticum* 13.12.3. According to Cicero the great antiquarian Varro had promised to write an honorific dedication for him, but had failed to do so.

121 Albus an ater sis nescio / I know not whether you are dark or fair

An adage often applied to a person who is completely unknown to you. Quintilian in book eleven of his *Principles of Rhetoric*: 'One of the poets says that he does not much care whether Caesar is dark or fair.'[1] He is pointing to Catullus no doubt, among whose poems this verse can be found: 'I know not whether thou art dark or fair.'[2] Apuleius in his *Defence against Charges of Witchcraft*: 'Up till quite recently I was very glad not to know whether you were dark or fair. And, heavens above, I hardly know even now.'[3] Jerome in *Against Helvidius*: 'Pray tell me, who even knew of you before this blasphemy of yours? Who thought you worth a penny? You have achieved what you wanted. You have made yourself a reputation – in crime. Even I, who write against you and live in the same city in which you stutter and blush, have no idea whether you are dark or fair, as the saying goes.'[4] I think, however, that there is something wrong in these words of Jerome.[5]

122 Mala de sese attrahens, ut Caecias nubes / Attracting troubles as the north-easter draws clouds

There is a wind called *Caecias* that Pliny says blows 'midway between north and east.'[1] He writes that unlike other northerly winds this one attracts clouds rather than drives them away. These are his words: 'The coldest of the winds are those that blow from the north, as we have said. The *Corus* 'north-west wind' is close to them. These hold the others in check and drive off rainstorms. In Italy the *Auster* 'south wind' and the *Africus* 'south-west

* * * * *

121 *Adagia* I vi 99. Erasmus draws on Filippo Beroaldo's *Annotationes centum* 36 (see C 3n), where the four sources mentioned by Erasmus can also be found. Polydore Vergil 77; Otto 50
   1 Quintilian 11.1.38. Erasmus usually gives the title of the work in the plural, although the correct form is in the singular (*Institutio oratoria*).
   2 This is the second line of a couplet (Catullus 93) directed at Caesar. In *1500* and *1506* the poet's name is wrongly given as Catulus.
   3 Apuleius *Apologia* 16
   4 Jerome *Adversus Helvidium* 16 PL 23 210B
   5 In his edition of Jerome Erasmus later omits the clause 'in which you stutter and blush,' regarding it as an intrusive gloss. This may be what Erasmus is referring to in the final sentence.

122 *Adagia* I v 62, which correctly offers *ad sese* instead of *de sese* (see n3). Niccolò Perotti refers to the adage in his *Cornucopiae* (340:15–18), but Aulus Gellius is Erasmus' probable source (see n3). Polydore Vergil 150
   1 Pliny *Naturalis historia* 2.120

wind' are the damp winds, especially the former. It is said that in the Black Sea the *Caecias* draws the clouds to itself.'[2] Aulus Gellius says the same in his *Nights* book two chapter twenty-two: 'There is also a wind called *Caecias*. According to Aristotle it blows in such a way that it attracts clouds instead of blasting them away. This, Aristotle says, is the source of the proverbial verse Κακὰ ἐφ᾽ ἑαυτὸν ἕλκων ὡς ὁ Καικίας νέφος "Attracting troubles about himself (*de sese*) as the north-easter draws clouds."'[3] It suits a person who takes pleasure in disputes and unrest and brings these things with him wherever he goes.

123 Equum habet Seianum. Aurum Tolosanum / He must have Seius' horse. Gold from Toulouse

An adage referring to those who suffer great misfortune, taken from a horse that got its name from its owner Gnaeus Seius[1] and had a curse laid on it. The horse was believed to descend from the horses of Diomedes,[2] and was a very handsome animal. However, the curse on it was that whoever owned it 'would be utterly destroyed along with his whole household.'[3] This was because Gnaeus Seianus[4] himself was sentenced to death and horribly executed.[5] Then Dolabella was killed in war, and after him Cassius was slain by the enemy.[6] Then later Antony died a shameful

* * * * *

2 Pliny *Naturalis historia* 2.126
3 Gellius *Noctes Atticae* 2.22.24, citing Aristotle *Problemata* 26.29 (943a32). Gellius is Erasmus' source for the Greek version of the proverb, the origin of which is uncertain. Nauck gives it as a fragment of tragedy (*Adespota* 75 Nauck), but E. Diehl, in *Anthologia lyrica graeca* 3 (Leipzig 1949) 75 (fragment 15), thinks that it is from an iambic poem. This proverb is one of the seven that George Hermonymus added to his manuscript of Diogenianus (Oxford, Bodley Grabe 30; see 7 n10 above, and Bühler 1.208 n109). It is also to be found as Diogenianus 4.66 in a slightly different form: ἕλκων ἐφ᾽ αὑτὸν ὥστε Καικίας νέφος. Erasmus adopts the Latin translation (with *de sese* for the more accurate *ad sese*) that accompanied the Greek verse in the early editions of Gellius (see C 6 n1).

123 *Adagia* I x 97 and 98; Erasmus draws on Gellius *Noctes Atticae* 3.9.1–7 for both proverbs. Polydore Vergil 15 and 16; Otto 1620 and 1793
1 Hardly anything is known of this person, who is described as a *scriba* 'secretary' in the sources.
2 The Thracian king whose horses Hercules had to capture as one of his Labours
3 Gellius *Noctes Atticae* 3.9.3
4 A slip for 'Seius'
5 Mark Antony, mentioned below, brought about Seius' death, probably in 44 BC.
6 Dolabella, who was consul with Antony in 43 BC, was killed in Syria after

death.[7] These events proved the validity of the curse. From them sprang the proverb relating to those who seem destined to perish: 'He must have Seius' horse.' If anyone wants more details about what I have said, he will find them in Aulus Gellius in his *Nights* book three, chapter nine.

'He has gold from Toulouse,' which Gellius gives in the same context, has a similar origin and meaning. 'For when the consul Quintus Caepio[8] pillaged the town of Toulouse, a huge amount of gold was found in the town's temples. Whoever even touched a piece of gold from the booty died a wretched and painful death.'[9]

124 Non cuiusque est Corinthum petere / Not everyone can make for Corinth

This means that not just anyone can mingle in high society or seek to attain the heights of success. The adage originated with Lais, a Corinthian woman of outstanding beauty. Great waves of visitors came from the whole of Greece to see her, but she admitted no one to her presence unless they paid a huge, extravagant price. Hence the very popular trimeter that became proverbial in Greece: Οὐ παντὸς ἀνδρὸς ἐς Κόρινθον ἔσθ' ὁ πλοῦς 'Not everyone can sail to Corinth.' Horace used this adage in his *Epistles* in a very apt way: 'To have pleased great men is not the finest praise, / 'Tis not for every man to go to Corinth – / He stayed at home who feared lest he should fail.'[1]

This is a clear allusion to Aristippus, who is known to have been intimate with Lais.[2] Demosthenes, however, was put off by the amount

* * * * *

being besieged by Cassius, the murderer of Julius Caesar. Cassius himself took his own life at the battle of Philippi, according to Gellius. Erasmus has had a lapse of memory here in saying that he was killed by the enemy.

7 According to Gellius Antony got possession of the horse after the death of Cassius. Like Cassius, he committed suicide, in Alexandria in 30 BC.

8 Quintus Caepio was consul in 106 BC.

9 Gellius *Noctes Atticae* 3.9.7

124 *Adagia* I iv 1 (where the Latin version is in verse and therefore worded differently). Here, Erasmus closely follows the Latin translation that followed the Greek quotation in Aulus Gellius (see n3 below and c 6 n1 above). The commentary is also greatly expanded and has a different interpretation. The proverb also appears at Diogenianus 7.16. Polydore Vergil 56; Otto 431

1 Horace *Epistles* 1.17.35–7 (translation from CWE 31 318)

2 Aristippus (c 435–366) was a philosopher from Cyrene. He founded the Cyrenaic school of hedonism. This sentence is drawn from Pseudo-Acron's comments on the Horace passage (see n1). On Acron see c 241A n4.

of money she demanded and had no interest in her; he said that he was not laying out ten thousand drachmas for something he would regret.[3]

125 Asinus ad lyram / An ass to the lyre

A very old and popular Greek proverb directed at those who are unsuited to and incapable of learning any of the noble disciplines.[1] Marcus Varro gave this proverbial title to one of his satires.[2] The words of the same writer in his satire entitled *The Will* can be found in Gellius: 'If one or more sons will be born to me within ten months, they will be disinherited if they turn out to be Ὄνοι λύρας "Asses to the lyre."'[3] He means if they turned out to be unmanageable and unteachable. Jerome says about Vigilantius, 'And yet I am doing a stupid thing in seeking teachers for him who is everyone's teacher and in imposing limitations on the man who does not know how to speak and yet cannot be silent. There is truth in the Greek proverb Ὄνος λύρας "Ass to the lyre."'[4] These are his words.

126 Idem Accii quod Titii / Let Accius have the same rights as Titius

There was an old proverb that was often used to describe things that were exactly the same. Varro used it in the same passage that we have just touched upon.[1] He says, 'They will be disinherited if they turn out to be asses to the lyre. But if one is born in the eleventh month, as may happen, according to Aristotle,[2] "Let Accius have the same rights as Titius."'[3] He uses the proverb to indicate that a son born in the eleventh month will have the same rights as one born in the tenth.

* * * * *

3 Erasmus draws the story about Demosthenes and Lais (and probably also the Greek version of the saying) from Gellius *Noctes Atticae* 1.8.3–4. Polydore Vergil 57 gives *poenitere tanti non emo* 'I don't pay such a price for regret' as a separate proverb.

125 *Adagia* I iv 35. Polydore Vergil 9; Otto 184
  1 A translation of the Latin phrase *bonae disciplinae*
  2 Varro *Menippean Satires* 348–69 Buecheler
  3 Gellius *Noctes Atticae* 3.16.13, quoting Varro *Menippean Satires* 543 Buecheler
  4 Jerome *Letters* 61.4.1 CSEL 54 581

126 *Adagia* I x 77. Polydore Vergil 10; Otto 203
  1 Cited in Gellius *Noctes Atticae* 3.16.13, referred to in the preceding adage
  2 Aristotle *Historia animalium* 9(7).4 (584a–b). Aristotle is reckoning in lunar months.
  3 Gellius *Noctes Atticae* 3.16.14. In modern editions of Gellius the names are Attius and Tettius, which were convenient stock names used by lawyers.

127 Caput sine lingua pedaria est sententia / With no tongue in your head, you vote with your feet

This is a line in a mime of Laberius, exactly suiting those who have nothing to say in consultations or debates, but simply agree with the opinions of others.[1] Some senators were called *pedarii* 'footmen.' Although they sat in the senate, they were not asked for their opinions. Instead they walked from their seats to stand beside other senators whose views they supported. Aulus Gellius book three chapter eighteen.

128 Multa cadunt inter calicem supremaque labra. Inter os et offam / There's many a slip 'twixt cup and lip. Between mouth and morsel

There is a Greek verse that is παροιμιώδης 'proverbial': Πολλὰ μεταξὺ πέλει κύλικος καὶ χείλεος ἄκρου 'There is many a slip between cup and the tip of the lip.'[1] This means that nothing we hope for is so certain and nothing is so tightly within our grasp, so to speak, that some chance event cannot change the situation completely. The Greeks write that the saying originated from the following event. When a man was planting a vineyard, one of his slaves grew disgusted at the work and became angry with his master. He said that his master would never taste the wine from these grapes. And so when the vines had been harvested, the old man told this very slave to pour out his wine. When he was just about to put the chalice to his lips he began to upbraid the slave for his unfulfilled prophecy. Before he could drink the wine, however, another man came in and said that the old man's fields were being ravaged by a boar. He immediately rushed out and was killed by the boar when hunting it down.

* * * * *

127 *Adagia* I x 79; cf C 454. Drawn from Gellius *Noctes Atticae* 3.18.9. Polydore Vergil 245

  1 CRF Laberius 88, but with a different wording. Laberius (c 105–43 BC) was a writer of mimes. He was of equestrian rank, but was compelled by Julius Caesar to act in one of his mimes. This cost him his rank, but Caesar restored it.

128 *Adagia* I v 1, 2. See Diogenianus 7.46, where the story about the owner of the vineyard and his slave is told. Also in Zenobius 5.71, Zenobius Athous 2.86 (see Bühler 5.517–31) and *Suda* Π 1869. The proverb (with the explanatory story) is also discussed by Niccolò Perotti in his *Cornucopiae* (649.56–650.12), and he, like Erasmus, describes the owner of the vineyard in the story as *senex* 'old man,' although the age is not specified in Diogenianus and Zenobius. Gellius and Diogenianus may be Erasmus' sources by way of Perotti. Polydore Vergil 14; Otto 1311 (for the second proverb)

  1 This first sentence closely echoes Perotti (see introductory note), who is drawing on Gellius *Noctes Atticae* 13.18.3 for the Greek version of the proverb and the accompanying Latin translation (a dactylic hexameter); see C 6 n1.

What Cato the Elder says in slightly different words has the same meaning. This is in his speech about aediles who had been improperly elected and runs as follows: 'Nowadays they say that with respect to crops a good harvest can be seen even in the blade. Do not be too hopeful about that. I have often heard that much can happen "Between mouth and morsel."[2] It certainly takes a long time for the blade to become the morsel.' This is what Cato said, as quoted in Gellius.[3]

129 Ipsa dies quandoque parens quandoque noverca / One day's a stepmother and one's a mother

Favorinus, also quoted by Gellius, says, 'There is a verse that has won the approval of many generations: Ἄλλοτε μητρυιὴ πέλει ἡμέρα, ἄλλοτε μήτηρ "One day's a stepmother and one day's a mother." The meaning is that things cannot turn out well every day; rather, they go well on one day and badly on another.'[1]

130 Non quod pueri clamitent in faba se repperisse / Not what children cry out they have found in beans

Strophylus, a slave in Plautus' *Pot of Gold*, had stolen a pot full of gold that an old man had buried. Being very eager to let his master know about this, he said, 'I have found something.' When he was asked what he had found, he said, 'Not what children cry out they have found in a bean,' indicating by a proverb that his find was of great significance.[1] He says this since there

* * * * *

2 The word *offa* means a lump of food, such as dough.
3 Cato fragment 217 Malcovati, cited by Gellius *Noctes Atticae* 13.18.1

129 *Adagia* I viii 64. The source of the Greek version is Aulus Gellius (see n1), although it is also present in Diogenianus (2.76). The Latin translation (a dactylic hexameter) in the editions of Gellius is adopted by Erasmus, and becomes the adage itself. George Hermonymus also added this Latin version in the margin of his manuscript (Oxford, Bodley Grabe 30; see 7 n10 above). Bühler (1.227 n204) seems to believe that here Erasmus drew his Latin translation from Hermonymus' manuscript. It is more likely that both Hermonymus and Erasmus were drawing on the printed editions of Aulus Gellius. Otto 1241

1 Favorinus, a philosopher and friend of Gellius, quoted at Gellius *Noctes Atticae* 17.12.4. The verse is Hesiod *Works and Days* 825. For Favorinus see Holford-Strevens 72–92.

130 *Adagia* II ix 86. Erasmus draws from Ermolao Barbaro (see n2) for the whole commentary, supplying only the name of the Plautine slave. Otto 620

1 Plautus *Aulularia* 818–19. More correctly the slave's name is Strobilus. He is

is a worm called a *mida* that hatches inside beans and gnaws away at them, just like the *ips* in horns and vine, the *cis* in grain, the *trips* in wood, the *sis* in clothes, and the *is* in woad. The source is Ermolao.[2]

131 Ululas seu noctuas Athenas / Night-owls or screech-owls to Athens

Γλαῦκας Ἀθήνας, Owls to Athens, understanding 'you send' or 'you bring.'[1] In other words, you try to teach someone who is more learned than you, or you give gifts to a wealthy man, or you generously shower him with what he already has in abundance. Owls are plentiful in Athens because this bird is sacred to Minerva on account of the grey eyes with which it sees even in darkness. Cicero to Torquatus: 'But again, it's Γλαῦκας ἐς Ἀθήνας "Owls to Athens" when I send this to you.'[2] Also to his brother: 'And as for the verses that you ask for, I'll send them to you – an owl to Athens!'[3]

132 Sero sapiunt Phryges. Ictus sapiam / The Phrygians learn wisdom too late. Once stung, I will be wiser

This proverb, which comes from a very old tragedy of Livius entitled *The Trojan Horse*, is used by Cicero in his *Letters*. He says, 'You know the line in *The Trojan Horse*, "The Phrygians learn too late."'[1] It fits those who repent

* * * * *

the slave of the young man in the play who wishes to marry the old man's daughter.
2 Ermolao Barbaro in his *Castigationes Plinianae* on *Naturalis historia* 21.131 (Pozzi 857). Barbaro is actually defending the reading *ipsa* against a conjecture *ipa* of Sabellicus.

131 *Adagia* I ii 11. Polydore Vergil 161. The Latin version in *1500* is *ululas Athenas*.
1 In *1500* the proverb is given as Γλαύξ εἰς Ἀθήνας, 'Owl to Athens,' the form in which it appears in Diogenianus 3.81 (and in Zenobius 3.6). In *1506* Erasmus changed the nominative singular γλαύξ to the accusative plural γλαῦκας. The usual form is accusative singular. Erasmus may have taken the plural form from Cicero *Ad familiares* 6.3.4 or from the Aldine edition of the scholia on Aristophanes *Birds* 301. See Bühler 4.114–22 on Zenobius Athous 2.12.
2 Cicero *Ad familiares* 6.3.4
3 Cicero *Ad Quintum fratrem* 2.16(15).4. Cicero's brother was a dilettante poet. He wrote four tragedies in sixteen days while he was in Gaul (*Ad Quintum fratrem* 3.5.7).

132 *Adagia* I i 28 and 29. Erasmus probably drew the material for the first of these from Filippo Beroaldo's *Appendix annotamentorum* 4 (*Lampas* 1.313–14), where Beroaldo refers to Cicero's letter, Livius and Festus; see Heinimann 161 n17 and C 3n. Polydore Vergil 229; Otto 1410
1 Cicero *Ad familiares* 7.16.1. Nonius (762.10 Lindsay) attests that Livius Andronicus, a very early Roman tragic poet, wrote a play entitled *The Trojan*

too late of their foolish actions. Although the Trojans suffered so many calamities in the war, it was only in the tenth year that they began to think about returning Helen to the Greeks.[2] Similar in sense is the proverb in Diogenianus, Πληγεὶς ἁλιεὺς νόον ἕξει 'Once stung, the fisherman will be wiser,' which originated with a fisherman who suffered a wound when he was handling his fish.[3] He said, 'Now that I have been stung, I shall be wiser.' Not dissimilar is what Hesiod says: 'When a thing is done, a fool can see it.' Similar in sense is the Homeric expression παθὼν νήπιος ἔγνω 'only suffering instructs a fool.'[4]

All these sayings are directed at those who act wisely only after learning sense from some great misfortune of theirs. It would be more prudent to learn caution from the misfortunes of others.

133 Fulgur ex vitro / A flash in the pan

Ἀστραπὴ ἐκ πυελίου, A flash in the pan. It can be said of the anger and threats of those who are quite harmless. A flash comes from light that strikes water or polished vessels, and then is reflected onto opposing walls; it has no power of its own.

* * * * *

Horse, but it is not certain that this phrase comes from that play. Ribbeck (TRF p 271) ascribes it simply to a play of this title whose author is uncertain.

2 For this sentence Erasmus drew on Beroaldo, who acknowledged that he was drawing on Festus (460.36 Lindsay).

3 Diogenianus 2.31; also in *Suda* A 1218. The Greek version of the proverb was added in *1506*.

4 There is some confusion in these two sentences. Erasmus does not give the Greek original of the Hesiodic quotation and in fact translates into Latin not the words of Hesiod but a similar sentiment from Homer ('Ρεχθὲν δέ τε νήπιος ἔγνω, as at *Iliad* 17.31–2, 20.197–8 = *Adagia* I i 30). Erasmus is following an error in the manuscript tradition of Diogenianus. What he describes in the next sentence (cf *Adagia* I i 31) as a Homeric expression is actually a close quotation of Hesiod *Words and Days* 218, cited at Diogenianus 2.31. 'Homeric' is an addition of *1506*, perhaps intended by Erasmus to correct the reference to Hesiod in the previous sentence, but misapplied by the printer.

133 *Adagia* II vii 90. The source is Diogenianus 3.7. The Greek (given in *1500*) means literally 'flash from a pan / tub' but Erasmus renders the Greek word πυελίου with *vitro* 'glass.' From here to c 148 (excepting nos 137–9) Erasmus gives a series of adages that, in their Greek form, begin with *alpha*, and are all drawn from Diogenianus. He then returns to the *alpha*-entries in Diogenianus in c 161–3.

134 **Inanes culmos excussisti.** Ἀτὰρ ἐκ καθαρῶν ἀχύρων τετρύγηκας <σῖτον> /
**You have harvested empty stalks. From mere chaff you have harvested
your crop**
This is a Greek expression directed at those who get no profit at all from
their toil.

135 **Mali fontem repperit /** <Κακοῦ πηγὴν εὗρεν> / **He has found the source of
his woe**
Customarily said of those who bring upon themselves a multitude of misfortunes.

136 **Tristis scytale /** Ἀχνυμένη σκυτάλη / **A depressing despatch**
This is said of bad news that one receives. Taken from the Spartan custom
of using a *scytale* 'baton' to send messages.

137 **Duabus sedere sellis / To sit on two stools**
It was with this insulting jibe that Laberius criticized Cicero's treachery
and fickleness, the point being that sometimes Cicero supported one party,
sometimes the opposing one.[1] Macrobius tells of this in his *Saturnalian Feast*
in the following way.[2] When Laberius, the writer of mimes, had been appointed to the senate by Caesar,

* * * * *

134 Cf *Adagia* II vii 91. A Greek version of this proverb was added in 1506, but it
was a mistaken conflation of Diogenianus 3.13 and 3.18. After τετρύγηκας we
read κακοῦ πηγὴν κύρεν, a corrupt version of the Greek original for C 135 (see
below). The sense of the adage given at Diogenianus 3.13 is 'but it is from
mere chaff that you have threshed your wheat,' reading σῖτον, which has been
restored here.

135 *Adagia* I i 56. The entry in Diogenianus 3.18 reads Αὐτὸς γὰρ εὗρε τοῦ κακοῦ
τὴν πιτύαν (see C 617) and the rare word πιτύαν is glossed with πηγήν 'fountain / source.' The printer erroneously added κακοῦ πηγὴν εὗρεν to the Greek
of C 134. The words have been restored to their rightful place. Erasmus' Latin
version fails to convey fully the point of the adage, although his explanation,
based on Diogenianus, is correct. The sense is 'he was himself the cause of his
woes.'

136 *Adagia* II ii 1 (and cf C 113). The source is Diogenianus 3.25. The Greek version
of the proverb was added in 1506.

137 *Adagia* I vii 2. The source of the whole of the commentary is Macrobius (see
n2). Otto 1621
  1 For Laberius see C 127 n1.
  2 Macrobius 7.3.8; cf 2.3.10.

Cicero would not make room for him on the benches, and said, 'I would make room for you, if we were not so cramped.' Laberius snapped back at him, 'And yet you often used to sit on two stools,' casting up the fickleness of such a great man. However, Cicero's words 'if we were not so cramped' were meant as a jibe at Caesar, who admitted so many new persons into the senate indiscriminately that fourteen rows of seats could not accommodate them.'[3]

So writes Macrobius.

138 Harenam numeras / You are counting the grains of sand

Ἄμμον μετρεῖς, You are counting, or measuring, the grains of sand. The meaning is that you are undertaking a task that will never be completed.

139 Ad Graecas Calendas / At the Greek Calends

When we want to say that something will never happen, we say it will come about at the Greek Calends. The reason is that Greeks did not mark the first day of a month as the Calends, but used the new moon to do so.'[1]

140 Argenteis hastis pugnare / To fight with silver spears

Once an oracle gave this response: Ἀργυραῖς λόγχαις μάχου 'Fight with silver spears.' The god meant that nothing can withstand the power of money. This is a Greek saying.

* * * * *

3 This is a reference to the fourteen rows in the theatre that were reserved for those of equestrian rank (*equites*). The implication is that the number of Caesar's appointees to the senate was so large that not even the generous space allotted to the equestrians was large enough to hold them.

138 *Adagia* I iv 44. The Greek version (present in *1500*) is probably drawn from Perotti's *Cornucopiae* (15:47–50), and not from Diogenianus 2.27 where the verb is given in the present infinitive and not in the second person singular of the present tense, as in Perotti. Polydore Vergil 38; Otto 786

139 *Adagia* I v 84. Probably drawn from Perotti *Cornucopiae* 636:18–22, though the saying was a favourite one of the emperor Augustus, and Erasmus might have known the proverb from Suetonius *Augustus* 87. In the Roman calendar the month was broken up by three days: the Calends (1st), the Nones (5th or 7th) and Ides (13th or 15th) – a system peculiar to the Romans. Polydore Vergil 51; Otto 301

1 This sentence was added in *1506*, based on Jerome *Letters* 106.86.1 CSEL 55 289.

140 *Adagia* II vii 43. Based on Diogenianus 2.81. The Greek version of this proverb was added in *1506*, thus making the final sentence otiose.

141 **Alienam messem metis / Ἀλλότριον ἀμᾷς θέρος / You are reaping another's harvest**

This is said about those who take possession of things accumulated by the labour of others and also about those who are negligent when looking after someone else's affairs. Taken from an ancient custom whereby neighbouring farmers used to help each other when harvesting their crops. However, no one is ever thought to be conscientious when working for someone else.

142 **Simul et da et accipe / Ἅμα δίδου καὶ λάμβανε / Give and take at the same time**

These words were used as a warning for those about to do business with or trade with a man of doubtful honesty. In other words, do not give anything unless you get something back at the same time.

143 **Argiva calumnia / Argive calumny**

Ἀργεία φορά, Argive calumny. Taken from the behaviour of the Argives who, as we know from our reading, were litigious and were always bringing forward false charges.

144 **De artificio apparens deus / A god appearing by artifice**

Ἀπὸ μηχανῆς θεὸς ἐπιφανείς, A god appearing by artifice. Taken from the common practice in tragedies whereby the gods make a sudden appearance on the stage by the clever use of machines. The expression is used of those whom some great advantage suddenly befalls unexpectedly and unbelievably. Cicero appears to have alluded to this practice, more or less, in *On the Nature of the Gods* when he says that if a tragic poet could not bring the play to a satisfactory ending he often suddenly introduced a god.[1]

145 **Simplex veritatis oratio / Truth speaks plainly**

Ἀπλοῦς ὁ μῦθος τῆς ἀληθείας ἔφυ, The plain speech of truth. Those who tell

* * * * *

141 *Adagia* I iv 41. Diogenianus 2.75. The Greek was added in 1506. See also C 749. Otto 152

142 *Adagia* II viii 8. Diogenianus 2.77a. The Greek version was added in 1506.

143 *Adagia* III iv 11. Diogenianus 2.79. The Greek version was present in 1500.

144 *Adagia* I i 68. Diogenianus 2.84. The Greek version was present in 1500.
   1 Cicero *De natura deorum* 1.20.53

145 *Adagia* I iii 88. Diogenianus 2.85. The Greek version of the proverb was present in 1500. Otto 1873

the truth speak in a straightforward way. Poliziano tells us that it comes from some writer of tragedies.[1]

146 Alcynoi apologus / A story for Alcinous

Ἀπόλογος Ἀλκυνόου, A story for Alcinous. This is a long, rambling story about sheer nonsense. The tales of women are for the most part like this. Taken from the *Odyssey*.[1]

147 Rumpere filum / To break the string

It means to avoid what is inevitable.[1] Lucian: 'As the proverb says, we shall break the string.'[2] The form of the proverb in Greek is: Ἀπορρα-γήσεται τεινόμενον τὸ καλῴδιον 'A stretched rope will break.' It is said of those who are unwilling to perform some action but are compelled to do so.

148 Magistratus virum arguit / 'Tis the place that shows the man

This was a saying of Pittacus of Mytilene: Ἀρχὴ ἄνδρα δείκνυσι 'Leadership

* * * * *

1 Poliziano in *Miscellanea* 33 (1.254 Maier) where the Greek version is not given. The phrase occurs at Euripides *Phoenissae* 469, as Erasmus informs his readers in the 1508 edition of the *Adagia*.

146 *Adagia* II iv 32 (cf v i 82). Diogenianus 2.86. The Greek version was present in *1500*.
1 Alcinous was the king of the Phaeacians to whom Odysseus recounted his travels in books 9–12 of the *Odyssey*.

147 Cf *Adagia* I v 67 To stretch the rope till it breaks (with a quite different interpretation). A more appropriate form of the adage in the title would be *Frangetur tensa corda* 'A stretched rope will break,' the form given in the commentary. The source is Diogenianus 2.89, the Greek version being present in *1500*. Diogenianus says that the phrase 'the stretched string will break' applies to those who are engaged on something by constraint and necessity, close to what Erasmus says in his final sentence. See Otto 159, Otto *Nachträge* p 33.
1 Erasmus seems to be thinking of the use of the proverb to deter someone from doing something that will have inevitable results: 'you will stretch the string to breaking point (if you do this).' In other words, 'don't do this.'
2 Lucian *Dialogi meretricii* 3.3. This is cited at Diogenianus 2.89, but the quotation was incomplete in Erasmus' manuscript of this collection. The correct translation of the full quotation would be 'Take care lest, as the proverb says, we stretch the rope to breaking point.'

148 *Adagia* I x 76. Diogenianus 2.94, the Greek version being present in *1500*, and ending a series of adages taken from this source that started at C 133. Erasmus returns to Diogenianus for C 161–3 and 298–312.

shows the man.'[1] Do you want to know what a man is like? Give him a position of authority.

149 Dat veniam corvis, vexat censura columbas / The law forgives ravens and harasses doves

This is a saying based on an apophthegm of a certain philosopher.[1] He said that the laws of state were very like spiders' webs. Only the weak were trapped, while the more powerful just broke through them.

150 Optimum aliena insania frui / It is best to profit by another man's madness

It is best to derive pleasure and profit from the misfortunes and folly of others. So in Pliny the Elder.[1]

151 Contra Cretensem Cretizare / To play the Cretan against a Cretan

The untruthfulness of the Cretans is well known through the testimony of many authors, even in a verse of Epimenides, although he was himself a Cretan.[1] This is quoted by St Paul: Κρῆτες ἀεὶ ψεῦσται, κακὰ θηρία, γαστέρες ἀργοί 'Cretans were always liars, vicious brutes, lazy gluttons.'[2] This belief

* * * * *

1 The reference to Pittacus is taken over from Diogenianus. In addition to Diogenianus only in Diogenes Laertius (1.77) is the saying ascribed to Pittacus, who was regarded as one of the Seven Sages of Greece.

149 *Adagia* III v 73. The proverb is a quotation from Juvenal 2.63. In a Roman context *censura*, translated as 'law' in the title, refers to the office of the censor, a Roman magistrate, one of whose tasks was to regulate the morals of Roman senators. In the accompanying commentary Erasmus draws on Giovanni Campano *De regendo magistratu* (f d iiiir in the Rome 1495 edition of his works). For Campano (1429–77), to whom Erasmus refers in Ep 61 (in 1497) and Ep 101 (in 1499) see CEBR 1:252. See also *Adagia* I iv 47 To spin spiders' webs. Otto 446

1 The philosopher is either Solon (see Diogenes Laertius 1.58) or Anacharsis, cited in Plutarch *Solon* 5. Anacharsis sometimes appears in Greek lists of the Seven Sages. See *Apophthegmata* 7.24 CWE 38 771.

150 *Adagia* II iii 39. Polydore Vergil 4; Otto 61
1 Pliny *Naturalis historia* 18.31

151 *Adagia* I ii 29. Erasmus draws all of this, including the Greek passages (which were present in *1500*), from Poliziano (*Miscellanea* 35; 1.256 Maier) without acknowledgment. See Heinimann 176 n85. Cf also C 612, C 650 and Diogenianus 7.65. Polydore Vergil 108; Otto 463

1 Epimenides, a Cretan seer, gave his name to a famous paradox. The verse is a dactylic hexameter.

2 Tit 1:12

gave rise to a proverb among the Greeks: Πρὸς Κρῆτα κρητίζειν 'To play Cretan with a Cretan,'[3] in other words, one must employ lies against liars and treachery against traitors.

152 Hodie nullam lineam duxi / I haven't done a stroke today

This can be said by a craftsman or a scholar to mean that he has done absolutely no work or study on that day. Pliny in book thirty-five of his *Natural History* tells us in the following words the source of this adage: 'It was the constant habit of Apelles never to spend a day, however busy it was, without practising his art by drawing a line. The proverb originated with him.'[1]

153 Ne sutor ultra crepidam / Let the cobbler stick to his last

The meaning is that no one should pass judgment on matters of which he has no knowledge. This too originated with something Apelles said. Pliny mentions it in the same place, quite near to the previous passage. He says of Apelles:

> The same person used to display in his porch what he had completed so that passers-by could see it. He would hide behind his painting and listen to the flaws they pointed out since he preferred the stricter judgment of the general public to his own. The story is that a cobbler criticized him for having drawn too few loops on the inner side of sandals. On the next day, after seeing that his criticism had been attended to, the same man arrogantly found fault with how a leg had been drawn. Apelles showed himself from behind the painting and angrily told him that a cobbler should stick to sandals when passing judgment. These actual words became proverbial.[1]

154 Rixari de lana caprina / To quarrel about goat's wool

This means to dispute about some frivolous topic of no importance. On the subject of those who quarrel with their friends over some trivial thing

* * * * *

3 Diogenianus 7.65

152 *Adagia* I iv 12; the proverb appears in Perotti's *Cornucopiae* (235:41). Polydore Vergil 60; Otto 957
1 Pliny *Naturalis historia* 35.84

153 *Adagia* I vi 16. Literally 'let not the cobbler look beyond a sandal.' Otto 462
1 Pliny *Naturalis historia* 35.84–5

154 *Adagia* I iii 53. Here begins a sequence of six proverbs drawn from Horace's *Epistles*. Otto 340

on the slightest pretext Horace says, 'Another in dispute over goat's wool often engages,' in other words, over nothing.[1] For a goat is covered with hair rather than with wool.

155 Dente Theonino rodere *similiaque* / To gnaw with Theon's tooth *and similar expressions*

This means to tear someone to pieces with terrible abuse. Theon had a shamefully scurrilous, virulent, and voluble tongue. Horace: 'When he is gnawed away at by a Theonian tooth.'[1] In a similar way we find in Jerome more than once the phrase *canina eloquentia* 'the eloquence of a barking dog' to indicate verbal abuse.[2] He names Appius as the inventor of this expression.[3] There is also the expression 'A Hipponactean testimonial'[4] in Cicero in his *Letters to Friends*, when he writes this about Tigellius: 'And I think he has already been knocked down for a song by the Hipponactean testimonial of Licinius Calvus.'[5] Hipponax was an iambic poet with a vicious tongue who drove some of those whom he attacked to hang themselves.[6]

156 Tua res agitur, paries quum proximus ardet / It's your concern when next door's wall is burning

The misfortune of one friend affects another. Horace in his *Epistles*: 'Are you in any way aware that dangers will befall you soon? / For it's your concern when next door's wall is burning.'[1]

* * * * *

1 Horace *Epistles* 1.18.15. The expression is identified as a proverb in Pseudo-Acron's commentary on the Horatian verse (see C 241 n4).

155 *Adagia* II ii 55. Otto 507
  1 Horace *Epistles* 1.18.82
  2 Jerome actually uses the noun *facundia* not *eloquentia*; see *Letters* 119.1.3 (CSEL 55 447), 125.16.2 (CSEL 56.1 135), 134.1.1 (CSEL 56.1 261). It is Quintilian who has *eloquentia* (12.9.9). This becomes *Adagia* II iv 34 (with *facundia*); see Otto 317.
  3 Appius Claudius Pulcher, the censor of 312 BC
  4 *Adagia* II ii 56
  5 Cicero *Ad familiares* 7.24.1. Licinius Calvus, a contemporary and friend of Catullus, was renowned both for his oratory and for his poetry. Little of his verse has survived. Like Catullus, he engaged in invective.
  6 Hipponax of Ephesus was a poet of the sixth century BC. Two sculptors were supposed to have hanged themselves because of how the poet had lampooned them. Cf Pseudo-Acron on Horace *Epodes* 6.14.

156 *Adagia* III vi 71. Otto 1343
  1 Horace *Epistles* 1.18.82–4

157 Tineas pascere / To feed the worms

This refers to things that are never used and perish from neglect. Horace, addressing his book of poems: 'When you are handled and grow dirty from the paws of the common folk, / You will either lie silent and feed the idle worms / Or you will take flight to Utica or be sent, wrapped up, to Ilerda.'[1]

158 Pennas ultra nidum extendere / To spread your wings beyond your nest

This means to increase the modest status and patrimony you received from your ancestors. Horace: 'Born from a freedman father and of modest fortune, / You will say that I spread wings greater than the nest, / So that you add to my virtues what you take from my birth.'[1]

159 Asinum male parentem in rupes protrusit / He pushed the stubborn ass over the cliff

This refers to a person who refused to take good advice and was allowed to do what he himself wanted. By learning from his misfortune he realized his own foolishness. Taken from a fable.[1] Horace: 'In anger he pushed the stubborn ass over the cliff. / For who would work to save it against its will?'[2]

160 Fores aperire. Iacere fundamenta. Munire viam / To open doors.
To lay foundations. To build a road

'To open doors' means to demonstrate how something may be approached and to make a start to it. Pliny in his *History of the World*: 'Anaximander of Miletus is said to have understood its obliquity, in other words, to have opened the doors of the natural sciences.'[1] The expressions 'to lay foundations'[2]

* * * * *

157 *Adagia* II viii 96
  1 Horace *Epistles* 1.20.11–13. Utica and Ilerda were towns in Africa and Spain respectively.

158 *Adagia* I vi 93. Otto 1423
  1 Horace *Epistles* 1.20.20–2.

159 *Adagia* IV i 76
  1 This seems to be an assumption of Erasmus. He says nothing about a fable at *Adagia* IV i 76.
  2 Horace *Epistles* 1.20.15–16

160 *Adagia* III vi 70 (only 'To open doors')
  1 Pliny *Naturalis historia* 2.31. The reference is to the obliquity of the zodiac.
  2 Referred to at *Adagia* I ii 33 To put on the coping-stone. Poliziano uses the expression at *Epistolae* 3.10 (1.34 Maier).

and 'to build a road'³ have a very similar sense, their meaning being to describe the preparatory stages of an enterprise.

161 Apertae Musarum ianuae / The doors of the Muses are open
Ἀνεωγμέναι Μουσῶν θύραι, The doors of the Muses are open. This was a Greek proverb relating to those who had a sharp and quick intellect and who picked up immediately what they were taught. On the contrary those who are rather slow can justifiably be said to learn 'with the Muses' doors closed.'

162 Viri antiqui maxillae sunt baculus / Ἀνδρὸς γέροντος αἱ γνάθοι βακτηρία /
An old man's jaws are his crutch
A Greek proverb directed at greedy old men. For when they are old, men are sustained by food as if by a crutch. And even today old men often say, 'It's my teeth that keep me going.'¹

163 Ἀντιπελαργεῖν / Antipelargein / To cherish in one's turn
Antipelargein has the sense of repaying kindnesses received. Taken from storks. When these birds grow weak with old age, their young are said to look after them. In Greek the word for a stork is *pelargos*.

164 Auribus lupum teneo / I hold a wolf by the ears
Donatus attests that this was a Greek proverb, namely Τῶν ὤτων ἔχω τὸν λύκον, οὔτ' ἔχειν οὔτ' ἀφεῖναι δύναμαι 'I have the wolf by the ears and I can't hold it or let it go.'¹ It suits those who are involved in some kind of activity that they are unable either to abandon or finish. Antipho had a wife at home. He could not get rid of her because of a ruling of the magistrates and yet

* * * * *

3 Cf the list of examples given in Erasmus' discussion of *Adagia* I i 48 You are entirely on the wrong road.

161 *Adagia* II vii 41. Diogenianus 1.77, the Greek version being present in *1500*. Also in Zenobius 1.89 and *Suda* A 2283

162 *Adagia* II vi 15. Diogenianus 1.78 (also *Suda* A 2190). The Greek version of the proverb (added in *1506*) may be a fragment of comedy (*Adespota* 549 Kock), but is not included in PCG 8.
  1 Suringar 238

163 *Adagia* I x 1. Diogenianus 1.84, the Greek being present in *1500*. It may come from comedy (*Adespota* 939 Kock). Used by Poliziano at *Epistolae* 3.4 (1.30 Maier)

164 *Adagia* I v 25. Polydore Vergil 12; Otto 987
  1 Donatus, the ancient commentator on Terence, on *Phormio* 506. The Greek version is given in *1500*.

he could not keep her because of his father's angry threats. He says, 'There it is, I have a wolf by the ears, as the saying goes. For I cannot find a way to let her go and I don't know how I can keep her.'[2] The pimp says in an aside that the same thing was happening to him with respect to Phaedria. He could not keep him on as a client since he paid nothing, and yet he could not drive him away because he was terribly persuasive and promised much. Caecilius, as cited in Gellius, seems to have alluded to the same proverb: 'Here are the worst friends, happy on the outside, but ill-disposed within. You don't know how you can hold on to them or let them go.'[3]

165 Ad restim res rediit / It all comes down to the rope
This adage signifies complete and utter despair, the feeling we have when we contemplate taking our own lives. Terence in his *Phormio*: 'Thanks to you, my situation has very clearly come down to the rope.'[1]

166 Ita fugias, ne praeter casam / Run away, but not beyond the house
This proverb advocates following the middle path, lest we flee from one fault in such a way that we rashly fall into another. Terence: 'By our fault we make it profitable to be bad / When we strive too hard to be called good and kind. / Run away, but not beyond the house, as they say.'[1] These are the words of Demipho, an old man who is reproaching himself for getting the blame of being a fool while trying to avoid the reputation of being a miser. Donatus explains it in this way:

> 'Run away, but not beyond the house, which can be the safest place of refuge.' Or 'run away but not beyond your house, where a thief can be better watched

* * * * *

2 Terence *Phormio* 506–7. Antipho is a young man who has married a young girl by claiming to be her nearest male relative. When his father discovers this, he wishes his son to get rid of the girl. Antipho says these words to his friend Phaedria, who is a customer of the pimp Dorio, also onstage at this point.
3 CRF Caecilius 79–80, cited in Gellius *Noctes Atticae* 15.9.1. Caecilius Statius was a writer of Roman comedy of the 2nd century BC. Only fragments of his work survive. Erasmus' text differs from that in contemporary editions (including the Aldine of 1515) in reading *nam hic sunt amici pessimi* 'for here are the worst friends' instead of *nam ii sunt inimici pessimi* 'for those are the worst enemies.' This may be a silent emendation of Erasmus. The change makes sense, but is unnecessary. Modern editions ignore Erasmus' reading.

165 *Adagia* I v 21. Otto 1528
  1 Terence *Phormio* 685–6

166 *Adagia* I v 3. Polydore Vergil 35; Otto 353
  1 Terence *Phormio* 766–8, with Donatus' comments there

and caught and punished with a flogging.' Or the words are those of someone driving out a thief and thereby taking precautions in case he passes in front of the house and steals something from there as well.

I am surprised that such a learned man added all this on the phrase by way of a commentary.[2]

167 Saepe etiam est holitor valde opportuna loquutus / Even a gardener oft speaks to the point

Πολλάκι καὶ κηπωρὸς ἀνὴρ μάλα καίριον εἶπεν, Often even a gardener speaks to the point. According to Gellius this verse was a familiar proverb among the Greeks.[1] This is an exhortation to us that we should not dismiss helpful and useful advice as worthless simply because of the low status of the person giving it. Very similar to this is what Caecilius says, as cited by Cicero in his *Tusculan Questions*: 'Often there is wisdom even under a dirty coat.'[2] Plautus' words in *The Two Captives* are close in sense: 'How often the greatest talents lie hidden.'[3] Finally there is even an adage of our own time, 'Words of wisdom sometimes come from a foolish man.'[4]

168 Caninum prandium / A dog's dinner

In the final chapter of book thirteen Gellius explains this adage in the following words:

* * * * *

2 In the *Adagia* Erasmus states his preference for the first interpretation offered by Donatus.

167 *Adagia* I vi 1. The Greek version, present in *1500*, is probably drawn from Gellius (see n1), though it can also be found at Diogenianus 7.81. The Latin version (a dactylic hexameter) appears in the early editions of Gellius; see c 6 n1. Polydore Vergil 249, on the relationship of which to this adage of Erasmus see 19 above.
1 Gellius *Noctes Atticae* 2.6.9. The source of the verse is unknown. In the 1508 edition of *Adagia* Erasmus emends κηπωρός 'gardener' to καὶ μωρός 'even a fool,' following a suggestion of Paolo Bombace, who was public reader in rhetoric and poetry in Bologna at that time. Bombace's suggestion was confirmed in Erasmus' mind when he came upon Stobaeus 3.4.24, where καὶ μωρός was the reading.
2 Cicero *Tusculan Disputations* 3.23.56, citing CRF Caecilius 266 (see c 164 n3).
3 Plautus *Captivi* 165. In early printed editions the title is often given as *The Two Captives*.
4 Suringar 196

168 *Adagia* I x 39. Polydore Vergil 59; Otto 332

The words of the passage in which this proverb appears (in Marcus Varro's book of *Satires* called ὕδωρ κρύον 'Water Frozen Stiff')[1] are the following: 'Are you not aware of Mnestheus'[2] statement that there are three kinds of wine: dark, light and medium (which the Greeks call κυρόν[3] "tawny"), and new, old, and medium? Don't you know that the dark wine gives virility, the light one is a diuretic, and the medium one helps πέψις "digestion"? Don't you know that the new wine cools, the old wine heats, while the medium wine is "A dog's dinner"'?

I have long and anxiously investigated the meaning of 'A dog's dinner,' trifling though the question may be. An abstemious dinner where no wine is drunk is called 'A dog's dinner' since a dog does not need wine. When Mnestheus called wine 'medium,' because it was neither new nor old – and generally people speak of all wine as being either new or old – he meant that the medium wine had none of the powers of either the new or old wine. Because of this it ought not to be regarded as wine because it did not have the effect of either cooling or heating.[4]

169 Malum consilium consultori pessimum est / Bad advice is worst for the adviser

An adage derived from Etruscan diviners who were punished by the Romans because out of hostility they gave them treacherous advice. They suggested moving a statue of Horatius Cocles that had been struck by lightning to a lower site on which the sun never shone. As a result of what happened[1] 'this clever line is said to have been composed and chanted by boys throughout the whole city ... However, the verse seems to be a translation of a well-known line of the Greek poet Hesiod:

* * * * *

1 The title should be Ὑδροκύων 'Water-dog.' The mistake continues in the *Adagia*. The parenthesis marks Erasmus' own addition to the text, by way of explanation.
2 Mnesitheus (not Mnestheus, the name given in the manuscript tradition of Gellius) was a Greek physician of the 4th century BC.
3 An error for κιρρόν
4 Gellius *Noctes Atticae* 13.31.14–17

169 *Adagia* I ii 14. This adage is taken directly from Gellius *Noctes Atticae* 4.5.5 (it is an iambic senarius). Polydore Vergil 187; Otto 423
1 The treachery of the diviners was revealed (the statue should have been moved to a *higher* elevation for the expiatory rites) and they were put to death. Erasmus now proceeds to quote directly from Gellius *Noctes Atticae* 4.5.5–7 including the Hesiodic verse.

Ἡ δὲ κακὴ βουλὴ τῷ βουλεύσαντι κακίστη[2] "Bad advice is worst for the adviser."[3]

170 Vir fugiens et denuo pugnabit / He that fights and runs away may live to fight another day

Demosthenes was thought to have behaved disgracefully because he threw away his shield and took flight at the battle of Chaeronea where Philip defeated the Athenians. He made fun of[1] the accusation by using this very famous verse: Ἀνὴρ ὁ φεύγων καὶ πάλιν μαχήσεται 'He that fights and runs away may live to fight another day.'[2] This is true enough but it would be unpleasant to put it to the test again; rather let us imitate Davus, a character in Terence. He said, 'We didn't succeed doing it this way. We must try another way.'[3]

171 Curruca cuculus / A curruca, a cuckoo

In our times men whose wives are sleeping with other men are commonly called 'cuckoos,'[1] but Juvenal calls such a husband a *curruca*.[2] Domitius[3] thinks this is a bird that Aristotle calls a *hypolais* in his books *On the Nature of Animals*: 'The cuckoo lays its eggs in the nest of a *hypolais*, and this bird rears them'[4] as if they were its own. Pliny, however, writes that the *cocyx*

* * * * *

2 Hesiod *Works and Days* 266
3 The Latin translation of the Hesiodic verse that Erasmus provides after the Greek quotation (*consultum male consultori pessima res est*) is the same as in most 15th century editions of Gellius. It is in the form of a dactylic hexameter, as is the Hesiodic line; see c 6 n1.

170 *Adagia* I x 40. Drawn from Gellius *Noctes Atticae* 17.21.30–1. Otto 726
1 Erasmus follows the text in contemporary editions of Gellius in reading *illusit* 'he made fun of' instead of the correct *elusit* 'he parried / deflected.'
2 Menander *Sententiae* 456, the Greek being present in *1500*
3 Terence *Andria* 670

171 Cf *Adagia* IV v 84, where there is no reference to the passage in Juvenal and the corrupt word *curruca* is dropped.
1 A Dutch usage; see Wesseling 358–9. Suringar 48
2 Juvenal 6.276, where the correct reading seems to be *uruca* 'a caterpillar.' *Curruca* was the reading of Domizio Calderini in his commentary of Juvenal (see next note).
3 Domizio Calderini (1446–78), the prominent humanist who taught in Rome and published commentaries on Martial, Juvenal, Propertius, and Statius' *Silvae*. His commentary on Juvenal, first published in 1474, was frequently printed in editions of the satirist, often along with the commentary of Giorgio Valla (see n6 below). See CEBR 1:243–4.
4 Aristotle *Historia animalium* 6.7 (564a). Cf 9.29 (618a).

(for this is the Greek word for 'cuckoo') lays its eggs in wood-pigeons' nests.[5] But if the Latin word *curruca* is the same as the Greek *hypolais*, it is a marvellously suitable name for the husband of an adulteress. He loves as if she were his alone a woman who is having an affair with another man and he rears children fathered by someone else as his own. However, I think that what some other individual, called Valla, says about a *huruca* seems more accurate.[6] Plautus calls a fornicating husband 'a cuckoo' on the grounds that he was, so to speak, laying his eggs in another's nest. For this is what Arthemone says when she has caught her husband in the arms of his mistress and throws him outside: 'But even a cuckoo sleeps.' And a little later she says, 'You are a hoary-haired cuckoo whose wife is dragging you out of a brothel.'[7]

172 Digito compescere labellum. Harpocratem facere *et in eundem sensum alia* / To put a finger to the lips. To turn him into Harpocrates *and others having the same meaning*
This verse-ending, 'To put a finger to the lips,' has a proverbial flavour.[1] It means to refrain from divulging secrets and confidences. It is an allusion to Angerona, the goddess of silence (as Solinus tells us).[2] Her shrine at Rome was regarded as 'one of the most ancient holy places,' and she herself 'was represented with a sealed bandage over her mouth.' Or it refers to Harpocrates, an Egyptian god who was depicted with his fin-

* * * * *

5 Pliny *Naturalis historia* 10.26. The Greek word is κόκκυξ. The transliteration in the text is inexact.
6 Giorgio Valla (c 1447–1500) on Juvenal 6.276, where he says that the correct reading is *huruca*, which he takes to refer to a caterpillar, used metaphorically to denote a timid and weak husband cowed by his wife. For this Valla, a relative of the more famous Lorenzo Valla, see CEBR 3:371–2. The manner in which Erasmus refers to Valla suggests that in 1500 he may not have known very much about this individual, although he had published commentaries on a number of Latin authors and translated into Latin parts of Aristotle, Galen, and Hippocrates.
7 Plautus *Asinaria* 923, 934. The name of the character is usually Artemona in modern editions.

172 The first of these is recast at *Adagia* v i 13 as *Manum ad os apponere*. For the second, drawn from Poliziano *Miscellanea* 83, see *Adagia* IV i 52.
1 Juvenal 1.160. The verse ends *digito compesce labellum*, and this is why Erasmus talks of a *clausula* 'verse-ending,' though the proverb as quoted (with the infinitive *compescere*) does not scan as the ending of a dactylic hexameter.
2 Solinus 1.6, from whom Erasmus quotes in the next sentence. Erasmus also refers to Angerona and Harpocrates at *Adagia* I v 74.

gers on his lips, the gesture of someone enjoining a holy silence.[3] This is what Ovid refers to when he says, 'And he who suppressed speech and bade silence with his finger.'[4] From this we get 'to turn someone into Harpocrates,' meaning to make someone say nothing. Catullus: 'And he turned his uncle into Harpocrates.'[5] This notion is commonly found in the writers of comedy: 'You will have been speaking to a dead man,'[6] 'words are being spoken to a man that has been buried,' 'you are telling a story to a corpse.'[7] Similarly, 'you'll have spoken to a stone,'[8] 'you'll say he's a mute.'[9] You can also say something like the following on such occasions: 'You'll have been speaking to Harpocrates' or 'you'll say that I am Harpocrates' or 'Harpocrates will be no more faithful in keeping a confidence.'

173 **Pulcherrimum est athletan Herculi placere aut mimum Roscio /**
Most glorious it is for an athlete to please Hercules and a
mime-actor Roscius
Campano says that this is an old saying.[1] The highest praise is to win the approval in one's profession of its most skilful practitioners – not the plaudits of the common herd. As a fighter Hercules had the same standing as Roscius had in theatre. No actor was ever satisfactory in the eyes of the latter.

174 **Suis cuique avi plumis est usus / Each bird needs its own feathers**
An expression in common use, meaning that no one has anything left over to spare, no matter how wealthy he may be. For the greater the assets of the powerful, the greater are the demands on their spending; and an eagle has as much need of its feathers as a swallow has.

* * * * *

3 Based on Poliziano (*Miscellanea* 83; 1.296 Maier). The interpretation of the gesture seems to be wrong. See CWE 35 472 (IV i 52 n4).
4 Ovid *Metamorphoses* 9.692, from Poliziano (see n3)
5 Catullus 74.4. The context is obscene; the uncle is silenced by being made to perform fellatio.
6 Cf c 199.
7 All of these examples from comedy are similar to *Adagia* I iv 86. Cf Terence *Phormio* 1015, Plautus *Bacchides* 519, *Poenulus* 840.
8 Cf *Adagia* I iv 89 (with slightly different wording).
9 Terence *Heautontimorumenos* 748

173 Cf *Adagia* I vii 41 A second Hercules, and *Adagia* IV vii 69 A Roscius; also Otto 801, 1553
1 *Epistolae* 4.6. For Giovanni Campano see CEBR 1:252.

174 This did not appear in the *Adagia*. It is probably a proverb current in Erasmus' own time.

175 **Apertis tibiis / With all the stops out**

Quintilian in book ten of his *Principles* with respect to pronunciation: 'These true things he now uttered with almost every stop open, as the saying goes,' meaning 'with a clear and full voice.'[1] Taken from flute-players.

176 **Ubi amici, ibi opes. Conscientia mille testes / Where there are friends, there is power. Conscience is a thousand witnesses**

Both of these are given as proverbs by Quintilian.[1] The first one is directed at tyrants and leaders of factions, the second at those who are caught out lying.

177 **Simile simili gaudet / Like rejoices in like**

Cicero: 'Very readily do like flock together with like, as the old proverb goes.'[1] In Greek it is ἦλιξ ἦλικα τέρπει.[2] In book one of Plato's *Republic* Cephalus alludes to this proverb when he says, 'Often we who are about the same age meet together, validating the ancient proverb.'[3] He means that they who are old meet together, as also do young men. Very similar is the Greek expression 'God always leads like to like.'[4] Agathon in Plato's *Symposium*: 'According to an old shrewd proverb "Like always clings to like."'[5]

* * * * *

175 *Adagia* I v 96. Otto 1784
   1 Quintilian 11.3.50. The translation reflects Erasmus' text, which erroneously offers *vera* 'true things' for *vero* 'truly / assuredly.' The text is correct in the *Adagia*.

176 *Adagia* I iii 24 (Polydore Vergil 17; Otto 88) and *Adagia* I x 91 (Polydore Vergil 76; Otto 421)
   1 Quintilian 5.11.41

177 *Adagia* I ii 21, 22, and cf I ii 20. Otto 1335
   1 Cicero *De senectute* 3.7 cited by Quintilian 5.11.41 (see previous adage) as well as being cited in *Adagia* I ii 20
   2 Diogenianus 5.16. Erasmus does not give a translation of the Greek here, which means 'persons of the same age give pleasure to each other.' Cf *Adagia* I ii 20 Everyone loves his own age (*Aequalis aequalem delectat*).
   3 Plato *Republic* 1.329A; see C 2 n7.
   4 *Adagia* I ii 20. Erasmus does not give the Greek here, which appears in Diogenianus 5.16: ὡς αἰεὶ τὸν ὅμοιον ἄγει θεὸς ὡς τὸν ὅμοιον (= Homer *Odyssey* 17.218).
   5 Plato *Symposium* 195B. In Greek the proverb is Ὅμοιον ὁμοίῳ ἀεί πελάζει. Agathon was an Athenian tragic poet, who is one of the participants in the dialogue.

178 Emunctae naris / With a nose well wiped

This is said of a person who has keen and precise judgment, as though his nose has been cleared of mucus, and has a sharp tongue.[1] Horace of Lucilius: 'With nose well wiped, but harsh in the verse he wrote.'[2] Plato appears to have alluded to this adage in book one of his *Republic* when he makes Thrasymachus say, 'Tell me, Socrates, do you have a nurse?' To which Socrates answered, 'Why? You should have answered me instead of asking such a question.' The other says, 'Since she neglects you and doesn't clean your snotty nose, although you need it wiped, when you do not know the difference between a shepherd and his sheep . . .'[3]

179 Fames et mora bilem in nasum conciunt / Hunger and waiting fill the nose with bile

The Plautine character Sosia says in *Amphitryo*: 'There's an old proverb "Hunger and waiting fill the nose with bile,"' meaning that when the stomach barks for food the emotions are stirred up by any delay.[1] This is why when we encounter someone who is grouchy and ill-tempered we usually ask him, 'Haven't you eaten yet?'

180 Oculatae manus. Oculata dies. Caeca dies / Hands with eyes. A day with eyes. A blind day

In Plautus' *Comedy of Asses* a young man makes great promises to a bawd. She is quite unimpressed and says, 'My hands always have eyes in them; they only believe what they see.'[1] The same idea is expressed by Sannio in Terence: 'I was never cunning enough not to prefer to get whatever ready

* * * * *

178 *Adagia* II viii 59
1 What has been translated as 'has a sharp tongue' is expressed in Latin by *nasutus*, which literally means 'with a big nose' but has a metaphorical sense of 'censorious.'
2 Horace *Satires* 1.4.8. Lucilius was one of the early writers of satires in the history of Roman literature.
3 Plato *Republic* 1.343A, quoted in Latin; see C 2 n7.

179 *Adagia* II viii 60. Polydore Vergil 159
1 This is a line in a spurious passage that was added to Plautus' text of the play in the 15th century.

180 For the first of these see *Adagia* I viii 31 (Otto 1272); for the second and third see *Adagia* I viii 32 (Otto 538).
1 Plautus *Asinaria* 202

cash I could on the spot.'² The pimp Ballio in *Pseudolus*: 'Buy olives on a blind day, sell it on a day with eyes. Heavens, you can make two hundred minae in ready cash!'³ He means that you should buy on credit, agree upon a day for payment and then sell immediately for ready cash. Ready cash can be seen; promises are only for the ears, not for the eyes. This is why Chaerea in Terence says: 'Now let me *see* your promises.'⁴

181 Graeca fide. Attica fides. Ἀττικὴ πίστις / On Greek credit. Attic honesty
Because of their unreliability no one trusted the Greeks in antiquity when they made any promises unless they put up ready cash as well. This is why affairs are said to be conducted on Greek credit when verbal promises are excluded and business is done with ready cash. Claracta, a bawd, in Plautus' *Comedy of Asses*: 'Daylight and water, sun, moon and night – for these I lay out no money. Everything else that we want to use we buy on Greek credit.'¹ She means with ready cash. However, in the collections of Greek proverbs 'Attic honesty' means unwavering and unquestionable honesty, because of the temple to the goddess Honesty built by the Athenians.²

182 Altera manu lapidem ferre, altera panem ostentare / To bear a stone in one hand, and offer a loaf in the other
This means to flatter someone to his face but criticize him secretly, to play the part of a friend in public but that of an enemy in private, to lead a person on by flattery to destroy him. This is like scorpions with their tail. They lick their prey with their tongue, while injecting poison with the tail, which is curved over their victim like a bow. Euclio in Plautus: 'He bears a stone in one hand, and offers a loaf in the other.'¹ Jerome frequently used this adage, especially against Rufinus in a very neat allusion: 'Do I refuse you bread because I am smashing the brains of heretics with a

* * * * *

2 Terence *Adelphoe* 221–2
3 Plautus *Pseudolus* 301–2
4 Terence *Eunuchus* 311

181 *Adagia* I viii 26. *Adagia* I viii 27; Otto 770. In *Adagia* I viii 27 Erasmus interprets *Graeca fide* to express reliability (see what he says at the end of his discussion here). The Greek version of the proverb was added in *1506*. Otto 201
1 Plautus *Asinaria* 198–9. The correct form of the name is Clareta.
2 Diogenianus 2.80, from where Erasmus took the information about the Athenian temple.

182 *Adagia* I viii 29. Polydore Vergil 157; Otto 914
1 Plautus *Aulularia* 195

stone?'² This means, 'Is this the reason I do not praise you, that I am attacking these others?'

183 Melle litus gladius. Mellitum venenum / A sword smeared with honey. Honey poison

This also occurs in Jerome, writing to Augustine if my memory serves me. Although the latter was intending to criticize an interpretation of Jerome's, he had prefaced this with some rather flattering remarks that tempered the forcefulness of his criticism. Jerome calls these 'A sword smeared with honey,' pointing out also that this was a proverb.¹ 'Honey poison' has the same sense.²

184 Ventus navim deserit. Pulchre haec confertur ratis / The breeze deserts the ship. This ship is running very well

The first of these is an appropriate saying to use when someone's luck, so far favourable, begins to change and whenever, as often happens, good gives way to bad. In Plautus Tranio, in the absence of his master, had spent three years in a quite comfortable fashion, enjoying himself. When his master returned, all he could hope for was punishment. He says, 'Now, "The breeze deserts my ship." '¹ By contrast, when things are going well, we find in the same poet 'This ship is running very well.'²

185 Simul flare sorbereque difficile / It is hard to suck and blow at the same time

Whenever we mean that two activities cannot be performed at the same time. It suits persons who bustle around all over the place, engaged in several tasks at the same time, none of which, however, they can do well. This fault is called πολυπραγμοσύνη in Greek. According to Gellius this word

* * * * *

2 Jerome *Letters* 49.13.1 (CSEL 54 368), 81.1.4 (CSEL 55 107); *Adversus Rufinum* 3.38 PL 23 484B, CCSL 79 107

183 *Adagia* I viii 57 (Otto 1086) for the first of these; see n2 below for the second adage.
1 Jerome *Letters* 105.2.2 CSEL 55 243
2 Very similar to what becomes *Adagia* I viii 58 A deadly honey brew. The phrase does not seem to exist in classical Latin.

184 Not in the *Adagia* as independent entries, but both are mentioned in *Adagia* II v 16 With a fair wind.
1 Plautus *Mostellaria* 737
2 Plautus *Bacchides* 797

185 *Adagia* II ii 80. Otto 672

means 'undertaking many pieces of business at the same time and trying to complete all of them.'[1] The same Tranio[2] was chastized by his master for having been away from the house for too long. He said that he had been involved in something else and that he could not at the same time be with his master and do what he had been told to do. His words: 'Please consider this saying, "It is not easy to suck and blow at the same time."'[3]

186 Res in foro nostro verti / Things are moving in our market
This means that our situation is changing in the same way that goods in the marketplace are continuously being renewed. The same Tranio in Plautus: 'I see that things are moving in my market.'[1]

187 Uti foro / To take the market as you find it
This means to adapt your behaviour to the immediate circumstances around you and to accept with calmness what the times demand. Terence in his *Phormio*: 'You know how to take the market as you find it.'[1] No one would have any doubts about this being a common proverb even if Donatus had not told us this.[2] Seneca: 'Let us take the market as we find it and bear with equanimity what chance will bring.'[3] According to Donatus the proverb is a metaphor taken from the business world: 'Traders do not set the price of their goods before they get to their selling place, but decide whether or not they should sell their wares depending on the market prices that they find in the forum.'[4]

188 Inscitia est contra stimulum calces / It is folly to kick against the goad
In Greek Πρὸς κέντρα λακτίζειν 'To kick up your heels against the pricks.' This

* * * * *

1 Gellius *Noctes Atticae* 11.16.6 (the source of the Greek word)
2 Mentioned in c 184
3 Plautus *Mostellaria* 790–1

186 *Adagia* III vi 2. Otto 712
1 Plautus *Mostellaria* 1051. Tranio is referred to in the two immediately preceding adages.

187 *Adagia* I i 92. Polydore Vergil 182; Otto 710
1 Terence *Phormio* 79
2 Donatus, the ancient commentator on Terence, on *Phormio* 79. He says that it is a common proverb (*vulgare proverbium*).
3 From the apocryphal letters of Paul and Seneca (see *Epistolae Senecae ad Paulum et Pauli ad Senecam*, ed Claude E. Barlow [Rome 1938] Letter 11)
4 Donatus, again on Terence *Phormio* 79

188 *Adagia* I iii 46. The Greek version of the proverb, was added in *1506*, perhaps from Zenobius 5.70, which has the infinitive form λακτίζειν 'to kick.' Diogenianus 7.84 has λακτίζεις 'you kick.' Also in *Suda* Π 2725. Otto 1693

is a saying from the same play.[1] Donatus says, 'It is a παροιμία "proverb" with an ellipsis; for "to kick up" is missing.'[2] The meaning of 'to throw up your heels against the goad' is to fight back against those whom you provoke only at great cost to yourself, since you cannot get the better of them. Similar is 'you fight goads with your hands.' Plautus in *Truculentus*: 'If you fight goads with your fists, your hands get the worst of it. It is pointless to be angry about nothing with a woman who thinks you are worthless.'[3]

189 Aureos polliceri montes / To promise mountains of gold

This means to make immense and extravagant promises. Plautus in his *Stichus*: 'He would not do it to earn for himself the mountains of Persia, which are said to be made of gold.'[1] Terence in *Phormio*: 'He tempted the old man by means of a letter in which he promised almost mountains of gold.'[2] Donatus tells us this is an example of a proverbial hyperbole. Persius: 'To promise great mountains.'[3]

190 Bona Cylicum / Cilician profits

There is a Greek proverb Ἀγαθὰ Κυλίκων, which owes its origin to a certain Cilician who betrayed Miletus and suddenly became enormously rich. The adage is directed at those who acquire wealth as a result of shameful activities.

191 A mortuo petere tributum / To try to get taxes from a corpse

Ἀπὸ νεκροῦ φορολογεῖν, To try to get taxes from a corpse. This is said of

* * * * *

1 Terence *Phormio* 77–8, followed by what Donatus says on the passage
2 Donatus is referring to the Latin version of the proverb in Terence, which requires a verb such as *iactare* 'to throw up.'
3 Plautus *Truculentus* 768–9

189 *Adagia* I ix 15; Otto 1132, 1133, 1383. Although Erasmus gives a Greek version of the proverb in the *Adagia*, he may have coined it on the basis of the Latin form. It does not appear in the Greek collections of proverbs.
1 Plautus *Stichus* 24–5
2 Terence *Phormio* 67–8, followed by Donatus' comment on the passage
3 Persius 3.65

190 *Adagia* II v 9 Cillicon is doing very well. The Greek version was present in *1500*. In the version here (Ἀγαθὰ Κυλίκων) Erasmus sees a reference to the Cilicians (as does Diogenianus at 1.9, the source of the Greek version), when in fact the proper noun is the name of a person, either Cillicon or Callicoon. Erasmus gets it right in the *Adagia*.

191 *Adagia* I ix 12 To exact tribute from the dead; cf *Adagia* II i 69 (a virtual doublet). The Greek version, which appears in *1500*, is given in Diogenianus 1.9 as being similar in meaning to c 190.

rapacious men who pile up wealth in any way, by fair means or foul, and from any source. Also very like this is the Greek proverb 'He steals even from the dead.'[1]

192 Divitiarum pelagus. Opum cumulus. Bonorum formicarium / A sea of riches. A heap of money. An ant-hill of good things

The Greek proverbs are Ἀγαθῶν θάλασσα[1] 'A sea of good things,' Ἀγαθῶν σωρός 'A heap of good things,' Ἀγαθῶν μυρμηκία 'The most packed and most plenteous abundance of good things.' For a μυρμηκία is either an ant-hill or a column of ants, and the word suits those who have enormous riches heaped up in their home.

193 Ilias malorum. Lerna malorum / An Iliad of troubles. A Lerna of troubles

Κακῶν Ἰλιάς, An Iliad of troubles. Used when we wish to indicate that we are spared from no misfortune; for every kind of trouble is mentioned in the *Iliad*. Very similar is Λέρνη κακῶν 'A Lerna of troubles.' We use this expression whenever misfortune follows on misfortune, disaster on disaster, which happens quite often, as we see. Taken from the marsh at Lerna in which every kind of filth had accumulated.[1]

194 Lineam mittere / To let out the line

Plautus in *The Haunted House*: 'I will not show him immediately what I am aware of. I shall let out the line, I shall pretend I know nothing of these.'[1] A metaphor taken from painting.[2]

* * * * *

1 Cf Diogenianus 5.84. Given only in Latin in both *1500* and *1506*

192 *Adagia* I iii 29, 31, 32. All three Greek forms (present in *1500*) are given in Diogenianus 1.10.
   1 Ermolao Barbaro uses this in his correspondence (*Epistolae* 81; 1.102 Branca). This letter is Poliziano *Epistolae* 9.5 (1.127 Maier).

193 *Adagia* I iii 26 (Otto 849) and 27 (Polydore Vergil 114). The source of the Greek versions, present in *1500*, was probably Diogenianus (1.10, 5.26, 6.7). The first of the two adages also appears at Zenobius 4.43 and *Suda* I 314.
   1 Lerna was the site of one of Hercules' labours, his fight with the Lernaean Hydra.

194 Not in the *Adagia*
   1 Plautus *Mostellaria* 1070–1. Erasmus follows the current text (see n2). A translation of the correct text of the first sentences in the first sentence would be 'I will not show him the hook immediately.'
   2 This should be 'taken from fishermen' – *piscatoribus*, not *pictoribus* 'painters,' a typographical error. Even with the then current text of Plautus (which offers *ita meum* for *hamum* 'hook' at *Mostellaria* 1070) the sense of the Latin has little

195 De facie nosse / To know only by sight
This means to know someone slightly; it is as if you have never been in close contact with him. Cicero *Against Piso*: 'This is the nature of virtue, which you do not know even by sight.' He means that not only have you not perceived the true substance of virtue but you do not recognize even its reflection.[1]

196 Matura / Hurry slowly
Aulus Gellius tells us that Augustus 'often used in his conversation and his letters the expression Σπεῦδε βραδέως "Hurry slowly."'[1] Gellius thinks that its meaning can be conveyed in Latin by the single word *matura*. With this expression Augustus 'gave the advice that to accomplish anything we should employ not only our energy, which implies speed, but also carefulness, which implies taking one's time.' Similar to this are Sallust's words: 'Before you begin, take thought; when you have taken thought, you need to act quickly.'[2]

197 Lentius ambulando longum etiam iter conficitur / Even a long journey is completed when one walks rather slowly
A modern proverb of the Italians that recommends persistence and endurance.[1] For even demanding tasks are completed by steady work even if it is done less energetically.

* * * * *

or nothing to do with painting. In his edition of Plautus (Milan 1500), used by Erasmus (see 69 above), Giambattista Pio recognizes the fishing metaphor. It seems unlikely that the error arose through confusion with C 152 I haven't done a stroke today.

195 *Adagia* I ix 85
1 Cicero *In L. Pisonem* 32.81

196 Cf *Adagia* II i 1 Make haste slowly (*Festina lente*).
1 Gellius *Noctes Atticae* 10.11.5. Erasmus translates the Greek phrase (present in *1500*) as *festina lente*, literally 'hurry slowly.' The subject of Gellius' chapter is the adverb *mature*, which he says once had the meaning 'not too quickly'; hence the choice of the verbal form *matura* instead of the form of the proverb that becomes the usual one (*festina lente*).
2 Sallust *Catilina* 1.6

197 Not in the *Adagia*. Erasmus may have meant this adage and its explanation to be the final part of the preceding entry rather than to be a separate entry in its own right. It is not unique, however, in consisting only of a modern proverb (see, for example, C 254, C 404, C 405, C 500, C 723, C 724, and C 725).
1 See Suringar 105. Cf the Italian proverb *passo a passo si va a Roma* 'step by step one gets to Rome.' Exactly what proverb Erasmus was thinking of is not certain.

198 **Abronis vita. Sicula mensa. Sibaritica vita / ᾿Αβρωνος βίος. Σικελὴ**
τράπεζα. Συβαριτικὸς βίος / The life of Abron. A Sicilian table.
The Sybaritic life
These are Greek adages directed at those who live in luxury and spend their
money excessively. For the luxury of Abron gave rise to a proverb among
the Greeks just as Aesop's plate prompts one in Latin.[1] In addition, a Sicilian
table and a Sybaritic life[2] (for the inhabitants of both these places were
renowned for their luxury) became proverbial, as did also 'Persian trappings.' Of these Horace says in his *Odes*: 'I have no time, boy, for Persian
elegance.'[3]

199 **Mortuo verba facere** *et alia in eundem sensum* / **To speak to a corpse** *and*
other expressions with the same sense
This occurs when someone talks to a person who reacts to his words as if
he does not hear them. Plautus: 'I am speaking now to a corpse.'[1] Terence:
'A corpse is being spoken to.'[2] Similar is 'to sing to the deaf.'[3] Virgil: 'We
are not singing to the deaf.'[4] And 'to tell a story to a deaf ass,' which is
in Horace.[5] Plautus: 'It is no different from telling a joke to a corpse at
the graveside.'[6] There is also a Greek proverb Νεκρῷ λέγων μύθους εἰς οὖς
'Speaking words into a corpse's ear.'[7] Also Λιθῷ λαλεῖς 'You are speaking
to a stone' and Πρὸς τοῖχον λαλεῖς 'You are speaking to a wall.'[8]

* * * * *

198 *Adagia* II v 30; II ii 68; II ii 65 A Sybaritic table (Otto 129). Diogenianus 1.2.
The Greek versions of the proverbs were added in 1506.
   1 The reference is to Aesopus, the son of the famous Roman actor of the same
   name (c 100–55 BC). For his extravagance see Valerius Maximus 9.1.2. Erasmus
   refers to him at *Adagia* II v 30 and IV ix 16. This may be the same person
   referred to in Horace *Satires* 2.3.239. In his introduction to the *Adagia* Erasmus
   also lists him among historical characters who give rise to proverbial sayings
   (CWE 31 27).
   2 On 'a Sybaritic life' see Poliziano in *Miscellanea* 15 (1.239–40 Maier).
   3 Horace *Odes* 1.38.1; cf *Adagia* I vi 74.

199 *Adagia* I iv 86 (Otto 1145–6) and 87 (Otto 1715)
   1 Plautus *Poenulus* 840
   2 Terence *Phormio* 1015
   3 *Adagia* I iv 87. Otto 1715
   4 Virgil *Eclogues* 10.8
   5 Horace *Epistles* 2.1.199–200
   6 Plautus *Bacchides* 519
   7 Diogenianus 6.82. Erasmus does not give a Latin translation of the Greek
   proverb (present in 1500).
   8 *Adagia* I iv 89 and 90. In 1500 only the Latin forms of these two proverbs

200 Est sua et formicis ira / Even the ant has its wrath

Ἔνεστι καὶ μύρμηκι χολή, Even ants get angry. This is a Greek proverb and its meaning is that no one is so helpless and weak that he does not wish to avenge a wrong he has suffered. It also means that one should not take lightly anyone at all as an enemy, even if he seems to be of the lowest rank.

201 Oleum et operam perdidi / I've wasted oil and toil

An adage taken from the care and treatment of wrestlers. It was used to indicate that all the labour expended on some project had achieved nothing. An example is someone trying very hard for many years to instruct a blockhead; his pupil would not turn out one whit more clever than he was to start with. Plautus in *The Carthaginian*: 'Heavens, I've wasted both oil and toil.'[1] Cicero in his *Letters*: 'Why should I think you miss the athletes, since you thought little enough of the gladiators, on whom Pompey himself admits that he wasted both oil and toil?'[2] No different is the proverb that a raven had learned to say: 'Care and cost lost.' The story is told by Macrobius.[3]

The expression is a splendid one to apply to ingrates, who give no return for all the money spent on them.

202 Oleum perdit et impensas qui bovem mittit ad ceroma / He who sends his ox to the wrestling-ring wastes his oil and money

This suits a man who teaches someone who is unteachable or who tries to correct the incorrigible. Jerome, writing to Pammachius about the best kind of translators: 'That common proverb on the lips of everybody, "He who sends his ox to the wrestling-ring (*ceroma*) wastes his oil and money,"[1] suits

* * * * *

were given (*lapidi loqueris* and *ad parietem verba facis*). The Greek version of the first occurs at *Appendix proverbiorum* 3.68 (at CPG 1.430), an unlikely, if not impossible, source for Erasmus for the edition of 1506. For the Greek version of the second cf Diogenianus 4.31 'To talk through a wall.'

200 *Adagia* II v 31. Diogenianus 4.48 (also 1.12), the Greek being present in 1500. The correct reading is κἂν = καὶ ἐν 'even in' for καὶ 'even.'
201 *Adagia* I iv 62. Polydore Vergil 81; Otto 1284
  1 Plautus *Poenulus* 332
  2 Cicero *Ad familiares* 7.1.3
  3 Macrobius *Saturnalia* 2.4.29–30, where a full account of the story is given

202 This variation of the preceding proverb is also mentioned by Erasmus in his discussion of *Adagia* I iv 62. Otto 263
  1 Jerome *Letters* 57.12.3 CSEL 54 525

me perfectly.' The word *ceroma* actually refers to the unguent, made from olive oil, with which athletes used to anoint themselves.

203 Cerealis cena. Pontificalis cena. Dubia cena / A dinner fit for Ceres. A dinner for a pontiff. A doubtful dinner

This is how we indicate a feast that is sumptuously prepared and set out. Peniculus in Plautus' *Menaechmus*: 'He gives dinners fit for Ceres, so piled up is the food on the table. He prepares such heaps of dishes that you have to stand on the couch if you want something from the top.'[1] Horace in his *Odes*: 'A worthier heir will consume the Caecuban wine that you have kept locked up with a hundred keys; he will stain the pavement with exquisite wine, better than that served at pontiffs' feasts.'[2] Terence: 'A doubtful dinner is placed before us ... where you don't know which dish to take first.'[3]

204 Acum credo invenisses, si acum quaereres / I think you would have found a needle if you were looking for one

This occurs in the same play of Plautus.[1] It relates to someone who has been searching in vain for a girl for a long time all over the world.

205 Viam qui nescit qua deveniat ad mare, Eum oportet amnem quaerere comitem sibi / He who knows not the road to the sea, Should seek a river as his companion

This occurs in Plautus in *The Carthaginian*.[1] I find that it is used by scholars[2] in the sense that if one cannot complete a task easily, one must do so by any means. It can also be taken in the sense that he who has no knowledge of his own should consult others who have more knowledge. Another application

* * * * *

203 *Adagia* III ii 37 (where the second adage given here is the title and the first and third are mentioned in the discussion) and II iv 23, the title of which is the third adage; Otto 1573. The second adage is used by Ermolao Barbaro at *Epistolae* 96.1 (2.17 Branca).
  1 Plautus *Menaechmi* 101–3. The title of the play used by Erasmus here (in the singular) occurs in some manuscripts and printed editions.
  2 Horace *Odes* 2.14.25–8
  3 Terence *Phormio* 342–3

204 *Adagia* III vii 20. Otto 13
  1 Plautus *Menaechmi* 238–9

205 *Adagia* II vii 81 (but only the first part is given, with a different word-order). Otto 676
  1 Plautus *Poenulus* 627–8 (in iambic senarii)
  2 Presumably a reference (not identified) to the writings of Erasmus' fellow humanists

too is possible: he who does not know how to live a good life should think of those who have been praised for how they have lived.

206 **Lupo agnum eripere postulant; nugas agunt / They want to snatch the lamb from the wolf; they're wasting their time**
This means trying to pull a robber's booty out of someone's hands. The words are spoken by a pimp in the same play.[1]

207 **Austrum ego perculi / I have punched the South wind**
This means that my efforts have all been in vain. The expression occurs in the same play.[1] Paul also uses this adage in his *Epistles*, when he says 'like beating the air.'[2]

208 **Nos tibi palumbem ad aream adduximus / We have brought a pigeon for you to the fowling floor**
We have presented you with someone to trick if you wish. We have provided the opportunity; it is up to you to make use of it.

209 **Plumbea ira. Plumea gratia / Wrath of lead. Thanks like feathers**
Plautus: 'But this is the way of our rich men. / Help them and their thanks are lighter than a feather. / Wrong them, and their wrath is like lead.'[1] In the same author there is 'heavier by a feather scrap,' meaning by even a tiny amount.[2]

210 **Sine pennis volare haud facile est / It is not easy to fly without wings**
We can use this whenever we wish to indicate that we lack something that is needed to complete some task. Even today this expression is very

* * * * *

206 *Adagia* II vii 80. Cf C 325 and *Adagia* II vii 63 From the wolf's mouth. Otto 982
  1 Plautus *Poenulus* 776

207 *Adagia* I ix 84. Cf Otto 1437.
  1 Plautus *Epidicus* 592, not in *Poenulus*, as Erasmus' words imply. Erasmus follows an inferior text, based on the medieval manuscripts. The Ambrosian manuscript of Plautus, from late antiquity, offers the correct reading: *plaustrum* 'wagon' for *Austrum* 'South wind.' The sense is then something like 'I have given the cart a good shove' (see *Adagia* I vi 13).
  2 1 Cor 9:26

208 Not in *Adagia*. Plautus *Poenulus* 676; Otto 1328

209 The first of these two expressions is referred to in *Adagia* III x 47 Avoid the rancours of the powerful. Cf Otto 1440n.
  1 Plautus *Poenulus* 811–13
  2 Plautus *Bacchides* 513

210 *Adagia* III v 84. Plautus *Poenulus* 871; Otto 1424

popular.[1] Related is the phrase *alas accidere* 'to cut off one's wings,'[2] meaning to remove the tools and materials needed for attempting some task.

211 Lapis irrisibilis / Ἀγέλαστος πέτρα / A laughless rock
This is a Greek adage. It suits those whose worries cause them to waste away and who never laugh and relax. The expression is said to have come from some rock on which Ceres sat when she was looking for her lost daughter. The saying 'You might well pass through a ring' also applies to the same kind of person.[1]

212 Gravior Areopagita / Sterner than an Areopagite
Στεγανώτερος Ἀρεοπαγίτου, Sterner than an Areopagite.[1] This proverb was said of those who were excessively gloomy and stern.[2] We commonly say that such men drink vinegar.[3]

213 Proba est materia si probum adhibes fabrum / The raw material is good if you employ a good craftsman
This is said of those whose outstanding abilities promise something magnificent provided they receive proper instruction. A metaphor taken from timber that is in its natural state, but is still suitable for use in constructing something.

214 Ab asinis ad boves transcendere / To rise from ass to ox
This means moving up from humble circumstances to join the wealthy class.

* * * * *

1 Suringar 210
2 Cf Cicero *Ad Atticum* 4.2.5, where the verb is *incidere*, not *accidere* as here.

211 This becomes *Adagia* II v 62. Taken from Diogenianus 1.8, whence Erasmus also draws the mythological reference to the rape of Proserpina. The Greek version appeared in *1500*.
1 *Adagia* I ix 7, in a slightly different form ('You might well be dragged through a ring'). Diogenianus 4.30

212 The Greek version (present in *1500*) is given by Diogenianus (1.8) as being similar in meaning to C 211. At *Adagia* IV x 6 the Greek expression is translated into Latin as *Taciturnior Areopagita* 'More reserved than an Areopagite.'
1 The Areopagus was the senior court in Athens, trying cases of homicide.
2 This sentence is based on Diogenianus 2.91, where the proverb is simply Ἀρεοπαγίτης 'A member of the Areopagus' (cf *Adagia* I ix 41).
3 Suringar 85

213 *Adagia* III vi 14. From Plautus *Poenulus* 915; Otto 701, Otto *Nachträge* p 44

214 *Adagia* I vii 30. One may compare the Greek proverb Ἀπ' ὄνων ἐφ' ἵππους 'From asses to horses,' the opposite in sense to that of the immediately following adage. This had been lost at some point in the manuscript tradition of Diogenianus (see 1.55 in the epitome of Diogenianus [CPG 2.9]) and was apparently unknown to Erasmus. Otto 189

It was said by Euclio in Plautus.[1] He was very poor but a certain rich man wanted to forge a relationship with him by marriage. He said, 'This is a great risk for me, to rise from ass to ox.'

215 Ab equis ad asinos / Ἀφ' ἵππων ἐπ' ὄνους / From horses to asses
The opposite of the preceding adage is this Greek one, directed at those who turn from noble pursuits to shameful ones; for example, if a philosopher were to become a cook, or a merchant were to turn to inn-keeping, or a theologian were to become an actor.

216 Tu trium litterarum homo / You're a three-lettered man
This indicates either a thief or a freedman. But the former is more likely since it is followed by the words 'you too are a thief, a triple-thieving scoundrel.'[1]

217 Laterna Punica / A Punic lantern
This suits someone who cannot keep a secret, like Parmeno in Terence, who describes himself in this way: 'I am full of chinks. I leak everywhere.'[1] The point of the proverb is that a lamp scarcely keeps concealed whatever you hide in it.

218 In tuo luco et fano est situm / It's been put in your grove and shrine
This means 'in your power, within your discretion, under your protection,

* * * * *

1 Plautus *Aulularia* 235

215 *Adagia* I vii 29. Taken from Diogenianus 1.96, though it also is in Zenobius (2.33). The Greek version of the proverb was added in *1506*. Otto 1163

216 *Adagia* II viii 89 (where Erasmus gives an additional explanation). The adage is drawn from Plautus *Aulularia* 325. The point is that the Latin word for thief (*fur*) has three letters. Polydore Vergil 168
1 Plautus *Aulularia* 326. Plautus uses a favourite punning joke by coining the word *trifurcifer*, a combination of *tri-* 'triple' and *furcifer* 'scoundrel,' though this latter word has nothing to do with *fur* 'thief.' It literally means 'yoke-bearer,' from *furca* 'fork, yoke' and *ferre* 'to carry.'

217 Retained in the 1508 edition of the *Adagia*, but dropped after that. The expression comes from Plautus *Aulularia* 566, and it is surprising that Erasmus does not quote the verse. The sense of the line in question is 'it is as transparent as a Punic lantern,' referring to a sacrificial victim so emaciated that its entrails could be seen through the skin. Erasmus' interpretation is strange and the final sentence in his commentary decidedly odd, since a lamp seems an unlikely place in which to hide anything. Did Erasmus connect *laterna* (= *lanterna*) with the verb *lateo* 'to be hidden' and interpret 'Punic' to mean untrustworthy?
1 Terence *Eunuchus* 105

218 *Adagia* I vii 49 (with only a slight addition). The expression comes from Plautus *Aulularia* 615.

in your hands.' It is a metaphor taken from the groves and shrines that were dedicated to gods.

219 Albo rete aliena oppugnare bona / To set upon other people's goods with a white net
This seems to be a description of those who make an assault on other people's possessions by bringing trumped-up charges and providing false evidence. A parasite in *The Persian* of Plautus says, 'Let those who set upon other people's goods with a white net turn up.'[1] I am led to think that these words should be understood in the way I have suggested on the basis of the preceding verses, namely:[2]

> When a cheater has brought a charge against someone,
> Let the victim bring a charge in turn against him
> So that they can appear before the magistrates on equal footing.
> If this be done, I am pretty sure, I tell you, this will happen.

This too was characteristic of parasites, to drag someone into court on false charges if they had not been given anything.[3] Horace: 'From the cowardly supporters of his wicked ways.'[4]

220 Ebur atramento candefacere / To whiten ivory with ink
This refers to a person who wishes to improve the natural beauty of something by means of external decoration. The decoration, however, detracts from the object's beauty instead of enhancing it. This is what a bawd says when a young girl asks for white pigment to apply to her cheeks: 'You might as well ask for ink to whiten ivory!'[1] White pigment used to be applied to

* * * * *

219 *Adagia* III vii 18 (with different wording)
1 Plautus *Persa* 73–4
2 Plautus *Persa* 70–3. Erasmus here follows the corrupt text of the contemporary editions reading *inquam* 'I tell you' for *numquam* 'never.'
3 The main characteristic of the parasite was to live comfortably at another's expense by means of flattery. Good food was a particular preoccupation of this stock character of New Comedy.
4 Horace *Epistles* 1.15.33. Horace is describing a parasite who, when he receives little or nothing in the way of luxurious food from his patrons ('the cowardly supporters of his wicked ways') and is forced to eat simple food, launches an attack on epicures and gluttons! Without knowledge of the context the relevance and sense of the Horatian phrase is far from clear. How Erasmus understood the phrase is also uncertain. He dropped it in the *Adagia*.

220 *Adagia* I iii 70. Otto p 123n, and Otto·*Nachträge* p 18
1 Plautus *Mostellaria* 259

the face to produce a pale complexion, just as rouge was used to redden the cheeks.

221 Aliquid mali propter vicinum malum / Something bad from a bad neighbour

Πῆμα κακὸς γείτων, A bad neighbour is harmful, in Hesiod.[1] Dorippa in Plautus in *The Soldier*: 'Now I find out the truth of that old saying, "Something bad comes from a bad neighbour."'[2] These words advise us not to associate with wicked persons lest their sins redound on our head.

222 Viva vox / Ζῶσα φωνή / The living voice

What we do not learn from written material, which is voiceless,[1] we learn, by 'The living voice,' from what our teacher himself says to us. The point of the saying is that, although a written expression is indeed a kind of voice, it is a dead one; the actual enunciation of an expression, however, is a kind of voice that has its own special force, as Jerome writes.[2] Aulus Gellius: 'Since I lacked "The living voice," as it is said, I might gain knowledge "From silent teachers,"[3] as the common expression goes.'

223 Davus sum, non Oedipus / I am Davus, not Oedipus

This is to be found in *The Woman of Andros* of Terence.[1] It is suitable to use when we want to say that we have been listening to someone speaking in obscurities and riddles and that we can in no way understand him. The adage originated with the myth of the Sphinx and Oedipus.[2]

* * * * *

221 *Adagia* I i 32. Polydore Vergil 153; Otto 1893
  1 This sentence was added to the title of the adage in *1506*. Erasmus probably drew the Greek phrase directly from Hesiod *Works and Days* 346 (see 11 above). His Latin translation of it is *Noxa malus vicinus*.
  2 Not from *Miles Gloriosus*, but from Plautus *Mercator* 771–2, the words being spoken not by Dorippa but by Lysimachus to Dorippa. Both errors were corrected in the 1515 edition of the *Adagia*.

222 *Adagia* I ii 17. The Greek in the title was added in *1506*, taken from Cicero *Ad Atticum* 2.12.2 or a letter of Francesco Pucci in Poliziano's *Epistolae* (6.4; 1.77 Maier). The adage is referred to in C 465. Otto 1936
  1 A translation of *mutis litteris*, the reading in *1500*. The edition of 1506 offers *multis litteris* 'much written material.'
  2 Jerome *Letters* 53.2 CSEL 54 446
  3 Gellius *Noctes Atticae* 14.2.1. The saying 'From silent teachers' is C 465, which becomes *Adagia* I ii 18.

223 *Adagia* I iii 36. Polydore Vergil 93; Otto 1280
  1 Terence *Andria* 194
  2 A reference to the well-known story of how Oedipus solved the riddle posed

224 Obsequium amicos, veritas odium parit / Flattery wins friends and truth engenders hate

A very famous saying that, far from advising us how we should behave, simply points out what usually happens. Whoever wishes to have many friends should go along with everyone's behaviour, and, as Persius says, he should refrain 'from bruising tender ears with biting truth.'[1]

225 Nuces relinquere / To leave the nuts behind

This means turning away from childish pursuits and taking up more serious activities. It is a metaphor taken from ancient wedding ceremonies where the groom scattered nuts as he led his wife away. It signified a renunciation of his childhood. In addition, as Servius writes, 'Young catamites used to scatter nuts when they were giving up their disgraceful servitude. This was an indication that they rejected from this time on all such youthful activities.'[1] It is common knowledge that children played with nuts in antiquity. Catullus: 'Give nuts, boy, quickly. Give nuts, beloved slave.'[2] Virgil: 'Scatter nuts, bridegroom.'[3] This is why when Persius wished to indicate manhood in a proverbial way he says, 'Whatever we do, after leaving our nuts behind,' meaning 'when we are no longer children.'[4]

226 Sapere patruos / To assume the wisdom of an uncle

'We who assume the wisdom of an uncle,' which follows immediately in the same passage, also has the flavour of a proverb.[1] It means that we have become stern and grave.

227 Extra quaerere / To look beyond oneself

This appears in the same satire. Wishing to agree with everyone else, you

* * * * *

by the Sphinx to the people of Thebes, thereby saving the city and becoming its king. See c 370.

224 *Adagia* II ix 53. The adage comes from Terence *Andria* 68. Polydore Vergil 201; Otto 1875
1 Persius 1.107–8

225 *Adagia* I v 35. Otto 1257
1 Servius on Virgil *Eclogues* 8.29
2 Catullus 61.124 (131), 128 (135). The first part is quoted erroneously. The text of modern editions can be translated 'give nuts to the children.'
3 Virgil *Eclogues* 8.30
4 Persius 1.10

226 *Adagia* II iv 39. Otto 1357
1 Persius 1.11

227 *Adagia* II v 37

show one thing on your face and in your words, while having a quite different feeling in your mind. Persius: '[Do not] go up and adjust the pointer of their worthless scales; don't look beyond yourself.'[1]

228 Auro habet soccis suppactum solum / He has gold-plated soles

This is in Plautus and is directed at a man who is so enormously wealthy that he seems to tread on gold.[1] We take *solum* to refer to the underside of sandals, the part that we put our weight on.

229 In fermento iacere / To lie in the leaven

This means to be tormented and swollen up with rage. Plautus in *The Merchant*: 'Your wife totally lies in the leaven.'[1]

230 Aquam in cribrum gerere / To put water in a sieve

This means to undertake a completely futile task. Plautus in the same play: 'It is as profitable as putting water in a sieve.'[1] A similar expression is 'to draw water with a leaky barrel,'[2] which is taken from the myth of the Danaids, the grand-daughters of Belus. The Greek adage 'A jar that cannot be filled,' directed at misers, is also taken from the same story.[3]

231 Supercilium salit / My eyebrow twitches

This seems to have been taken from the superstitious beliefs of the ancients. They thought that something good was in store if their eyebrow twitched. In Plautus there are similar, frequent references to itching: 'My

* * * * *

1 Persius 1.6–7. Erasmus omits from the quotation an initial negative. Persius is referring to contemporary tastes in poetry, which he deplores. The words urge the addressee to be his own man and ignore the fashion of the times.

228 *Adagia* III vii 82. Otto 220
1 Plautus *Bacchides* 332

229 *Adagia* II x 76. Otto 651
1 Plautus *Mercator* 959

230 Cf *Adagia* I iv 60 To draw water in a sieve. See also C 368. Otto 466
1 Plautus *Pseudolus* 102 (not *Mercator*, as Erasmus implies). The line is misquoted; in its correct form it refers to catching a shower of rain (*imber*) in a sieve. Erasmus quotes the verse in *Adagia* I iv 60, though the correct form does not appear until the edition of 1520.
2 Cf Plautus *Pseudolus* 369.
3 Diogenianus 1.95 (though Erasmus does not give the Greek form of the proverb and Diogenianus says that the proverb is directed at gluttons, not at misers). It appears below as C 368 and eventually becomes *Adagia* I x 33.

231 *Adagia* IV ix 72; Otto 1713. This is taken from Plautus *Pseudolus* 107.

back itches so'[1] and 'Is it your teeth or cheeks that are itchy?'[2] And today women think that they are being talked about behind their backs
if their ears ring, and that this is being done in a complimentary way
if the ringing is in their right ear, in a derogatory way if it is in the
left.[3]

**232 In utramvis dormire aurem *aut* in oculum utrumlibet / To sleep soundly
on either ear *or* on either eye**
This means to be at ease and free from care. Plautus: 'On that matter sleep peacefully on either eye.'[1] Terence: 'I'll see to it that you
sleep soundly and at ease on either ear.'[2] Menander in *The Necklace*, as
cited in Gellius: 'She has her dowry; she may sleep soundly on either
ear.'[3]

233 Magno gemitu manus fit gravior / More pain, more gain
This is in Plautus.[1] The meaning is that pain and anger increase a man's
strength.[2]

234 Obtrudere palpum / To smother with caresses
The meaning is to deceive by treacherous flattery. Plautus: 'I've learned
how to do that to others; you can't smother me with caresses.'[1]

* * * * *

1 Plautus *Miles gloriosus* 397 (with a slightly different text)
2 Plautus *Poenulus* 1315
3 Suringar 156

232 *Adagia* I viii 19 (for the first part); IV i 43 (for the second); Otto 211. The first
is used by Poliziano (*Miscellanea* 9; 1.233 Maier).
1 Plautus *Pseudolus* 123. This is obviously a comic variation of 'To sleep soundly
on either ear' and should hardly be regarded as proverbial.
2 Terence *Heautontimorumenos* 342
3 Menander fragment 333 Körte-Thierfelder (from the *Plokion*), cited in Gellius
Noctes Atticae 2.23.9. Erasmus does not give the original Greek, but draws from
the Latin translation (lacking any manuscript authority) that accompanied the
passage in early editions of Gellius; see C 6 n1.

233 Not in *Adagia*
1 Plautus *Pseudolus* 785–6
2 This interpretation deviates from the sense of these words in the Plautine
context. There, the speaker, a young boy owned by a pimp, says that extra
sexual services bring him more money as well as more pain. In the next verse
(*Pseudolus* 787) he says that he somehow manages to grit his teeth and bear it,
and this has prompted Erasmus' explanation.

234 *Adagia* III vi 27. Otto 1327
1 Plautus *Pseudolus* 945

235 Rara avis / A rare bird

This is said about something that is extremely rare. Juvenal: 'A rare bird in the world, as rare as a black swan.'[1] Persius: 'If by chance something good comes out (and that would be a rare bird indeed), yet if it does, ...'[2] 'Rarer than a white crow' is found in Juvenal.[3] Because of its uniqueness the phoenix too was used proverbially to indicate rarity.[4]

236 Bonis avibus. Malis avibus / With good auspices. With bad auspices

Both of these were derived from the observations of the augurs.[1] 'I came here with good auspices,' meaning 'with favourable signs.'[2] Horace: 'Varius will sing of you as the brave conqueror of the enemy on the wings of Maeonian song.'[3] Also in Horace: 'It is with bad auspices that you bring her home'[4] and again 'with evil auspices the ship sets sail.'[5]

237 Suo iumento sibi malum arcessere / To fetch trouble for oneself on one's own beast

This means to be responsible for bringing about one's own misfortune. Mercury in Plautus' *Amphitryo*: 'That man is bringing trouble for himself from me on his own beast.'[1] The meaning is that he brings trouble on himself by his own efforts, by his own wagon, so to speak.

* * * * *

235 *Adagia* II i 21. Otto 232
1 Juvenal 6.165. The Juvenal quotation is found in the commentary of Josse Bade (Ascensius) on Persius 1.45–6, and this is probably Erasmus' source.
2 Persius 1.45–6. The quotation is incomplete.
3 Juvenal 7.202. Cf *Adagia* IV vii 35 A white crow.
4 *Adagia* II vii 10 As rare as the phoenix

236 *Adagia* I i 75. Cf *Adagia* II vii 20 To be given better auspices. The phrase *bonis avibus* occurs at Ovid *Metamorphoses* 15.640.
1 The augurs were priests who examined the sky and the appearance of birds there to decide whether any enterprise should be undertaken.
2 Erasmus seems to be quoting Terence *Andria* 807 (*auspicato huc me appuli*) from memory. His version of the line is *bonis avibus huc me appuli*.
3 Horace *Odes* 1.6.1–2 (from a poem where Horace declines to write of the exploits of Agrippa, Octavian's great general). Varius Rufus was a contemporary poet, more suited, according to Horace, to write an epic poem. 'Maeonian' is a reference to Homeric and epic verse.
4 Horace *Odes* 1.15.5 (referring to Paris' abduction of Helen)
5 Horace *Epodes* 10.1

237 *Adagia* I i 50. Otto 759
1 Plautus *Amphitryo* 327

238 A tergo ridere quomodo proverbialiter dicitur / How 'to laugh behind someone's back' is expressed proverbially

It would be surprising if the following images from Persius were not taken from everyday common speech:

> O Janus, whom no stork ever pecked from behind,
> Behind whom no nimble hand mimicked white donkey-ears.
> At whom no tongue stuck out the length of a thirsty Apulian hound's.[1]

It is certainly with such gestures that foolish and vainglorious men are laughed at behind their backs by those who praise them when face to face.

239 Postica sanna / Making a face behind someone's back

In the same passage we read 'turn round and confront the grimace made behind you,'[1] referring to being secretly mocked behind one's back.

240 Caput scabere. Ungues arrodere / To scratch one's head. To chew one's nails

Both these actions are typical of a man deep in thought who cannot hit upon what he is searching for. Horace in his satire about Lucilius:

> Often he would scratch his head and chew his nails,
> Often he would make changes, wanting to write
> Something that would deserve a second reading.[1]

* * * * *

238 The heading is not itself an adage, but is a generic description of the proverbs that follow (see c 93n). The proverbs are contained in the quotation from Persius. See *Adagia* IV i 78.
1 Persius 1.58–60. The verses are quoted at *Adagia* IV i 78 (see next entry). The Latin expressions are *ciconia pinsit* 'a stork pecked,' *imitari auriculas albas* 'to imitate white donkey-ears,' and *linguae quantum sitiat canis Apula tantum* "tongues [protruding] as far as the tongue of a thirsty Apulian hound.'

239 *Adagia* IV i 78; cf Otto 1578.
1 Persius 1.62

240 *Adagia* III vi 96. Otto *Nachträge* p 92
1 Horace *Satires* 1.10 71–3. Erasmus' text deviates from that in modern editions, where the second line marks the beginning of a new sentence and the subject changes from the third person to the second. The sense of the second and third lines is 'often you should make changes if you want to write . . .' The error is corrected in the *Adagia*.

Persius on the subject of poets who are lazy and carefree in their writing: 'No banging on desk or biting one's nails to the quick.'[2] The same poet: 'So says Chaerestratus, gnawing his nails to the quick.'[3]

241 Genuinum infigere / To gnaw with one's molars

This means to snipe at and criticize someone in secret, tearing him to pieces, so to speak, with a hidden tooth (as our molars are). Persius on the subject of Lucilius: 'And he broke his molars on them.'[1] Jerome: 'I can reply if I wish, I can fasten my molars on him who has injured me.'[2]

241A Foenum habet in cornu / He has hay on his horn

This is an adage that we use to indicate the need to beware of someone because he is foul-mouthed, violent, and wild. Horace, on the subject of a poet who was prone to give sharp criticism: 'Keep well away from him; he has hay on his horn.'[1] Jerome applies the proverb to himself on several occasions.[2] Plautus has the same notion in mind when he says, 'You are assailing a horned beast,'[3] meaning a person whom one would not attack unjustly and get away with it. The adage relates to a bull that is given to goring, either because beasts that are well pastured are often more wild, or because, as a sign, straw was customarily tied to the horns of bulls that might gore you (like a bell being put on dogs and horses that might bite). The latter is the view of Acron.[4]

* * * * *

2 Persius 1.106
3 Persius 5.162

241 *Adagia* II ii 59. The first sentence draws on the commentary of Josse Bade (Ascensius) on Persius 1.115. Otto 507
1 Persius 1.115
2 Jerome *Letters* 50.5.2 CSEL 54 393. This seems to be the only apparent example.

241A *Adagia* I i 81; Polydore Vergil 58; Otto 438. This adage is erroneously numbered CCXLI, like the preceding one. Cf 65A.
1 Horace *Satires* 1.4.34
2 Jerome *Letters* 50.5.2 CSEL 54 393. This seems to be the *only* occasion.
3 Not Plautus, but Jerome (*Adversus Rufinum* 1.31 PL 23 423, CCSL 79 32). This becomes *Adagia* I i 82. See C 54 n7.
4 Acron was an ancient commentator on Horace, to whom many scholia that have come down to us have been falsely attributed. See O. Keller ed *PseudAcron: Scholia in Horatium vetustiora* 2 (Stuttgart 1967) 54 (on *Sermones* 1.4.34).

242 Naso suspendere / To turn up the nose

In antiquity the nose was associated with mocking. Because of this those
who knew how to mock others cleverly and wittily were described as *nasuti*
'sharp-nosed.'[1] Martial: 'And children have the nose of a rhinoceros.' Also:
'Not all can have a critic's nose.' Again: 'You may be sharp-nosed, you may
be all nose.'[2] From this idea came 'To turn up the nose at' in the sense of
making contemptuous fun of someone. Horace: 'You turn up your nose and
hang them on it.'[3] And elsewhere: 'A nuisance of a fellow, turning up his
nose at everything.'[4] Persius, writing about Horace, whom he wishes to be
thought of as subtle in his mockery: 'Skilled he was in wiping his nose clean
and hanging the populace on it.'[5] The same poet: 'You scoff, he says, and
curl up your nostrils too much.'[6]

243 Aurem vellicare / To tweak an ear

Just as the ancients associated the nose with mockery, so they linked the
ear with the memory. This is why when they were going to bring a lawsuit
against someone they tweaked the ear of a bystander if they wished to call
him as a witness.[1] Then we find 'To tweak someone's ear' in the sense of 'to
remind someone' among the learned poets. Virgil: 'Cynthius tweaked my
ear and reminded me.'[2]

* * * * *

242 *Adagia* I viii 22. The source for the Latin expression is Horace *Satires* 1.6.5 (see
n3). In chapter 8 of his *Ex tertio libro observationum* (see 13 and C 120n above)
Domizio Calderini explains *nasutus* as meaning 'expressing strong derision'
and also cites the Horatian line (Campanelli 119). Erasmus may also have consulted Calderini's commentary on Martial at the appropriate points (see n2).
Perotti *Cornucopiae* 201–2 is another possible source for Erasmus here. Otto
1198
   1 An adjective formed from *nasus* 'nose.' See C 178 n1.
   2 Martial 1.3.6, 1.41.18, 13.2.1
   3 Horace *Satires* 1.6.5 (literally 'you hang them on your hooked nose')
   4 Horace *Satires* 2.8.64
   5 Persius 1.118. Erasmus reads *exterso* 'wiped clean' for *excusso* 'stuck out.' This
      is probably a lapse of memory.
   6 Persius 1.40–1

243 *Adagia* I vii 40. Otto 214
   1 This sentence is based on Porphyrion and Pseudo-Acron on Horace *Sermones*
      1.9.76.
   2 Virgil *Eclogues* 6.3–4. See also Poliziano in *Miscellanea* 80 (1.288 Maier) and 42
      (1.261 Maier).

244 Premere pollicem. Convertere pollicem / Thumbs down. Thumbs up

In antiquity the thumb indicated interest and support. And so it used to be said of a supporter that he turned his thumb down, and of one who did not support that he turned his thumb up. Pliny in book twenty-eight: 'When we support someone we are told to turn our thumbs down, and there is actually a proverb about this.'[1] Horace: 'If he thinks that you are in sympathy with his tastes, he'll be your supporter and praise your game with both thumbs.'[2] Juvenal about turning thumbs up: 'If the mob has turned thumbs up, they kill anyone at all and thus please the people,'[3] the phrase 'to turn thumbs up' meaning to move from support for someone to hatred for him.

245 Frontis perfrictae / A brow wiped clean

The forehead is a marvellous indicator of modesty and a person's morality. This is why those who have abandoned all sense of what is right and who are not ashamed of anything they do are said to have wiped shame off their forehead. Such unprincipled men are said to have a bold front and a bold face. The Elder Pliny: 'I put a bold face on it and yet I have not made any progress since I encounter your greatness in another way.'[1] The same metaphor occurs in 'How do you have the face to dare to say this?' or 'How do you have the face to accuse your own son?' Shameless persons are said to have a cruel face or no face at all, meaning that they have no brow. Ovid: 'Not more heart you have, but less sense of shame.'[2] Pliny book eleven: 'Other animals have brows, but only for humans is it an indicator of sadness, joy, contentment, or sternness.'[3] When we want to describe someone who is stern and angry we say he has a gloomy and

* * * * *

244 *Adagia* I viii 46. Drawn from Poliziano *Miscellanea* 42 (1.261 Maier). Polydore Vergil 74; Otto 1445
  1 Pliny *Naturalis historia* 28.25
  2 Horace *Epistles* 1.18.65–6
  3 Juvenal 3.36–7

245 *Adagia* I viii 47. There is no close equivalent in English. The source is Niccolò Perotti in his letter to Francesco Guarmieri (*Cornucopiae* 1039:10–12). Polydore Vergil 231; Otto 631
  1 Pliny *Naturalis historia* praefatio 4
  2 Ovid *Heroides* 17.104
  3 Pliny *Naturalis historia* 11.138

wrinkled brow.[4] Plautus: 'His brow is wrinkled with sternness,'[5] obviously a metaphor drawn from a goat's horns.[6] Again, when we wish to indicate happiness we say 'with an unwrinkled brow.' 'Speak with a less wrinkled brow,' meaning 'with a happier countenance.'[7]

246 Adducere supercilium. Superciliosus / To knit one's eyebrows. To give the eyebrow

After referring to the previous expression Pliny goes on immediately in this way: 'A man's eyebrows can be moved together and separately, reflecting our thoughts; for with them we say "No" or "Yes." They especially indicate disdain. While pride originates elsewhere within us, its home is in the eyebrows. It is born in the heart, but it rises up to live here, and here it hangs suspended. It has found no loftier or steeper abode in the body where it can live its lonely life.'[1] So much for Pliny. This is why we say 'raising one's eyebrows' to indicate disdain and 'relaxing one's eyebrows' when we refrain from contempt. And we call arrogant men 'supercilious.' In Latin *supercilium* 'eyebrow' is used by itself in the sense of 'disdain.'[2]

247 Connivere / To wink at, shut one's eyes to

This is a very fine metaphor that we use when someone deliberately, whether out of generosity or partisanship, does not reveal another's guilt of which he is aware, like parents who close their eyes to some minor faults of their children and jurymen who accept a bribe to shut their eyes to evidence in a trial. You will find many examples of the word in this sense in the speeches of Cicero.[1]

* * * * *

4 *Adagia* I viii 48 To smooth the forehead, To wrinkle the forehead
5 Plautus *Epidicus* 609
6 It is unclear what Erasmus means by 'drawn from a goat's horns.' The verb in the Plautine passage is *capero* 'to be wrinkled,' and was accordingly linked with *caper* 'goat.' Nonius Marcellus (13.25–6 Lindsay) says, in an etymological explanation and one that is more specific than Erasmus', that the verb comes from the 'ruffled brow of a goat' (*a frontibus crispis caprorum*). In modern editions the verb is usually spelled *caperro*, not *capero*. Perhaps Erasmus is thinking of how a goat's horns may lean towards each other.
7 Plautus *Casina* 281; cf Terence *Adelphoe* 839.

246 Cf *Adagia* I viii 49.
1 Pliny *Naturalis historia* 11.138
2 As at Juvenal 6.169 and Martial 1.4.2

247 *Adagia* I viii 50. More a metaphor than a proverb
1 For example Cicero *Pro M. Caelio* 24.59

248 **Rubo arefacto praefractior / ᾿Αγναμπτότερος βάτου αὔου / As stubborn
as a dried-up bramble bush**
This is a Greek proverb directed at stubborn, difficult, and inflexible men.
One may be able to break them, but one certainly cannot make them
bend.

249 **Aquam e pumice postulare / To ask for water from a pumice stone**
This is to seek to obtain from someone what that person himself has
the greatest need of; for example, if one were to ask an ignoramus
for instruction, or seek advice from one who never thinks before acting. Plautus: 'For you are asking for water from a pumice stone, which
is itself thirsty for it.' Also: 'A pumice stone is not as dry as this old
man is.'[1]

250 **Tibiam tubae comparas / You match flute against trumpet**
Αὐλὸν σάλπιγγι συγκρίνεις,[1] You match flute against trumpet. Used when
insignificant things are compared with great ones: 'Thus I knew that pups
were like hounds, and kids like their dams; thus I used to compare great
things with small.'[2] Τέττιγι μέλιτταν συγκρίνεις 'You match a cricket against
a bee,'[3] relating to musicians and orators who are superior in talent to their
colleagues, has much the same sense. A cricket is tuneful, while a bee makes
hardly any sound.

251 **Claudus loripedem ridet, Aethiopem Maurus, luscum luscus /
The lame man mocks the cripple, the Moor mocks the Ethiopian,
the one-eyed mocks the one-eyed man**
Used whenever someone taunts another with a fault that he himself has.
Juvenal: 'Let the straight-legged man mock the cripple, the white man mock

* * * * *

248 *Adagia* II i 100. The Greek version added in *1506* had the incorrect superla-
tive form of the adjective (as in Zenobius 1.16, which is therefore Erasmus'
probable source for the Greek; see c 26n). Diogenianus 1.13 offers the correct
comparative form ἀγναμπτότερος. Also *Suda* A 278

249 *Adagia* I iv 75. Otto 1487, and the following entry (wrongly numbered 1486)
  1 Plautus *Persa* 41–2, *Aulularia* 297

250 *Adagia* I viii 74
  1 The Greek version, present in *1500*, comes from Diogenianus 1.15.
  2 Virgil *Eclogues* 1.22–3
  3 Cited at Diogenianus 1.15. This becomes *Adagia* I viii 75.

251 Cf *Adagia* III ii 21 (which consists of the first part of the verse of Juvenal
quoted here).

the Ethiopian.'[1] Persius: 'The man who would call out "Old one-eye" to the one-eyed.'[2] And yet I am quite aware that Persius wrote this with a different meaning.[3]

252 Dii tibi tuam dent mentem / May the gods give you the mind you deserve

This is a proverbial prayer relating to those who are insane. Martial: 'May the gods give you the mind that suits you, Philenus.'[1] Horace, alluding to this proverb: 'What are you to do with him? Tell him to be miserable, since he enjoys that state.'[2] We pray that those who we think are not sane get better sense, as in Terence: 'I want you to get better sense.'[3]

253 Sub alia quercu collige / Gather from under another oak-tree

Ἄλλην δρῦν βαλάνιζε, Gather acorns from another oak-tree. An adage that goes back to very ancient times. For in the beginning humans lived on acorns, which they gathered after shaking them from oak trees. And so if they saw that a tree had been stripped bare, they said that another oak tree had to be shaken. The expression suits those who shamefully and too often solicit the same person for a favour or a service.

254 Strenuos equos non esse opere defatigandos / Don't wear out a hard-working horse

This is a modern proverb of our own times;[1] it advises us to treat with moderation and respect friends who freely help us and are always ready to oblige.

* * * * *

1 Juvenal 2.23. As the next line of the poem shows ('Who would tolerate the Gracchi complaining about sedition'), the point is that we should not mock someone who has our own faults.
2 Persius 1.128
3 Persius is referring to the kind of reader / listener that he does not want, one without taste or wit.

252 *Adagia* IV i 91; see notes there. Erasmus is drawing from Domizio Calderini's commentary on Martial 7.67.16 (see C 171 n3).
1 Martial 7.67.16. The correct name of the addressee is Philaenis. The wish refers to Philaenis' depraved sexual behaviour.
2 Horace *Satires* 1.1.63–4
3 Terence *Adelphoe* 432

253 *Adagia* I v 34. The Greek version, present in *1500*, comes from Diogenianus 1.19.

254 Not in *Adagia* (see C 197n)
1 Suringar 215

255 Polypi mentem habe / Have the outlook of the polyp

Πολύποδος νόον ἴσχε, Have the outlook of the polyp. This means that we should be prepared to act in different ways in accordance with a particular time and place. The adage is drawn from a peculiarity of this fish. Pliny tells us that it changes its colour to suit its surroundings, especially when it is afraid.[1] St Paul took over the gist of this adage: 'He became all things to all men.'[2] Chrysalus in *The Bacchis Sisters* of Plautus articulated the sense of this proverb in a wonderful way. He says:

> No one can be a man of any worth unless he knows how to do good
> > and bad.
> He must be a rogue with rogues, with robbers he should plunder and
> > steal what he can.
> A man with any sense, of any worth, should be able to change his skin.
> He should be good with good men, wicked with wicked. He must
> > adopt the character that the situation demands.[3]

256 Genio sinistro / An evil genius

Those things that we say we encounter through the malevolence of the gods or through an evil genius are misfortunes. For a bad genius as well as a good genius accompanies each one of us.

257 Dextro Hercule / With Hercules as a helper

This suits those who are very lucky in accumulating wealth. The story is that when Hercules was on the point of death he said that whoever consecrated a tenth of his possessions to him would become rich.[1] Horace: 'Rich through the friendship of Hercules.'[2] Persius: 'O, if only I could

* * * * *

255 *Adagia* I i 93. The source of the Greek version, present in *1500*, is Diogenianus 1.23.
  1 Pliny *Naturalis historia* 9.87
  2 1 Cor 9:22
  3 Plautus *Bacchides* 654–62

256 *Adagia* I i 72. This is probably based on Persius 4.27, where the phrase *dis iratis genioque sinistro* occurs. Otto 519

257 *Adagia* I i 73
  1 This sentence is drawn from Iohannes Britannicus' commentary on the Persius lines (see n3). On Britannicus see 12 above.
  2 Horace *Satires* 2.6.12–13, also adduced by Britannicus in his commentary on the Persius lines (see n3)

hear the sound of a jar of money under my rake, with the help of Hercules!'[3]

258 Movere bilem. Facere stomachum / To stir the bile. To upset the stomach
Both of these expressions are very common, meaning to provoke anger in someone.

259 Sonat vicium percussa maligno, respondit viridi percussa fidelia limo / A pot, made of green mud, sounds out its flaw in answer to a blow
This is in Persius, and is undoubtedly a proverbial metaphor.[1] It can be said of those who give a foolish reply when asked anything and whose words betray their ignorance as well as their foolishness.

260 Ad populum phaleras! ego te intus et in cute novi / To the mob with your trappings! I know you inside and out
Jerome frequently uses this verse of Persius as a proverb.[1] It is suitably directed at those who brag in the company of the uninformed, but who can in no way deceive learned men.

261 Theta praefigere / To prefix a theta
This is in Persius and means 'to condemn': 'And on guilt the black *theta* he can plant.'[1] This is taken from the ancient procedure in the courts where each juryman dropped his lot into an urn. *Theta* designated condemnation, *kappa* acquittal, and *lambda* deferment.[2]

* * * * *

3 Persius 2.10–12

258 Not in *Adagia*. Cf Plautus *Bacchides* 537 (*movere bilem*); Cicero *Ad Atticum* 5.11.2 (*facere stomachum*).

259 This did not get into the *Adagia*.
1 Persius 3.21–2, with a corrupt text

260 See *Adagia* I ix 89, which (like C 461) consists only of the last part of the quotation here: 'inwardly and in the buff.' Otto 492
1 Persius 3.30. Jerome *Letters* 58.7.2 CSEL 54 537; *Adversus Rufinum* 2.16 PL 23 438C

261 *Adagia* I v 56. The name of the Greek letter is spelled as *thita* throughout.
1 Persius 4.13, with a slight variation from the modern text (the verb in the third person instead of the second). What follows is based on Iohannes Britannicus' commentary on the Persius passage (see 12 above), but Erasmus (or the printer) has misread 'n l' (for *non liquere*) as the Greek letter *lambda* to signify deferment.
2 At *Adagia* I v 56 the three letters are *theta*, *tau*, and *delta*. Cf also *Adagia* IV x

262 **Metus sine metu / Fear where there is no fear**

Ἀδεὲς δέος, Fear without fear. This is a Greek adage.[1] It is said of those who are afraid when there is no cause for fear. The expression in Plato, 'to be afraid of one's own shadow,' is similar.[2]

263 **Cornix scorpium. Leonem pungis / The crow seized the scorpion. You are goading the lion**

Κορώνη τὸν σκορπίον. This is a metaphor with ellipsis of 'seized' or 'ate,' the sense being 'The crow seized the scorpion.' It suits those who attack or try to destroy someone in such a way that they too must perish. Or they revile someone from whom they will suffer as much, or even more, discomfiture. What Plautus writes is not dissimilar: 'That's a hot dinner you have eaten today,'[1] meaning that a person has done something that is going to cause him great trouble. Almost the same sense is conveyed by Λέοντα νύττεις 'You are goading a lion.'[2] This is said of a man who provokes those who, if angered, will strike him dead on the spot. An example is if someone attacks a tyrant or a prince.

264 **Ede helleborum / Eat hellebore**

We tell those whom we wish to mark out as insane to sail for the Anti-cyras,[1] to sacrifice a pig,[2] or to eat hellebore. The reason is that this plant, which everyone agrees purges the brain, grows in these islands. In Plautus

* * * * *

85, where the third element is given as 'n l' (= *non liquet* 'not proven'). See Pseudo-Ascanius on Cicero's *Verrines* (T. Stangl ed *Ciceronis orationum scholiastae* [Vienna / Leipzig 1912] 193, 231).

262 *Adagia* II iii 80
  1 The Greek version, taken from Diogenianus 1.16, appears in *1500*.
  2 *Adagia* I v 65. Plato *Phaedo* 101D. This became C 400.

263 *Adagia* I i 58. The Greek version, taken from Diogenianus 1.52, is present in *1500*.
  1 Plautus *Poenulus* 759, which becomes *Adagia* I i 59
  2 Also in Diogenianus 1.52 and printed in its Greek form in *1500*. This became *Adagia* I i 61 (with *stimulas* instead of *pugnis*).

264 The correct form of the adage would be 'Drink hellebore' as at *Adagia* I viii 51. Erasmus seems to have concocted this version on the basis of the next adage 'Eat nasturtium.' See Otto 596 and Polydore Vergil 43 ('He's sailing to Anticyra').
  1 *Adagia* I viii 52 (Otto 117). Two towns called Anticyra are attested, one in Phocis and the other in Thessaly. The description of the places as islands is inaccurate, the error occurring in Pliny *Naturalis historia* 25.52.
  2 *Adagia* I viii 55. Otto 1448

a madman is ordered to sacrifice a sound and suitable pig.[3] Horace: 'He should sail for the Anticyras.'[4] The same poet: 'If you never entrust to the barber Licinus a head that three Anticyras could not cure.'[5] Persius: 'Better to swallow whole islands of pure hellebore.'[6] Plautus: 'Three acres of hellebore won't settle this.'[7]

265 Ede nasturtium / Eat cress

Ἔσθιε κάρδαμον, Eat cress. This is a Greek adage directed at idle, lazy, and stupid persons.[1] For, according to Pliny in book twenty, cress is a plant that excites the mind and stimulates the intellect just as rocket heightens sexual desire but blunts the mind.[2]

266 Quantum non miluus oberret / More than a hawk could fly around

This is said of extremely wealthy men who own such a great estate that a hawk could not pass over all of it even if it never stopped flying. Persius: 'That rich man at Cures ploughs more land than a hawk could fly over.'[1] Juvenal: 'Your great pastures tire out hawks.'[2]

267 Caedimus inque vicem praebemus crura flagellis / Now it is we who strike, now it is we who expose our shins to whips

A proverbial metaphor taken from a battle between archers. It can be

* * * * *

3 Plautus *Menaechmi* 289–90. Erasmus draws on this for *Adagia* I viii 55 Sacrifice a pig.
4 Horace *Satires* 2.3.166
5 Horace *Ars poetica* 300–1
6 Persius 4.16
7 Plautus *Menaechmi* 913. Erasmus' text differs from that in modern editions.

265 *Adagia* I viii 54. The Greek version was present in *1500* (see n1). Polydore Vergil 54; Otto 1197
1 The Greek proverb is not found in Diogenianus (or, indeed, in any of the Greek collections of proverbs). It seems to be a creation of Niccolò Perotti; see *Cornucopiae* (202:44–8). See also Heinimann 164 and 17 above.
2 Pliny *Naturalis historia* 20.126–7

266 *Adagia* III vi 5. Otto 1116
1 Persius 4.26
2 Juvenal 9.55, referred to by Britannicus in his commentary (see 12 above) on the Persius line.

267 *Adagia* III vi 6. The adage is Persius 4.42, where the correct reading is *sagittis* 'arrows' for *flagellis* 'whips.' The verse is correct in the *Adagia*. The initial sentence of the commentary suggests that Erasmus actually read *sagittis* and that *flagellis* was printed by a printer's error or by a slip on Erasmus' part. Otto 279

applied to those who attack the faults of others but who do not see their own ones. The result is that they in turn are criticized by others for their flaws. Horace: 'We are whipped and wear out our enemy with as many blows,'[1] meaning that we criticize others only to be criticized in turn by other persons.

268 Tuo te pede metire. Tecum habita / Measure yourself by our own foot. Be your own lodger

This adage occurs in Horace in his *Satires*[1] and advises us not to extend ourselves beyond our station in life, and not to assess ourselves on the basis of flatterers' compliments or the opinion of the common herd or the enjoyment of good fortune. Rather we should do so on the basis of our character and morals.

What Persius says is of equal weight: 'Be your own lodger, so that you may recognize how little your possessions come to.'[2]

269 Bullatae nugae / Trifles and bubbles

Things that are trifling and worthless, even though they are often exalted in extravagant language as being very important, are called 'Trifles and bubbles.' Inexperienced preachers exemplify this. Although they spout pure rubbish, they deliver their words in a portentous tone and with grand gestures. It is as if they had learned their words with St Paul in the third heaven and not from compilations.[1] Horace describes as 'tuneful rubbish' a speech that is constructed in a pretentious style, but is devoid of any solid content.[2] Persius: '... that my page should swell with trifles and bubbles.'[3]

* * * * *

1 Horace *Epistles* 2.2.97. Horace is talking of his response to those who criticize his work. Erasmus reads *caedimus* 'we whip' instead of the correct *caedimur* 'we are whipped.' The error persists into the *Adagia*.

268 The first becomes *Adagia* I vi 89 (Otto 1107), the second I vi 87 (Polydore Vergil 101; Otto 1929).
1 Horace *Epistles* (not *Satires*) 1.7.98 (the reference for only the first adage given, which is Erasmus' primary concern)
2 Persius 4.52

269 *Adagia* III vi 98. The source is Persius (see n3).
1 For 'third heaven' see 2 Cor 12:2. The third heaven refers to paradise and the dwelling place of God. Compilations or summaries (*summae* or, as here, *summulae*) of extensive or difficult works were popular in medieval and Renaissance times. Erasmus often refers to them in derogatory terms: see Epp 396:89–92, 531:165–9, 575:33–5.
2 Horace *Ars poetica* 322
3 Persius 5.19–20

270 Aceto perfundere / To drench with vinegar

This means to direct rather biting abuse at someone. Horace: 'Persius, our Greek, drenched with Italian vinegar, cries out.'[1]

271 Sambucam citius caloni aptaveris alto / You would sooner supply a war-machine to a lanky soldier's servant

This is a proverbial verse in Persius, taken from warfare.[1] For the *sambuca* is a war-machine that can be used only with the greatest skill and the only thing that soldiers' servants do is to carry timber for fortification, since they have no experience in fighting.[2] The sense is the same as if you were to say 'you have a better chance of turning an ox into a tightrope walker than of transforming this extremely stupid old man into a learned philosopher.' The expression also makes good sense if you take *sambuca* to refer to a musical instrument and *calo* to a simple peasant. For each word is found in both senses.

272 Creta notare. Carbone notare / To mark with chalk. To mark with coal

Things we approve of we mark with chalk since they are auspicious and favourable. We mark things we disapprove of with coal because they are sordid and contemptible. Persius: 'What to follow and what to shun you marked, one with chalk, the other with coal.'[1] Horace in his *Satires*: 'How do they come off? Are they sane, to be marked with chalk, or are they to be marked with coal?'[2]

273 Edentulus invidet dentato. Talpa caprearum contemnit oculos / The toothless man envies those who have teeth. The mole thinks lightly of the roe-deer's sight

* * * * *

270 Cf *Adagia* II iii 52 He has vinegar in his bosom, in the discussion of which *aceto perfundere* is mentioned. Cf c 90. Otto 9
1 Horace *Satires* 1.7.32–3

271 See *Adagia* III v 43, where Erasmus takes *sambuca* to refer primarily to a musical instrument and only secondarily to a war-machine – the reverse of what he does here. Otto 1576
1 Persius 5.95
2 This sentence is based on the humanist commentaries of Ascensius (Josse Bade) and Britannicus (see 12 above) on Persius 5.9.

272 *Adagia* I v 54. Otto 299. Cf c 664.
1 Persius 5.107–8
2 Horace *Satires* 2.3.246, referred to by Britannicus in his commentary on Persius 5.107–8 (see 12 above)

273 *Adagia* III i 7, where the first adage constitutes the heading and the second is cited in the discussion. Otto 1739

Jerome closed his well-known and very learned letter to the orator Magnus with a fine proverb. He says, 'I beg you, advise him not to be like the toothless man who envies those who have their teeth or like the mole who does not think much of the roe-deer's keen sight.'[1] Jerome means that a person should not grudge in others what he himself cannot match. For it is very much like human nature for all to praise what they hope they can accomplish, but if they feel that something is beyond their abilities, they say that it is not worth learning.

274 Tota erras via. Toto erravit coelo / You are entirely on the wrong road. He was quite wrong, by the whole sky

Whenever we wish to indicate that someone is guilty of a gross error, we say that he is entirely on the wrong road and that the scope of his error is the whole sky. Terence in *The Eunuch*: 'You are entirely on the wrong road.'[1] This is very similar to what Euangelus says in Macrobius in his *Saturnalia* book 3: 'Did it never occur to you, Praetextatus, that Virgil was quite wrong – wrong by the whole sky, as they say?'[2] Most probably the second adage is taken from the story of Phaethon or of Ceres.[3]

275 Equis albis praecedere / To lead the way with white horses

When the ancients wished to indicate that someone was far superior in some activity and surpassed others by a great degree, they would say that he led the way with white horses. The reason was that in antiquity either white horses were thought to be more noble and faster than the rest or those celebrating triumphs (the conquerors of the enemy) were drawn by white horses. Horace, writing about a certain Persius: 'A cruel man and one who could surpass a king in hatred, / Arrogant, presumptuous and so bitter in his words / That over a Sisenna and a Barrus he led the way with white horses.'[1] Sisenna and Barrus were renowned for their skill in

* * * * *

1 Jerome *Letters* 70.6.2 CSEL 54 708

274 The first proverb becomes *Adagia* I i 48 (Otto 1885), the second I i 49 (Polydore Vergil 264; Otto 283).
1 Terence *Eunuchus* 245
2 Macrobius *Saturnalia* 3.12.10, referring to Virgil's description of Dido's sacrifice for marriage.
3 Phaethon drove the chariot of his father, the sun god, in the heavens before crashing to earth. Ceres searched the earth for her abducted daughter Proserpina.

275 *Adagia* I iv 21. In part of the first sentence Erasmus paraphrases the commentary of the humanist Cristoforo Landino on the Horace passage (see n1). See 12 above for the Horace edition that Erasmus used. Otto 1498
1 Horace *Satires* 1.7.6–8

insulting others, though Acron read *barros*, as if it were an adjective describing *Sisennas*.[2]

An expression in Plautus in his *Comedy of Asses* is quite similar: 'For if he lets this opportunity slip, he will never get it again, by heavens, even if he has a chariot and four white horses.'[3] The same author in *The Pot of Gold*: 'Let him hurry to do on a chariot with four swift horses what the other tells him to do.'[4] Plautus uses this metaphor on different occasions.[5] The Horatian passage, however, seems to be based more on a horse race than on the triumphal celebrations, and we are to take the sense to be that white horses are lucky and successful.

276 Ubi non sis qui fueris, non est quur velis vivere? / When you are not the man you were, why wish to live?

This comes from a letter of Cicero to Marius, where the expression is specifically named as a proverb. He says, 'There is an old saying that when you are not the man you were there is no reason for wishing to live.'[1] The point of this is that it is more acceptable to live in exile among strangers than to remain, stripped of all honour and as an object of contempt, in a society in which you once commanded the greatest respect.

277 Plautina eloquentia. Attica lepos / Plautine eloquence. Attic wit

Although Horace did not approve,[1] the ancients derived so much pleasure from the comedies of Plautus that 'Plautine eloquence' became proverbial just like 'Attic wit' and 'the eloquence of the Muses.' Jerome to Pammachius says, 'This is Plautine eloquence, this is Attic wit, comparable, as the saying goes, to "the eloquence of the Muses."'[2] What he says about the eloquence of the Muses is an allusion to Varro's praise of Plautus. Varro said,

* * * * *

2 An accusative plural, agreeing with *Sisennas*, in the sense of 'slanderous.' There are contradictory notes in the commentary ascribed to Acron, on whom see C 241A n4. One note correctly takes the word to be a proper noun.
3 Plautus *Asinaria* 278–9
4 Plautus *Aulularia* 600
5 Plautus *Amphitryo* 450–1, *Poenulus* 369

276 *Adagia* I viii 45. Otto 1928
1 Cicero *Ad familiares* 7.3.4

277 *Adagia* I ii 57. There Erasmus quotes the passages from Jerome and Varro that illustrate the phrase 'Plautine eloquence,' but does not include it in the title. Otto 200 and 1177
1 Horace *Ars poetica* 270–2
2 Jerome *Letters* 57.12.3 CSEL 54 525

'If the Muses had wished to speak Latin, they would have spoken like Plautus.'[3]

278 Bos lassus fortius figit pedem / The weary ox treads more firmly

Jerome also[1] used a witty adage when writing to Augustine, advising him, as a young man, not to challenge an old one. The reason he gave was that although older men are more slowly roused to battle, they fight more fiercely when they are annoyed and become heated with anger. These are his words: 'Remember Dares and Entellus,[2] and the common proverb, that the weary ox treads more firmly.'[3] It is taken from the old way of threshing. For carts were driven round over the sheaves and the grain was shaken out, partly by the cart's wheels, partly by the hooves of the oxen. The proverb warns us not to provoke those who are slow to anger since such persons, once enraged, can scarcely be appeased; for 'patience too oft provoked is turned to rage.'[4]

279 Per nebulam, per caliginem, per somnium / Through a cloud, through darkness, as in a dream

To know, think, or understand through a cloud means to think or know something slightly, darkly, and with difficulty. The expression is found on several occasions in Plautus.[1] Jerome said 'to think as in a dream' in the same sense.[2] When we are old, we sometimes remember what we did when very young, but we do so 'through a cloud,' and 'as if in a dream.' The phrase 'through darkness' is found in the same sense.[3]

280 Qui vestitu ac creta sese occultant / Those who hide behind clothes and chalk

Euclio in Plautus' *The Pot of Gold* talks about thieves whose clothes and

* * * * *

3 Cited by Quintilian 10.1.99

278 *Adagia* I i 47. Otto 264
  1 Erasmus is referring to his citation of Jerome in the preceding adage.
  2 Cf c 803 and *Adagia* III i 69.
  3 Jerome *Letters* 102.2.2 CSEL 55 236
  4 Publilius Syrus 208 (Loeb edition of *Minor Latin Poets*), cited by Gellius *Noctes Atticae* 17.14.4

279 *Adagia* I iii 63. Otto 1210
  1 As at Plautus *Captivi* 1023–4 and *Pseudolus* 463
  2 Jerome *Letters* 70.3.2 CSEL 54 703
  3 As at Cicero *Philippics* 12.2.3 and *De finibus* 5.15.43

280 Not in the *Adagia*. Cf Otto 1377.

appearance suggest that they are honest. He says, 'They hide behind clothes and chalk and sit as if they are fine men.'[1] This is suitably directed at those who are unprincipled inside and are 'attractive in their outside skin, to no avail.'[2]

281 In vado est omnis res / Everything is in shallow water
The meaning is that one is out of danger. Terence: 'Everything is in shallow water.'[1] Plautus in *The Pot of Gold*: 'This business seems now to be in shallow water and to be safe.'[2] A metaphor taken from those crossing a river or, if not that, at any rate from those sailing. Not very different from this is a phrase, also in Terence, in *The Woman of Andros*: 'I am sailing in harbour,' meaning that what is being done is free of danger. He says, 'Now he is the one at risk. As for me, I am sailing in harbour.'[3]

282 Omnes sibi melius esse malunt quam alteri *et alia eodem in sensu* / Everyone wants things to go better for himself than for others *and other similar ones*
In the same play: 'True is the saying on everyone's lips, "Everyone wants things to go better for himself than for others." '[1] Plautus' words, 'The tunic is nearer than the cloak,' have the same sense.[2] Terence elsewhere: 'Hey you there, the nearest person to myself is me.'[3] We must realize that this adage does not advocate what we ought to do but is critical of what is customarily and commonly done.

283 Quando id fieri non potest quod vis, id velis quod possis / When you can't do what you want, let what you can do determine your wants
This is a saying that offers advice on how we should live and is most charmingly expressed. It is made more attractive by the use of the figure of speech

* * * * *

1 Plautus *Aulularia* 719. As chalk was used to clean cloth, there is perhaps here a hendiadys, the sense being 'sparkling clothes.'
2 Persius 4.14

281 *Adagia* I i 45. Polydore Vergil 133; Otto 1843
1 Terence *Andria* 845
2 Plautus *Aulularia* 803
3 Terence *Andria* 480, which becomes *Adagia* I i 46 (Otto 1455)

282 *Adagia* I iii 91. Polydore Vergil 166; Otto 72
1 Terence *Andria* 426–7
2 Plautus *Trinummus* 1154, which becomes *Adagia* I iii 89 (Otto 1324)
3 Terence *Andria* 636

283 *Adagia* III vi 4. The source is Terence *Andria* 305–6. Otto 1456

called *conversio*.[1] Laberius' words are similar in sense: 'What can't be cured, must be endured.'[2]

284 **Facile, quum valemus, recte consilia aegrotis damus. Tu, si hic sis, aliter sentias / Good counsel to the sick is cheap enough when we ourselves are well. In my place you would think differently**

A weighty sentiment expressed by a young man,[1] despite his not being very intelligent. The sense is that it is much easier to give good advice to others than to look after your own interests. Those who give advice can easily see what is right since they are free of the emotions that hamper those whom they are addressing.

285 **Monstrum alere / To breed a monster**

This adage means that something foul and awful is being kept secret. We shall use it whenever we suspect that some deceit or secret misfortune is afoot. When that young man[1] had first been rejected as a son-in-law and then was being sought after, he made the following surmise: 'Once rejected, now I am sought. Why? Unless it's what I suspect. / They are breeding some monster. They can't pass her off on someone else. / And so they turn to me.'[2]

286 **Bona verba quaeso / Watch what you say, please**

This is an expression that is used not to make fun of someone[1] but when one wishes to avert disaster. Spoken when someone is thought to have uttered words of ill omen. Terence: 'Watch what you say, please!'[2] Donatus also

* * * * *

1 The figure of speech called *conversio* involves the repetition of the same word, sometimes exactly the same, sometimes with minor variation, in different clauses. See Quintilian 9.1.33–4.
2 The author of these words is not Laberius but the other famous writer of mimes, Publilius Syrus (the line is no 206 in the Loeb volume *Minor Latin Poets*). This became *Adagia* I iii 14. It is cited by Gellius *Noctes Atticae* 17.14.4, who also mentions Laberius there; hence Erasmus' error.

284 *Adagia* I vi 68 (only the first line). Terence *Andria* 309–10. Otto 22
1 Charinus in Terence's *Andria*

285 *Adagia* II iv 98
1 Erasmus implies that the speaker of this phrase is the same as that of the preceding adage, but in fact the speakers are different.
2 Terence *Andria* 249–51

286 This did not survive into the *Adagia*.
1 As might be its purpose, if the expression *bona verba*, literally 'fine words,' was an ironic comment on what has just been said.
2 Terence *Andria* 204

gave a similar comment on the phrase.[3] Cicero: 'Watch what you say about Socrates!'[4] He meant, 'May it not be true what you say about Socrates!' And as told in Plato, book one of *The Republic*, Sophocles was asked when he was quite an old man whether he still had sex with women. His answer: 'My friend, watch what you say, please. Very gladly have I escaped from that, which is like a raging, savage taskmaster.'[5]

287 In portu impingere / To run aground in the harbour
This appears in both Quintilian and Jerome in the sense of failing in something immediately one makes a start to it.[1] Taken from sailing.

288 Claudi more pilam tenere / To grasp a pillar like a lame man
The sense is to find or acquire nothing at all by one's own abilities, but to adhere to and follow all that one has learned from one's teachers, whether that is sensible or foolish. Cicero in his speech against Piso: 'The Greek began to distinguish and analyse how the words were used, but that fellow swore allegiance to what he had been taught, like the lame man holding onto a pillar, as the saying goes.'[1]

289 Mansum in os inserere *sive* Praemandere / To feed with pre-chewed food *or* To chew before feeding
This means to teach a subject in a very simplified way and impart information piece by piece at a time. This is the method of those who have little confidence in the abilities of their listeners. A metaphor taken from babies' nurses, who chew food before putting it in the mouth of the child in their care. Cicero in *The Making of an Orator*: 'To feed with pre-chewed food, as the saying goes.'[1]

* * * * *

3 Donatus on *Andria* 204
4 Not Cicero. See Macrobius *Saturnalia* 2.1.4.
5 Plato *Republic* 1.329C, quoted only in Latin (see C 2 n7)

287 *Adagia* I v 76. Otto 1454
  1 Quintilian 4.1.61; Jerome *Adversus Rufinum* 2.15 PL 23 437C, CCSL 79 48, *Letters* 57.12.2 CSEL 54 525

288 *Adagia* III ii 20. Otto 394. The correct interpretation, suggested in *Adagia* III ii 20, is to take *pila* in the sense of 'ball' rather than 'pillar,' the notion being that a lame man would be unable to take part successfully in a game of ball because of his disability.
  1 Cicero *In L. Pisonem* 28.69

289 *Adagia* II x 33 (translated as 'Spoonfeeding' at CWE 34 140). The verb *praemandere* comes from Gellius *Noctes Atticae* 4.1.11. Otto 1254
  1 Cicero *De oratore* 2.39.162. This is the source of the first adage.

290 Bis pueri senes / Old men have a second childhood

The Greek form of the proverb is Δὶς παῖδες οἱ γέροντες.[1] Marcus Varro gave one of his satires this title.[2] Although the phrase in itself has the appearance of a proverb, I am more confident in believing that it is one because Varro used proverbs for the titles of many of his satires, as, for example, 'An Ass to the Lyre,'[3] 'Know Thyself.'[4] The proverb suits old men who behave like young boys, so that it looks as if they have returned to their childhood. Seneca says, 'We are not children twice, as is commonly said. No, we are always children. The difference, however, is that we play with bigger toys.'[5]

291 Dignum propter quod vadimonium deseratur / Worth breaking bail for

This is what the ancients said when they wanted to indicate an extremely important matter that could not be neglected without great expense. For bail was not customarily broken except for the most serious of reasons. Pliny the Elder in his preface of his *Natural History* talks of 'titles that were worth breaking bail for.'[1]

292 Nostro Marte / By our own prowess

Whenever we complete something without anyone's help, using only our own talents and strength, we are said to do so 'By our own prowess.' Cicero in *On Moral Obligations* book three: 'This gap we shall fill with no help from someone else but, as the saying goes, by our own prowess.'[1] Based on the practice of supreme commanders of waging war with the aid of the auxiliary troops of kings and allies.[2]

* * * * *

290 *Adagia* I v 36. Polydore Vergil 105; Otto 1625
  1 This sentence, present in *1500*, is printed as part of the title of the adage.
  2 Drawn from Gellius *Noctes Atticae* 7.5.10, where the adage title is given in Greek (= Varro *Menippean Satires* 91 Buecheler). It also occurs in Diogenianus (4.18).
  3 C 125 (*Adagia* I iv 35)
  4 C 108 (*Adagia* I vi 95)
  5 Seneca fragment 121 Haase, cited by Lactantius *Divinae institutiones* 2.4.14

291 *Adagia* I viii 18. Polydore Vergil 100
  1 Pliny *Naturalis historia* praefatio 24, from which the adage is drawn. Cf Niccolò Perotti in a letter to Francesco Guarnieri (*Cornucopiae* 1046:44–8).

292 *Adagia* I vi 19. Polydore Vergil 240; Otto 1063
  1 Cicero *De officiis* 3.7.34
  2 This is rather odd, since it contradicts the sense of the adage, as given in the first sentence. One would expect 'without the aid of' instead of 'with the

293 Nequicquam sapit qui sibi nihil sapit / He is wise in vain who is not wise for himself

They say that some people used to have on their lips what all now know in their hearts, that 'He who is not wise for himself is wise in vain.' This was taken from Ennius' *Medea*, as Cicero points out in his correspondence. He wrote to Trebatius in the following words: 'Since I have begun to take the part of Medea, always remember those words: "He whose wisdom helps not himself is vain to no avail."'[1] The sense of the adage is expressed by a Greek verse: μισῶ σοφιστὴν ὅστις οὐχ αὑτῷ σοφός 'I hate a wise man who is not wise for himself.'[2]

294 Oleum flammis addere / To add oil to fire

The meaning is to goad on someone who is already ablaze with anger, or to worsen someone's troubles by giving him more. Horace in his *Satires*: 'Add poems now, that is, add oil to fire.'[1] Jerome to Eustochius: 'Wine and youth fan the fires of pleasure two times over. Why are we adding oil to the flames?'[2]

295 Munus levidense / A threadbare present

In his *Letters to his Friends* Cicero calls the speech in which he had defended king Deiotarus 'A threadbare present,' using a proverbial metaphor.[1] He wanted his correspondent to think that his speech was written in a rather crude style and had been put together in a rough and ready manner. He was describing it metaphorically with reference to the nature of Deiotarus' toga. He says that he wanted to repay an old friend with even a modest gift, like the presents that Deiotarus had often sent to him.

* * * * *

aid of.' Cf *Adagia* I vi 19 (CWE 32 16): 'A metaphor ... from supreme commanders, who fight a campaign on their own initiative and with their own forces.'

293 *Adagia* I vi 20. Polydore Vergil 106; Otto 1579
    1 Cicero *Ad familiares* 7.6.2, citing Ennius *Scaenica* 273 Vahlen (TRF Ennius 240)
    2 Euripides fragment 905 Nauck, which is cited in Cicero *Ad familiares* 13.15.2. Erasmus' source for the Greek version (present in *1500*) was the commentary of the humanist Hubertinus Crescentinas on the Ciceronian passage.

294 This is a slight variant of *Adagia* I ii 9, which refers to this form of the proverb. Otto 1283
    1 Horace *Satires* 2.3.321
    2 Jerome *Letters* 22.8.2 CSEL 54 154

295 *Adagia* III v 22
    1 Cicero *Ad familiares* 9.12.2

296 Mordere frenum / To bite on the bit

This means to resist and rebel against being enslaved. Decius Brutus to Cicero in book two: 'If you bite on the bit, I'd stake my life on it that all of them, no matter how many, will not be able to face you if you try to speak.'[1] He means, 'if you give even the slightest indication that you will not tolerate servitude.' This is a metaphor taken from a horse that has not been broken. 'To shake the yoke' is very similar.[2] Juvenal: 'They have learned in the school of life not to shake the yoke.'[3]

297 Suum cuique pulchrum / What is one's own is beautiful

An adage based on human nature. For all of us are vain and think that our possessions are more beautiful than those of others even if they are ugly. It seems to be taken especially from suitors, all of whom vie with each other in praising their brides-to-be. This is similar to what we read about the Tarquin family.[1] Cicero to Atticus: 'For every man his own bride, mine for me. For every man his own love, mine for me.'[2] The same author in his *Tusculan Questions*: 'Everyone thinks that what is his own is beautiful.'[3] Plautus expressed the same sentiment in a very elegant way: 'Every queen thinks her king handsome,'[4] meaning that every wife thinks more highly of her husband than of anyone else. Very similar to these is 'no wonder if an old man takes an old bride.'[5]

298 Coepisse dimidium facti / Well begun is half done

Ἀρχὴ ἥμισυ παντός, Well begun is half done. This is an expression of Hesiod's

* * * * *

296 *Adagia* I iv 14. Otto 715
  1 Cicero *Ad familiares* 11.23.2 (not book 2)
  2 *Adagia* III vii 78
  3 Juvenal 13.22

297 *Adagia* I ii 15. Cf C 601 and C 809. Otto 1726
  1 Two members of the ruling Tarquin family in Rome boasted that their wives were the most virtuous. They went to Rome unexpectedly to see what their wives were doing. According to the story, this eventually led to the rape of Lucretia, one of the wives, and her suicide. See Livy 1.57–8.
  2 Cicero *Ad Atticum* 14.20.3, citing CRF Atilius 1
  3 Cicero *Tusculan Disputations* 5.22.63
  4 Plautus *Stichus* 133
  5 Varro *De lingua Latina* 7.28. See C 809 (and, more extensively, *Adagia* I ii 62). The word for 'old' is *cascus* and *casca*, but these are also proper names.

298 *Adagia* I ii 39. See Diogenianus 2.97, where Hesiod is named as the source. The Greek version of the proverb appears in *1500*. Otto 557. Here begins a series of adages (down to 312, excluding 307) taken from Diogenianus, resuming the alphabetical series in C 133–48, 161–3; see also C 341n.

that has had proverbial status even from ancient times.'[1] Horace expressed it in this way: 'He who starts a task has half completed it.'[2]

299 Atticus martyr / An Attic witness
Ἀττικὸς μάρτυς, An Attic witness. When used literally this is said of someone telling the truth. It can be used ironically of a liar.

300 Currus bovem trahit / Ἡ ἅμαξα τὸν βοῦν ἕλκει / The cart before the horse
Used when we want to indicate that something is done in the opposite way to what is normal; for example, if a servant gives instructions to his master, or a pupil tries to teach his instructor, or if a hare chases a hound.

301 Haec retia nihil traxerunt / These nets have caught nothing
Αὕτη ἡ μύρινθος[1] οὐδὲν ἔσπακεν, These nets have caught nothing. A metaphor from fishing, applied to those who have tried to catch something without success.

302 Homo Euripus / Man's a Euripus
Ἄνθρωπος Εὔριπος, Man's a Euripus. This is said of those who are inconstant and always changing. Taken from the nature of the Euripus sea, which ebbs and flows seven times a day with incredible force.[1]

* * * * *

1 Cf Hesiod *Works and Days* 40 (= c 6, *Adagia* I ix 95).
2 Horace *Epistles* 1.2.40

299 *Adagia* I viii 25. Diogenianus 3.11. The Latin title is given as *Atticus martir* in *1500*, *Atticus martyr* in *1506*, the noun being a Latinization of the Greek noun μάρτυς. In *1500* the Greek read Ἀττικὸς μάρτηρ, in *1506* it is changed to Ἀττικὸς μάρτυρ.

300 *Adagia* I vii 28. Diogenianus 3.30. The Greek version of the proverb was added in *1506*.

301 *Adagia* I ix 45. Diogenianus 3.35 is the source of the Greek version, which is present in *1500*.
1 The form μύρινθος is an erroneous reading found in Bodley Grabe 30 that was also in Erasmus' manuscript (see 7 above). The correct form is μήρινθος, meaning 'line' rather than 'nets.'

302 *Adagia* I ix 62. Diogenianus 3.39 is the source of the Greek version, which is present in *1500*. Otto *Nachträge* pp 21, 247
1 Cf Pliny *Naturalis historia* 2.219, where Pliny describes the Euripus of Euboea in a similar way to what Erasmus says here. See also Pseudo-Seneca *Hercules Oetaeus* 779–80 and Pomponius Mela 2.108. The proper noun is commonly used in the general sense of 'channel.'

303 Rana Seriphia / A Seriphian frog

Pliny in his *Natural History* book eight chapter fifty-eight wrote that on Seriphos even cicadas were mute.[1] In this passage Ermolao has replaced 'cicadas' with 'frogs,' adding that according to Stephanus there was a Greek proverb Βάτραχος Σερίφιος 'A Seriphian frog.' Applied to those who are excessively quiet.

304 Bos in lingua. Argentanginam patitur / An ox on his tongue. He has largesse-itis

Βοῦς ἐπὶ γλώσσης, An ox on his tongue. Customarily said of those who have been bribed and are not able to speak freely. Similar is what the people said of Demosthenes: 'He has largesse-itis.'[1] In the first proverb 'ox' has the sense of money, since Athenian coins had upon them the image of an ox.[2]

305 Bos Cyprius / A Cyprus ox

Βοῦς Κύπριος, A Cyprian ox. This is said of persons who live in squalor and eat the foulest of food. According to Pompeius, oxen in Cyprus ate human excrement.[1]

* * * * *

303 *Adagia* I v 31. Diogenianus 3.44 is the probable source of the Greek version, which is present in *1500*. Polydore Vergil 8
  1 Pliny *Naturalis historia* 8.227. Erasmus draws on Ermolao Barbaro's *Castigationes Plinianae* on this passage (Pozzi 597) for the emendation of the text in Pliny and for the reference to Stephanus. The latter is Stephanus of Byzantium (sub Σέριφος), for whom see 46–7 above.

304 *Adagia* I vii 18 and 19. Diogenianus 3.48 is probably source of the immediate Greek version of the first proverb (present in *1500*). The most famous use of the proverb in Greek literature, at Aeschylus *Agamemnon* 36, was not adduced by Erasmus until *1523*, at *Adagia* I vii 18.
  In the second adage, also in Polydore Vergil (no 48), the word *argentangina* is a coined compound based on the Greek ἀργυράγχη (see Plutarch *Demosthenes* 25.5). The coined form is drawn from contemporary editions of Aulus Gellius, where it appears as a gloss on the Greek word at *Noctes Atticae* 11.9.1.
  1 The story that Demosthenes was thought to have taken a bribe from the Milesians is told at Gellius *Noctes Atticae* 11.9, Erasmus' probable source. Cf also Plutarch *Demosthenes* 25.
  2 This is drawn from Diogenianus 3.48.

305 *Adagia* I x 95. Diogenianus 3.49 is the source of the Greek version, which is present in *1500*. Cf C 715. Otto 269
  1 Pompeius Festus 51.23–6 Lindsay

306 Ranis propinas / You pour wine for frogs

Βατράχοις οἰνοχεῖς, You pour wine for frogs, meaning that you give
something to those who actually have plenty of what they are being
offered.[1] In a letter to Pico, Ermolao[2] used this proverb in the following
way: 'That fellow Pico has put on shoes too huge for a tiny foot.[3] For why
does he use so many rhetorical figures, or why does he pour wine for
frogs? And, to put it more strongly, I would say "pour wine for Seriphian
frogs."'[4] In this one passage Ermolao has mentioned three adages, the first
about shoes that are too big for one's feet, the second about pouring wine for
frogs, and the third relating to Seriphian frogs. Yet in this context there may
be another meaning present; Ermolao may have said that Pico has poured
wine for frogs because he has used rhetorical figures to defend those who
take no pleasure in rhetoric, just as frogs have no interest in the taste of
wine. In addition Seriphian frogs are like the most inarticulate of men, and
these are not suited to be defended by the most eloquent of speakers.

307 Acanthia cicada / An Acanthian grasshopper

In Aeolia there is a city called Acanthon[1] where the cicadas are silent,

* * * * *

306 *Adagia* II iii 20. The adage is in Diogenianus (3.57), Erasmus' probable source
for the Greek version, which is present in *1500*. Ermolao Barbaro (see n2)
gives only a Latin version of the proverb.
  1 In the *Adagia* Erasmus drops this interpretation in favour of the one he mentions here at the end of his discussion, that the proverb relates to those offering
  something to those who have no need of what they are being offered.
  2 Ermolao Barbaro *Epistolae* 81.15 (1.102 Branca). The letter was published in
  editions of Poliziano's *Omnia opera* (*Epistolae* 9.5; 1.127 Maier), where Erasmus
  would have read the letter. The reference is to Giovanni Pico della Mirandola's
  playful defence of contemporary philosophers in answer to a criticism of them
  by Barbaro. With this proverb Barbaro is imagining the reaction of one of these
  philosophers to Pio's defence. See C 407 n1.
  3 C 781. Cf *Adagia* II v 46 Let not the shoe be too big for the foot.
  4 *Adagia* I v 31 A Seriphian frog. Seriphian frogs were quite mute. See C 303.

307 *Adagia* I v 14. This adage interrupts the sequence of sayings drawn by Erasmus from the third century of Diogenianus' collection, although this one is
also in Diogenianus (1.49). It is likely that Erasmus drew the adage and the information about Stephanus of Byzantium from Ermolao Barbaro *Castigationes
Plinianae* on *Naturalis historia* 4.6 (Pozzi 182–3). The Greek version in the accompanying text was present in *1500*. The adage also occurs at Zenobius 1.51
and *Suda* A 798.
  1 *Aeolia* in Erasmus' text is a misreading of *Aetolia* in Barbaro. However, the
  town of Acanthos (not 'Acanthon') is in Thrace, as Stephanus of Byzantium
  (see next note) tells us.

according to Stephanus.² This gave rise to the proverb Ἀκάνθιος τέττιξ 'An Acanthian cicada,' directed at persons who hardly spoke at all.

308 **Ranae aquam. Cato pingue / Βατράχῳ ὕδωρ. Γαλῆ τὸ στέαρ / Water to a frog. Suet to a weasel**
Whenever we give something that is most welcome to the receiver, we say that we have given water to a frog or suet to a weasel (or cat).

309 **Malis percutere / Βάλλειν μήλοις / To pelt with apples**
This means the same as to bribe with gifts. Taken from the story of Atalanta and Hippomanes.¹ The latter won a victory over the girl by dropping golden apples. Otherwise she would never have been defeated.

310 **Noctua volavit / Γλαὺξ ἵπταται / The owl has taken flight**
When an enterprise goes well, we say that the owl has taken flight. To the Athenians the sight of an owl in flight was a sign of victory.

311 **Annosam arborem transplantas / You are transplanting an aged tree**
Γεράνδριον μεταφυτεύειν, To transplant an old tree. This is said of someone who tries to persuade someone, now an old man, to take up a new way of life. Even nowadays it is commonly said that it is difficult to train an old dog to get used to the leash.¹ In the past we ourselves have 'wasted much oil and money'² in attempting such things.

* * * * *

2 Stephanus of Byzantium sub Ἄκανθος. For Stephanus see 46–7 above.

308 *Adagia* III vi 16 and I iv 11. The source is Diogenianus 3.58 (containing both adages). The Greek versions were added to the title in *1506*. Erasmus translates the Greek term in the second adage (γαλῆ) by *catus*, but the accompanying commentary shows that he was not certain of the identity of the animal. In the Greek original the term applies to a weasel.

309 *Adagia* II iv 70. The source is Diogenianus 3.63, the Greek version being added in *1506*.
  1 Atalanta's suitors had to defeat her in a race in order to win her. If they failed, they lost their lives. Hippomanes is the name of the suitor given here; in other versions the name is Milanion.

310 *Adagia* I i 76. Diogenianus 3.72 is the source; the Greek version was added in *1506*.

311 *Adagia* I iv 43. Diogenianus 3.77 is the source, the Greek version being present in *1500*. Otto 154
  1 Suringar 206.36. Also cited in *Adagia* I ii 61.
  2 Cf C 202.

312 **Terrae onus / A burden on the earth**

Γῆς βάρος, A burden on the earth. This refers to persons who are utterly useless.

313 **In silvam ligna ferre / To carry wood to the forest**

This means to wish to give something to those who already have a very abundant supply of it. Horace in his *Satires*:

> When I, born overseas, was writing Greek verses,
> Quirinus appeared after midnight, when dreams are true,
> And bade me stop with these words:
> 'Carry not wood into a forest.'[1]

314 **Tertius Cato. Sapientum octavus / A third Cato. An eighth Sage**

This is said ironically of men who have an austere disposition and who are convinced that they know what is right. Juvenal: 'A third Cato has fallen from the skies'[1] (for it was generally believed that the two Catos had come from heaven to wage war on vice). Horace: 'Stertinus, an eighth sage, taught me this.'[2] The point of this latter saying is that the number of sages honoured by the Greeks was seven.

315 **Secunda meliora / Better luck next time**

Δευτέρων ἀμεινόνων, Better the second time. A metaphor taken from those performing a sacrifice. These were in the habit of repeating a sacrifice if they did not receive a favourable response from the first offering. Cicero provides the evidence in book two of *On Divination*.[1] This Greek proverb gives us the same advice as the parable in the Gospel about the man who

* * * * *

312 *Adagia* I vii 31B. The source is Diogenianus 3.90, the Greek version being present in *1500*. Also in *Suda* Γ 258. This adage brings an end to a series of proverbs drawn primarily from Diogenianus, beginning at C 298.

313 *Adagia* I vii 57. Erasmus uses the proverb in Ep 27:43–4. This begins a series of sayings (down to 320, excluding 315) drawn from Horace's *Satires* or *Epistles*. Otto 1649
　1 Horace *Satires* 1.10.31–4

314 *Adagia* I viii 89 and 90. Otto 358 and 1581
　1 Juvenal 2.40. Cato the Elder railed against dissolute behaviour. Cato the Younger was renowned for his frugal and upright way of life.
　2 Horace *Satires* 2.3.296

315 *Adagia* I iii 38 (with a slightly different Latin translation – *posterioribus melioribus*). The Greek version (Diogenianus 4.15) did not appear until *1506*, when it was added (with a Latin translation) to the heading itself. Otto 404
　1 Cicero *De divinatione* 2.17.38. This sentence was added in *1506*.

knocked at his friend's door in the middle of the night, and finally received three loaves by his shameful persistence.[2]

316 Eadem pensaberis trutina / You will be weighed on the same scales

You will be treated in the same way that you treat others. Horace in his *Satires*: 'This granted, he will be placed on the same scales.'[1] Also in his *Epistles*: 'Roman writers are weighed in the same scales.'[2] Similar is the metaphor in the Gospels: 'Whatever measure you deal out to others will be dealt back to you.'[3] The two metaphors in these examples are both very appropriately used. In fact, Persius also says, 'Adjust the pointer of their worthless scales.'[4] Here Persius is following Horace, as he often does.

317 Nil intra est oleam, nil extra est in nuce duri / Olive no kernel hath, nor nut no shell

This is a proverbial line in Horace's *Epistles* that is directed at those who assert the truth of what is clearly false and who deny the truth of what everyone knows to be true.[1] It is impossible to have an argument with such persons. All sane people are agreed that a nut has a hard shell and that an olive contains a hard stone.

318 Ire per extentum funem / To walk the tightrope

The meaning of this is to do something that is very difficult. The source of the metaphor is not very clear, even though Acron thinks that it is taken from tightrope walkers;[1] they walk along a tautly stretched rope. Horace: 'The poet who can touch my heart with idle words / Can walk a tightrope, to my way of thinking.'[2]

319 Propria vineta caedere / To cut down one's own vineyards

This is said of the man who is quick to criticize himself and his associates.

* * * * *

2 Luke 11:5–8 (dropped in the *Adagia*)

316 *Adagia* I v 15
1 Horace *Satires* 1.3.72
2 Horace *Epistles* 2.1.29–30
3 Matt 7:2, Mark 4:24, Luke 6:38
4 Persius 1.6, where the command is actually in the negative; cf C 227 n1.

317 *Adagia* I ix 73. Otto 1256
1 Horace *Epistles* 2.1.31

318 *Adagia* II v 3. Otto 741
1 Pseudo-Acron (see C 241A n4) on Horace *Epistles* 2.1.208
2 Horace *Epistles* 2.1.210–11

319 *Adagia* I vi 84. Otto 1898

Horace: 'Much is the harm we poets inflict upon ourselves; I cut down my own vineyards.'[1]

320 Zonam perdidit / He has lost his belt

A military proverb, directed at those who are penniless. Acron tells us that it was taken from a Greek fable, while Porphyrion says it comes from the soldiers' habit of carrying whatever they had in their belt.[1] It occurs in Horace in his *Epistles*: '"He who has lost his belt will go wherever you want," he says.'

321 Taurum tollet qui vitulum sustulerit / He who has borne a calf will carry a bull

Poliziano in his *Miscellanea*: 'I think the proverb that says he who has carried a calf can carry a bull had its origin from this.'[1] In this context he reports the words of Quartilla from Petronius: 'May I incur the wrath of Juno if I ever remember being a virgin. For when I was child I was defiled along with those of my age, and as I grew older I attached myself to older boys, until I reached this age.'[2] The sense of the proverb is clear from this, namely that the person who has become accustomed to committing minor crimes as a child will commit greater ones when he is older.

322 Narthecophori multi, Bacchi vero pauci / Πολλοὶ μὲν ναρθηκοφόροι, παῦροι δέ τε Βάκχοι / Many bear the wand, but few feel the god

This can be found in Plato in his *Phaedo*.[1] It is taken from the Bacchanalian rites, in which all the participants carried a *thyrsos*, a spear or wand with vine-shoots, which was a distinctive feature associated with Bacchus, but they were not all devotees of Bacchus. It suits those who wear the markings of virtue and learning, but are neither virtuous nor learned. It is the same

* * * * *

1 Horace *Epistles* 2.1.219–20

320 *Adagia* I v 16. Otto 1950
  1 In the ancient commentaries on Horace ascribed to Acron and Porphyrion (here on Horace *Epistles* 2.2.40, which is quoted in the next sentence)

321 *Adagia* I ii 51. Polydore Vergil 289; Otto 1744
  1 *Miscellanea* 89 (1.300–1 Maier)
  2 Petronius *Satyricon* 25.4–6

322 *Adagia* I vii 6. The Greek version of the adage (Diogenianus 7.86) was added in 1506. Erasmus took the Latin version from Filippo Beroaldo *Appendix annotationum* 6 (*Lampas* 1.316). Cf Otto 391.
  1 Plato *Phaedo* 69c

as if you were to say that not all are theologians who wear the gown of
a doctor of divinity, not all who wear a graduate's cap are competent in
letters, not all are monks who wear the cowl.

323 Iustitia iustior. Libra aequior / More just than justice. As fair as a pair of scales

Δικαιότερος σταχάνης and Δίκης δικαιότερος. Both expressions refer to those
whom we wish to mark out as being exceedingly just and fair.

324 De pilo pendet / It hangs by a hair

Ἐκ τριχὸς κρέμαται, It hangs by a hair. About a situation that is very precarious and dangerous. Even nowadays the expression is very common in
our own language.[1]

325 E lupi faucibus eripui / I snatched it from a wolf's jaws

Ἐκ λύκου στόματος ἀφείλω. Said of those who unexpectedly recover something that is virtually lost. An example would be if I recovered my money
from the customs officer on the shore at Dover.[1]

326 Non capit murem elephantus / The elephant does not catch mice

Ἐλέφας μῦν οὐχ ἁλίσκει, The elephant does not catch mice. The meaning is
that those who are powerful pay no attention to tiny things.

327 Elephantum ex musca facis / You make an elephant out of a fly

Ἐλέφαντα ἐκ μυίας ποιεῖς, You make an elephant out of a fly. This applies

* * * * *

323 *Adagia* IV i 12 (for the first proverb) and *Adagia* II v 82 (for the second). The
source of the Greek versions (present in *1500*) is Diogenianus (4.22 and 4.28).
The second of these adages occurs also at Zenobius 3.16, Zenobius Athous 2.64
(see Bühler 5.257–65), and *Suda* Δ 1076.

324 *Adagia* I ix 72. The source of the Greek version (present in *1500*) is Diogenianus
4.41. Otto 662
  1 Suringar 56

325 *Adagia* II vii 63 (with slightly different wording). The Greek version (present
in *1500*) is taken from Diogenianus 4.42. Cf Otto 982.
  1 In January 1500 most of Erasmus' money was confiscated by English custom
officials when he was crossing from Dover to France (see 6 and n6 above, and
Ep 119).

326 *Adagia* I ix 70. Diogenianus 4.45 is the source of the Greek version, present in
1500.

327 *Adagia* I ix 69. Diogenianus 4.46 is the source of the Greek version, present in
1500.

to someone who uses big words about little things and exaggerates them. Similar is 'To put huge sandals on small feet.'[1]

328 De lapide emptus / Bought from the block

This is said of an unknown and worthless fellow, since bought slaves were of the lowest quality. Cicero: 'With the exception of two who were bought from the block,'[1] the origin being the auctioneer's block. Very similar is the Greek expression 'Bought with salt.'[2]

329 In eadem es navi / You are in the same boat

The meaning is that you are sharing danger with others. Taken from those who travel on the same ship and who are all exposed together to every danger. This expression occurs in Cicero in his *Letters*.[1]

330 Lari sacrificant. Proterviam fecit / They are sacrificing to the Lar. He has made a clean sweep

This can be said about greedy guests at a dinner who leave nothing of the food served up to them. It was regarded as wrong for any part of a sacrifice to the Lar to be removed from the house.[1] Very similar to this is what Cato says of a person who had spent all that he had inherited, with the exception of one house, which was then destroyed by fire.[2] Cato said that the fellow had made a *protervia* 'a clean sweep' since a *protervia* was a sacrificial banquet where all the food that was left over had to be consumed by fire.[3]

* * * * *

1 c 781. Cf *Adagia* II v 46, III vi 67.

328 *Adagia* III i 67; cf II x 77. The source is Giambattista Pio's *Annotationes priores* 10 (*Lampas* 1.382); see also c 11n, c 28 n1.
  1 Cicero *In L. Pisonem* 15.35
  2 This is c 420 (see notes there). 'Bought with salt' is actually given in Latin.

329 *Adagia* II i 10. Otto 1206
  1 Cicero *Ad familiares* 2.5.1; cf 12.25.5.

330 The first of these reappears as c 580 in a slightly different form. *Adagia* I ix 43 and 44. Cf Diogenianus 4.68 ('He sacrifices to Hestia').
  1 The Lar was the Roman god who looked after the household.
  2 The story is told in Macrobius *Saturnalia* 2.2.4, where it is clearer that the individual concerned had himself burned down his house. From 'Very similar' to the end Erasmus is drawing from Niccolò Perotti (*Cornucopiae* 497:57–62). The adage is based on a faulty text. Modern texts read *propter viam* 'on account of a journey' for *proterviam*, the usual meaning of which is 'shamelessness.' The spendthrift says that he has burned down (*combussisse*) what he could not make use of (*comesse*).
  3 Cato *Dicta memorabilia* fragment 83 Jordan

331 **Delphinum cauda alligas / Δελφῖνα πρὸς τὸ οὐραῖον δέεις / You are tying a dolphin by the tail**

A Greek adage relating to those who cannot be held fast.[1] Nowadays too this idea is expressed by 'you hold an eel by its tail.'[2]

332 **Invento urso vestigia insequeris / Ἄρκτου παρούσης τὰ ἴχνη ζητεῖς / Having come upon the bear you still look for its tracks**

Taken from cowardly hunters and directed at those who engage in some trifling activity when they are face to face with the person whom they must punish. Similar is what Plato says in his *Laws* about a dog that savagely attacks a stone that has been thrown at it and ignores the person who threw it.[1]

333 **Cocta numerabimus exta / We shall count the entrails when they are cooked**

The grammarian Diomedes gave this as an example of a proverb and said the sense of it was that 'we shall only know what will happen from the outcome.'[1]

334 **Nescis quid vesper serus vehat / Who knows what evening in the end will bring?**

According to Gellius 'there is a very charming book of Marcus Varro's, one of his *Menippean Satires*, entitled "You know not what the late evening will bring."'[1] I do not think that anyone will doubt that this title, like many others of Varro's *Satires*, is proverbial.[2] This is a stern warning to us not to

* * * * *

331 *Adagia* I iv 93. The Greek version, probably from Diogenianus (see n1), was added in 1506.
  1 Diogenianus 4.37. Also Zenobius 3.38 and *Suda* Δ 212
  2 Suringar 54. Despite being a modern proverb, this becomes *Adagia* I iv 94.

332 *Adagia* I x 34 (with different wording). The Greek version (from Diogenianus 2.70) was added in 1506. Also Zenobius 2.36 (in a slightly different version) and *Suda* A 3954. According to Zenobius the expression comes from the lyric poet Bacchylides (see *Bacchylides* ed R. Jebb [Cambridge 1905] frag 5).
  1 Plato *Republic* (not *Laws*) 5.469E. Cf *Adagia* IV ii 22 A dog getting angry with a stone.

333 *Adagia* I v 17. Otto 618
  1 Diomedes in H. Keil ed *Grammatici latini* 1 (Leipzig 1855) 462

334 *Adagia* I vii 5. Otto 1881
  1 Gellius *Noctes Atticae* 13.11.1. See Varro *Menippean Satires* 333 Buecheler. A very similar expression also occurs at Virgil *Georgics* 1.461 'The sun will tell you what the late evening will bring.'
  2 Many of the titles of Varro's *Menippean Satires* are proverbial, as Erasmus frequently mentions (see C 7, 125, and 290).

be so elated by our present good fortune that we give no thought to what may happen in the future.

335 Ad vivum. Summo iure / To the quick. By the letter of the law
The meaning is 'right to the skin.'[1] We use the expression to refer to actions that are conducted with the utmost precision, as when we pursue something with excessive keenness. In Plato Thrasymachus calls Socrates a false accuser, meaning a pettifogger, because he applies a very narrow interpretation to what has been said, distorting the sense of words whose meaning is clear rather than showing how somewhat carelessly expressed words can be given a better sense. He adds, 'Therefore, according to your precise mode of interpretation (since you cut right to the quick) no craftsman can make a mistake.'[2] Similar to this is what Cicero says when defending Caecina: 'All the others turn to that way of speaking when they think they have a fair and good defence to make in a case. If, however, there is a wrangling about words and phrases, and, as the saying goes, the letter of the law is applied, they are in the habit of using such fine words as "fair" and "good" to counter such wickedness.'[3] To fight *Summo iure* 'By the letter of the law' means to cut back the laws to the quick and to apply a very narrow interpretation. From this we get 'Extreme right is extreme wrong.'[4]

336 Boni ad bonorum convivia vel invocati accedunt / Good men with good men dine, even when not invited
Αὐτόματοι δὲ ἀγαθοὶ ἀγαθῶν ἐπὶ δαῖτας ἵενται. This is a Greek adage that occurs in Plato's *Symposium*. Socrates brings Aristodemus along with him to the banquet hosted by Agathon and says, 'Follow me and let us adapt the proverb that good men attend the dinners of the good even when uninvited.'[1]

* * * * *

335 For the first phrase in the title cf *Adagia* II iv 13 To cut to the quick (where the sources adduced are quite different). Cf Polydore Vergil 65; Otto 1933. For the second see n4 below.
  1 Cf *Adagia* III iii 34.
  2 Plato *Republic* 1.340D–E (see C 2 n7). Socrates says that if a craftsman makes an error he really cannot be a craftsman. A statement such as 'the craftsman makes a mistake' is therefore inadmissible.
  3 Cicero *Pro A. Caecina* 23.65
  4 C 560 (= *Adagia* I x 25)

336 *Adagia* I x 35. The Greek version was added in 1506. In the *Adagia* Erasmus refers to Zenobius 2.19, and Erasmus may have taken the Greek version in 1506 from the edition of Zenobius that was printed in 1497; see C 26n. The proverb is mentioned in Diogenianus (at 1.60), though it is not the main entry there.
  1 Plato *Symposium* 174B. The point is the connection between ἀγαθός, the Greek

337 **Canis a corio nunquam absterrebitur uncto / A dog will never
be driven away from a greasy hide**
This is in Horace's *Satires* and is directed at those who are so eager to make
money that they enjoy committing shameful acts.[1]

338 **Crescentem tumidis infla sermonibus utrem / Inflate the bladder
so that it grows big with your hot air**
This occurs in the same satire and relates to those who use flattery and false
praise to make fools think well of themselves.[1]

339 **Cristae surgunt / His crest rises**
Said of foolish men who are vain and admire themselves. Taken from birds.
Juvenal: 'What could be more patent flattery? Yet his crest began to rise.'[1]

340 **Subsidunt pennae / Its feathers droop**
This is said of those who become dispirited and lose their self-confidence.
Taken from the behaviour of peacocks. Juvenal: 'The result is that all its
feathers droop.'[1]

341 **Gygis anulus / Γύγου δακτύλιος / The ring of Gyges**
A proverb taken from Gyges and the story that Glaucon tells of him in
Plato's *Republic* book two.[1] Said of those who achieve their ends by the use
of marvellous objects and secret tricks.

* * * * *

word for 'good' and the host's name Agathon and the connection between
ἄριστος, the Greek word for 'best,' and Aristodemus' name. Plato is cited in
Latin; see C 2 n7. Otto 5

337 Cf *Adagia* II iv 22 It is risky for a dog to taste guts, in the commentary on
which this proverb is quoted. Otto 325
  1 Horace *Satires* 2.5.83. Porphyrion, the ancient commentator on Horace, says
  that the expression is proverbial.

338 Not in *Adagia*. Otto 1841
  1 Horace *Satires* 2.5.98

339 *Adagia* I viii 69 (with a different verb). Otto 467
  1 Juvenal 4.69–70

340 Not in *Adagia*
  1 Juvenal 6.197–8

341 *Adagia* I i 96. The Greek version of the adage, taken from Diogenianus 3.99,
  was added in 1506. Here begins another series of adages drawn from Diogenianus in alphabetical order, running to C 364; see C 298n.
  1 Plato *Republic* 2.359D. Gyges was a shepherd who became king of the Lydians
  by means of a magic ring that made him invisible. He seduced the queen and
  killed her husband.

342 **A duce muliere ducitur mulier** / Γυνὴ στρατηγεῖ καὶ γυνὴ στρατεύεται /
A woman general leading a woman soldier
A Greek adage referring to cowards.

343 **Tam nudus quam ex matre** / **As naked as he came from his mother**
Γυμνὸς ὡς ἐκ μητρός, Naked as from his mother. This is said of someone who
is extremely poor.

344 **Anus vulpes non capitur** / Γραῦς ἀλώπηξ οὐχ ἁλίσκεται / **An old vixen**
is not caught
The Greeks used this of those who were sharp-witted from long experience
or of those who could not be bribed.

345 **Iovis cerebrum** / Διὸς ἐγκέφαλος / **Jove's brain**
This expression was used to refer to those who lived luxuriously, the reason being that this was what the Persians called sumptuous and costly
banquets.

346 **Rusticanum oratorem ne contemnas** / Ἀγροίκου μὴ καταφρόνει ῥήτορος /
Do not despise a country speaker
The meaning is that you should not look down on someone, however much
beneath you in station he may be. This too is Greek.

347 **In tenebris saltas** / Ἐν σκότῳ ὀρχεῖσθαι / **You dance in the dark**
The meaning is that no one sees your efforts.

* * * * *

342 *Adagia* II v 81 (with different wording in the Latin title). The Greek version
in the title (Diogenianus 4.1) was added in *1506*. Also in the *Suda* (Γ 502)

343 *Adagia* II viii 44; cf *Adagia* v i 57. The source is Diogenianus 4.2 The Greek was
correctly printed in *1500* as ἐκ μήτρας, 'from the womb' but Erasmus did not
know the word and the phrase was changed to ἐκ μητρός 'from one's mother'
in *1506*. Otto 1248

344 *Adagia* I x 17. The Greek version of the adage (Diogenianus 4.7) was added in
1506. Also in Zenobius 2.90 and *Suda* Γ 202. The reference to bribery in the
interpretation of the adage is based on a textual error in Erasmus' manuscript
of Diogenianus (χρυσίου 'of gold' for χρόνου 'of time'), also in Bodley Grabe
30; see 7 and 10 n23 above.

345 *Adagia* I vi 60. The Greek version of the adage (Diogenianus 4.24) was added
in *1506*. Also *Suda* Δ 1204 and Zenobius 3.41. Otto 882

346 *Adagia* II vi 45; cf I vi 1. The Greek version (Diogenianus 1.12, but more probably taken from 4.48 where it is not the main entry) was added in *1506*.

347 *Adagia* I ix 40. The Greek version of the adage (Diogenianus 4.50) was added
in *1506*.

348 Sibi canere / To sing your own song

This means to act in accordance with one's own desires, and not to do what others wish of you. Jerome: 'Worthy of singing only his own song and that of the Muses.'[1] And in Plato's *Symposium* a flute-girl is told to play only for herself.[2]

349 Aestate vestem deteris / Ἐν θέρει τὴν χλαῖναν κατατρίβεις / You wear out your clothing in summer

This is directed at the foolishly prodigal who spend their money for no good reason and have nothing left when they need it.

350 In trivio sum / Ἐν τριόδῳ εἰμί / I am at the crossroads

This suits those who are in a quandary and are unsure of what they should do first.

351 Mercurius non doctus / Ἑρμῆς ἀμύητος / An unlettered Mercury

An insulting proverb directed at those whose wisdom is based on experience and not on education. What Horace says about Ofellus is similar: 'A rustic, a self-taught philosopher, and quite uncultivated.'[1]

352 Dormientis rete cepit / Εὕδοντι κύρτος αἱρεῖ / The sleeper's net made a catch

Taken from fishermen whose nets catch fish even when they are sleeping. It suits either a person whose project turns out well even though he sets it up in a stupid way or a person who enjoys success without working for it.

* * * * *

348 *Adagia* III v 80. Cf c 26. Otto 1178
  1 Jerome *Letters* 50.2.3 CSEL 54 390
  2 Plato *Symposium* 176E

349 *Adagia* I x 100 (where the Latin version is a more exact translation of the Greek, *paenula* 'cloak' being used for the more general *vestis* 'attire' in the *Collectanea*). The Greek version of the adage (Diogenianus 4.51) was added in *1506*.

350 *Adagia* I ii 48. The Greek version of the adage (Diogenianus 4.59) was added in *1506*.

351 Erasmus draws the Greek version, literally 'An uninitiated Hermes,' and the interpretation from Diogenianus 4.63. The Greek was added in *1506*. Cf *Adagia* II x 10, where Erasmus reads ἀμύθητος, which means 'wonderful,' but which Erasmus misunderstands, taking it to mean 'voiceless' or 'illiterate.'
  1 Horace *Satires* 2.2.3

352 *Adagia* I v 82 (with a different Latin rendering of the Greek original). The source is Diogenianus 4.65, the Greek being added in *1506*. Otto 579

353 Cothurno instabilior / Εὐμεταβολώτερος κοθόρνου / As changeable as a buskin

This is applied to a fickle and unreliable person. The *cothurnus* is a kind of shoe that fits either foot.[1]

354 In vino veritas / Wine speaks the truth

Ἐν οἴνῳ ἀλήθεια, the point being that wine reveals everyone's true nature. Alcibiades in Plato's *Symposium*: 'What I am going to tell you next, you will not hear without my first invoking the proverb "Wine and children tell the truth" – and wine does so on its own!'[1]

355 Ab asino lanam / Ἀπὸ ὄνου πόκος / Wool from a donkey

This is similar to what we find in Plautus: 'You are asking for water out of a pumice stone.'[1] For we cannot expect to get wool from a donkey.

356 Spartano liberior / Ἐλευθεριωτέρα Σπάρτης / As freeborn as a Spartan

The Spartans are known for being noble-minded and free of any servile disposition.

* * * * *

353 *Adagia* I i 94 (with *versatilior* for *instabilior*). The source is Diogenianus 4.72, the Greek being added in *1506*. Also Zenobius 3.93, Zenobius Athous 2.63 (see Bühler 5.244–56), and *Suda* E 3582.
  1 The explanation is greatly expanded in the *Adagia*. The *cothurnus* was the footwear used by the actors of tragedy.

354 *Adagia* I vii 17. The Greek version (from Diogenianus 4.81 and present in *1500*) is not printed as part of the title and is not followed by a Latin translation. Otto 1900
  1 Plato *Symposium* 217E, of which Erasmus, as usual, gives a Latin version; see C 2 n7. For the idea that only drunkards and children tell the truth cf Suringar 101.

355 *Adagia* I iv 79. The Greek version of the adage (Diogenianus 4.85) was added in *1506*. In Diogenianus the heading reads ἐπ' ὄνου πόκος and the reading, ἐπί for ἀπό, accounts for the position of the adage here, in a series where the Greek versions begin with epsilon. The preposition ἀπό may be a slip on the part of Erasmus, influenced perhaps by a sentence in Diogenianus' explanation: 'we cannot get wool ἀπ' ὄνου "from an ass."'
  1 C 249, drawn from Plautus *Persa* 41

356 *Adagia* II viii 61 (with *generosior* 'more noble-minded' instead of *liberior*). The source is Diogenianus 4.87, the Greek being added in *1506*. The reading, ἐλευθεριωτέρα (feminine singular) for the correct ἐλευθεριώτερος (masculine singular), appears in Bodley Grabe 30, the source of Erasmus' own manuscript of Diogenianus (see 7 and 10 n23 above).

357 **Ventus neque navigare sinit neque manere /** ″Ενθ′ οὔτε
πλεῖν ἄνεμος οὔτε μίμνειν ἐᾷ **/ The wind lets me neither sail
nor stay**
This has the same sense as the expression we find in Terence, 'I hold the
wolf by the ears.'[1]

358 **Jupiter absque filiis /** Ζεὺς ἄγονος **/ Jupiter has no children**
Suitable when people say inconceivable and unbelievable things. It is similar
to what Horace writes: 'Olive no kernel hath, nor nut no shell.'[1]

359 **Ollae amicitia /** Ζῇ τῇ χύτρᾳ φιλία **/ Cupboard love**
Customarily used of those who become friends for the sake of their bellies.
A certain wise man calls them table-friends.[1]

360 **Doliaris vita /** Ζωὴ πίθου **/ Life in a tub**
This refers to a frugal and abstemious life. The adage arose from Diogenes'
barrel.[1]

* * * * *

357 *Adagia* II v 21. The source is Diogenianus 4.88, the Greek version of the adage
being added in *1506*. Erasmus reverses the position of πλεῖν and μίμνειν from
the version in Diogenianus. Apostolius (7.22), inaccessible to Erasmus until he was preparing the vastly expanded *Chiliades* of 1508, gives the adage
in a slightly different form and identifies it as a fragment from Aeschylus
Philoctetes (TrGF 3 fragment 250).
  1 Terence *Phormio* 506–7 (C 164 = *Adagia* I v 25)

358 *Adagia* I ix 74. The source of the Greek version, added in *1506*, must be the
manuscript of Diogenianus used by Erasmus (see 7 and 10 n23 above), since
the adage is found only in Bodley Grabe 30 and its descendants; see Bühler
1.226 n204. In CPG 1 the adage appears as Diogenianus 4.95b.
  1 C 317, drawn from Horace *Epistles* 2.1.31

359 *Adagia* I v 23. The Greek, added in *1506*, means literally 'friendship lives in the
pot.' The correct text reads Ζεῖ χύτρα, ζῇ φιλία 'A pot boils, friendship lives'
(Diogenianus 4.96). Erasmus follows the erroneous text in his own personal
manuscript of Diogenianus, also in Bodley Grabe 30; see 7 and 10 n23 above.
Otto 1286
  1 Jesus, son of Sirach, at Ecclus 6:10

360 *Adagia* I viii 61. The Greek version, from Diogenianus 4.98, was added in
1506.
  1 Diogenes of Sinope was a famous Cynic philosopher of the 4th century, who
championed self-sufficiency and eschewed luxury. He lived simply and de-
fied many of society's conventions, but the story of his walking around in a
barrel may be apocryphal. For many other stories about Diogenes see Erasmus
Apophthegmata 3.164–388 CWE 37 271–334.

361 **De gustu iudicare / Ἐκ γεύματος γινώσκειν / To judge from a mere taste**
This means coming to a judgment on important matters on the basis of the slightest of evidence.

362 **Vel ter sex vel tres taxilli / Either three sixes or three ones**
Ἢ τρὶς ἓξ ἢ τρεῖς κύβοι, Either three sixes or three ones. This is customarily said by those who wish to run extreme risks and either win everything or lose everything. In dicing complete victory went to a throw of three sixes, a throw of three ones won nothing.

363 **Sylosontis chlamys / Ἡ Συλόσωντος χλαμύς / Syloson's cloak**
This was said about luxurious clothing. When Darius was still a private citizen, Sylon had given him a garment of inestimable value. Darius remembered the gift when he became king and allowed him to return to Samos from exile.[1]

364 **Equus me portat, rex alit / A horse to carry me, a king to feed me**
Ἵππος με φέρει, βασιλεύς με τρέφει, A horse carries me, a king feeds me. A Greek adage, referring to those who live in comfort and luxury at someone else's expense. It is said to have originated with a soldier in the service of king Philip. When his mother advised him to seek a discharge, he replied

* * * * *

361 *Adagia* I ix 37. The source of the adage is Diogenianus 4.92 (also cited in Diogenianus 5.15). The Greek was added in *1506*. Also in the *Suda* (E 676)

362 *Adagia* II iii 66. The source is Diogenianus 5.4, the Greek being present in *1500*. Also in Zenobius 4.23, Zenobius Athous 2.29 (see Bühler 4.224–32), and the *Suda* (H 635). The Greek word κύβος can refer to the whole die or to the side of the die that had the value of one (see Bühler 4.228).

363 *Adagia* I x 84. The source is Diogenianus 5.14, the Greek being added in *1506*. Also in the *Suda* (X 333). In *1500* the name in the Latin version was erroneously given as Sylon, reflecting a corruption (Συλώοντος) in Erasmus' manuscript of Diogenianus, also in Bodley Grabe 30 (see 7 and 10 n23 above, and Bühler 4.172–6). This was corrected in the title in *1506* but the erroneous name in the accompanying text persisted. Polydore Vergil 123

1 The Darius referred to is Darius the Great, king of the Persians, who tried unsuccessfully to conquer Greece, his forces being defeated at the battle of Marathon. In the *Adagia* Erasmus gives a longer (and slightly different) version of the story from Herodotus and Strabo. The last sentence closely resembles in its wording Niccolò Perotti's explanation of the expression in his *Cornucopiae* (216:34–9); see Heinimann 167 n46.

364 *Adagia* I vii 20. The source is Diogenianus 5.31, the Greek being present in *1500*. Otto 608

with these words. In his *Epistles* Horace credits Aristippus with the same notion: 'It is much better and finer for a horse to carry me and a king to feed me.'[1] In his commentary on this passage Acron mentions this proverb.[2]

365 Corcorus in lachanis. Graculus inter Musas. Anser inter olores / Blue pimpernel among the vegetables. A jackdaw among the Muses. A goose among the swans

Κόρκορος ἐν λαχάνοις, Blue pimpernel among the vegetables. This is customarily said of those who wish to be regarded as the equal of the most powerful persons, even though their status is very low. According to Pliny blue pimpernel is the most worthless kind of vegetable.[1] Not dissimilar to this are 'A jackdaw among the Muses' and the Virgilian phrase 'A goose among the swans.'[2]

366 Aderit Temessaeus Genius / Παρέσται Τεμεσσεῖος δαίμων / The spirit of Temesa will be at hand

In his book on Elis, Pausanias writes that a companion of Ulysses whom

* * * * *

1 Horace *Epistles* 1.17.20. Aristippus (c 435–366 BC) founded the Cyrenaic school of hedonism. Here Horace quotes his response to the Cynic philosopher Diogenes.
2 According to modern editions it is Porphyrion and not Pseudo-Acron (on Horace *Epistles* 1.17.20) who identifies Horace's words as a proverb and gives the Greek version. In early editions, however, Pseudo-Acron does say that this is a proverb.

365 *Adagia* I vii 21 (for the first proverb, also cited in *Adagia* II i 62); *Adagia* I vii 22 (for the second). The third is cited in the discussion of *Adagia* I vii 22. The first of the three appears in Diogenianus 5.36a (also in Zenobius 4.57), but Erasmus is probably also drawing from Ermolao Barbaro's *Castigationes Plinianae* (Pozzi 570–1), on Pliny *Historia naturalis* 7.208; see Heinimann 172. The usual form of the noun is κόρχορος. But κόρκορος is the reading in Bodley Grabe 30, and so, presumably, was also the reading in Erasmus' manuscript of Diogenianus; see 7 and 10 n23 above. Polydore Vergil 253 (the first of the three) and 181 (the third).
1 Pliny *Historia naturalis* 21.89 and 21.183, but Pliny does not say what Erasmus reports here.
2 Virgil *Eclogues* 9.36

366 *Adagia* I i 88. The Greek version of the adage, probably Erasmus' own invention, was added in 1506, but does not appear in the *Adagia*. Erasmus draws, without acknowledgment, almost all of this material from Ermolao Barbaro's *Castigationes Plinianae* (on *Naturalis historia* 7.152 [Pozzi 557–8]); see Heinimann 172. The name of the town (on the west coast of the toe of Italy) usually appears in the form 'Temesa,' not 'Temessa,' as in the heading. Polydore Vergil 18

the hero was to meet at Temesa had been put to death for having raped
a girl and that because of this his ghost walked abroad and brought destruction to all ages and both sexes unless it was placated by the yearly
offering of a virgin. He was thought to be the guardian spirit of the place.
Euthymus, a *pyktes* 'a boxer,' overcame him when he returned to Temesa,
setting free and marrying the virgin whom the people had given for sacrifice.[1] Aelian says this about the same person: 'Euthymus, a Locrian, was a
famous boxer from Italy and was of outstanding strength. He could lift a
massive stone (now on display at Locri). He compelled the hero of Temesa
to give back with interest what he had extorted from the people. This
gave rise to the adage, the sense of which is that people who make im-
moral and unjust gains will have the spirit of Temesa beside them,'[2] meaning that they must pay back with interest whatever they have plundered
illegally.

367 In lenticula unguentum / Perfume on lentils

In Aulus Gellius, book thirteen chapter twenty-seven, there is an adage
given in a corrupt form: Τὸν ἐν τῇ φακῇ μῦθον 'The story on lentils.'[1] Ermolao emends it to read Τὸ ἐν τῇ φακῇ μύρον 'Myrrh on lentils.' Lentils are
a kind of legume, very similar to the *lens*, but different nevertheless. The
adage suits those who engage in some activity that in itself is quite proper,
but do so in an inappropriate fashion or at an inappropriate time. For this
is what Fronto says according to Gellius: 'Take care, however, not to think
that *mortales multi* 'many mortals' is to be used in the sense of *multi homines*
'many persons' lest that Greek proverb from one of Varro's satires Τὸ ἐν τῇ
φακῇ μύρον 'Myrrh on lentils' may be readily applicable.'[2] But perhaps we
should prefer to take *lenticula* in the sense of *vasculum* 'small container'; for
the word has both meanings.[3]

* * * * *

1 Pausanias 6.6.7–10
2 Aelian *Varia historia* 8.18

367 *Adagia* I vii 23 (also mentioned in *Adagia* II iv 77). Polydore Vergil 36
  1 Gellius *Noctes Atticae* 13.29.5, the source of the Greek in Erasmus' discussion
  2 Erasmus is drawing from *Glossemata* L 21 of Ermolao Barbaro's *Castigationes
    Plinianae* (Pozzi 1407). Filippo Beroaldo also makes the same emendation in
    his *Appendix annotamentorum* 13 (*Lampas* 1.320), invoking Cicero *Ad Atticum*
    1.19.6.
  3 Cf Perotti *Cornucopiae* 672:33–5, who makes the same point about the meaning
    of *lenticula*.

368 **Inexplebile dolium. Pertusum dolium /** ᾿Άπληστος πίθος **/**
A jar that cannot be filled. A jar full of holes.
Both of these are taken from the punishment of the Danaids.[1] The first of
these is used of the greedy and rapacious. The second refers to those who
are very forgetful; every piece of learning that is poured into them immediately flows away. The same myth is also the origin of the saying that even
today continues to be in common use, 'To draw water with a sieve.'[2] Plato
in his *Republic* book two: 'In the underworld they cover the wicked with
dung and compel them to carry water in a sieve.'[3]

369 **Odi memorem compotorem / I hate a pot-companion with**
a good memory
Since the poet of the *Epigrams* inserted this adage in its Greek form in one
of his poems,[1] I do not think that there can be any doubt about its having
the status of a proverb. In the same way the poet inserted the well-known
saying of Pythagoras into a poem, 'O Candidus, as for your possessions,
Πάντα κοινὰ φίλων "Between friends all is common."'[2] Juvenal too introduced an oracle of Apollo in a poem: 'The saying γνῶθι σεαυτόν "know thyself"' came down from heaven.'[3] Martial's epigram directed at Procillus is
very well known. When Procillus had been invited during a carousal to
come to dinner the next day, he actually came, as if what a man says in
his cups should carry any weight. That epigram closes with this verse μισῶ
μνήμονα συμπότην, the meaning being 'Procillus, I hate a pot-companion
with a good memory.'

* * * * *

368 *Adagia* I x 33. The source of the Greek is Diogenianus 1.95 (see also 7.27). Cf
    C 230, where the Danaids are also mentioned, and the adages given here
    are referred to. The Greek version in the title was added in *1506*. Otto
    466
  1 The Danaids are here called the *Belides* 'descendants of Belus' after their grand-
    father Belus.
  2 *Adagia* I iv 60 and Suringar 91
  3 Plato *Republic* 2.363D, quoted only in Latin; see C 2 n7.

369 *Adagia* I vii 1. Erasmus took as the adage the Latin translation of the Greek
    phrase at Martial 1.27.7 that was given in the commentaries accompanying the
    text in early editions.
  1 Martial 1.27.7, cited at the end of the discussion
  2 Martial 2.43.1. Erasmus quotes the verse with πάντα as the last word in the
    line, instead of κοινά, as in modern editions. C 94 and *Adagia* I i 1
  3 Juvenal 11.27. C 108 and *Adagia* I vi 95

370 Aenigma Sphingis, Oedipo propositum / The riddle of the Sphynx (that was set to Oedipus)

What walks first on four feet, then on two and finally on three? The answer is a human being; for as a child he uses his hands as well as his feet to get himself about, then he supports himself on two feet until decrepit old age gives him a third foot, a walking stick.

371 Contra retiarium ferula / A rod against a net-man

Domizio Calderini points out that this was a proverb directed at those who fought with poor resources against someone who was exceptionally well equipped.[1] If this is true, the expression 'you try to kill a lion with a straw' is very similar to it.[2] However, a little later Calderini takes a different approach, saying that in antiquity gladiators were accustomed to be beaten with rods and thrown out of the arena if they did not please the spectators. The words occur in a letter of Martial: 'Consider whether you take pleasure in watching a rod against a net-man,'[3] meaning that one should not think acceptable something that everyone else condemns and treats with catcalls.

372 Patres nostri comederunt uvam acerbam / Our fathers ate a bitter grape

In the books of the prophets there is the following Jewish proverb: 'Our fathers ate a bitter grape, but it is our teeth that are benumbed.'[1] We can use this whenever we wish to indicate that one person is guilty of something but that a different person pays the penalty. Sometimes punishment is exacted not from those who have offended us but from those who cannot retaliate.

* * * * *

370 This hardly constitutes an adage and it does not appear as a separate entry in the *Adagia*. For the riddle, briefly referred to in C 223 and described more fully at *Adagia* II iii 9 'Boeotian riddles,' see for example Athenaeus 10.456B. Here, Erasmus' explanation is based on Domizio Calderini's commentary on Martial 1.90.9 (*Thebano aenigmate*).

371 *Adagia* II v 80; Otto 1531
   1 Domizio Calderini, in his commentary on the preface to Martial book 2, the source of the proverb
   2 A source for this expression has not been identified. ASD II-9 157:536–7n compares *subula leonem excipit* 'he tries to capture a lion with an awl.' See Seneca *Letters* 82.24 and cf Otto 938.
   3 The letter to Decianus that serves as the preface to Martial book 2

372 Not a separate entry in the *Adagia*, but cited by Erasmus as a proverb in the introductory material to the *Adagia* (CWE 31 13:68).
   1 Jer 31.29; Ezek 18:2

The same meaning is expressed by the common saying that a piglet usually suffers for a sow's misdemeanours.[2]

373 In expuentem recidit quod in coelum expuitur / Εἰς τὸν οὐρανὸν τοξεύειν / What is spat into the sky falls back on the spitter. To shoot at heaven

Filelfo is the authority for the following Greek proverb: 'Whatever is spat into the sky falls back on the spitter's face.'[1] This is humorous but important advice, warning us not to vilify either those who are of higher rank or those who are powerful. Such words usually result in death. It is not safe to provoke by insults those who have the power to destroy us with the nod of their head.

374 Scindere glaciem / To break the ice

This occurs in the same author and has the sense of undertaking something that has not yet been tried.[1] Taken from ship-captains; the boldest of these was accustomed to be the first to drive his ship through a river that was frozen over.

375 Manum de tabula / Hands off the tablet!

'Hey you there, hands off the tablet; the master is here sooner than we thought.'[1] This is found in Cicero's *Letters* and there is no doubt that it is

* * * * *

2 Suringar 167

373 *Adagia* III iv 87. The Greek adage (cf *Adagia* I iv 92) is not discussed here by Erasmus, and has a quite different meaning – of engaging in a useless task – from the Latin one. It was added in *1506*, being drawn from Zenobius (3.46); see c 26n. It is also to be found in the *Suda* (EI 300), but is absent from Diogenianus.
1 This saying, with a slight variation ('on the spitter's beard'), occurs in Francesco Filelfo's *Epistolae* 15 (202v in the Paris edition of 1501) and is probably of medieval origin; see Heinimann 178 n93. The Greek original is ἐς οὐρανὸν πτύεις. For Filelfo (1398–1481), whose correspondence continued to be printed on many occasions after his death, see CEBR 2:31–3.

374 *Adagia* III v 95. Erasmus uses the expression in Ep 20:10.
1 Francesco Filelfo *Epistolae* 12.45 (158r in the Paris edition of 1501), where Filelfo uses the verb *frangere* 'to break' in place of *scindere* 'to cut'

375 *Adagia* I iii 19, where the erroneous interpretation given here is corrected with the help of Pliny. The sense of *tabula* is 'picture' rather than 'writing tablet,' and the point of the proverb is that one should stop making changes to something that is essentially complete in the hope of improving it. Otto 1038
1 Cicero *Ad familiares* 7.25.1

proverbial. However, its sense and origin are far from clear. Nevertheless I think it originates in the schools. Boys who are to deliver a speech fear that their teacher may interrupt them; they are afraid they may be caught still writing when they ought to be already prepared to declaim.

376 Nihil cotio est / A broker's word is worthless

About those who make promises for the future but give nothing on the spot. Plautus: 'It's an old saying, a broker's word is worthless.'[1] Gellius explains the meaning of *cotio*: 'The ancients commonly called a *cotio* "broker" an *arulator* "haggler." '[2]

377 Transversum unguem. Latum digitum / A nail's breadth. A finger's breadth

This too is read in Cicero's *Letters*: 'Urge him therefore not to stray from the sea by a nail's breadth, as they say.'[1] It is not surprising that we do not understand this when we read it since the writer himself wished it to be understood by only one person. Everyone is aware that the smallest distance possible is often indicated proverbially by the finger, as in Cicero in *Against Verres*: 'They did not yield a finger's breadth.'[2] And Euclio in Plautus' *Pot of Gold*: 'By Hercules, if you move from this place by the width of a finger or a nail.'[3]

This expression seems to have been taken over from craftsmen, who, as is well known, measure their work by finger-widths, just as land surveyors measure fields by feet.

378 Scyllam defugiens in Charybdim incidi / Escaping Scylla I encountered Charybdis

A very well-known adage which indicates the foolishness of those who take

* * * * *

376 *Adagia* IV iii 23. This adage first appeared in *1506*, replacing one in *1500* that was dropped (*Cato in Catonem*; see Appendix A1 358 below). Otto 402
   1 Plautus *Asinaria* 203. Modern editions read *coactio*; *cotio* is a variant spelling for *cocio* or *coctio*.
   2 Gellius *Noctes Atticae* 16.7.12. Modern editions read *arillator*.

377 *Adagia* I v 6; Otto 1825
   1 Cicero *Ad familiares* 7.25.2, quoted incompletely, with the Latin for 'not to stray' omitted. The text that Erasmus gives is also corrupt in that it offers *a salo* 'from the sea' for *a stilo* 'from the pen.' The sense is 'press on and do not let the breadth of a finger-nail part you from your pen,' as the passage is translated in the Loeb edition of Cicero.
   2 Cicero *Verrines* 2.4.15.33
   3 Plautus *Aulularia* 56–7

378 *Adagia* I v 4 (reversing Scylla and Charybdis). In mythology Scylla and Charybdis were both monstrous beings. In natural terms Scylla refers to reefs

extreme action in everything they do. In trying to avoid one fault they fall into one more serious. An example is if someone gets the reputation of being a miser because he does not wish to be thought extravagant. Horace: 'For in vain one fault you may avoid if to another you will turn.'[1] It also fits those who in their zeal to escape one disaster land in another one. The proverb is taken from sailors who avoid rocks without due caution and are pulled into a dangerous whirlpool. Each presents a danger at sea, but one is quite different from the other. For Scylla protrudes from the sea and smashes a ship to pieces, while Charybdis sucks it down into its great depth.

379 Iungere vulpes. Mulgere hircos / To yoke foxes. To milk billy-goats

What appears in Virgil in his *Thyrsis*, 'and let the same man yoke foxes and milk he-goats,'[1] may be thought to have been in antiquity a shepherds' proverb; for it smacks of the countryside, not of the city. It is appropriately used of those who try to undertake some insane and quite absurd task. For the words are preceded by 'who hates not Bavius let him like your songs, Maevius.'[2] It would be equally insane to admire Bavius and to take pleasure in Maevius. No less insane is it to yoke foxes together to the plough like bulls or to want to get milk from a billy-goat.

380 Caligare in sole / To be in the dark in sunlight

This is found in Quintilian.[1] It suits perfectly those persons who through their own deficiencies are blind about things that are as clear as daylight but seem very difficult to them. An example is those for whom Cicero's style of writing is usually shrouded in darkness. The better the writer, the less such persons comprehend. They claim that the books they read are full of obscurity, although it is they themselves who carry darkness around in their eyes. The result is that everything is obscure to them. This saying is taken from blind persons, or, if not them, at least from owls, or from those

* * * * *

or rocks, while Charybdis is used in the sense of a whirlpool. Erasmus uses the proverb in Ep 113:115–16. The more common form of the proverb has *cupiens vitare* 'wishing to avoid' for *defugiens* 'escaping.' Polydore Vergil 246; Otto 382, and Otto *Nachträge* p 54
1 Horace *Satires* 2.2.54–5, quoted in *Adagia* I v 5 Fleeing from the smoke I fell into the fire

379 *Adagia* I iii 50 and I iii 51; Otto 1942 and 812
  1 Virgil *Eclogues* 3.91
  2 Virgil *Eclogues* 3.90. Bavius and Maevius were both bad poets, contemporaries of Virgil.

380 *Adagia* II v 77 (translated as 'To blink in the sunlight'); Otto 1663
  1 Quintilian 1.2.19

with poor eyesight, in whose eyes even the light of the sun is dim. Indeed, those who suffer from this weakness see more at night than in the day.

381 Balbus balbum rectius intellegit / One stammerer better understands another

Jerome in a letter to Domnio criticizes the foolishness of a certain monk with this saying, whether in a humorous manner or scathingly I am not sure. He says, 'And the reason for his thinking that he is a scholar is that he alone understands Jovinian. There is of course the proverb that "One stammerer better understands another." '[1] Jerome also makes fun of Jovinian's pretentious and obscure style with marvellous wit in the preface to the books in which he refutes Jovinian's errors.[2] Everyone can see that this proverb is based on the actual nature of things. It is suitably directed at those who have been poorly educated and understand nothing but books that are the products of poor intellects.

382 Camelum saltare / The camel dances

Whenever we want to indicate that something is being done in a quite absurd manner, 'Against Minerva's will,'[1] and ungracefully, we say that 'A camel is dancing.' An example is someone who is stern and serious by nature but who tries to get a reputation for being witty and humorous. We find the following in St Jerome: 'We laughed at you when you exemplified the proverb of a camel dancing.'[2]

383 Ut canis e Nilo / Like a dog drinking from the Nile

This proverb seems to have originated with the following apophthegm mentioned by Macrobius in book one of his *Saturnalia*: 'After the rout at Modena, when people were asking what Antony was doing, a friend of his replied, "He's doing what a dog does in Egypt, drinking on the run." In that country it is well known that dogs drink on the run since they are frightened that crocodiles may snatch them.'[1] We can use it if we want to indicate that

* * * * *

381 *Adagia* I ix 77. Otto 237
   1 Jerome *Letters* 50.4.1 CSEL 54 392
   2 Jerome *Adversus Iovinianum* 1.1 PL 23 211–12

382 *Adagia* II vii 66; Otto 310
   1 *Adagia* I i 42, but not an entry in the *Collectanea*
   2 Jerome *Adversus Helvidium* 18 PL 23 202A

383 *Adagia* I ix 80. This is used by Ermolao Barbaro in his *Epistolae* ('Epistole non datate VIII': 2.92 Branca). Polydore Vergil 23; Otto 333n
   1 Macrobius *Saturnalia* 2.2.7 (not from book 1). Erasmus *Apophthegmata* 6.430 CWE 38 715–16

someone has glanced at some poetry in a cursory and superficial way.[2] We would say that he has drunk from the poets but like dogs drinking from the Nile.

384 Herbam dare *vel* porrigere / To give *or* offer grass
This means that you accept your defeat and that your opponent is the victor. It occurs everywhere in our authors.[1] The expression is taken from a military custom. For in antiquity 'the chief token of victory'[2] was if the conquered offered grass to the conqueror. This meant that the conquered 'were giving up the very country and the land that nourished them.'

385 Dare manus / To put one's hands up
This too is a military proverb. Those who surrender to the victors voluntarily hold out their hands to be bound. Horace in his *Odes*: 'I hold out my hands to your powerful skill.'[1]

386 Hastam abiicere. In harenam descendere. Harena cedere / To throw away one's spear. To descend into the arena. To leave the arena
This occurs in Cicero in his speech for Murena.[1] It means that you have lost faith in your cause and are giving up the struggle.

'To descend into the arena' means to enter the fray.[2] 'To leave the arena' means to abandon the struggle. Both of these adages are too well known for me to make a strong case for them. Both were taken from gladiatorial combat.[3]

* * * * *

2 Poliziano had earlier applied this proverb to a cursory reading of poetry in the epilogue of his *Miscellanea* (1.310 Maier).

384 *Adagia* I ix 78. Polydore Vergil 190; Otto 799
  1 An exaggeration. See Pompeius Festus 88.10–15, citing Plautus (the phrase *herbam do* is listed among the fragmentary *vocabula* in the Oxford Classical Text of Plautus by Lindsay); Servius on *Aeneid* 8.128. Used by Battista Guarini in a letter to Pico della Mirandola (Poliziano's *Epistolae* 1.19 [1.13 Maier]).
  2 Erasmus is paraphrasing in this and the next sentence Pliny *Naturalis historia* 22.8.

385 *Adagia* I ix 79. This occurs in Poliziano's *Epistolae* 4.6 (1.52 Maier). Otto 1040
  1 Horace *Epodes* (not *Odes*) 17.1

386 *Adagia* I ix 81, 83 and 82; Otto 795
  1 Cicero *Pro L. Murena* 21.45; Erasmus is referring to only the first of the three expressions. The other two do not seem to be attested in classical Latin.
  2 Erasmus uses this expression in *Antibarbarus* 1.1 CWE 23 54:21. This work was not published until 1520 but Erasmus worked on it before he produced the *Collectanea*.
  3 See for example Horace *Epistles* 1.1.6 and *Odes* 3.8.23–4.

387 In tua ipsius te harena supero / I beat you at your own game

The meaning is that I get the better of you even in your own skill and subject. An example is if a physician defeated a theologian in a theological argument. Poliziano: 'And they defeated them in their own arena, as the saying goes.'[1]

388 Amor nullo magis emitur quam se ipso / Nothing buys love more readily than love itself

This expression is as witty as it is sound advice. Seneca, pointing out that love is the most powerful agent, says, 'Do you wish to be loved? Show love.'[1] Ovid: 'To be loved, be lovable.'[2]

389 In amore mutuum non reddere turpissimum est / In love it is a great disgrace not to repay your love

Just as the preceding adage was taken from buying, so this one comes from lending: 'In love it is disgraceful not to repay your love.' For kindnesses often cannot be repaid even by those who wish to do so, but there is no one who cannot repay love to those who love them. Both of these are cited as proverbs by the most learned authors.[1]

390 Si vultur es, cadaver expecta / If you are a vulture, wait for your carcase

This is used by Seneca, and is customarily said of legacy-hunters who, like vultures, feast, as it were, on the dead.[1] Martial's words are directed at the same persons: 'Which vulture will have this carcase?'[2]

391 Ultra cornices vivax / Outliving crows

Ὑπὲρ τὰς κορώνας βεβιωκώς, He outlived the crows. An adage referring to

* * * * *

387 *Adagia* III vi 62
1 Poliziano *Epistolae* 12.6 (1.168 Maier)

388 Not in *Adagia*. Drawn from Poliziano *Epistolae* 2.10 (1.24 Maier). Tosi 1423. Cf Otto 75.
1 Seneca *Letters* 9.6: *si vis amari, ama*
2 Ovid *Ars amatoria* 2.107: *ut ameris, amabilis esto*

389 Not in *Adagia*
1 The source of this adage has not been identified.

390 *Adagia* I vii 14. Polydore Vergil 210; Otto 1946
1 Seneca *Letters* 95.43, the reference being taken from Giorgio Merula's commentary on Martial 6.62.4. For Merula see CEBR 2:437.
2 Martial 6.62.4

an old man who keeps on living. The authority is Merula.[1] A crow is very long-lived like a stag. That is why a certain satirist described extreme old age as 'like that of a stag.'[2] Martial: 'Outliving all crows.'[3] Horace: 'Lyce matching in years an old crow.'[4]

392 **Non omnibus dormio / I'm not asleep for everyone**
Cicero in book seven of his *Letters*: 'In times past it was "I'm not asleep for everyone," but for me, my dear Gallus, "I'm not a slave to everyone."'[1] Cicero is making the point that 'I'm not asleep for everyone' was an old saying, while 'I'm not a slave for everyone' was new and his invention. Festus Pompeius tells us that 'I'm not asleep for everyone' was a proverb.[2] Merula thinks it originated with husbands who prostituted their wives to make money and feigned sleep to give a man the opportunity to have sex with his wife.[3] Juvenal: 'He's learned to look at the ceiling, and to pretend to snore with goblet beside him.'[4]

393 **Et nos ferulae manum subduximus / We too have drawn back our hand from the cane**
This is a suitable saying for those who wish to indicate that they too have had teachers and have learned their letters. Juvenal: 'We too have drawn back our hand from the cane.'[1] Jerome to Domnio: 'We too have learned our letters. We too have often drawn back our hand from the cane.'[2] This saying's figurative nature and also its frequent use by Jerome make me believe that it was a proverb.

* * * * *

391 *Adagia* I vi 64 (with the comparative *vivacior*); Otto 434. The Greek is present in *1500*.
  1 Giorgio Merula in his commentary on Juvenal 10.247, Erasmus' source for both the Greek and Latin forms of the adage
  2 Juvenal 14.251
  3 Martial 10.67.5
  4 Horace *Odes* 4.13.25

392 *Adagia* I vi 4. Polydore Vergil 94; Otto 580
  1 Cicero *Ad familiares* 7.24.1
  2 Pompeius Festus 174.34–5 Lindsay
  3 This is the explanation given in Festus (see n2), which is adduced in Giorgio Merula's commentary on Juvenal 1.56–7.
  4 Juvenal 1.56–7

393 *Adagia* II vi 64. Identified as a proverb by Giorgio Merula (see C 390 n1) in his commentary on Juvenal 1.15. Otto 658
  1 Juvenal 1.15
  2 Jerome *Letters* 50.5.2 CSEL 54 393. Also 57.12.2 CSEL 54 525

394 Nullus comatus qui non idem cinaedus / All long-haired men are homosexuals

Οὐδεὶς κομήτης ὅστις οὐ περαίνεται, No one who is long-haired is not a homosexual. Synesius is our source for taking this to be a well-known Greek proverb.[1] It is directed at those who are more obsessed with their appearance than befits a man and who take pleasure in womanly adornments.

395 Nos nostrum onus, vos clitellas / We carry our burden, you carry the saddles

Quintilian gives this as a proverb in book five of his *Principles*, though what he says is somewhat obscure.[1] It seems to have originated in some old fable. The proverb is noted by that man who purges the text of Quintilian of corruptions and who remarks that the meaning of this proverb is that neither party gets off without doing his share.[2]

396 Ovum ovo simile *et cetera similitudinis adagia* / One egg is like another *and all the other adages that indicate similarity*

In proverbs we indicate complete resemblances in the following ways. 'As like as one egg to another,' is in Quintilian.[1] 'As like as milk to milk'[2]

* * * * *

394 Not in *Adagia*. For *cinaedus* (from the Greek κίναιδος) Erasmus offers *cynoedus*. Erasmus took the reference to Synesius (with the proverb) from the commentary of Giorgio Merula (see C 390 n1) on Juvenal 2.15, the proverb being given in both Greek and Latin. The Greek version in *1500* had the verb βι-νητιᾷ, which was then replaced by the rare περαίνεται in *1506*. The source of the latter was probably *Suda* O 821. The proverb was also used by Pico della Mirandola in a letter to Ermolao Barbaro (Poliziano *Epistolae* 9.4; 1.122 Maier).
  1 Synesius *Letters* 104, *Laus Calvitii* 85D

395 *Adagia* II ix 84. In the *Adagia* of 1508 it appears as *non nostrum onus: bos clitellas* 'Not my burden: a saddle on an ox'; This is now the accepted text of the passage in Quintilian, though the credit for the change of *vos* to *bos* is given not to Erasmus but to later scholars; see Grant 170–1. Otto 262
  1 Quintilian 5.11.21, where the adage is linked to a fable. See also O. Crusius, *Paroemiographica* p 62 (in CPG *Supplementum*).
  2 The reference is to Raffaele Regio who published *Ducenta problemata in totidem Quintiliani depravationes* in 1492, on which see Michael Winterbottom, 'In praise of Raphael Regius' in *Antike Rhetorik und ihre Rezeption* (Stuttgart 1999): 99–117. Erasmus also refers to his contribution at *Adagia* II ix 84. See CEBR 3:134.

396 *Adagia* I v 10; Otto 1318
  1 Quintilian 5.11.30
  2 Plautus *Amphitryo* 601, *Bacchides* 6, *Menaechmi* 1089, *Miles gloriosus* 240. This appears later as *Adagia* I v 11 (Otto 899).

and 'As like as water to water'[3] are found on several occasions in Plautus. Poliziano uses 'Of the same flour'[4] as a proverb: 'And completely of the same flour, as the saying goes,' meaning 'of the same kind.'

397 Contemptus proverbia / Proverbs indicating contempt

We shall usually indicate contempt with the use of worthless things in this way: 'I care not a wisp of wool';[1] 'I care not a mite.'[2] Both of these occur in Plautus.[3] 'I count it not worth a hair,'[4] as in Catullus: 'They count their staff not worth a hair.'[5] Cicero to his brother: 'I shall love you not even a hairsbreadth the less.'[6] 'It's not worth a snap of the fingers to me' in *The Brothers*.[7] Plautus: 'I wouldn't buy your life for a rotten walnut.'[8] I did not think the following should be overlooked, but I think it sufficient just to mention them. Plautus used the expression 'a three-ha'penny man' for some wretched and worthless fellow.[9] Persius: 'A lackey not worth three pennies,' and 'He offers a broken hundred-pence piece for a hundred Greeks.'[10]

398 Iterum ad eundem lapidem offendere / To stumble twice over the same stone

A Greek proverb, Δὶς πρὸς τὸν αὐτὸν προσκρούειν λίθον. It is a suitable metaphor to mean making the same error twice. For, as in the Greek adage, to make an error for the first time can be put down to inadvertence, but to repeat it does not deserve forgiveness.[1] Horace expressed the same idea

* * * * *

3 Plautus *Menaechmi* 1089, *Miles gloriosus* 551–2. This appears later as *Adagia* I v 12 (Otto 132).
4 *Adagia* III v 44. Poliziano *Epistolae* 12.13 (1.174 Maier)

397 The title is obviously not a proverb itself but a general heading for the adages mentioned in the accompanying discussion; see C 93n.
1 *Adagia* I viii 6 *Flocci non facio*
2 *Adagia* I viii 5 *Nauci non facio*
3 For example Plautus *Menaechmi* 423 (for the first) and *Bacchides* 1102 (for the second)
4 *Adagia* I viii 4 *Pili non facio*. Otto 1420n
5 Catullus 10.13
6 Cicero *Ad Quintum fratrem* 2.16.5
7 Terence *Adelphoe* 163. *Adagia* I viii 7 *Huius non facio*
8 Plautus *Miles gloriosus* 316. *Adagia* I viii 8 *Vitiosa nuce non emam*. Otto 1258
9 Plautus *Poenulus* 381, 463. *Adagia* I viii 10 *Homo trioboli*. Otto 1799
10 Persius 5.76 and 5.191. *Adagia* I viii 11 *Homo tressis*

398 *Adagia* I v 8. The Greek, from Diogenianus 4.19, is present in *1500*. Otto 915
1 Erasmus seems to be thinking of an expression that he quotes in *Adagia* I ix 62 (where he also refers to *Adagia* I v 8): συγγνώμη τῷ πρῶτον ἁμαρτόντι 'forgive

differently with a metaphor drawn from music: 'And the lute-player who is forever striking the same wrong note is mocked.'[2] And so to play the wrong note many times means to make the same mistake again and again.

399 Penelopes telam retexere / To unravel Penelope's web
I remember reading this in Plato. It has the sense of taking up a pointless task.[1] For Penelope is said to have tricked the suitors by offering to marry one of them when she had completed the web that she was weaving. She was in the habit of unravelling at night what she had woven during the day.[2] It can also be appropriately applied to someone who tries to improve and change any part of a splendid object when any change can only be for the worse. Such a person may be said to be unravelling Penelope's web. An example is if someone attempts to write down afresh in his own way the precepts of rhetoric that have been established in the most complete way by the writers of old.

400 Umbram suam metuere / Τὴν αὑτοῦ σκιὰν δειμαίνειν / To be afraid of one's own shadow
This is said of a person who is needlessly afraid and, like a child, fears danger where none exists. It is given in Plato as a proverb.[1] Cicero to his brother about seeking the consulship: 'As for the other one, in heaven's name, what distinction does he have? First, he has the same social rank as Catiline. Does he have greater? No, but he surpasses him in his accomplishments. For this reason you will indeed despise Manius, who fears his own shadow.'[2]

401 Manum non vorterim / I would not turn a hand
This is in Apuleius in his *Defence against the Charge of Sorcery* in the sense of 'it does not trouble me at all' or 'it is no concern of mine.'[1] An example

* * * * *

a first offence (but not a second),' though this does not have the status of a proverb in its own right in the *Adagia*.
2 Horace *Ars poetica* 355–6. The phrase in question (*eadem oberrare chorda*) becomes *Adagia* I v 9 To strike the same wrong note.

399 *Adagia* I iv 42. In the *Adagia* the explanation is more clear: 'to take up a pointless task, and then to undo what one has done.' Otto 1379
1 Plato *Phaedrus* 84A
2 See Homer *Odyssey* 2.96–105.

400 *Adagia* I v 65 (and mentioned in C 262). The Greek title, probably Erasmus' invention, was added in 1506. Otto 1817
1 Plato *Phaedo* 101D
2 Quintus Cicero *Commentariolum petitionis* 2.9. On the error in authorship see C 37 n2. The text of the passage translated here by Erasmus is in a corrupt state.

401 *Adagia* I iii 21. Otto 1041
1 Apuleius *Apologia* 56

is if someone were to say, 'Should ignorant men praise me or abuse me, I would not turn a hand.' Plautus used the expression *susque deque* 'upwards, downwards' in the same sense.[2]

402 Pingui Minerva / With a stupid Minerva

Aulus Gellius in book fourteen chapter one of his *Attic Nights* says, 'But a few things may be conjectured παχυμερέστερον, to use his own word, the Greek word meaning "more stolidly and *pingui Minerva.*"'[1] The same author in chapter five of book two: 'You know, I believe, that ancient and common saying, ἀμαθέστερον εἶπε καὶ σαφέστερον,' meaning "speak more roughly and less eruditely and express yourself more clearly and openly."'[2] Horace in his *Satires*: 'A rustic sage, attached to no school *crassaque Minerva* "and with a crass Minerva,"' referring to a philosopher who practised his philosophy in an unsophisticated and crude manner.[3] We often find in stylish writers[4] the expression *pinguiore formula* meaning 'more plainly and more intelligibly.' Such a description applies to those who teach their pupils the philosophy of Aristotle using their own methods and their own words – which are certainly more plain than Aristotle's.

403 Emere malo quam rogare / I would rather buy than beg

Cicero himself, who used this expression in his *Verrines*, provides the evidence that it was proverbial.[1] To explain it one might use the words

* * * * *

2 Plautus *Amphitryo* 885–6. This becomes *Adagia* I iii 83, translated as 'Neither here nor there' (see Otto 1723). See also C 458.

402 *Adagia* I i 37 (cf I i 38). An alternative form of the adage is *crassa Minerva*, as in the Horace example given below (n3), with the same meaning. The phrase *pingui Minerva* comes from Theodore Gaza's Latin translation of the Greek word in the early editions of Gellius (see C 6 n1), not from Gellius himself. However, the phrase is attested in Latin literature, in Columella, adduced by Erasmus at *Adagia* I i 37. Polydore Vergil 66; Otto 1119, 1120

1 Gellius *Noctes Atticae* 14.1.5. The Greek adverb, as printed, first appeared in Schürer's 1513 edition of the *Collectanea*. It means 'rather coarsely,' and is the form found in most early editions of Gellius. It replaced a corrupt and irregular form in 1500 and 1506 that may have been the result of a printer's error. The last part of the sentence (from 'the Greek word meaning . . .') was Theodore Gaza's Latin translation of the Greek work and was printed as part of the text of Gellius in early editions. The same is true for the last part of the next sentence.

2 Gellius *Noctes Atticae* 12.5.6 (not book 2). The Greek phrase is the Greek version of *Adagia* I i 39 More roughly and more plainly.

3 Horace *Satires* 2.2.3

4 For example, Ermolao Barbaro on Pliny *Naturalis historia* 2.119 (Pozzi 51)

403 *Adagia* I iii 20. Otto 597
1 Cicero *Verrines* 2.4.6.12

of Apuleius in his *Florida*: 'For the man who pleads for something buys at enormous cost, and the man who gives it gets no small price. The result is that you should prefer to buy in all that you need instead of having to plead for it.'[2] It was the custom in antiquity to ask one's neighbours to lend you household objects that you did not have in your home, as we can tell from Plautus' *The Pot of Gold* and *The Ropes*.[3]

404 Vino vendibili suspensa hedera nihil opus / Good wine needs no hanging bush

This saying seems to have originated in everyday life and to be quite modern. For nowadays such signs are hung up at wine shops. The expression is to be found in Poliziano.[1] In *The Carthaginian* Plautus expressed the same sentiment in a very agreeable manner: 'For wares that are difficult to sell a buyer you yourself must seek. Good products readily find a buyer, even when located in an out-of-the-way place.'[2] The sense is that true quality needs no advertisement by others. Those things that by their nature are not at all distinguished require someone to praise them.

405 Amicitiae personam oportet detrahi / Friendship needs no mask

This very appealing saying is found in the same author.[1] A mask represents the human face, but conceals its true appearance and gives a false representation. This prompted Seneca to make a very facetious criticism of an emperor when he said, 'He prefers a mask to true appearance.'[2] This too seems to have been taken from everyday life; it advises us that between friends there should be no falsehood, and that everything between them should be true and free of deception.

406 In se descendere. Manticam in tergo videre / To venture down into oneself. To see the bag on our backs

* * * * *

2 Apuleius *Florida* 16
3 Plautus *Aulularia* 90–7, *Rudens* 133–6 (see C 70 n2)

404 *Adagia* II vi 20. Literally the sense is 'good wine needs no ivy hung up.' For the inclusion in the collection of modern proverbs see C 197n.
1 Poliziano in *Epistolae* 1.11 (1.8 Maier)
2 Plautus *Poenulus* 341–2

405 *Adagia* III vii 6. The literal sense is 'we should remove the mask from friendship.' This adage too, like C 404, may be modern (see C 197n). Otto 1385
1 This refers to Poliziano (*Epistolae* 1.11, as in the preceding adage)
2 Seneca *De beneficiis* 2.13.2 (referring to Caligula)

406 *Adagia* I vi 86 and I vi 90. Both expressions were used by Erasmus in Ep 113:128–9. Otto 1032

Persius: 'None, I say, none dare venture down into themselves. They cast their eyes on the bag that hangs on the back of him they follow.'[1] The satirist used both of these expressions in a proverbial way; 'To venture down into oneself,' means 'to look at one's own faults,' and 'to cast one's eyes on the back of the man who walks before' means 'to see the faults of others.' The source of the former is not quite clear, but perhaps it is drawn from mining. Poliziano demonstrated that the second expression originated in a fable of Aesop;[2] Aesop writes 'that each man has two bags, one carried on his chest, and the other hanging from his shoulders on his back. He says that we put other person's faults into the former, our own faults into the one behind us.'[3] We continually look at the bag on our chest, but we pay no attention to the one on our backs, even though it is much bigger, because we never see it. Catullus: 'But we see not the satchel that is on our back.'[4] Horace: 'He will learn to look at what hangs on the back that he never sees.'[5] Jerome: 'But this is true cause for friends to correct each other: we do not see our own actions and concentrate, as Persius says, on the bags of others.'[6] The adage in the Gospels about the beam and the mote has the same sense.[7] On someone who is criticizing the faults of others and feigning ignorance of his own Jerome says, 'Despite the beam in his own eye he would strive to remove the mote in another's.'[8]

407 Aethiopem dealbare / To turn an Ethiopian white

There is a Greek adage Αἰθίοπα λευκαίνειν 'To turn an Ethiopian white,' with the sense of wanting to make something that is disgusting attractive with fine words,[1] like those who apply their rhetorical skills to disreputable

* * * * *

1 Persius 4.23–4
2 Angelo Poliziano, in his *Praelectio in Persium* (*Opera omnia* 1.512 Maier). The fable is Aesop 266 Perry, Babrius 66, Phaedrus 4.10.
3 Erasmus is here drawing from Poliziano (see n2).
4 Catullus 22.21
5 Horace *Satires* 2.3.299
6 Jerome *Letters* 102.2.1 CSEL 55 236
7 Matt 7:3–4, Luke 6:41. *Adagia* I vi 91 To cast a mote out of another man's eye
8 Jerome *Letters* 50.1.2 CSEL 54 388. Cf Jerome *Adversus Rufinum* 1.31 PL 23 443A, CCSL 79 31.

407 *Adagia* I iv 50, where two Latin adages (C 407 and 414) comprise its title. The Greek versions of these, given there, are Αἰθίοπα λευκαίνεις 'You are turning an Ethiopian white' and Αἰθίοπα σμήχεις 'You are washing an Ethiopian.' The source is Ermolao Barbaro at *Epistolae* 81.42 (1.109 Branca); the letter is *Epistolae* 9.5 in Poliziano's *Omnia opera* (1.130 Maier). Otto 32
1 The verb λευκαίνειν does not appear in Diogenianus' version of the proverb (see next note). Erasmus' source, Ermolao Barbaro (see introductory note) ex-

cases or those who praise things that are worthy of the utmost censure. The Greek proverb Αἰθίοπα σμήχεις 'You are washing an Ethiopian' is the very same proverb, or is at least a very similar one.[2]

408 Quibus inanem operam significamus / Proverbs indicating pointless labour

Lavare laterem 'To wash a brick'; in Greek Πλίνθον πλύνειν.[1] *Arare harenam* 'To plough sand'[2] (or *Arare litus* 'To plough the seashore'[3]). These are found in appropriate authors[4] in the sense of taking on a pointless task. Also the expression found in comedy: *Actum, aiunt, ne agas* 'don't re-open a closed subject, as they say.'[5] And Plautus: *Rem actam agis* 'You are pleading a case already finished.'[6] *Nugas agere* 'To play the fool'[7] and *nugas terere* 'to devote your life to trifles' are found very frequently in the writers of comedy but also appear elsewhere in the sense of achieving nothing.[8]

409 Os sublinere. Dare verba. Addere manum / To smear someone's face. To give empty words. To use sleight of hand

The first appears quite frequently in Plautus in the sense of deceiving someone by trickery: 'My face was well and truly smeared.'[1] 'To give empty

* * * * *

plains the sense of the proverb as 'wanting to defend a crude and foolish mode of philosophizing,' which is close to Erasmus' explanation here. The context of Barbaro's letter is that he had criticized contemporary philosophers who were hostile to the rhetorical emphasis in humanistic education. Giovanni Pico della Mirandola, the recipient of the letter, had wittily composed a defence of these philosophers, using the very techniques that they abhorred. See C 306.

2 This is C 414. The Greek version of this proverb (Αἰθίοπα σμήχεις = Diogenianus 1.45) was added in 1506. In 1500 only the Latin version (*Aethiopem lavas*) is given.

408 A descriptive tag for the adages that follow (see C 93n)

1 *Adagia* I iv 48. The Greek, added in 1506, is probably taken from Diogenianus 7.50. The proverb appears in Terence *Phormio* 186. Otto 922

2 This is not found in the *Adagia* or in the proverb collections. Otto 789

3 *Adagia* I iv 51. The proverb appears in Ausonius *Epistolae* 13.4 Green. Otto 789

4 He probably means authors in whose works one commonly finds proverbs, such as epistolographers and the writers of comedies.

5 Terence *Phormio* 419. *Adagia* I iv 70. Otto 42

6 Plautus *Pseudolus* 260

7 *Adagia* I iv 91

8 The first phrase (*nugas agere*) is common (cf Plautus *Menaechmi* 621–5), but the second (*nugas terere*) is very rare.

409 *Adagia* I v 48 (Otto 1312), 49, and 50 (Otto 1057). The meaning of all three is similar: 'to trick.'

1 This seems to be a conflation of Plautus *Epidicus* 491 and *Captivi* 783.

words' is very well known in the sense of deceiving.[2] What is found in Plautus in *The Persian* is more uncommon: 'Look here, you jailbird, you wearer out of whips. How you roasted me today! What embarrassments have you led me into! How you used sleight of hand on me (*manus mihi addita est*) about the Persian!'[3] Also in Plautus in *The Carthaginian*: 'I'll see to it that from now on all the other gods and goddesses will be more contented and less greedy when they find out how the pimp put a hand (*addiderit manum*) to Venus.'[4] However, in this last passage our texts read *adierit*, not *addiderit*.[5]

410 Ut possumus, quando ut volumus non licet / We live as we can, since we cannot live as we wish

Ζῶμεν γὰρ ὡς οὐ θέλομεν, ἀλλ' ὡς δυνάμεθα, We live not as we wish, but as we can. So says Mysis in Terence in *The Woman of Andros*. When asked by Crito what kind of life they lived in Athens, she shamefacedly admitted to the old man that she earned her living as a courtesan: 'As the saying goes, as best we can since as we would we may not.'[1]

411 In astu aliud ex alio malum venit / One evil after another comes into the city

In cities men of good character are drawn to villainy and each day sees evil springing from evil.

412 Sine capite fabula / A story without a head

Ἀκέφαλος μῦθος, A story without a head. This is used to describe a tale that is lewd and shameless, as if it had immodest body parts like the

* * * * *

2 As, for example, at Terence *Andria* 211
3 Plautus *Persa* 795–6, where *addita est* is the reading of the MSS, corrected by Camerarius to *adita est*
4 Plautus *Poenulus* 460–2 (quoted in *Adagia* I v 50, also with the reading *addiderit*; see n5).
5 The reading *addiderit* in *Poenulus* 462 seems to be a (mistaken) emendation of Erasmus. Modern editions use the verb *adire* (literally 'to approach') in this expression in both passages quoted, not *addere* 'to add.'

410 *Adagia* I viii 43. The Greek, present in *1500*, was taken from Diogenianus 4.100. The correct form (γὰρ οὐχ ὡς for γὰρ ὡς οὐ) was introduced later in the *Adagia* on the basis of Zenobius 4.16 and *Suda* Z 133. The adage is Menander fragment 45 Körte-Thierfelder. Otto 1456
1 Terence *Andria* 805, quoted inaccurately from memory

411 Cf *Adagia* III ix 97. The adage is a quotation from Terence *Eunuchus* 987. Otto 1019

412 *Adagia* I i 14 (with a different, and correct, interpretation of the adage, that it refers to a story that is imperfect and incomplete). The source is Diogenianus

belly and the buttocks but did not have a head. Plato: 'I leave our talk headless.'[1]

413 Alius sementem fecit, alius messem / Ἄλλοι μὲν σπείρουσι, ἄλλοι δὲ ἀμήσονται **/ Some sow, others will reap**

This is a Greek proverb directed at those who possess what belongs to others or to those who win glory for themselves on the basis of other persons' labours.

414 Aethiopem lavas / You are washing an Ethiopian

Αἰθίοπα σμήχεις, You are washing an Ethiopian. This suits those who take up a pointless task.

415 Pulverem edis / You must eat dust

Κόνιν σιτίζεις, You eat dust.[1] This is said of men who are greedy and have an enormous appetite but who do not get any fatter from their diet.

416 Vulpizas, sed contra vulpem / Ἀλωπεκίζεις πρὸς ἑτέραν ἀλώπεκα **/ You play the fox, but only against a fox**

This is also a Greek adage. Applied to those who fight guile with guile. Even today there is a common saying, 'The monkey tries to trick the fox,' both animals being extremely crafty.[1]

* * * * *

2.9, the Greek being present in *1500*. Erasmus' interpretation here is based on a corruption in his manuscript of Diogenianus (see 7 and 10 n23 above). In the explanation of the proverb the manuscript offered ἀσελγῆ 'wanton, lewd' for the correct ἀτελῆ 'incomplete.' Also in *Suda* A 853. Otto 344

1 Plato *Laws* 6.752A, quoted in Latin; see C 2 n7.

413 *Adagia* I v 32. The Greek title was added in *1506*. It is derived from Diogenianus 2.62. Otto 152

414 *Adagia* I iv 50. A doublet of C 407. The source is Diogenianus 1.45, the Greek being present in *1500*. Also Zenobius 1.46 and *Suda* AI 125. Otto 32

415 This must be based on an error in Erasmus' MS of Diogenianus (see 7 and 10 n23 above) at 2.8. It offered, instead of the correct ἀκόνην 'whetstone,' κόνην, which is meaningless and was taken by Erasmus to be a mistake for κόνιν 'dust.' The proper sense is 'You feed a whetstone' (see *Adagia* I iv 71, where the saying has the same explanation as the one Erasmus offers here for 'You must eat dust'). Note that the adage in its given form interrupts a sequence of entries beginning with alpha (412–14 and 416–20), all drawn from Diogenianus.

1 Erasmus mistranslates the verb, which really means 'to feed,' not 'to eat.'

416 *Adagia* I ii 28. The Greek title was added in *1506*. The source is Diogenianus 2.17. Also Zenobius 1.70. Otto 1939

1 Suringar 243

417 Ventos colis / You are tilling the winds

Ἀνέμους γεωργεῖν, To till the winds. It means to undertake a pointless task.

418 Carbonum thesaurus / A treasure of coals

Ἄνθρακες ὁ θησαυρός, A treasure of coals. This is said of those who have great hopes that are not realized. Lucian: 'You have shown me a treasure of coals.'[1]

419 Ex tardo asello equus prognatus / Ἀπὸ βραδυσκελῶν ὄνων ἵππος ὤρουσεν / A slow donkey has produced a stallion

It suits the man who is born from a humble family but achieves great distinction.

420 Inemptum mancipium *vel* Cum sale emptum / A slave no one will buy *or* A slave bought for salt

If ever we wish to indicate a cheap and worthless man we say 'A slave no one will buy,' in Greek Ἀνώνητον ἀνδράποδον.[1] Menander: 'What a noble Thracian you are, bought with salt!'[2]

* * * * *

417 *Adagia* I iv 58. The source is Diogenianus 1.88, the Greek being present in 1500. See also Zenobius 1.99 and *Suda* A 2261. Cf Otto 27.

418 *Adagia* I ix 30. The source of the adage is Diogenianus 1.90, the Greek version being present in 1500. It is found also in Zenobius 2.1 and *Suda* Λ 521. Otto 350
  1 Lucian *Hermotimus* 71; *Philopseudes* 32. Erasmus' quotation is in Latin, but the original Greek of *Hermotimus* 71 is quoted in Diogenianus.

419 Cf *Adagia* II viii 47. The Greek version of the adage (taken from Diogenianus 1.94) was added in 1506.

420 Instead of two similar, but different, expressions there should be only one, the second, which becomes *Adagia* I vii 79 and was drawn from Diogenianus 1.100. The first expression is based on an error in many of the MSS of Diogenianus at this point; see Bühler 5.439 (ii). These read ἀνώνητον, a form that does not exist in Greek and one that Erasmus translated by *inemptum*. The correct form is ἁλώνητον 'bought with salt,' as is suggested by the conclusion of the verse of Menander, quoted by Diogenianus (also at 1.100): πρὸς ἅλας ὠνημένος 'bought for grains of salt' (here, however, ὠνημένος is an unmetrical error for the correct ἠγορασμένος, also meaning 'bought').
  1 Apart from Diogenianus 1.100 (with the corrupt form as just mentioned), the adage is found at Zenobius 2.12, Zenobius Athous 2.86 (see Bühler 5.439–45), and *Suda* A 1384.
  2 Menander fragment 805 Körte-Thierfelder

421 Calabri hospitis munera / Gifts of a Calabrian host

This is said of those who give their friends gifts that they themselves think worthless. Since the Calabrians have a surfeit of pears, they serve them up in abundance to their guests, and when these are stuffed full they are told to take more pears away with them. If they decline to accept the fruit, it is scattered on the ground for pigs to consume. Horace in his *Epistles*:[1]

> Not in the way a Calabrian host bids one feed on pears
> Have you enriched me. 'Please eat.'
> 'No, thanks.' 'But take as many as you want.' 'No, thanks.'
> 'You will be taking gifts that your small children will like.'
> 'I am as much obliged by your gift as if I leave laden down.'
> 'As you please. What you leave will be devoured today by our pigs.'

422 Semper ad pocula Leontini / Ἀεὶ Λεοντῖνοι πρὸς τοὺς κρατῆρας / Always at their cups, the Leontini

The Leontines[1] constantly took great pleasure in drinking bouts. When Phalaris defeated them in war, he threw away their cups.[2] This gave rise to the proverb 'Always at the mixing bowls, the Leontini.' The adage is Greek.

423 Inaniter aquam consumes / You will waste the water

Originally this was directed at speakers in court who were garrulous and incompetent. It is well known that the length of their speeches was customarily controlled by water clocks. Then the expression was transferred from these speakers to all bletherers and chatterers. The Greek form of the saying is Ἄλλως ἀναλίσκεις ὕδωρ.[1]

* * * * *

421 *Adagia* III vi 94
1 Horace *Epistles* 1.7.14–19

422 *Adagia* I iii 22. The Greek form of the adage (from Diogenianus 2.50) was added in *1506*.
1 The people of Leontini, a town in Sicily
2 Erasmus' interpretation is a misunderstanding of the text of Diogenianus at this point. In the *Adagia* Erasmus correctly says that Phalaris (a tyrant who ruled Agrigentum) defeated the Leontines and deprived them of their weapons, and this made them turn to drinking.

423 *Adagia* I iv 73. The source is Diogenianus 2.61 (also *Suda* A 1400)
1 The Greek was omitted, by accident, in *1500*, the final sentence being incomplete in that edition.

424 Utrem verberas / You are beating a wineskin

The Greeks described those who were doing something in a foolish manner in these words: Ἀσκὸν δέρεις 'You are skinning a wineskin'[1] and Ἀσκῷ
φλαυρίζεις.[2]

**425 Tandem mus picem gustavit / Ἄρτι μῦς πίσσης γεύεται / Finally
the mouse has tasted the pitch**

This was said of those who were so eager to try something that they encountered some great misfortune. The point of the saying is that a mouse
cannot escape if ever it falls into pitch.

426 In mari aquam quaeris / You seek water in the sea

You are looking in the sea for something as if it were difficult to find when
in fact it is the only thing you can find there. For what else is there in the
sea but water? This suitably applies to those who search for one or two
faults in authors whose writings are packed full of flaws.

**427 Ignorat quid intersit inter aes et lupinum / He knows not
the difference between money and lupins**

The meaning is that a person cannot discriminate between what is of the
greatest value and what is worthless. Nothing is more valuable than money,
nothing is cheaper than lupins. 'Yet he well knows the difference between
bronze coins and lupins.'[1]

* * * * *

424 *Adagia* I iv 68n (CWE 31 364) holds that Erasmus' interpretation is wrong here,
the expression meaning something like 'to flay a man until he becomes no better
than a wineskin.' Erasmus, however, is simply following Diogenianus (see n1).
  1 Diogenianus 3.3
  2 Diogenianus 2.100. This was added, without a Latin translation, in 1506. The
   text and meaning are uncertain. ASD reads φαυρίζεις, the reading in Bodley
   Grabe 30, the source of the manuscript of Diogenianus used by Erasmus, but
   this verb is not in LSJ. At *Adagia* I vi 39 You terrify with a wineskin (CWE 32 31)
   Mynors translates the phrase as 'to rout with a wineskin,' reading φαυλίζειν
   for φλαυρίζειν (see LSJ sub φλαυρίζω).

425 *Adagia* II iii 68. The Greek version (added in 1506) comes from Diogenianus 2.64.

426 *Adagia* I ix 75, where Erasmus gives a Greek version, but its source has not
been identified and it may be Erasmus' invention. For the Latin form of the
adage Erasmus may have been thinking of Propertius 1.9.16: *insanus medio
flumine quaeris aquam.* Otto 674

427 *Adagia* I iii 79. Otto 978
  1 Horace *Epistles* 1.7.23. Lupin seeds were used for stage money in the Roman
   theatre.

428 Cantilenam eandem canis / You sing the same old song

The meaning is that you say the same thing a thousand times. Terence in *Phormio*: 'You sing the same song.'[1] This comes from incantations that are very ancient and have often been heard.

429 Aliquid suo assuet capiti / He will stitch together a cap for his own head

Used when we advise caution against someone (or something) potentially harmful. Terence: 'Oh, I fear the pimp may stitch together a cap for his own head.'[1]

430 Sui similis est / He is true to himself

This expression can be used when persons do something that is consistent with their usual behaviour. It can be said and understood in both a good and bad sense. Examples are when a courtesan talks shamelessly, a pimp commits perjury, an impostor dissembles, a detractor engages in abuse, a braggart shows off, a good friend gives good advice, a scholar talks in a learned fashion, an honest man talks sincerely and a humble man talks modestly. If on the contrary a perjurer has at some point to stand by what he has sworn, he can be said to be untrue to himself. Terence: 'How true both are to themselves.'[1] This was said about a pimp and Phaedria, the latter being very much a flatterer and the former being extremely avaricious.[2]

431 Defraudare genium / To cheat one's genius

This means to deprive oneself of some of the necessities that your nature requires. It appears in the same writer of comedy.[1]

* * * * *

428 *Adagia* II v 76. Otto 338
  1 Terence *Phormio* 495

429 *Adagia* III i 58. Otto 347
  1 Terence *Phormio* 491. Erasmus' use of the compound verb *assuet* reflects the text of contemporary editions. Modern editions offer the simple verb *suet*.

430 Cf *Adagia* III x 32 A different face (*Sui dissimilis*).
  1 Terence *Phormio* 501
  2 In the play Phaedria is a young man who at this point is trying to persuade the pimp to have pity upon him.

431 This is referred to in *Adagia* II iv 74 To indulge one's genius (= C 510).
  1 Terence *Phormio* 44

432 **Naturam expellas furca, tamen usque recurret / Though you cast out nature with a fork, it ever returns**
This is a verse in Horace's *Epistles*.[1] The things that nature has implanted in us are not easily unlearned. Terence: 'He returns to his true nature.'[2]

433 **Caelum, non animum mutant qui trans mare currunt / Those who rush across the sea change only the sky they see, not their disposition**
The meaning is that if anyone has not also changed his disposition he has wasted his time changing his location.

434 **Vilis amicorum est annona bonis, ubi quid deest / The price of friends is cheap for the prosperous when something is needed**
Friends who want something are easy to keep. Those who give are very few.

435 **Optat ephippia bos piger, optat arare caballus / The sluggish ox wants the trappings of a horse, the nag wants to pull the plough**
A splendid saying for those who dislike what they do and are familiar with and desire something new and different.

436 **Cura esse quod audis / Strive to be what you are said to be**
Take care to be the kind of person that all men say you are when they compliment you. Horace to Quintius: 'You live a good life if you strive to match your reputation. / We and all Rome have long boasted that you are blessed, / But I fear you place more weight on what is said than on how you live.'[1]

* * * * *

432 *Adagia* II vii 14. This entry (used by Erasmus at Ep 109:169) and the next eight are all quotations from Horace's *Epistles*. Otto 743 and 1200
  1 Horace *Epistles* 1.10.24
  2 Terence *Adelphoe* 71

433 Not in the *Adagia* as a proverb in its own right, but cited in *Adagia* I i 49. It is taken from Horace *Epistles* 1.11.27.

434 Quoted at *Adagia* II viii 81. It is taken from Horace *Epistles* 1.12.24. Erasmus' punctuation has misled him. The word *bonis* goes with *ubi quid deest* and the sense is 'Friends are cheap when men of substance need something,' that is, 'men readily become friends when there is hope of reward.'

435 *Adagia* I vi 71. The adage is from Horace *Epistles* 1.14.43. Otto 261

436 *Adagia* IV i 92
  1 Horace *Epistles* 1.16.17–19

437 Cautus enim metuit foveam lupus accipiterque suspectos laqueos, adopertum milvius hamum / A wolf carefully fears the pit, and the hawk the suspected nooses, the pike the covered hook

Three very elegant metaphors, splendidly suiting those who refrain from crime only through fear of punishment. Otherwise they would be eager to do wrong.

438 Caecus caeco dux / Τυφλὸς τυφλοῦ ἡγεμών / The blind leading the blind

An adage from the Gospels referring to men who, though ignorant themselves, attempt to teach other ignoramuses.[1] What Horace says is similar: 'The blind man leads the way.' For this is what he writes to Scaeva: 'Look all the same, though a blind man wishes to show the way.'[2] Porphyrion points out that this saying is just the same as 'The sow teaches Minerva.'[3]

439 Odit cane peius et angue / He hates worse than dog and snake

Horace: 'The other fellow will shun a cloak woven in Miletus more fiercely than dog and snake.'[1]

440 Sed tacitus pasci si posset corvus, haberet Plus dapis et rixae multo minus invidiaeque / If a raven could feed in silence, it would have A better feast, less trouble and less ill will

Some think that this originated in a fable about a raven and a fox,[1] even though Porphyrion does not agree.[2] The meaning is this, that if we receive a gift from the rich we should enjoy it in silence without making any fuss, since in this way we will receive gifts more often and keep them without the ill will of others.

* * * * *

437 *Adagia* IV i 93. Horace *Epistles* 1.16.50–1. Otto 985

438 *Adagia* I viii 40. The Greek version in the title was added in *1506*. Otto 277
  1 Matt 15:14; Luke 6:39
  2 Horace *Epistles* 1.17.3–4
  3 C 782 (= *Adagia* I i 40). Porphyrion was an ancient commentator on Horace's poems. See the scholia on Horace *Epistles* 1.17.3–4.

439 *Adagia* II ix 63. Used by Poliziano in *Miscellanea* 49 (at end; 1.265 Maier). Otto 108
  1 Horace *Epistles* 1.17.30–1, where the verb is *vitabit* 'he will avoid,' not *odit* 'he hates'

440 *Adagia* IV i 94. This is drawn from Horace *Epistles* 1.17.50–1. See C 438 n3.
  1 Aesop 124 Perry. In the *Adagia* Erasmus adduces Apuleius' reference to the fable in *De deo Socratis* 4.
  2 In the scholia on Horace *Epistles* 1.17.50

441 Sine cortice nabis / You will swim without cork

Acron tells us that this was a proverb used by Horace and that it was taken from those first learning to swim.[1] They keep afloat by means of cork tied round their waist. Then when they become more skilled they begin to swim without this aid. Plautus in *The Pot of Gold*: 'Just as boys learning to swim have a raft of reeds, so that they have less trouble; they can then swim more easily and move their arms.'[2] Horace: 'Once time has strengthened your mind and body, you will swim without cork.'[3] He means by these words that you will have control of yourself and be your own master, without need of a supervisor or tutor.

442 Aegrotus dum spirat, sperat / As long as a sick man draws breath, he has hope

Cicero writing to Atticus: 'They say a sick man has hope as long as he draws breath. For my part I did not give up hope as long as Pompey was in Italy.'[1] The adage, based on actual experience, can be applied to those who never abandon hope even in the most desperate situation.

443 Patere et abstine / Bear and forbear

The philosopher Epictetus summed up the whole way in which we should live in two words: Ἀνέχου καὶ ἀπέχου 'Bear and forbear.'[1] One of these verbs advises us to endure misfortune with fortitude, the other tells us to refrain from forbidden pleasures. Epictetus also has a saying that refers to the common herd of philosophers: ἄνευ τοῦ πράττειν μέχρι τοῦ λέγειν 'they speak but do not act.' This means literally 'far from deeds, limited to words.'[2] This saying can also be applied to those who flatter us but are false friends.

* * * * *

441 *Adagia* I viii 42. Used proverbially by Poliziano at *Epistolae* 8.16 (1.113 Maier). Polydore Vergil 211; Otto 444
   1 For Acron see C 242 n4. The reference here is to the comments on the passage cited later (see n3).
   2 Plautus *Aulularia* 595–6
   3 Horace *Satires* 1.4.119–20

442 *Adagia* II iv 12. Used by Erasmus at Ep 123:34. Otto 1681
   1 Cicero *Ad Atticum* 9.10.3

443 Cf *Adagia* II vii 13 (with *sustine* for *patere*). Erasmus' unacknowledged source, including the Greek, is Aulus Gellius (see following notes). The Greek phrases are present in *1500*.
   1 Gellius *Noctes Atticae* 17.19.5–6
   2 Gellius *Noctes Atticae* 17.19 1. Cf *Adagia* III x 53.

444 **Aedibus in nostris quae prava aut recta gerantur / The good or ill that's wrought in our own halls**

Aulus Gellius writes that the following Homeric verse was always on Socrates' lips (as if it were proverbial): "Οττι τοι ἐν μεγάροισι κακῶν ἀγαθῶν τε τέτυκται 'The good or ill that's wrought in our own halls.'[1] The verse advises us to concern ourselves only with those things that relate to us, and warns us not to inquire into things that are external to us and relate to others.

445 **Coturnix Herculem servavit / Ὄρτυξ ἔσωσεν Ἡρακλῆ / A quail saved Hercules**

This was usually said when someone had been saved unexpectedly.

446 **Ira tardissime omnium senescit / Resentment is the last thing to grow old**

A Greek adage: Ὁ θυμὸς ἔσχατον γηράσκει[1] 'Anger grows old last of all.'

447 **Ne in cena quidem laudaberis / Οὐκ ἐπαινεθείης οὐδὲ περὶ δείπνῳ / Not even at a funeral feast will you be praised**

Applied to a person who is deeply hated. At funeral feasts the dead were given praise even if they would not have deserved it while they were alive. In addition, the Greeks seemed to have had the practice of praising each other at drinking parties, in the way that Alcibiades lauds Socrates in Plato.[1]

* * * * *

444 *Adagia* I vi 85. The Greek is present in *1500* (see n1).
- 1 Gellius *Noctes Atticae* 14.6.5, citing Homer *Odyssey* 4.392. Gellius does not say that the verse was proverbial; that is Erasmus' interpretation.

445 *Adagia* I i 71. Diogenianus 7.10, whose brief explanation Erasmus replicates. The Greek version of the adage, probably from Diogenianus, was added in *1506*. Also Zenobius 5.56, used by Erasmus in the *Adagia*, and Zenobius Athous 2.84 (Bühler 5.424–9).

446 *Adagia* I vii 13. Cf Alcaeus fragment 442 in *Poetarum Lesbiorum fragmenta*, E. Lobel and D. Page eds (Oxford 1955). The Greek is present in *1500*.
- 1 This Greek adage appears between 7.21 and 7.22 in the lower margin of a page in Bodley Grabe 30 and is also to be found in Bodley Laud 7 and Vienna, Supplementa Graeca 83; see 7 and 10 n23 above. It is absent from the other branches of the manuscript tradition of Diogenianus. See Heinimann 160 n12; Bühler 1.208 n109, 209–10, 212. The adage is also to be found in Apostolius (8.93), but Erasmus did not have a copy of this collection until he was in Venice, preparing the 1508 edition of the *Adagia*.

447 *Adagia* II vii 11. The Greek version (from Diogenianus 7.24) was added in *1506*.
- 1 Plato *Symposium* 215A

448 **Asinus in apibus /** ῎Ονος ἐν μελίτταις **/ An ass among bees**
Of those who suffer misfortune.

449 **Omnem movebo petram / I shall leave no rock unturned**
I shall leave no stone unturned. I have come across both forms of the proverb
in Greek.[1] The meaning of Πάντα κινήσω πέτρον 'I shall move every rock' is
that I shall try everything and never give up until I achieve what I want.

450 **Ante victoriam laudes canis / You sing of your exploits before
you have won**
Πρὸ τῆς νίκης τὰ ἐγκώμια.[1] Of those who praise achievements that have not
yet come to pass.

451 **Frustra canis /** Πρὸς κενὸν ψάλλεις **/ You sing in vain**
About those who give advice to no avail. Taken from singers whose songs
are ignored by everyone.

452 **Imperatorum multitudo Cariam perdidit /** Πολλοὶ στρατηγοὶ τὴν Καρίαν
ἀπώλεσαν **/ An excess of generals destroyed Caria**
A Greek adage meaning that those who disagree among themselves and do
not yield to anyone else on any point do a bad job of the task in which they
are engaged.

453 **Sine rivali diligere / To love without a rival**
To love something that no one else would want. An example is a monkey

* * * * *

448 *Adagia* I v 42. The Greek version of the title (from Diogenianus 7.32) was
added in 1506. Also in the *Suda* (O 388)

449 *Adagia* I iv 30. Erasmus' source is Diogenianus (see n1), the Greek being
present in 1500. Also in Zenobius 5.63, Zenobius Athous 2.24 (on which see
Bühler 4.190–8), where the verb is in both cases in the imperative: κίνει 'move'
[every stone], and *Suda* Π 223. Cf Otto 1596.
 1 Diogenianus 7.42, who offers the two forms of the proverb, one with 'rock'
  and one with 'stone.'

450 *Adagia* I vii 55
 1 From Diogenianus 7.56, the Greek being present in 1500. Erasmus omits from
  the Greek the verb ᾅδεις 'you sing,' added in the *Adagia*. Also *Suda* (Π 2880).

451 *Adagia* I iv 88. The Greek version of the title (from Diogenianus 7.60) was
added in 1506.

452 *Adagia* II vii 7. The Greek version of the title (from Diogenianus 7.72) was
added in 1506.

453 *Adagia* II i 17. The probable source is Poliziano in the preface to his *Miscellanea*
(1.216 Maier); see also *Epistolae* 6.5 (at end; 1.85 Maier). Otto 1546

that is alone in admiring and embracing its young. It is found in Ausonius.[1]

454 Pedibus in sententiam discedere / To vote with one's feet

Taken from a practice of the Roman senate.[1] The expression means the same
as supporting someone's views simply by indicating one's agreement with
him.

455 Mus malus / Μῦς κακός / A bad mouse

A Greek saying directed at a lecherous and lustful man. For Aelian tells us,
on the authority of many authors, that mice are very lecherous creatures.[1]
This is why lovers, who use as an endearment terms such as 'lovebird' or
'little dove,' also use 'mouse' in the same way. Martial: 'Call me mouse,
and the light of your life.'[2]

456 Nunquid et Saul inter prophetas? / Is Saul also among the prophets?

A very well-known story about Saul in the books of Kings[1] became proverbial among the Jews.[2] While he was searching for his father's asses,

* * * * *

1 The reference to Ausonius, taken from Giambattista Pio's *Annotationes priores*
8 (*Lampas* 1.374) has not been identified.

454 *Adagia* II vii 12. Taken from Pico della Mirandola's letter in Poliziano's *Omnia
opera* (*Epistolae* 1.5; 1.5 Maier). Cf C 127. Otto 1399
1 Some members of the Roman senate hardly ever had the opportunity to speak
in debates. They showed their views by walking to a speaker whose proposals
they supported.

455 Cf *Adagia* II vii 8 A white mouse. Diogenianus 6.45, where the adjective is
λευκός 'white' not κακός 'bad' in most of the manuscript tradition. However,
the Oxford manuscript that was ultimately Erasmus' source for Diogenianus
(Bodley Grabe 30; see 7 and 10 n23 above) actually offers κακός at this point.
The Greek title was added in *1506*. The verse in Martial is the subject of chapter 96 in Poliziano's *Miscellanea*. Poliziano also quotes the relevant passage
from Aelian (see next note). See 1.306–7 Maier.
1 Aelian *De natura animalium* 12.10. Aelian cites, among others, Epicrates and
Philemon, two writers of Greek comedy, as authorities.
2 Martial 11.29.3

456 *Adagia* II i 64
1 Erasmus uses *Malachon*, a Grecized form of the Hebrew word *Malachim* meaning 'of the kings,' to refer to the four books of Samuel and Kings. Jerome used
the Hebrew word in the preface to his translation of these four books (see PL
28 590, 598), and this must have been Erasmus' source.
2 1 Sam 10:1–12; 19:24. Saul's behaviour prompted the question that becomes
proverbial according to Erasmus.

he was suddenly overcome with prophetic frenzy; he then danced naked among the other prophets and began to prophesy. We can suitably apply the proverb to those who change suddenly or to those who consort with those who are quite different from them, for example if a soldier were to associate with monks or a poet with modern, fashionable[3] theologians.

457 Facies tua computat annos / Your years are counted in your face

This is to be found in Juvenal, said of an old woman who was acting as if she had the sexual longings of a young girl.[1] It can be used of those who wish to appear young when the furrows on their brow deny it. I thought that it should be included in the collection because it had the appearance of a proverb.

458 Mare coelo confundere / To mingle sea and sky

This means to throw everything together in complete confusion. This is the same as the Greek expression ἄνω κάτω 'upwards, downwards' (*sursum deorsum*).[1] Some Latin writers used the expression *susque deque* 'upwards, downwards,' meaning that whatever was happening was of no relevance.[2]

459 Ignorat quid intersit inter caput et inguen / Not knowing the difference 'tween head and groin

Juvenal said of a drunken woman, 'She knows not the difference 'tween head and groin.'[1] If this expression is not a proverb, it is certainly very like one.

460 Qui semel scurra, nunquam paterfamilias / Once a buffoon, never an upright head of a family

In his commentary on Horace Porphyrion tells us this was a proverb.[1] Cicero uses it in a speech, saying that there was a common expression that

* * * * *

3 For what is translated as 'modern, fashionable' Erasmus uses the pejorative adjective *neotericus* 'in the new style.'

457 *Adagia* II vii 9
1 Juvenal 6.199

458 *Adagia* I iii 81. Juvenal 6.283–4. Otto 280
1 *Adagia* I iii 85 Up and down. There Erasmus gives several examples of the Greek phrase ἄνω καὶ κάτω.
2 *Adagia* I iii 83, translated in CWE 31 303 as 'Neither here nor there.' This is referred to in C 401.

459 *Adagia* II vii 6
1 Juvenal 6.301

460 *Adagia* II iv 11. Otto 1614
1 Porphyrion on Horace *Epistles* 1.17.58

rightly said a buffoon could become a wealthy man but not the respectable head of a family.[2]

461 Intus et in cute / Inside and out

A proverbial expression meaning the same as *penitus* 'completely, to the core.' Persius: 'The trappings are for the mob. I know you inwardly and in the buff.'[1]

462 Iovem lapidem iurare / To swear by Jupiter the stone

This means to swear a very solemn oath. Taken from the ritual of treaty-making. This was performed according to a fixed formula by the *pater patratus*, holding a stone in his hand.[1]

463 Circulum absolvere / To complete the circle

The meaning is to complete something in every detail and part. It can be thought to derive from the so-called circle and ring of which all branches of knowledge are part.[1]

464 Cimeriae tenebrae / Cimerian gloom

The region of Cimeria is placed by geographers in Scythia. It was con-

* * * * *

2 Cicero *Pro P. Quinctio* 17.55

461 *Adagia* I ix 89. This is a doublet of the second part of C 260. Drawn from Giambattista Pio's *Annotationes priores* 10 (*Lampas* 1.382). Otto 492
1 Persius 3.30

462 *Adagia* II vi 33. Like the preceding adage this is drawn from Pio's *Annotationes priores* 10. Cf Otto 883n.
1 See Livy 1.24.6. The *pater patratus* was a special priest who ratified treaties.

463 *Adagia* II vi 86. The wording of the adage is not attested and seems to have been created by Erasmus on the basis of Poliziano *Miscellanea* 4 (1.229 Maier). Poliziano talks about scholars who *doctrinae illum orbem faciunt quae vocamus encyclia* 'create that circle of learning that we call *encyclia*.' At *De copia* II (ASD I-6 19) Erasmus uses the phrase *cyclopaediam absolvit*, translated as 'he completes a thoroughly comprehensive education' at CWE 24 572.
1 At *Adagia* II vi 86 Erasmus refers to the Greek expressions ἐγκύκλιος παιδεία 'complete general education' and κυκλοπαιδεία (which does not exist in Greek). Quintilian 1.10.1 gives ἐγκυκλοπαιδεία (hence our encyclopedia).

464 *Adagia* II vi 34, where Erasmus spells the place name with a double *m*, the usual spelling according to him in Greek literature. He seems inclined, however, to prefer on etymological grounds the spelling with a single *m*. Erasmus draws some material from Filippo Beroaldo's *Annotationes centum* 84, including the inaccurate reference to Lactantius (see n3 below). Polydore Vergil 69; Otto 387

demned to be in eternal darkness and, according to Homer, the sun never rose there.[1] It was here that the learned poet Ovid built a place for the god of sleep in a very fine passage.[2] The darkness of this region became proverbial and Lactantius used it in a very suitable way in book four of his *Divine Institutions*: 'What a blind heart, what a mind, darker, as the saying goes, than Cimerian gloom.'[3] As if emulating him Jerome says, 'What blindness is this, wrapped in Cimerian gloom, as the saying goes?'[4]

465 Muti magistri / Silent teachers

By way of a proverb the ancients called books 'silent teachers.' Books can teach though they cannot speak. Those who have acquired eloquence just by reading tracts on rhetoric can boast that they have learned the art of speaking from silent teachers. Aulus Gellius book fourteen chapter two: 'Since there was a dearth of "The living voice,"[1] as they say, I learned from the so-called "silent teachers."'[2] He was referring of course to books.

466 Non omnia pari filo conveniunt / The same length of thread does not join everything together

Pico della Mirandola wrote this with the implication that it was a proverb.[1] Taken perhaps from everyday use. We use it to mean that all men cannot say all things, that 'All men cannot do everything,' as the bucolic poet wrote,[2] though the words are not at all bucolic in tone.

467 Intra tuam pelliculam te contine / Keep inside your own skin

Porphyrion thought that the origin of this proverb was the fact that generals used to sleep on skins.[1] One may also think that it has been taken from the

*****

1 Homer *Odyssey* 11.16
2 Ovid *Metamorphoses* 11.592–6
3 Lactantius *Institutiones* 5.3.23 (not book 4)
4 Jerome *Contra Iohannem Hierosolymitanum* 44 PL 23 412A, CCSL 79A 81

465 *Adagia* I ii 18. Otto 945
  1 C 222
  2 Gellius *Noctes Atticae* 14.2.1

466 Not in the *Adagia*. In *1500* and *1506* the verb in the proverb was wrongly in the singular (*convenit*). The plural appears in later editions. Otto 1268
  1 Giovanni Pico della Mirandola in a letter to Ermolao Barbaro (*Epistolae* 9.4 in Poliziano's *Opera omnia*; 1.122 Maier)
  2 *Adagia* II iii 94; from Virgil *Eclogues* 8.63

467 *Adagia* I vi 92. Polydore Vergil 198; Otto 1376
  1 Porphyrion (see C 438 n3) on Horace *Satires* 1.6.22. Erasmus' text is a corrupt version of what is in Porphyrion. For *ductores* 'generals' Erasmus gives *doctores*

very well-known fable in which an ass put on a lion's skin, an action that cost it dearly.[2] Horace: 'And quite right too, since I had not stayed within my own skin.'[3] The proverb advises us to conduct ourselves in keeping with our status. Martial addresses a cobbler who had risen to great riches by good fortune and then had hoisted his sails to enjoy the favouring winds.[4] Later however, he was reduced to his former poverty by extravagant spending and he was again nothing but a poor cobbler. Martial says, 'Now, cobbler, stay within your own skin.'[5] Plautus writes of his boastful and swaggering soldier that he was 'clad in elephant's hide, not his own.'[6] The point of this description is either that the soldier spoke of achievements beyond his powers or that Plautus wanted to show that the soldier was stupid.

468 Siculae gerrae. Persae nugae. Lyrae lyrae / Sicilian trash. Persian nonsense. Stuff and nonsense

Festus Pompeius wrote that *gerrae* was a Greek work meaning wicker hurdles and that it came to be commonly used to mean nonsense or trifling and unimportant things in the following way. He says, 'When the Athenians were besieging Syracuse and were frequently calling out for *gerrae*, the Sicilians made fun of them by shouting back *gerrae*.'[1] After this *gerrae* began to be used in the sense of nonsense. Ausonius writes to Symmachus:

> When I was considering, not 'To whom shall I give my smart new book?' as Catullus asks himself, but much more selfishly and more sincerely, 'To whom shall I give my dowdy, unsophisticated book?' I did not search for long. For you came to mind and I would always choose you from all my friends if

* * * * *

'teachers' and for *dormirent* 'used to sleep' he gives *dormitent* 'sleep.' These may have been errors of the printer. Erasmus gets the text right in the *Adagia*, although he takes the skins to refer to skin-tents.
2 Babrius 139 (Loeb, ed B.E. Perry) and *Aesopica* 188 Perry. The ass passed itself off as a lion for a while, but its true nature was eventually revealed and the ass was beaten to death (cf C 792).
3 Horace *Satires* 1.6.22. Horace is referring to the ill will he faced because he was the son of a freedman.
4 This metaphor (Erasmus', not Martial's) is often used proverbially; see *Adagia* II iii 24 To hoist topsails.
5 Martial 3.16.6
6 Plautus *Miles gloriosus* 235

468 *Adagia* II iv 10. Polydore Vergil 195 (for the first of the three expressions); Otto 755
1 Pompeius Festus 83.11–14 Lindsay

I could. I have sent you therefore this stuff, more worthless than Sicilian trash.[2]

Plautus in *The Carthaginian*: 'What you say is clever for the occasion, even though we have heard it before. For I regard your flattering words as *gerrae germanae* "pure trash" and *lyrae lyrae* "stuff and nonsense." '[3] From these words of Plautus I suspect that *lyrae* too was used in a proverbial way to mean trifling matters. This is why old men are said *delyrare* 'to be crazy' when their age leads them to do silly things.[4] We read on several occasions in the same poet *Persolae nugae* and *Persae nugae* 'Persian nonsense.'[5] The word *congerro* 'crony,' referring to a friend or to someone engaged with another person in the same kind of trifling affairs, is found quite often in Plautus as well as in other authors.[6]

469 E plaustro loqui / Ἐξ ἁμάξης / Wagon-language
Taken from the licence granted to Old Comedy. Young men performing the comedy on wagons used to hurl insults and abuse at anyone they encountered. Because of this, when the Greeks wanted to indicate that someone had railed at another in an intemperate and excessive manner, they said that he had been speaking Ἐξ ἁμάξης 'Wagon-style.'[1]

* * * * *

2 Ausonius *Griphus*, preface (p 111 Green), quoting Catullus 1.1
3 Plautus *Poenulus* 135–7. The words *lyrae lyrae* are the corrupt remains of a Greek phrase. In the *Adagia* Erasmus connects it with the Greek words λῆροι 'trifles' and ληρήματα 'silly talk.'
4 Erasmus' etymology of the Latin verb *delyrare* (= *delirare*) is 'stuff and nonsense.' The verb is connected with the noun *lira* 'furrow' or 'ridge between furrows.' The verb literally meant 'to deviate from a straight line' and then acquired its metaphorical sense of 'to be deranged.' Erasmus gets the etymology correct in *Adagia* I iv 91.
5 For *Persolae nugae* Erasmus is thinking of Plautus *Curculio* 192, but there the reading is *persolla* 'person,' which is not an adjective but a noun, unconnected in syntax with *nugae*. For *Persae nugae* he is thinking of Plautus *Persa* 718, where similarly there is no syntactic connection between *Persae* and *nugae*. The text there can be translated as 'To the Persians? Stuff and nonsense!' The expression 'Persian nonsense' does not exist.
6 See for example Plautus *Mostellaria* 931, 1049, and *Persa* 89. The word seems to be peculiar to Plautus.

469 *Adagia* I vii 73. The Greek title was added to the heading in 1506. The source of the Greek in the body of the text is drawn from Poliziano (*Praelectio in Persium*; 1.513 Maier); see n1.
1 The Greek phrase at the end of the discussion appeared as ἐξ ἁμάξω in 1500 since this was how the word was printed (instead of ἐξ ἁμαξῶν) in the 1498

470 **Non remulco, sed plena velificatione invectus / Attacking not by tow-rope, but at full sail**

This expression is very similar in meaning to that of the immediately preceding one. It is taken from naval battles in which ships equipped with battering rams attack each other. Similarly those who have criticized someone with great licence, either verbally or on paper, are said to have attacked "Not by tow-rope but at full sail."[1] The verb itself, *invehi*, which we are using here in its literal sense,[2] comes either from chariots in which the ancients used to fight, or, if that is not right, certainly from ships.

471 **Ad Aristophanis lucernam lucubrare / To study by the lamp of Aristophanes**

The lamp of Aristophanes, the writer of comedies, has been proverbial for a long time because of the man's painstaking diligence.[1] This is why we say that a person who has devoted most of his nights to scholarly work has studied by the lamp of Aristophanes. For the same reason the lamp of Demosthenes also became part of everyday language.[2] Because he usually spoke from a script and his speeches had been carefully planned before they were delivered, his enemies made the criticism τὰ τοῦ ἐκείνου ἐλλύχνιον ὄζειν 'that his work smelt of the lamp.' And why should we not add

* * * * *

edition of Poliziano's *Opera*. In *1506* Erasmus corrected the form to ἐξ ἁμάξης (genitive singular). See Heinimann 177 n90.

470 Cf *Adagia* IV vi 72 Not by poles or branches, which is based on the same passage of Ammianus Marcellinus as here (see n1). Erasmus draws from Poliziano's *Miscellanea* 9 (1.233 Maier), but the (correct) reading *remulco* comes from the *Miscellanea* as printed in the composite volume published in Brescia in 1496 (see 13 above). In the 1498 edition of Poliziano's works the reading was *remulo* 'by branch.' Otto 428
1 Ammianus Marcellinus 18.5.6, but *invectus* 'attacking' comes from Poliziano.
2 Literally 'to be carried against,' 'to attack,' as opposed to the metaphorical sense of 'to inveigh against.'

471 *Adagia* I vii 72 and cf I vii 71.
1 As Erasmus says in *Adagia* I vii 72, the Aristophanes mentioned here is the Alexandrian scholar Aristophanes of Byzantium, not, as he states here, the famous writer of comedy. Erasmus' source is Poliziano's *Miscellanea* 4 (1.229 Maier), which was drawing on Varro *De lingua latina* 5.9.
2 The story is told in Plutarch *Demosthenes* 8. Erasmus drew the Greek phrase in the next sentence (present in *1500*) from Niccolò Perotti's *Cornucopiae* (482:21–6).

the lamp of Cleanthes[3] as a third example to enlarge the collection of our adages?[4] If anyone wants 'To complete the circle'[5] and orb of all fields of knowledge, he must study by the lamps of all these persons.

472 **Vel cum pulvisculo / Dust and all**
We use this verse-ending[1] to mean that everything has been completely removed and that nothing at all has been left. It seems to have been taken from those who sweep up the grain on the threshing floor. Plautus in *The Ropes*: 'He will sweep me up completely, dust and all.'[2] Plautus in *Truculentus*: 'So that she may sweep away more quickly all his money, dust and all.'[3] Juvenal seems to have alluded to this metaphor when he said, 'If he gives back your old leather purse, rust and all.'[4]

473 **A limine salutare / To greet from the threshold**
This is said of the person who does not devote constant or strenuous effort to theology or philosophy or any other field of knowledge and does not have any close familiarity with the subject. Rather he greets it from the threshold, that is, his doorway, just as if it were a passer-by.

474 **Summis degustare labiis / Ἄκρου χείλεος / To taste with the tip of the tongue**

* * * * *

3 Cleanthes was a Stoic philosopher of the 3rd century BC. This is drawn from Varro *De lingua latina* 5.9 by way of Poliziano (see n1).
4 Cleanthes is added to the version of the adage at *Adagia* I vii 72 The lamp of Aristophanes and Cleanthes.
5 Cf c 463.

472 *Adagia* II viii 85. One may compare the English expression 'a clean sweep.' The phrase comes from the preface to Poliziano's *Miscellanea* (1.213 Maier). The references, however, are the work of Erasmus.
1 Erasmus uses the term *clausula*, which in rhetoric often refers to the prosodic patterns at the end of sentences and syntactic breaks within sentences. Here it refers to the final part of an iambic senarius.
2 Plautus *Rudens* 845. For the title see c 70 n2. Otto 1485
3 Plautus *Truculentus* 19
4 Juvenal 13.61

473 *Adagia* I ix 91. The expression is drawn from the preface to Poliziano's *Miscellanea* (1.213 Maier). It occurs at Seneca *Letters* 49.6. Otto 953

474 *Adagia* I ix 92. The Greek version of the adage, which requires a preposition such as ἀπό, was added in 1506. Erasmus may have coined it, with imperfect recollection of Lucian *Dialogi meretricii* 7.3 or *Apologia* 6. This and the following adage are given separate numbers. More often Erasmus

475 **Extremis digitis attingere / Ἄκρων δακτύλων / To touch with the fingertips**
Expressions that everyone knows, 'To taste with the tip of the tongue' and 'To touch with the fingertips,' are close in meaning to the preceding adage. Cicero, defending Caelius:[1] 'I myself have seen and heard many in this city who had not only tasted this kind of life with the tip of their tongue and touched it, as the saying goes, with their fingertips, but who had given over their whole youth to pleasures. Yet they had finally escaped from them and had returned, as the saying goes, to good harvests.'[2]

476 **Bonae frugis / Of good harvests**
Cicero tells us that this proverb was customarily used whenever the ancients wished to indicate that a man was upright and completely free from iniquity.[1] By contrast they called an unprincipled and worthless fellow 'a man of no harvests,'[2] a metaphor drawn from trees or fields. This gave rise to an expression common in comedy, *frugi es* 'you are a fine man,'[3] used when someone is praised for having done his duty in a fine fashion.

477 **De calcaria in carbonariam decurrimus / We go from the lime-kiln into the charcoal-burner's fire**
This is to be found in Poliziano where it is referred to as a proverb.[1] I think this expression denotes a speech that wanders off topic. When we leave the topic we have proposed and suddenly slip into another one that is quite

* * * * *

combines adages of similar meaning under the same number (cf C 268, 304). Otto 892

475 *Adagia* I ix 94; cf *Adagia* IV ix 73 With the tips of two fingers. The Greek version was added in *1506*, and, like the preceding one, may be Erasmus' invention. It should have a preposition or be in the dative case as in Diogenianus 2.10 or Zenobius 1.62. Polydore Vergil 265 (lacking the Greek version); Otto 546
   1 Cicero *Pro M. Caelio* 12.28
   2 See C 476.

476 *Adagia* IV v 27. The phrase *bonae frugis* occurs at Poliziano's *Miscellanea* 9 (1.233 Maier) and 95 (1.306 Maier). Polydore Vergil 275; Otto 722
   1 Cicero *Pro M. Caelio* 12.28
   2 Here the Latin phrase is *nullius frugis*, but this does not seem to be found in classical Latin.
   3 As at Plautus *Casina* 327; Terence *Eunuchus* 608

477 *Adagia* II iv 96. Otto 295
   1 Poliziano, who is directly quoted in the final sentence, in the preface to his *Miscellanea* (1.214 Maier), referring to Tertullian *De carne Christi* 6.1

different, 'we almost go from the lime-kiln into the charcoal-burner's fire, as the saying goes.'

478 Pulverem ob oculos offundere. Glauconiam ob oculos obiicere / To throw dust in someone's eyes. To cast a cataract in someone's eyes
The meaning is to deliberately treat some topic in an obscure fashion and thus to deprive one's listeners of the ability to make any judgment about it. In a speech Cicero boasts that he has thrown dust in the jurymen's eyes.[1] Jerome too says against a certain monk, who had more than a modest amount of loquacity but no eloquence,[2] 'Immediately he would have cast darkness over jurymen's eyes.'[3] 'To cast a cloud over someone's eyes' has the same sense.[4] No different is Plautus' phrase 'To cast a cataract in someone's eyes.'[5] Cataracts are a disease of the eyes and frequently cause blindness.

479 Sybaritae per plateam / Sybarites in the streets
The Sybarites are included among the examples of those who had extravagant tastes in food and dress. They gave rise to the common saying among the ancients Συβαρῖται διὰ πλατείας 'Sybarites in the streets,' directed at those who parade themselves in an arrogant fashion. Africanus in his speech entitled *Cestis*: 'But Sybarites swollen with pride.'[1]

* * * * *

478 *Adagia* II ix 43. The first part of the heading is drawn from Poliziano's *Miscellanea* 9 (1.232 Maier); the second part does not attain status as an adage in its own right in the *Adagia*, but is mentioned in *Adagia* II ix 43. Erasmus' text of it is faulty, the correct reading being *glaucumam* or *glaucoma*. Otto 1483
  1 Quoted by Quintilian 2.17.21, who is more specific, saying that it was in a speech for Cluentius
  2 This seems to be a variation of a saying of the historian Sallust, quoted in Gellius *Noctes Atticae* 1.15.18: 'a certain amount of eloquence but little discretion.'
  3 Jerome *Letters* 50.2.2 CSEL 54 390
  4 Cf *Adagia* I iii 63 and C 279.
  5 Plautus *Miles gloriosus* 148

479 *Adagia* II ii 67. Diogenianus 8.10 (the source of the Greek, present in *1500*). Also Zenobius 5.88, *Suda* Σ 1271 and Apostolius 15.77. Polydore Vergil 89; Otto 1727
  1 Julius Africanus, an obscure historian of the 2nd / 3rd centuries AD who wrote in Greek and whose work survives in fragmentary form. Erasmus derived this information from Poliziano (*Miscellanea* 15; 1.239 Maier), getting the title and the nature of the work wrong at the same time. The title should be *Cesti* (= Κεστοί) and Poliziano says the work is about military matters,

480 Domi, non hic, Milesia / Follow your Milesian ways at home, not here

The Milesians were famous for their luxury and effeminacy. This prompted the proverb Οἶκοι Μιλήσια, οὐ γὰρ ἐνθάδε 'At home, not here, your Milesian ways,'[1] which suits 'those who parade their domestic luxury in a place where it is not deemed acceptable. These words were spoken to a Milesian who was visiting Sparta and was praising the delights of his own city. The source is Apostolius of Byzantium.'[2] This expression has moral force, advising us that we are all free to live at home as we wish, but that outside the home we should conform to how others live.

481 Surdis agere testimoniis / To plead a case on deaf testimonies

Those who use the written evidence of tablets are said 'To plead a case on the basis of deaf testimonies.' The reason for the expression is that such evidence cannot be cross-examined because tablets are deaf. Even now those who cite many great authors without giving either author's name or the passages they are using are said 'To plead a case on deaf testimonies.' Poliziano: 'Let there not be pleading on the basis of deaf testimonies, as they say.'[1]

482 Ansam quaerere, arripere, praebere / To look for, snatch, or provide a handle

This is an attractive metaphor, meaning to look for or provide an opportunity. Plautus: 'Don't you see that he is looking for a handle?'[1] He means that the person is seeking an opportunity to rescind an agreement. 'Let us not

* * * * *

though it covered other subjects. Poliziano does not give the Greek version of 'Sybarites in the streets.' See Heinimann 175 n82.

480 *Adagia* I iv 8. Erasmus draws (see n2), again without acknowledgment, from Poliziano (*Miscellanea* 16; 1.240 Maier). Polydore Vergil 90
  1 Cf also *Adagia* I ix 49.
  2 Taken directly from Poliziano (see introductory note). In *1500* the name is given as 'Apostolus Byrrantius'; in *1506* we read 'Apo. Byzantius.' The usual Latin version of the name is Apostolius. The proverb is to be found at Apostolius 12.37 (in CPG 1). Erasmus himself did not have access to Apostolius' collection of proverbs until 1508 when he was preparing the new *Chiliades*.

481 *Adagia* III v 75
  1 *Miscellanea* 23 (1.245 Maier)

482 *Adagia* I iv 4. Erasmus uses the phrase *ansam praebere* at Allen Ep 113:131–3.
  1 Plautus *Persa* 670–1

provide our enemies with a handle to abuse us.'[2] You will come across 'to snatch, take hold of a handle,' meaning 'to seize an opportunity' in scholars' writings.[3]

483 Occasionem arripere / To seize Opportunity

The phrase 'To seize Opportunity' has the flavour of a proverb. The divinity Opportunity was represented in the following way.[1] She stood on a freely turning wheel with wings on her feet, spinning around very quickly. The forepart of her head was covered in thick hair; the back of her head was bald, so that it could not be caught hold of. Whoever wrote the verse 'long in the forelock, Opportunity is bald behind' was making a learned allusion to this kind of representation.[2] In Greek this divinity is called Καιρός 'Timeliness.'[3]

484 Fenestram aperire / To open a window

This is a similar metaphor to the preceding adage, meaning to provide an opportunity and access. Terence: 'Oh, what a great window onto wickedness you will have opened.'[1] I rather think that the metaphor used by Cicero in his speech for Plancus was taken from everyday language: 'Although I entered into the case by a door I did not wish to use.'[2]

485 In sinu gaudere / Ἐν κόλπῳ χαίρειν / To rejoice in one's own bosom

The meaning is to be happy without saying anything about it and not to

* * * * *

2 This sentence is a close paraphrase of a sentence in Poliziano *Epistolae* 9.13 (1.135 Maier).

3 The phrase *ansam arripere* (or *ansam apprehendere*) is not attested in TLL. The reference must be to the humanists.

483 This made its way into the 1508 edition of the *Adagia* (no 301), but was dropped thereafter as an independent adage. Erasmus refers to it at *Adagia* I vii 70 (CWE 32 109). Otto 1262

1 This sentence and the two following ones draw on Poliziano's words at *Miscellanea* 49 (1.265 Maier)

2 Cato *Disticha* 2.26

3 The Greek word Καιρός was accidentally omitted in 1500. This sentence was also drawn from Poliziano (see n1 above).

484 *Adagia* I iv 3. Cf c 160 and *Adagia* III vi 70.

1 Terence *Heautontimorumenos* 481

2 Cicero *Pro L. Plancio* 3.8. Erasmus gives the name as Plancus instead of Plancius.

485 *Adagia* I iii 13. The Greek version was added in 1506, but it does not appear in the *Adagia*. It may be Erasmus' own translation of the Latin phrase. Otto 1655

expect the applause of others. This is the behaviour of those who are at ease with themselves because of a good conscience and do not care a whit about the opinion of others. Cicero in his *Tusculan Questions* book five: 'Since these things will not win applause, let them rejoice in their own bosoms and cease to speak so boastfully.'[1] Tibullus: 'Let the wise man keep his joy hushed in his heart.'[2] Propertius: 'Silently keep your joy locked up in your bosom' and 'to weep silently in another's bosom,'[3] the sense being that I feel the pain of your misfortune and you in turn feel mine.

486 Satis de quercu / Enough about the oak

Ἅλις δρυός, Enough of the oak, or Enough about the oak. This was a Greek proverb, relating to those who rose from a very humble station in life to much more affluent circumstances. As soon as early primitive society discovered the use of grain, people ceased to live on acorns. This gave rise to the proverb.[1]

487 Testudinem Pegaso comparas / You match a tortoise against Pegasus

Χελώνην Πηγάσῳ συγκρίνεις, You match a tortoise against Pegasus. Applied to things that are quite different. Nothing is slower than a tortoise, while Pegasus is depicted as a winged horse.

488 Semper feliciter cadunt Iovis taxilli / Ἀεὶ γὰρ εὖ πίπτουσιν οἱ Διὸς κύβοι / The dice always fall well for Jove

A Greek adage, usually said of those who experience all that they wish or of those whose good fortune matches their virtues. Jupiter is an auspicious planet, favouring honourable pursuits and piety.[1] And probably it was ob-

* * * * *

1 Cicero *Tusculan Disputations* 3.21.51 (not book 5)
2 Tibullus 3.19.8
3 Propertius 2.25.30; 1.5.30

486 *Adagia* I iv 2. The Greek version, present in *1500*, comes from Diogenianus 1.62 (it is also in Zenobius 2.40). Otto 762
  1 Cf also *Adagia* IV iii 1 Milled fare.

487 *Adagia* I viii 76. The Greek version, present in *1500*, comes from Diogenianus 1.56.

488 *Adagia* I iii 9. The source is Diogenianus 1.58. The Greek version of the adage was added in *1506*. Also in Zenobius (2.44) and the *Suda* (A 607). See also *TrGF* 4 Sophocles fragment 895.
  1 Cf Marsilio Ficino's *Theologica Platonica* in *Opera omnia* (Basel 1576) 1.861, where Ficino says that Mars will yield soon to Jupiter, and then the *religiosi* 'devout' and the *pii* 'holy' will rule.

served in antiquity that a throw of the dice in the name of Jupiter[2] was a luckier one. But we may prefer to see in the expression a reference to the myth of Jove and Juno.[3]

489 Simulare cupressum / To paint a cypress

Acron tells us that this was a Greek proverb, 'directed at a dreadful painter who could paint only a cypress. When a shipwrecked sailor requested him to paint his portrait, he asked the sailor whether he wanted part of a cypress tree to be added to the picture.'[1] This gave rise to a proverbial expression. It suits those who are proficient in only one thing, like preachers who have learned by heart one or two sermons and are incapable of contributing anything of their own. They always 'Sing the same song.'[2]

490 Delphinum sylvis appingit, fluctibus aprum / He paints a dolphin in a landscape and a boar in the sea

This is a verse of Horace and one that in my opinion is proverbial.[1] It fits a person who says or does something that is quite inappropriate and completely out of place.

491 Parturient montes, nascetur ridiculus mus / Ὤδυνεν ὄρος, εἶτα μῦν ἀπέκτεκεν / The mountains will labour, but a ridiculous mouse will be born

This is another verse of Horace that Porphyrion attests was proverbial and had been taken from a fable of Aesop.[1] Said of boastful and showy per-

* * * * *

2 In the *Adagia* Erasmus adds the point that before throwing dice the thrower uttered the name of a god.
3 It is not clear to which myth Erasmus is referring, but it may be the story of how Jupiter managed to seduce Juno, as told in *Adagia* IV iv 23.

489 *Adagia* I v 19. The expression is taken from Horace *Ars poetica* 19–20. Polydore Vergil 213; Otto 483
1 Erasmus is following Pseudo-Acron's commentary on the passage in Horace. For Acron see C 242 n4.
2 C 428; *Adagia* II v 76

490 *Adagia* II iv 77
1 Horace *Ars poetica* 30

491 *Adagia* I ix 14. The Greek version of the title (from Diogenianus 8.75) was added in *1506*. Otto 1173.
1 Horace *Ars poetica* 139. In the commentary ascribed to Porphyrion (on this passage) we are told that it was a Greek proverb, but Erasmus gets the information that the source is a fable of Aesop's from Cristoforo Landino's commentary (see 12 above). The fable is *Aesopica* 520 Perry and Phaedrus 4.24.

sons who stir up wonderful expectations by their great promises and the magisterial air of their expression and clothes but when it comes to the point they produce pure rubbish.

492 Omne tulit punctum / He obtained every point

An adage borrowed from electoral practice. At elections a wax tablet was customarily carried around, and on it voters marked with a dot or point the candidates whom they supported. That is why any person who wins the support and approval of everyone is said to have obtained every point. Those who write entertaining material satisfy only those who read for pleasure; those who write to give useful advice are favoured only by those who wish to be informed about what is useful and do not wish to read for pleasure. The writer who combines entertainment and usefulness will win praise and support from all. Horace in his *Art of Poetry*: 'He who has mingled usefulness with pleasure obtained every point.'[1] Horace too in his *Epistles*: 'I come off as an Alcaeus by his vote.'[2]

493 Non missura cutem nisi plena cruoris hyrudo / The leech that will not let go until full of blood

This verse too has certainly the look of a proverb.[1] It should be used of dreadful and persistent men who act excessively in whatever they do and become extremely annoying. They have forgotten a very common saying, that you should leave a party at its height lest later unpleasantness spoils your enjoyment.

494 Sat cito, si sat bene / Soon enough if well enough

Taken from a speech of Cato.[1] The saying warns us against being precipitate in performing any task; for it does not matter how quickly something is done provided it is done well. Jerome to Pammachius: 'That too is a fine remark of Cato: "Soon enough if well enough." This made us laugh when we were young and heard an accomplished orator say it in some brief preface.

* * * * *

492 *Adagia* I v 60. As in C 491, Erasmus follows the commentators on Horace (Porphyrion and Cristoforo Landino), here for the first three sentences.
1 Horace *Ars poetica* 343
2 Horace *Epistles* 2.2.99. The word 'vote' is a translation of *punctum*.

493 *Adagia* II iv 84; Otto 814
1 Horace *Ars poetica* 476

494 This is referred to at the end of *Adagia* II i 1 Make haste slowly, but does not earn itself an independent entry in the *Adagia*. Otto 367
1 Cato *Dicta memorabilia* 80 Jordan. Also CRF *Incerta* 74

I think that you remember that we both went wrong when the whole lecture room resounded with the students' voices as they shouted out "Soon enough if well enough."'[2]

495 Bona nomina nonnunquam fieri mala si nunquam interpelles / Good names sometimes become bad ones if you never call them in

These are the words of Alphius, a moneylender, cited in Columella,[1] and they have become a common saying. By the term 'names' Alphius was referring to debtors. We can apply this to our friends or to those who are obliged to us, taking it in the sense that good and close friends can become distant ones unless we constantly renew our affection for each other by social contact and by letters and unless we remind each other of our mutual obligations.

495A Pueros astragalis, viros iure iurando fallendos esse / Cheat children with counters, men with oaths

This is an apophthegm of Lysander.[1] It meant that those who wished to be thought of as mature men should regard an oath as the most sacred thing. Dice and worthless rubbish can deceive children; only an oath can deceive a man of stature.[2]

496 Quarta luna nati / Born on the fourth day of the new moon

Those born on the fourth day of the new moon are destined to suffer mis-

* * * * *

2 Jerome *Letters* 66.9.2 CSEL 54 659

495 This does not have independent status in the *Adagia* but it is cited and explained in *Adagia* II i 26 Many's the friendship silence hath undone. Taken from Filippo Beroaldo *Annotationes centum* 31
1 Columella *Res rustica* 1.7.2

495A *Adagia* III iii 43. This is given, by error, the same number as the preceding entry. Taken from Filippo Beroaldo (see n1)
1 Erasmus *Apophthegmata* 1.292 CWE 37 134. It is recorded in Plutarch *Moralia* 229B (*Apophthegmata Laconica*), but Erasmus is drawing, without acknowledgment, from Filippo Beroaldo *Annotationes centum* 27.
2 Because such a man would not believe it possible for someone to break an oath

496 *Adagia* I i 77. Erasmus' source for this entry in the *Collectanea* is Angelo Poliziano (see n1). In *Adagia* I i 77 he does not mention Poliziano, referring instead to Eustathius. The most common Greek form of the proverb is τετράδι γέγονας, as at Zenobius 6.7 and *Suda* T 338. See also Zenobius Athous 2.78 and Bühler 5.381–8. The Greek sources relate the expression to the fact that Heracles, who was enslaved to Eurystheus, was supposed to have been born

fortune because according to the astrologers this day is inauspicious as far as conducting any business is concerned. Poliziano: 'Let us not be thought to have been born on the fourth day of the new moon, as the proverb goes.'[1]

497 Copiae cornu / A horn of plenty

'Αμαλθείας κέρας, Amalthea's horn. Taken from the myth about the she-goat that fed Jove. The expression is used of those who have a supply of every kind of thing in their home and whom you could ask for anything. A parasite in Plautus calls a letter 'A horn of plenty.'[1] Aulus Gellius and Pliny attest that some writers gave this as a title to their commentaries, meaning that they contained everything and were a source for anything that anyone wanted to know.[2]

498 Aquila non capit muscas / Ἀετὸς μυίας οὐχ ἁλίσκει / An eagle does not catch flies

The meaning is that very important men sometimes make slips over trivial matters, not because they misunderstand them, but because they do not pay any attention to them.

499 Aquilam volare doces / Ἀετὸν ἵπτασθαι διδάσκεις / You teach an eagle to fly

This is said of those who try to give instruction to a learned man or who give a reminder to someone who has a very good memory. 'You teach a dolphin to swim' and 'You teach a fish to swim' have the same meaning.[1]

* * * * *

on such a day. Contrast Polydore Vergil 262 This man was born on the fifth day of the new moon.
1 *Miscellanea* 80 (1.289 Maier)

497 *Adagia* I vi 2. The Greek version, present in *1500*, comes from Diogenianus 1.64. Also in Zenobius 2.48 and the *Suda* A 1478. Otto 441
1 Plautus *Pseudolus* 671
2 Gellius *Noctes Atticae* praefatio 6; 1.8.1. Cf Pliny *Naturalis historia* praefatio 24.

498 *Adagia* III ii 65. The Greek version of the title was added in *1506*, perhaps invented by Erasmus on the basis of c 326 (= Diogenianus 4.45). A slightly different version occurs at Apostolius 1.44, with θηρεύει 'hunts' for ἁλίσκει 'captures.'

499 *Adagia* I iv 98. The Greek version of the title (Diogenianus 1.65) was added in *1506*.
1 *Adagia* I iv 97 (quoted in Diogenianus 1.65, its probable source for Erasmus here, but also an independent entry at Diogenianus 4.33) and III vi 19 (Diogenianus 5.33)

500 Aquam culpat ardea / The heron blames the water

This is a common expression and one that is modern,[1] but it deserves to be included with the ancient ones. It suits those who usually blame something in order to cast a cloak over their own ignorance. An example is of someone who cannot read very well and gives as an excuse illegible writing.

501 Aquilae senecta / Ἀετοῦ γῆρας / An eagle's old age

'A proverb referring to old men who drink more than they eat,' according to Donatus in his commentary on Terence.[1] Taken from a physical characteristic of the eagle. For Pliny in book ten of his *Natural History* tells us an eagle died, not through old age or sickness, 'but through hunger.' 'The upper beak grew so large that the bird could not open its mouth.'[2] Because of this in its old age an eagle could only drink or suck blood from its prey. Terence in *The Self-Tormentor*: 'You say you drank not to excess! It seemed to me like an eagle's old age, as the saying goes.'[3]

502 Palinodiam canere / To sing a palinode

This means to say the opposite of what you have said before and adopt a contrary position. Taken from the very famous story about Stesichorus.[1] Chrysostom used this phrase[2] specifically as a proverb.[3] Also Augustine

* * * * *

500 Not in *Adagia*, as there is apparently no ancient equivalent (see C 197n)
  1 Suringar 17. The point may be that a heron blames the water for its failure to catch fish.

501 *Adagia* I ix 56. The Greek version of the proverb, added in 1506, occurs at Diogenianus 1.56. Polydore Vergil 122; Otto 143
  1 The ancient commentary of Aelius Donatus on Terence's *Heautontimorumenos*, the source of the adage, has been lost. Erasmus is drawing from Johannes Calphurnius, who composed a commentary on this play to accompany Donatus. This appears in many 15th-century editions. The quotation is from Calphurnius' comment on *Heautontimorumenos* 521.
  2 Pliny *Naturalis historia* 10.15
  3 Terence *Heautontimorumenos* 520–1

502 *Adagia* I ix 59. Otto 1323
  1 Stesichorus, a lyric poet of the 7th/6th centuries BC, is said to have become blind because he had vilified Helen of Troy. On learning of the cause of his blindness he recanted and praised Helen. See Plato *Phaedrus* 243B. The story could have been found by Erasmus in Perotti's *Cornucopiae* 515:27–30.
  2 For what is translated as 'phrase' Erasmus uses the word *clausula* (see C 472n).
  3 The Greek version of the phrase occurs near the beginning of John Chrysostom's essay *Quod nemo laeditur nisi a se ipso*. Erasmus, however, did not in 1500

to Jerome: 'Therefore I beg you to apply a fair and true spirit of severity, tempered with Christian charity, to correcting and emending that work and to sing your palinode, as the saying goes.'[4] Plato in his *Letters*: 'If you admit this, consider the wisdom of Stesichorus, imitate his palinode, abandon a false story and take up a true one.'[5] Cicero to Atticus: 'Expect a wonderful palinode.'[6]

503 Contra fluminis tractum niti / To strive against the river's flow

This means to dispute with more powerful opponents whom you cannot defeat if you take them on. The waters of a river flowing downstream become much rougher if you fight against them or if they encounter some impediment. In the same way, some persons become more violent unless you do what they want. One should yield to those whom it is pointless to resist. Juvenal praises this example of good sense on the part of Crispus in giving way before Domitian's violent temperament and not trying to swim against the torrent: 'He therefore never struck out his arms against the torrent.'[1] Augustine to Jerome: 'Why therefore do I try to go against the river's flow and not seek forgiveness instead?'[2]

504 Illotis pedibus / Ἀνίπτοις ποσίν / With unwashed feet

When something is done with too much confidence and stupidity we say it is done 'With unwashed feet.' An ignorant but arrogant person who tried to deal with the mysteries of theology in unscholarly language could be said to be disputing about theology with unwashed feet. Aulus Gellius in his *Attic Nights*: 'He criticizes the argument of a most learned men with unwashed feet, as they say, and unwashed language.'[1] Macrobius in book one of his

* * * * *

have access to the original Greek version, and he is drawing on a printed Latin translation. The presence there of *ut dicitur* 'as it is said' in conjunction with the expression, as well as in St Augustine's letter (see next note), prompted him to take the expression as proverbial.

4 Augustine *Letters* 40.7 CSEL 34 78 (= Jerome *Letters* 67.7.1 CSEL 54 672)
5 Plato *Letters* 3.319E, quoted in Latin; see C 2 n7.
6 Cicero *Ad Atticum* 2.9.1

503 *Adagia* III ii 9. Otto 680
  1 Juvenal 4.89–90
  2 Augustine *Letters* 73.3 CSEL 34 266 (= Jerome *Letters* 110.3.1 CSEL 55 358)

504 *Adagia* I ix 54. The Greek was added in 1506, probably from Zenobius 1.95 (see C 26n), though Erasmus may have provided it himself on the analogy of Diogenianus 1.43 (see n3). Erasmus is drawing primarily on Aulus Gellius (see n1), but Gellius gives only the Latin form of the saying. Otto 1390
  1 Gellius *Noctes Atticae* 17.5.14

Saturnalian Feast: 'They pass by with unwashed feet.'[2] He is referring to the teachers of literature who ignore the profound learning embedded in Virgil's poetry. Also the expression is used to describe obscene, irreverent, and offensive language, the metaphor being taken from those who are about to perform a sacrifice. For these are not accustomed to begin a sacrifice unless their feet have been washed. 'With unwashed feet' therefore means much the same as 'in a profane and unholy manner.' The Greeks have a proverb Ἀνίπτοις χερσίν 'With unwashed hands' with the same meaning.[3]

505 **Dignus quicum in tenebris mices / A man with whom you could play morra in the dark**
Cicero reveals that there was a very old, rustic proverb commonly used of men who were completely honest and trustworthy. Cicero in book three of *On Moral Obligations*: 'Surely it is disgraceful that philosophers have doubts where not even simple country people have them. For it was the latter who invented this proverb, which is very ancient and has thereby become almost a cliché. When they praise a man's honesty and goodness, they say he's "A man with whom you could play morra in the dark."'[1] I suspect that morra is the kind of game in which some men are in the habit of cheating.[2]

506 **Rem acu tangere / To touch the issue with a needle-point**
This means to solve a problem without any error. One can think that this saying too has been taken from a pleasurable game in which one person guessed and touched with a needle-point the spot that another person had marked. In this game the person who was successful in touching a counter or some other thing was said to have touched it with the point of a needle. Plautus: 'You have touched the issue with the point of a needle.'[1]

507 **Sic est ad pugnam properandum / That's the way to hurry to a battle**
This is said of those who, as cowardly fighters are wont to do, arrive as if in great haste, but only when the whole issue has been settled. Callicles

* * * * *

2 Macrobius *Saturnalia* 1.24.12
3 *Adagia* I ix 55, from Diogenianus 1.43, the Greek being added in *1506*

505 *Adagia* I viii 23. Polydore Vergil 165; Otto 1109
1 Cicero *De officiis* 3.19.77
2 In this game each player had to guess how many fingers his opponent would hold up.

506 *Adagia* II iv 93. Otto 16
1 Plautus *Rudens* 1306

507 *Adagia* II ix 52

in Plato's *Gorgias* to Socrates, who arrived in a hurry but was already late: 'This is the way, Socrates, one should enter the fray, as they say.'[1]

508 Post festum venire / Κατόπιν ἑορτῆς ἥκεις / To come too late for the feast
Socrates immediately responded to the preceding proverb with another one, understanding of course what the other one meant. He said, 'Surely we have not come too late, when the feast is over, as the saying goes.'[1]

509 Purgatis auribus / With well-washed ears
This means the same as being attentive and not at all distracted. Horace: 'I have a friend whose voice often resounds in my well-washed ears.'[1] Plautus: 'We give you our attention, both of us with well-washed ears.'[2] Persius: 'This Stoic here, with his ears well washed with biting vinegar.'[3]

510 Indulgere genio. Curare cutem / To indulge one's genius. To care for one's skin
'To indulge one's genius' means to give free play to what you want and to devote yourself to pleasure. Persius: 'Indulge your genius.'[1] We say 'To care for our skin' with the same meaning. Those who devote themselves to pleasure care only for this, that their complexion will shine, and to achieve this they enjoy hot baths, perfumes, sunshine, sleep, and drinking parties. Persius: 'Your pretty skin, nourished by constant sunning.'[2]

511 Qui quae vult dicit, quae non vult audit / He who says what he would will hear what he would not
A very well-known adage. Terence: 'If he proceeds to say what he likes to me, he will hear what he does not like.'[1] Plautus: 'If you hurl abuse at me,

* * * * *

1 Plato *Gorgias* 447A, quoted in Latin; see c 2 n7.

508 *Adagia* I ix 52. The Greek, from Diogenianus 5.73, was added in 1506. Cf Otto 369.
1 Plato *Gorgias* 447A, quoted in Latin; see c 2 n7.

509 *Adagia* II iv 94. Otto *Nachträge* p 134
1 Horace *Epistles* 1.1.7
2 Plautus *Miles gloriosus* 774
3 Persius 5.86

510 *Adagia* II iv 74 and II iv 75. Polydore Vergil 160 (for the first, on which see 19 n56 above); Otto 494
1 Persius 5.151
2 Persius 4.18

511 *Adagia* I i 27. Otto 205
1 Terence *Andria* 920

you will get it back.'[2] Caecilius in *Chrysion*, quoted in Gellius: 'If you speak
ill of me, I will speak ill of you.'[3]

512 Nodum in scyrpo quaeris / You seek a knot in a rush
This proverb is to be found in exactly the same form in both Plautus, in
Menechmus,[1] and in Terence, in *The Woman of Andros*.[2] To seek a knot in
a rush means to carry out an investigation into something where none is
needed. Donatus says that a rush is a kind of reed that is smooth and has
no knots. An alternative meaning is to be captious and excessively conscientious in some trifling and insignificant matter, treating it as if it were of
great importance.

**513 Pridie caveas ne facias quod pigeat postridie / Take care yesterday lest
you do something that will vex you tomorrow.**
Nothing could be more proverbial than these words. They appear in the
play entitled *Stichus*, one that is included among those ascribed to Plautus
even if the style smacks of a different author. There Pinacium wants to
dissuade her father, the old man, from marrying and uses these words: 'Let
him who can avoid women, avoid them. Everyday let him beware yesterday
doing something that will bring him grief tomorrow.'[1]

    The meaning is that though he is a slave to his current desires he
should not do now what he may later regret.

**514 Stultitia est venatum ducere invitas canes / 'Tis folly to take reluctant
hounds to the hunt**
In the same play the sister Panegyris wants to warn her father not to find
husbands for them against their will. She uses a very humorous adage,

* * * * *

2 Plautus *Pseudolus* 1173
3 On Caecilius see C 164 n3. This is CRF Caecilius 24, quoted in Gellius *Noctes
   Atticae* 6.17.13.

512 *Adagia* II iv 76. This begins a series of adages drawn from Plautus (to C 525).
   Polydore Vergil 49; Otto 1607
1 Plautus *Menaechmi* 247. For the title see C 203 n1.
2 Terence *Andria* 941, followed by Donatus' comment on the line

513 This did not survive into the *Adagia*, despite what Erasmus says in the first
   sentence.
1 Plautus *Stichus* 121–2. In modern editions the speaker is named Pamphila or
   the sister of Panegyris, not Pinacium, the name of a male slave. Erasmus is
   following the corrupt text of the early printed editions.

514 *Adagia* I vii 65. Otto 326

saying, 'It is folly, father, to take hounds to the hunt if they do not want to go.' And she goes on to explain the metaphor with this maxim: 'The woman who is married off to a man against her will becomes his enemy.'[1] The saying can be applied to those who compel men to work for them and demand their services against their will. Even today a proverb survives among our own peoples that it is very difficult to drive a carriage when the horses do not want to move.[2]

515 Actum est / It is all over

This is an expression of someone in despair. It is taken from a practice in the courts, so Donatus says.[1] When both parties had been heard and the jurymen had delivered their verdict, a herald called out, 'It is all over.' This is why whenever we mean that all hope is gone we say that it is all over; we say, for example, 'It is all over for me,'[2] or 'It's all over for your safety.' Plautus: 'Unless you provide real help, this affair is all over. I am resolved to die.'[3]

516 Aedilitatem gerere sine populi suffragio / To be a self-appointed aedile

This means to give orders on some matter when no one has given you the right to do so. Plautus in *Stichus*: 'Although he has not been elected by the people, he acts as if he is an aedile!'[1]

517 Lupus in fabula / The wolf in the story

Whenever we are talking about someone and he suddenly appears as we are conversing, we say that he is 'The wolf in the story.' We mean that the very person about whom we are telling a story is at hand. Donatus thinks that it originates with the belief that a wolf can render speechless a person it sees first.[1] But I think this explanation is pointless and irrelevant. A second view of Donatus, relating to nurses' tales, is certainly reasonable,

* * * * *

1 Plautus *Stichus* 139–40
2 Suringar 102

515 *Adagia* I iii 39; Otto 42n
1 Donatus on Terence *Eunuchus* 54
2 Plautus *Pseudolus* 85 (*actum est de me*)
3 Plautus *Rudens* 683–4

516 *Adagia* III i 4. See Otto p 5n.
1 Plautus *Stichus* 352–3. The aedileship was one of the magistracies of the Roman *cursus honorum*. It was held after the quaestorship, and before the praetorship.

517 *Adagia* IV v 50. Cf *Adagia* I vii 86, III viii 56. Polydore Vergil 42; Otto 988
1 Donatus, the ancient commentator on Terence, at *Adelphoe* 537

but I would especially accept the third explanation that he adds, had he not said that it was based on something that never took place. At the part of a play of Naevius that dealt with how a wolf had fed Romulus and Remus a real wolf suddenly appeared. This gave rise to an adage, so that when someone absent was being talked about and he suddenly appeared unexpectedly, it was said that the wolf in the play was at hand. When Syrus in Terence was telling a young man how he was tricking his father Demea, whom he thought was in the country, the father suddenly appeared. Syrus said, 'Oh, oh! Here's your wolf in the play.'[2] Similarly in Plautus in *Stichus*, the brothers are chatting about the parasite Gelasimus, and suddenly he makes an appearance. They say, 'There you are, the hungry wolf in the story is here.'[3]

518 Nota mala res optima est / A known evil is the best evil

What appears in Plautus in *The Three-Shilling Day*, 'A known evil is the best evil,'[1] is somewhat enigmatic. These are the words of an old man, who is advising his friend not to get rid of his wife, even though she is a dreadful woman, and marry another. The reasons are firstly that generally those who exchange one thing for another get something worse than they had, secondly that they take on the unknown for something they know, finally that the evils we are used to are no longer evils, while, on the other hand, blessings that we have not appreciated may turn into evils. This adage discourages us from making great changes, so that we do not wish too readily to get rid of a king, a teacher, a friend, or a wife in the hope of getting a better one.

519 Gladium dedisti qui se occideret / You gave him the sword with which he could kill himself

The meaning is that you have provided help and materials for someone's destruction. An old man in Plautus is castigated for having done this when he had given his young son money to buy a house, money that he would lose while ruining himself at the same time. The speaker says: 'Haven't you given him in this way a sword to kill himself with? / That is no different from putting money / In the hand of a young man in love.'[1]

* * * * *

2 Terence *Adelphoe* 537
3 Plautus *Stichus* 577

518 *Adagia* II ix 85. Otto 1022
1 Plautus *Trinummus* 63

519 *Adagia* III i 4. Otto 758
1 Plautus *Trinummus* 129–31

520 **A stirpe / From the root**

This is the same as saying 'from the source,' meaning the point from which all things have come – from the root, as it were.[1] For all branches are engendered by the roots. Plautus: 'But if the identity of the inventor is investigated right from the root,'[2] meaning the source from which these rumours sprang.

521 **Nunquam edepol temere tintinnabulum. Nisi qui illud tractat acuet, mutum tacet / Never for nothing does a bell sound. It is dumb and silent unless its handler sharpens it**

This is said of talkative persons who can keep a secret only as long as they have no one to talk to or no opportunity to speak.

522 **Lucrum pudori praestat / Profit before shame**

Κέρδος αἰσχύνης ἄμεινον is the Greek form. 'What causes shame is far easier to bear than what causes annoyance': so Plautus in *Pseudolus*.[1] He expresses the same idea in different words in *The Three-Shilling Day*. 'By Pollux, better to be ashamed than annoyed, even though the words have the same number of letters.'[2] This is a sentiment unworthy of a fine man, and this is why the first of these is spoken by a pimp, and the second by an old man, who eagerly and profitably made use of this disreputable saying to persuade his son. It is better to incur the loss of money than the loss of reputation.

523 **Quod habeas ne habeas, et illud quod nunc non habes habeas malum / Lose what you have, and get the misfortune you do not now have**

Customarily said of a wealthy but miserly man who does not dare to use

* * * * *

520 Not a proverb in its own right in the *Adagia*, but referred to at the end of *Adagia* III vii 12
  1 Cf *Adagia* v ii 37 and II iv 86.
  2 Plautus *Trinummus* 217

521 Not in *Adagia*. This is Plautus *Trinummus* 1004–5, but the lines are quoted in a corrupt form. For *acuet* 'will sharpen' in the second line modern editions read *aut movet*, the sense of the last part of the quotation being 'unless someone handles or moves it.'

522 *Adagia* III vii 14. Diogenianus 5.42 is the source of the Greek version, which was added in 1506. The Latin version is Erasmus' own translation of the Greek proverb.
  1 Plautus *Pseudolus* 281
  2 Plautus *Trinummus* 345. The Latin words with the same number of letters are *pudere* 'to feel shame' and *pigere* 'to be vexed.'

523 Not in *Adagia*

his wealth himself and does not allow others to do so either. This occurs in the same play.[1]

524 Efficimus pro opibus nostris moenia / We build the walls we can afford

This is said of poor men who nevertheless live as comfortably as their resources allow. Plautus in *Stichus*: 'Rich men from gilded cups and goblets drink, / We from our Samian crocks – and yet we live, / We live and build the walls we can afford.'[1]

The same idea is expressed in a common saying that little birds build little nests.[2]

525 Ne musca quidem / Not so much as a fly

When we wish to indicate that hardly anyone at all lives in some place we say that there is not so much as a fly there. Plautus in *Truculentus*: 'What women do you mean? There is not so much as a female fly in the house.'[1] The expression provided Crispus with a witticism of double meaning directed against the emperor.[2] When he was asked whether there was anyone with the emperor in his study, Crispus replied that there was not so much as a fly. He was clearly alluding to a habit of Domitian's; for whenever the emperor was on his own he hunted flies, and when he caught them he pierced them with a very sharp pen.

526 Semper adfert Libya mali quippiam / Ἀεὶ φέρει ἡ Λιβύη τι κακόν / Libya is always bringing forth something evil

This is the same as or at least very similar to the expression from Pliny that 'Africa is ever bringing forth something new.'[1] I suspect that this adage arose from the fact that Libya produces every kind of poison and monstrosity. It is applied to wicked men; for they are always devising new kinds of crime.

* * * * *

1 Plautus *Trinummus* 351. Erasmus seems to have taken *malum* as a noun meaning 'misfortune' in the accusative case, when in fact it is in the vocative case, meaning 'you scoundrel.'

524 *Adagia* I vii 62. Otto 1126
1 Plautus *Stichus* 693–5. The translation of the lines is taken from CWE 32 104.
2 Suringar 65

525 *Adagia* II i 84. Otto 1180
1 Plautus *Truculentus* 283–4
2 This sentence, as well as what follows, comes from Suetonius *Domitian* 3. Crispus is Vibius Crispus, an orator referred to in Quintilian 10.1.119.

526 *Adagia* III vii 9. The Greek, from Diogenianus 1.68, was added in *1506*. Otto 35
1 Pliny *Naturalis historia* 8.42. Cf *Adagia* III vii 10 and see C 46.

527 Aceassei luna / The moon of Aceasseus

'Ακεασσάου σελήνη, The moon of Aceasseus. Applied to procrastinators who always find a new reason to put off some business. Taken from the behaviour of a certain seaman called Aceasseus. In order to spend less time at sea he would say that he was waiting for a more propitious moon.

528 Pluris est oculatus testis unus quam auriti decem / One eyewitness is worth more than ten ear-witnesses

What we have seen with our eyes is more certain than what we have heard with our ears. This is in Plautus in *Truculentus*.[1] The saying is based on the fact that we often think that what we are told by others is false, while what we ourselves have actually seen we believe to be absolutely true because we are witnesses to it. Nevertheless things heard are often more certain than what we think we saw, and our eyes often deceive us.

529 Prudens in flammam mitto manum / I put my hand into the flame intentionally

The meaning is that I deliberately expose myself to unavoidable and terrible danger. This is in Jerome.[1] Similar is what Terence says: 'Deliberately and intentionally, though alive and seeing, I am done for.'[2]

530 Omnium rerum vicissitudo est / All things do change

This saying comes from a character in Terence[1] and even today[2] so retains its proverbial force that it is put everywhere on windows and doorposts. It can very aptly be applied to those whose good fortune has made them arrogant and who annoyingly insult those who are weaker.

* * * * *

527 *Adagia* I v 85. The Greek version, present in *1500*, is from Diogenianus 1.57 (reading -αίου). The correct form of the person's name seems to be Acessaeus, the form found in the *Adagia*.

528 *Adagia* II vi 54. Otto 1273
1 Plautus *Truculentus* 489. In *1500* the commentary on the adage ends here. What follows (from 'The saying') was added in *1506*.

529 *Adagia* III vi 13. Otto 671
1 Jerome *Adversus Rufinum* 2.32 PL 23 429, CCSL 79 69; *Letters* 54.2 CSEL 54 467
2 Terence *Eunuchus* 72–3, quoted also in *Adagia* IV iii 75

530 *Adagia* I vii 63 and cf III ix 72. Here begins a series of adages, down to C 543, excluding C 537, where the main or only source is Terence. Otto 1292
1 Terence *Eunuchus* 276
2 Suringar 161

531 Ne nimium callidum hoc sit modo / It may be too cunning this way

Donatus tells us that this is a proverb.[1] The reading is doubtful however. For both *calidum* 'hot' and *callidum* 'cunning' can be read, the former referring to hasty decision, the other to a plan that is over-ingenious.[2] For both approaches often turn out badly, either doing things in heat (meaning actions that are undertaken too hastily) or using excessively bold deceitfulness.

532 In me haec cudetur faba / These beans will be pounded on me

The meaning, according to Donatus, is that 'this trouble will fall on me and I will get the blame.'[1] This is taken from the striking of beans, referring to when they are beaten with flails and the pods are stripped open. Another possibility is that it comes from beans that are hard and badly cooked. In this case it was sometimes the custom for angry masters to pound the beans on the cook's head with a rock, as if they were punishing the beans and not the cook, although the cook got the worst of it.

533 Tute hoc intristi: omne tibi est exedendum / You made this dish and you must eat it all up

Donatus points out that this expression is similar to the preceding one and that it is taken from a relish or a country dish of crushed garlic.[1] The sense is the following: 'You were the instigator of this affair, and you must bear whatever unpleasantness comes out of it.' Or: 'You began it and you should also finish it.' This is what Phormio, who had advised the young man to take a wife, says: 'The whole affair redounds on you alone, Phormio. / You made this dish and you must eat it all up.'[2]

* * * * *

531 *Adagia* II v 50. Otto 302
  1 Donatus on Terence *Eunuchus* 380, the Terentian line being the source of the proverb
  2 In *Adagia* II v 50 Erasmus gives preference to *calidum*, correctly so. Metrical considerations in fact exclude *callidum*, though Erasmus does not use this as a reason for his choice.

532 *Adagia* I i 84. Otto 621
  1 Donatus on Terence *Eunuchus* 381, the source of the expression

533 *Adagia* I i 85. The source is Terence *Phormio* 318. Otto 869
  1 Donatus adduces this as a proverb in his commentary on Terence *Phormio* 318.
  2 Terence *Phormio* 317–18

The same expression is still a common one even now and there are other similar ones: 'You got it ready for the distaff and you must spin it yourself.'[3]

534 Eone ferox es, quia habes imperium in beluas? / Are you so bold because you are in charge of the beasts?
This is a rather vulgar and low-class adage that was often directed in the past at ostlers, grooms, or mule-drivers. In Terence in *The Eunuch* a stupid soldier says it to Strato, who was in charge of the elephants.[1]

535 E flamma cibum petere posse / To be capable of trying to snatch food out of the flames
This suits men who are like parasites and are extremely hungry. They can put up with even the vilest of abuse provided they fill their bellies. In the same play these words are spoken to a parasite: 'Shut up, you. I think you are the lowest of the low. / For now that you are disposed to flatter this man / I think you can try to snatch food out of the flames.'[1]

536 Domini similis es / You are like your master
A facetious remark directed at the bad slave of a bad master.

537 Dignum patella cooperculum / The cover is worthy of the dish
This is in Jerome.[1] The sense is that bad Christians may deserve a bad pope just as bad people get a bad king and a bad man gets a bad wife. Also to Pammachius: 'And straightaway the cover found its cup.'[2]

538 Quod scio nescio / I do not know what I know
An adage by which we indicate an unwavering pledge to keep quiet. It is like saying that we will always not know what we know. Terence in *The*

* * * * *

3 Suringar 230

534 Not in *Adagia*
  1 Terence *Eunuchus* 415

535 *Adagia* IV i 51. This adage is also quoted in *Adagia* II iii 55. Otto 669
  1 Terence *Eunuchus* 489–91

536 Not in *Adagia* in this form, but cf *Adagia* IV v 63. Drawn from Terence *Eunuchus* 496

537 *Adagia* I x 72. Otto 1355
  1 Jerome *Letters* 7.5 CSEL 54 30
  2 Jerome *Letters* 127.9.1 CSEL 56.1 152 (but the addressee's name is Principia)

538 *Adagia* III v 99. Polydore Vergil 170; Otto 1605

Eunuch: 'By Pollux, if you are wise, you would not know what you know.'[1]
Also in *The Self-Tormentor*: 'Do not know what you know if you are wise.'[2]
Donatus thinks that this proverb has been borrowed from the games dia-
lecticians play; they are in the habit of making riddling statements such as
'I do this and I do not do this' and 'I am a friend and I am not a friend'
and 'I hear and I do not hear' and countless others of this kind.[3]

**539 Sine Cerere et Baccho friget Venus / Without Ceres and Bacchus
Venus grows cold**
Chremes in *The Eunuch*: 'By Hercules, this is a true saying, "Without Ceres
and Bacchus Venus grows cold."'[1] It is a very well-known notion that sexual
desire is stimulated by food and drink and fades away if these are removed.
Jerome uses this proverb frequently.[2]

**540 Ovem lupo commisisti / Τὴν ὄϊν τῷ λύκῳ πεπίστευκας / You have
handed the sheep over to the wolf**
The meaning is that you have entrusted something to be guarded by a person when this is the very person you should be guarding against. Terence
in *The Eunuch*: 'You scoundrel of a woman, you have entrusted the sheep
to the wolf.'[1] The reference is to Chaerea, into whose sole care a young girl
was being given because he was thought to be a eunuch. Cicero: 'What a
fine guardian of sheep is the wolf, as the saying goes.'[2]

541 Quid si aliquis deus voluit / Some god may have wished this
A proverb that offers consolation in a cruel and difficult situation that cannot be accounted for in any acceptable way. The same Chaerea: 'Perhaps
some god wished this to happen.'[1]

* * * * *

1 Terence *Eunuchus* 721–2
2 Terence *Heautontimorumenos* 748
3 Donatus on Terence *Eunuchus* 722

539 *Adagia* II iii 97. Polydore Vergil 134; Otto 1868
1 Terence *Eunuchus* 732
2 Jerome *Letters* 54.9.5 CSEL 54 476; *Adversum Iovinianum* 2.7 PL 23 297A

540 *Adagia* I iv 10. The Greek title (probably Erasmus' own invention) was added
in 1506. Polydore Vergil 135; Otto 983
1 Terence *Eunuchus* 832
2 Cicero *Philippics* 3.11.27

541 *Adagia* III ix 89
1 Terence *Eunuchus* 875. The speaker, Chaerea, is referred to in the preceding
adage.

542 In tranquillo esse / In calm water

This means the same as to be safe and free of danger. It is similar to 'In shallow water,'[1] though 'In calm water' is more expressive. Both are taken from sailing. Terence: 'Then I am glad that my brother Phaedria's love affair is in calm water.'[2]

543 Saxum volvere / To roll a stone

The meaning is to tire oneself out with inexhaustible toil. Terence: 'I have been rolling this stone for long enough.'[1] Donatus says that this was a proverb 'referring to those who had been afflicted with tasks from which they could not escape.' He also thinks that it originated with the myth of Sisyphus.

544 Claudiana tonitrua / Claudian thunder

This can be said of noisy and very obstreperous persons. 'Claudius Pulcher began the practice, at games held behind the stage,[1] of crashing stones together in such a way that the sound of real thunder was produced. Previously very slight and insignificant sounds were created by throwing nails and stones[2] into a bronze pan.'

545 Aiantis risus / Αἰάντειος γέλως / To laugh like Ajax

This is said of those who laugh for no good reason and laugh like a madman.[1]

* * * * *

542 *Adagia* II ii 6
  1 C 281
  2 Terence *Eunuchus* 1037–8

543 *Adagia* II iv 40. Otto 1596
  1 Terence *Eunuchus* 1085, followed by Donatus' comment on the line

544 *Adagia* III ii 19. After the first sentence the rest is taken, without acknowledgment, from Pompeius Festus 50.1–5 Lindsay, complete with corruptions (see nn1 and 2).
  1 Erasmus follows the contemporary text. The sense should be 'the practice, at the public games, of crashing stones together off-stage . . .'
  2 In *1506* the text, perhaps as a result of a printer's error, reads *clausi lapides* 'wrapped stones,' a corruption of *clavi et lapides* 'nails and stones' or of *claves et lapides* 'keys and stones.'

545 *Adagia* I vii 46. Diogenianus 1.41 is the source of the Greek version, present in *1500*; see also Zenobius 1.43 and *Suda* AI 8.
  1 Ajax, the great Greek hero, went mad after he lost the armour of Achilles to Odysseus and then took his own life.

546 **Audiendum cui quattuor sint aures /** Ἄκουε τοῦ τέσσαρα ἔχοντος ὦτα /
We should listen to him who has four ears

A Greek adage that tells us to follow the advice of those who have heard
very many things and are therefore very knowledgeable. The Spartans had
a statue of Apollo with four ears.[1]

547 **Incultior Libethrio / As uncultured as Libethrion**

Ἀμουσότερος Ληβηθρίων, meaning 'as unpleasant or as harsh as Mount Libethrion,' which is both bleak and barren.[1] The expression suits those who
are unsophisticated and uncultured.

548 **Pulchrorum etiam autumnus pulcher est / Even the autumn of beauty
is beautiful**

This is an apophthegm of Archelaus, said when Euripides was kissing
Agathon, who was then growing into a young man.[1] It suits those who
carry their age well.

549 **Aquila in nubibus /** Ἀετὸς ἐν νεφέλαις **/ An eagle in the clouds**

This is said of those who want what they cannot acquire.[1]

* * * * *

546 *Adagia* I iii 8 (much expanded). Cf C 723, which Erasmus says (in *Adagia* I iii 8)
has a similar meaning. The Greek version (from Diogenianus 2.5) was added
in 1506. Also Zenobius 1.54 and Zenobius Athous 2.39 (see Bühler 4.291–8 for
discussion of the adage)
  1 This information is drawn from Diogenianus.

547 *Adagia* I vi 48 As rude as any Libethrian (*Inelegantior Libethriis*). The source
of the Greek version, present in *1500*, is Diogenianus 2.26. Erasmus follows
fairly closely the interpretation in Diogenianus, but the text is probably corrupt. Libethrion is a mountainous region in Thrace, and the proverb refers to
those who live there, not to the mountain itself. See n1.
  1 In the sources other than Diogenianus (Zenobius 1.79, Zenobius Athous 3.1)
there is no mention of a mountain. Instead they refer to a people called the
Libethrians, and this is clearly correct.

548 *Adagia* I iii 72
  1 Erasmus *Apophthegmata* 5.89 CWE 38 481. Archelaus was king of Mace-
donia. The story is in Plutarch (*Moralia* 177B), but Erasmus' immediate
source is Francesco Filelfo's Latin translation of Plutarch (see ASD II-9 205:
540n).

549 *Adagia* I ix 20. The source is Diogenianus 1.67, the Greek being added in *1506*.
  1 The point, as Diogenianus tells us, is that an eagle cannot be captured in the
clouds.

550 **Vulpes non accipit munera / Ἀλώπηξ οὐ δωροδοκεῖται / A fox takes
no bribes**

A Greek adage directed at those who are extremely greedy but are very
reluctant to accept gifts that are offered them. It is as if they take them
unwillingly and are forced to do so.

551 **Scitum est periculum ex aliis facere / It is shrewd to profit from
others' mishaps**

This means to become more prudent by drawing on what has happened
to others. This is how Terence expressed it.[1] Plautus, in different words:
'Happy is he who learns at another's cost.'[2]

552 **Annus est / A whole year has gone by**

This is a proverb of exaggeration by which we indicate a very protracted
delay. Terence in *The Mother-in-Law*: 'You know what women are like. While
they get ready, while they adorn themselves, a whole year has gone by!'[1]
We can say this with reference to anyone who is always unpunctual.

553 **In tempore adire omnium est maximum / To come at the right time
is the most important thing of all**

If you want someone to grant a request, the time when you make an approach is extremely important.

554 **Dies aegritudinem adimit / Time tempers grief**

* * * * *

550 *Adagia* I x 18. The Greek, present in *1500*, is from Diogenianus 2.18. Also
Zenobius 1.71 and *Suda* A 1391.

551 Not in the *Adagia* in this form, but cf II iii 39 It is best to profit by another
man's madness. Here starts another series of adages taken from Terence (see
C 530n). This runs from C 551 to C 572, excluding C 555.
  1 Terence *Heautontimorumenos* 210
  2 The line appears in a spurious scene added in the Renaissance to Plautus'
Mercator; see L. Braun, *Scenae suppositiciae* (Göttingen 1980) 194 line 73, but
here Erasmus probably draws it directly from Poliziano *Miscellanea* 9 (1.233
Maier). Erasmus also cites it in *Adagia* I i 31 and II ix 71. It is medieval in
origin; L. Walther *Lateinische Sprichwörter des Mittelalters* no 8927.

552 *Adagia* II v 4. Otto 115
  1 Terence *Heautontimorumenos* 239–40 (not from *Hecyra*). Erasmus follows a different text (*comuntur* 'adorn themselves') from that printed in modern editions
(*conantur* 'try to get ready').

553 Not in *Adagia*. It is based on Terence *Heautontimorumenos* 364–5.

554 *Adagia* II v 5. Polydore Vergil 71; Otto 535

Terence: 'Either I was born for misery, or there is no truth in what I commonly hear men say, that time tempers grief.'[1]

555 Asinum sub freno currere doces / You teach a donkey to race with the bit

That is, you are wasting your time. Horace: 'You would be wasting your time, poor fellow. It's as if one were trying to teach a donkey to be a racehorse, obeying the bit.'[1] Acron indicates that this is a proverbial saying about donkeys.[2]

556 Provinciam capere. Tradere provinciam / To take over a province. To hand over a province

Both of these are drawn from the Roman practice of magistrates drawing lots for their provinces. Terence in *The Self-Tormentor*: 'That slave of Clinias is clearly rather slow. That's why the province has been handed over to this man of ours.'[1] He means that the task of organizing the deception has been given to his slave. Terence in *Phormio*: 'O Geta, that's a difficult province you have taken over,' meaning that he has taken on an onerous task.[2] Menander, as quoted in Gellius about the husband of a bossy wife: 'You have a quite unmanageable province.'[3] The Greek for this is πρᾶγμα ἄμαχον λέγεις.[4]

557 Bolus ereptus e faucibus / A morsel snatched from one's jaws

We say that a morsel is snatched from our throat whenever some gain that was almost within our grasp is suddenly and unexpectedly snatched

* * * * *

1 Terence *Heautontimorumenos* 420–2

555 *Adagia* I iv 40. Otto 181
  1 Horace *Satires* 1.1.90–1
  2 Pseudo-Acron on Horace *Satires* 1.1.88

556 *Adagia* II iv 41
  1 Terence *Heautontimorumenos* 514–16
  2 Terence *Phormio* 72–3
  3 Erasmus is being misleading here, since there is no mention of a province or anything similar in Menander. The proverb is in fact drawn from Theodore Gaza's Latin translation of a fragment of Menander (fragment 334.6 Körte-Thierfelder) that Aulus Gellius cites at *Noctes Atticae* 2.23.12; see C 6 n1 and C 31 n2.
  4 This sentence was added in 1506, without the Greek being translated. The literal sense of the Greek phrase, taken from Menander by way of Aulus Gellius (see n3), is 'you tell of something you cannot contend with.'

557 *Adagia* III vi 99. In the Latin form of the proverb the sense is 'throat' rather than 'jaws.' Otto 257

away. Calphurnius thinks that this saying is a metaphor drawn from animals that have lost their prey. Terence in *The Self-Tormentor*: 'It tortures me that such a morsel has been snatched so suddenly from my jaws.'[1]

558 Quid si nunc caelum ruat? / What if the heavens should fall now?

This refers to those who are fearful by nature and think that everything that is worse will come to pass. Terence in *The Self-Tormentor*: 'What if I return to those who say "What if the heavens should fall now?"'[1]

559 Dictum ac factum / Said and done

When we mean that nothing has been overlooked in attending to some task we say 'Said and done.' Terence: 'I have carried it out, said and done.' The same author in the same play: 'Clitipho went in here, said and done.'[1]

560 Summum ius summa malitia / Extreme right is extreme wrong

To avoid the charge that I am gathering together maxims instead of proverbs I would not have included this saying if it were not explicitly named as an adage by a slave in comedy: 'But it is true what they say, Chremes. "Extreme right is often extreme wrong."'[1] This proverb advises us to do what is equitable rather than follow the letter of the law.

561 Quod abs te allatum erat, id est relatum / Whatever you brought will be given back to you

This appears in the prologue of *Phormio*.[1] Donatus tells us that it is a

* * * * *

1 Terence *Heautontimorumenos* 673 and Johannes Calphurnius' comment on the line. For Calphurnius see c 501 n1 above.

558 *Adagia* I v 64. Otto 286
1 Terence *Heautontimorumenos* 719

559 *Adagia* III vi 85. Otto 529
1 Terence *Heautontimorumenos* 760 and 904. The sense in the second passage is closer to 'no sooner said than done,' referring to the speed with which something is carried out.

560 *Adagia* I x 25 (with slightly different wording). Cf c 335. Polydore Vergil 110; Otto 884
1 Terence *Heautontimorumenos* 795–6

561 This does not appear in the *Adagia* as a separate entry, but it is quoted at *Adagia* I i 35 To render like for like.
1 Terence *Phormio* 21 and the commentary of Donatus on the line

proverb; it is clearly directed at those who pay in kind for the evil they
have done. It seems to derive from moneylending.

562 Tradunt operas mutuas / They help each other out

This was customarily said of those who protect or praise each other. It occurs
in *Phormio*.[1] It seems to have been taken from craftsmen or neighbouring
farmers who help each other out.

**563 Ne in nervum erumpat fortitudo / I fear your courage may break
a string**

This is said of those who are rash and thoughtlessly bold, a trait that generally leads to great trouble. Donatus thinks that it is taken from archers,
who sometimes break a bowstring by drawing it back to an excessive degree. Terence in *Phormio*: 'But I often fear this, Phormio, that your courage
may in the end break a string.'[1]

564 Pedum visa est via / That path has been seen

Taken from travellers who travel more safely on pathways with which they
are familiar. Similarly, we are more adventurous in those activities in which
we have previously engaged. Terence in *Phormio*: 'Ah, not so. We have done
that. That path has already been seen.'[1]

**565 Rete non tenditur accipitri aut miluo / A net is not spread for a kite
or a hawk**

No one brings trumped-up charges against pettifoggers. Rather, trickery
is used against naive persons who do not know how to deceive, and can
therefore be deceived. In the same play:

> Because a net is not spread for a kite or a hawk.
> These birds can harm us. It is spread for those who are harmless.[1]

* * * * *

562 *Adagia* I vii 97. Cf Otto 1162.
1 Terence *Phormio* 267

563 *Adagia* II vi 36. Polydore Vergil 272; Otto 1222
1 Terence *Phormio* 324–5 and Donatus on line 324

564 *Adagia* III v 55. Otto 1891
1 Terence *Phormio* 326

565 Cited at *Adagia* III v 73, but not given an entry of its own. Cf c 149. Otto
446
1 Terence *Phormio* 330–1

566 Amico amicus / A friend to his friend

'This fellow is unique as a friend to a friend.' Donatus points out that this is a proverb.[1] Said of those who are in no way false friends. It appears in Apollodorus, who wrote the Greek version of *Phormio*, in this way: Μόνος ἐπίσταται φιλεῖν τοὺς φίλους 'He alone knows how to love his friends.'[2]

567 Ipsa senectus morbus est / Old age itself is sickness

Old men are never free of illness. Horace: 'Many good things advancing years will bring, many they remove as they recede.'[1] Apollodorus expresses this in Greek in these words: Τὸ γῆράς ἐστιν αὐτὸ νόσημα.[2]

568 Sudabis satis / You will break a good sweat to no avail

These words indicate in a proverbial way a pointless undertaking. Terence in *Phormio*: 'Ah! You will break a good sweat to no avail if you tangle with that fellow.'[1]

569 Vorsuram solvis / You pay off a loan with a loan

This is said of someone who manages to extricate himself from a predicament he is facing, but does so in such a way that he will create even more serious trouble for himself from another source. Donatus says that *vorsuram facere* means 'to pay a debt by taking on additional debt' or 'to borrow money at a high rate and invest it at a lower one.'[1] Terence in *Phormio*:

* * * * *

566 *Adagia* I iii 17. The source is Terence *Phormio* 562. Otto 97
 1 Terence *Phormio* 562. Donatus' commentary gives in full the Greek original of the Latin words but there is no mention of the expression being proverbial in modern editions. Its identification as such rests on an intrusive gloss (παροιμία 'proverb') in Erasmus' text of Donatus. The Greek is present in *1500*.
 2 PCG 2 Apollodorus of Carystus fragment 23. The title of the Greek original was *Epidikazomenos*.

567 *Adagia* II vi 37. Drawn from Terence *Phormio* 575. Otto 1623
 1 Horace *Ars poetica* 175–6
 2 PCG 2 Apollodorus of Carystus fragment 24, cited by Donatus on Terence *Phormio* 575

568 Not in *Adagia*
 1 Terence *Phormio* 628–9

569 *Adagia* I x 23. The source is Terence *Phormio* 780. See Otto 994.
 1 Donatus on Terence *Phormio* 780. Erasmus' interpretation of the proverb that it refers to someone's situation going from bad to worse is based on a corruption at this point in contemporary editions of Donatus. The sense of Donatus' explanation, in the text as emended by Robert Estienne in his edition (Paris 1529), is actually 'to borrow money at a low rate and invest it at a higher one,' the very opposite of the meaning of the corrupt text.

'You are stuck in the same mud.[2] You will pay a loan by another loan. Your present problem has gone for the moment, but the burden increases.'[3] Seneca: 'Paying loans by other loans begins at home, as they say.'[4]

570 Animam debet / He owes his own soul

This suits a person who is in the grip of excessive debts. Terence: 'What if he owes his own soul?' Donatus also give the Greek form of the proverb: Τὴν ψυχὴν ὀφείλει.[1]

571 Eodem in ludo docti sunt / They were taught in the same school

Even today this is a common saying, directed at those who are extremely alike in how they behave.[1]

572 Suo sorex indicio periit / The shrew-mouse gave itself away

This relates to a person who has given himself away, like Parmeno in *The Eunuch*.[1] Jerome: 'He who is angry and writes back in response will be betrayed, like a mouse, by his own revelation.'[2]

573 Quodcunque in solum venis / On whatever ground you fall

Cicero *On the Nature of the Gods* book one: 'For all these matters you make use of the lawless rule of atoms. From these you fashion and produce ... "On whatever ground you fall," as they say.'[1]

* * * * *

2 See C 44.
3 Terence *Phormio* 780–1
4 Seneca *De beneficiis* 5.8.3

570 *Adagia* I x 24; cf *Adagia* IV ix 20. Polydore Vergil 199; Otto 109
  1 Terence *Phormio* 661 and Donatus' commentary on it. Erasmus follows the text of early editions for the Greek version. The sense of the text printed in modern editions is 'He [Terence] spurned the Greek proverb εἰ δὲ ὤφειλε τὰς χεῖρας "what if he owes his *hands*?"'

571 *Adagia* II viii 50. Drawn from Terence *Hecyra* 203. Otto 975
  1 Suringar 67

572 *Adagia* I iii 65. The last of the series of adages drawn from Terence. Otto 1676
  1 Terence *Eunuchus* 1024, the source of the proverb, which Parmeno applies to himself
  2 Jerome *Letters* 133.11.6 CSEL 56.258

573 *Adagia* III vi 3. Otto 1671
  1 Cicero *De natura deorum* 1.23.65. Erasmus' text differs from the one found in modern editions. The correct text reads *venit* for *venis*. The meaning is then 'whatever falls to the ground,' being the object of 'fashion and produce.' Erasmus gives the correct form in the *Adagia*. Cicero is talking about the Epicurean theory of atoms in relation to the nature and existence of the gods.

574 **Mancipii capillus / Ἀνδραποδώδης θρίξ / A slave-haircut**
This is said of harsh-minded men. When we wish to indicate that someone
has a rough, uncivilized, and boorish disposition, we say that he has a slave-
haircut. Plato writes that such men have a slave-haircut mind.[1]

575 **Lac gallinaceum** *seu* Γάλα ὀρνίθων. **Lac gallinarum / Hen's milk**
A Greek adage referring to something extremely rare. When we mean that
some object or other contains absolutely everything, even something that does
not actually exist, we say that even hen's milk could be drunk from it. Pliny:
'Other writers call their works "Amalthea's horn," meaning a horn of plenty,
as if one may expect to find a draught of hen's milk from their volumes.'[1]

576 **Suspendio arbor deligenda / Choose your tree and hang yourself**
When we indicate that something is very shameful and quite intolerable
we say that one should choose a tree and hang oneself. The Elder Pliny
writes that this adage came from an attack on Theophrastus, the prince of
philosophers, that a courtesan named Leontium dared to write. This is what
Pliny says on this matter: 'As if I do not know that a mere woman vilified
Theophrastus (a man of such eloquence that he achieved an immortal reputation for it), and that this gave rise to a proverb that one should choose a
tree and hang oneself.'[1]

577 **Minervae felem / Minerva against a cat**
Directed at those who match inferior things with much superior ones simply because they agree in one slight detail. For what does Minerva have in

* * * * *

574 *Adagia* II iii 28. Diogenianus 1.73 is the source for the Greek version (present
   in *1500*) and the information about Plato.
 1 Plato *Alcibiades* 120B, referred to in Diogenianus 1.73

575 *Adagia* I vi 3. In the *Adagia* the interpretation of the proverb is different, being
   based on Apostolius 5.19. In the *Collectanea* Erasmus draws from Diogenianus
   3.92 for the Greek version, present in *1500*, and for the interpretation given in
   the first sentence of the commentary. The saying occurs in Poliziano *Epistolae*
   11.2 (1.148 Maier) and Perotti's letter to Guarnieri (*Cornucopiae* 1046:23–4). It
   is also used by Ascensius (Josse Bade) in his commentary on Persius 5.144–5.
   Polydore Vergil 233; Otto 748
 1 Pliny *Naturalis historia* praefatio 24. For 'Amalthea's horn' see C 497.

576 *Adagia* I x 21. Polydore Vergil 248; Otto 1722.
 1 Pliny *Naturalis historia* praefatio 29. The name of the courtesan comes from
   Ermolao Barbaro's *Castigationes Plinianae* (Pozzi 22).

577 *Adagia* I x 22, where Erasmus informs his readers that they must understand
   'you match' to understand the expression.

common with a cat other than the grey-green colour of their eyes? In Greek the proverb is Ἀθηνῇ τὸν αἴλουρον.[1]

578 **Attici Eleusinia (*subaudi* 'celebrant') / The Athenians their Eleusinia (*understanding* 'celebrate')**
This is said of something that is terribly secret and must be kept concealed. For among the Athenians it was a capital offence to reveal the mysteries of Ceres of Eleusis. This gave rise to a proverb applied to anything kept secret, Ἀττικοὶ Ἐλευσίνια,[1] meaning that only the Athenians celebrate (for this is the verb that is to be understood) the Eleusinia.

579 **Sal unde venerat rediit / Ἀλῶν δὲ φόρτος ἔνθεν ἦλθεν ἔνθ' ἔβη / Salt to water whence it came**
This is a Greek proverb, taken from what happened to a certain merchant. When he received a cargo of salt as a gift and was shipping it, the level of the bilge-water in the ship rose to such an extent that, while the merchant was sleeping, it got into the salt, completely dissolving and ruining it. And so what had been derived from seawater as a result of evaporation returned to the sea to be dissolved again in it. Very similar in meaning is what Plautus says: 'Ill gotten, ill spent.'[1]

580 **Lari sacrificare / Ἑστίᾳ θύειν / To sacrifice to the Lar**
This means to do something in a very secret way. It was forbidden for anyone to remove anything from such sacrifices out of the house.

581 **Cantharus aquilam quaerit / A dung-beetle seeks out an eagle**
An adage taken from a fable.[1] A dung-beetle pushed an eagle's eggs out of its nest to avenge the contempt the eagle had shown it. The saying suits

* * * * *

1 The Greek version, present in *1500*, is from Diogenianus 2.37, but Erasmus gives an erroneous form αἴρουλον for 'cat,' instead of αἴλουρον. This reflects an error in his manuscript of Diogenianus (see 7 and 10 n23 above). The proverb can be found also in Zenobius 2.25 and *Suda* A 726.

578 *Adagia* II v 66
1 The Greek version, present in *1500*, from Diogenianus 2.38; also Zenobius 2.26

579 *Adagia* I vii 80. The Greek version of the proverb (Diogenianus 2.34 and Zenobius 2.20) was added in *1506*.
1 Plautus *Poenulus* 844, which becomes *Adagia* I vii 82

580 *Adagia* I ix 43 and C 330. The Greek, literally 'to sacrifice to Hestia,' was added in *1506*. Diogenianus 2.40 and 4.68. Also Zenobius 4.44 and *Suda* E 3214

581 *Adagia* III vii 1 (greatly expanded in *1515* into one of Erasmus' most famous essays in the *Adagia*)
1 *Aesopica* no 3 Perry

those who are angered by some wrong they have suffered and prepare to exact punishment in return. The Greek form of the proverb is Ἀετὸν κάνθαρος μαιεύεται.[2]

582 Pastillos Rufillus olet, Gorgonius hircum / Rufillus smells of lozenges, Gorgonius reeks of billy-goat
Individual sayings of famous poets can be used as proverbs, but nothing has a more proverbial air than this verse of Horace.[1] It is directed at men suffering from opposite vices, for example a man who hardly says a word and a man who never stops talking, someone who is very jovial even at inappropriate times and someone who is very austere, a miser and a spendthrift, a proud man and one who lacks spirit and is excessively modest.

583 Capra Syra / Αἲξ Σκυρία / A Syrian she-goat
This suits those who taint their fine achievements by the addition of some flaw and who have a sorry ending to a good beginning in what they do. This is like a Syrian [*Syra*] she-goat that fills its pail with milk, then knocks it over; in this way it undoes the good service that it has rendered.

584 Canis per phratoras ductus / Ἀγόμενος διὰ φρατόρων κύων / A dog brought before the phratry-members
This was customarily applied to those who finally pay the penalty for their crimes. The Phratores are peoples who immediately kill dogs that are brought before them.

585 Inexperta aut expers nuptiarum / Ἀγνὴ γάμων / A stranger to wedlock
In its literal sense this refers to women who are pure and unwed. Fig-

* * * * *

2 The Greek means 'a dung-beetle plays midwife to an eagle,' and Erasmus has mistranslated the verb, confusing it with μαίεται 'seeks out'; see CWE 35 180 nn1–2. It is taken from Diogenianus 2.44, being present in *1500*. See also Zenobius 1.20.

582 *Adagia* II ix 48
1 Horace *Satires* 1.2.27

583 *Adagia* I x 20. In both editions of the *Collectanea* the proverb is given as *capra Syra* 'A Syrian she-goat' even though the correct Greek version, with Σκυρία 'A Scyrian she-goat,' appears in both *1500* and *1506*. *Syra* looks like a printer's error that was not caught until the *Adagia*. The source is Diogenianus 2.33.

584 *Adagia* III vi 93. Erasmus does not understand the sense of *phratores*, who were members of a phratry, a sub-division of the Athenian tribal structure. He corrects his error at *Adagia* III vi 93 in *1515*. The source of the Greek version, present in *1500*, is Diogenianus 2.45.

uratively, it refers to shameless women who engage every day in sexual congress, though unmarried. Cicero says of these, 'Her mother takes delight in daily consummation.'[1]

586 Cum larvis luctari / To wrestle with ghosts

This means to revile the dead and find fault with the writings of those who are buried.

587 Cum mortuis non nisi larvae luctantur / Only ghosts wrestle with the dead.

Pliny the Elder in his preface: 'When Plancus heard that Asinius Pollio was working on speeches against him that were to be published by him or his children after Plancus' death so that he would be unable to reply, Plancus wittily remarked that only phantoms wrestle with the dead. With these words he dealt Pollio and his family such a blow that in scholarly circles they were thought to be the most shameless of persons.'[1]

588 Mola salsa litant qui thura non habent / Those who have not incense offer salted spelt to the gods

It is proper to respect and honour any offering however small, if given sincerely. Pliny in the same preface: 'I know that even those who greet you approach you with great trepidation. For you have attained the highest pinnacles of human achievement and are endowed with great eloquence and learning. For that reason they are extremely anxious that what is dedicated to you befits you. But peasants and many peoples who have no incense pray to the gods with offerings of milk and offer only salted spelt.'[1]

* * * * *

585 *Adagia* II ix 26. The Greek version of the title, present in *1500*, is drawn from Diogenianus 2.46. The Latin version is based on Horace *Carmina* 3.11.11.
   1 *Rhetorica ad Herennium* 4.34.45. This work was commonly ascribed to Cicero in the Renaissance. Raffaele Regio (see C 395 n2) had challenged the ascription in a short tract published in 1492.

586 *Adagia* I ii 53. This is a shorter version of the adage that immediately follows. Otto 1147

587 Cited in *Adagia* I ii 53. It occurs in a letter of Filippo Beroaldo (Poliziano *Epistolae* 6.2; 1.76 Maier), where Beroaldo is concerned with how he should respond to the attacks of Giorgio Merula, now that he has just died. Polydore Vergil 5; Otto 1147
   1 Pliny *Naturalis historia* praefatio 31. Erasmus' text differs somewhat from that in modern editions.

588 Not in *Adagia*; Otto 1128
   1 Pliny *Naturalis historia* praefatio 11

589 Murus aheneus / A wall of bronze

This is found in book one of Horace's *Epistles* in the sense of a sure and immutable resolve: 'Let this be your wall of bronze, to have a conscience clear, and have no guilt to make you blanch.'[1]

590 Quo teneam vultus mutantem Protea nodo? / With what knot can I bind the ever-changing Proteus?

These are splendid words of Horace,[1] directed at persons who continually change their minds. According to a very well-known myth Proteus was in the habit of transforming himself into all kinds of things to escape his chains.[2]

591 Syncerum est nisi vas, quodcumque infundis acescit / Whatever you pour in a dirty pot turns sour

This is an apophthegm of the same author.[1] It suits those whose folly turns their blessings into misfortune or those who misapply good and sensible advice and encounter disaster and destruction. This is the view of Epictetus, whose words directed at a philosopher of bad character are cited in Gellius: 'Consider, fellow, whether the vessel in which you store these topics is clean. For if you pour them into an empty head, they are lost. If they are spoiled, they will turn into piss or vinegar, or something worse if that is possible.'[2]

592 Quo semel est imbuta recens, servabit odorem testa diu / Long will a pot retain the taste of what was placed within it when it was new

'So important it is to instil good habits in the young.'[1]

* * * * *

589 *Adagia* II x 25. A series of adages drawn from Horace (down to C 602, but excluding C 596 and C 597) begins here.
　1 Horace *Epistles* 1.1.60–1

590 Cf *Adagia* II ii 74. Otto 1478
　1 Horace *Epistles* 1.1.90. Pseudo-Acron commenting on the passage calls this a proverb.
　2 The most famous accounts of Proteus' ability to take on different appearances occur in Homer's *Odyssey* book 4, where Menelaus tells of his encounter with this sea god (lines 450–570), and in Virgil *Georgics* book 4, where Aristaeus also has to subdue the god (lines 437–46) to extract information.

591 Not in *Adagia* as a separate entry but cited in I i 2 (CWE 31 40). Otto 1849
　1 Horace *Epistles* 1.2.54.
　2 Gellius *Noctes Atticae* 17.19.3, where the quotation is given only in Greek. Early editions gave a Latin translation of all Greek passages (see C 6 n1), and this is what Erasmus uses here, giving no Greek at all. See Erasmus *Apophthegmata* 7.286 CWE 38 837.

592 *Adagia* II iv 20. The adage is drawn from Horace *Epistles* 1.2.69–70. Otto 1770
　1 Virgil *Georgics* 2.272

593 Cornix furtivis plumis exornata *vel* Cornix alienis plumis superbit / The crow decked out with stolen plumage *or* The crow prides itself in plumage not its own

This was taken from a fable[1] and has been proverbial for some time. Horace: 'When flock of birds come perchance to claim their feathers, / Let not the poor crow inspire laughter / When stripped of its colours.'[2] This suits those who claim the discoveries of others as their own and thereby promote themselves.

594 Corpus sine pectore / Body without soul

This refers to a boorish and coarse man lacking intelligence. Horace to Albius: 'You were not a body without soul. The gods had given you good looks and riches, and the art to enjoy them.'[1]

595 Cerite cera digni / Worthy to be registered in Caere

Those who deserved to be publicly disgraced were said to be worthy of being registered in Caere. According to Acron and Porphyrion the reason for this is that when the Romans had defeated Caere in war they imposed sanctions: the citizens of Caere did not have the right to vote and they could not make or possess any laws of their own. This gave rise to a well-known proverb whereby ignominy was referred to as the register of Caere. Horace: 'They are oblivious of what is right and what is not, fit for the Caere register.'[1]

596 Aranearum telam texere / To spin spiders' webs

This is to expend endless labour on something that is frivolous and worthless. It is found in Basil at the beginning of his *Hexameron*.[1]

597 Utramque paginam facit / She fills both pages

Pliny the Elder in his *Natural History* book two chapter seven, talking of

* * * * *

593 Cf *Adagia* III vi 91 Aesop's jackdaw. Otto 64
  1 *Aesopica* 101 Perry; Phaedrus 1.3. Pseudo-Acron (on Horace *Epistles* 1.3.18–20) identifies the source as a fable of Aesop's.
  2 Horace *Epistles* 1.3.18–20

594 *Adagia* I x 80. Otto 1365
  1 Horace *Epistles* 1.4.6–7

595 *Adagia* I x 81
  1 Horace *Epistles* 1.6.62–3. The explanation comes from the commentaries of Pseudo-Acron and Porphyrion on the passage.

596 *Adagia* I iv 47 (with the plural form *telas* for the singular here). Otto 151 and Otto *Nachträge* p 96
  1 Basil *Homiliae in Hexameron* 1.2 PG 29 8B

597 *Adagia* II iv 15

the goddess Fortune, says, 'To her all expense is debited, to her all that is received is credited. In their reckoning of all that happens, mortals believe she alone fills both pages.'[1] The meaning is that whenever something good befalls mortals, they praise Fortune as if she is responsible; whenever something bad happens, they rail at her as if she is the source of all misfortune.

598 Ulyssis remigium / Ulysses' crew

Said of weak and debauched men, like the comrades of Ulysses.[1] They could not abstain from the drinks that Circe offered them nor could they resist the singing of the Sirens.

599 Ab ovo usque ad mala / From the eggs to apples

This is another way of referring to a whole banquet; for the ancients began a feast with eggs and finished it with dessert. Horace in his third satire: 'If it pleased him, he would shout out "O Bacchus" from egg to apples.'[1]

600 Neglectis urenda filix innascitur agris / Neglected fields beget fern that must be burned away

Taken from the same satire.[1] A splendid metaphor, whose meaning is the following: vices naturally grow of their own accord within us unless they are weeded out by noble pursuits, just as uncultivated land is overrun by fern, a useless plant.

601 Balbinum polypus Agnae delectat / Balbinus loves the polyp on Agna's nose

This suits a person who is blinded by zeal and love, and praises with admiration a fault as a virtue. Even the polyp on Agna's nose was attractive to Balbinus, her lover. Horace: 'Unsightly faults deceive the

*****

1 Pliny *Naturalis historia* 2.22

598 *Adagia* II x 62
  1 Drawn from Horace *Epistles* 1.6.63. Erasmus' brief commentary is taken from Porphyrion's. Strictly speaking, Ulysses did not allow his crew to hear the Sirens, as he filled their ears with wax.

599 *Adagia* II iv 86. Otto 1319
  1 Horace *Satires* 1.3.6–7

600 *Adagia* II ix 97. Otto 661
  1 Horace *Satires* 1.3.37. Erasmus' comments are similar to those in the commentary of Cristoforo Landino (see 12 above).

601 This is cited in *Adagia* I ii 15 What is one's own is beautiful (= C 297).

blind or even give pleasure, like the polyp on Agna's nose that delights Balbinus.'[1]

602 **Qui ne tuberibus propriis offendat amicum Postulat ignoscet verrucis illius / Who his friend's pardon for his boils demands, 'Tis fair that his friend's warts he should forgive.**
Whoever wishes his own considerable faults to be forgiven should put up with the lesser faults of others.

603 **Cygnaea cantilena / Κύκνειον ᾆσμα / Swan-song**
Often said of those who manage to speak for the last time at the point of death. For swans are said to sing when they are dying. Jerome: 'They sang some kind of swan-song when death was near.'[1] He is speaking about poets who have reached old age; the closer they are to death, the more sweetly they sound in their works.

604 **Communis Mercurius / Κοινὸς Ἑρμῆς / Share Mercury**
This is said of the proceeds of theft. Mercury, the patron of stealing, taught that all should share in these.

605 **Mali corvi malum ovum nascitur / Κακοῦ κόρακος κακὸν ᾠὸν ἔφυ / A bad egg comes from a bad crow**
The sense is that bad parents produce a bad son, or an ignorant teacher produces an ignorant pupil. Gellius[1] tells us that bystanders called this out

* * * * *

1 Horace *Satires* 1.3.39–40. The correct name is Hagna rather than Agna, a variant in the manuscript tradition.

602 Not in *Adagia* as an independent entry, but quoted at *Adagia* I vi 91. This is drawn from Horace (*Satires* 1.3.73–4) and is the last of the Horatian series that begins at C 589.

603 *Adagia* I ii 55. The Greek version of the title (from Diogenianus 5.37) was added in *1506*. This adage marks the beginning of a series drawn from Diogenianus, running to C 651 (excluding C 629 and C 631).
1 Jerome *Letters* 52.3.5 CSEL 54 418. Otto 497

604 *Adagia* II i 85. The Greek version of the adage (from Diogenianus 5.38) was added in *1506*.

605 *Adagia* I ix 25. The source of the Greek version, present in *1500*, is Diogenianus 5.39, but the disputants are not named (see n1).
1 Gellius *Noctes Atticae* 5.10.3–15, though there Gellius is referring to a dispute between Protagoras and his pupil Euathlus, and says nothing about this adage. Corax and Ctesias, named here by Erasmus, were involved in a similar dispute. The names given by Zenobius 4.82, who also refers to the origin of the

when Corax and Ctesias were in a dispute, and were using the same argument against each other, the argument being 'convertible.'[2]

606 Sacram movere ancoram / Κινεῖν τὴν ἀφ' ἱερᾶς / To move the sheet-anchor. To move the counter from the sacred line
This means to use extreme measures and to leave nothing untried. For in antiquity the heaviest anchor was called 'sacred' and this was dropped only in extreme danger.[1]

607 Cassioticus nodus / Κασσιωτικὸν ἅμμα / The Cassius knot
This was applied to clever and crooked men. The people of Cassius[1] are said to have invented certain knots that were very difficult to disentangle.

* * * * *

adage, are Corax and Teisias. It is doubtful, however, whether Erasmus had access to Zenobius for the 1500 edition of his *Collectanea*. He may have been drawing the names from Perotti's *Cornucopiae* (966:1ff) or Quintilian 1.7.17. In the *Adagia* Erasmus cites as his source for the story of Corax and Tisias (he gives the correct name there) the introduction to the *Rhetoric* of Hermogenes (actually Sopatros' commentary on that work; see *Rhetores graeci* ed C. Walz 5 [Leipzig 1833] 6–7, and 154.25).

2 The chapter in Gellius *Noctes Atticae* deals with arguments that in Greek were described as ἀντιστρέφοντα and were called *reciproca* 'convertible' in Latin. These are arguments that could be turned advantageously against the one who first used them. In this particular case a pupil was refusing to pay the fees that he had promised he would pay when he first won a case in court. The teacher went to court to get the money. The teacher said that if the court found against his pupil, the pupil would have to pay. If, however, the court found against the teacher, his pupil would still have to pay since he would have won his first case. The pupil's answer was that if the jury found in his favour, he would not have to pay the fees. If the court gave a verdict against him, he also would not have to pay since he had not won a case.

606 Cf *Adagia* I i 24 and I i 25. In *1500* the adage appeared as *Sacra movere*, literally 'To move sacred things,' without a Greek version, which was added in *1506* (from Diogenianus 5.41, with τήν, as in Bodley Grabe 30, for τόν in the rest of the tradition). The Greek title, is in fact the equivalent of *Adagia* I i 25 I will move the counter from the sacred line. This is different, however, from 'To move the sheet-anchor.'
1 This second sentence was added in *1506*, and seems to have been drawn from *Suda* K 1642.

607 *Adagia* II v 34. The Greek version (from Diogenianus 5.44) was added in *1506*. Also *Suda* K 454
1 A town in Egypt, as Erasmus explains at *Adagia* II v 34

608 **Colophonia contumelia** / Κολοφωνεία ὕβρις / **Colophonian wantonness**
Used of powerful men who treat the poor unjustly. Plato in his letter to
Dionysius: 'To all of your promises, most honourable sire, you applied the
Colophonian vote, as they say, and renounced them in a most glorious way.'[1]

609 **Ventis secundis navigat** / Κατὰ ῥοῦν φέρεται / **He sails
with a fair wind**
Often said of those enjoying good fortune.

610 **In aqua scribere** / Καθ᾽ ὕδατος γράφειν / **To write on water**
The meaning is to take on a useless task.

611 **Camelus vel scabiosa multorum asinorum portat onera** / Κάμηλος
καὶ ψωριῶσα πολλῶν ὄνων ἀνατίθεται φορτία / **Even a mangy camel
bears the load of many donkeys**
Often used of those old men who, despite their age, are much stronger than
many young ones.

612 **Cretensis contra Aeginitam** / Κρῆς πρὸς Αἰγινίτην / **A Cretan against an
Aeginetan**
The meaning is that one rogue is dealing with another one. For both Cretans
and Aeginetans are liars and tricksters.[1]

613 **Pedetentim** / Κατὰ ποδὸς βάσιν / **One step at a time**

* * * * *

608 *Adagia* II i 13. The Greek version (from Diogenianus 5.79) was added in 1506.
Cf c 680 n1.
1 Plato *Letters* 3.318B, which Erasmus cites only in Latin (see c 2 n7). This passage, not really appropriate here, is referred to in *Adagia* III x 82 The Colophonian vote.

609 Cf *Adagia* II v 16 With a fair wind. A Greek version of the adage (from Diogenianus, seemingly 5.82) was added in 1506, but in a corrupt form: κατὰ νοιν
φέρεται for κατὰ ῥοῦν φέρεται 'He is carried by a following tide,' ῥοῦν or ῥόον,
meaning 'tide' or 'current' (see *Adagia* II v 15). Clearly, there is a discrepancy
with the Latin version, which refers to favourable winds. The Greek form of
Adagia II v 16 is Ἐξ οὐρίου φέρεσθαι 'To be carried by a fair wind,' and is based
on *Suda* E 1818.

610 *Adagia* I iv 56. The Greek version (from Diogenianus 5.83) was added in 1506.
Otto 135

611 *Adagia* I ix 58. The Greek version (from Diogenianus 5.81) was added in 1506.

612 *Adagia* I ii 27. The Greek version (from Diogenianus 5.92) was added in 1506.
1 Cf c 151 and c 650 for Cretans, c 682 for Aeginetans.

613 *Adagia* II i 2. The Greek (from Diogenianus 5.95) was given in 1500. Otto 1372

Taken from those who walk on ice with caution. Terence: 'May the gods grant you success in what you do, but do it one step at a time.'[1] He means that one should proceed gradually and gently.

614 Cancer leporem venatur / Καρκίνος λαγωὸν αἱρεῖ. *Item* **lupus ovem servat / The crab pursues the hare.** *And* **the wolf guards the sheep**
Both of these expressions are used of something that is quite improbable.

615 Fictiles divitiae / Κεράμειος πλοῦτος **/ Wealth made of clay**
This is said of things that are fragile and at risk, like objects that are easily destroyed.

616 Homo fictilis / Κεράμειος ἄνθρωπος **/ A man of clay**
The meaning is that a man is soft and very weak. The saying is taken from earthenware pots.

617 Invenit mali coagulum / Αὐτὸς ἀνεῦρε τοῦ κακοῦ τὴν πιτύαν **/ He found the curd of his evil**
This suits a man who pays the penalty he deserves.

618 Lepus dormiens / Λαγὼς καθεύδων *vel* **Leporis somnus / A hare asleep** *or* **The sleep of a hare**
This fits perfectly a man who is pretending to be doing what he is not doing

* * * * *

1 Terence *Phormio* 552

614 The first of these adages becomes (with a slight change of wording) *Adagia* II iv 78. The Greek version, added in *1506*, comes from Diogenianus (5.96). For the second adage cf c 540 You have handed the sheep over to the wolf (= *Adagia* I iv 10). Otto 983

615 *Adagia* I x 56. The Greek, with κεράμεος (an oddity) for κεράμειος, is based on Diogenianus 5.97 and was added in *1506*, but the correct Greek form may be Κεραμέως πλοῦτος 'a potter's wealth,' as printed at ASD II-9 219.

616 *Adagia* II x 90. The Greek is based on Diogenianus 5.98 (where the text reads κεραμεὺς ἄνθρωπος 'man is a potter'), and was added in *1506*. At *Adagia* II x 90 Erasmus prints the adjective κεράμιος 'man is made of clay,' which accords better with the Latin adjective *fictilis*. The form κεράμειος is an orthographic variant.

617 *Adagia* I i 56. The Greek version, added in *1506*, is mentioned in Diogenianus 5.99, the probable source for Erasmus, although it has its own entry at Diogenianus 3.18. The word πιτύαν, meaning 'curdled milk' is far from common. The idea seems to be that a man's misdoings curdle against him. Cf c 135, of which this is a doublet.

618 *Adagia* I x 57. The source is Diogenianus 6.1, the Greek being added in *1506*. Also Zenobius 4.84 and *Suda* Λ 29

or is pretending not to do what he is doing. For it is well known that a hare sleeps with its eyes open.[1]

619 Lemnium malum / Λήμνιον κακόν / A Lemnian evil

This was applied to a sullen and unmanageable woman. For Lemnos is said to have produced an abundance of very bad women.

620 Lepus pro carnibus / Λαγὼς περὶ κρεῶν / A hare because of its meat

This saying suits those who are endangered because of their wealth or some other advantage they possess. We hunt hares not because they do us harm, like the wolf, but because they have meat we can eat.

621 Libyca fera / Λιβυκὸν θηρίον / An African beast

This was said of a crafty man, one who was shrewd, changeable, and hypocritical in his behaviour. According to Cicero, Catiline was such a monster.[1] The point of the saying is that in Libya different species of animals interbreed.[2]

622 Album suffragium / Λευκὴ ψῆφος / A white vote

This refers to a happy outcome of events; for in antiquity votes were cast with white and black pebbles. Because of this Pliny uses 'white pebble' in the sense of 'support,'[1] and Plautus says 'to insert a black pebble instead of a white one,' meaning 'to bring misfortune and harm.'[2]

* * * * *

1 See Pliny *Naturalis historia* 11.147.

619 *Adagia* I ix 27. The Greek is from Diogenianus 6.2, being added in *1506*. Also Zenobius 4.91 and *Suda* Λ 451

620 *Adagia* II i 80, where Erasmus explains that 'run risks' is to be understood. The source is Diogenianus 6.5, but the Greek version does not appear until *1506*. Also Zenobius 4.85 and *Suda* Λ 30, where the verb 'runs' appears.

621 *Adagia* III vii 8. The Greek is from Diogenianus 6.11, being added in *1506*. Cf also *Adagia* III vii 9 and 10.
  1 As at Cicero *Catilinarians* 2.1.1–2 and *Pro M. Caelio* 5.12
  2 See *Adagia* III vii 10 Africa always produces something novel, and C 46.

622 *Adagia* I v 53. The source is Diogenianus 6.9, the Greek being added in *1506*. See Otto 299, 300.
  1 Pliny *Letters* 1.2.5
  2 Plutarch (not Plautus) *Alcibiades* 22.2. Also Erasmus *Apophthegmata* 5.189 CWE 38 513

623 Lindii sacrificium / Λύνδιοι τὴν θυσίαν **/ A Lindian sacrifice**
Lactantius tells a story about how Hercules snatched two oxen by force
from a Lindian and sacrificed them.[1] The old man cursed Hercules at great
length as he was eating the animals but he simply made Hercules laugh, so
much so that Hercules said that he had never had a more enjoyable dinner. This saying can be adapted to refer either to those who sacrifice with
something they have stolen or to those who have suffered wrong but are
actually mocked by those who did them harm.

624 Linum lino copulas / Λίνῳ λίνον συνάπτεις **/ You join thread with thread**
You join what is weak with what is weak. Ctesippus in Plato's *Euthydemus*:
'Euthydemus, it is not a case of your connecting one thread to another one,
as the saying goes. It is a serious thing you say if your father is the father
of all.'[1]

625 Locrense pactum / Λοκρῶν σύνθημα **/ Locrian loyalty**
Said of treaty-breakers, which is what the Locrians are said to have been.

626 Lupi alas quaeris / Λύκου πτερὰ ζητεῖς **/ You are seeking the wings of a wolf**
In other words, you are looking for what does not exist.[1]

627 Lupus hiavit. Lupus puteum circumit / Λύκος ἔχανεν. Λύκος περὶ φρέαρ
χορεύει **/ The wolf's jaws are gaping. The wolf dances round the well**
Said of those who gape in vain at something they desire. When a hungry

* * * * *

623 *Adagia* II v 19. The Greek version, from Diogenianus 6.15, was added in *1506*.
Grammatically *Lindii* is nominative plural and *sacrificium* is accusative. A verb
meaning 'offer' or 'perform' must be understood. Cf *Adagia* III i 82 Cretans
[perform] the sacrifice.
1 Lactantius *Institutiones* 1.21.31–5

624 *Adagia* I viii 59. Diogenianus 6.16, the Greek being added in *1506*. Also Zenobius 4.96 and *Suda* Λ 566
1 Plato *Euthydemus* 298c. Erasmus quotes this in Latin (see C 2 n7).

625 *Adagia* II v 33. Diogenianus 6.17, the Greek being added in *1506*. Also Zenobius
4.97, *Suda* Λ 668, and Zenobius Athous 2.3. See Bühler 4.61–6.

626 *Adagia* I iv 81. Diogenianus 6.4, the Greek being added in *1506*. The presence of the verb ζητεῖς seems to be confined to the branch of the Diogenianus-
tradition represented by Bodley Grabe 30 (see 7 and 10 n23 above). According
to CPG 1 270 the other branches of the tradition have no verb in the proverb.
Also in *Suda* Λ 822.
1 Cf C 575 Hen's milk.

627 *Adagia* II iii 58 and II ii 76. Diogenianus 6.20 (also *Suda* L 816) and 6.21 (also
Zenobius 4.100 and *Suda* Λ 817), the Greek being added in both cases in *1506*.

wolf does not get its prey, it walks around with jaws agape. When the same animal is thirsty, it runs round a well, showing what it wants, but to no avail. 'A dog sniffing offal' has the same sense.[1]

628 Leonem tondere / Λεόντα ξυρᾶν / To shave a lion

This means to practise deceit on the powerful. Socrates in *The Republic* book one, with reference to the wild and ferocious Thrasymachus says, 'Do you think I am so mad that I would dare to shave a lion and lay a trap for Thrasymachus?'[1] To be sure, lambs are shorn with no risk, but lions are not willing to be handled in the same way.

629 Quavis incantatione melius / Better than any spell

This was said about a plan of action that was extremely effective. Plato in his *Letters*: 'For I think that, unless some important point is involved, fair and respectful letters sent by us will be more effective than any spell, as the saying goes, and will restore you to your former amity and partnership.'[1]

630 Lucernam in meridie accendere / Λύχνον ἐν μεσημβρίᾳ ἄπτειν / To light a lantern at midday

This means using something at an inappropriate time, when there is no need to do so.

631 Soli lumen inferre / To hold a candle to the sun

This means to wish to explain things that are very clear and obvious in themselves. It appears in Quintilian.[1]

632 Laconicae lunae / Λακωνικὰς σελήνας / Spartan moons

The Spartans were in the habit of postponing the making of treaties, using

* * * * *

1 *Adagia* II iv 24

628 *Adagia* II v 11. The source is Diogenianus 6.25, the Greek for both sayings being added in *1506*. Cf Otto 935.
1 Plato *Republic* 1.341C, quoted in Latin; see C 2 n7.

629 *Adagia* IV viii 19
1 Plato *Letters* 6.323B, quoted in Latin; see C 2 n7.

630 *Adagia* II v 6. Diogenianus 6.27, the Greek being added in *1506*. Also in *Suda* Λ 880. Cf Otto 1665.

631 *Adagia* II v 7. Otto 1665
1 Quintilian 5.12.8

632 *Adagia* II v 25. The Greek version, from Diogenianus 6.30 and given in the accusative case, was added in *1506*; we must understand a phrase such as 'using the pretext of.'

the phase of the moon as a pretext. This gave rise to the adage 'Spartan moons,' referring to very shaky agreements of doubtful value.

633 **Lychno pinguior. Lecytho crassior** / Λιπαρώτερος λύχνου. Λιπαρώτερος ληκύθου / **Oilier than a lamp. Sleeker than an oil-bottle**
Said of parsimonious men[1] or of those living in the lap of luxury.

634 **Megarensium lachrymae** / Μεγαρέων δάκρυα / **Megarian tears**
These are forced tears. For the people of Megara were all compelled to weep together for their king when he died. 'To shed tears at the grave of a stepmother,' which we have given elsewhere, has the same sense: Πρὸς σῆμα μητρυιᾶς θρηνεῖν.[1]

[635] See C 634n

636 **Ad mensuram aquam bibunt, sine mensura offam comedunt** / Μέτρῳ ὕδωρ πίνοντες, ἀμετρίᾳ μᾶζαν ἔδοντες / **They drink water by the measure and eat barley-cake without measure**
This suits those who act perversely in being extremely parsimonious when there is no need and being extravagant when they should be careful.

637 **Ne puero gladium** / Μὴ παιδὶ μάχαιραν / **No sword to a boy**
Understand 'should be given.' The meaning is that one should beware of en-

* * * * *

633 *Adagia* II v 26. Greek versions (from Diogenianus 6.31) were added in *1506*.
  1 Presumably when used in an ironic sense. According to Diogenianus the saying is applied to extravagant persons. The Latin word, translated here as 'parsimonious,' could also mean 'humble' or 'living in squalor.'

634 *Adagia* II v 20. Diogenianus 6.34, the Greek version, with the erroneous Μεγαρείων for Μεγαρέων, being added in *1506*. Also *Suda* M 383, Zenobius 5.8, and Zenobius Athous 2.95. On the last of these see Bühler 5.507–16. The printer has added 'DCXXXV' immediately after the Greek at the end of the commentary, taking it by mistake to be an independent adage on its own at this point, with the result that there is no C 635.
  1 C 786, cited at Diogenianus 6.34. Erasmus gives only a Latin version of this proverb in *1500*, but adds the Greek version in *1506*.

636 *Adagia* II v 27. The Greek (from Diogenianus 6.43) was added in *1506*. Also in *Suda* A 1561, Zenobius 5.10, and Zenobius Athous 2.35. The meaning of the adage is very uncertain. Our sources tell us that it was linked with an oracle given to the Sybarites, relating to their defeat at the hands of the neighbouring city of Croton. See Bühler 4.264–9.

637 *Adagia* II v 18. The Greek (from Diogenianus 6.46) was added in *1506*. Otto 757

trusting important business to those who are inexperienced, lest they misuse the powers they have been given and bring about their own or others' ruin.

638 **Non una hirundo ver efficit** / Μία χελιδών ἔαρ οὐ ποιεῖ / **One swallow does not make a summer**
The meaning is that no single thing is sufficient when many other factors are required; for example one inference is not enough basis for passing judgment in a case.

639 **Ne temere Abydum** / Μὴ εἰκῇ Ἄβυδον / **Not rashly to Abydus**
We must understand 'you should sail.' The meaning is that no great danger should be faced without good cause.

640 **Malum bene quiescens ne commoveris** / Μὴ κινεῖν κακὸν εὖ κείμενον / **Do not disturb a sleeping evil**
An evil that has been lulled to sleep should not be re-awakened. Similar to this adage are 'stir not a fire concealed beneath the ash,'[1] 'rub not this sore,'[2] 'do not rub open this old scar.'[3]

641 **Neque natare neque litteras** / Μήτε νεῖν μήτε γράμματα / **Neither to swim nor to read**
Understand either 'he has learned' or 'he has the ability.' In Athens young boys first learned these two skills of swimming and reading. It is therefore said of those who have learned nothing in the way of good skills in their childhood. Plato in book three of *The Laws*: 'Those of the contrary sort

* * * * *

638 *Adagia* I vii 94. This proverb is to be found only in the branch of the Diogenianus tradition to which Erasmus' MS of Diogenianus belonged (see 7 and 10 n23 above; Heinimann 160 n12; Bühler 1.208 n109, 210, 308 n26). George Hermonymus added it to his manuscript between 6.47 and 6.48. The Greek version was added in *1506*. Also in Zenobius 5.12 and *Suda* M 1030. The season mentioned in the Greek proverb is spring, not summer. Polydore Vergil 225 (taken from Perotti's *Cornucopiae* 340:50–3)

639 *Adagia* I vii 93. The Greek (from Diogenianus 6.53) was added in *1506*. The danger posed by Abydus is unclear. See commentary on *Adagia* I vii 93.

640 *Adagia* I i 62. The Greek (from Diogenianus 6.54) was added in *1506*.
  1 Cf Horace *Odes* 2.1.7–8 and Virgil *Aeneid* 5.743.
  2 Cf c 92 and *Adagia* I vi 79.
  3 Cf c 766 and *Adagia* I vi 80.

641 *Adagia* I iv 13. The Greek (from Diogenianus 6.56) was added in *1506*. Also in *Suda* M 989.

should be thought of as wise, even if, as the saying goes, they know not how to either swim or read.'[1]

642 **Ne caprea cum leone pugnam ineas / Do not fight with a lion if you are a roe**
Μὴ πρὸς λέοντα δορκάς, Let not a roe go against a lion. Do not compete on unequal terms against someone much stronger. The word *dorcas* refers to a wild goat.[1]

643 **Parvum malum, magnum bonum / Μικρὸν κακόν, μέγα ἀγαθόν / A small evil can be a great good**
The greatest benefits can be won at the cost of a small inconvenience and modest exertion. Unless we prefer to take it in the sense of what Terence says, that the greatest friendships have been forged from a bad beginning.[1]

644 **Ne gladium tollat mulier / Μὴ μάχαιραν αἴρει θῆλυ / A woman should not draw sword**
The sense is that a person who is incapable of giving assistance should not try to do so.

645 **Midas auriculas asini habet / Μίδας ὄνου ὦτα / Midas has ass's ears**
This can be said of stupid persons or of rulers who can hear things even at a long distance, since they send agents to eavesdrop. In Persius there is a half-verse: 'Who does not have the ears of an ass?'[1] This is said to have replaced what was originally written: 'King Midas has the ears of an ass.'[2] The adage comes from a very well-known story.

* * * * *

1 Plato *Laws* 3.689D, quoted in Latin; see C 2 n7.

642 *Adagia* II iv 79. The Greek version, from Diogenianus 6.59, was present in *1500*. Otto 931
1 The word refers to a wild deer.

643 *Adagia* II v 65. From Diogenianus 6.62, the Greek version being added in *1506*.
1 Terence *Eunuchus* 873–5, here paraphrased by Erasmus

644 *Adagia* II v 51.The Greek (from Diogenianus 6.72) was added in *1506*. The correct form is αἶρε, not αἴρει.

645 *Adagia* I iii 67. From Diogenianus 6.73, the Greek version being added in *1506*. Otto 1111
1 Persius 1.121
2 According to the scholia on the passage and the *Vita Persii* ascribed to Valerius Probus

646 **Ignem igni ne addas / Μὴ πῦρ ἐπὶ πῦρ / Do not add fire to fire**
This is said to have originated with a charcoal burner who set himself on fire.[1] The meaning is that you should not add one misfortune to another.

647 **Nebulas detexis / Νεφέλας ξαίνεις / You are carding clouds**
Said of someone attempting a pointless task.[1]

648 **Asinus mysteria vel sacra portat / Ὄνος ἄγει μυστήρια / An ass that carries the mysteries or the sacred objects**
The origin of this saying is that sacred objects and other things necessary for rituals were placed on the backs of asses. Apuleius gives abundant evidence of this when he was in the service of those foulest of priests.[1] The saying is used of someone being given an honour when he is not worthy of it. 'An ape in purple' has the same sense,[2] as is what is said nowadays, 'to gild the shells of nuts,'[3] and 'to wrap a stake in purple.'[4]

649 **De asini umbra / Περὶ ὄνου σκιᾶς / About an ass's shadow**
Understand 'they are disputing' or 'they are quarrelling.' The story is that a man rented an ass, and then because of the sweltering heat he lay underneath the animal, protecting himself from the sun. The lessor started a quarrel about this, saying that he had not rented out the ass's shadow, but the ass itself.[1] Very similar to this is 'About goat's

* * * * *

646 *Adagia* I ii 8. From Diogenianus 6.71, the Greek being added in *1506*. Also in Zenobius 5.69 and *Suda* P 3211. Otto 844
   1 This reflects what is in Diogenianus 6.71.

647 *Adagia* III vi 38. The Greek, taken from Diogenianus 6.83, was added in *1506*. Also in *Suda* N 274
   1 The metaphor is from spinning, suggested by the resemblance of clouds to wool.

648 *Adagia* II ii 4. Diogenianus 6.98. Erasmus follows the interpretation of Diogenianus in taking the Greek verb to mean 'carry,' but the proverb could be translated as 'An ass celebrates the mysteries.' The Greek was present in *1500*.
   1 Apuleius *Metamorphoses* 8.24–5, where the hero has been transformed into an ass
   2 *Adagia* I vii 10, cited in Diogenianus 6.98
   3 Suringar 158
   4 Suringar 158B

649 *Adagia* I iii 52. The Greek title (Erasmus' variation on Diogenianus 7.1) was added in *1506*. Otto 187
   1 The story is in Diogenianus 7.1 (under Ὄνου σκιά) and Zenobius 6.28 (under Ὑπὲρ ὄνου σκιᾶς). Also *Suda* O 427, Υ 327

wool.'[2] Apuleius also mentions that he prompted the spread of this common proverb.[3] In the form of an ass he poked his head out of a window and was caught, betrayed by his shadow.

650 **Cretizare / Κρητίζειν / To play the Cretan.**
Similiter Graecari / Similarly To play the Greek
The sense is to engage in deceit. In the same way Plautus used the terms *Graecari* 'To play the Greek' and *pergraecari* 'To thoroughly play the Greek'[1] in the sense of devoting oneself to a life of pleasure.[2] Both expressions are based on the character and behaviour of the two groups.

651 **Frater adesto viro / Ἀδελφὸς ἀνδρὶ παρείη / Let a man's brother stand by him**
In Plato in book two of *The Republic* Adamantus[1] takes over the role of Glaucon, who is arguing with Socrates, and says, 'Socrates, we have not yet dealt satisfactorily with this topic. You ask me why? The particular point that should have been settled has not been settled.' Then Socrates answers, 'Let a man's brother stand by him, as the proverb has it. And so, if he has left anything out, help him.'[2] Plato also points out the origin of the proverb in *Protagoras*. There Socrates calls on Prodicus to protect his fellow citizen Simonides from being maligned by Protagoras. He says, 'I think I am appealing to you in the way Homer says Scamander appealed to the Simoeis when hard pressed by Achilles: "Dear brother, let us both together stem this man's strength." '[3] When he was stabbing Caesar, Cassius used the same words (and that too in Greek, according to Plutarch) to ask his brother to help him.[4]

* * * * *

2 C 154 (= *Adagia* I iii 53)
3 In the *persona* of the narrator of his *Metamorphoses* (see *Metamorphoses* 9.42). The passage is quoted more fully at *Adagia* I iii 64, where it is more relevant than it is here.

650 For the first adage cf C 151 and *Adagia* I ii 29 where it is explained that the Cretans were renowned liars. The source is Diogenianus 5.58, the Greek being added in 1506. Polydore Vergil 108; Otto 463
1 *Adagia* IV i 64
2 Plautus *Mostellaria* 22, *Truculentus* 88

651 *Adagia* I vii 92. The Greek version (from Diogenianus 3.29) was added in 1506. Also in the *Suda* A 442. This adage marks the end of the series drawn from Diogenianus that started at C 603.
1 An erroneous form of the Greek name, which should be Adeimantus
2 Plato *Republic* 2.362D. Erasmus gives only a Latin version; see C 2 n7.
3 Plato *Protagoras* 340A, again quoted in Latin
4 Plutarch *Caesar* 66. According to Plutarch it was Casca, not Cassius, who made this appeal.

The saying refers to a man helping out someone who is weak and unequal to a task by adding his strength to the other's.

652 Sine obsonio convivas fecisti / No relishes for your dinner-guests
This refers to those who undertake a plan without calculating what is needed to execute it. In Plato when Socrates gave nothing but bread and wine in the way of victuals to his imaginary citizens, Glaucon said, 'Apparently, there are no relishes for your feasters.'[1]

653 Lynceus / Λυγκεύς / A Lynceus
The eyesight of Lynceus[1] has long been proverbial. Plato in his *Letters*: 'Not even Lynceus could make such a person see.'[2] Horace in his *Epistles*: 'You may not see as far as Lynceus, yet you would not for that reason refuse a salve for sore eyes.'[3] The Elder Pliny, talking about the moon: 'The last of the old moon and the new moon can be seen on the same day only in Aries, and only a few mortals have the ability to see this. Hence the fable about Lynceus' eyesight.'[4] Pliny also says more about Lynceus elsewhere. In the opposite sense we call a blind man a Tiresias.[5] Juvenal: 'Neither a deaf man nor a Tiresias is one of the gods.'[6]

654 Tricae, Apinae / Stuff and nonsense
Martial: 'The games I played in my youth and childhood, our *Apinae* "silly tricks."'[1] The same author elsewhere. 'It is *Apinae* "nonsense" and *tricae*

* * * * *

652 Not in *Adagia*
1 Plato *Republic* 2.372C, quoted in Latin; see C 2 n7.

653 *Adagia* II i 54 More clear-sighted than Lynceus. The Greek for this was added in 1506. This saying is used by Poliziano both at *Epistolae* 8.14 (1.112 Maier) and in a letter to Bartholomaeus Scala on Epictetus (1.407 Maier). Otto 1003
1 Lynceus was a Greek hero who participated in the Calydonian boar hunt and the expedition of the Argonauts for the golden fleece. According to Apostolius 10.78 (used by Erasmus in the *Adagia*) Lynceus could see with clarity things underground, especially metals.
2 Plato *Letters* 7.344A, quoted in Latin; see C 2 n7.
3 Horace *Epistles* 1.1.28–9
4 Pliny *Naturalis historia* 2.78
5 *Adagia* I iii 57 As blind as Tiresias
6 Juvenal 13.249

654 *Adagia* I ii 43. Cf C 468. Used by Poliziano at *Miscellanea* 77 (1.286 Maier). This adage begins a series drawn from Martial (654–68, except for 657 and 658). Polydore Vergil 45; Otto 127
1 Martial 1.113.1–2

"trifles" and worse, if that can be.'[2] This expression is used to describe very cheap and worthless things. According to Pliny, the expression originated when the ancients used the name of the destroyed city of Apina to refer to something that was a laughing-stock.[3]

655 In toga saltantis personam inducere / To put a dancer on the stage wearing a toga

This refers to bringing something serious into what is humorous, or, in the opposite sense, to introducing laughable material into what is solemn. The Jewish proverb 'music in grief' is very similar.[1] Martial: 'Do not, then, if you consider it, do something ridiculous and put a dancer on the stage wearing a toga.'[2]

656 Rem factam putare / To consider a thing done

This occurs here and there in Martial in the sense of regarding something as certain and indubitable. To Procillus: 'You immediately thought the whole thing was done';[1] 'Do you think, Bythinicus, that you now take the thing as done?'[2]

657 Echino asperior / Ἐχίνου τραχύτερος / Rougher than an urchin

A Greek adage directed at moody and truculent persons. According to Pliny the sea urchin is a kind of fish that is completely covered by a shell with sharp prickles.[1]

658 Odium Vatinianum / A hatred deserved by Vatinius

Vatinius was so hated by the Roman people that his name became proverbial. Whoever wished to indicate extreme and bitter hatred said 'A hatred

* * * * *

2 Martial 14.1.7, quoted by Domizio Calderini (see C 171 n3) in his commentary on the previous passage
3 Pliny *Naturalis historia* 3.104

655 *Adagia* II v 28. Otto 1386
1 Sirach 22:6
2 Martial 2 *praefatio*

656 *Adagia* I iii 40
1 Martial 1.27.4
2 Martial 2.26.3. The correct form of the name is 'Bithynicus.'

657 *Adagia* II iv 81. The Greek, perhaps devised by Erasmus himself, was added in 1506.
1 Pliny *Naturalis historia* 9.100

658 *Adagia* II ii 94. The phrase comes from the Catullan verse (see n1).

deserved by Vatinius.' Catullus: 'For that gift I would hate you with hatred I feel for Vatinius.'[1]

659 Fumos vendere / To sell smoke

The meaning of this expression is to try to win popularity by ostentatious flattery. In Martial: 'You cannot sell empty smoke around the palace, or applaud Canus and Glaphyrus.'[1] It originated with a certain Thurinus. The emperor Alexander Severus ordered him to be put to death by suffocation from smoke. The reason was that in return for money Thurinus lied to someone, saying that he had won for him the good will of the emperor and an introduction to him. The emperor himself had suborned this man to approach Thurinus. Because of Thurinus' actions a herald was told to proclaim, 'He who sold smoke perishes by smoke.' This is what Spartianus writes in his life of that emperor.[2] The gospel phrase 'to sell oil' is similar.[3] This one is taken from anointers, while 'to sell smoke' comes from those burning incense.

660 Pellem caninam rodere / To gnaw dogskin

The meaning is to hurl abuse at those who hurl abuse at others. Martial on a critic who barked at him like a dog: 'Yet in this city there may be perhaps / One or two or three or four / Who are willing to gnaw dogskin. / We hold our nails far from this mange.'[1]

* * * * *

1 Catullus 14.3. The Catullan poem is addressed to the poet's friend, Caius Licinius Calvus, who prosecuted Vatinius on three occasions, and the phrase in question is better translated here 'with the hatred Vatinius shows for you,' but that is not how Erasmus understood it. His interpretation agrees with that found in the commentary of Antonius Parthenius (Venice 1487) on Catullus.

659 *Adagia* I iii 41. In *1506* Erasmus reworked the essay on this expression as it appeared in *1500* (see n2). Otto 730
1 Martial 4.5.7–8
2 *Severus Alexander* 36.2 (by Aelius Lampridius, not Aelius Spartianus) in the *Historia Augusta*. In *1500*, where the incident is recounted more briefly, Erasmus names and draws on Domizio Calderini as his source for this story (in the latter's commentary on Martial; see C 171 n3). For *1506* Erasmus himself consulted the section in the *Historia Augusta* (mentioned by Calderini), and gave a somewhat fuller account.
3 Matt 25:8–10

660 *Adagia* II iv 80. Otto 316n
1 Martial 5.60.8–11

661 Oleum aure (*vel* ore) ferre / To carry oil in the ear (*or* in the mouth)

If you like to believe Domizio, in antiquity there was a proverb according to which those who could not speak well were said to carry oil in their mouth. This is why Martial says of someone who has an ear that was hard to please and who did not wish to listen to anyone, 'It's a pretty jest he's said to have made, Marullus, who said you carried oil in your ear.'[1]

662 Vivi ursi fumantem nasum ne tentaveris / Do not touch the fuming nose of a bear

Do not anger someone more powerful than yourself, not even in jest. Martial:

> Wretch with foaming mouth,
> Touch not the fuming nose of a living bear.
> Though a bear be calm and lick your fingers and hands,
> If driven by pain and bile or real anger
> It will be a bear. Wear out your teeth on an empty skin.[1]

Taken from dogs hunting down a bear.

663 Alia voce psittacus, alia coturnix loquitur / Parrot and quail speak with different voices

Said of musicians or poets of differing ability. Martial, with reference to an anonymous poet who was publicly distributing his verses under Martial's name: 'Is this what you think, Priscus, that the parrot speaks with the voice of the quail?'[1]

664 Dies albo lapillo notandus / A day to be marked with a white pebble

If the ancients wanted to indicate that a day had turned out luckily and

* * * * *

661 *Adagia* I v 63. Otto 210
1 Martial 5.77.1–2, preceded by Domizio Calderini's commentary on the passage; see C 171 n3.

662 *Adagia* III v 67. Otto 1837
1 Martial 6.64.27–31

663 *Adagia* II v 59
1 Martial 10.3.6–7

664 This did not have an entry of its own in the *Adagia*, but cf *Adagia* I v 54, which includes the material that Erasmus gives here on this adage. Cf also C 272, *Adagia* II viii 18, and Otto 299.

propitiously they said it should be marked with a white pebble,[1] or with a white pearl, a snowy-white counter, or a clear precious stone. In the opposite way an unlucky day should be indicated with charcoal and a black pebble. Examples of these are too well known and common among authors for them to be added here.[2]

665 **Calvus comatus / A bald man with long hair**
This is applied to a person who flaunts himself, using artificial aids for his appearance. Martial: 'There is nothing more disgusting than a long-haired bald man.'[1]

666 **Barbam leoni mortuo vellere / To tug at the beard of a dead lion**
Domizio tells us that this was a proverb referring to a man who tried to cajole into action someone who was incapable of doing anything. Martial: 'Therefore, Legella, if you have any shame, do not tug at the beard of a lion that is dead.'[1]

667 **Congregare cum leonibus vulpes / To group foxes with lions**
This means to bring together things that are unequal and dissimilar. Martial: 'Why bring together foxes and lions?'[1]

668 **Aquilam noctuae comparare / To match eagle and owl**
To wish to make things that are quite different seem similar. Martial: 'You seek to make owls appear like eagles.'[1]

669 **Ne mihi Suffenus essem / Not to be my own Suffenus**
The meaning is that one should not be vain and self-satisfied. Suffenus was

* * * * *

1 Cf Martial 10.38.4–5.
2 As at Persius 2.1. See also the discussion in *Adagia* I v 54.

665 *Adagia* II v 60
   1 Martial 10.83.11

666 This is cited in *Adagia* II iv 69 and II v 11. Cf *Adagia* IV vii 82. Polydore Vergil 214; Otto 239
   1 Martial 10.90.9–10, with Domizio Calderini's commentary on the lines; see C 171 n3.
667 *Adagia* I ix 19. Otto 932, 933
   1 Martial 10.100.3

668 *Adagia* I ix 18. Here ends the series of adages drawn from Marial; see C 654n. Otto 146
   1 Martial 10.100.4

669 *Adagia* II v 12

a very incompetent poet who had much to say on the faults of others, but was blind to his own. Catullus describes his behaviour and talent: 'The same man is duller than the dull countryside / As soon as he lays his hand to verse; yet he is never / Happier than when writing poetry, so much joy in his talent / Does he feel, so much admiration for himself does he have.'[1]

In the same poem: 'You can see something of Suffenus in yourself,' meaning that you overlook your failings. In the same way we can say, 'Do not be your own Maevius.' Horace writes of him, 'Maevius says he pardons his own deficiencies.'[2]

670 Siculus vel Samia furatur / Σικελὸς ὀστρακίζεται / A Sicilian steals even Samian sherds

A Greek expression directed at those thieves who cannot keep their hands off even the most worthless of things.

671 Vitae pugillus / Ἡ σπιθαμὴ τοῦ βίου / Just a handspan of one's life

This signifies a very small amount. Plautus used 'a little salt-cellar of life' in the same way.[1]

672 Syri contra Phoenices / Σύροι πρὸς Φοίνικας / The Syrians against the Phoenicians

This refers to one crafty person dealing with another one. For both of these races are well known for their deceitfulness.

* * * * *

1 Catullus 22.14–17 and then line 19
2 Horace *Satires* 1.3.23

670 This becomes *Adagia* II v 13, but with a different text. Here begins another series of adages drawn from Diogenianus that runs to C 692. The Greek version of this proverb was added in 1506. Erasmus' manuscript of Diogenianus (see 7 and 10 n23 above) was corrupt at this point (8.15), offering ὀστρακίζεται. This should mean something like 'is ostracized,' based on the use of pieces of earthenware (*ostraka*) on which citizens wrote the name of anyone they wished to be banished. Erasmus has taken the verb to mean 'steal sherds,' and for sherds has inserted *Samia* in the title, a reference to Samian earthenware, which was fragile. The correct text, which has nothing to do with earthenware or ostracism, is ὀμφακίζεται 'picks unripe grapes.'

671 *Adagia* II ii 69. The Greek version, taken from Diogenianus 8.17, is present in 1500.
1 Plautus *Trinummus* 492, which becomes *Adagia* v i 8

672 Not in *Adagia*, but cited as an adage in the introduction to the work (CWE 31 6) and in *Adagia* I viii 56 Syria is not short of herbs. From Diogenianus 8.19, the Greek version being added in 1506.

673 **Ex tripode / Ἐκ τοῦ τρίποδος / Straight from the tripod**
This is the same as saying 'from the oracle of Apollo,' which gives rise to
the line in comedy 'Apollo's oracle did not speak more truly.'[1] Therefore if
anyone wants to indicate that he is telling the truth he can use these words:
'Consider it said straight from the tripod.'

674 **Pelopis vel Tantali talenta / Πέλοπος ἢ Ταντάλου τάλαντα / The talents
of Pelops or Tantalus**
This is used by the Greeks to refer to immense wealth. 'Not Pelops' gold
nor his many talents do I crave.'[1]

675 **Talpa caecior / Τυφλότερος ἀσπάλακος / Blinder than a mole**
This is a hyperbolic expression referring to those who are very short-
sighted.

676 **Ephyraeum (seu Dodonaeum) aes / Τὸ Δωδωναῖον χαλκεῖον /
Ephyraean (or Dodonean) bronze**
In antiquity this was said of noisy and garrulous persons. The reason is that
Ephyrean bronze makes a very loud ringing noise when struck.

* * * * *

673 *Adagia* I vii 90. The Greek version, based on Diogenianus 8.21, was added in
    1506. Otto 130
  1 Terence *Andria* 698, quoted inaccurately by Erasmus from memory

674 This is divided into two separate entries in the *Adagia* (I vi 22 The talents of
    Tantalus, and I vi 23 The talents of Pelops). The source of the latter is Theocri-
    tus (see n1) and it does not seem to be in the proverb collections. The former
    is drawn from Diogenianus 8.23, but it occurs also at Zenobius 6.4 and Zeno-
    bius Athous 2.66 (see Bühler 5.273–80). Also *Suda* T 81, 147. The Greek was
    added in *1506*.
  1 A Latin version of Theocritus 8.53–4, the original Greek of which is not
    given

675 *Adagia* I iii 55. From Diogenianus 8.25 (the Greek being present in *1500*). In
    1500 only the title is given, the brief commentary being an addition in *1506*.
    Otto 1739

676 *Adagia* I i 7 Dodonean bronze, with no mention of Ephyrean bronze. The
    source of the Greek version, present in *1500*, is Diogenianus 8.32. The er-
    roneous presence of Ephyrean bronze in the title here is owed to Ermo-
    lao Barbaro's commentary on Pliny *Naturalis historia* 4.6 (Pozzi 180). Ephyra
    was an old name for Corinth, which was famous for bronze work. The
    adage refers to the bronze vessels or instruments used at the oracle of
    Dodona in Epirus. The words *seu Dodonaeum* were added to the title in
    1506.

677 **Parni scaphula / Τὸ Πάρνου σκαφίδιον / Parnus' skiff**
This suits those who are very bothersome for little cause. A certain Parnus
is said to have become an extreme nuisance to his fellow citizens because
of the loss of a tiny boat.

678 **Hylam vocas / Τὸν "Υλαν κράζεις / You are calling for Hylas**
This is said of those searching and shouting for someone in vain. The adage
is taken from a myth. Hylas was one of Hercules' comrades. He went ashore
to a spring to fetch water and was lost there. He is supposed to have been
snatched from the spring by nymphs. Sacred rites were established for
him, during which dancers called out his name through the mountains and
around springs.[1] Hence Virgil:

> To these he adds Hylas, whom the sailors had left and had shouted for,
> So that the whole shore resounded with the call 'Hylas, Hylas.'[2]

679 **Turture loquacior / Τρυγόνος λαλίστερος / As garrulous as a turtle-dove**
A very well-known metaphor aimed at those who never stop talking. Even
today a common saying is 'as garrulous as a magpie.'[1]

680 **Colophonium suffragium / The Colophonian vote**
In the collection of Greek proverbs I find the following adage: Τὸν Κολοφῶνα
ἐπέθηκεν ἐπὶ τῆς βεβαίας ψήφου 'He set up Colophon for an irrevocable
decision.'[1] On the basis of this we can understand Plato's irony in his words
to the tyrant Dionysius:

* * * * *

677 *Adagia* II v 17. The Greek version is drawn from Diogenianus 8.27, being
present in *1500*. Also *Suda* M 971 and Zenobius Athous 2.10. On the latter
see Bühler 4.103–7, who suggests that the *scaphula* refers to a small container,
rather than a small boat.

678 *Adagia* I iv 72. The Greek version is drawn from Diogenianus 8.33, being
present in *1500*. The Greek verb κράζεις reflects what is found in much of the
manuscript tradition of Diogenianus. The correct form is κραυγάζεις, which appears in *Adagia* I iv 72. The saying is also found in Zenobius 6.21 and *Suda* Υ
90. Polydore Vergil 247
  1 Servius on Virgil *Eclogues* 6.43
  2 Virgil *Eclogues* 6.43–4

679 *Adagia* I v 30. The source is Diogenianus 8.34, the Greek being present in *1500*.
  1 Suringar 229

680 *Adagia* II iii 45 and III x 82. Cf c 608.
  1 Diogenianus 8.36. Only the first three words of the Greek version comprise

For when you were selling all the possessions of Dion without his consent, although you had said that this was only to be done with his agreement, O most honourable sire, you applied the Colophonian vote, as they say, to all your promises, renouncing them in a most glorious way.[2]

681 Tithoni senectus / Τιθωνοῦ γῆρας / The old age of Tithonus
Taken from the myth of Tithonus, which is too well known to be recounted here.[1]

**682 Primum optimos Aegina alit / Τὰ πρῶτ' ἀρίστους Αἴγινα τρέφει /
Of old, Aegina rears the finest men**
The origin of this saying lies in how cities naturally develop. After they are first formed, they grow strong through strict morals and thrifty ways. Then as cities grow wealthy, vices appear and gradually make their way into them. The saying is directed at those who initially lived frugally but then turned to extravagant luxury.

**683 Fumum fugiens in ignem decidit / Τὸν καπνὸν φεύγων εἰς τὸ πῦρ
ἐνέπεσον / Fleeing from the smoke he fell into the fire**
This means avoiding one misfortune only to encounter a worse one.

* * * * *

the adage 'he put the colophon [the word is masculine] upon ...' The remaining words explain its significance: 'relating to an irrevocable vote.' The expression has nothing to do with the city of Colophon (which is feminine by gender), as Erasmus and most of the ancient sources understand it (the common explanation is that the city was called in to cast the deciding vote if the votes in a pan-Ionic assembly were equal). The word simply means 'finishing touch.' See next note.

2 Plato *Letters* 3.318B. The Colophonian vote is a phantom, being based on Marsilio Ficino's erroneous Latin translation of the passage in Plato, which means 'you put the finishing touch (τὸν κολοφῶνα) to your promises.' See Bühler 4.47–55.

681 *Adagia* I vi 65. The Greek version, from Diogenianus 8.37, was added in *1506*. Also Zenobius 6.18 and *Suda* T 578. Otto 1789
1 Tithonus was the mortal spouse of the goddess Dawn. She asked Zeus to grant Tithonus eternal life. The request was granted but without eternal youth. Tithonus suffered all the physical effects of extreme old age; he finally turned into a grasshopper. In the *Adagia* Erasmus follows a somewhat different version according to which 'Tithonus was taken up into heaven and bathed with some heavenly elixir, as a result of which he lived to such an immense age that at length he prayed to be turned into a grasshopper' (CWE 32 46).

682 *Adagia* II v 61. The Greek, from Diogenianus 8.38, was added in *1506*.

683 *Adagia* I v 5. The Greek version, from Diogenianus 8.45, was added in *1506*.

684 Titanas vocas / Τιτᾶνας καλεῖς / You call for the Titans
The meaning is that you call for help. Taken from the myth of the Titans, who came to help Jupiter against the Giants.[1]

685 Fricantem refrica / Τὸν ξύοντα δὲ ἀντιξύειν / You scratch my back and I'll scratch yours
This means to do someone a favour in return for his doing you one, to repay a compliment with a compliment, to flatter someone who flatters you.

686 Ficulno folio anguillam / Τῷ θρίῳ τὴν ἔγχέλυν / An eel in a fig-leaf
The meaning is that you are holding an eel in a fig leaf. A fig leaf has a rough surface and is therefore suited for holding an eel, which is slippery by nature. The saying is applied to an unscrupulous trickster, who is held fast by being bound with knots tight enough to prevent his escape.

687 Sub omni lapide scorpius dormit / Ὑπὸ παντὶ λίθῳ σκορπίος εὕδει / Under every stone sleeps a scorpion
This was said of ill-tempered persons and those who were very timid by nature.

688 Sus seipsam laudat / Ὗς ἑαυτὴν ἐπαινεῖ / A sow praises itself
Said of those who actually boast about their misdeeds.

* * * * *

In the Greek version, and in the *Adagia*, the proverb is given in the first person: 'I fell into the fire.' Otto 667

684 *Adagia* II iii 47. The Greek version, from Diogenianus 8.47, was added in 1506. Only the first sentence of the commentary reflects what is in Diogenianus, where there is no mention of the Titans (see n1).

1 In most versions the Titans were enemies of Zeus in Greek mythology. In the *Suda* (T 677) the saying is related to humans calling to the Titans. The sense of the saying may be to do something in vain.

685 *Adagia* I vii 99. The Greek version, from Diogenianus 8.48, was added in 1506. Also in *Suda* T 767

686 *Adagia* I iv 95. The Greek version, which is found in Diogenianus 8.55, was added in 1506.

687 *Adagia* I iv 34. The Greek version (Diogenianus 8.59) was added in 1506. Also in Zenobius 6.20 and *Suda* Υ 534. Otto 1613

688 Cf *Adagia* III v 72 A swine revelling. Erasmus originally misunderstood his source, Diogenianus 8.60 (Ὗς ἐκώμασεν 'A swine revelled'), and invented a Greek version for 1506 that reflected his erroneous interpretation.

689 **Hydram inficis / You give poison to a Hydra**
You prompt someone who is wicked by his own nature to engage in further
wickedness.

690 **Suem provocat / ῏Υν ὀρίνει / He is provoking a boar**
Said of someone who is eager for a fight.

691 **Phalaridis imperium / Φαλάριδος ἀρχαί / To rule like Phalaris**
Said of those who misuse their powers in an excessively arrogant and cruel
manner.[1]

692 **Phoenicum conventa / Φοινίκων συνθῆκαι / Phoenician
agreements**
Based on the character of that nation.[1] Used of those who break treaties.

693 **Δάθος ἀγαθῶν / Dathos agathon (et similia) / A Dathos of good things
(and similar expressions)**

* * * * *

689 This adage is an oddity, seemingly an invention of Erasmus. In this series of sayings drawn from Diogenianus, this one should be the Latin version of Diogenianus 8.61 "Υδραν τέμνεις 'You behead the Hydra' (= Adagia I x 9; cf Otto 837), the meaning of which is to designate an impossible task, since the Hydra grew two heads to replace a head that was cut
off. In fact the Latin version of Diogenianus 8.61 (*Hydrae caput amputas*)
appears as c 735. The verb *inficere* must here mean 'infect with poison,'
the point being that that the Hydra was in its very nature a poisonous
serpent.

690 *Adagia* II vii 100. For the Greek version, present in *1500*, Erasmus followed
his manuscript of Diogenianus (see 7 and 10 n23 above) at this point (8.64),
which mistakenly offered ὖν (accusative case) for ὖς (nominative). The correct
sense is something like 'A charging pig.' Erasmus did not correct his error in
Adagia II vii 100.

691 *Adagia* I x 86. The Greek version (Diogenianus 8.65) was added in *1506*. Otto
1405
1 Phalaris was tyrant of Agrigentum, and was famous for his cruelty.

692 *Adagia* III v 56. The Greek version (Diogenianus 8.67) was added in *1506*.
Also in Zenobius (Aldus) column 167 and *Suda* Φ 796. Here ends the series of adages drawn from Diogenianus that started at c 670. Cf Otto
1490.
1 Cf *Adagia* I viii 28 Punic faith.

693 The source is Ermolao Barbaro (see n1). *Adagia* I iii 33. Erasmus does not give a
Latin translation of the proverb, simply transliterating the Greek. The correct

As cited in Ermolao Barbaro,[1] 'Eustathius tells us that Dathos was such a populous colony of the Thasians[2] near the Strymon that the wealth of its citizens became proverbial: "A Dathos of good things."[3] This is like Ἀγαθῶν Ἀγαθίδες "An Agathides of good things."[4] This is also treated as a proverb by the Greeks, so that the word "Agathides" must be the name of a place.' According to the same author[5] 'A Thasos of good things' was also used in the same sense.[6]

694 Calauriam insulam / The island of Calauria

There is a story that Neptune took possession of the island of Calauria in return for giving Latona the island of Delos and similarly received Taenarus in return for Pytho. This then became proverbial for an exchange or an agreement that is conducted with the words 'I give on condition that you give.'[1]

It makes no difference whether you live on Delos or Calauria.
Or on lofty Pytho or windy Taenarus.[2]

695 Psyrice facta / Ψυρικῶς πραχθέντα / As they do in Psyra

According to Pliny in book five Psyra or Psyria is the name of an

*****

form is probably 'Datos' (rather than 'Dathos'), an emendation of Ermolao Barbaro. Also in Zenobius 3.11 and *Suda* Δ 91

1 In his *Castigationes Plinianae*, on Pliny *Naturalis historia* 4.42 (Pozzi 247)
2 Both 1500 and 1506 erroneously read 'Tharsians.'
3 Barbaro is drawing from Eustathius' commentary on Dionysius Periegetes 517 (*Geographi Graeci minores* ed C. Müller, 2 [Paris 1882] page 315). In turn, Erasmus draws from Barbaro for all of the information in his discussion.
4 *Adagia* II iv 92
5 That is, Ermolao Barbaro (see the introductory note and n1 above)
6 *Adagia* I iii 34. From Zenobius 4.34. Cf Zenobius Athous 2.20. See Bühler 4.164–71, who thinks that 'Thasos' is a corruption of 'Datos.'

694 *Adagia* IV iii 20, where references from Pausanias and Strabo are added. Almost the whole essay here in the *Collectanea* is drawn, virtually word for word, from Ermolao Barbaro's *Castigationes Plinianae* (on *Naturalis historia* 4.56; Pozzi 263).
1 A translation of the Latin legal formula *do ut des*
2 Ἴσον τοι Δῆλόν τε Καλαυρίαν τε νέμεσθαι / Πυθὼ δ' ἠγαθέην καὶ Ταίναρον ἠνεμόεσσαν. This quotation, present in 1500, is from Ephorus, a Greek historian (FGrHist 70F 150 fragment 59), but Erasmus' source for it is Ermolao Barbaro. Erasmus does not give a Latin translation.

695 *Adagia* I x 94. The Greek version of the title was added in 1506, probably invented by Erasmus. Polydore Vergil 251

island so undistinguished that its obscurity became proverbial.[1] What was thought to have been done in a mean and sordid way was said to have been done as they do in Psyra. Cratinus: Ψύρα τὸν Διόνυσον ἄγοντες 'taking Dionysus to Psyra' and Ψύρα τὴν Σπάρτην ἄγεις 'you take Sparta to Psyra.'[2]

696 **Felix qui nihil debet / "Ολβιος ὁ μηδὲν ὀφείλων / Lucky is he who is free of debt**
A Greek proverb according to Merula as cited in Ermolao Barbaro.[1] The sentiment is very familiar.

697 **Myconium caput / A Myconian head**
Strabo tells us that this was a proverbial expression for a baldpate. He says: 'It is customary to call Myconians baldpates, because baldness is very much an endemic defect in this island.'[1]

698 **Clematis Aegyptia / An Egyptian clematis**
Demetrius of Phalerum said, 'An Egyptian clematis became proverbial, being applied to those who were tall and had a dark complexion.'[1] It is a plant whose many species are mentioned by Pliny in his History of the

* * * * *

1 Pliny *Naturalis historia* 5.134, but Erasmus is drawing from Ermolao Barbaro's *Castigationes Plinianae* at this point (Pozzi 421). Barbaro emends *Psere* in his text to *Psyra* (neuter plural) and also refers to the place name 'Psyrie' at Homer *Odyssey* 3.171.

2 PCG 4 Cratinus fragments 347 and 119, quoted by Ermolao Barbaro (see preceding note). The first becomes *Adagia* III iv 39. They are also cited by Stephanus of Byzantium sub Ψύρα.

696 *Adagia* II vii 98. The Greek version was added in 1506. Polydore Vergil 255

1 Ermolao Barbaro's *Castigationes Plinianae* on *Naturalis historia* 7.119 (Pozzi 549). Barbaro gives the proverb identified by Giorgio Merula (see C 391 n1) only in Latin. Merula gives the Greek version in his *Emendationes in Plinium*, but he has εὐδαίμων for ὄλβιος. Erasmus may have created the Greek version on the basis of the Latin form.

697 *Adagia* II i 7. Polydore Vergil 185; Otto 1190

1 Strabo 10.5.9, cited in Latin by Erasmus, and taken almost word for word from Ermolao Barbaro's *Castigationes Plinianae* on Pliny *Naturalis historia* 11.130 (Pozzi 666). The original Greek version of Strabo did not appear in print until 1516.

698 *Adagia* I i 22. Polydore Vergil 88

1 Demetrius *De elocutione* 172, drawn from Ermolao Barbaro's commentary on Pliny *Naturalis historia* 24.141 (Pozzi 898)

World book twenty-four, chapter fifteen.[2] He says that one of them 'has the name "Egyptian clematis." Some call it *daphnoides*, some *polygonides*; it has a long thin, black leaf.' The reading in Pliny, however, is *clamatis*, not *clematis*.

699 Optimum non nasci, aut ocissime aboleri / Not to be born is best or to be extinguished as soon as possible

Pliny in the preface to book seven put together a list of the many perils encompassing our birth and later life and used a proverbial expression. He says, 'And so there have been many who thought it best not to be born or to be extinguished as soon as possible.'[1] The Greeks express this in two trimeters in the following way: 'Not to be born is ever best of all. / But when born, 'tis best for death to come with speed.'[2]

Theognis in his *Words of Warning*: 'The best for mortals is never to have been born, / But, if born, to pass quickly through the gates of Hades.'[3]

Lactantius in his *Institutions* writes that this sentiment originated with some Silenus or other, and that Cicero used it in his book *On Consolation*, adding for effect a metaphor to each part in the following way: 'Not to be born is far the best, and not to run aground on these reefs of life; next to that, if you have been born, to die with speed and escape the violence of fortune, like escaping from a fire.'[4]

700 Ἀδώνιδος κῆποι / Adonidis horti / Gardens of Adonis

Pausanias the grammarian says, 'Adonis-gardens were packed with lettuce and fennel, and were dedicated to Venus. Seeds would be planted in them just as in pots. Because of this the Adonis-gardens became a proverbial ex-

* * * * *

2 Pliny *Naturalis historia* 24.141

699 *Adagia* II iii 49

1 Pliny *Naturalis historia* 7 praefatio 4

2 PCG 2 Alexis fragment 145.15–16: Τὸ μὴ γενέσθαι μεντ' ἄριστόν ἐστ' ἀεί. / Ἐπὰν δὲ γένηται, ὡς τάχιστ' εἶναι τέλος. Erasmus gives, somewhat inaccurately, the Greek without a Latin translation. He has drawn the quotation and the following one from Theognis directly from Ermolao Barbaro's comments on Pliny *Naturalis historia* 7 praefatio 4 (Pozzi 533).

3 Theognis *Elegeia* 1.425 and 427: Ἀρχὴν μὲν μὴ φῦναι ἐπιχθονίοισιν ἄριστον, / Φύντα δ' ὅπως ὤκιστα πύλας Ἀΐδαο περῆσαι. Erasmus gives only the Greek, taking it from Barbaro (see previous note).

4 Lactantius *Institutiones* 3.19.14, citing Cicero *De consolatione* fragment 11

700 *Adagia* I i 4. Diogenianus 1.14 is the source of the Greek, which is present in *1500*. Cf also Zenobius 1.49 and Zenobius Athous 2.90, both of which

pression, directed at worthless and shiftless men.'[1] On Adonis see Pliny book twenty-one, chapter ten.[2] Plato also mentions these gardens, in pointing out that flowers gathered from them immediately die.[3]

701 Bonae leges a malis moribus procreantur / Evil ways produce good laws

A very well-known sentiment and one that is familiar because of its being an old proverb.

702 Homo bulla / Man is but a bubble

An old adage that indicates the fragility of human life.

703 Crocodili lachrymae / Κροκοδείλου δάκρυα / Crocodile tears

A crocodile is said to shed tears when it spots a man in the distance before devouring him shortly afterwards. This gave rise to a proverb 'Crocodile tears,' referring to those who pretend that they deeply regret the misfortune of those whose misfortune they themselves cause.[1]

* * * * *

are given in a fuller form, 'More unfruitful than a garden of Adonis.' See Bühler 5.463–73.

1 Pausanias was a lexicographer of the 1st or 2nd centuries of the Christian era. Erasmus draws this, without acknowledgment, from Ermolao Barbaro's *Castigationes Plinianae* on Pliny *Naturalis historia* 21.60 (Pozzi 1480, in Barbaro's *Annotamenta*). Barbaro in turn drew the fragment of Pausanias from *Suda* A 517, but misunderstood the Greek. The seeds were actually planted in pots, and the plants that sprouted from them were short-lived. On Pausanias see H. Erbse *Untersuchungen zu den attizistischen Lexica* (Berlin 1950: Abhandlungen der deutschen Akademie zu Berlin, phil.-hist. Klasse 1949.2) and Heinimann (1992) 81.

2 Pliny *Naturalis historia* 21.60

3 Plato *Phaedrus* 276B

701 *Adagia* I x 6. The source is Macrobius *Saturnalia* 3.17.10 by way of Perotti's *Cornucopiae* (181:45). Polydore Vergil 52; Otto 944 *Nachträge* pp 177, 239, 275

702 *Adagia* II iii 48. The source is Varro *Res rusticae* 1.1.1 by way of Perotti's *Cornucopiae* (211:15–17). Polydore Vergil 25; Otto 275

703 *Adagia* II iv 60. Only Apostolius (10.17) among the paroemiographers has this proverb, but he is an impossible source for Erasmus when he was preparing the 1500 edition of the *Collectanea*. Erasmus' source was Perotti's *Cornucopiae* (see n1). Polydore Vergil 230

1 Erasmus' (and Polydore Vergil's) interpretation follows that of Niccolò Perotti in his *Cornucopiae* (342:61–343:2). In other versions the crocodile is believed to weep when it has devoured all or most of its victims. See Heinimann 163–4.

704 Minimo provocare / To challenge with the little finger

This means to challenge someone to an evenly balanced contest, but in a contemptuous fashion. Horace in a satire: 'Look, / Crispinus challenges me with his little finger, "Take these, if you wish. / Take these tablets now. We have a place, a time, scrutineers. / Let's see which of us can write more." '[1]

705 Mandare laqueum. Medium unguem ostendere / To tell someone go hang. To show the middle fingernail

Both adages express the utmost contempt. We tell those to go hang when we want to show that we think so little of them that even if they hanged themselves it would be of no concern to us. Juvenal about Democritus: 'He laughed at the troubles and the pleasures of the common throng, / Sometimes too at their tears. But he himself would tell menacing Fortune / Go hang herself and would show her the middle fingernail.'[1]

The second expression, 'To show the middle fingernail,' has the same meaning as the first, that is, it shows contempt. Martial too used it in the same sense: 'And I would offer him the middle finger.'[2] This expression is certainly based on a gesture, and perhaps the same is true for the immediately preceding saying.

706 Illi alabastrus unguenti plena putet / To him an alabaster vase full of perfume smells bad

This is suitable when something that is really of excellent quality is thought by some to be very poor. It occurs in Cicero.[1]

707 Crocodilus in fugientem / A crocodile attacks the man who flees

This is taken from the animal's natural behaviour. Pliny writes that the

* * * * *

704 *Adagia* III vi 45. Otto 547
  1 Horace *Satires* 1.4.13–16

705 *Adagia* II iv 67 and 68
  1 Juvenal 10.51–3
  2 A reference to Martial 2.28.2, which is loosely paraphrased. The reference is perhaps owed to a humanist commentary on Juvenal 10.51–3; Giorgio Merula, for example, adduces it in his commentary.

706 Not a separate entry in *Adagia*, but quoted in I iv 38 A pig has nothing to do with marjoram, as being similar in sense. Erasmus' source is the preface to Poliziano's *Miscellanea* (1.214 Maier).
  1 Cicero *Academica* 2 fragment 11, cited by Nonius Marcellus 87.13–14 Lindsay

707 Not in *Adagia*

crocodile becomes savage towards those who flee from it, while it retreats from those who pursue it.[1]

708 Promusque quam condus magis / And a spender more than a saver

Used by Ausonius of a man of lavish disposition who knows how to spend what he has acquired but does not know how to acquire more.[1] The *promus* is a servant in charge of dispensing the supplies, while the *condus* is responsible for laying them in.

709 Pistillo retusius / As blunt as a pestle

Used in Jerome more than once to refer to someone who is thickheaded and stupid: 'O how stupid he is, and blunter than any pestle, as the saying goes.'[1]

710 Puppis et prora / Stem and stern

This means both the beginning and end, the whole amount. It is found in Ermolao Barbaro. He says, 'So that the stem and stern of Latin lies in this one thing.'[1] The wholeness of a ship depends on these two parts.

711 Ut Praenestinis gonea est ciconia / A stork is a 'tork in Praeneste

This is found in Plautus in *Truculentus*.[1] Said of those who pronounce words in a distorted and truncated fashion, cutting off the first letters. In that play when a young man from the country is rebuked for saying *rabo* instead of *arrabo* 'pledge,' he replies, 'That's a saving for me, just as a stork is a 'tork in Praeneste.'

712 Mea est pila / The ball is mine

The meaning is that I have won and done what I wanted to do. This is taken from a ball game and appears in the same comedy.[1]

* * * * *

1 Pliny *Naturalis historia* 8.92

708 *Adagia* II iv 73
  1 Ausonius *Epistles* 20b.20 Green. Filippo Beroaldo referred to this at *Annotationes centum* 19, and he may be Erasmus' source here.

709 *Adagia* III vi 21. Otto 1431
  1 Jerome *Letters* 69.4.5 CSEL 54 686

710 *Adagia* I i 8. Otto 1477
  1 In Barbaro's *Castigationes Plinianae* Epilogus (Pozzi 1208). A variation of the adage (*prora et puppis*) occurs at Cicero *Ad familiares* 16.24.

711 Not in *Adagia*
  1 Plautus *Truculentus* 690–1 where the reading is *conia* in modern editions

712 *Adagia* II iv 85. Otto 1417
  1 Plautus *Truculentus* 706

713 **Clurinum pecus. Rus merum / A pack of apes. Pure country**

Also in Plautus in this play.[1] Both expressions are directed at a thick-headed man: 'This fellow is pure country. He would put a pack of apes to shame.'

714 **Conlatinus venter / A belly like Conlatinus**

Plautus applies this to a huge swollen man.[1] I think he is alluding to the name Collatinus, calling a huge belly into which everything could be placed 'Conlatinus.' The source is Festus Pompeius.[2]

715 **Cyprio bovi merendam / Luncheon for a Cyprian ox**

This is a sotadean verse in Ennius which tells of a custom in the island of Cyprus, that oxen were fed human excrement. Pompeius is also the source.[1] It can be appropriately used whenever a despicable guest is fed disgusting food.

716 **Quandoque bonus dormitat Homerus / Sometimes the noble Homer sleeps**

An allegorical expression that has become proverbial. We use it when we want to indicate that no one is so flawless in his skill that he does not falter on some occasion and seem quite different from what he really is. So Horace in his *Art of Poetry*: 'Sometimes the noble Homer sleeps, / But we can forgive his falling asleep over such a long work.'[1]

* * * * *

713 Not in *Adagia*. *Rus merum* was added in 1506.
 1 Plautus *Truculentus* 269

714 Not in *Adagia*
 1 Plautus *Curculio* 231, but Erasmus' text differs from that in modern editions, which offer *collativus* 'capacious enough to hold everything.' To link the expression with Collatinus (perhaps Lucius Torquatus Collatinus, whose wife was the famous Lucretia), or with the town Collatia, is therefore groundless.
 2 Pompeius Festus 51.15–16 Lindsay

715 *Adagia* I x 96. Cf c 305. Polydore Vergil 39; Otto 269
 1 Pompeius Festus 51.23–5 Lindsay, citing Ennius *varia* 26 Vahlen. The information about the metre (named after Sotades, a poet of the 3rd century BC) is drawn from Festus.

716 Not in *Adagia*
 1 Horace *Ars poetica* 359–60. Modern editions offer a different text from Erasmus: 'but it is permitted for sleep to creep over a long work' (*obrepere* for *ignoscere*).

717 **Quam curat numerum lupus / As little as the wolf cares**
about counted sheep
A proverb of the countryside. It appears in Virgil,[1] and we use it when
we want to indicate that nothing can be done and that nothing makes any
difference. Even today our own people have a well-known saying, 'A wolf
devours sheep even if they have been counted.'[2]

718 **Alia vita, alia diaeta / Ἄλλος βίος, ἄλλη δίαιτα / Different life,**
different style
This saying suits those who have seized upon a new way of life or those who
experience good fortune and change their mode of life and habits accordingly. This gives rise to a sentiment that is extremely common everywhere,
'fortune determines life-style.'

719 **De sale et faba / About salt and beans**
Those who share secrets with each other are said to be concerned Περὶ ἁλὸς
καὶ κυάμου 'About salt and beans.' Taken from the ancient custom of the
spreading out of salt and beans by prophets.

720 **Capra gladium (seu machaeram) / Αἲξ τὴν μάχαιραν / The goat**
[found] the sword (or the dagger)
Understand 'found.' The saying suits those who find something that will
bring about their own ruin. It originated in Corinth when a goat that was to

* * * * *

717 *Adagia* II iv 99. Otto 984
  1 Virgil *Eclogues* 7.51–2
  2 Suringar 146

718 *Adagia* I ix 6. The source of the Greek version, present in *1500*, is Diogenianus
  1.20. Also in Zenobius 1.22 and *Suda* A 1357. Otto 66

719 *Adagia* I i 12. The source of the Greek version, present in *1500*, is Diogenianus 1.50. Also Zenobius 1.25. In the *Adagia* Erasmus points out a different
  (and better) text of the proverb found in two places in Plutarch: Περὶ ἁλὸς
  καὶ κύμινου 'About salt and cummin.' This is also the text in Zenobius Athous
  2.43; see the lengthy discussion in Bühler 5.62–72. See also *Adagia* III v 20 Salt
  and a bean.

720 *Adagia* I i 57. The source of the Greek version, present in *1500*, is Diogenianus
  1.52. Also Zenobius 1.27. See Bühler 4.233–45 on Zenobius Athous 2.30 Οἷς
  τὴν μάχαιραν 'The sheep [found] the dagger.' Bühler accepts the view that the
  proverb and the story surrounding it originated in an ancient Indic source
  and was taken over from there by the Greeks. The phrase *seu machaeram* in
  the title was added in 1506.

be sacrificed to Juno scratched on the ground and unearthed a sword that had been hidden there and that was to be used to kill it.

721 Semper graculus cum graculo congregatur / Αἰεὶ κολοιὸς πρὸς κολοιὸν ἱζάνει / **Jackdaw ever joins up with jackdaw**
Like gathers with like, scoundrel with scoundrel.

722 Complurium foliorum ficulnorum strepitum audivi /
Πολλῶν θρίων ψόφον ἀκήκοα / **I have heard the sound of many fig leaves**
This will be a useful saying for someone who wants to indicate that he cares nothing for another's anger or threats. Fig leaves make a great cracking sound when they are set on fire but that is all they do.

723 Prospectandum vetulo cane latrante / **Look out when an old dog barks**
Lest we seem to have taken nothing from ordinary people and to have completely ignored our own times, this is a proverb that lacks only ancient provenance and a specific source.[1] The sense is metaphorical: we should be especially on our guard when old men point out some dreadful danger. Taken from watchdogs that always have good reason to bark when they are old.

724 Canes qui plurimum latrant perraro mordent / **Barking dogs rarely bite**
This too is a saying of this day and age, about men who curse and threaten but are timid cowards when it comes to doing anything.[1]

* * * * *

721 *Adagia* I ii 23. The source of the Greek version, present in *1500*, is Diogenianus 1.61. Also in Zenobius 2.47 and *Suda* K 1968

722 *Adagia* I x 88. In *1500* the adage read *complurium ferarum fremitum audivi* 'I have heard the roaring of many wild beasts,' a translation of the corrupt text of Diogenianus 1.70 (θηρίων 'wild beasts' instead of θρίων 'fig leaves'). In *1506* the new adage, with accompanying Greek, came from a scholion on Aristophanes *Wasps* 436. The final sentence of Erasmus' comment, added in *1506*, is also taken from this scholion.

723 Cited in *Adagia* I iii 8. For other contemporary, non-classical proverbs see C 197n.
  1 Suringar 70

724 Cf *Adagia* III vii 100 Nervous dogs bark louder. Otto 321
  1 Suringar 34

725 **Canes omnibus ignotis allatrant / Dogs bark at all things strange
to them**

Said of those who condemn and criticize anything they do not understand.[1]

726 **Azanaea mala / Ἀζαναῖα κακά / Azanian ills**

This applies to an insuperable task involving endless toil, yet one that is
worthless anyway. Ἀζαναῖα in Greek refers to land that is covered with
briers and is hard to cultivate, so that farmers who work it have no success.

727 **Anagyrum irritas / Ἀνάγυρον κινεῖς / You are provoking Anagyrus**

Customarily said of someone unjustly assailing a person who will thus be
provoked into inflicting great harm upon him. Taken ἀλληγορικῶς 'allegori-
cally' from a certain Anagyrus, a rich man who was provoked by his neighbours' wrongdoing and then completely destroyed them.

728 **Ipsis placet / Αὐτοῖς ἀρέσκει / That is how they like it**

Plato in book three of *The Laws*: 'Then the story was (and this is how they
liked it, as the saying goes) that they should divide their army into three parts
and they should inhabit three cities: Argos, Messene, and Sparta.'[1] Terence
in *The Woman of Andros*: 'That's their story, and that is how they like it.'[2]

* * * * *

725 Not in the *Adagia*. Another contemporary proverb, with no apparent ancient
source (see C 197n). Erasmus took it from Pico della Mirandola *De hominis
dignitate* (page 154 in Garin's edition of 1942).
  1 Suringar 33

726 *Adagia* II vi 9. Diogenianus 1.24 is the source of the Greek title, which was
present in *1500*.

727 Cf *Adagia* I i 65. The source of the Greek version, present in *1500*, is Diogenianus 1.25, but the explanation given there differs in some details from what
Erasmus says here. According to Diogenianus Anagyros was a local deity on
whose shrine the neighbouring people committed an outrage. This was the
cause of their downfall. Perotti (*Cornucopiae* 772:14–16) simply says that the
proverb refers to our doing or saying something that brings public disgrace.

728 *Adagia* II iv 100. The Greek was added in *1506*, but there is no known source in
the collection of proverbs, not surprisingly since Erasmus is dependent here on
a mistranslation of Marsilio Ficino of the Platonic passage, and Erasmus simply translated the Latin phrase into Greek. There is no reference to a proverb
in the original Greek. The passage means 'then they determined (*ipsis placet*),
so the story goes, to divide their army into three parts ...'
  1 Plato *Laws* 3.683D, taken from Marsilio Ficino's Latin translation
  2 Terence *Andria* 225

729 Pulchre narras. Belle dicis / Καλῶς ἔλεξας / Fine words! A likely story!

A proverbial expression directed at those who make great promises. Socrates in Plato's *Euthydemus*: 'All right, Euthydemus. As the proverb goes, all these are fine words.'[1]

730 Iovis Corinthus / Διὸς Κόρινθος / Corinthus son of Jove

In the same dialogue Socrates says, 'What good will these men be, and how useful to us? Are we to say that they will make other good men, and then these creations will create more? How they will be good for us is not at all clear, since we have paid no heed to the so-called political arts, and as the proverb goes, we have a case of "Corinthus son of Jove."'[1] So much for Plato. This expression seems to be customarily applied to great wealth and to many different and rare achievements.

731 Corvum hiantem delusit / He tricked the gaping crow

Since this bird hovers over corpses, the saying especially suits a person who has deceived a legacy-hunter by his will, which has been keenly and long awaited. Horace tells us of Coranus, who tricked his father-in-law Nasica with hopes of a legacy but when he died he left him 'nothing but tears.'[1] He says, "Very often a lowly police officer will be cooked up into a notary, and will deceive the gaping crow.'

732 Tragice loqui / To speak like a tragedian

This means to speak in a rather obscure fashion. It is to be found in Plato book three of *The Republic*.[1] The style of tragedy is exalted and by no means that of ordinary speech.

* * * * *

729 *Adagia* I x 55. The Greek version of the proverb was added in 1506, probably Erasmus' own translation of the Latin.
  1 Plato *Euthydemus* 293D, quoted in Latin; see C 2 n7.

730 *Adagia* II i 50, where different interpretations from the unsatisfactory one given here are offered. The Greek version of the title did not appear until 1506, and it may have been Erasmus' invention.
  1 Plato *Euthydemus* 292E, quoted in Latin; see C 2 n7.

731 *Adagia* I vii 15. The proverb appears in Poliziano *Epistolae* 6.3 (1.76 Maier). Otto 448
  1 Horace *Satires* 2.5.69, then lines 55–6

732 *Adagia* II v 39
  1 Plato *Republic* 3.413B

733 **Mida locupletior / As rich as Midas**
This occurs in the same book,[1] denoting unlimited wealth.

734 **Corinthius luxus / Κορίνθια ἀσέλγια / Corinthian luxury**
The following expressions are to be found in the same dialogue:[1] 'A Syra-
cusan table,'[2] 'Sicilian dishes,' 'Attic pastries and spices.'[3]

735 **Hydrae caput amputas / Ὕδραν τέμνεις / You cut off the head of the Hydra**
The sense is that you remove one evil only to have to encounter many others.
It occurs in Plato.[1]

736 **Vitilitigatores / Captious critics**
An unusual word, first coined by Cato and composed of *vitia* 'faults' and
litigator 'litigant.'[1] It acquired almost proverbial status among the learned.[2]
Those who deserve this name do absolutely nothing themselves, but are
eager to criticize the accomplishments of others. It is as if they suffer from
some addiction to making accusations.

737 **Dionysius Corinthi / Ὁ Διονύσιος ἐν Κορίνθῳ / Dionysius in Corinth**
An allegory with proverbial force, very popular in antiquity with the
Greeks, about those who had been reduced from the highest position
possible to the lowest. Quintilian talks about this adage in book eight in the

* * * * *

733 *Adagia* I vi 24. Otto 1110
    1 Plato *Republic* 3.408B. Also Diogenianus 8.53

734 Cf *Adagia* IV iii 68. The Greek title, which mistakenly transforms luxury into
    licentiousness, was added in *1506*.
    1 Plato *Republic* 3.404D
    2 *Adagia* II ii 68
    3 *Adagia* II iii 100

735 *Adagia* I x 9. The Greek version, added in *1506*, was taken from Diogenianus
    8.61. Otto 837 *Nachträge* pp 58, 105–6, 238
    1 Plato *Republic* 4.426E

736 *Adagia* II vi 19
    1 This is taken from Pliny *Naturalis historia* praefatio 32.
    2 For example, Poliziano in the preface of his *Miscellanea* (1.216 Maier)

737 *Adagia* I i 83. The Greek title was added in *1506*. The phrase does not appear
    in the collections of proverbs, and is probably Erasmus' own translation of
    the Latin phrase. The Greek expression occurs at Plutarch *Moralia* 511A and
    Cicero *Ad Atticum* 9.9.1. The subject of the adage is Dionysius II, the tyrant of
    Syracuse, who was expelled from that city and went to live in Corinth as a
    private citizen. Otto 559

following words: 'Historical instances are a source of allegory if they are
not used in a speech for some specified reason. "Dionysius in Corinth" is
used by all Greeks, and many similar phrases can be used.'[1]

**738 Architectus invidet architecto / Τέκτων τέκτονι φθονέει / Builder envies
builder**
This is a sentiment expressed by Hesiod.[1] Virgil made witty use of it against
Cornificius, an envious and secret critic.[2]

**739 Iovi fulmen, Herculi clavam extorquere / To wrench his thunderbolt
away from Jove, and his club from Hercules**
Both expressions are said of extremely difficult tasks. Both also come from
Maro.[1]

740 Hunc cespitem circumdemus / Let us surround this thicket
The meaning is that we should closely examine this question. Taken from
how huntsmen search out their prey by surrounding a covert where they
think an animal is hiding. This appears in Plato in book four of *The Republic*.[1]

**741 Alga vilior. Rusco horridior. Sardois herbis amarior / As worthless
as seaweed. A rough as gorse. As bitter as Sardinian herbs**
These comparisons, found in Virgil's *Thyrsis*, also have the feel of proverbs:
'Nay, may I seem to you more bitter than Sardinian herbs, / Rougher than
gorse, more worthless than cast-up seaweed.'[1]

742 Arcem tenere / To occupy the citadel
This means to hold the highest rank and have the greatest acclaim in some

* * * * *

1 Quintilian 8.6.52

738 Cf *Adagia* I ii 25. The Greek version (see n1) was added in *1506*. Otto 660
  1 Hesiod *Works and Days* 25–6. Erasmus has not given a precise quotation.
  2 The source of this is a life of Virgil in the so-called *Donatus auctus*.

739 *Adagia* IV i 95. Otto 804, *Nachträge* p 170
  1 Macrobius (not Virgil, named here as Maro) *Saturnalia* 5.3.16 (talking about
    Virgil)

740 Not in *Adagia*
  1 Plato *Republic* 4.432B

741 The first (see Otto 58) appears in the introduction to the *Adagia* (CWE 31 25:123).
    The third (see Otto 1586) is cited in *Adagia* III v 1.
  1 Virgil *Eclogues* 7.41–2. The first verse is quoted in *Adagia* III v 1 A Sardonic
    laugh.

742 Not in *Adagia*, but the metaphorical use of 'citadel' is mentioned at *Adagia* II i

activity, like Cicero in eloquence and Plato in philosophy.

743 Humi serpere / To crawl on the ground
A style that is plain and very simple is said to crawl on the ground. Horace: 'Too set on safety and fearful of the storm it crawls upon the ground.' And elsewhere: 'Conversations crawling along the ground.'[1]

**744 Venereum iusiurandum irritum / Ἀφροδίσιος ὅρκος οὐκ ἐμποίνιμος /
Lovers' oaths are null and void**
Plato in his *Symposium*: 'It is commonly said that the gods forgive only lovers for perjury.'[1] The general view is that a lover's oath is worthless.

**745 In dolio figulinam / Ἐν πίθῳ τὴν κεραμείαν / To learn the potter's art
on a big jar**
Plato in *Laches*, talking about those who put their skill to the test on some huge project rather than on easy ones as they should, says, 'And to be sure, as the proverb has it, if you practise your potting skill on a big vase, you risk breaking it.'[1]

**746 Γηράσκω δὲ αἰεὶ πολλὰ διδασκόμενος / Consenesco quotidie addiscens
aliquid / With age I learn something new every day**
Solon's words are also cited as a proverb by Plato,[1] and even today it is a very common expression. People say, 'While we live, we learn.'[2]

* * * * *

61. The phrase *arx eloquentiae* 'citadel of eloquence' occurs at Tacitus *Dialogus de oratoribus* 10 and Quintilian 12.11.28.

743 *Adagia* II x 88
1 Horace *Ars poetica* 28 and *Epistles* 2.1.251

744 *Adagia* II iv 90. The Greek version of the title, literally 'a lover's oath carries no penalty,' was added in *1506*, probably from Diogenianus 3.37 (see TrGF 2 Adespota 525). Otto 77
1 Plato *Symposium* 183B, cited in Latin; see C 2 n7.

745 *Adagia* I vi 15. The Greek, probably from Diogenianus 4.44, was added in *1506*. Erasmus used the proverb in Ep 108:102–3 (in 1499) and in Ep 188:8 (in 1506).
1 Plato *Laches* 187B, in Marsilio Ficino's Latin translation. Plato is talking about the danger of applying educational theories immediately to young men before finding out more about them. Erasmus gives this specific context in *1500*, but drops it in *1506*.

746 *Adagia* I viii 60. In *1500* the heading was simply *Solonis dictum* 'A saying of Solon.' This was replaced by the actual adage in *1506*, with the Greek version, closer to Zenobius 3.4 than to Diogenianus 3.80, preceding, rather than following, the Latin version. Otto 1627. Cf Polydore Vergil 294.
1 Plato *Laches* 189A, quoting Solon fragment 18 West, and *Republic* 7.536D
2 Suringar 43

747 Difficilia quae pulchra / Δύσκολα τὰ καλά / Good things are difficult
Plato gave this as a proverb in his *Cratylus* as well as elsewhere. He says, 'According to the old proverb good things are difficult.'[1]

748 Tamquam meum nomen, tamquam digitos teneo / As well as I know my own name, and my fingers
This was said proverbially about certain unwavering knowledge. Martial: 'You tell me this, Afer, all day, every day. / I know it better than I know my own name.'[1] Juvenal: 'As well as his fingers and his nails.'[2] Conversely, when we want to indicate that someone is extremely forgetful we say he has forgotten his own name. Ovid: 'Sooner will we forget our own name.'[3] Jerome: 'So that I almost forgot my own name.'[4]

749 Falcem in messem alienam mittere / To apply the scythe to someone else's harvest
The meaning is to concern oneself with someone else's business.

750 Canis reversus ad vomitum / A dog returns to its own vomit
This is in the Epistles of the apostles, and refers to someone who has attained purity but then slips back again into his old way of life.[1] 'A washed pig wallows in the muck,' which appears in the same verse, has the same meaning.[2]

751 Homunculus ex Caria / Ἀνθρωπίσκος ἐκ Καρίας / A fellow from Caria
This refers to someone who is of low status and of little value. Socrates in

* * * * *

747 *Adagia* II i 12. The Greek version, probably Erasmus' own translation, was added in 1506. The usual form of the proverb in Greek has χαλεπά (Zenobius 6.38) for δύσκολα, but the latter appears in Apostolius 6.39a.
  1 Plato *Cratylus* 384A; also *Hippias maior* 304E, *Republic* 4.435D, 6.497D

748 *Adagia* II iv 91 and cf II iii 96. Otto 543 and 1234
  1 Martial 4.37.6–7
  2 Juvenal 7.232
  3 Ovid *Epistulae ex Ponto* 2.11.5, quoted in *Adagia* II iii 96
  4 Jerome *Letters* 126.2.1 CSEL 56.1 144, also quoted in *Adagia* II iii 96

749 This is a doublet of C 141 You are reaping another's harvest, with slightly different wording.

750 Cf *Adagia* III v 13.
  1 2 Peter 2:22
  2 *Adagia* IV iii 62

751 Cf *Adagia* I vi 14. The Greek was added in 1506. Erasmus seems to have made it up himself, a back formation from the Latin phrase in Marsilio Ficino's translation, as it is not found in the collections of proverbs. Otto 348 *Nachträge* pp 98, 146

Euthydemus tells his interlocutors to conduct the experiment in transformation on him, as if he were a fellow from Caria, meaning someone who is worthless and unimportant.[1] If you destroy such a person, you will incur no loss.

752 Carica Musa / Καρικὴ μοῦσα / Carian music
This refers to something crude and unsophisticated. It is listed as a Greek proverb.[1]

753 Sequitur ver hiemem / Spring follows winter
Ausonius in the preface of his *Monosyllables*: 'Like the old proverb, spring follows winter, I shall now add similar trifles of a more disgusting nature.'[1]

754 Sacra haec non aliter constant / These rites cannot be performed otherwise
The meaning is that this business cannot be conducted in any other way. It appears in Ausonius. In excusing the indecency of the wedding song he has composed he says, 'The subject is a wedding and, like it or not, these rites cannot be conducted otherwise.'[1] If anyone does not think that these concluding words of his are proverbial, let them be noted under some other heading or other.

755 Tenui filo. Divite vena. Paupere vena / With a slender thread. In a rich vein. In a poor vein gap
Each of these figurative expressions appears as a proverb in important writers. 'With a slender thread'[1] refers to a style that is compressed and pointed;

* * * * *

1 Plato *Euthydemus* 285c

752 *Adagia* I viii 79. The Greek title, almost certainly from Diogenianus, was added in *1506*.
1 Diogenianus 5.86

753 *Adagia* II iv 89, where Erasmus says that Ausonius does not use the proverb in the proper sense.
1 Ausonius *Technopaegnion* 4 (p 177 Green), but the text used by Erasmus is corrupt, and a different proverb occurs there.

754 *Adagia* II iv 88
1 Ausonius *Cento nuptialis* (at the end; p 139 Green)

755 *Adagia* II vi 75 (Otto 662) and *Adagia* II vi 76. The source of the first is Horace *Epistles* 2.1.225 (cf Ausonius *Gratiarum actio* 13.61 [p 155 Green]). For the second see Quintilian 11.3.167.
1 The reading of *1500* and *1506* (*stilo* 'pen'), in both title and commentary, is replaced by *filo* 'thread,' in ASD II-9, following the text in Schürer's 1512 edition.

'In a poor vein' or 'In a rich vein' refers to abilities that are barren or fruit-ful respectively. The first image is taken from weaving,[2] the other two from water-courses.

756 Tua voluntate coactus / Compelled willingly

Charinus in Terence says, 'You have been compelled willingly.'[1] This saying suits those who do something gladly and eagerly but wish to appear to be acting under compulsion.

757 Saguntina fames / A Saguntine hunger

Extreme hunger, the kind that a long siege usually brings. Ausonius: 'May sausages free me, wasting away as I am, from this Saguntine hunger.'[1]

758 Faber quas fecit compedes ipse gestat / The smith who made the fetters wears them

That this expression was a proverb is indicated not only by its style but also by an additional argument. In Ausonius, a careful poet, it is linked to a Terentian proverb, so that it gives the same sense as it, but in different words. These are Ausonius' verses:

You who are annoying me with your demands, read these verses
annoying to you.

You made this dish and you must eat it all up.[1]
This is what the old proverb says.
So the smith who made the fetters should wear them.[2]

* * * * *

In *Adagia* II vi 76 Erasmus substitutes *vena* for *filo*, and says that the image comes either from water-courses or from metals.
2 Reading *nentibus* for *mentibus* in *1500* and *1506* with ASD, again on the basis of Schürer's 1512 edition

756 Not in *Adagia*
1 Terence *Andria* 658

757 *Adagia* I ix 67. See Otto 1568n and Otto *Nachträge* p 21.
1 Ausonius *Epistles* *20b.43–4 Green. One part of the text used by Erasmus, *pere-sam* 'wasting away,' is no longer printed by editors, having been replaced by *Perusina* 'of Perusia.' Saguntum was a town in Spain that was besieged by the Carthaginians at the beginning of the Second Punic War between Rome and Carthage.

758 *Adagia* I i 86. Otto 623
1 An adaptation of Terence *Phormio* 318 (= C 533)
2 Ausonius *De bissula* 1.4–6 Green

**759 Tollat te qui non novit / Let him who does not know you
pull you out**

In book six of his *Institutions* Quintilian says, 'What is called a παροιμία
"an adage" is very similar, as are proverbs that can be applied to particular
circumstances, like the reply given to a man who had fallen into the water
and was asking to be lifted out: "Let him who does not know you pull
you out."'[1] So writes Quintilian. But Horace mentions the same proverb
in his *Epistles*, in reference to a impostor called Planus[2] who would often
fall down and pretend he had broken his leg.[3] In pitiful words he would
implore passers-by to lift him up. Any stranger who went to aid him was
fleeced by the trickster. However, his deception became known to many.
Once when the fellow had really broken his leg, he pleaded to be lifted up,
but no one came to his help, since everyone thought that he was playing
his usual tricks. These are Horace's words:

> A man once tricked has no thought to lift an impostor at the crossroads,
> Even if his leg is broken. Though many a tear flow down his cheeks,
> Though he swears by holy Osiris, 'Trust me I am not joking.
> Lift up a man who cannot walk, you cruel people.'
> 'Find a stranger,' that's what his rasping neighbours reply.

And so when we want to indicate to someone that we know his tricks and
that we cannot be deceived by him ever again, we shall say to him, 'Let
him who does not know you pull you out,' or 'Find a stranger.'

760 Nebulae in pariete pictae / Shadows painted on a wall

This is found in Ausonius in a letter addressed to his son Gregorius, in the
sense of something that is empty and trivial.[1] He says, 'Have you ever seen
a shadow painted on a wall.' He uses the proverbial expression 'Shadow

* * * * *

759 *Adagia* I vii 75. Otto 1792
   1 Quintilian 6.3.98. What is translated as 'into the water' reflects Erasmus' text
     (*in aquam*). The correct reading is *nequam* 'bad, worthless.' The translation
     would be 'like the reply given to a worthless man who had fallen and was
     asking to be lifted up.'
   2 The word *planus* means impostor, but Erasmus seems to have taken this for a
     name, as does Pseudo-Acron on Horace *Epistles* 1.17.59.
   3 Horace *Epistles* 1.17.58–62

760 *Adagia* II iv 38. Otto 1212
   1 Ausonius *Cupido cruciatus* (preface, p 109 line 1 Green)

painted on a wall' as a heading for the poem that is attached to the letter, meaning that the content is shallow, frivolous, and as insubstantial as a dream. A shadow is too insubstantial a thing to be depicted in colour.

760A Omnium horarum homo / A man for all hours

This means someone 'who can accommodate himself to seriousness and jesting alike.' According to Quintilian this was said in antiquity of Asinius Pollio.[1]

761 In caelo sum / I am in heaven

This is just as if one were to say 'I am a god.'[1] Cicero to Atticus: 'If what has been agreed about me is not adhered to, I am in heaven.'[2]

762 Deum facere / To make a god of someone

This means to exalt someone with extravagant praise. Terence: 'I make you a god.'[1]

763 Omnibus vestigiis inquirere / To investigate every trace

This means to examine something with the greatest care and thoroughness.

764 Ne sis patruus mihi. Ne sis mihi tutor / Don't play the uncle with me. Don't play the guardian with me

The sternness that uncles show to their nephews gave rise to a proverb that appears in Horace: 'Whether I was right or wrong in choosing to do this, do not play the uncle with me,' meaning 'do not chastise me.'[1] In his *Odes* the same poet referred to an uncle's threatening and censorious language:

* * * * *

760A *Adagia* I iii 86. By error this adage is given the same number as the immediately preceding one. Otto 830
   1 Quintilian 6.3.110, from where Erasmus also draws the interpretation of the saying. Asinius Pollio (76 BC–AD 4) was an accomplished politician, general and writer. He wrote a history of the period 60–42 BC, covering the civil war.

761 *Adagia* I v 100. Otto 288
   1 *Adagia* I v 99
   2 Cicero *Ad Atticum* 2.9.1

762 *Adagia* I v 9. Otto 515
   1 Terence *Adelphoe* 535

763 *Adagia* IV ii 18. The source may be a humanistic text. No instance of the expression has been found in classical Latin.

764 *Adagia* II iv 39. Otto 1357 and 1807
   1 Horace *Satires* 2.3.87–8

'Fearing the lashes of his uncle's tongue.'[2] Cicero against Herennius: 'In this case he was like an uncle, a censor, a schoolmaster. He chastised Marcus Caelius in a way that no parent ever chastised his son.'[3] Similar is what Persius writes: 'But you are even paler. Don't play the guardian with me.'[4]

765 **Aristarchi obelisci asteriscique. Censoria virgula / The obelus and asterisk of Aristarchus. A mark of censure**
In the same way the obelus and asterisk of Aristarchus entered everyday language.[1] We use 'to obelize' in the sense of 'to strike out and remove,' and 'to mark with an asterisk' (that is, 'with a star') in the sense of 'to accept,' or 'to give the mark of approval from on high, so to speak.' Some think it is taken from navigation,[2] for sailors plot the position of the shore-line or of a harbour by means of a star. In Jerome we find everywhere the expression 'O you who are the Aristarchus of our generation.'[3] He means 'you who take the role of judge about the talents of all, praising some and condemning others.' This is what Aristarchus did with respect to Homer's verses. Horace: 'He will become an Aristarchus.'[4] 'A mark of censure' has the same meaning, and Jerome makes joking reference to it on many occasions.[5]

766 **Refricare cicatricem. Vulnus recrudescere / To rub open a scar. A wound that breaks open again**
When pain that has diminished with time breaks out again, we say proverbially that the scar is being rubbed open.[1] Similarly, when mental

* * * * *

2 Horace *Odes* 3.12.3
3 Cicero *Pro M. Caelio* 11.25. Herennius was one of the speakers on the opposite side.
4 Persius 3.96

765 Cf *Adagia* I v 57 and 58, and, for 'A mark of censure,' IV viii 26 The obelus of censure. Otto 370 *Nachträge* p 23
  1 Aristarchus was one of the greatest of the Alexandrian scholars, renowned for his work on the Homeric corpus. He became head of the library in Alexandria c 153 BC.
  2 Perhaps a reference to Diogenianus 2.66. See also *Suda* A 4257. Cf Cicero *Academica* 1.2.66.
  3 Jerome *Adversus Rufinum* 1.17 PL 23 410B, CCSL 79 15; *Letters* 57.12 CSEL 54 525
  4 Horace *Ars poetica* 450
  5 Jerome *Letters* 61.2.5 CSEL 54 578; 50.4.1 CSEL 54 392

766 *Adagia* I vi 80. For the second cf *Adagia* I vi 79.
  1 Cicero *De lege agraria* 3.2.4

anguish returns, we say that the wound is flaring up again. Both of these expressions use a very fine metaphor. Examples are too frequent for there to be any need to cite them here. Cicero used this metaphor in a very elegant fashion against Clodius. When the common people were already angered by a shortage of food, Clodius goaded them on to further fury by seditious speeches. Cicero said, 'You were the fingernail that broke open this ulcer.'[2] The verb *suffricare* means to re-open by gentle rubbing; and so we have the expression *suffricare memoriam* 'to jog the memory.'[3]

767 Domi habet / He has it at home

We are said to have at home that which is part of our own resources and for which we do not need to go elsewhere. It seems to have arisen from the custom of borrowing equipment from outsiders; we have already spoken about this.[1] 'He has philosophers of his own.'[2] 'He has his own resources from which to learn.'[3] 'This conclusion is all home-grown.'[4] 'I test this at home,'[5] meaning from his own resources. 'You have the means at home to be happy.' 'You have the plan at home; do not seek it from outsiders.' 'To be at home' (*in domo esse*) means that what is needed is ready and at hand, and stored, as it were, at home. It often occurs in Plautus.[6]

768 Obviis ulnis / With open arms

This is taken from a common gesture and then applied to the mind, meaning 'with great affection and eagerness.' This is how we usually greet dearest friends whom we have deeply missed when we see them in the

* * * * *

2 Cicero *De domo sua* 5.12, cited in *Adagia* I vi 79

3 Erasmus may be thinking of *refricare memoriam* (cf Cicero *Philippics* 3.7.18). No example of *suffricare memoriam* has been identified.

767 *Adagia* I x 49, also I x 48. Otto 573 and 574

1 See C 403.

2 Terence *Adelphoe* 412–13. Erasmus follows the corrupt text of early editions in reading *philosophos* 'philosophers' (printed as *phōs* in the editions) for the correct *phy!* – an uncommon interjection. Terence should read 'Fi! He has [resources?] of his own.'

3 Jerome *Letters* 60.10.2 CSEL 64 559, but this is also similar to Terence *Adelphoe* 413 (see n2).

4 Plautus *Casina* 224 and *Cistellaria* 204

5 Cf Plautus *Amphitryo* 637. The next two examples may simply be Erasmus' own invention.

6 As at Plautus *Epidicus* 653

768 *Adagia* II ix 54. Cf Otto 1049.

distance. It occurs in Quintilian: 'There was no one who did not accept your work eagerly and, as the saying goes, "With open hands" or "With open arms." '[1]

769 Bellicum canere. Receptui canere / To give the signal for battle. To sound the retreat

Both of these are taken from military practices. Those who are about to go into the fray sound the signal for battle, and a signal to retreat is given to those who are about to return to camp, in other words, the retreat is sounded. This is why by means of a proverbial metaphor we use the phrase 'To give the signal for battle' in the sense of urging and encouraging. 'To sound the retreat' means to put an end to something. This is especially true if the aim of our urging or if what we wish to be ended has some similarity with the tumult of battle. There is no need for us to make use of examples for such a well-known matter. In Martial 'let them sound the trumpet' means the same as 'let us join battle.'[1]

770 Stilum vertere. Stilo infigere. Stilo appetere / To reverse the pen. To stick in the pen. To attack with the pen

The stilus, the writing instrument of the ancients, gave rise to several proverbial expressions. They use the phrase 'To reverse the stilus' in the sense of changing what one has written, or even of attacking what one has previously praised. Jerome *Against Rufinus*: 'As long as I did not reject your praise, you followed me as if I were your master, you called me brother and colleague, and claimed that I was orthodox on all points. Now that I do not accept your praise and think that I am unworthy of the support of such a great man, you immediately reverse your pen and attack what you previously praised, bringing forth both sweetness and bitterness from the same mouth.'[1] 'To stick in the pen' means to use one's writings to inveigh against someone, 'To attack with the pen' means to censure someone in writing.

* * * * *

1 Not in Quintilian. Perhaps from a humanist text

769 *Adagia* III v 88. These expressions are used figuratively in Poliziano's *Epistolae* (1.14, 64, 175, 177 Maier). See also Cicero *Philippics* 7.1.3. Otto 1510
1 Martial 11.20.8

770 *Adagia* I v 59; Otto 1692. According to TLL the last two expressions in the heading are not found in classical Latin.
1 Jerome *Adversus Rufinum* 1.31 PL 23 424A, CCSL 79 32

771 **Iacere aleam. Extra omnem aleam / To throw the dice.**
Beyond the fall of the dice
Since dice are subject to luck and chance, we use them to denote an uncertain outcome. When Caesar was about to lead his troops over the Rubicon, he said, 'Let the whole die be cast.'[1] He meant that they should entrust to chance how everything turned out, but that they would at least put everything to the test.[2] Pliny in the preface to his *History of the World*: 'Cicero uses this procedure, even though the question of his genius is beyond the fall of the dice.'[3] And when we use the phrase 'beyond the fall of the dice' there can be no intervention of chance; things cannot turn out contrary to expectations. A metaphor taken from the throw of dice. Quintilian expressed the same idea, using a different metaphor: 'Let us entrust our sails to the wind, and as for those setting sail, let us wish them well.'[4] Horace also said the following in a proverbial sense: 'Very rarely does chance deceive us,' meaning that hardly ever did things turn out badly.[5] And in his *Odes*: 'A work full of risky chance.'[6]

772 **Ad unguem / To the fingernail**
A metaphor taken from workers in marble who test the joints in the marble by drawing their fingernail over the surface. Therefore, anything on which the utmost care is expended so that nothing escapes the diligence of the craftsman is said to be made 'To the fingernail.' Horace: 'Cocceius, a man finished to the fingernail.'[1] And elsewhere:

* * * * *

771 *Adagia* I iv 32. Polydore Vergil 40; Otto 55
  1 Plutarch *Moralia* 206c; Erasmus *Apophthegmata* 4.206 CWE 37 403. For the form of the proverb that he gives here Erasmus uses the Latin translation of Plutarch by Franceso Filelfo (*iacta sit omnis alea*). Cf Suetonius *Divus Iulius* 32 where the proverb is transmitted as *iacta alea est* 'the die has been cast,' though Erasmus suggested emending *est* to *esto* 'let it be' in his edition of Suetonius.
  2 Suetonius *Divus Iulius* 32
  3 Pliny *Naturalis historia* praefatio 7. Poliziano uses the expression *extra aleam* at *Epistolae* 1.19 (1.13 Maier) and 12.15 (1.175 Maier), as does Erasmus (Allen Ep 111:145–7).
  4 Quintilian *Epistula ad Tryphonem* 3. This is the prefatory letter to *Institutio oratoria*.
  5 Horace *Satires* 2.5.50
  6 Horace *Odes* 2.1.6

772 *Adagia* I v 91. The phrase is used by Poliziano (*Miscellanea* 11; 1.237 Maier) and by Erasmus Allen Ep 20:115. Polydore Vergil 278; Otto 1827
  1 Horace *Satires* 1.5.32–3. The phrase is actually applied to a man called Fonteius, the correct name finally appearing in the 1533 edition of the *Adagia*.

Find fault with the poem that
Many a day and many a change has not refined,
And ten-fold shaping has not smoothed it to the fingernail.[2]

Persius marvellously combined this metaphor and the one that follows
it in one passage:

Since each joint accepts smoothly the test
Of the demanding fingernail, he knows how to draw his verse
As if setting straight the red cord with one eye shut.[3]

773 Ad amussim. Ad perpendiculum / By rule. By the square.

Whenever we want to indicate the utmost diligence of a craftsman and the
perfect state of an object we say that the thing was made *Ad amussim* 'By
rule' or *examussim* 'by exact rule' (for we find both forms of the expression) or *amussatim* 'in accordance with a rule.' The measuring rule is the
cord used by tradesmen to ensure that their stones and floors run square.[1]
'By the square' means the same as 'By rule,' and today when we want to
indicate that something has been made faultlessly we say it is made 'on
the line or cord.'[2] In addition when the ancients wished something to be
thought of as having been made with the closest attention and finest judgment, they said it had been made *pensiculate* or *pensiculatim* 'with careful
consideration.'[3] This word is taken from the word for a paymaster.[4]

In giving all this information, however, I rather think that I have dealt
with the topic at somewhat excessive length.

* * * * *

2 Horace *Ars poetica* 292–4
3 Persius 1.64–6, with a text that varies slightly from the usual one, since Erasmus reads *effundit* for the correct *effundat*. The correct sense would be 'so
  that each joint may accept ...' The image of the red cord in the last verse
  does not get an entry of its own in the *Adagia*, but is quoted at I v 88 (at the
  end).

773 *Adagia* I v 90 (with examples from Aulus Gellius, Pompeius Festus and Nonius
  Marcellus); Otto 102
  1 The first two sentences in the commentary are drawn from Perotti's *Cornu-
    copiae* 446:23–6.
  2 Suringar 2
  3 The adverb *pensiculate* is very rare. It occurs in Gellius *Noctes Atticae* 1.3.12,
    from where Erasmus probably took it.
  4 The word for this occupation, *libripendens*, indicates that the paymaster had to
    weigh or count out the pay owing to the soldiers, and this had to be done
    very carefully.

774 Elimare. Prima et suprema manus. Ad umbelicum / To polish with the file. The first touch and the final touch. To the scroll's end

These are taken from craftsmen's workshops: to polish a book with the file and to apply the file; to add the final touch,[1] meaning the last part of a task after which nothing else needs to be done. 'All this task needs is the final touch.'[2] Horace used the phrase 'to bring something to the scroll's end' in the sense of completing it.[3] The first attempt at making an artefact is called 'The first touch,' meaning that the object is still in a rough and crude state.

775 A teneris unguiculis / From when their nails were soft

Cicero attests that this was a Greek proverb. He says, 'From when their nails were soft, as the Greeks say.'[1] Horace: 'And she dreams of impure sex, from when her nails were soft.'[2] 'From the cradle' has the same sense, meaning right from early childhood.[3]

776 Pandere *vel* contrahere vela / To spread *or* to draw in the sails

These are metaphors that are used everywhere. 'To spread sails' means doing something boldly and confidently,[1] 'To draw in the sails' means doing something in a modest and niggardly way.[2]

777 Plumbeo gladio iugulare / To cut a man's throat with a sword of lead

This means to refute someone despite using a weak and worthless argument. Cicero to Atticus: 'Although he said that his throat would be cut,

* * * * *

774 The first of these adages is mentioned in *Adagia* I v 58, but does not have independent status. For the second and third adages cf *Adagia* I ii 34 (Otto 1051) and I ii 32 (Otto 1816). Cf Polydore Vergil 306 (for the third).
1 Used by Ermolao Barbaro regarding the completion of his *Castigationes Plinianae* at *Epistolae* 153.1 (2.71 Branca)
2 This quotation is Erasmus' invention.
3 Horace *Epodes* 14.8

775 *Adagia* I vii 52; Otto 1826
1 Cicero *Ad familiares* 1.6.2. The Greek equivalent (Ἐξ ἁπαλῶν ὀνύχων) occurs only in Apostolius (7.51a), but this collection was not accessible to Erasmus until he was in Venice in 1508.
2 Horace *Odes* 3.6.23–4
3 *Adagia* I vii 53 (Otto 478). Cf Livy 4.36.5.

776 *Adagia* v i 32 (Otto 1857) for the second adage. For the first cf *Adagia* I iv 33 and IV vi 1.
1 As at Quintilian 6.1.52
2 As at Cicero *Ad Atticum* 1.16.2

777 *Adagia* II v 10. Otto 1440

even with a sword made of lead.'[1] Elsewhere Cicero calls a poor argument 'a dagger of lead.'[2]

778 Lupi illum priores viderunt / The wolves have seen him first

What is found in Virgil in his eclogue entitled *Moeris*, 'The wolves have seen Moeris first,' is said by a man of no little learning to be a proverb.[1] And it may be that it was a proverb among rustics, who applied it to a person who had lost his voice. Servius does not actually say that this was a proverb, but we have Terence's expression, 'The wolf in the story,'[2] which originates in the belief, according to the natural philosophers, that a wolf deprives a man of the ability to speak if it sees him before he sees it.

779 Πανικός / Panicus casus / A panic attack

What Cicero writes in his letters to Atticus has the look of a proverb. He says, 'I think there will be a most horrible war, unless, as you write, there is a wave of panic.'[1] This comes from the god Pan, who often causes sudden, strange, mental confusion and makes people change their intentions.[2] Cicero means therefore that war will break out unless there is sudden change of mind, like a panic attack.

780 Celerius elephanti pariunt / Elephants give birth faster

Some[1] think that what we find in Pliny the Elder in the preface of his *History of the World* should be regarded as a proverb: 'As for erudite men, I always

* * * * *

1 Cicero *Ad Atticum* 1.16.2
2 Cicero *De finibus* 4.18.48

778 *Adagia* I vii 86. Polydore Vergil 42; Otto 989
 1 Virgil *Eclogues* 9.54. The 'man of no little learning' is Niccolò Perotti (see *Cornucopiae* 160:25–6).
 2 This sentence and the two that follow are based on Servius in his commentary on *Eclogues* 9.54. The Terentian allusion is to *Adelphoe* 537. See C 517.

779 *Adagia* III vii 3, where Erasmus draws on Poliziano (*Miscellanea* 28; 1.249–50 Maier). In *1500* the adage is given as *Parthicus casus* 'A Parthian incident' or 'A Parthian collapse.' At the end of his commentary in *1500* he suggests that a textual change to *Panicus casus* is possible. See n1.
 1 Cicero *Ad Atticum* 7.26.3. The correct text is *Parthicus casus* 'a Parthian collapse.' Cicero means that that there will be a terrible war unless either Caesar or Pompey retreats in the manner of the Parthians.
 2 This sentence is a paraphrase of one in Poliziano's *Miscellanea* 28 (1.249–51 Maier).

780 *Adagia* I ix 11. Polydore Vergil 62; Otto 594
 1 Probably a reference to Perotti (*Cornucopiae* 723:54)

expected them to give birth to something that would oppose the books that I published on scholarly matters, and yet there have been miscarriages, one after the other, for ten years now. Even elephants would give birth faster.'[2] Plautus in *Stichus*, on the gestation of elephants: 'I have often heard it said that an elephant is pregnant for ten years.'[3] Pliny also says in book eight, 'It is a common belief that their pregnancy lasts ten years, even if Aristotle believes that the period of gestation is two years and that they produce only one offspring on only one occasion.'[4]

781 **Parvo pedi magnos calceos circumdare / To put large sandals on small feet**
What is written in Quintilian in his *Institutions* is surely proverbial. He says that those who talk grandiloquently in some trivial case are putting the boots of Hercules on a child.[1] This seems to come from an apophthegm of Agesilaus. 'When someone was lavishing excessive praise on a sophist for making the most trifling matter seem the most important by his style of oratory, Agesilaus said that he judged a man who put big shoes on a small foot to be in no way a good cobbler.'[2]

782 **Sus Minervam / Ὗς Ἀθηνᾶν / The sow teaches Minerva**
This is a very well-known adage, directed at ignorant persons who try to

* * * * *

2 Pliny *Naturalis historia* praefatio 28
3 Plautus *Stichus* 167–9
4 Pliny *Naturalis historia* 8.28

781 This adage becomes *Adagia* III vi 67. It is also cited at C 327. Cf *Adagia* II v 46. The Latin form of the proverb is probably taken from Ermolao Barbaro (*Epistolae* 81.15 = Poliziano *Epistolae* 9.5; 1.102 Branca). Otto 1387
　1 Quintilian 6.1.36
　2 Plutarch *Moralia* 208c; Erasmus *Apophthegmata* 1.5 CWE 37 22. Agesilaus was king of Sparta from 398 to 360 BC. The quotation, given in Latin, resembles Francesco Filelfo's translation of this passage in his printed edition of this work of Plutarch. For Erasmus' defence of his use of translations, specifically Filelfo's, see CWE 37 7–8 with n22.

782 *Adagia* I i 40. The Greek version of the title was added in 1506. It does not appear to be in the collections of Greek proverbs. Erasmus' source may have been Plutarch *Moralia* 803D *Praecepta gerendae reipublicae* 'Precepts of Statecraft,' but this passage is not used by Erasmus in the *Adagia* until 1515. Cf also Theocritus 5.23. and Plutarch *Demosthenes* 11.5. On balance, it looks as if Erasmus may have formed the Greek version himself from Jerome's Latin. Ermolao Barbaro used the proverb, in its Latin form, in a letter to Giorgio Merula (*Epistolae* 29; 1.44 Bianca). See also Pompeius Festus 408.14–17 Lindsay. Polydore Vergil 67; Otto 1118

give instruction to someone who should instead be teaching them. Jerome *Against Rufinus*: 'I pass over the Greeks whose wisdom you brag about. In pursuing foreign things you have almost forgotten your native tongue, in case it should seem, as the old proverb says, that the sow is teaching Minerva.'[1] The origin of the proverb seems to have been some ancient fable.

783 Multi Manni Ariciae / There are many men called Mannius at Aricia

In honour of Diana of Aricia Mannius is said to have consecrated a grove, which itself was called after the town. So Festus Pompeius tells us.[1] This Mannius had very many illustrious descendants, also called Mannius. This gave rise to the proverb that there are many men called Mannius at Aricia.

784 Diomedis et Glauci permutatio / The exchange between Diomede and Glaucus

The exchange of armour between Diomede and Glaucus that is told by Homer became proverbial, like many other parts of that poet's work. The story is recounted in book six of *The Iliad* in the following fashion.[1] Diomede and Glaucus advanced to take up position between the two armies, ready to join battle in single combat. Glaucus told of his ancestry and then Diomede suggested that they become guest-friends instead of enemies. So that the rest of the armies would realize what was happening he said that they should exchange their armour. Glaucus was the first to give his armour to Diomede. This was made of gold and was worth one hundred cattle. Diomede then handed over his armour, made of bronze, worth no more than nine cattle. When this unequal exchange was complete, Diomede was thought to have been clever and Glaucus stupid. Because of this whenever we want to indicate an exchange of gifts that is extremely imbalanced we say that it is an exchange between Diomede and Glaucus. Pliny the

* * * * *

1 Jerome *Adversus Rufinum* 1.17 PL 23 410B, CCSL 79 15; cf *Letters* 46.1.1 CSEL 54 329.

783 *Adagia* II x 24. How the proverb is used is left unexplained here by Erasmus. Later, in the 1515 edition of the *Adagia*, he reports one interpretation according to which the expression was applied to those who were physically deformed. Polydore Vergil 242; Otto 1030
  1 Pompeius Festus 128.15–18 Lindsay by way of Filippo Beroaldo (*Annotationes centum* 44)

784 *Adagia* I ii 1. Much of the discussion (with references) was taken directly from Filippo Beroaldo *Annotationes centum* 47; see Heinimann 168. Polydore Vergil 102; Otto 384
  1 Homer *Iliad* 6.212–36

Younger, in a letter to Flaccus: 'You are getting therefore letters that bear
no fruit and are frank in their ingratitude. They do not even imitate the
shrewdness of Diomede when he made his exchange with Glaucus.'² When
Aulus Gellius in his *Nights* book two compares Caecilius' translation with
the Greek passage in Menander and points out that it is far below the
original in quality, he says, 'I swear that the disparity between the armour of Diomede and Glaucus was no greater.'³ The same exchange is
mentioned in the introduction to the *Digest* in these words: 'In our times
the difference between the new laws and the old is as great as between
what Glaucus and Diomede offered each other in Homer, the father of
all virtue, when they exchanged what was quite dissimilar.'⁴ Martial: 'You
were never so stupid, Glaucus, I think, as when you gave gold in return
for bronze.'⁵

785 Non sus quivis intellegit / Not every pig knows this
This refers to something that is extremely difficult to understand. Plato in
Laches: 'And so, as the proverb has it, not every pig would know this.'¹

**786 Flere novercae tumulum / Πρὸς τὸ σῆμα μητρυιᾶς θρηνεῖν / To weep
over your stepmother's grave**
This means to feign distress with false tears, when in fact you are very
happy. It is a Greek proverb.¹

787 Homo non homo / A man who is not a man
This suits a weak and effeminate man. Plato mentions a riddle of this
kind in *The Republic* book five.¹ Even if he says it is a children's riddle,
I thought I should include it. A man (who is not a man), who can see

* * * * *

2 Pliny *Letters* 5.2.2. The context is that Pliny is unable to show his gratitude in
a material way for a gift he has received from his correspondent.
3 Gellius *Noctes Atticae* 2.23.7
4 Digest *Constitutio 'Omnem'* section 11 (at the beginning of the *Digest*)
5 Martial 9.94.3–4

785 Cited in *Adagia* III iv 6 Nobody who is wicked shall know this
1 Plato *Laches* 196D, quoted in Latin; see C 2 n7.

786 *Adagia* I ix 10. The Greek, taken from Diogenianus 6.34, was added in 1506.
The source of the Latin form is probably Ermolao Barbaro *Epistolae* 81.15 (=
Poliziano *Epistolae* 9.5), 1.102 Branca.
1 In addition to being cited at Diogenianus 6.34, under 'Megarian tears,' the
adage has its own entry at Diogenianus 7.66 (with different wording).

787 Not in *Adagia*
1 Plato *Republic* 5.479C

(but cannot see), struck (but struck not) a bird that was not a bird, with a stone that was not a stone, on a tree that was not a tree. The answer is a one-eyed eunuch struck with a pumice stone a bat's wing on an elderberry bush.[2]

788 Polypus / Πολύποδος ὁμοιότης / A polyp. The camouflaging polyp
In *The Pot of Gold* Plautus calls thieves and men with sticky fingers 'polyps,' proverbially, in my opinion, and certainly wittily. He says, 'I know those polyps; they hold fast to whatever they touch.'[1] He was referring to the octopus; with its suckers and whip-like tentacles it draws in and holds fast by suction whatever it attacks.

789 Victitant succo suo / They live on their own juice
This is a marvellous adage to apply to parasites.[1] When they happen to be given a sumptuous dinner, they gorge themselves, but they can endure long periods of not eating when they fail to get a meal. The notion is taken from snails; in the heat they shrink inside their shells and live off their own juice until rain comes. The expression occurs in Plautus in *The Two Captives*.[2]

790 Nucleum amisi, reliquit pignori putamina / I've lost the kernel, he's left the shell as a pledge
A verse of Plautus from the same play, spoken by Hegio.[1] When he discovered he had been tricked, and had released[2] the master instead of the

* * * * *

2 The scholia on the Platonic passage give fuller versions of the riddle that is mentioned in Plato's text. The tree that was not a tree is identified as a fennel stalk.

788 *Adagia* II iii 91. The Greek version, from Diogenianus 7.73, was added in *1506*. The adage refers to the ability of the polyp to change colour in keeping with its surroundings. It has little to do with what Erasmus says of the polyp here. Otto 1446
1 Plautus *Aulularia* 198

789 *Adagia* II viii 80. Otto *Nachträge* pp 30–1, 247
1 One of the stock characters of New Comedy was called a parasite. His main characteristics were poverty and an obsession with getting free meals.
2 Plautus *Captivi* 83. The play was also entitled *Duo captivi* 'The Two Captives' in early editions.

790 *Adagia* II ix 75. Otto 1247
1 Plautus *Captivi* 655
2 The text in *1500* and *1506* reads *emisse* 'had bought.' This makes no sense, and is a printer's error for *emisisse* 'to have sent away,' a reading found in

slave (keeping the latter, who he thought was the master), he said, 'I have lost the kernel, and he's left the shell as a pledge.' The meaning is that the person from whom he was expecting to make a profit has escaped, leaving behind someone who was worth nothing.

791 Exordiri telam / To set up the web
The meaning is to initiate some enterprise skilfully. Plautus in *The Bacchis Sisters*: 'I've set up this web not at all badly.'[1]

792 Leoninam pellem indutus / Τὴν λεοντῆν ἐνδυόμενος / Wearing a lionskin
In Plato's *Cratylus* Socrates says, 'But now that I have put on the lionskin, I should not be frightened. Nay, these terms are splendid, as you say,'[1] the sense of the expression being 'now that I have taken over the arrogant role of teacher.' In the printed texts, however, *Leontinam* 'from Leontini' is read.[2] The adage seems to have come from a fable about a runaway ass that covered itself with a lionskin and terrified wild beasts that did not know any better.[3]

793 Vallum caveamve supergredi / Ὑπὲρ τὰ ἐσκαμμένα πηδᾶν / To leap over rampart or trenches
This means to go beyond what is proper and permitted. Socrates in the same dialogue: 'I seem now to be making excessively tiresome demands

* * * * *

Schürer's 1513 edition. In the *Adagia* the idea is expressed slightly differently, but the verb used is *amitto* 'to lose.'

791 *Adagia* II vi 68; Otto 1749
　1 Plautus *Bacchides* 350

792 *Adagia* I iii 66. The Greek, probably from Diogenianus 4.54, was added in 1506. Also in Zenobius 3.75 and *Suda* E 1190. Here begins a series (792–801, excepting 799) of adages drawn from Marsilio Ficino's Latin translation of the Platonic corpus.
　1 Plato *Cratylus* 411A, cited in Latin. The quotation is incomplete.
　2 This is a reference to printed editions of Marsilio Ficino's translations of Plato.
　3 The story about the ass at Cumae, as told by Lucian *The Fisherman* 32, is very similar. See *Adagia* I vii 12. For the fable see *Aesopica* 358 Perry, Babrius 139 (*Babrius and Phaedrus* ed B.E. Perry [Cambridge, Mass 1955]). See c 467.

793 Cf *Adagia* I x 93. The Greek was added in 1506. The verb used by Plato, however, is ἅλλεσθαι, not πηδᾶν. The latter verb appears in some MSS of Zenobius at 6.23, Erasmus' probable source, though he could have found it in *Suda* Υ 364 or in a scholion to Lucian *Gallus* 6.

and to be leaping over the rampart or palisade, as the saying goes.'[1] This is taken from the enclosed area in which men fought each other.

794 Ex tua officina. Ex aliena officina / From your own workshop. From someone else's workshop

We are said to draw from our own workshop those things that we have devised by ourselves. Taken from traders who sell goods made by others. Hermogenes in *Cratylus*: 'Socrates, I think that you have heard this from someone and are not drawing, in a rather crude way, from your own workshop.'[1]

795 A se ipso decipi perniciosissimum / There is nothing worse than self-deception

A sentiment of Socrates in Plato that deserves to be ever on our lips and ever in our thoughts. Socrates gives an explanation that could itself be regarded as a proverb. He says, 'It is a very dangerous situation when the deceiver never leaves you and is always your closest companion.'[1]

796 A fronte pariter atque a tergo contemplari / To examine from front and back both at once

This means to examine something carefully and closely. Socrates in Plato's *Cratylus*: 'And so I should often consider these previous remarks and, as the poet says, "look fore and aft."'[1]

797 Ab hac mensa non potes abesse / You cannot leave this table

The meaning is that you cannot do without a pleasure that you deeply crave. Socrates in *Phaedrus*: 'For how could I leave this table?'[1] Although Socrates was extremely eager to hear discourses, Phaedrus had just sworn

* * * * *

1 Plato *Cratylus* 413A, quoted in Latin; see C 2 n7.

794 *Adagia* II vi 66
  1 Plato *Cratylus* 413D. The metaphor 'from your own workshop' is Ficino's translation of the verb αὐτοσχεδιάζειν 'to extemporize' in Plato.

795 Not in *Adagia*. Like the preceding examples, this is taken from Marsilio Ficino's Latin translation of Plato.
  1 Plato *Cratylus* 428D, quoted in Latin

796 *Adagia* III i 53
  1 Plato *Cratylus* 428D, quoting Homer *Iliad* 1.343, 3.109

797 Cf *Adagia* II i 37.
  1 Plato *Phaedrus* 236E, given in Latin

that he would never deliver one unless Socrates explained what he had meant. Socrates is jokingly saying that he is driven on by this one thing, his inability to do without the pleasure of hearing Phaedrus.

798 Dulcis ancon / A sweet bend

Socrates in *Phaedrus*: 'My dear Phaedrus, it has escaped your notice that "A sweet bend" (a proverb, *ancon* meaning literally "elbow")[1] comes from the long bend in the Nile, and in addition you are unaware that the citizens renowned for their wisdom[2] are very eager to write speeches and to bequeath them to posterity. They are so fond of the admirers of their works that they refer to those who always praise them at the beginning of their speeches.'[3] This is certainly what Socrates says at this point. In the meantime, however, we shall mark this adage with a *lambda* until the situation becomes more clear.[4]

799 A caelo ad terram / From heaven to earth

In Plautus when a buyer asked whether he might ask some questions of a girl, the vendor gave him permission to ask as much as he wanted, saying, 'From heaven to earth, whatever you want.'[1]

800 Ante pedes. Ad pedes revolvi / At one's feet. To roll at one's feet

This refers to what is present and at hand. What presents itself of its own

* * * * *

798 *Adagia* II i 38. There Erasmus explains the phrase as a euphemism, a way of averting harm in a dangerous situation, since this stretch of the Nile in question was hazardous. The various interpretations are discussed by Bühler 5.572–81 on Zenobius Athous 2.102. The interpretation of the phrase in Plato's *Phaedrus* (257D) is bedevilled by textual problems there. The proverb is found in Zenobius 2.92 and *Suda* A 249.
1 What is in parentheses is Erasmus' addition to the quotation.
2 The sense of the Greek original is rather 'the most ambitious of politicians.' Erasmus is following Marsilio Ficino's translation.
3 Plato *Phaedrus* 257D. Many scholars have thought that the text of the original has suffered interpolations. 'Sweet elbow' may have stood alone, as a way of rebutting what Phaedrus has just said, that politicians are reluctant (not 'are eager') to write speeches. It would be similar to our 'yes, and pigs can fly' in response to some statement that we do not believe.
4 That is, as to whether the expression is really a proverb or not. At C 261 the letter *lambda* is taken to mean deferment of a case in the judicial system.

799 *Adagia* II v 95. Otto 281
1 Plautus *Persa* 604

800 *Adagia* III vii 17. Otto 1389

accord is said to roll at one's feet, an expression that occurs more than once in Plato.[1]

801 In easdem ansas pervenisti / You are caught in the same grip
Plato in *Phaedrus*: 'On this point, my friend, you are caught in the same grip.'[1] 'The meaning is that he cannot slip away in the way he wants. Rather, he is caught and cannot escape without speaking.

802 Herculem insimulas ignaviae / You are accusing Hercules of cowardice
The meaning is that you are accusing someone of a fault that could not be more inappropriate. It is as if someone were to accuse Cato of being unprincipled, Lucretia of licentiousness, Socrates of intemperance, Cicero of lacking eloquence.[1] I remember reading this in Plutarch.[2]

803 Dares Entellum provocas / You are Dares challenging Entellus
In *Aeneid* book five Virgil introduces Dares, who exults in his strength and youth, and is arrogant and boastful. He challenges Entellus to a boxing match. Entellus was an old man, but with good experience for such a contest. Dares was soon defeated by him.[1] Jerome, writing to Augustine, says, 'Remember Dares and Entellus.'[2] The meaning is that Augustine should beware of provoking him to a fight because he was young and brash and Jerome was old and had had enough of such disputes. Augustine would discover, perhaps to his great cost, what Jerome could accomplish when angered.

* * * * *

1 As at *Republic* 4.432D; cf *Theaetetus* 174A.

801 *Adagia* II i 36. This ends the series of adages from Plato that began with C 792.
  1 Plato *Phaedrus* 236B, cited in Latin as usual, though the Latin form of the adage is a fairly literal translation of the original Greek (εἰς τὰς ὁμοίας λαβὰς ἐλήλυθας), which is not given in the heading.

802 Not in *Adagia*
  1 Probably the Elder Cato, who was renowned for his strict morals and stern disposition (but see n2). Lucretia stabbed herself in shame after being raped by the son of Tarquinius Superbus.
  2 Plutarch *Cato Minor* 52.5, where Plutarch uses the 'proverb,' part of a quotation from Euripides, as a comment on Caesar's accusation of avarice, directed at the Younger Cato.

803 *Adagia* III i 69
  1 Virgil *Aeneid* 5.368–460
  2 Jerome *Letters* 102.2.2 CSEL 55 236. Cf C 278.

804 In aere meo est / He is in my pay

When wè want to indicate that someone is bound to us by our kindnesses
to him we say that he is in our pay. It appears in Cicero.[1]

**805 Amici mores noveris, non oderis / Know a friend's failings,
but hate them not**

Porphyrion informs us that these words were proverbial.[1] No one should
be ill-tempered about the minor failings of his friends.

806 Bithus contra Bacchium / Bithus against Bacchius

Bithus and Bacchius were a well-known pair of gladiators, mentioned by
Suetonius.[1] They matched each other in skill and bravery. Consequently
whenever two rogues, equally dishonest, are in contention with each other,
with neither wishing to yield to the other, we can use this allegorical expression. Horace in his *Satires*: 'Never was Bacchius better matched with
Bithus.'[2] He meant that Rupilius and Persius were equally unscrupulous.

**807 Commodandum amicis, sed usque ad aras / One must oblige a friend,
but only as far as the altar**

As Gellius tells us in his *Nights*, when Pericles was asked by a friend to
commit perjury in some case, he replied in the following way: Δεῖ με συμ-
πράττειν τοῖς φίλοις, ἀλλὰ μέχρι θείων 'I must oblige my friends, but not
beyond the altars of the gods.'[1]

808 Vel caeco appareat / Even a blind man could see that

A proverbial exaggeration relating to what is extremely obvious.

* * * * *

804 *Adagia* I vii 51. Otto 30
  1 Cicero *Ad familiares* 13.62; 15.14.1

805 *Adagia* II v 96. The adage is an iambic senarius and appears among the verses
  ascribed to Publilius Syrus, a writer of mimes of the first century BC (see n1).
  Erasmus edited Publilius Syrus in 1514 along with the *Disticha Catonis*. Otto 96
  1 Porphyrion on Horace *Satires* 1.3.32, quoting Publilius Syrus (A 56 in the Loeb
  edition of *Minor Latin Poets*). Cf Poliziano at *Epistolae* 3.13 (1.36 Maier).

806 *Adagia* II v 97
  1 Suetonius, in the fragments (p 280 Roth), by way of Pseudo-Acron on Horace
  Satires 1.7.20
  2 Horace *Satires* 1.7.19–20

807 *Adagia* III ii 10. The Greek, present in *1500*, is derived from Aulus Gellius (see
  n1).
  1 Gellius *Noctes Atticae* 1.3.20. Modern editions offer θεῶν 'gods' for θείων 'divine
  things.'

808 *Adagia* I viii 93. Erasmus' source for this adage is not clear. Closest in wording

809 Cascus cascam duxit / An old man takes an old bride

Whenever an old bride marries an old man, or a cripple marries a cripple. This is used μεταφορικῶς 'metaphorically' when ugly persons like ugly
things or fools take delight in foolish things.

810 Mopso Nisa datur / Mopsus gets Nisa for a wife

When marvellous good fortune befalls someone who is unworthy of it.

**811 Floribus austrum immisisti / You have let in the south wind
to the flowers**

A metaphor from the countryside, directed at those who use what is harmful
instead of what is beneficial or at those who have prayed for disasters.

812 Apros fontibus immittere / To let in boars to the springs

This has the same meaning as the immediately preceding metaphor. Both
occur in Virgil's *Eclogues*: 'Alas, what have I done? The south wind on my
flowers / I've admitted, and boars to my clear-watered springs.'[1]

813 Ibyci grues / The cranes of Ibycus

Αἱ Ἰβύκου γέρανοι, The cranes of Ibycus. This became a proverb among the
Greeks. Whenever crimes came to light by some strange and unforeseen
chance and the criminals then paid the penalty, it was said that the cranes of
Ibycus were at hand. The general belief is that it is an allegory arising from
the following event. When a certain Ibycus was being murdered by robbers,
he called to witness cranes that happened to be flying overhead. Much later
the robbers were sitting in a marketplace[1] and when cranes flew over them

* * * * *

is a passage in Livy 32.34.3 (*apparet id quidem ... etiam caeco*), but this example did not appear in the *Adagia* until the 1528 edition. Plutarch records the
saying as a *bon mot* of Antigonus I (Antigonus the One-eyed) at *Moralia* 633C
(*Apophthegmata* 4.130 CWE 37 375). The presence of the phrase *ut aiunt* 'as they
say' (often sufficient for Erasmus to infer the presence of a proverb) at Quintilian 12.7.9, quoted at *Adagia* I viii 93, may suggest that this was Erasmus'
source, but the text that Erasmus read was *caecis hoc, ut aiunt, satis est*, rather
different from the Latin of the adage. Otto 276

809 *Adagia* I ii 62. Cited at C 297. The source is probably Varro *De lingua latina* 7.28.

810 *Adagia* II v 100. The source is Virgil *Eclogues* 8.26.

811 *Adagia* III vi 72. The source is Virgil *Eclogues* 2.58–9 (cited in the next adage).

812 *Adagia* III vi 72. Polydore Vergil 200
   1 Virgil *Eclogues* 2.58–9

813 *Adagia* I ix 22. The Greek version, present in *1500*, comes from Diogenianus
   1.35. Also Zenobius 1.37 and *Suda* I 80
   1 Diogenianus and Zenobius place the robbers in a theatre.

they said to each other, 'Look, the cranes of Ibycus.' These words roused suspicion in those sitting beside them. Having given themselves away in this manner, the robbers confessed and were punished.

814 **Ipsi testudines comedite qui cepistis** / Αὐτοὶ χελώνας ἐσθίετε οἵπερ εἵλετε / **You caught the turtles, you eat them**
It is very similar to what Terence writes: 'You made this dish and you must eat it all up.'[1] It is thought to come from a fable according to which some fishermen caught a turtle and shared it among themselves. Since they shrank from eating it, they invited Mercury to join them for the meal. He, however, refused and told them that since they had caught the turtle, they themselves should eat it. It is a perfect saying for those persons who embark on some badly planned venture and then try to involve others in it. You should reply to such persons in the following words: 'You began it without me, complete it without me.' 'You caught the turtle, you eat it.'

815 **Ventres** / Γαστέρες / **Guzzle-guts**
We call men who are greedy and think only of their stomachs 'Guzzle-guts.' Epimenides calls the Cretans 'idle bellies.'[1] Lucilius called parasites and carousers 'bellies.'[2] Terence: 'Punch that belly,' meaning the parasite as a whole.[3]

816 **Rudem accipere. Rude donatum** / **To be given the wooden sword. Presented with the wooden sword**
Gladiators who were allowed to retire from their profession were said to have been presented with the wooden sword. This retirement was granted with a wooden staff that was called a *rudis*. That is why those who were released in this way were called *rudiarii*. Those who, because of age, are allowed to retire from their occupation and enjoy a quiet life, as if they have done everything that they are capable of, are said to have

* * * * *

814 *Adagia* I i 87. The Greek version (present in *1500*) is taken from Diogenianus 1.36. Also Zenobius 2.29
  1 Terence *Phormio* 318. This is c 533.

815 *Adagia* II viii 78. Cf c 151. The Greek was added in *1506*.
  1 Titus 1:12, quoted by Jerome *Letters* 70.2.2 CSEL 54 701
  2 Lucilius fragment 75 Marx (67 Krenkel), taken from Donatus' commentary on Terence *Phormio* 988
  3 Terence *Phormio* 988. Erasmus' interpretation follows that of Donatus (see n2).

816 *Adagia* I ix 24. The first two sentences in the commentary were drawn from Perotti's *Cornucopiae* 156:23–7. Otto 1557

been given the wooden sword, by a metaphorical use of the proverb. Horace in his epistle: 'Oft I have proved myself and have been given the wooden sword. You try, / Maecenas, to take me back again into the old squad?'[1]

817 Albae gallinae filius / A son of the white hen

This suits a person who is of lucky birth. Juvenal: 'Because you are the son of the white hen.'[1]

818 Demulcere caput / To stroke a man's head

This means to agree with someone in a flattering way, taken from a common action of toadies. Jerome to Augustine: 'I say nothing of the blandishments with which you stroke my head.'[1]

819 Oedipi imprecationes / Οἰδίποδος ἀρά / The curses of Oedipus

This comes from Aeschylus, in the sense of bitter and dreadful misfortunes.[1] For Oedipus destroyed his two sons and his whole family with his curses.

820 Novi Simonem, et Simon me / Οἶδα Σίμωνα καὶ Σίμων ἐμέ / I know Simon and Simon knows me

Said of rogues who know each other.

821 Tuis te pingam coloribus / I shall paint you in your true colours

The sense is that I shall describe you just as you really are, meaning in an uncomplimentary way. Jerome against Rufinus: 'I could also paint you

* * * * *

1 Horace *Epistles* 1.1.2–3

817 *Adagia* I i 7. Used by Poliziano at *Epistolae* 3.19 (1.41 Maier). Otto 749
1 Juvenal 13.141

818 *Adagia* III i 37. This was the final adage in *1500*.
1 Jerome *Letters* 112.2.5 CSEL 55 369

819 *Adagia* I vii 61. This and all the following adages first appeared in *1506*. The Greek title probably comes from Zenobius 5.43, whose wording Erasmus follows (Diogenianus 2.51 gives the Greek as αἱ Οἰδίποδος ἀραί with the definite article and ἀραί in the plural for ἀρά in the singular). Zenobius also has a reference to Aeschylus (not present in Diogenianus). For Erasmus' use of Zenobius see C 26 n. See also Bühler 5.452–8 on Zenobius Athous 2.88.
1 Aeschylus *Seven against Thebes* 833; cf also 775–91.

820 *Adagia* II v 49. Probably from Zenobius 5.41 because of its proximity to the source for 819. Also in Diogenianus 7.26 and *Suda* OI 26

821 *Adagia* I iv 6. Otto 64

in your true colours and rave against a raving man.' Also against Rufinus: 'You say you will proclaim this publicly and that I must be painted in my true colours.'[1]

822 Simia vel pulcherrima deformis est / Even the most beautiful monkey is ugly

This is said of those who by their very nature are wicked and contemptible. It is just as if one were to say that the most honest Carthaginian is still a liar. It is given by Plato in *Greater Hippias*, being credited to Heraclitus.[1]

823 Vespa cicadae obstrepit / A wasp buzzing against a cricket

When a person challenges someone who is by far his superior in erudition. Theocritus in his *Bucolics*: Σφὴξ βομβῶν τέττιγος ἐναντίον.[1]

824 E dolio hauris / You draw from the cask

About a man who gets everything he desires. Theocritus: Ἐκ πίθου ἀντλῆς δῆλον 'You clearly drink from the large jar.'[1]

825 Graviora Sambico patitur / Δεινότερα Σαμβίκου πάσχει / He suffers worse tortures than Sambicus

This suits those who suffer terrible and chronic misfortune. If I remember clearly, it appears in Plutarch's *Problems*.[1] It originated with a certain Sambicus, a criminal who stole and sold statues from Olympia, and then set fire to the temple of Diana at Elis (called the Aristarcheum). He was captured and subjected to the most horrible torture for a whole year to make him betray his associates in crime.

826 Oleo tranquillior / As smooth as oil

Plautus in *The Carthaginian*: 'I'll see to it that you find this dog more tranquil

* * * * *

1 Jerome *Adversus Rufinum* 3.42 and 41 PL 23 510 and 509, CCSL 79 111

822 *Adagia* II v 54
1 Plato *Hippias maior* 289A, quoting the philosopher Heraclitus of Ephesus (fragment 22 B82 Diels-Kranz)

823 *Adagia* I viii 71
1 Theocritus *Idylls* 5.29, taken directly by Erasmus from a printed edition

824 *Adagia* II i 87
1 Theocritus *Idylls* 10.13, taken directly by Erasmus from a printed edition

825 *Adagia* I i 80
1 Plutarch *Moralia* 302C *Quaestiones Graecae* 'Greek Questions,' the direct source of the Greek version

826 *Adagia* I vii 35. Otto 1282

than oil.'[1] Oil floats on the surface of water quietly and gently. Plato uses the same expression in his dialogue on knowledge.[2]

827 Auricula infima mollior / Softer than the ear lobe
This is very similar to the preceding adage. Cicero in his letters to Atticus: 'As for how you think I should behave in public life and in my private feuds, rest assured that I am and will be softer than the tip of the ear.'[1]

828 Manu facere / To fashion by hand
This means to fashion and mould everything with great care and with little help from nature. Cicero in his *Letters*: 'Some natures are easy and straight-forward, some must be fashioned by hand, as the saying goes.'[1]

829 Ficos dividere / Σῦκα μερίζειν / To split figs
This was said of miserly persons in antiquity. Martial: 'He who says σῦκα μέριζε "divide the figs" cuts up his four hundred thousand.'[1]

830 Cumini sector / A cummin-splitter
This is given by Aristotle.[1] It has the same meaning as the preceding adage.

831 Res est in cardine / Things are at the crucial point
The meaning is that the completion of some business must be seen to im-mediately. Servius tells us that this was a proverb, in his commentary on Virgil's words 'in such a turn of things she will not tarry.'[1] Cicero: 'The matter hinges on this.'[2]

* * * * *

1 Plautus *Poenulus* 1236
2 Plato *Theaetetus* 144B

827 *Adagia* I vii 36. Otto 209
1 Cicero *Ad Quintum fratrem* (not *ad Atticum*) 2.14.4

828 *Adagia* II v 32. Otto 1056
1 Seneca (not Cicero) *Letters* 52.6

829 *Adagia* II i 6. Polydore Vergil 206
1 Martial 5.38.3 (where the Greek version of the proverb is given). The point is that Martial's subject has the property qualification for equestrian status in Rome (400,000 sesterces), but gives his money, at least nominally, to his brother so that he too can be a knight (*eques*). As Martial says, 'Do you believe that two men can ride on one horse?'

830 *Adagia* II i 5. The Greek version of the proverb is not given.
1 Aristotle *Nicomachean Ethics* 4.1 (1121b27)

831 *Adagia* I i 19. Polydore Vergil 257; Otto 351
1 Servius, the ancient commentator, on Virgil *Aeneid* 1.672
2 Not in Cicero. Cf Lactantius 2.8.55 and Jerome *Letters* 57.4.2 CSEL 54 507.

832 Matura satio saepe fallit, sera nunquam non fallit / Early sowing oft brings regrets, late sowing ever

A proverb of the countryside. It advises us that it is better to anticipate the proper time for doing something than to delay and do it too late. Columella reports the saying in these words: 'There is an old farming proverb to the effect that an early sowing often disappoints, while a late sowing never fails to turn out badly.'[1]

833 Γέλως Ἰωνικός / An Ionian laugh

An Ionian laugh. This was directed at homosexuals in antiquity, since the effeminacy of Ionians, like that of the Milesians and Sybarites, became proverbial.[1]

834 Purior clavo / Ἁγνότερος πηδαλίου / As clean as a rudder

Ὑπερβολὴ παροιμιώδης 'a proverbial exaggeration' used of incorruptible men with an impeccable character. A rudder is always being washed by the waves.

835 Dorica musica / Δωρικὴ μουσική / The Dorian Muse

This can be said of men who are eager to accept bribes. There is a double allusion, one to the word for a gift (δῶρον), and the other to famous kinds of music: the Dorian, Lydian, Phrygian, and Boeotian modes. In his *Knights* Aristophanes makes a joke against Cleon for never having learned any form of music other than the Dorian; οὗτος οὐ δύναται μαθεῖν, ἢν μὴ δωροδοκῇστί 'this man can only learn how to play the gift receiver.'[1] He uses δωροδοκῇστί 'gift receiver' as a distortion of δωριστί 'in the Dorian mode.'

836 Neque terram attingens neque coelum / Οὔτε γῆς οὔτε οὐρανοῦ ἁπτόμενος / Touching neither heaven nor earth

* * * * *

832 *Adagia* I ix 65. Otto 1590
  1 Columella *De re rustica* 11.2.79–80

833 *Adagia* I v 69. The Greek probably came from Diogenianus 3.87.
  1 For the Milesians see *Adagia* I ix 49; for the Sybarites see C 198 and *Adagia* II ii 65.

834 *Adagia* II iv 95. The Greek version appears in Diogenianus 1.11. Also in *Suda* A 281

835 *Adagia* II v 45. The whole commentary is based on Aristophanes *Knights* 989–96 and the scholia thereon.
  1 Aristophanes *Knights* 995–6, taken directly from the Greek play

836 *Adagia* I v 44. Otto 281

This refers to things that are far removed from the topic. Lucian uses this as a proverb in his *False Prophet*.[1]

837 Nihil ad chordam / Μηδὲν πρὸς τὴν χορδήν / Nothing to do with the lutestring

About those who are far removed from what is going on. Taken from dancing where the movements ought to correspond with the notes of the lute.[1]

838 Haud iterum capitur laqueo vulpes / No fox is caught twice in a trap

Ἀλλ' οὐκ αὖθις ἀλώπηξ, But not a second time is a fox, understanding 'led into a trap.'[1] Said of clever persons whom you try in vain to trick a second time.

Here concludes the ancient and well-known adages
as so far collected by the most eloquent
Erasmus of Rotterdam, canon and theologian.*

* * * * *

1 Lucian *Alexander* 54, which may be Erasmus' source for the Greek since he published a translation of this work in 1506.

837 *Adagia* I v 46
1 The source of the proverb and the Greek version is probably Lucian *De saltatione* 80.

838 *Adagia* II v 22. Zenobius 1.67 (see n1). Also in Diogenianus 2.15, Zenobius Aldine column 24, and *Suda* A 1354.
1 The closest in wording to Erasmus' explanation here is Zenobius 1.67, which is probably his source. See c 26n.

* A more pretentious ending than the one found in *1500*, which simply announced the end of the collection without naming Erasmus at all. The phrase 'so far' suggests that Erasmus or Josse Bade, the printer of *1506*, was already contemplating an even more expanded edition, one that was to come to fruition in the 1508 edition of the *Adagia*, but it was published by the Aldine press in Venice.

Appendix

The following three adages appeared in the first edition of the *Collectanea*, but were dropped in the second.

A1 Cato in Catonem / Cato meets Cato

No less obscure is what we read in the same letter *vereor ne in Catonem*[1] 'I fear that Cato will meet Cato.' The meaning is that a critic and accuser himself encounters an accuser. For Cato was not only a very stern critic, he was also a very fierce accuser (However, others read *vereor ne in Catonem Catonius* 'I fear that he will encounter Cato in the guise of another Cato.' They are troubled by the words which follow, namely *in nos* 'against us,' which makes the construction somewhat harsh.)[2] Horace in his *Satires*: 'And seeking to strike against what is fragile he will break his tooth on something solid.'[3] By this proverb Cicero seems to criticize the tyrannical power of Caesar, to write against whom would be very dangerous.

A2 Festus dies / A holiday

Whenever we mean that some turbulent business is being undertaken for someone, with much expense and preparation, or that something out of the ordinary is being done for him, we say that a holiday is being held on his behalf. Pamphilus in *The Mother-in-Law*: 'I don't want holidays on my behalf.'[4]

A3 Quae haec est fabula / What is all this tall story about?

About something strange and unheard of. It appears in Terence in both *The Woman of Andros* and *The Eunuch*.[5]

* * * * *

A1 This was positioned after c 375 in *1500* and was replaced by a new adage, the current c 376.
1 Cicero *Ad familiares* 7.25.1
2 The point seems to be that Erasmus' text read *vereor ne in Catonem Cato in nos*, where, as Erasmus says, *in nos* is difficult, if not impossible, to construe and that this was emended by someone into *vereor ne in Catonem Catonius*.
3 Horace, *Sermones* 2.1.77–8

A2 This adage was positioned after c 509 in *1500*.
4 Terence *Hecyra* 592–3. Erasmus misunderstands the passage because of mispunctuation. What Pamphilus says is that he does not want Sostrata to give up her friends, relatives, and holidays for his sake.

A3 This adage was positioned after c 528 in *1500*.
5 Terence *Andria* 747, *Eunuchus* 689

Concordance of the *Adagia* to the *Collectanea*

Adages listed here in parentheses, whether from the *Adagia* or from the *Collectanea*, are not the title of the adage but are referred to in the essay.

Adagia	Collectanea	Adagia	Collectanea	Adagia	Collectanea
I i 1	94	I i 57	720	I ii 17	222
I i 2	95, 99, 100,	I i 58	263	I ii 18	465
	101, 102, 104,	I i 59	(263)	I ii 20	(177)
	105, 106, 107,	I i 60	54	I ii 21	177
	591; cf 103	I i 61	263	I ii 22	(177)
I i 4	700	I i 62	640	I ii 23	721
I i 7	676	I i 65	92, 727	I ii 25	738
I i 8	710	I i 68	144	I ii 27	612
I i 12	719	I i 69	91	I ii 28	416
I i 14	412	I i 70	63	I ii 29	151, 650
I i 15	28	I i 71	445	I ii 32	774
I i 19	831	I i 72	256	I ii 34	774
I i 22	698	I i 73	257	I ii 37	82
I i 24	606	I i 75	236	I ii 38	10
I i 25	606	I i 76	310	I ii 39	298
I i 27	511	I i 77	496	I ii 43	654
I i 28	132.	I i 78	817	I ii 44	112
I i 29	132	I i 80	825	I ii 48	350
I i 30	(132)	I i 81	241A	I ii 51	321
I i 31	(132)	I i 82	(241A)	I ii 53	586, 587
I i 32	221	I i 83	737	I ii 55	603
I i 33	5	I i 84	532	I ii 57	277
I i 35	(58)	I i 85	533	I ii 62	809, (297)
(I i 35)	561	I i 86	758	I ii 69	64
I i 37	402	I i 87	814	I ii 71	65
I i 38	402	I i 88	366		
I i 39	(402)	I i 92	187	I iii 8	546
I i 40	782, (438)	I i 93	255	(I iii 8)	723
I i 42	(382)	I i 94	353	I iii 9	488
I i 45	281, (542)	I i 96	341	I iii 13	485
I i 46	(281)			I iii 14	(283)
I i 47	278	I ii 1	784	I iii 17	566
I i 48	274	I ii 4	50	I iii 19	375
I i 49	274	I ii 5	51	I iii 20	403
(I i 49)	433	I ii 8	646	I iii 21	401
I i 50	237	I ii 9	294	I iii 22	422
I i 51	53	I ii 11	131	I iii 24	176
I i 52	53	I ii 14	169	I iii 26	193
I i 53	(53)	I ii 15	297	I iii 27	193
I i 56	135, 617	(I ii 15)	601	I iii 29	192

Adagia	Collectanea	Adagia	Collectanea	Adagia	Collectanea
I iii 31	cf 192	I iv 15	40	I iv 93	331
I iii 32	192	I iv 16	40	I iv 94	(331)
I iii 33	693	I iv 17	(41)	I iv 95	686
I iii 34	(693)	I iv 18	41	I iv 97	(499)
I iii 36	223	I iv 21	275	I iv 98	499
I iii 38	315	I iv 24	40	I iv 99	44
I iii 39	515	I iv 30	449	I iv 100	45
I iii 40	656	I iv 32	771		
I iii 41	659	I iv 33	cf 776	I v 1	128
I iii 46	188	I iv 34	687	I v 2	128
I iii 50	379	I iv 35	125	I v 3	166
I iii 51	379	I iv 37	3	I v 4	378
I iii 52	649	I iv 38	3	I v 5	683
I iii 53	154	(I iv 38)	706	I v 6	377
(I iii 53)	649	I iv 39	25	I v 8	398
I iii 55	675	I iv 40	555	I v 9	(398)
I iii 57	(653)	I iv 41	141; cf 749	I v 10	396
I iii 63	279	I iv 42	399	I v 11	396
I iii 64	(649)	I iv 43	311	I v 12	396
I iii 65	572	I iv 44	138	I v 14	307
I iii 66	792	I iv 47	596	I v 15	316
I iii 67	645	I iv 48	408	I v 16	320
I iii 70	220	I iv 50	407, 414	I v 17	333
I iii 72	548	I iv 51	408	I v 19	489
I iii 75	16	I iv 56	610	I v 20	66
I iii 79	427	I iv 58	417	I v 21	165
I iii 81	458	I iv 60	230, (368)	I v 23	359
I iii 83	(458)	I iv 62	201, 202	I v 25	164, (357)
I iii 85	(458)	I iv 68	424	I v 30	679
I iii 86	760A	I iv 70	(408)	I v 31	303
I iii 88	145	I iv 72	678	I v 32	413; cf 749
I iii 89	(282)	I iv 73	423	I v 34	253
I iii 91	282	I iv 74	56	I v 35	225
		I iv 75	249	I v 36	290
I iv 1	124	I iv 76	57	I v 37	19
I iv 2	486	I iv 79	355	I v 38	20
I iv 3	484; cf 160	I iv 81	626	I v 39	21
I iv 4	482	I iv 83	27	I v 41	30
I iv 6	821	I iv 86	(172), 199	I v 42	448
I iv 8	480	I iv 87	(199)	I v 44	836
I iv 10	540, 614	I iv 88	451	I v 46	837
I iv 11	308	I iv 89	(199)	I v 48	409
I iv 12	152	I iv 90	(199)	I v 49	409
I iv 13	641	I iv 91	(408)	I v 50	409
I iv 14	296	I iv 92	cf 373	I v 52	37

Adagia	Collectanea	Adagia	Collectanea	Adagia	Collectanea
I v 53	622	I vi 65	681	I vii 35	826
I v 54	272, (664)	I vi 68	284	I vii 36	827
I v 55	38	I vi 69	(109)	I vii 40	243
I v 56	261	I vi 71	435	I vii 46	545
I v 57	765	I vi 79	92; cf 766	I vii 49	218
I v 58	cf 774	I vi 80	766, (640)	I vii 50	70
I v 59	770	I vi 81	cf 88	I vii 51	804
I v 60	492	I vi 82	78	I vii 52	775
I v 62	122	I vi 84	319	I vii 53	(775)
I v 63	661	I vi 85	444	I vii 55	450
I v 64	558	I vi 86	406	I vii 57	313
I v 65	400, (262)	I vi 87	268	I vii 58	631
I v 67	147	I vi 89	268	I vii 61	819
I v 69	833	I vi 90	406	I vii 62	524
I v 74	34	I vi 91	(406)	I vii 63	530
I v 76	287	(I vi 91)	602	I vii 65	514
I v 82	352	I vi 92	467	I vii 69	(79)
I v 84	139	I vi 93	158	I vii 70	483
I v 85	527	I vi 95	(108)	I vii 71	(471)
I v 88	23, (24)	I vi 96	(108)	I vii 72	471
I v 90	773	I vi 97	(108)	I vii 73	469
I v 91	772	I vi 99	121	I vii 75	759
I v 96	175			I vii 79	420
I v 99	762	I vii 1	369	I vii 80	579
I v 100	761	I vii 2	137	I vii 82	(579)
		I vii 3	114	I vii 86	778; cf 517
I vi 1	167	I vii 4	(114)	I vii 90	673
I vi 2	497	I vii 5	334	I vii 92	651
I vi 3	575	I vii 6	322	I vii 93	639
I vi 4	392	I vii 10	(648)	I vii 94	638
I vi 6	(117)	I vii 13	446	I vii 96	7
I vi 7	117	I vii 14	390	I vii 97	562
I vi 14	751	I vii 15	731	I vii 98	8
I vi 15	745	I vii 17	354	(I vii 98)	9
I vi 16	153	I vii 18	304	I vii 99	685
I vi 19	292	I vii 19	304		
I vi 20	293	I vii 20	364	I viii 4	397
I vi 22	674	I vii 21	365	I viii 5	397
I vi 23	674	I vii 22	365	I viii 6	397
I vi 24	733	I vii 23	367	I viii 7	397
I vi 43	120	I vii 28	300	I viii 8	397
I vi 48	547	I vii 29	215	I viii 10	397
I vi 60	345	I vii 30	214	I viii 11	397
(I vi 62)	62	I vii 31B	312	I viii 18	291
I vi 64	391	I vii 34	12	I viii 19	232

Adagia	Collectanea	Adagia	Collectanea	Adagia	Collectanea
I viii 22	242	I ix 7	(211)	I ix 79	385
I viii 23	505	I ix 10	(634), 786	I ix 80	383
I viii 25	299	I ix 11	780	I ix 81	386
I viii 26	181	I ix 12	191	I ix 82	386
I viii 27	181	I ix 14	491	I ix 83	386
I viii 29	182	I ix 15	189	I ix 84	207
I viii 31	180	I ix 18	668	I ix 85	195
I viii 32	180	I ix 19	667	I ix 89	260, 461
I viii 33	119	I ix 20	549	I ix 91	473
I viii 34	39	I ix 22	813	I ix 92	474
I viii 40	438	I ix 24	816	I ix 93	474
I viii 42	441	I ix 25	605	I ix 94	475
I viii 43	410	I ix 27	619	I ix 95	6
I viii 45	276	I ix 30	418		
I viii 46	244	I ix 34	22	I x 1	163
I viii 47	245	I ix 35	(22)	I x 9	689, 735
I viii 48	245	I ix 36	(22)	I x 17	344
I viii 49	246	I ix 37	361, (22)	I x 18	550
I viii 50	247	I ix 38	(22)	I x 20	583
I viii 51	cf 264	I ix 39	(22)	I x 21	576
I viii 54	265	I ix 40	347	I x 22	577
(I viii 56)	672	I ix 41	cf 212	I x 23	569
I viii 57	183	I ix 43	330, 580	I x 24	570
I viii 58	cf 183	I ix 44	330	I x 25	335, 560
I viii 59	624	I ix 45	301	I x 33	(230), 368
I viii 60	746	I ix 49	18	I x 34	332
I viii 61	360	I ix 50	17	I x 35	336
I viii 64	129	I ix 52	508	I x 39	168
I viii 66	55	I ix 54	504	I x 40	170
I viii 69	339	I ix 55	(504)	I x 47	115
I viii 71	823	I ix 56	501	I x 48	(767)
I viii 74	250	I ix 58	611	I x 49	767
I viii 75	(250)	I ix 59	502	I x 50	76
I viii 76	487	I ix 60	42	I x 51	75
I viii 77	81	I ix 62	302	I x 55	729
I viii 78	(84)	I ix 65	832	I x 56	615
I viii 79	752	I ix 67	757	I x 57	618
I viii 84	118	I ix 69	327	I x 61	701
I viii 86	43	I ix 70	326; cf 498	I x 71	1
I viii 89	314	I ix 72	324	I x 72	537
I viii 90	314	I ix 73	317, (358)	I x 76	148
I viii 93	808	I ix 74	358	I x 77	126
		I ix 75	426	I x 79	127
I ix 4	35	I ix 77	381	I x 80	594
I ix 6	718	I ix 78	384	I x 81	595

Adagia	*Collectanea*	*Adagia*	*Collectanea*	*Adagia*	*Collectanea*
I x 84	363	II ii 59	241	II iv 23	203
I x 86	691	II ii 65	cf 198	II iv 24	(627)
I x 88	722	II ii 67	479	II iv 32	146
I x 91	176	II ii 68	198	II iv 33	116
I x 93	793	II ii 69	671	II iv 34	(155)
I x 94	695	II ii 74	590	(II iv 37)	231
I x 95	305	II ii 76	627	II iv 38	760
I x 96	715; cf 305	II ii 80	185	II iv 39	226, 764
I x 97	123	II ii 82	32	II iv 40	543
I x 98	123	II ii 83	49	II iv 41	556
I x 100	349	II ii 94	658	II iv 51	33
				II iv 58	80
II i 1	196	II iii 20	306	II iv 59	77
(II i 1)	494	II iii 26	110	II iv 60	703
II i 2	613	II iii 28	574	II iv 67	705
II i 5	830	II iii 30	48	II iv 68	705
II i 6	829	II iii 31	47	II iv 69	cf 666
II i 7	697	II iii 39	150	II iv 70	309
II i 10	329	(II iii 39)	551	II iv 73	708
II i 12	747	II iii 45	cf 680	II iv 74	431, 510
II i 13	608	II iii 47	684	II iv 75	510
II i 17	453	II iii 48	702	II iv 76	512
II i 21	235	II iii 49	699	II iv 77	490
II i 26	495	II iii 52	90, 270	II iv 78	614
II i 29	15	II iii 58	627	II iv 79	642
II i 30	26	II iii 66	362	II iv 80	660
II i 36	801	II iii 68	425	II iv 81	657
II i 37	797	II iii 72	(77)	II iv 84	493
II i 38	798	II iii 74	111	II iv 85	712
II i 50	730	II iii 80	262	II iv 86	599
II i 54	653	II iii 91	788	(II iv 86)	520
(II i 61)	742	II iii 94	(466)	II iv 88	754
II i 64	456	II iii 97	539	II iv 89	753
II i 69	191	II iii 100	(734)	II iv 90	744
II i 80	620			II iv 91	748
II i 84	525	II iv 10	468	II iv 92	(693)
II i 85	604	II iv 11	460	II iv 93	506
II i 87	824	II iv 12	442	II iv 94	509
II i 100	248	II iv 13	86, 335	II iv 95	834
		II iv 14	58	II iv 96	477
II ii 1	136; cf 113	II iv 15	597	II iv 98	285
II ii 4	648	II iv 16	14	II iv 99	717
II ii 6	542	II iv 17	31	II iv 100	728
II ii 55	155	II iv 20	592		
II ii 56	(155)	II iv 22	337	II v 3	318

Adagia	Collectanea	Adagia	Collectanea	Adagia	Collectanea
II v 4	552	II v 82	323	II viii 18	cf 664
II v 5	554	II v 95	799	II viii 41	161
II v 6	630	II v 96	805	II viii 44	343
II v 7	631	II v 97	806	II viii 47	419
II v 9	190	II v 100	810	II viii 50	571
II v 10	777			II viii 59	178
II v 11	628	II vi 9	726	II viii 60	179
II v 12	669	II vi 15	162	II viii 61	356
II v 13	670	II vi 19	736	(II viii 78)	(815)
II v 15	609	II vi 20	404	II viii 78	815
II v 16	609, (184)	II vi 33	462	II viii 80	789
II v 17	677	II vi 34	464	(II viii 81)	434
II v 18	637	II vi 36	563	II viii 85	472
II v 19	623	II vi 37	567	II viii 86	89
II v 20	634	II vi 45	346	II viii 88	83
II v 21	357	II vi 54	528	II viii 89	216
II v 22	838	II vi 64	393	II viii 96	157
II v 25	632	II vi 66	794		
II v 26	633	II vi 68	791	II ix 13	52
II v 27	636	II vi 75	755	II ix 26	585
II v 28	655	II vi 76	755	II ix 35	67
II v 30	198	II vi 86	463	II ix 43	478
II v 31	200			II ix 48	582
II v 32	828	II vii 6	459	II ix 52	507
II v 33	625	II vii 7	452	II ix 53	224
II v 34	607	II vii 8	455	II ix 54	768
II v 37	227	II vii 9	457	II ix 59	657
II v 39	732	II vii 11	447	II ix 62	(47)
II v 45	835	II vii 12	454	II ix 63	439
II v 49	820	II vii 13	443	(II ix 71)	(551)
II v 50	531	II vii 14	432	II ix 75	790
II v 51	644	II vii 20	cf 236	II ix 84	395
II v 54	822	II vii 41	161	II ix 85	518
II v 59	663	II vii 43	140	II ix 86	130
II v 60	665	II vii 63	325	II ix 97	600
II v 61	682	II vii 66	382		
II v 62	211	II vii 69	109	II x 10	351
II v 65	643	II vii 80	206	II x 24	783
II v 66	578	II vii 81	205	II x 25	589
II v 72	68	II vii 90	133	II x 33	289
II v 74	69	II vii 91	134	(III x 47)	209
II v 76	428, (489)	II vii 98	696	II x 62	598
II v 77	380	II vii 100	690	II x 76	229
II v 80	371			II x 77	11
II v 81	342	II viii 8	(5), 142	II x 88	743

Adagia	Collectanea	Adagia	Collectanea	Adagia	Collectanea
II x 90	616	III v 75	481	III vii 18	219
		III v 80	348	III vii 19	60
III i 1	13	III v 84	210	III vii 20	204
III i 4	516	III v 88	769	III vii 55	84
III i 7	273	(III v 88)	72, 73	III vii 78	(296)
III i 37	818	III v 95	374	III vii 82	228
III i 41	519	III v 99	538	III vii 100	724
III i 53	796				
III i 58	429	III vi 2	186	III viii 56	517
III i 67	328	III vi 3	573		
III i 69	803, (278)	III vi 4	283	III ix 68	40
		III vi 5	266	III ix 72	530
III ii 9	503	III vi 6	267	III ix 89	541
III ii 10	807	III vi 13	529	III ix 97	cf 411
III ii 19	544	III vi 14	213		
III ii 20	288	III vi 16	308	(III x 47)	209
III ii 21	251	III vi 19	(499)	III x 53	(443)
III ii 37	203	III vi 21	709	III x 82	680
III ii 60	87	III vi 27	234		
III ii 65	498	III vi 38	647	IV i 12	323
III ii 75	71	III vi 45	704	IV i 43	232
		III vi 62	387	IV i 51	535
III iii 43	495A	III vi 63	74	IV i 52	172
		III vi 67	781	IV i 64	650
III iv 6	785	III vi 70	160; cf 484	IV i 74	59
III iv 11	143	III vi 71	156	IV i 75	79
III iv 39	cf 695	III vi 72	811, 812	IV i 76	159
III iv 87	373	III vi 77	85	IV i 78	239; cf 238
		III vi 85	559	IV i 91	252
III v 1	2	III vi 91	593	IV i 92	436
(III v 1)	741	III vi 93	584	IV i 93	437
III v 13	750	III vi 94	421	IV i 94	440
III v 20	719	III vi 96	240	IV i 95	739
III v 22	295	III vi 98	269		
III v 27	65A	III vi 99	557	IV ii 18	763
III v 43	271			IV ii 19	812
III v 44	(396)	III vii 1	581	IV ii 22	(332)
III v 55	564	III vii 3	779		
III v 56	692	III vii 6	405	IV iii 20	694
III v 67	662	III vii 8	621	IV iii 23	376
III v 71	cf 246	III vii 9	46, 526	IV iii 62	750
III v 72	cf 688	III vii 10	46; cf 526	IV iii 68	734
III v 73	149	(III vii 12)	520	IV iii 75	(529)
(III v 73)	565	III vii 14	522		
III v 74	36	III vii 17	800	IV v 27	476

Adagia	Collectanea		Adagia	Collectanea		Adagia	Collectanea
IV v 50	517		IV vii 69	173		IV x 6	212
IV v 63	cf 536		IV vii 82	cf 666			
IV v 71	(69)					v i 8	(671)
IV v 84	171		IV viii 19	629		v i 32	776
			IV viii 26	765		(v i 57)	343
IV vi 72	cf 470		IV viii 38	29		v i 82	146
IV vi 74	773						
			(IV ix 20)	570		v ii 37	cf 520
IV vii 35	(235)		IV ix 72	231			

Collectanea adages not used in the Adagia

The Collectanea adages in this list are not mentioned in the Adagia, either as title adages or in the commentary to an adage. They are therefore not given in the Concordance above.

4	259	470	711
61	280	500	713
96	286	513	714
97	338	521	716
113	340	523	725
174	368	534	740
194	370	536	741
197	372	553	756
208	388	568	787
217	389	588	795
233	394	652	802
254	415	688	
258	430	707	

INDEXES TO ERASMUS' ADAGES

by

WILLIAM BARKER

Erasmus' 1528 Note on Indexes

From the start of the expanded editions of 1508 onwards, indexes were treated by Erasmus as integral to the overall structure and use of the *Adagia*. His approach is made clear in this short note that first appeared in the Froben edition of 1528 (fol aa2v, immediately following Ep 2022). Here he outlines the care he took in personally preparing his two indexes: an alphabetical index of proverbs (*per ordinem alphabeti*) and an index according to places and matters (*iuxta locos et materias*). He recognizes the need for some redundancy in listing the listing of proverbs to help the reader in locating material, so that there are multiple points of access to the proverbs. And he warns the reader that there are many more proverbs and proverb variations in the *Adagia* than are actually implied by the titles of the essays. The topical listings, he admits, are necessarily incomplete, in large part because proverbs have multiple meanings and applications, as he shows in the essay 'What is a proverb?' that introduces the work (CWE 31 3–28). The following was translated by John Grant.

DESIDERIUS ERASMUS OF ROTTERDAM TO THE READER
ON THE SUBJECT OF THE TWO INDEXES
My hopes were quite dashed when I discovered that the alphabetical index was marked by confusion and incompleteness, the result of the reluctance of men of some learning to lower themselves to such humble tasks. Since this state of affairs has been inconvenient to me as well as to others – so much so that because of this some items have had to be crammed into places to which they do not belong – we have taken on this wearisome task, the result being that the index is now fuller than it was and has been carefully organized in terms of the alphabetical order.[1] We have not been content

* * * * *

1 The alphabetical index of proverbs titles was expanded in 1526.

with this and have added topics that arise in passing when one is discussing a proverb, material that is compatible with the nature of the proverb or in other ways worthy of being noted. We have added the three letters *p*, *m* and *f*, which indicate that the item stands at the beginning, middle and the end of a page respectively[1] (for it is very easy to divide a page into these three parts even without a measuring tool).

Sometimes the same adage is offered in different ways, sometimes I group several adages under the same heading. This too is the result of the diligence I have exerted in this matter. Moreover, lest any confusion be caused by the order of words in the adages, which sometimes differs in the index from that in the titles in the work itself, be advised that in the index I indicate the sense of the proverb by starting with those words that are important and distinctive. Especially significant are words that specifically refer to persons, places, animals, or things; next comes anything that is quite out of the ordinary in the context. An example of the first is *Pasetis obolus* as well as *Obolus Pasetis* ('Pases' penny'),[2] of the second is *Abydum ne temere* as well as *Ne temere Abydum* ('Not rashly to Abydus'), and *Corinthum appellere non est cuiusvis* as well as *Non est cuiusvis Corinthum appellere* ('It is not given to everyone to land at Corinth'),[3] of the third is *Elleborum bibe* as well as *Bibe elleborum* ('Drink hellebore'),[4] and of the fourth is *Olitor opportuna loquutus* as well as *Saepe etiam est olitor valde opportuna loquutus* ('Even a gardener oft speaks to the point').[5] Some proverbs that lack a significant word we have included twice. If you follow what we have aimed to do in the index, you cannot fail to find what you are looking for. However, the words have not been changed to such

* * * * *

1 He uses these letters (for *in principio*, *in medio*, and *in fine*) primarily as an aid to locate proverbs that are not title-adages but are cited in the commentaries that accompany each adage (as, for example, 'He hopes some breeze will blow from this direction' in *Adagia* III vii 45). The letters appear more frequently in the alphabetical index of proverbs than in the index by topic.

2 'Pases' being the name of a person. Erasmus' memory fails him here since the proverb, as it appears in the *Adagia* (II vii 31), does in fact begin with the proper noun, and the actual proverb is *Pasetis semiobolus* (not *obolus*), the form in which it appears (once) in the index.

3 That is, these two proverbs contain a proper noun referring to a place. The first is I vii 93, the second is I iv 1. They appear twice in the alphabetical index, once under the initial word and a second time under the proper noun.

4 The proverb is I viii 51. It occurs twice in the index.

5 This is I vi 1. The proverb is striking (or 'out of the ordinary') because of its quasi-paradoxical nature. In his essay on I vi 1 Erasmus actually preferred the form 'Even a fool oft speaks to the point.'

a degree as to prevent even a modestly educated reader from finding a proverb. And this has not been done in very many cases, as there was no need to do so.

The second index, the order of whose headings reflects some connection of meaning from one to another, was put together by us very hastily some time ago in Venice.[6] We have left it as it is, apart from adding many items that had been omitted. More headings could have been added and there are many adages that would fit several headings; for example, *Dolium pertusum* ('A leaky tub')[7] can refer to an avaricious man[8] or to a spendthrift or to a forgetful one, but the index would have grown to an immense size. We have given a great deal of information; as for what remains we have left that to the intelligence of the reader. To get more profit from this index, you ought to read through the list of headings that have been arranged on the principle of similarity and difference in meaning, doing so several times and with great care.

* * * * *

6 In the 1508 edition of the *Adagia*. This remained the basis for the topical index in all subsequent editions, being constantly expanded by the addition of new topics and of new examples for most of the headings. An example of the latter is afforded by the number of proverbs listed under *Absurda* (74 in *1515* against 107 in *1536*).

7 This expression is not actually a title-adage in the *Adagia* but it is cited (from Plautus *Pseudolus* 369) in *Adagia* I x 33 (*Inexplebile dolium* 'A great jar that cannot be filled') and I iv 60. It is found as a title in *Collectanea* 368 (alongside *Inexplebile dolium*). It is listed in the subject-index under *Inanis opera* 'Pointless action' in *1536*.

8 Because, as Erasmus says in *Adagia* I x 33, 'the more they [grasping men] are filled with riches, the emptier they seem.'

Greek Index
of Erasmus' Adages

An asterisk indicates that the Greek is not given in CWE 31–6, the proverb being simply translated into English. A raised plus sign (⁺) indicates that the adage is to be found in the *Collectanea* (87–358 in this volume); see the Concordance (359–66) to find the appropriate C number(s) corresponding to the *Adagia* number the ⁺ is attached to. The index does not include the Homeric quotations that run from III viii 1 to III x 75 (see CWE 35 281). All nouns and verbs (except εἶναι) and most adjectives and adverbs have been indexed; most conjunctions, particles, pronouns, and pronominal adjectives have not. This index was prepared by John Grant.

εἰργάσατο see βόθρον
εἴρηκας see Ῥόδα
εἰρημένα see δεδραμένα
Εἷς see ἀνήρ, θεός, οἰωνός
εἴσεται see κακός
εἰσίν see σελίνοις
εἰσίτω see Ἀγεωμέτρητος
εἰσκρούειν see λίθον
εἰσόμεσθα see μάντεων
εἰσορᾶν see ἐρᾶν
Εἶτα see ἐξηγρόμην
εἶχεν see Ἀρμένην
εἴχετο see Γέλως
εἶχον see τυρόν
Ἐκκαίδεκα see ποδῶν
ἐλέσθαι see Ὄνους
ἐλθόν see Πῦρ
ἐλθόντας see ὄρους
ἕλκειν see τριχῶν
ἕλκεσι see ἰατρός
ἕλκομαι see Ἴυγγι
ἐκαθέζετο see βύρσης
ἔκαμ' see οὐρανός
Ἕκαστος ἡμῶν οὐχ αὑτῷ μόνον γέγονεν
    IV vi 81
– see also βδέμα, ποδῶν, τέχνην
Ἑκάτειον see Θεαγένους
Ἑκάτερος ἀμφότερος, ὁ δὲ Ἀμφότερος
    οὐδέτερος, Ὁ μὲν IV iii 55
Ἑκατὸν δέ τε δούραθ' ἁμάξης IV iii 88
– see also ἄραιντ'
ἐκβάλλειν see ὀφθαλμοῦ
ἐκβάλοις τὴν ἔνθεσιν, Εἴθε φαύλως
    ὥσπερ εὗρες II viii 76
ἐκδιδάσκεται see Αἰσχροῖς
ἐκδύς see γῆρας
Ἐκεῖ see βλέπουσα
Ἕκητι see Συλοσῶντος
ἐκθανεῖν see Γέλω
Ἐκκέκοφθ' see μουσική
ἐκκρούειν see Ἤλω
ἔκλεισε see Λυδός
ἐκλελοιπότος see Γλυκεῖ'
Ἐκλινίσαι III v 38
Ἐκπερδικίσαι III v 21
ἐκπίοι see ἐλέφας
ἐκποδών see φίλοι
ἐκράτει see Μόνος

ἐκρίνετο see Δύσκωφος
ἔκρυψαν see παγίδι
ἐκτίνειν see τόκον
ἐκτραγών see βοῦν
ἐκτρέφει see πρῶτ'
ἐκφοβεῖς see λέοντα
ἐκφυγών see Χάρυβδιν
Ἐκφυλλοφορῆσαι IV x 27
ἐκώμασας see μελίττας
ἐκώμασεν see Ὗς
Ἑκὼν ἀέκοντί γε θυμῷ II vii 82
ἔλα see σαυτόν
ἐλαίαν ἔσθι', Μή ποτε IV vii 28
ἔλαιον ἐπιχέουσιν, Οἱ τοῦ λύχνου χρείαν
    ἔχοντες IV vii 63; Ἔλαιον οὐκ ἔνεστιν
    ἐν τῷ ληκύθῳ III vii 72
– see also ἄλα, ὀφθαλμοῖσιν
ἐλαίου see στέμφυλα
Ἐλαίῳ see πῦρ
ἐλαιῶν φέρεται, Ἐκτὸς τῶν II ii 10
ἐλάσειας see ἀράχνια
ἔλασσον ἢ δύνασθαι δεῖ μεῖζον, Ἢ
    φρονεῖν IV ii 90
ἐλάττονα see Διθυραμβοποιῶν
ἔλαυνε see ἄμαξαν, βοῦν
ἐλαύνει see Ἀλώπηξ, ἄμαξα, μάστιξ
ἐλαύνειν see κώπην
ἐλαύνεσθαι see Γῆν
ἐλαύνομεν see θέομεν
Ἐλάφειος ἀνήρ II vii 36
ἔλαφοι τὰ κέρατα ἀποβάλλουσιν, Ὅπου
    αἱ II v 71
ἔλαφος see κύνας
ἔλαχε see Πενία
Ἔλαχες see Μῦ, Σπάρτην
ἐλείφθη see πυρφόρος
ἐλεῆσαι see ἐχθρόν
Ἑλένη, Αὕτη I iii 69
ἔλεξας see Καλῶς
ἔλεσι see Λάρος
Ἐλευθέρα see Κόρκυρα
Ἐλεύθεραι see αἶγες
Ἐλευθεριώτερος see Σπάρτης
Ἐλευσίνια see Ἀττικοί
Ἐλέφαντα ἐκ μυίας ποιεῖς I ix 69+
ἐλέφαντας ὑπὸ μάλης κρύψειας ἢ ἕνα
    κίναιδον, Θᾶττον ἂν πέντε II v 56*
ἐλέφαντι παραβάλλειν, Κώνωπα III i 27

καθεύδων see Λαγώς, Ὀνειροπολεῖ
Καθημέριος see βίος
Καθῆσθαι προσκυνήσοντας ι i 2
καικίας καὶ συκοφαντίας πνεῖ, Ὡς οὗτος
    ἤδη IV viii 92*
– see also νέφος
Καινεύς, Ἄτρωτος ὑπάρχεις ὡς III iv 25
Καινέως δόρυ, Τὸ IV i 80
καιομένης see δάφνης
καίρια see πολλά
καίριον see Πολλάκι
καιρόν, Γνῶθι ι vii 70
καιροῦ see Κακόν
κακὰ καὶ μὴ διζημένοισι, Παραγίνεται τὰ
    IV ii 62; Κακὰ μὲν θρῖπες, κακὰ δὲ ἶπες
    II x 35; κακὰ τεύχει ἀνὴρ ἄλλῳ κακὰ
    τεύχων, Οἷ τ' αὐτῷ IV viii 56*
– see also Ἀζαναῖα, ἀνθρώπους, Βράχιστα,
    Θάλασσα, Ἰλίῳ, κέρδεα, κρητῆρι,
    Μαγνήτων, Πῦρ, Τερμέρια, Τρίς,
    Ὠγύγια
κακαί see ἤθη
κακή see βουλή
κακῆς see Ἀρχῆς, κυνός
Κάκιον see Βάβυς
κάκιστα see κάππα
κακίστη see βουλή
κάκιστος οὔτε πρᾶτος, Οὔτε IV iv 22
κακοδαίμονα see πατέρ'
κακοί, Οἱ μὲν γὰρ οὐκέτ' εἰσίν, οἱ δ'
    ὄντες II ix 37
– see also Ἐσθλοί, Λέριοι, πίνουσι
κακοῖν, Ἐνὶ γὰρ ξυνέχεσθαι κρεῖττον ἢ
    δυοῖν IV ii 36
κακοῖς see Πᾶσιν, Τρίς
κακοῖσιν see Δέδοται
Κακὸν ἄγγος οὐ κλᾶται IV ii 99;
    κακόν, Διωλύγιον II vi 79; κακόν,
    Ἐπίσπαστον IV ii 5; κακὸν εὖ
    κείμενον, Μὴ κινεῖν ι i 62+; Κακὸν εὖ
    κείμενον μὴ κινεῖν III vi 83*; κακὸν
    κακῷ θεραπεύειν, Τὸ ι ii 6; Κακὸν
    τὸ καλὸν ἦν τι μὴ καιροῦ τύχῃ IV
    iii 2
– see also Ἀναγκαῖον, Ἀρχῆς, δῶρον,
    εὖρον, Κίχλα, κόρακος, κυνός, Λεύσσω,
    Λήμνιον, Λιβύη, Μικρόν, Πύρραν,
    Ταινάριον

κακὸς εἴσεται τοῦτο, Οὐδεὶς III iv 6;
    Κακὸς κακῷ γὰρ συντέτηκεν ἡδονῇ II
    iii 75
– see also Θρασύς, ἰατροῦ, ἰχθύς, Μῦς,
    Πῆμα, Πυλωρός, ὕδωρ
κακοῦ see βουλή, κόρακος, πατρός, πηγήν,
    χρώς
κακούργει see μουσικήν
κακῷ see κακόν, Κακός, παρωνυχίας,
    Σκύθη
κακῶν, Κύρβεις II v 91; Κακῶν πανήγυ-
    ρις II x 27; κακῶν τ' ἀγαθῶν τε τέτυκ-
    ται, Ὅττι τοι ἐν μεγάροισι ι vi 85+
– see also ἥκομεν, θάλασσα, Θησαυρός,
    Ἰλιάς, Κρατήρ, Λέρνη, Στέργει, τριῶν
κακῶς see δρομῆσαι, κόρη, μάντιν, τίτθαι,
    φίλοι
καλά, Δύσκολα τὰ II i 12+; καλά, Ἔρρει
    τὰ III v 59; Καλὰ δὴ πάντα λέγεις IV
    viii 97
καλάμης γινώσκειν, Ἐκ τῆς ι x 41;
    καλάμης ὁ τεθερισμένος στάχυς, Ἐκ
    IV ii 3
– see also ἀροῦν
Καλαμοβόας IV vi 33
καλαπόδι πάντας ὑποδέουσιν, Ἑνὶ IV iv
    56
Καλαυρίαν see Δήλου
καλέεσθαι see πολύξεινον
καλεῖς see Τιτᾶνας
καλεῖσθαι see ἰατροῦ
καλεῖται see μητέρος
καλή see Ἄβδηρα, ὀπώρη, Ῥοδῶπις
καλιάς see θέρος
Καλλίας πτερορρυεῖ IV vii 74
Καλλικράτους, Ὑπὲρ τὰ II viii 71
Καλλικυρίων πλείους III ii 32
Καλλιπίδης ι vi 43
Καλλίπυγοι IV vii 15
κάλλιστ' see λιμός
κάλλιστον see Ὄνος
Καλλιφάνης IV i 31
κάλλος see πλοῦτος
καλοῖσιν ἀνδράσιν πρέπει, Ἅπαντα τοῖς
    II ix 60
Καλόν γ' ἀποθανεῖν πρὶν θανάτου δρᾶν
    ἄξιον IV ix 11; καλὸν φίλον, Τὸ IV
    vii 81

κύβοι, Ἀεὶ γὰρ εὖ πίπτουσιν οἱ Διὸς
   I iii 9⁺; κύβοι, Ἦ τρὶς ἓξ ἢ τρεῖς II
   iii 66⁺
κύβοισιν see Μίδας
κύβος, Πᾶς ἀνερρίφθω I iv 32
κύβω see Ἀχιλλεύς
Κύδου see δίκην
Κύδωνος, Ἀεί τις ἐν II ii 15
Κυζικηνοὶ στατῆρες III i 73
Κυζικηνόν see Βάμμα
Κυθνώδεις συμφοραί III i 71
Κυθωνύμου αἶσχος III i 72
κυκᾷς, Οὐ μάλα IV ii 55
Κυκλοβόρου φωνή III ii 16
κύκλον ἀποτελεῖν, Τὸν II vi 86
κύκλω περιελθών, Ἅπαντας ἐν II iii 38;
   Κύκλω περιέλκεσθαι IV vii 52
Κυκλώπειος βίος I x 69
Κυκλωπικῶς IV viii 40*
Κύκλωπος δωρεά I iv 5
Κύκνειον ᾆσμα I ii 55⁺
κύκνοι ὅταν κολοιοὶ σιωπήσωσι, Τότ'
   ᾄσονται III iii 97
κύκνοισι see θεμιτόν
κυληκτής see Μέγας
κύλικος καὶ χείλεος ἄκρου, Πολλὰ μεταξὺ
   πέλει I v 1*⁺
– see also πιεῖν
Κυλίκων ἐρέται IV vii 41
κυλινδόμενος see Λίθος
κύλιξ see Βαθυκλέους
κύλισμα see Ὗς
Κυλλοῦ see πήρα
κῦμ' ὅπως, Ὀχλεῖς μάτην με
   III iii 64
Κῦμα κωφόν IV vi 40; κῦμα τὸ δ'
   ἐγκατελάμβανεν, Τὸ μὲν μ' ἔλιπεν
   I vi 34
– see also ἄλλεσθαι, θαλάσσης
Κυμαῖοι, Ὀψὲ αἰσθάνονται οἱ I v 61
Κυμαίους, Ὄνος παρὰ I vii 12
Κύματα see μετρεῖς, Πολλά, φοβοῖτο
κύματος see καπνοῦ
κυμάτων, Ἀπὸ δὶς ἑπτά III ii 88;
   Κυμάτων ἐν ἀγκάλαις IV vi 39
Κυμινοπρίστης II i 5
κύνα γεῦσαι, Χαλεπὸν χορίων II iv 22;
   Κύνα δέρειν δεδαρμένην II iii 54; κύνα

τρέφει ξένον, τούτω μόνον λίνος μένει,
   Ὃς III iii 46
– see also γραῦν, ὄνος
κύνας, Εἷς οἶκος οὐ δύναται τρέφειν τοὺς
   δύο II ii 24; κύνας ὁ ἔλαφος ἕλκει,
   Τοὺς IV iv 11; κύνας τρέφεις, Αὐτὸν
   οὐ τρέφων II v 88
κύνες ἐσθίουσιν, Τὸ εὔωνον κρέας οἱ IV
   iii 37; κύνες μιμούμεναι, Τὰς δεσποίνας
   αἱ II vi 13
– see also Προμέρου
κυνῆ see Ἄϊδος, Πλοῖον
κυνηγετεῖν see βοΐ
Κυνὶ δίδως ἄχυρα, ὄνω δὲ ὀστέα III v 14;
   κυνὶ καὶ βαλανείω, Τί κοινόν I iv 39⁺;
   κυνὶ καὶ τὸν ἱμάντα, Σὺν τῷ IV iii 26
κυνίδιον see Μελιταῖον
κυνὸς ἄρσενος εὐναί, Πολλαὶ II x 18;
   Κυνὸς δίκην I vii 47; κυνὸς κακὸν
   ὗς ἀπέτισεν, Τὸ III iii 99; κυνὸς
   πρωκτοῦ, Ἐκ IV ii 20; κυνὸς πυγὴν
   ὁρᾶν, Ἐς II ii 36*; κυνὸς σῦν ἀπαιτεῖς,
   Ἀντὶ κακῆς III vi 12
Κυνόσαργες, Ἐς III i 70
κυνόσβατος see ῥόδα
κυνῶν τε καὶ λίνων, Ἄνευ IV viii 78
Κυπαρίττου καρπός IV iii 10
Κύπριδος κεστόν, Τὸν III ii 36; Κύπριος
   βοῦς I x 95⁺
Κύρβεις see κακῶν
κυρία, Αὕτη I vi 28
Κυρνία ἄτη III vii 92; Κυρνία γῆ III i
   74
κύρτος see Εὕδοντι
κυσὶ μάχεσθαι, Ἐν φρέατι I x 36
κυσὶν ἄρνας, Προβάλλειν τοῖς II ix 73
κύων, Ἀγόμενος διὰ φρατόρων ὁ III
   vi 93⁺; κύων ἄρτως μαντεύεται, Ἐν
   ὕπνοις πᾶσα III x 86*; Κύων εἰς τὸν
   λίθον ἀγανακτοῦσα IV ii 22⁺; κύων
   ἐν τῇ φάτνη, Ἡ I x 13; Κύων ἐπὶ
   δεσμά II vii 67; Κύων ἐπὶ σῖτον IV
   vi 92; Κύων ἐπὶ τὸ ἴδιον ἐξέραμα
   III v 13; Κύων ζῶν ἀπὸ μαγδαλιᾶς
   IV i 23; κύων θρόνου, Ἀξία ἡ II
   vi 4; Κύων παρ' ἐντέροις II iv 24;
   κύων σπεύδουσα τυφλὰ τίκτει, Ἡ II
   ii 35; κύων τοῦ βρώματος, Ἀξία ἡ

πίστευε see Γυναικί
πιστεύσαι see Ἑρμῇ
πίστις see Ἀττικῇ, βωμός
πιστότεροι see ὀφθαλμοί
Πιτάνη εἰμί   III vi 20
πιττεύει see ψελλῇ
πιών see Γλαῦκος
Πλακιάδαι καὶ στέλαιον   IV i 10
πλακοῦντες see Λαγῷ
Πλαταγῇ δοκιμάσεις   IV ii 47
– see also Ἀρχύτου
πλάτει, Ἐν   IV vii 75
πλατείας see Συβαρῖται
Πλάτων φιλωνίζει ἢ Φίλων πλατωνίζει
   II vii 71*
πλατωνίζει see Πλάτων
Πλάτωνος φθεῖρες, Οἱ   IV x 65
πλέα see Ψευδῶν
πλεῖ see Αἰγαῖον
πλείῃς see Γαστρός
πλεῖν see Ἄνεμος, γῇ, Κοντῷ, λιμένι,
   Μυσῶν, Σίδηρον
πλεῖον see ἀλώπεκος
πλειόνων see ψῆφος
Πλείους see ἥλιον, Καλλικυρίων
πλέκειν see Δεινοί, σχοινίον
πλέκεις, Λεπτὴν   II ix 3
πλέκω, Τοὺς ἐμοὺς κορύμβους   III ii 96
Πλέον ἥμισυ παντός   I ix 95+
– see also Εὔχου
Πλεόνων see ἔργον
πλέων see Ἄδεις
πλευρά see Ἄθως
Πλεύσειας see Μασσαλίαν, Τροιζῆνα
Πλεύσεις see Ἀντικύρας
πληγαῖς see δρῦς, πουλύπους
πληγάς see αὐλητήν
πληγείς see Πίθος, Φρύξ
πλῆκτρον see Αἶρε, σκῆπτρον
πλήρη see Ἀσκόν
πλησιάζων ἥδεται, Ἐν οἷς ἂν ἀτυχῇσ'
   ἄνθρωπος, ἥκιστα τούτοις   IV i 57
πλησίον see Εὔχου
πλήττειν see Ὕδωρ
Πλίνθον πλύνεις   I iv 48+
πλινθοφόρος see Αἰγύπτιος
πλοεῖς see νυκτί
Πλοῖον ἢ κυνῇ   II ix 100

– see also Μηλιακόν
πλοίῳ see Θᾶττον
πλοκάμους, Περικείρειν τοὺς   I v 51
πλοῦς, Δεύτερος   III iv 71; πλοῦς μὲν
   ὁ παρὰ γῆν, περίπατος δ' ὁ παρὰ
   θάλατταν ἥδιστός ἐστιν   I ii 91*
– see also Κόρινθον
πλούσιος see γεωργός
πλουσιώτερος see Μίδου
πλουτεῖν see Φρουρεῖν
πλουτεῖς see Λυσιστράτου
πλοῦτον see Λυσιστράτου, Πακτωλοῦ
πλοῦτος, Ἄριστον ὑγιαίνειν, δεύτερον
   δὲ κάλλος, τρίτον δὲ   III i 90*;
   Πλοῦτος δὲ βάσανός ἐστιν ἀνθρώπων
   τρόπων   II iv 51*; πλοῦτος, Δειλὸς
   ὁ   III vii 2; πλοῦτος, Κεράμειος
   I x 56+
– see also Ἄζηλος, Κινύρου, Μίδου
πλουτοῦντα see γῇ
πλουτῶν οὐκέθ' ἥδεται φακῶν, Ἔπειτα
   II viii 36
πλύνειν see Ὄνου
πλύνεις see Πλίνθον
πλῶμες see Ἱππολέκτας
πνεῖ see καικίας
πνεύματος see Ἀσκόν, κώπας
πνίγῃ see ὕδωρ
πνίξ see Μερίς
πόαν see Γλαῦκος
πόδα, Μηδὲ τὸν ἕτερον   I x 44; πόδα,
   Περὶ   II ix 18; πόδα ἐν τῷ πορθμείῳ
   ἔχων, τὸν ἕτερον   II i 52*; πόδα
   τίθεσθαι, Ἐν ἀλλοτρίῳ χορῷ   II ii 51;
   πόδα τὸ ὑπόδημα, Μὴ ὑπὲρ τὸν   II v
   46; πόδα χειρὶ πιέζοις, Λεπτῇ δὲ παχὺν
   IV iii 85; πόδ' ἔχων, Ἐν τούτῳ πεδίλῳ
   δαιμόνιον   IV viii 70
– see also ἀναχωρεῖ, ἀνόστεος, διώκει
ποδάγρας ἀπαλλάττει Καλτίκιος, Οὔτε
   IV iv 77
πόδας ἐκ κεφαλῆς, Ἐς   I ii 37*+; πόδας
   ἔχεις, Ἐκ τοῦ πηλοῦ   I ii 81
πόδε see καθεύδειν
πόδες φέρωσιν, Ἔνθ' ἂν οἱ   I x 68
ποδί, Ἄκρῳ   IV ix 59; ποδί, Ἡσύχῳ
   II i 4; ποδί, Ὅλῳ   III i 34; ποδὶ
   ἐπιβαίνειν, Ἄκρῳ   IV iii 66

Latin Index
of Erasmus' Adages

All the Latin proverbs found in the *Adagia* are listed here, cross-referenced by all salient words (excluding prepositions, conjunctions, most pronouns and pronominal adjectives, and a number of other common words). A raised plus sign (⁺) indicates that the adage is to be found in some form in the *Collectanea* (87–358 in this volume); see the Concordance (359–66) to find the appropriate c number(s) corresponding to the *Adagia* number the ⁺ is attached to. When multiple versions of an adage (separated by /) are given, the first is the title of the adage as found in cwe, followed by alternative versions from the beginning of the essay of the same proverb.

Abdera pulchra Teiorum colonia II
  iv 53
Abderitica mens IV vi 28
abeat *see* bibat
abegerunt *see* Nunquam
aberret a ianua?, Quis I vi 36
abesse *see* possim
abest *see* Dulce, Praesens
Abhorrentis, ac detestantis III x 31
abi aut exuere, Aut IV vii 86
abigendae *see* Primum
Abiecit hastam. Rhipsaspis II ii 97
abiicere *see* Hastam
Abiiciendum procul IV iv 67
abiicit animum, Non III ix 96
abiiciunt *see* Ubi
Abiit et taurus in sylvam I i 43
– *see also* Salis
abluit *see* Marinam
Abominandus scarabaeus II x 5
abominor *see* Scellii
Abronis vita II v 30⁺
abrumpere *see* Funem
Absit clamor in colloquio, aut lusu III
  ix 37

– *see also* Procul, Somnus
absolvenda *see* Sacra
absolvere *see* Circulum
absolvit *see* nimium
abstergas *see* vacuam
absterseris *see* Sellam
abstine *see* Sustine
abstineas *see* gallo
Abstinenda vis a regibus III x 43
– *see also* sacris
abstineto *see* fabis, piscibus
abstulerit *see* Argivum
absumit *see* Delphis
absumpseris *see* Nemini
absunt *see* Fluvius
absurde locutum, In III viii 6
Abydena illatio II v 23a
Abydenus *see* Abydus
Abydum *see* temere
Abydus, Abydenus IV vi 17
Academia venis, Ex III iv 19
Acanthia cicada I v 14⁺
Acanthida vincit cornix I viii 83
Acarnanius *see* Porcellus
Acarnici equi IV ii 70

bibens *see* Aquam

Bibere mandragoram IV v 64; bibere poculo, Eodem I viii 81

– *see also* Gallam, mulctro, poculo

biberint *see* Parthi

bibisti *see* amphitheto

bibit *see* Fecem, Strychnum, Vinum

bibunt *see* Mali, mensuram

bilem *see* Fames, Movere

bilis *see* Inest, nare

Bipedum nequissimus I vii 42

bipennis *see* Tenedia

Bis ac ter, quod pulchrum est I ii 49; Bis dat qui cito dat I viii 91; Bis interimitur, qui suis armis perit IV i 96; Bis pueri senes I v 36⁺; Bis septem plagis polypus contusus II v 99; bis septem undis, A III ii 88

– *see also* Crambe, licet

Bithus contra Bacchium II v 97⁺

Blace *see* Inutilior

blandiri *see* Cauda

Blandius alloqui III viii 43

Bocchyris II vii 65

Boeotia auris III ii 48

Boeotica aenigmata II iii 9; Boeotica cantilena II iii 8; Boeotica sus I x 6

Boeoticum ingenium II iii 7

– *see also* Moschus

Boeotis vaticinare II iii 11

Boeotissare v i 77

bolis *see* Tribus

Boliti poenam II ii 13

Bolus ereptus e faucibus III vi 99⁺; bolus quidem relictus, Ne III v 40

bombylius *see* Homo

Bona Cillicon II v 9⁺; Bona etiam offa post panem / Maza post panem bona II iv 61; Bona nemini hora est IV v 7; Bona Porsenae I vii 88; Bona spes ostensa III x 36; Bona terrae III i 24; Bona verba quaeso c 286

– *see also* Albo, Baeta, Novit, parvula, Perierunt, respiciens, Sapiens, Ultro

Bonae fortunae sive Boni genii I vi 53; Bonae leges ex malis moribus procreantur I x 61⁺

bonam frugem, Ad IV v 27⁺

Boni ad bonorum convivia ultro accedunt I x 35⁺; Boni pastoris est tondere pecus, non deglubere III vii 12⁺; Boni viri lachrymabiles II vii 64

– *see also* adest, adsunt, Aquam, Bonae, Multi, Praesentem

Bonis avibus, malis avibus I i 75⁺; bonis bona disce, A IV viii 37; bonis glomi, Pro III v 83

bono in bonum traductus sum, Ego ex III vi 78

– *see also* mala, Malum

Bonorum glomi II iv 92⁺; Bonorum myrmecia I iii 32⁺; bonorum virorum est morbus, Hic III vii 74

– *see also* Acervus, Boni, Dathus, Gargara, Mare, Thasos

bonos *see* Corrumpunt, Omnia, spina

Bonum est duabus niti ancoris IV viii 72

– *see also* bono, Bonus, Effugi, Exiguum, habitu, Malum, Nullus, paucis, Signum

Bonus cantor, bonus cupediarius II v 35; bonus dormitat Homerus, Quandoque c 716; Bonus dux bonum reddit comitem I viii 100; Bonus e pharetra dies II viii 18

– *see also* Brasidas, Imperator, Lucri, Malus, Nunquam

boreas *see* cessat

Bos ad praesepe II i 39; Bos adversus seipsum pulverem movet II v 78; Bos alienus subinde foras prospectat I x 62; Bos apud acervum III ii 53; Bos Cyprius I x 95⁺; Bos Homolottiorum III ii 52; Bos in civitate III iv 16; Bos in lingua I vii 18⁺; Bos in quadra argentea IV vi 93; Bos in stabulo IV vi 91; Bos lassus fortius figit pedem I i 47⁺; Bos marinus IV vi 90; Bos porrecto ultra Taygeton capite IV ii 59; bos quidem pereat, Ne IV v 1; bos quidem vocem edat, Ne si III i 46; Bos sub iugum II vi 74

Calcar addere currenti I ii 47
- *see also* Tolle
calcaria in carbonariam, De II iv 96⁺
calce *see* Arena
calceamento pedem habet, In hoc IV
    viii 70
calcem, Extra IV vi 73; calcem per-
    venire, Ad III v 35
- *see also* capite
calceo *see* Dextrum
Calceos mutare IV viii 13
calces *see* stimulum
calceum omni pedi inducere, Eundem
    IV iv 56
Calceus *see* liberat, Pedem
calciamentum consuit Histiaeus,
    Aristagoras induit, Hoc III iv 42
- *see also* Colophonium
calcibus *see* Pugnis
calculi *see* Aequales
calculis *see* Omne
Calculo mordere III vii 40
Calculum reducere I v 55⁺
- *see also* Album
calculus *see* Connae, Plurium
calendas *see* Graecas
calicem *see* Multa
Calicum remiges IV vii 41
Calidam veruti partem II vi 87
calidis *see* Teneri
Calidum mendacium IV v 68; Calidum
    prandium comedisti I i 59⁺
- *see also* Cor, ore
Caliga Maximini I i 21
Caligare in sole II v 77⁺
caliginem *see* nebulam
Calliae defluunt pennae IV vii 74
Callicratis, Ultra res II viii 71
Callicyriis plures III ii 32
callidum *see* nimium, quaestum
Calliphanes IV i 31
Callipides I vi 43⁺
Callipygos IV vii 15
Callum ducere III i 35
callus *see* Socratis
caloni *see* Sambucam
calumnia *see* Argiva
calumniari *see* Domesticum

calumniosior *see* Pattaecione
calvaria *see* Viri
calvior *see* Pistillo
Calvum vellis II viii 37
Calvus comatus II v 60⁺; Calvus quum
    sis IV vii 6
- *see also* Myconius
Camarinam *see* Movere
Camarine loqui IV v 98
Camelus desiderans cornua, etiam au-
    res perdidit III v 8; Camelus saltat
    II vii 66⁺; Camelus vel scabiosa
    complurium asinorum gestat onera
    I ix 58⁺
- *see also* Formica
camino *see* Oleum
Campana superbia IV viii 14
Campanica *see* Peristromata
Campanos *see* Plus
campi *see* Fors
campum *see* Herniosi
campus *see* Famis, Martis, Oblivionis,
    Venti
canali *see* Tenui
Cancer leporem capit II iv 78⁺
cancri *see* Nunquam
Cancros lepori comparas I viii 85
Cancrum ingredi doces III vii 98
candefacere *see* Ebur
candela *see* Accepta
candido *see* gallo
candidorum *see* Nulla
Candidum linum lucri causa ducis III
    ii 77
Candidus sermo IV vii 100
cane simul et lorum, Cum / Lorum
    una cum cane IV iii 26; Cane Tellenis
    cantilenas II vi 8
- *see also* malo, Odit, Tetigit
canem alit externum, Qui III iii 46;
    Canem excoriatam excoriare II iii 54
- *see also* Agninis, asinus, canis, Litem,
    magis, Periculosum, Praestat
Canens vitae palmum IV ii 34
- *see also* Excubiarum, Moschus
canent *see* Cicadae, Tunc
canere, Sibi III v 80⁺; Canere ad myr-
    tum II vi 21; Canere de Telamo /

nondum peperit, haedus autem
ludit in tectis II vi 10; Capra Scyria
I x 20[+]; Capra gladium I i 57[+]
- *see also* Matris
caprae *see* Liberae
Capram coelestem orientem con-
spexerunt III x 76; Capram portare
non possum, et imponitis bovem II
vii 96
Caprarius in aestu II vi 95
capras sylvestres, In III ii 78
- *see also* agro
caprea contra leonem, Ne II iv 79[+]
caprina *see* lana
captant *see* Undecunque
Captantes capti sumus I x 14
captare *see* Anguillas
captas *see* Impossibilia
captat *see* Aquila
capti *see* Captantes, Tibicines
captivis *see* Similes
captus *see* laqueo
Caput II i 61; caput, In tuum ipsius
IV vi 88; Caput artis, decere quod
facias IV v 2; caput, nec pedes, Nec
v i 11; caput praecipitari, In III
iii 83; Caput scabere III vi 96; Caput
sine lingua I x 79[+]; Caput vacuum
cerebro III iv 40
- *see also* allii, Asini, Demulcere,
pedes, Polypi, Summo, Tertium,
Unico
cara *see* Cicada
carbonariam *see* calcaria
carbone *see* Creta
carbones *see* Thesaurus
carcere, A II v 94
carceribus, A I vi 58
Carcini poemata III ii 30
- *see also* Fortunatior
cardine, Res est in I i 19[+]
Care Carizas, Cum I ii 30; Care
periculum, In I vi 14[+]
Cares *see* Foras, Lydi
caret *see* Venter, Vinum
Cariam *see* Multitudo
Carica musa I viii 79[+]; Carica victima
III ii 31

Carico *see* More
Caricum sepulchrum IV iii 3; Caricum
vinum IV vi 41
Caricus hircus III vi 97
carior *see* Discordia
Carizas *see* Care
Carne *see* Delphis
carnes *see* adsunt, Dasypus, Delphis,
Oportet, Parvo
carnibus *see* Lepus
Carpathius leporem II i 81
Carpet citius aliquis quam imitabitur
II ii 84
carpito *see* Coronam
carum *see* opus, Vale
carycae *see* Lydorum
carycas *see* Lydorum
casae *see* Fores
casam *see* Ita
cascam *see* Cascus
Cascus cascam ducit I ii 62[+]
caseolus *see* Xenocratis
caseum haberem, non desiderarem
opsonium, Si III iv 89
- *see also* Salem
Cassa glande v i 17
Cassioticus nodus II v 34[+]
castior *see* Melanione
casus *see* Panicus
catalogum, Ultra III v 61
Catastrophe fabulae I ii 36
Catella Melitaea III iii 71
Cato dicat, Etiam si IV v 61
- *see also* Tertius
Catone hoc contenti sumus IV x 3
Catulae dominas imitantes II vi 13
catuli *see* Aliter
catulos *see* Ale, Canis
catulum *see* Leonis
catulus *see* Melitaeus
Cauda blandiri IV i 32; Cauda de
vulpe testatur I ix 35[+]; Cauda tenes
anguillam I iv 94[+]
- *see also* Asini, Delphinum, gustaris,
Toto
Caudae pilos equinae paulatim vellere
I viii 95
caudata *see* Simia

equinis *see* Procul

equis ad asinos, Ab I vii 29⁺; Equis albis praecedere I iv 21⁺

equisque *see* Velis

Equitandi peritus ne cantet IV ix 34

equitum *see* modus

Equo senescenti minora cicela admove II viii 52

equorum *see* Salvete

equos *see* Nunquam, Strenuos

equum et virginem, Apud IV ix 69; Equum habet Seianum I x 97⁺

– *see also* Incita, planiciem

Equus me portat, alit rex I vii 20⁺

– *see also* Anus, Ibyci, tardigradis, Testudinem

eradere *see* Imis

Erasinade *see* Militavit

Erecti IV v 18

ereptus *see* Bolus

Eretriensium *rho* II viii 53

Ergini cani III iii 86

erigere *see* Senem

Erinnys ex tragoedia IV ii 95

eripere *see* Lupo

eriphus *see* Anus

Erisichthonis *see* Mutabilior

erithacos *see* Unicum

errare *see* Toto

erras *see* Tota

erratum *see* textoris

erro *see* Accipit

eruditus *see* Pauciloquus

erumpat *see* nervum

escam *see* nassa

esculenta *see* Omnia

Esernius cum Pacidiano II v 98

esuriens *see* Asinus

Esurienti leoni praedam exsculpere v i 58; Esurienti ne occurras IV x 53

– *see also* Lepori, Viro, Vulpi

Eteobutadis ducit genus, Ab III iii 85

Eucrates *see* Vias

euntibus *see* Duobus

Euparyphus ex comoedia IV iv 95

Euripus homo I ix 62⁺

Eurybatizare I ii 86

Eurycles IV i 39

Eurymnus IV ii 6

Evenit malo male III viii 49

eveniunt *see* Bonis, Mala, omnia

Eventus praeter exspectationem III ix 4

– *see also* Anceps

Evitata Charybdi in Scyllam incidi I v 4⁺

Exacta via viaticum quaerere III iv 45

exactum *see* Fatale

exaequatur *see* alibi

excavat *see* Assidua

excepit *see* Alio

excideret *see* Citius

excipere *see* heros

excipio *see* Divinum

excitandus *see* Temulentus

excitas *see* Octipedem

excitat *see* Anus

excludere *see* Oculum

excogitavit *see* Dea

excoquat sevum, Unde III vii 77

excoriare *see* Canem

excorias *see* Priusquam

excoriatam *see* Canem

Excubiarum causa canens I vii 78

Excubias agere / ditari II x 70

Excubias agere in Naupacto I ii 83

– *see also* Nudo

excusationes *see* Certamen

excute *see* Aliam

Execestides quidem rectam viam invenerit, Ne II vi 49

exedundum *see* Tute

Exemplum utile v i 98

– *see also* vicinis

exerceat *see* norit

Exercitatio potest omnia II ii 53

exhauris *see* Mare

exhauritur *see* Influit

exigere *see* mortuo

Exigit et a statuis farinas III ii 89

Exigua res est ipsa iustitia II i 67

– *see also* Iustitia

exiguae *see* Concordia

Exiguum malum, ingens bonum II v 65⁺; Exiguum oboli precium III v 54

Magna civitas, magna solitudo II
  iv 54; Magna de re disceptatur III
  ix 29; magna loquaris, Ne II ii 52
  – see also pusillis
magnam see Papyri
magnes see Omnes
Magnetis see Omnes
Magnetum mala II x 17
magnifica see sero
magnis et voluisse sat est, In II
  viii 55
magnitudine see Colossi
Magno flumini rivulum inducis III
  i 44; Magno gemitu manus fit
  gravior C 233
Magnorum fluminum navigabiles
  fontes I iii 73
Magnum os anni II vii 17
  – see also calceum, Multa, Semper
Magnus versator in re pusilla / Versator ingens in negocio levi III
  iv 82
  – see also Nullus
maio see Mense
maior thylaco accessio, Ne IV ii 69
  – see also Calceus, Chorus
maiore see Fuge
maiores see Pennas
māla see Hesperidum, ovo
mala, animo si bono utare, adiuvat, In
  re III iv 68; Mala attrahens ad sese,
  ut caecias nubes I v 62⁺; Mala malis
  eveniunt V ii 31; Mala proditio II
  x 34; mala prudentior, Post I iii 99;
  Mala senium accelerant III x 62;
  Mala ultro adsunt IV ii 62
  – see also Azanaea, Conciliant, Ex-
  trema, Hominum, Ignis, Magnetum,
  Malis, Mare, Matura, Niobes, Nota,
  Novit, Ogygia, ovo, Samiorum,
  Semper, Termeria
malae see Mense
malam segetem serendum est, Et post
  IV iv 62
Male coniugati III ix 88; Male parta
  male dilabuntur I vii 82
  – see also Bene, Evenit, Nutricum,
  Parit, Satius, Utinam

Maleam legens quae sunt domi
  obliviscere II iv 46
mali, Nam iam illi non sunt, at qui
  sunt, II ix 37; Mali bibunt impro-
  bitatis fecem II x 36; Mali comma-
  tis III ii 6; Mali corvi malum ovum
  I ix 25⁺; mali fontem reperit, Ipse sibi
  I i 56⁺; mali, in Pyrrham, Si quid III
  ii 1; Mali principii malus finis IV
  ix 86; mali, propter vicinum malum,
  Aliquid I i 32⁺; Mali thripes, mali
  ipes II x 35
  – see also Lerii, Lydi, Semper, tempore,
  Tollenda
maligno see Sonat
malim see Citius
mālis see Punicis
Malis ferire II iv 70⁺
Malis mala succedunt III ix 97⁺; malis
  neque sine malis, Neque cum II
  ix 92; Malis ter mala III iii 98
  – see also Assuevit, Bonae, Bonis,
  cedendum, Celeritas, Contigit,
  Duobus, Lecythum, luctu, tribus
malleum et incudem, Inter I i 16
Malo accepto stultus sapit I i 31; Malo
  asino vehitur IV vii 8; malo cane
  suem reposcis, Pro III vi 12; Malo
  nodo malus quaerendus cuneus
  I ii 5⁺
  – see also Emere, Evenit, Malum,
  Malus, Nunquam, Praestat
Malorum assuetudo III ix 91; malorum memineris, Ne II i 94; Malorum oblivio III viii 22; Malorum
  panegyris II x 27
  – see also Cyrbes, Ilias, Iucunda, Lerna,
  Mare, Thesaurus
Malum bene conditum ne moveris
  I i 62⁺; Malum bono pensatum III
  x 12; Malum consilium consultori
  pessimum I ii 14⁺; Malum est
  bonum IV iii 2; Malum Hercules
  II x 30; malum lunam deduces, In
  tuum ipsius III ii 2; Malum malo
  medicari I ii 6; Malum munus IV
  iii 4; malum repperit, Sibi III x 65;
  Malum vas non frangitur IV ii 99

nocentem *see* capra, Reperit

nocere potest, et idem prodesse, Qui III ix 74

– *see also* Deo, tempestas

nocte consilium, In II ii 43; Nocte lucidus, interdiu inutilis IV iii 29A

– *see also* pluit

noctem *see* decet, pluet

Noctes diesque I iv 24⁺

noctu *see* navigas

Noctua volat I i 76⁺

– *see also* Aliud

Noctuae Laurioticae II viii 31

– *see also* Aquilam

Noctuinum ovum II i 44

Nocuit et nocebit III viii 80

nodo *see* Malo

Nodum in scyrpo quaeris II iv 76⁺; Nodum solvere I i 6

nodus *see* Cassioticus, Herculanus

Nolens volens I iii 45

nolente *see* Volens

nolentem *see* Vinum

nolit *see* mori

nollem *see* dedi

nomen quidem, Ne IV iv 10; nomen, Tanquam meum / Tanquam digitos II iv 91⁺

– *see also* patris

Nomine tantum notus I ix 87

nominis *see* Proprii

nondum *see* apio, Capra, chytropode, Prius, Septennis

noris *see* Multa

norit artem, in hac se exerceat, Quam quisque II ii 82⁺

Nosce teipsum I vi 95⁺; Nosce tempus I vii 70⁺

nosse *see* facie

nosti *see* tria

Nota res mala optima II ix 85⁺

notare *see* Creta, Stellis

Notari ungui I v 58

noti *see* Principes

Notum lippis ac tonsoribus I vi 70

notus *see* Domestice, Nomine

Nova hirundo I vi 59; Nova Hymettia, Falerna vetera II ii 71

Novacula in cotem I i 20

– *see also* Fortunae

novaculae *see* acie

novam aggredior, Rem III x 67

novem *see* Septem

noveram priusquam Theognis natus est, Hoc IV iii 100

noverca *see* dies

novercae *see* Flere

novercale *see* Odium

novercam queri, Apud IV v 52

noveris *see* Mores, Vivum

Novi nummi IV viii 51; Novi Simonem et Simon me II v 49⁺

– *see also* Semper

novilunium *see* Attagenae

Novit haec Pylaea et Tyttygias II vii 57; Novit mala et bona III x 57; novit natos, Non I vi 100; Novit quid album, quid nigrum I vi 98

– *see also* Bestia, Invitus, Iupiter, Multa, Tollat, umbram, Vias

novitas *see* Grata

Novos parans amicos ne obliviscere veterum III iii 80

Novum cribrum, novo paxillo V i 64

– *see also* Semper

Nox humida III vi 30

noxa *see* Litem, Sponde

noxae *see* Heroum

noxam *see* Litem

noxia *see* Cunctatio

nubem *see* Serenitati

nubes *see* Mala

nubibus *see* Aquila

nubunt *see* Mense

nuce nucleum esse vult, frangit nucem, Qui e II ix 35⁺

– *see also* Nil, Vitiosa

nucem *see* nuce

Nuces relinquere I v 35⁺

Nucleum amisi, reliquit pignori putamina II ix 75⁺

– *see also* nuce

Nudae Gratiae II vii 50

Nudior leberide I i 26; Nudior paxillo II x 100

– *see also* Pistillo

nudius *see* Heri

Nudo capite III iv 67; Nudo mandas excubias II ix 76; Nudo vestimenta detrahere I iv 76[+]

Nudus tanquam ex matre II viii 44[+]

Nugae theatri IV ix 90

– *see also* Bullatae, Siculae

Nugas agere I iv 91[+]

nugis *see* Lusciniae, Omissis, Tragoedias

Nulla candidorum virorum utilitas III vi 29

– *see also* Exitii

Nullam corporis partem IV x 29; Nullam hodie lineam duxi I iv 12[+]

nulli sis amicus, neque multis, Neque III vi 37

Nullius coloris IV ix 100; Nullius indigens Deus II ix 74

Nullo scopo iaculari III v 45

Nullum animal. Quod animal? II i 83; nullum negocium erat, Harmenen muro cinxit, Cui IV vi 44; Nullum ocium servis II iii 46

Nullus comatus qui non idem cinaedus C 394; Nullus delectus III viii 34; Nullus dies omnino malus IV x 88; Nullus emptor difficilis bonum edit obsonium III iii 50; Nullus malus magnus piscis II iii 92; Nullus sum I iii 44; v i 86

– *see also* Hodie, Inopi, Nemo, Occultae, Ovium, Unus

Numenius *see* Convenerat

numerabimus *see* Cocta

numeras *see* Undas

numerato, In IV iii 82

Numeris Platonicis obscurius III vi 32

Numero dicis III vii 58

– *see also* Superis

numerum pervenire, In v ii 44

– *see also* curat

Numerus II iii 23

num *see* properas

Numinis ira inevitabilis v ii 32

nummi *see* Novi

Nummo addicere IV ix 1

nummus quidem plumbeus, Ne III

vii 52; Nummus plumbeus v i 9

– *see also* Faba

numquam *see* nunquam

Nunc bene navigavi, cum naufragium feci II ix 78; Nunc contingat servari II ix 77; Nunc dii beati II vii 24; Nunc illa advenit Datidis cantilena II ix 80; Nunc in regionem veni II ix 79; Nunc ipsa floret Musa III iii 24; Nunc ipsa vivit sapientia III iii 23; Nunc leguminum messis II vii 23; Nunc meae in arctum coguntur copiae I i 17; Nunc pluit et claro nunc Iupiter aethere fulget / Iupiter aliquando pluit, aliquando serenus est I viii 65; nunc sunt homines, Ut III viii 59; Nunc tuum ferrum in igni est IV iv 100

– *see also* I modo

nunciat *see* Siren

nunciavit *see* municeps

Nuncio nihil imputandum v ii 1

Nuncius *see* Procul

Nunquam efficies, ut recte ingrediantur cancri III vii 38; Nunquam enim meas boves abegerunt nec equos II vii 97; Nunquam edepol temere tintinnabulum C 521; Nunquam ex malo patre bonus filius I vi 33

– *see also* Coeno, semel, Timidi

nuntius *see* Procul

nuptiae *see* Aegypti

nuptiis *see* Pura

nutans *see* Utroque

nutrias *see* uncis

nutricationis *see* Aries

Nutricis pallium v i 68

– *see also* lacte

Nutricum more male III v 30

Nutu atque renutu IV ix 39

nyssam *see* Incita

obambulat *see* Buthus

obdis *see* Ceram

obdite *see* Ostium

obducitur *see* Saxum

Obedientia felicitatis mater IV v 59

Romanus sedendo vincit I x 29
Rore pascitur IV iv 16
ros *see* Psecas
rosa *see* squilla
Rosam cum anemona confers II vi 41;
 Rosam quae praeterierit ne quaeras
 iterum II vi 40
Rosas loqui II vi 42
– *see also* Sus
Roscius IV vii 69⁺
rotae *see* Multae
ruat *see* coelum
rubidus *see* Semel
Rubo arefacto praefractior II i 100⁺
Rude *see* Rudem
Rudem accipere. Rude donare I ix 24⁺
rudentem *see* Omnem
Rudentes et remos cum armis commu-
 tavit III iii 32
Rudius ac planius I i 39
Rufillus *see* Pastillos
Ruminare negocium III vii 68
Rumor publicus non omnino frustra
 est IV viii 34
rumpere *see* Columnas
rumpitur *see* Arcus
rupes *see* Asinum
Rupta ancora IV i 41
Ruris fons II vi 62
rursus *see* Mortuos
Rus civitas II vi 46; Rus merum
 C 713
Rusticanum oratorem ne contempseris
 II vi 45⁺
Rusco horridior C 741
Ruta caesa IV iv 38

Saburratus III vii 57
sacco adire, Cum IV vi 7
Sacer manipulus IV vi 51; Sacer piscis
 IV vi 64
Sacra celerius absolvenda III ix 48;
 sacra consultor, Res II i 47; Sacra
 haec non aliter constant II iv 88⁺;
 Sacra nihil sunt III v 93
– *see also* Commovere, Miscebis,
 Movebo, Persaepe
Sacram ancoram solvere I i 24⁺

sacri *see* Nihil
sacrificandum *see* Superis
sacrificant *see* Cereri, Lari
sacrificata *see* Persaepe
sacrificato sine farina, Ne I i 2 (Pythagoras) CWE 31 47
sacrificatum *see* chytropode
sacrificaverit *see* Delphis
sacrificium *see* Phaselitarum, Rhodii
sacris abstinenda manus, A III ix 45;
 sacris haereditas, Sine I iii 59
sacrorum *see* Sursum
sacrum et saxum, Inter I i 15⁺; Sacrum
 sine fumo I x 11
– *see also* Cretenses, Lindii, Nephalium
Saepe etiam est olitor valde opportuna
 locutus I vi 1⁺
– *see also* Matura, Vultu
saeviens *see* Canis
saevum *see* Mustelae
saga, Ad IV viii 10
sagittis *see* Caedimus
Sagram *see* Veriora
Saguntina fames I ix 67⁺
Sal et mensa IV ix 80
Salacones V i 79
Salaminia navis III iii 4
Sale emptum mancipium I vii 79⁺;
 Sale et aceto V i 16; Sale nihil
 utilius IV ix 68; Sale perunctus hic
 adiuvabitur III iv 26
– *see also* Piscis
Salem apponito I i 2 (Pythagoras)
 CWE 31 47; Salem et caseum edere
 IV v 87; salem et fabam, Qui circa
 I i 12⁺; Salem et fabam III v 20⁺;
 Salem et mensam ne praetereas
 I vi 10; Salem lingere III vii 33
– *see also* Oleum
Sales vehens dormis I vii 81
Saliares dapes IV ix 81
Salillum animae V i 8
Salis onus unde venerat, illuc abiit
 I vii 80⁺
– *see also* Nemini
salit *see* Oculus, Supercilium
Salivam imbibere II iv 19
salsa *see* Mola

est cur velis vivere I viii 45⁺; Ubi paveris impera IV iv 24; Ubi per Harma fulgurarit I v 86; Ubi quis dolet, ibidem et manum habet II ii 44; Ubi timor, ibi et pudor I ii 64; Ubi tu Caius, ibi ego Caia IV viii 33
– see also adsunt, finem, Libera, Pedem, pila, Sus
ulcere see hulcere
ulceribus see Aliorum
ulciscetur see Deus
ulcus see Tangere, hulcus
ulnis see Obviis, Undarum
ulti see beneficentia
ultimas terras, In IV x 67
ultimum see primum
ultimus see Mysorum
Ultro citroque I iii 84; Ultro Deus subiicit bona II viii 77
– see also Boni, Mala
ultronea see Merx
Ululas Athenas I ii 11⁺
Ulysses pannos exuit IV iv 47
Ulysseum commentum II viii 79
Ulyssis remigium II x 62⁺
umbilicum ducere, Ad I ii 32⁺
umbra in solem, Ex I ii 82; Umbra pro corpore III ii 98; umbra sequi, Velut III vii 51
– see also asini, Decempes, Fumi, Vulturis
Umbrae I i 9
– see also Scarabei
Umbram metiri II ii 80A; umbram quidem eius novit, Ne I ix 86; Umbram suam metuere I v 65⁺
– see also capillus
Una domus non alit duos canes II ii 24; Una hirundo non facit ver I vii 94⁺; Una lavabor II vii 85; una manu capere, Non IV v 31; Una pertica IV v 36; Una scutica omnes impellit II x 65; una vehit navis, Non IV i 61
– see also Omnia
unam see Omnia
uncis sunt unguibus, ne nutrias, Quae I i 2 (Pythagoras) CWE 31 43

unda see Obturbas
undam see fumum
Undarum in ulnis IV vi 39
Undas numeras I iv 45
Undecunque lucrum captant III ix 81
– see also Deus
undis see bis
unguem, Ad I v 91⁺; Unguem medium ostendere II iv 68⁺
– see also Latum
unguenti see Plus
unguento see Asinus, Mortuum
unguentum see lente, Lenti
Ungues see Caput
ungui see Notari
unguibus incipere, Ab IV vii 42
– see also Leonem, Summis, uncis
unguiculis see teneris, Toto
Unguium criniumque praesegmina ne commingito I i 2 (Pythagoras) CWE 31 42
Uni cum duobus non est pugnandum V ii 30; uni navi facultates, Ne IV iv 6
– see also Mus, Praestat
Unica filia duos parare generos I vii 4
Unico digitulo scalpit caput I viii 34⁺
Unicum arbustum haud alit duos erithacos II ii 22
Uno digitulo IV iv 78; uno dignus, Nec I viii 13; Uno fasce complecti I vi 9; uno multa facere, Ex II i 49; uno omnia specta, Ex I ii 78; Uno ore I ix 17; Uno tenore I x 2
– see also Culleo, Oscitante, saltu
unquam arcet ostium, Haud II ii 14; unquam Megarensibus, Ne quis III vi 28; unquam viri senis, Ne II vii 73
– see also Lignum
Unum ad unum II ii 42; Unum augurium optimum tueri patriam III i 57
– see also Multa, tribus
Unus Deus et plures amici III iv 88; Unus multorum instar III viii 53; Unus vir, nullus vir I v 40
– see also capillus, Pluris

Index of Early Modern
English Proverbs

This index lists Early Modern English proverbs that correspond either precisely or in close parallel to proverbs in the *Adagia*.

Our two sources are Morris Palmer Tilley's *A Dictionary of Proverbs in England in the Sixteenth and Seventeenth Centuries* (Ann Arbor 1959) and F.P. Wilson's revision of *The Oxford Dictionary of English Proverbs* 3rd ed (Oxford 1970). These proverbs came into English from classical sources, often via Erasmus in Latin or in English translation (see Erica Rummel 'The Reception of Erasmus's Adages in Sixteenth-Century England' *Renaissance and Reformation/Renaissance et Reform* 18 [1994] 19–30).

The proverbs are listed alphabetically in the order they appear in Tilley or ODEP. Tilley proverbs are located by the key word and by a special identifier: an italic capital letter followed by a number, eg *A* 366. The proverbs in ODEP are listed alphabetically by key word and page number. The majority of these English proverbs are also cross-indexed in our main English Index of Erasmus' Adages (635–766).

Most of the adages listed here are the subject of an essay by Erasmus and are identified by the regular adage number. But here and there he slips in other 'unofficial' adages that also entered Early Modern English; these are indicated by parenthetical citations (listing the proverb essay in which they appear followed by the CWE volume and page number). As might be expected, given the way proverbs are transmitted from one language to another, many English proverbs are parallels, not precise translations; these are indicated by 'cf.' Often a note in the translator's commentary will provide a rationale for the parallel. The index is a revision of an earlier draft prepared by the late R.A.B. Mynors.

Abundance of things engenders disdainfulness, The *A* 12; ODEP 12; III vii 53

Acorns were good until bread was found *A* 21; ODEP 3; cf I iv 2; IV iii 1

Adversity makes men wise *A* 42; ODEP 5; cf I iii 99

Africa is always producing something new *A* 56; ODEP 5; III vii 10

Age is sickness of itself, Old *A* 73; ODEP 587; II vi 37

Ajax, As mad as *A* 95; ODEP 498; cf I vii 46

All are of the same dust *A* 119; cf I vii 27

All is lost, both labour and cost *A* 140; ODEP 485; cf I iv 62. *See also* Labour

All is well that ends well *A* 152; ODEP 879; cf I iii 37

All is well, the old man dances *A* 155; III i 40

All and found myself, I have lost *A* 195; ODEP 486; cf II ix 78n (CWE 34 356)

Breeks off a bare arse, It is ill to take B 650 (and B 644); cf I iv 76. *See also* Raiment

Bridle, To bite upon the B 670; ODEP 62; I iv 14

Brim than at the bottom, Better spare at the B 674; cf II ii 64

Bull that hath borne a calf, He may bear a B 711; I ii 51

Bull (he-goat), To milk a B 714; I iii 51

Buskin that will serve two legs, A B 758; I i 94

Buy than to beg, Better to B 783; I iii 20

Cabbage twice sodden. *See* Coleworts

Caesar's wife must be above suspicion ODEP 97; (*Adagia* introduction iv CWE 31 9)

Camel, going to seek horns, lost his ears, The C 27; ODEP 99; III v 8

Camel to dance, It becomes him as well as it becomes a C 30; II vii 66

Candle, It smells of the C 43; ODEP 745; cf I vii 71. *See also* Lamp

Captain should not sleep the whole night through, A C 69, II vii 95

Cart before the horse, To set the C 103; ODEP 104; I vii 28

Cat for lard, Send not a C 164; ODEP 108; cf I iv 11

Censure, which spares the raven, torments the dove C 210; III v 73

Ceres and Bacchus Venus grows cold, Without C 211; ODEP 112, 521; II iii 97

Chameleon, As changeable as a C 221; ODEP 114; III iv 1

Chance than by any good cunning, More by C 225; ODEP 321; (I v 82 CWE 31 455)

Change is sweet C 229; ODEP 858; cf I vii 64

Change of all things, There is C 233; I vii 63

Chapman that comes after the fair, He is a fond C 237; cf I ix 52

Charity begins at home C 251; ODEP 115; cf I iii 89–91

Chickens before they are hatched, To count one's C 292; ODEP 147; cf I vii 55

Child dreads the fire, A burnt C 297; ODEP 92; cf I i 29

Child that knows its own father, It is a wise C 309; ODEP 899; cf II x 14

Children and fools must not play with edged tools ODEP 120; II v 18. *See also* Jesting, Sword

Chink, we'll bear with the stink, So we get the C 350; ODEP 121; III vii 13. *See also* Gain

City a great solitude, A great C 398; ODEP 333; II iv 54

Claw me and I'll claw thee C 405; ODEP 125; I vii 99

Coals to Newcastle, To carry C 466; ODEP 104; cf I ii 11; I vii 57

Coat lies wisdom, Under a ragged C 476; ODEP 130; cf I vi 1

Cobbler go beyond his last, Let not the C 480; ODEP 130; I vi 16

Cock is proud on his own dunghill, Every C 486; ODEP 130; cf IV iv 25

Codrus, Poorer than C 503; I vi 76. *See also* Irus

Coleworts (*or* Cabbage) twice sodden C 511; ODEP 97; I v 38

Come, first served, First C 530; ODEP 262; (II x 15 CWE 34 134)

Communications corrupt good manners, Evil C 558; ODEP 232; cf I x 74

Conscience is a thousand witnesses C 601; ODEP 140; I x 91

Cooks spoil the broth, Too many C 642; ODEP 831; cf II vii 7

Counsel uncalled, Come not to C 678; ODEP 135; I ii 90

Counsel is worst to the counsellor, Ill C 691; cf I ii 14

Cover is worthy of such a cup, The C 742; I x 72. *See also* Cup

Cow does a cart saddle, He becomes (suits) it as well as a C 758; ODEP 38; cf II ix 84

Coward changes colour, A C 773; ODEP 151; I ii 89

Hand and not with the whole sack,
Sow with the *H* 91; ODEP 757; III i 52

Hand to mouth, To live from *H* 98;
ODEP 474; cf I viii 62

Hands make light work, Many *H* 119;
ODEP 509; II iii 95

Hands, With unwashed *H* 125; ODEP
348; I ix 55

Hare has crossed your way, A *H* 150;
II x 45

Hare sleeps with his eyes open, A
H 153; ODEP 742; I x 57

Hare and hunt with the hounds, To
run with the *H* 158; ODEP 689; cf I
vii 3 and n (CWE 32 308)

Hare will look fair seven days after,
He who eats a *H* 159; ODEP 354; cf II
i 15

Hares loses both, He that hunts two
H 163; ODEP 688; III iii 36

Hares may pull dead lions by the
beard, So *H* 165; ODEP 354; (II iv 68
CWE 33 226); IV vii 82

Harm I know than that I know not,
Better the *H* 166; ODEP 55; II ix 85

Harpocrates, To be a *H* 177; IV i 52

Haste slowly, Make *H* 192; ODEP 510;
II i 1

Haste than good speed, More *H* 197;
ODEP 356, 543; cf II i 1

Haste less speed, More *H* 198; ODEP
356; cf I i 1; III v 60

Hate like to brothers' if they fall at
debate, No *H* 211; I ii 50

Haven, To shipwreck in the *H* 219; I v
76

Hay on his horn, He has *H* 233; ODEP
359; I i 81

Heads as Hydra, As many *H* 278; ODEP
361; I x 9

Heads are better than one, Two *H* 281;
ODEP 851; cf III i 51

Heart never won fair lady, Faint *H* 302;
ODEP 238; cf II vi 25

Heart conquers ill fortune, A good
H 305; cf III iv 68

Heart is in his heels, His *H* 314; ODEP
363–4; cf I viii 70

Heart out, Do not eat your *H* 330; ODEP
214; I i 2 (Pythagoras) CWE 31 37

Heart of the sober man is in the mouth
of the drunkard, What is in the
H 333; ODEP 749; II i 55

Heaven, To be in *H* 350; ODEP 365; I v
100

Heaven, To spit against *H* 355; III iv 87

Heaven, it falls in his face, Who spits
against *H* 356; cf I iv 92

Heed of the wrath of a mighty man,
Take *H* 383; ODEP 923; III viii 38

Helps little that helps not himself, He
H 412; ODEP 368; cf I vi 20

Hercules himself cannot deal with two
H 436; ODEP 370; I v 39

Hog, A Hampshire *H* 488; ODEP 346; cf
I x 6

Hold to be taken of his word as of a
wet eel by the tail, There is as much
H 508; ODEP 377; cf I iv 94

Home is home be it never so homely
H 534; ODEP 629; III iii 38

Honours nourish arts *H* 584; ODEP 383;
I viii 92

Hook, To fish with a golden *H* 591;
ODEP 14; II ii 60

Hope is the poor man's bread *H* 603;
ODEP 384; IV iv 63

Hornets' nest, To stir up a ODEP 869; I
i 60. *See also* Wasps

Horns, Pull in your *H* 620; ODEP 201;
opposite of I viii 68 (*see* n CWE 32 343)

Horse, Do not spur a free *H* 638; ODEP
768; cf I ii 47

Horse and foot, He is undone *H* 655;
ODEP 386; (I iv 17 and n, CWE 31
332)

Horse in the mouth, Look not a given
H 678; ODEP 301; IV v 24

Horse needs no spur, A running *H* 688;
ODEP 768; cf I ii 47

Horse's heel nor a dog's tooth, Trust
not a *H* 711; ODEP 842; cf I iii 95

Horses to the asses, From the *H* 713; I
vii 29

House dry overhead is happy, A *H* 767;
cf IV iii 38

House and a chiding wife make a man run out of doors, A smoking H 781; ODEP 817; cf II ii 48

Hunger is the best sauce H 819; ODEP 392; II vii 69

Hunger makes a man leap at a crust H 820; cf I iii 77

Hurts another hurts himself, He that H 830; ODEP 394; IV viii 56

Ice, To break the I 3; ODEP 83; III v 95

Ignorance is bliss, Where ODEP 396; II x 81

Iliads of woe I 22; I iii 26

Iron whetteth iron I 91a; ODEP 406; I vii 100

Irons in the fire, He has many I 99; ODEP 509; IV iv 100

Irus, As poor as I 101; I vi 76. See also Codrus

Janus two-faced, Like J 37; IV ii 93

Jay is unmeet for a fiddle, The J 38; cf I iv 37

Jesting with edged tools J 45; II v 18. See also Children, Sword

Joan is as good as my lady in the dark J 57; ODEP 412; cf III iv 77

Job, As poor as J 60; ODEP 638; I vi 76

Jove, far from lightning, Far from J 81; ODEP 244; I iii 96

Jove laughs at lovers' perjuries J 82; ODEP 414; cf II iv 90

Joy is that of the pyrausta [fire-worm], Your J 89; cf I ix 51; III iii 8

Juice of the mandrake, To drink the J 101; IV v 64

Jupiter himself cannot please all J 103; II vii 55

Justice comprises all other virtues J 105; II iii 73

Kernel, let him crack the nut, He that will eat the K 19; ODEP 215; II ix 35

Kindness is lost that is done to an old man or young child K 47; ODEP 425; cf I x 52

King to do well and hear ill, It belongs to a K 58; (II vii 89 CWE 34 42)

King loves the treason but hates the traitor, A K 64; ODEP 426; (II x 34)

King like people, Like K 70; ODEP 426; cf I viii 100

Kings have long arms K 87; ODEP 428; I ii 3

Kings have long ears K 87; ODEP 428; I ii 2

Knees of the gods, On the ODEP 432; cf II viii 58

Knot in a rush, To seek a K 168; ODEP 433; II iv 76

Know thyself K 175; ODEP 435; I vi 95

Knows not himself happy, He is not happy that K 182; IV v

Knowing nothing is the sweetest life, In K 188; II x 81

Labour is pleasant L 7; II iii 43

Labour, You lose your L 9; ODEP 485; I iv 62. See also All

Lamp than of wine, It smells more of the L 44; ODEP 745; cf I vii 71. See also Candle

Land, To see L 56; ODEP 441; IV viii 18

Land, To dig (or water) another's L 57; III i 42

Latchet of his shoes, Not worthy to loose the (Mark 1:7) L 84; cf I v 94

Law and country L 100; III vi 55

Law in one's own hand, To have the L 111; IV vii 50

Learning in the breast of a bad man is as a sword in the hand of a madman L 156; ODEP 451; cf II v 18

Letters of Bellerophon L 214; ODEP 44; II vi 82

Liar should have a good memory, A L 219; ODEP 457; II iii 74

Lie is the best, A hot (sudden) L 232; IV v 68

Life is a pilgrimage L 249; ODEP 461; IV x 74

Life is a span L 251; ODEP 461; cf II ii 69

Life, there's hope, While there's L 269; ODEP 462; II iv 12

Like I say sits with the jay, The L 283; I ii 23

Like will to like L 286; ODEP 465; I ii 21

Line to the wall, not your wall to the line, Bring your L 304; ODEP 466; cf II v 36

Lion fears no bugs, A L 310; cf I vi 40

Lion is known by his claws, A L 313; ODEP 467; I ix 34

Lion, Wake not a sleeping L 317; ODEP 863; I i 61

Lion's share, The ODEP 467; I vii 89

Lion's skin cannot, the fox's shall, If the L 319; ODEP 467; III v 81

Lips like lettuce, Like L 326; ODEP 468, 813; I x 71

Liquor a vessel is first seasoned, it will long keep the scent of it, With what L 333; ODEP 105; cf II iv 20

Little and little, By L 340; ODEP 469; cf II i 2

Little is known the much, By the L 342; I ii 78

Live long, Too soon wise to L 384; ODEP 832; cf III ix 43

Look before you leap L 429; cf II iii 70; II i 1; v ii 28; v ii 75

Love and it will flee; flee love and it will follow, Follow L 479; ODEP 272; (II v 27 CWE 33 255)

Love, Looks breed L 501; ODEP 484; I ii 79

Love is the true price of love L 515; ODEP 491; C 388

Love and be wise, It is impossible to L 558; ODEP 488; (II ii 80 CWE 33 118)

Love is without reason L 517; (I i 2 CWE 31 37)

Man is, so is his talk, As the M 75; ODEP 783; I vi 50

Man should judge no colours, A blind M 80; ODEP 68; (I vi 16 CWE 32 14)

Man might see that, A blind M 82; I viii 93

Man does nothing good until he dies, A covetous M 85; IV v 6

Man has his delight, Every M 115; ODEP 229; I ii 15

Man has his faults, Every M 116; ODEP 229; (II iv 29 CWE 33 205)

Man likes his own thing best, Every M 131; ODEP 230; I ii 15

Man can give good counsel to the sick, The healthful M 182; ODEP 362; I vi 68

Man to go to Corinth, It is not given to every M 202; ODEP 143–4; I iv 1

Man says, It is true that every M 204; ODEP 841; cf I vi 25

Man carries his treasure about with him, A learned M 207; IV v 9

Man is a god to man M 241; ODEP 505; I i 69

Man is a wolf to man M 245; ODEP 505; I i 70

Man is but a bubble M 246; ODEP 505; II iii 48

Man must ask excessively to get a little, A M 272; cf II iii 26

Man must not leave the king's highway for a path, A M 281; ODEP 506; I i 2 (Pythagoras) CWE 31 42

Man need not look in your mouth to know how old you are, A M 287; cf II vii 9

Man of three letters, A M 295; ODEP 816; II viii 89

Man proposes, God disposes M 298; ODEP 506; cf III i 19 and n (CWE 34 377)

Man all things can, No living M 315; ODEP 476; II iii 94

Man happy until he is dead, Call no M 333; ODEP 352; (II viii 25 CWE 34 58)

Man is wise at all times, No M 335; ODEP 571; II iv 29

Man loses (wins) but another wins (loses), No M 337; cf IV v 7

Man loves his fetters, though made of gold, No M 338; ODEP 499; II iv 25

Man is sought after to be rifled, No naked M 345; ODEP 554; cf I iv 76

Remembrance of past sorrow is joyful, The R 73; ODEP 671; II iii 43; IV ix 27

Repentance too dear, To buy R 81–2; ODEP 672; (I i 30 CWE 31 78)

Riding at two anchors, Good R 119; ODEP 323; I i 13; IV viii 72

Riding in a good haven, It is safe R 121; ODEP 691; cf I i 46

Right is extreme wrong, Extreme R 122; ODEP 235; I x 25

Ring, Do not wear a tight R 129; I i 2 (Pythagoras) CWE 31 36

Ring of Gyges, The R 132; ODEP 678, I i 96

River and you'll get to the sea, Follow the R 137; ODEP 272; cf II vii 81

Rope of sand, To twist (make) a R 174; ODEP 684; I iv 78; II vi 51

Salve for all sores, He has but one S 82; ODEP 698; IV viii 21

Sand, He sows the S 87; ODEP 757; I iv 52

Sand, To build on S 88; ODEP 698; I iv 57

Sand, To plough the S 89; ODEP 635; I iv 52; cf IV viii 16

Sands of the sea, As difficult as to number the S 91; I iv 44

Saul also among the prophets? Is S 104; ODEP 700; II i 64

Says what he would hears what he would not, He that S 115; ODEP 762; I i 27

Said than done, No sooner S 117; ODEP 574; II ix 72; cf III vi 85; (IV ix 19 CWE 36 432)

Sceptre is one thing and a ladle another, A S 131; ODEP 704; (II ii 82 CWE 33 120)

Scratch my back and I'll scratch yours ODEP 706; cf I i 33

Scratches his head with one finger, He ODEP 706; I viii 34

Scylla and Charybdis, Between S 169; ODEP 707; I v 4

Sea every man may be a pilot, In a calm S 174; ODEP 99; IV iv 96

Sea with a spoon, To lave (empty) the S 183; ODEP 707; cf III vii 99

Seas and mountains, He promises S 187; ODEP 649; I ix 15

Seeing is believing S 212; ODEP 710; cf I i 100; I viii 31. *See also* Credit

Seem to be, Be what thou wouldst S 214; ODEP 33; cf IV i 92

Self-love is a mote in every man's eye S 218; ODEP 712; cf I iii 92

Sepulchres, Whited S 225; (III vi 23 n3 CWE 35 136)

Serpent must eat another serpent before he can become a dragon, A S 228; ODEP 714; III iii 61

Servant before one can be a master, One must be a S 237; ODEP 714; I i 3. *See also* Master, Served

Servants, so many enemies, So many S 242; ODEP 715; II iii 31

Serves everybody is paid by nobody, He that S 244; ODEP 716; III ix 82

Served knows not how to command, He that has not S 246; ODEP 323; I i 3. *See also* Master, Servant

Service stinks, Preferred S 252; ODEP 648; cf I ix 53

Seven at a feast, nine at a fray S 257; I iii 97

Shadow and lose the substance, Catch not at the S 951; ODEP 110; III ii 98

Shadow, To be afraid of his own S 261; ODEP 5; I v 65

Shadow, To fight with one's own S 262; ODEP 256; IV vi 48

Shapes as Proteus, As many S 285; ODEP 720; II ii 74

Shepherd must fleece his sheep, but not flay them, A good S 329; ODEP 323; III vii 12

Shoe fits not every foot, Every S 364; ODEP 597, 725; IV iv 56

Shoe will not fit a little foot, A great S 366; ODEP 334; II v 46; cf III vi 67

Shoes, Not worthy to wipe his S 378; ODEP 922; cf I v 94

Sickle into another man's corn, Put not thy S 420; ODEP 732; I iv 41

Erasmus' Index of Topics

Erasmus provided his first *Index proverbiorum iuxta locos* or 'index of proverbs according to topics' in the edition of 1508. A *locus* is a commonplace, a general conceptual term under which proverbs could be classified and retrieved by the reader. Erasmus continued to add to this index and by the final edition of 1536 there were 278 different topics. His work was a bit rough in places and certainly incomplete, as he himself acknowledges in his short introductory note of 1528 (369–71 above). Nevertheless this index is a marvellous introduction to the way Erasmus classified proverbs, and also a guide to the way his readers might also gather them topically in a commonplace book or other collection. Indeed, later editions of *Adages* in the sixteenth and seventeenth centuries often used these topical headings to re-organize the proverbs in a less random structure.

Erasmus' topics, beginning with *Divitiae* or 'Riches,' followed by *Paupertas* or 'Poverty,' and so on, are presented here in the same non-alphabetical order in which they appeared in the edition of 1536. We also provide separate alphabetical listings of these topical headings in English (621–7) and Latin (628–34).

The adages listed under the topical heading are now presented in the order they appear in the book (in 1536 there was no apparent order to the listings). We have not listed duplicates, but otherwise we have kept to the text of the edition of 1536.

As elsewhere in the English indexes, a proverb that is embedded in the essay of another proverb is listed in parentheses (the host proverb number followed by the cwe volume and page number).

Proverbs in this index are also identified in the main English index of proverbs (635–766), which provides the topic number (eg T 178, directing you to topic 178), essentially indexing this index for your convenience.

[1] **Riches (*Divitiae*)**   1 i 73 With Hercules at my side; 1 vi 22 The talents of Tantalus; (1 vi 22 cwe 32 18) Tantalic wealth; 1 vi 23 The talents of Pelops; 1 vi 24 The riches of Midas; 1 vi 74 As rich as Croesus; (1 vi 74 cwe 32 51) Persian splendours; (1 vi 74 cwe 32 51) Treasures of Arabia; 1 vi 75 The wealth of Pactolus; 1 ix 31 Eight-feet; 1 ix 47 A rich man is either wicked himself or the heir of a wicked man; 11 iii 27 Up to both ears; 11 iv 45 Not a tenth part of the Syracusans; 11 vii 17 A good year talks big; 11 viii 31 Lauriotic owls; 11 viii 35 Money makes the man; 11 viii 71 Beyond the standard of Callicrates; 11 ix 74 God is in need of nothing; 11 x 64 The talents of Zopyrus; 111 i 60 Clothes

make the man; III i 75 The riches of Cinyras; III iv 78 A second Lysicrates; III iv 79 You have the wealth of Lysistratus; III vi 5 More than a hawk could fly around; III vii 53 Luxury breeds brutality; III vii 77 He could get dripping from it; III viii 68 Very wealthy; III ix 99 Wealth is not always the lot of the best; III x 55 The comforts of life; IV iii 73 A francolin's new moon; IV iii 83 Each is only as good as he's worth; IV iv 95 Like Euparyphus in comedy; IV vi 5 At my feet, up to my head; IV vi 16 Pit-rich; IV x 93 Hercules' profits; V i 53 Put on an appearance (see also CWE 33 55 To show one's face)

[2] **Poverty** (*Paupertas*) I i 26 As bare as a snake's sloughed skin (also at CWE 31 282); I iii 48 He hasn't a farthing left to buy himself a rope; I v 7 He has no place to set his foot; I v 16 He's lost his belt; I v 22 Poverty has drawn wisdom as her lot (also at CWE 33 320); (I v 22 CWE 31 401) Harsh hunger is the teacher of many men; I vi 76 As poor as Irus *or* Codrus; (I vi 76 CWE 32 52) As poor as Hecale; I ix 66 A Melian famine; I ix 67 Famine at Saguntum; I ix 68 Famine field; I x 24 He owes his own soul; II ii 78 Wagtail; II vi 2 Water-drinkers are not powerful thinkers; II viii 44 Naked as he came from his mother; II ix 6 Theagenes' wealth; II ix 38 Seek riches first, then virtue; II ix 93 Not even in skin; III iv 62 He is wearing all his wealth; III vii 49 Limodorians; (III vii 49 CWE 35 246) Gutter-snipes; III x 45 The needy man should keep with the crowd; III x 51 Poor but talented; IV ii 48 Hunger teaches many things; IV ii 51 For a beggar not even parents are friends; (IV iii 29 CWE 36 22) Two-footers; IV iii 31 As poor as Telenicus; IV iii 48 As naked as a pestle; IV iii 53 Cleomenes is too big for his bed; IV iii 58 There is no dithyramb if he drinks water; IV iii 60 As poor as

Pauson; IV iii 85 Thin hand, swollen foot; IV iii 87 When a polypus gnaws its own foot; IV iii 89 To cast out spider's webs; (IV iv 95 CWE 36 124) Tunicked; IV v 81 The surest poverty; IV vii 67 To a standstill; IV vii 68 Limited by centre and radius; IV ix 20 Everything bar the soul; IV ix 46 Not even a storm can harm; IV ix 48 Seriatim, in detail; IV x 63 He hasn't a thing to sleep on

[3] **Bribery with gifts** (*Munerum corruptela*) I iii 18 Even the gods are won over by gifts; I iii 87 Everything bows to money; I vii 18 An ox on the tongue; I vii 19 He has the silver-quinsy; I vii 86 The wolves have seen him first; I x 18 A fox takes no bribes; II ii 72 He who helps himself on a grand scale, and gives his backers little, will be all right; II iii 10 He carries an ox in his mouth; II iv 70 To pelt with apples; II iv 87 Virtue and wisdom bow before the turtles; II v 45 The Dorian muse; II vii 43 To fight with silver spears; III viii 35 Gifts get the business done; III ix 8 Corrupt judgments; III ix 83 Bribery with gifts; IV viii 29 A rich man cannot be found guilty; IV viii 54 Hail, daughters of stallions; IV x 89 Add a drop of dressing; V i 36 Bean-currency

[4] **Beauty, ugliness** (*Forma, deformitas*) I iii 72 Even the autumn of beauty is beautiful; I iii 100 He came out of an egg; I vii 11 An ape is an ape, though clad in gold; II i 7 Myconian baldpate; II i 15 He has not eaten hare; II ii 29 Legs like Mr. Partridge; II iii 99 Take ship for Troezen; II v 54 The prettiest ape is hideous; III ii 8 As ugly as Corytheus; III vi 57 You're carrying a lot of undergrowth; IV ii 7 Børn of the Furies; IV ii 17 Pronomus' beard; IV ii 54 Anyone who sees you will read it as an omen; IV iii 49 As bald as a pestle; IV iii 80 The look of Thersites; IV iv 31 Mere outlines;

IV vii 15 Beautifully-buttocked; IV vii 81 What is beautiful is also loved

[5] Boredom through repetition (*Taedium ex iteratione*) I v 38 Twice served cabbage is death; I v 89 Over and over again; I vi 5 Sardinians for sale; I viii 59 You join thread with thread; I ix 98 To pound the same anvil; II i 50 Corinthus son of Jove; II ii 5 Again I spy a calm; II iv 84 The leech that won't let go till full of blood; II v 17 Parnus' skiff; II v 76 You sing the same song; II vi 44 An oracle for the Rhodians; II viii 2 The twirling of a pestle; II x 57 Over and again the Pytho road; III i 68 Give me a basin; III ii 32 More than the Callicyrians; III v 19 Cord to rope; IV vii 31 God Lentil; IV viii 18 I see land; IV viii 96 The preamble is long when one is eager to hear

[6] Repetition without boredom (*Iteratio citra taedium*) I ii 49 Beauty bears repeating twice and thrice; (I ii 49 CWE 31 191) Never too much of the beautiful; (I ii 49 CWE 31 191) One-bite

[7] Annoying people and ailments that are intolerable (*Molesti, intolerabiles*) II viii 65 As warts grow on the eye; II x 29 With fetters that gnaw the arm; III ii 90 Athos darkens the flanks of the Lemnian cow; III iii 25 A burden on the ship; III v 47 They wouldn't be lifted by a hundred Egyptians; III v 48 An Egyptian brick-carrier; III vii 32 Driving and carrying off; III vii 46 I become a year older; III viii 95 The depravity of the fly; III ix 95 He causes havoc everywhere; IV iii 71 To plough among the stubble; IV iv 39 An Etna, an Athos; IV ix 40 Not even wild beasts could stand it; IV x 75 The whole thing is a festering sore; IV x 100 Like a runny eye (also II ii 44 CWE 33 97); V i 27 Beat one's brow; V i 81 All-spiny

[8] Things that are unpleasant because of their age (*Ingrata ob vetustatem*) I ii 98 A fish put by; I v 24 You are talking of things older than the diphthera; II viii 19 Cannacas' things; II viii 40 Older than Chaos and the age of Saturn; III iii 17 A tunic Pellene-style; III v 58 In olden time; IV i 13 As old as the Bacchanalia; IV i 46 Since Nannacus; (IV i 46 CWE 35 469) Going back to the time of the Aborigines; IV i 74 A fish is no good unless it is fresh

[9] Recent things (*Nupera*) II v 42 Yesterday and the day before

[10] Errors repeated (*Iteratus error*) I v 8 To stumble twice over the same stone; I v 9 To strike the same wrong note; I ix 61 Let a beginner off lightly; II v 22 No fox is caught twice in a trap; III i 31 In war it is not permitted twice to err; III v 13 A dog goes back to his vomit; III viii 51 Beware of the man who has cheated once; IV iii 62 A washed pig rolls in muck; IV v 62 A once-deceiver

[11] Errors made initially (*Error in initio*) I v 76 To be shipwrecked in the harbour; I v 77 To fall or stumble on the threshold; I v 78 The gelding at the gate

[12] Garrulousness (*Garrulitas*) I i 7 Dodonean bronze; I i 14 A story without a head; I ii 99 Speaking much and speaking well are not the same thing; I iii 3 Intoxication without wine (repeated also in Greek); I v 30 As garrulous as a turtle-dove; I v 72 Whatever came into his mouth; (I v 72 CWE 31 447) Whatever comes into the head; I v 73 Whatever may come on the tongue; I vi 44 A bathman; (I vi 70 CWE 32 49) Teetotal drinking parties; (I vi 70 CWE 32 49) Talking-places; I vii 16 To croak; I vii 32 An Arabian piper; I ix 100 As noisy as a cricket; II i 92 Vain repetition.

Spartan brevity; II ii 2 Swallow choirs; II ii 3 Nightingales perching on trifles; II ii 39 Tongue, whither wouldst thou?; II iv 58 To stuff a patchwork coat; II vi 8 Sing Tellen's songs; II vii 44 Archytas' rattle; II ix 32 As talkative as the seashore; II x 12 A Melian vessel; III i 18 Words are the lightest of things; III iii 76 Moschus singing a Boeotian strain; III iii 100 The music is cut off; III iv 47 An unbridled mouth; (III iv 47 CWE 35 30) With a mouth lacking a door; III vi 26 Like cork; III vi 53 As garrulous as reef; III vi 88 A Daulian crow; III vii 57 Full of ballast; IV i 94 If the crow can eat quietly; IV iii 32 An echo of Telenicus; IV v 51 As long-winded as the Iliad; IV vi 4 Birds of the Muses (also IV x 87 Birds of the Muses' flock); IV vi 36 Nonsense-spouter; IV vii 13 It is human never to stop arguing; IV viii 44 Citeria (also *Adagia* introduction xiii CWE 34 23); IV viii 49 As much as a man of sense; IV ix 70 Orators over the bottle; V i 75 The cicadas will sing to themselves

[13] Laconicism (*Breviloquentia*) I vi 9 To bundle together; II i 92 and II x 49 Spartan brevity; III vi 46 To enclose with a smaller pomoerium, and sayings like these; III vii 50 In three throws; III vii 58 You talk like 1 2 3; III viii 77 Sparing of words, but knowledgeable; IV iv 84 In three words; IV v 25 Brevity has charm; IV ix 91 In brief

[14] Noisiness (*Clamosus*) I iii 97 Seven make a feast, nine make a fray; I v 96 Using all the holes (With all the stops out); II iii 37 Noisier than Stentor; II v 23 Interruption, Abydos fashion; II vii 22 As noisy as burning bay-leaves; II ix 19 Sarpedon shore; III ii 16 A voice like the Cycloborus; III ii 19 Claudian thunder; III viii 91 Against people who shout; III ix 37 Against brawling in conversation or in games; IV i 70 Till I'm

hoarse; IV iii 77 Shattering columns; IV vi 33 Pen-shouter; IV ix 96 To roar

[15] Quarrelsomeness (*Rixosus*) I viii 98 He will have the law on you, if an ass has so much as bitten his dog; II iv 31 We have a mad baytree among us; II iv 34 The eloquence of a barking dog; II v 19 A Lindian sacrifice; II vi 43 A Rhodian sacrifice; II vii 60 A band from Syrbene; II viii 53 The Eretrian rho; III vi 7 Ptolemaic dispute; III viii 41 To start a dispute; IV i 17 Eat neither garlic nor beans; IV iii 61 Worse than Hyperbolus; IV v 17 He has touched a stone that a dog has bitten; IV viii 92 Blowing north-easterlies

[16] Taciturnity censured (*Taciturnitas illaudata*) I ii 18 Silent teachers; I v 14 The grasshopper of Acanthus; I v 29 As dumb as the fishes; (I v 29 CWE 31 408) Silence [of fishes]; I v 31 A Seriphian frog; I vi 45 Like a Bacchant; I viii 3 Not a grunt; I ix 1 Silence destroyed Amyclae; I x 78 A walk-on part; I x 79 No tongue in your head; II vii 93 Hipparchion loses his voice; II viii 43 As dumb as a boat; IV i 52 He turned him into Harpocrates; IV iii 72 As silent as the Pythagoreans; IV iii 99 As mute as a statue; IV v 14 Like a bodyguard; IV ix 71 With a dry rush

[17] Taciturnity praised (*Taciturnitas laudata*) I iii 13 To rejoice in one's own bosom; III v 3 Safety is silence's reward; III v 99 What you know, you do not know; III ix 11 One who falls silent; III x 20 Some things must be trusted to others, some concealed; III x 66 The man who keeps a secret; IV i 97 Silence becomes a woman; IV v 69 Sooner will a dumb man speak; IV x 6 Closer than an Areopagite

[18] Inarticulateness (*Infacundia*) II vi 21 To sing to the myrtle-branch; II vii 34 Babys plays the flute even worse; II x 86 Tedious as a dirge; III vii 76 To be a Battarist

[19] **Eloquence (*Facundia*)** I ii 55 Swan song; I ii 56 The eloquence of Nestor; I ii 57 Attic wit, Attic eloquence; (I ii 57 CWE 31 197) Attic honey; I viii 80 The Attic Muse; III iii 23 Now wisdom itself is alive; III iii 24 Now is the Muse herself in flower; III iii 97 The swans will sing when the jackdaws are silent; III vi 33 Your words are never rustic; IV vi 4 Birds of the Muses; IV x 87 Birds of the Muses' flock; IV viii 19 More effective than any spell

[20] **Gifts that are not gifts (*Munus non munus*)** I iii 35 Gifts of enemies are no gifts; (I iii 35 CWE 31 264) Harm and not good must come from gifts of an evil man; (I iii 35 CWE 31 264) In giving to the rich man the poor man begs; I iv 5 The gifts of the Cyclops; II x 58 After offering sacrifice at Delphi, he eats the meat himself; IV iii 4 A bad gift is as good as a loss

[21] **An honourable death (*Exitium honestum*)** II ii 8 If you must be hanged, let it be on a fair gallows; IV vii 94 More quickly than Heraclitus' sun; IV ix 32 Not even a vestige or trace

[22] **Evil uncurable (*Malum immedicabile*)** I x 90 The arse beats all efforts to wash it; II vi 59 Treated by Acesias; II viii 21 A wound for Chiron; IV iv 77 A sandal does not cure gout

[23] **Industriousness (*Industria*)** I ii 41 Do not hesitate to plant; I ii 82 Out of the shadow into sunlight; I vi 17 The gods help those who help themselves; I vi 18 Invoke Minerva, but use your own strength too; I vi 62 No bees, no honey; I vii 33 Skill fills your hand in every land; (I vii 33 CWE 32 87) Skill

is a man's best harbour in distress; II i 11 He who ploughs an olive-grove; II ii 81 Set your hand to the work before you appeal to Fortune; II v 32 To mould by hand; II ix 88 Unless you clean and grind, you'll have nothing to eat; III iii 42 Unless you pound the clay, you get no jar; III iii 59 He who runs away from the mill runs away from the meal; III iii 65 Hard work best earns a dinner for old age; III vi 14 The material is good, if only you engage a good workman; III vii 28 What in the end cannot be done with hands?; III ix 55 God helps those who work hard; IV iii 35 To add your hand to; IV iv 79 Marian mules; IV ix 53 Labour costs, fee

[24] **Laziness and ignorance (*Ignavia et inscitia*)** I iv 12 I haven't done a stroke today; I iv 13 Neither swim nor read; I vi 48 As rude as any Libethrian; I vii 31A Fallen off the donkey; (I viii 21 CWE 32 136) Supine, at ease; (I viii 21 CWE 32 136) A little folding of the hands to sleep; II i 20 A barbarian from the roadside; II i 32 A horse's old age; II v 52 No use to himself nor to others; II v 53 Neither wet with the rain, nor scorched by the sun; II vi 12 For sluggards it is always a holiday; II vi 18 Strangers to the Muses; II vi 27 You have not even thumbed your Aesop; II viii 13 As an old woman you will have a deep grave, like a horse; II viii 70 Neglected corner; II ix 94 You don't know even Stesichorus' triplet; II ix 97 Fern to be burnt grows in neglected fields; II x 40 She-goats are free from the plough; III ii 20 To grasp a pillar like a lame man; III vi 50 A woman's rump; IV ii 32 To drink at one draught; IV iii 38 Not even God pities the man who is rained upon in his own house; IV iv 13 He has never even laid eyes upon oil; IV viii 75 As aggressive as a cock in his own backyard

[25] Ingratitude (*Ingratitudo*) I i 2 (Pythagoras) CWE 31 44 You shall not have swallows under the same roof; I x 52 Never do a kindness to an old man; II i 86 Keep wolf-cubs; II iv 1 Nobody sacrificed an ox to his benefactor except Pyrrhias; II v 92 The ram paid for its upbringing; II vi 6 Scorpion instead of perch; II vi 7 In return for kindness the Achaeans punished Agamemnon; III i 83 No sooner is he pitied than his gratitude is dead; III iii 46 He who feeds a stranger's dog; III iv 63 No enemy, but still an enemy; III ix 82 Public ingratitude; IV vi 87 Doing a good turn to a ram; IV x 99 Know a man while he's alive

[26] Gratitude (*Gratitudo*) I x 1 To cherish in one's turn; I x 84 Syloson's cloak; III v 83 Reels for good deeds; III vii 42 The tongue is cut out separately; (III vii 42 CWE 35 241) The tongue for the herald; III ix 79 Invoking past deserts; III x 68 The memory of good deeds; IV vii 63 Those who need a lamp pour oil in it; IV viii 36 Let the price be agreed for a friend

[27] Pretence, concealment (*Simulatio, dissimulatio*) I ii 31 The Cretan and the sea; I ii 95 Bearded, therefore wise; I vi 4 I'm not asleep to everyone; (I vi 4 CWE 32 7) I'm not a slave to everyone; I vi 63 A cough for a fart; I vii 6 Many bear the wand, few feel the god; I vii 7 Not all that hold the lyre can play it; I vii 8 Many the casters of lots, but few can you find that are prophets; I vii 9 Few men can plough, though many ply the goad; I vii 10 An ape in purple; I vii 12 An ass at Cumae; (I vii 12 CWE 32 72) A fool's prosperity is hard to bear; I viii 50 To wink; I viii 57 A sword smeared with honey; I ix 10 To weep at your stepmother's funeral; I x 57 A hare asleep; II ii 86 Lacon one thing, his ass carries others; II ii

99 To feign indifference; II ii 100 The Scythian fighting shy of the donkey; II iv 60 Crocodile tears; II v 20 Megarian tears; II v 37 To seek outside oneself; II vi 55 The hungry fox grows drowsy; II ix 45 A singer in difficulties means a cough; III ii 7 Well-wishing murderer; III iii 1 The Sileni of Alcibiades; III iii 31 The dead man lies there farting; III v 20 Salt and a bean; III v 53 The opportunity of Patroclus; III v 79 A monkey with a beard, or with a tail; (III v 79 CWE 35 113) Monkeys of the people; III vi 15 You may look back that way, but pass the goods this way; III vi 23 A whited wall; III vi 91 Aesop's jackdaw; III vii 62 A painted monkey; (III vii 63 CWE 35 254) To disguise with pretences and allurements; III viii 17 For someone revealing what he has long concealed; III ix 35 He has ears and hears not; IV iii 50 There's copper beneath the gold; IV iv 74 He carries water in one hand, etc.; IV vi 43 To squawk like a jay; IV vi 52 To leave by the back door; IV vii 88 Imitating a curlew; IV ix 21 He complains of a whitlow

[28] Freedom, truth (*Libertas, veritas*) I iii 88 The plain speech of truth; I vii 17 Wine speaks the truth; (I vii 17 CWE 32 76) Wine and truth; (I vii 17 CWE 32 76) What is in the heart of the sober man is in the mouth of the drunkard; (I vii 17 CWE 32 76) Bronze the face mirrors, and strong drink the mind; (I vii 17 CWE 32 76) A slip of the tongue is wont to tell the truth; I vii 73 Wagon-language; I x 46 Listen to man who speaks from the heart; II iii 5 He calls figs figs and a spade a spade; II ix 5 Thrice; II ix 53 Flattery wins friends and truth engenders hate; II ix 70 So ran the tale, and such you were; III i 48 Poets and painters are not subject to audit; III i 80 So speak the Curetes; III v 34 Open-heartedly; III viii 4 Of one who commends frank speech; III ix 71 Speaking literally and simply; III ix 75 Speaking out firmly; III x 29 I cannot help speaking; IV i 21 Corcyra is free, shit where you will; IV ii 11 The freedom of Byzenus; IV ii 23 A deep furrow; IV ii 60 Pronouncements according to the sieve; IV iii 56 The speech has bones; IV ix 2 Truer than truth; IV x 69 With honest brow; IV x 80 Speak oracles; V i 14 If you want to give orders, you must buy a slave; V i 47 Nothing nicer than a bed to oneself

[29] Servitude (*Servitus*) IV iii 47 A man under the yoke; IV v 73 A lion tied up with a thread; IV v 91 To swim to shore with your baggage; IV vi 14 Lettered Samians; IV ix 35 Nowhere more a slave than at Sparta; V i 24 I took the money, sold my authority

[30] Things that are worthless or pointless (*Vanitas*) I ii 29 To play Cretan with a Cretan; I iii 41 To sell smoke; (I iii 41 CWE 31 272) Court incense; I iv 82 The things in Hades; II i 46 Gardens of Tantalus; II i 62 A dream; II ii 98 Singers tell many lies; II iii 74 A liar should have a good memory; II iv 9 A Hiberian rigmarole; III i 26 A Cilician finds it hard to speak the truth; III i 46 Not if an ox were to speak; III i 66 And then I awoke; III ii 58 The deaths of a donkey; III vii 16 Ravings of silly old women; III vii 21 His progeny are full of wind; (III vii 21 CWE 35 229) To speak words of wind; (III vii 21 CWE 35 229) Airy nothings; IV ii 28 Small grapes; IV iii 10 The fruit of the cypress; IV iii 42 A blind dream; IV v 68 A hot lie; IV v 92 Shall-givers; IV vi 6 Lie pimples; IV vii 85 No firm notion; IV viii 53 Never said and never done; IV ix 63 A winter dream; IV ix 83 He doesn't tell the truth even by accident; IV x 24 No deception in the market-place; V i 82 A story for Alcinous

[31] Curiosity (*Curiositas*) I ii 2 Many are the eyes and ears of kings; I ii 44 A Corycaean was listening; II iv 76 You seek a knot in a rush; II vii 52 Mylus hearing everything; IV iv 23 He knows how Jupiter married Juno; IV vii 27 You are a Zeno even if you are cooking lentils; IV vii 51 Nothing is more useless than much knowledge; IV ix 51 Hunting dogs; V i 42 Nothing nicer than being in the know

[32] Cruelty (*Crudelitas*) I x 85 Plenty of room thanks to Syloson; I x 86 To rule like Phalaris; I x 87 Manlian orders; II ii 27 We shall give them no more quarter than we would to wolves; II vii 64 Good men are prone to tears; II x 39 Clay kneaded with blood; II x 44 With Lemnian hand; III ii 47 In ox-flaying style; III iii 93 Every master speaks to his slave in words of one syllable; III iv 41 Bacchus is cruel; III vii 72 There's no oil in the bottle

[33] Timidity, cowardice (*Timiditas, ignavia*) I ii 89 The coward changes colour; I iii 78 To keep to the clothes one's mother gave one; I v 65 To be afraid of one's own shadow; I v 66 He is afraid of the very flies fluttering past; I viii 2 He does not even dare say *mu*; I viii 70 My heart is in my boots; I ix 2 You are as frightened as the peeper; I ix 3 As big a coward as Pisander; I x 34 Confronted with the bear you go looking for his tracks; I x 40 He that fights and runs away may live to fight another day; I x 92 The Mysians are fair game; II i 82 To grumble (cf also I viii 3 CWE 32 130); II ii 26 He cowers like a cock; II ii 97 He threw away his spear; II v 81 A woman as a commander-in-chief and women soldiers; II vi 25 Faint hearts never set up a trophy; II vii 36 A man with the heart of a deer; II viii 48 As great a coward as Epeus; II viii 69 You're frightened before you hear the trumpet sound; II ix 27 As frightened as the Rhegians; II x 47 To fight with the tongue; III iii 22 The cock jumps in; III iv 4 He calls on God for a flea bite; III iv 12 Bold at the start, timid in the act; III v 98 A lion's skin over a saffron dress; III vi 29 White-skinned men are no use; III vii 2 Plutus is a coward; III viii 42 For a man dismayed; III ix 16 You are fighting with words, not facts; III ix 21 For a runaway; IV i 44 Troy is not angry with the Corinthians; IV i 85 Liver-pale; IV ii 2 When the road is before you, you look for a track; IV ii 82 He's going back on his tracks; (IV v 34 CWE 36 164) Such a man will never capture a city; IV v 66 To cast a small stone; IV v 80 Peace-time lions; IV vi 13 Like squids; IV vi 32 You are not walking on fire

[34] Fear that is groundless (*Inanis metus*) I vi 39 You terrify with a wine-skin; (I vi 39 CWE 32 31) You terrify with a shadow; II iii 80 You were afraid where no fear was; II x 19 Many are the illusions of war; III ii 60 You've sprinkled me with water; III iii 54 Theagenes and his shrine of Hecate; (III iv 4 CWE 35 5) Like someone who is afraid of everything, even if a mouse makes a noise; III vii 3 A panic attack; III vii 100 Nervous dogs bark louder; IV viii 66 Give the rock a kick

[35] Boldness (*Audacia*) I vii 41 A second Hercules; (I vii 41 CWE 32 92) Achilles; (I vii 41 CWE 32 92) Achillean argument; III ii 64 Water pours by; III iv 31 A fledgling of Mars; III viii 72 Those who attack with no regard for their life; III viii 84 A crisis reveals who is a man; III viii 85 Never yield to misfortunes; III viii 95 The depravity of the fly; III ix 17 Don't be put off by loud words; III ix 96 Not losing heart; III x 5 A firm mind; IV i 19 A heart of seven ox-hides; IV viii 12 He fears neither earthquake nor raging sea

[36] Bravery (*Fortitudo*) (I vii 41 CWE 32 92) Achilles; (I vii 41 CWE 32 92) Achillean argument; I vii 43 Adamantine; (I vii 43 CWE 32 94) Naxian emery; III i 57 One omen is best of all: to fight for one's country; III iv 7 Walls of iron, not earth; III v 10 He must stay and conquer or die; (III v 10 CWE 35 71) With this, or on this; III viii 28 Rejecting talk of fear; III ix 6 Prove yourselves men; IV ii 84 You fight in Lypsidrium; IV iii 17 Only Spartan women produce men; IV iii 65 Land a plough punch; IV vi 61 A rushing resolve; IV x 59 Masculine

[37] Yielding to the masses (*Cedendum multitudini*) I i 2 (Pythagoras) CWE 31 42 Do not walk outside the public highway; I v 39 Not even Hercules can take on two; (I v 39 CWE 31 419) It is hard to fight against two opposite things; (I v 39 CWE 31 419) It is difficult for one to hold off many; I v 40 One man, no man; III ix 60 Yield to numbers; IV iii 44 The vote of the majority prevails; V ii 30 One should not take on two

[38] Generosity (*Liberalitas*) I vii 88 Porsena's property; I viii 91 He that gives quickly gives twice; I ix 16 To take with both hands; II i 16 In handfuls; II i 85 Share Mercury; II iv 73 More spender than saver; III ii 11 Codalus' measure; III v 63 Like a virgin the first time; III vi 59 A gull in the swamps; III vi 61 By the granaryful; III x 50 Generous with others' goods; IV viii 98 What's once given

[39] Miserliness (*Tenacitas*) IV v 6 A miser does nothing right except when he dies; V i 3 As in the grave

[40] Hospitality (*Hospitalitas*) I i 99 To tear the cloak; II ii 14 The door is never barred; II ii 15 There's always someone in Cydon's house; II x 84 He has a doorway as well trodden as a shepherd's cottage; III ix 98 A stranger must be cared for

[41] **Extravagance (*Profusio*)** I ii 69 Wasteful in holiday time; I ii 92 The purse of desire is fastened with a leaf of leak; I iii 5 Leave something for the Medes too; I ix 44 He has made a clean sweep; I x 32 Bounty has no bottom; II i 16 In handfuls; II i 87 You draw from the cask; II i 88 Basket and all; II x 97 To blame cock's guts; III i 10 A hail of drachmas; III ii 50 To kill oxen; III iii 37 The man who has plenty of pepper sprinkles it even on the salad; III vi 61 By the granaryful; IV ii 27 We are not sailing to the Hippolaïtas; IV ii 72 Another Glaucus; IV iii 3 A Carian tomb; IV iv 58 Spoils of war; IV vii 74 Callias is shedding his feathers; IV x 54 Toil on toil

[42] **Rapacity, greed (*Rapacitas, avaritia*)** I ii 70 A Tartessian cat; (I ii 70 CWE 31 210) As rapacious as cats; I vi 27 Snatch not food as yet unblest out of the dish; (I vi 27 CWE 32 21) Straight from the pan; (I vi 27 CWE 32 21) Straight out of the pan; (I vi 27 CWE 32 21) Snatching it from the spit; I vii 88 Porsena's property; I ix 12 To exact tribute from the dead; I x 33 A great jar that cannot be filled; II ii 33 Seamew; II iii 84 Greedier than purple; II iii 87 Offerings unblest full oft devours (Cf I vi 27 Snatch not food as yet unblest out of the dish); II iii 91 Polyps; II iv 16 Not everything, nor everywhere, nor from everybody; II iv 24 A dog sniffing offal; II iv 64 Greedy as a racing-car; II iv 99 The wolf heeds not your counting; II v 24 A beggar's satchel is never filled; II v 74 To swallow the hook; II vi 26 Sheaves and all; II vi 72 Buthus walks to and fro; II vii 18 Megarian sphinxes; II vii 46 An Athenian holds his hand out on his deathbed; II vii 57 Pylaea knows this and Tyttygias; II vii 83 A vulture's

shadow; II vii 94 Love of money will be Sparta's undoing, and nothing else; II viii 85 Dust and all; II x 11 Beggars' wallets are always empty; II x 48 A cormorant open-mouthed; II x 55 A Milesian bass; III ii 77 You marry white flax for the sake of gain; III ii 89 He makes even the statues give him food; III iii 61 A serpent, unless it devours a serpent, will not become a dragon; III v 30 Badly, like foster mothers; III vi 1 You devour the commons even before you get your share; III vi 22 Don't choke, share; III vii 12 A good shepherd should shear his sheep, not skin them; (III vii 12 CWE 35 222) I hate the herbalist who pulls out the herb root and all; III vii 13 Profit smells good whatever it comes from; (III vii 13 CWE 35 223) Urging people to seek superiority of possessions, but to praise equality; III vii 14 Profit before shame; (III vii 14 CWE 35 225) Nothing is bad that brings profit with it; III vii 41 A Charybdis. A Barathrum; III vii 81 Rifling wallets; III vii 93 Pillage at the Cotytia; III ix 81 No matter where from, it's profit they're after; IV i 3 Argive thieves; (IV i 3 CWE 35 441) Laverniones; IV i 84 Like children admiring a peacock; IV ii 45 Pamphilus pilfering; IV iv 4 Daysleeper; IV vi 37 Gnawer of beans; IV vii 93 What is useful is virtuous; IV viii 7 Jointly owned like Sisapo; IV x 8 Trot out the same stale prophecy; IV x 28 Fill up the gap; IV x 29 No part of his body

[43] **Meanness and niggardliness (*Sordes et parsimonia*)** I i 2 (Pythagoras) CWE 31 33 Do not sit on the grain-measure; I ix 43 They sacrifice to the Lar; I x 11 A smokeless sacrifice; I x 39 A dog's dinner; I x 94 As they do in Psyra; I x 96 Luncheon for a Cyprus ox; II i 5 A cummin-splitter; II i 6 To split figs; II iv 36 He spends three minas and charges twelve; II vi 14 The punishment of Tantalus; II vii 33 A sacrifice

Phaselite-fashion; II viii 80 They live on their own juice; II ix 95 Nephalian wood; II ix 96 A nephalian sacrifice; II x 3 A dung-cake for the beetle, quick as quick!; II x 32 To have one's hand in one's bosom; III ii 31 A Carian victim; III iii 50 No hard bargainer eats good meat; III iii 92 As sordid as Patroclus; III iv 39 Bacchus to Psyra; III v 93 The sacrifices are nothing; III vii 33 To lick salt; III vii 61 You're combing it out thinly; III ix 80 Invited but not to take part; IV i 71 They sacrifice to Ceres; IV i 82 Dirty knuckles; IV ii 34 Singing brief life away; IV iii 37 Cheap meat feeds the dogs; IV iii 51 None of the yoke; IV iv 16 Feeding on dew; IV iv 33 To live on charlock; IV iv 40 To come empty-handed; IV iv 57 A snail's life; IV iv 60 He comes from the house of Patrocles; IV v 56 As skinny as Philippides; IV vi 26 Single-diners; IV vi 70 Drinkers of dregs; IV vi 83 A figleaf-eater; IV vii 23 As skinny as Leotrephides; IV vii 64 To kick in the belly; IV x 11 Fouler than filth; IV x 23 To come from Phelleus; IV x 65 Plato's lice

[44] **Completing or finishing (*Perficiendi sive absolvendi*)** I i 6 To undo the knot; I ii 32 To bring to the scroll's end; I ii 33 To put on the coping-stone; I ii 34 To add the final touch; I ii 35 To add a last act to the play; (I ii 35 CWE 31 177) It is for a stitcher of patches to sew his last bit of patchwork best; I ii 38 I hand on the torch in the race; I iii 37 Look to the end of life; I vi 26 When you make your house, leave it not un-planed; I vii 26 All eights; I ix 24 To be given a wooden sword. To present with a wooden sword; I ix 29 An axe from Tenedos; I x 65 Had I held the pen; II iii 45 He added the colophon; II iv 41 To take on a department. To entrust a department; II iv 49 He has sailed as far as Phasis; II vi 86 To complete the circle; II viii 1 A third to the Deliverer; III

iii 68 He ate the whole ox and stopped short when he got to the tail; III v 24 To the pillars of Hercules; (III v 24 CWE 35 80) The regions beyond Gades are inaccessible; III v 88 To give the signal for war. To sound the retreat; (III v 88 CWE 35 118) Sound the trumpet; III ix 59 He will never finish; III x 82 The Colophonian vote; IV v 37 Windproof and watertight; IV vi 20 Right to the final flourish; IV vi 47 One finished the web, the other took it apart; IV vii 5 You have spun the thread, now you want a needle; IV vii 73 Moon beams do not ripen grapes; IV viii 4 Nothing can be either added or taken away; IV viii 35 A four-square man

[45] **From beginning to end (*Ab initio ad finem*)** I i 8 Stem and stern; I ii 37 From head to heel; I ii 39 Well begun is half done; I iv 3 To open a window, and similar metaphors (also at III vi 70 CWE 35 160); I vi 57 To start from scratch; I vi 58 From the start; (I vi 81 CWE 32 54) First taste; I vi 83 Begin at home; I vii 52 Since the time their nails were soft; I vii 53 From the cradle; I x 89 They are not even in the celery; II i 25 Such is the web now woven; II i 61 The head; (II ii 10 CWE 33 83) Whitebait glory; II iv 86 From the eggs to the apples; II v 94 From the starting-pen; II v 95 From heaven to earth; II vi 68 To set up a web; II viii 14 Whitebait glory; III i 38 With a full range; III i 53 Forward and backward; III v 35 To reach the chalk mark; (III v 35 CWE 35 87) To be called back to the starting boxes from the line; (III v 35 CWE 35 87) Right up to the call for applause; III v 95 To break the ice; III vi 3 Whatever falls on the ground; III vi 70 To open doors; III vii 56 We have come to the final line

[46] **Similarity and likeness (*Similitudinis et congruentiae*)** I i 98 Fools in their folly speak; I ii 4 To drive out one

nail by another; I ii 5 A hard wedge must be sought for a hard knot; I ii 20 Everyone loves his own age; (I ii 20 CWE 31 166) Like readily comes together with like; I ii 21 Like rejoices in like; I ii 22 God always leads like to like; I ii 23 Jackdaw always sits by jackdaw; I ii 24 Cicada loves cicada, ant is dear to ant; I ii 27 A Cretan with a man of Aegina; I ii 28 To play the fox with the fox; I ii 29 To play Cretan with a Cretan; I ii 30 You are Carizing with a Carian; I ii 62 An old man takes an old bride; (I ii 62 CWE 31 202; see IV viii 33) Where you are Gaius, I am Gaia; I v 10 As like as one egg to another; I v 11 As like as milk to milk; I v 12 As like as water to water; I v 13 As like as bees to bees; I v 68 To make water in a chamber-pot; I v 95 Loose broomtwigs, To untie a broom; I vii 27 All is the same dust; I vii 34 You were not on this roster; I vii 60 The pot picks its own greens; I viii 1 Seek a wife of your own sort; (I viii 1 CWE 32 129) An aged groom is mastered by his bride; I x 2 Even tenor; I x 35 Good men with good men dine, nor wait for an invitation; I x 71 Like lips like lettuce; I x 72 The cover is worthy of such a cup; I x 77 Accius and Titius take alike; II i 28 A suitor of the selfsame Muse; II iii 21 Hatched from the same egg; II iii 63 Thief knoweth thief and wolf to wolf is known; II iii 64 Earth loves the rain; II iii 75 Bad man with bad man fused in mutual glee; II iv 47 One Myconos to cover everything; II iv 89 Spring follows winter; II v 35 A good fiddler or a good pastrycook, all's one; II v 48 I'm not one of that class of heroes; II v 49 I know Simon and Simon knows me; II v 97 Bithus against Bacchius; II v 98 (also at v i 52 CWE 36 571) Esernius versus Pacidianus; II vi 13 A lapdog takes after its mistress; II vii 51 Crobylus' yoke; II vii 68 Chiot against Coan; II viii 7 As like as two figs; II viii 50 Taught in the same school; II viii 57 One and the same wax; II ix 58 They're all the same; II x 2 Nauson to Naucrates; II x 35 Worm's bad, grub's bad; III i 8 Eating the same onions; III ii 4 Attabas and Numenius have met; III ii 13 To navigate with a pole; III iii 45 Mountains never meet; III iv 29 Mars never shuffles his own weapons about; (III iv 48 CWE 35 31) To bear the yoke equally; III iv 83 Hard-of-hearing vs Nearly deaf; III v 29 Futile advice from futile people; III v 44 Same flour as we are; (III v 44 CWE 35 94) Same flock as I am; (III v 44 CWE 35 94) Of the same stamp; (III vi 86 CWE 35 169) It is one of that herd; (III vi 86 CWE 35 169) From that gang; (III vi 86 CWE 35 169) They are from your herd; (III vi 86 CWE 35 169) Members of the herd; III ix 34 It was either you or someone very like you; IV i 24 Figs after fish; IV iii 25 Human character matches habitat; IV iii 36 He is his father's son; IV iv 45 In one key; IV iv 46 You are not the son of Achilles; IV iv 56 Putting the same shoe on every foot; (IV iv 56 CWE 36 100) To treat the eyes of all with the same salve; IV v 20 A perch follows a cuttlefish; IV v 23 Smelling of fish or flower; IV v 43 An asp borrows poison from a viper; IV v 63 Like mistress, like maids; IV v 85 The ploughman is no ploughman unless he is bent; IV vii 86 Either go off or strip off; IV viii 33 Where you are Gaius, there I am Gaia (see also I ii 62 CWE 31 202); IV ix 62 Dorians may speak the Doric; IV x 30 Clean and clear; IV x 32 Tread in the tracks of; IV x 64 Ass looks lovely to ass and pig to pig; v i 64 A new sieve on a new peg

[47] Dissimilarity and unlikeness (*Dissimilitudinis et incongruentiae*) I i 2 (Pythagoras) CWE 31 40 Do not put food in a chamber-pot; I ii 72 A party-frock for the cat; (I ii 72 CWE 31 211) Hercules wearing the *crocoton*; I iii 66 You are dressing me up in the lionskin; (I iii 66

CWE 31 291) An ass covered with a lionskin; (I iii 66 CWE 31 291) His lion's skin covered a silly ape; I iv 35 An ass to the lyre; (I iv 35 CWE 31 345) A bull at the lyre; (I iv 35 CWE 31 345) The ass twitching its ears; I iv 37 A jackdaw has no business with a lute; I iv 38 A pig has nothing to do with marjoram; (I iv 38 CWE 31 348) To him an alabaster vase full of scent smells bad; (I iv 38 CWE 31 348) Beetles flee from perfume but pursue a foul smell; I iv 39 What has a dog to do with a bath?; (I iv 39 CWE 31 350) As a dog in a bath; I v 43 A donkey wearing perfume; I v 45 Nothing to do with the verse; I v 46 Nothing to do with the lyre; I vii 10 An ape in purple; I vii 22 A jackdaw among the Muses; I vii 23 Perfume on the lentils; I vii 25 A leaden sword in an ivory sheath; I viii 77 Dogs and hogs smell very different; I ix 19 To group foxes with lions; I x 13 Dog in the manger; I x 45 Diametrically opposite. Distant by a diameter; II i 64 Is Saul also among the prophets?; II ii 4 An ass that bears the mysteries; II ii 10 Beyond the olive-trees; II ii 47 Out of tune; II iv 57 What has this to with Bacchus? II v 18 A sword in the hand of a child; II v 59 Parrot and quail speak with very different voices; II v 60 A bald man with long hair; II ix 21 You wear your hair long, though you're a slave; III i 36 Beyond the instrument; III ii 55 Keep a dancer of hornpipes away from the oar; III ii 74 The owl has one cry and the raven another; III iii 73 Not being a Syrian, do not behave like one; III vii 54 What's a blind man doing with a mirror?; IV i 47 An ass to the flute; IV i 56 A sceptre is one thing, a plectrum is another; IV v 57 Once a servant, never a mistress; IV v 88 Like goats in a young orchard; v i 1 You in camp, I in the kitchen

[48] Suitable or unsuitable gifts (*Munus aptum aut ineptum*) II iii 20 You are offering wine to frogs; II

iii 83 Rotting salt fish is fond of marjoram; II v 47 Do not make a Mercury out of any and every wood; II vi 74 An ox under the yoke; II vii 15 An old ship will not sail the open sea; II ix 18 To fit the foot; II ix 84 Not my burden: a saddle on the ox?; III i 30 He has sacrificed a pig to Venus; III ix 9 A suitable function; III ix 78 An unsuitable undertaking; III x 46 An unworthy office; IV i 67 Ship-shape; IV i 90 Using the spoils of the pygmies for the Colossus; v ii 13 Fashioned by heaven; (v ii 13 CWE 36 605) They seem to be not just born, but fashioned by some divinity

[49] Misfortune or ruination (*Infortunii sive exitii*) I i 20 The razor against the whetstone; I i 72 An evil genius; I i 80 He suffers worse tortures than Sambicus; I ii 68 Luckier than the Strobili of Carcinus; I ii 73 You have a weasel in your house; I ii 83 To keep watch in Naupactus; I iii 26 An Iliad of troubles; I iii 27 A Lerna of troubles; I iii 28 A sea of troubles; I iii 30 A store of evils; I v 41 A donkey among apes; (I v 14 CWE 31 421) An owl among the crows; I v 42 A donkey among bees; I vi 34 One wave left me and another caught me up; I vi 54 A rascal at the water; I ix 7 You might well be dragged through a ring; I ix 27 As bad as Lemnos; I x 36 To fight with dogs in a well; I x 97 He must keep Sejus' horse; I x 98 He has gold from Toulouse; II i 31 To the quarries; II i 90 By the darkness around the oak; II i 96 Off with you to the crows; II i 97 Throw him in the water; II i 98 To blessedness; II ii 66 A Sybarite calamity; II v 91 Whole statute-books of wrong; II vi 79 A resounding disaster; II vii 47 Argus' hill; II vii 67 The dog asks for his chain; II viii 22 Charon's gate; II viii 23 He has made water on the ashes of his ancestors; II viii 34 A Cadmean victory; II ix 4 Subterranean baths; II ix 41 With what a portent fortune has embroiled me!; II ix 50 Ogygian disasters; II x 17 The misfortunes of the Magnesians; II x 20 He fought under Erasinades; II x 27 A throng of misfortunes; II x 45 A hare appearing makes your path unlucky; II x 52 In labour laborious; II x 68 May you fall into Orcus' anus; II x 73 You have charged into the bees; II x 78 The sorrows of Ino; II x 98 A blazing robe; III i 3 Aegyptus' wedding; III i 70 Off with you to Cynosarges; III i 71 Cythnian disasters; III iii 7 May you say your three words from the court; III iii 29 An Archidamian war; III iii 33 The woes of Niobe; III iii 88 Of ultimate disasters the ultimate; III iv 59 Antiope's sorrow; III iv 64 Unpropitious days; III v 69 One of three penalties; III vi 60 Issa!; III vi 75 To be pitied even by an enemy; III vii 85 A Taenarian bane; III vii 92 A Cyrnian disaster; III vii 94 What comes from the old city; III viii 26 Absolutely hostile fortune; III ix 15 Wrong-headed; III ix 97 One misfortune after another; III x 80 You will keep watch on the ox; IV i 20 Troy is ill-fated ever; IV i 41 His hook has broken; IV ii 62 Evils come of their own accord; IV ii 64 You have drawn M; IV iii 9 A shipwreck shared; IV iii 75 Though alive and seeing; IV iv 72 As precarious as a bean on the edge; IV v 40 He who did great harm as an enemy; IV v 59 Obedience is the mother of prosperity; IV vii 8 Riding on a wretched ass; IV vii 26 As doleful as a duellist; IV vii 48 May you become water and earth; IV vii 56 A thorny life; IV viii 46 Nothing's going right today; V i 49 A stormy situation

[50] Good fortune, abundance, of good auspices (*Bonae fortunae, copiae, felicitatis, aut ominis*) I i 74 With the applause of gods and men; I i 75 With good auspices; I i 76 The owl flies; I i 78 A son of the white hen; I i 79 I bear the

staff of bay; I i 96 The ring of Gyges; I i 97 The magic wand; I iii 9 The dice always fall out well for Jove; (I iii 26 CWE 31 257, ironic inversion of An Iliad of troubles) An Iliad of all good things; I iii 29 A sea of good things; I iii 31 A heap of good things; (I iii 31 CWE 31 261) A heap of services rendered; I iii 32 An ant-hill of good things; (I iii 32 CWE 31 262) A swarm of virtues; (I iii 32 CWE 31 262) A wainload of good things; I iii 33 A Dathos of good things; I iii 34 A Thasos of good things; I v 99 To be a god. To make a god of someone; (I v 99 CWE 31 469) A godlike man; (I v 99 CWE 31 469) Equal to a god; (I v 99 CWE 31 469) Absolutely divine; (I v 99 CWE 31 469) A mortal god; I v 100 To be in heaven; (I v 100 CWE 31 470) Fallen from the stars; I vi 2 A horn of plenty; I vi 3 Hen's milk; I vi 5 Sardinians for sale; I vi 53 Here's to good luck, *or* A blessing on it!; II i 39 An ox at the manger; II ii 93 Home is everywhere; II iv 37 My right eye twitches; II iv 92 Reels of good things; II iv 97 The day of Datylus; II v 2 Rascals are sometimes lucky in the hunt; II v 15 With a following tide; II v 16 With a fair wind; II v 58 A donkey on the straw; II vii 77 Light has dawned; II vii 87 Procris' weapon; II viii 46 Achilles has thrown two threes and a four; II ix 80 Now is the moment come for Datis' tune; II ix 86 I've made a find, and it's not what children find in beans; II ix 87 Midas on the dice gives the best advice; II x 74 The helmet of Orcus; III i 2 I have escaped evil, I have found good; III i 24 Earth's bounty; III i 90 Good health first, next good looks, and in the third place wealth; III ii 51 Oxen looking towards harvest-time; III ii 53 An ox at the heap; III ii 71 It rains black-puddings; III viii 13 An enormous number of things; III viii 14 Things which come by divine providence; III viii 55 On one whose wish is fulfilled; III viii 94 Everything is happening as planned; III ix 50 God's help is everywhere, if only he is so inclined; III ix 56 A lucky outcome; III x 6 The profits of the wealthy; III x 36 Appearance of hope; III x 40 Prestige divinely given; III x 76 They have seen the heavenly she-goat rising; IV i 62 This year's harvest; IV ii 91 Success comes from God; IV iv 96 In a calm sea anyone can be a pilot; IV v 9 The wise man carries his resources with him; IV v 23 Smelling of fish or flower; IV vi 24 Heaps of possessions; IV ix 68 Nothing more beneficial than salt; IV ix 72 My eyebrow twitches; IV x 44 I'm a king (also III v 41 CWE 35 92); IV x 47 Guided by virtue, fortune attending; v i 16 With salt and vinegar

[51] Evils brought upon oneself or diverted (*Malum accersitum aut retortum*) I i 50 To fetch trouble for oneself on one's own beast; I i 51 I am cutting his throat with his own sword, with his own weapon; I i 52 He fell into the pit which he had made; I i 53 He was caught in his own noose; I i 54 You constructed this device against yourself; I i 55 The thrush's droppings are its own harm; I i 56 He himself discovered the source of his woe; I i 57 The goat (found) the sword; I i 58 The crow (caught) the scorpion; I i 59 You have eaten a hot dinner; I i 60 To stir up hornets; I i 61 You are goading the lion; I i 62 Do not disturb a well-suppressed evil; I i 63 You are waking up Eightfeet; I i 64 To move Camarina; I i 65 You are moving Anagyrus; I i 66 The goat (turns) its own horns against itself; I i 67 Atlas (supported) the sky; I i 82 You attack a horned beast; I i 85 You made this dish and you must eat it all up; I i 86 Let the smith who made the fetters wear them; I i 87 Eat the turtles you caught yourselves; I ii 14 Bad advice; I ii 77 To make the leash from the bull's own hide; I iii 65 The shrew-

mouse gave itself away; I v 62 Attracting trouble as the north-easter draws clouds; I vi 52 We are shot with our own feathers; I vi 73 He must drink the dregs that drank the wine; I vii 56 Attracting all men, like the magnet stone; I vii 60 The pot picks its own greens; I ix 28 You have taken a grasshopper by the wing; I ix 51 The death of a fireworm; I x 14 We were made prisoners as we prisoners made; I x 15 The hunt was her undoing; II i 81 The Carpathian and the hare; II i 86 Keep wolf-cubs; II ii 41 The child and the ice; II iii 11 Prophesy to the Boeotians; II iii 88 The man from Chios has bought his master; II iv 35 The man from Ilium hired the tragic actors; II iv 56 Oenoë and the ravine; II iv 82 The urchin puts off the birth of its young; II v 11 To shave a lion; II v 78 The ox raises the dust to its own harm; II vi 82 A Bellerophon letter; II vi 83 Foul the clear water with mud and you'll never find any to drink; II vi 87 The hot end of the spit; II vii 72 A man from Lydia was free of troubles; II vii 100 He provokes the boar; II viii 39 Phocus' dinner-party; III i 58 For fear he might stitch a cap for his own head; III i 69 You are Dares challenging Entellus; III ii 2 You will bring down the moon to your own hurt; III ii 61 You ask me for Arcadia; III iii 8 Your joy is that of the fire-worm; III iv 84 I taught you how to dive; III iv 87 You are spitting against heaven; III v 8 The camel asked for horns and lost his ears too; III vi 13 To put one's hand in the flame intentionally; (III vi 34 CWE 35 141) No one is hurt except by himself; III vi 72 Pigs to springs, the south wind to flowers; III viii 86 He brought calamity on himself; III x 65 He invented his own misfortune; IV i 39 Eurycles; IV i 59 To pull down the moon; IV i 79 Crow and serpent; IV i 96 He dies twice who dies by his own arms; IV ii 5 Evil brought on oneself; IV ii 40 Nourishing a serpent in one's bosom; IV ii 57 Basin and all; IV v 8 Trouble of one's own making; IV v 33 An enemy within; IV vi 80 Whoever spits on an ants' nest . . .; IV vi 88 On your own head may it fall; IV viii 56 He that plots ill for another lays up ill for himself; IV ix 67 Lay the axe; IV x 68 Such things are born of war

[52] **Repentance that is too late (Sera poenitentia)** I i 28 The Phrygians learn wisdom too late; I i 29 Once stung, the fisherman will be wiser; I i 30 When a thing is done, a fool can see it; I i 31 Trouble experienced makes a fool wise; (I ii 60 CWE 31 199, also III vi 17 CWE 35 133) Doctoring the dead; I v 61 The people of Cumae learn wisdom late; I ix 32 Better run backwards than run all awry; II ii 64 It's too late to spare when the bottom is bare; II iii 39 It is best to profit from another man's madness; II iii 68 A mouse tasting pitch; II iv 59 I'm sorry I gave what I did; III iv 18 Ivy after the Anthisteria; III iv 28 But the place for deliberation is not before the altar; III vi 17 Help when the war is over; IV iii 59 Sadder but wiser

[53] **Cures that are too late or are in time (Serum remedium aut tempestium)** I ii 40 Doctoring is better first than last; (I ii 60 CWE 31 199) Doctoring the dead; III iv 20 Correcting an old man; III vi 17 Help when the war is over; (III vi 17 CWE 35 133) Water onto ashes; IV iii 97 You have come too late

[54] **Condemnation (Damnandi)** (I v 54 CWE 31 430) This man is black, beware of him, thou Roman!; (I v 54 CWE 31 431) To be marked with coal; I v 56 To prefix a theta; (I v 57 CWE 31 435) To mark with an obelus; (I v 57 CWE 31 435) To affix a marginal sign; (I v 57 CWE 31 436) The Aristarchus of his speeches; (I v 57 CWE 31 436) I was terrified of those little red wafers of

yours; I v 58 To mark with the fingernail; (I v 58 CWE 31 437) To correct with a sponge; (I v 58 CWE 31 437) To have been under the file; II v 80 A rod against a net-man; II vii 16 Were you not my father; III vi 76 Votes equal; III vii 40 To bite with a voting token; III viii 1 For a dissenter; III viii 6 Against one who has spoken out of place; IV iv 10 Not even the name; IV iv 67 It must be cast far away; IV x 85 The sinister letter

[55] **Approval (Approbandi)** I v 53 To add a white stone, and similar metaphors; I v 54 To mark with chalk; (I v 54 CWE 31 431) To mark with a pearl; (I v 54 CWE 31 431) White day; (I v 54 CWE 31 431) White bean; I v 60 He obtained every point; With everyone's votes; (I v 60 CWE 31 439) To gather in these things vote by vote; I v 74 To satisfy Momus, and the like; I viii 46 Thumbs down. Thumbs up; I ix 17 With one voice; II i 33 If it's agreeable to you, it's not disagreeable to me; II vii 12 To vote with one's feet; II vii 55 Even Jupiter does not please everybody; III vii 89 I maintain no servant; IV x 90 You're on the right track

[56] **Judging (Iudicandi)** I iv 36 The pig heard the trumpet; I v 87 The Lydian, or Heraclian, stone; I v 88 An unmarked rule; I v 93 By the Lesbian rule; (I vi 81 CWE 32 54) To have a keen nose; I vi 98 He knows white from black; II i 60 Set-square and right rule; II i 74 Purple should be judged against purple; II iv 51 What the touchstone is to gold, gold is to men; II vi 64 I have withdrawn my hand from the cane; II viii 58 It lies on the knees of five judges; II viii 59 With nose well wiped. Thick in the head; III i 32 The judgment of Panides; III viii 34 No discrimination; III x 57 He knows the bad and the good; IV i 6 A man of Tenedos; IV i 7 A Tenedian defender; IV vi 35 A Dutch ear; IV vii 35 A white

crow; IV vii 58 The orders of a blind man; IV viii 26 The obelus of censure

[57] Difference of taste (*Alia aliis placent*) I ii 15 What is one's own is beautiful; (I ii 15 CWE 31 159) Balbinus loves the polyp that on Agnes' nose he sees; (I ii 15 CWE 31 160) You are charmed with your work, I with mine; (I ii 15 CWE 31 160) To every queen her king is fair; (I ii 15 CWE 31 160) Beautiful in your own eyes; (I iii 6 CWE 31 240) Each has his own desires; I iii 7 So many men, so many opinions; II v 57 Corinth is a fine town, but Tenea for me; IV x 64 Ass looks lovely to ass and pig to pig

[58] Making errors (*Aberrandi*) I i 48 You are entirely on the wrong road; I i 49 To be entirely astray (by the whole sky); I vi 36 Who could miss the gate?; IV vi 73 Off course

[59] Blindness of vision (*Caecutientia*) I iii 55 As blind as a mole; I iii 56 As blind as a sloughed skin; I iii 57 As blind as Tiresias; I iii 58 As blind as Hypsea; I viii 40 The blind leading the blind; I viii 41 A blind man's watch; II i 29 They live on darnel; II i 75 Saturnian rheums; II i 76 Your eyes run pumpkins; II i 77 Your eyes run pots; II ii 36 To look into a dog's anus; II vi 34 Cimmerian gloom; II ix 43 To throw dust in a man's eyes; III i 6 You see three in place of two; III iii 78 Neither a blind guide nor a witless counsellor; III vi 30 A damp night; III vii 59 Groping in the dark

[60] Clear-sightedness (*Perspicacitas*) I vi 81 Scenting out, and sundry metaphors of this kind; I ix 96 A serpent's eye; II i 54 More clear-sighted than Lynceus; IV vii 75 In a broad way

[61] What is obvious and clear (*Perspicuitas*) I i 39 More roughly and more plainly; I vi 70 Known to blear-

eyed men and barbers; I viii 93 A blind man might see that; II i 42 Even a child can see it; II iii 50 As though in a mirror. As though in a picture; IV iii 95 As if from a watch-tower; IV iv 71 As clear as amber; IV v 12 The mind sees, the mind hears; IV v 95 Archimedes could not describe it better; IV vii 100 White speech

[62] Obscurity (*Obscuritas*) I iii 36 I am Davus, not Oedipus; (I iii 36 CWE 31 265) I am no seer; I iii 63 Through cloud, through darkness, as in a dream; I vi 29 A Delian diver; II ii 36 To look into a dog's anus; II iii 9 Boeotian riddles; III vi 32 As obscure as Plato's maths; IV v 78 Not even Apollo would understand it

[63] Deafness (*Surditas*) II ix 8 As deaf as the harbour at Torone; II ix 9 As deaf as a starling

[64] Attentiveness and its opposite (*Attentio et contra*) II iv 94 With well-washed ears; II vii 84 Though present he is far away; III ii 56 With ears pricked up; III vi 47 A mind elsewhere; III viii 11 Consider well and take advice; III viii 45 Pay heed and consider; IV iii 7 Your ears are stopped with wax; IV v 18 To one's full height; V i 19 Attend to the business at hand

[65] Compliance (*Obsecundantis*) II ii 38 Follow God; II vii 99 At the snap of a finger; II ix 82 I'll not be set up as a lioness on a sword-hilt; III vi 55 Law and country; III viii 19 When each yields to the other; IV v 59 Obedience is the mother of prosperity; IV vii 14 To take on the madness of the mad

[66] Correction of a word or deed (*Correctio dicti aut facti*) III viii 57 For one who corrects what someone else has said; III viii 90 Mending what we say; III x 1 Where have I transgressed, etc.?

**[67] Profit at another's expense (Com-
modum interversum)** I iii 4 To bear
the palm; I v 32 Some sow, others will
reap; II x 1 He baked the sponge cake
I kneaded

[68] Impossible things (Impossibilia)
I iii 15 The springs of the sacred rivers
flow backwards; I iii 25 The earth flies;
I iv 78 (also II vi 51) You are twisting a
rope of sand; I iv 79 Wool from a donkey; I v 64 What if the sky should fall?; I
viii 84 Ere that, the tortoise shall outrun
the hare; I x 7 You pursue the impossible; II i 89 Sooner shall a grasshopper
bring forth a cow; II ii 80 It is hard to
suck and blow at the same time; II iii 16
Sooner would a man fall in a ship and
not fall on wood; II iv 21 To cleanse the
stable of Augeas; II iv 71 Sooner will
vines grow in the sea; II iv 83 Sooner
would two urchins make friends; II v
56 Sooner hide an elephant under your
arm; II vii 80 They want to snatch the
lamb from the wolf; II vii 96 I cannot
carry a she-goat and you load me with
an ox; III iv 56 You are trying to drink
a statue; III v 43 Sooner tune a harp;
III v 52 You've got hold of the lentil by
the point; III v 84 It is not easy to fly
without feathers; III vi 77 A nightingale
without a song; (III vi 77 CWE 35 163) A
woman without words; III vii 36 Sooner
a wolf would mate with a sheep; III vii
38 You'll never make crabs walk forwards; IV ii 56 An ass' tale; IV ii 59 An ox
putting its head over Taygetus; IV ii 94
You are putting a cloak round a fire; IV
viii 17 Sooner will a dung-beetle make
honey; IV viii 76 Neither god nor man;
IV viii 94 You would sooner persuade
a dung-beetle; IV ix 3 Live on the wind

**[69] Ridiculousness, improprieties,
topsyturviness (Absurda, indecora,
praepostera)** I i 2 (Pythagoras) CWE 31
43 Do not make water facing towards
the sun; I i 40 The sow (teaches) Min-

erva; I i 41 A sow competed with Minerva; I ii 54 To cut a dead man's throat;
I ii 90 Come not to counsel before you
are called; I iii 50 To yoke foxes; I iii
51 To milk a he-goat; I iii 70 To whiten
ivory with ink; I iii 71 To daub a sound
vessel; I iv 74 To fish in the air, to hunt
in the sea; I iv 76 To drag the clothes
off a naked man; I iv 81 You are looking for the wolf's wings; I v 65 Afraid
of one's own shadow; I vi 6 A hairyfoot
hungry for meat; I vi 7 A hare thyself,
and goest in quest of game?; I vi 21
Donkey in a ditch; I vi 51 The girl who
stammers doesn't b-believe; I vii 24 A
gold ring in a pig's snout; (I vii 24 CWE
32 81) I hate the rogue who speaks like
an honest man; (I vii 24 CWE 32 82) A
stinking sheatfish on a silver dish; I vii
28 The cart before the horse; I vii 58
You lend light to the sun; I vii 59 The
springs themselves are thirsty; I vii 67
Slow catches up with fast; I vii 68 Tortoise defeats eagle; I vii 83 Who does
not own himself would Samos own; I
viii 71 Wasp buzzing against cricket;
I viii 72 Jay strives with nightingale,
hoopoe with swans; I ix 69 You make
of a fly an elephant; I ix 73 Olive no
kernel hath, nor nut no shell; I ix 74
Jupiter childless; I ix 75 You seek water in the sea; II i 8 When water chokes
you; II i 56 To cross the Aegean in a
wicker boat; II iii 54 To skin a dog that's
skinned already; II iv 78 The crab catching the hare; II v 6 You use a lantern at
midday; II v 7 To hold a candle to the
sun; II v 27 They drink water by measure and eat meat without measure; II v
28 To put a dancer on the stage wearing a toga; II v 38 You physic others,
full of sores yourself; II v 46 Let not the
shoe be too big for the foot; II v 77 To
blink in the sunlight; II v 88 You keep
hounds though you cannot keep yourself; II vi 10 The she-goat has not yet
given birth, but the kid is playing on
the roof; II vi 28 Fox driving ox; II vi 81

To split logs with a key and open the door with an axe; II vii 45 You shoot with a plough (also at IV iv 44 CWE 36 91); II vii 66 The camel dances; II viii 10 An aged kid; II viii 11 An old woman dancing; II ix 68 I tell you your own dream; II ix 76 You post a naked man on sentry-duty; II x 10 Mercury tongue-tied; III i 43 A river waters what is far away; III i 54 Why castrate Galli?; III ii 68 Water out of a ditch into the sea; III iii 10 Before you've grown your beard you teach old men; (III iii 10 CWE 34 285; also at III iii 86 CWE 34 311) Sooner than your beard; III iii 13 You flay the beast before you've killed it; III iii 14 Before the meal is roasted; III iii 30 You smear ointment over a corpse; III iii 69 He digs a well alongside the river; III iii 79 The mouse that did not run into its hole was carrying a gourd; III iv 30 An emerald, dark in the light; III iv 45 To seek money for the journey already completed; III iv 54 Talking through a wall; III iv 65 The old woman is in her cups; III v 14 You are giving chaff to the dog and bones to the ass; III v 72 A swine danced; III v 98 A lion's skin over a saffron dress; III v 100 I neither hear nor touch; III vi 16 Water to a frog; III vi 19 You are teaching a fish to swim; III vi 67 To put Hercules' boots on a baby; III vii 24 The ass is a bird; III ix 20 Possessions are worthless if not used; III x 91 Straining at a gnat; IV i 100 I hate striplings who are precociously wise; (IV i 100 CWE 35 502) Child in age but endowed with mature wisdom; IV ii 39 Stealing the sands of the sea-shore; IV ii 44 Adding stars to the heavens; IV iii 29A Bright at night, useless in daylight; IV iii 93 You are a carpenter, stick to your trade; IV iii 94 Mixing fire and water; IV iii 98 Antidote before poison; IV iv 11 The stag drags off the hounds; IV iv 21 While our knees are fresh; IV iv 30 Bringing clouds to a clear sky; IV iv 44 To hunt a hare with an ox (also at

II vii 45 CWE 34 24); IV v 2 The secret of artistic success is doing what suits you; IV v 80 Peace-time lions; IV vi 77 In Carian fashion; IV vi 94 With candle in hand; IV vii 39 Wool to a fuller's workshop; IV vii 80 To dance eloquently; IV viii 21 One salve for all sores; IV viii 39 Play in order to be serious; IV viii 25 Add light to the sun with torches; IV viii 57 Carrying the plank; IV ix 94 Tie up a dog with lamb's chitterlings; IV x 2 Turn birthday into funeral day; V i 5 To start reckoning up when the money's been squandered; V i 30 Back to front; V i 80 Archilochus' song; V ii 8 Throw the first spears; V ii 9 Ignore the fountain-head and follow along the stream; V ii 11 Hired labourers; V ii 22 Rank growth

[70] Pointless action (*Inanis opera*)

I ii 11 Owls to Athens; I ii 12 You are reminding the mindful, teaching the taught, etc.; I ii 53 To wrestle with ghosts; I ii 60 A teacher of the old; (I ii 60 CWE 31 199) Doctoring a dead man and teaching an old one are the same thing; I ii 61 To teach an old man a new language; (I ii 61 CWE 31 200) The old parrot takes no notice of the rod; I ii 75 From a lot of chaff I got little grain; I ii 96 They fought among stones but could not pick one up; I iii 46 You are kicking against the goad; I iii 52 About an ass' shadow; I iii 53 About goat's wool; I iii 54 To dispute about smoke; I iii 64 About the ass that poked its head in; I iv 40 You teach a donkey to race with a bit; I iv 42 To unravel Penelope's web; I iv 44 You are measuring the sands; I iv 45 You are counting the waves; I iv 46 To break wind in front of a dead man; I iv 47 To spin spiders' webs; I iv 48 You are washing a brick; I iv 49 You are boiling a stone; I iv 50 You are washing, or whitening, an Ethiopian; I iv 51 To plough the seashore; I iv 52 You are sowing seed in the sand; I iv 53

You are sowing seed in water; I iv 54 You are sowing among the rocks; I iv 55 To cleave fire; I iv 56 You write in water; I iv 57 You are building on the sand; I iv 58 You are tilling the winds; I iv 59 You are teaching iron to swim; I iv 60 To draw water in a sieve; (I iv 60 CWE 31 361) Emptying pitchers into the jars of the Danaids; (I iv 60 CWE 31 361) Pouring words into a leaky tub; I iv 61 You are sprinkling scent on manure; I iv 62 I have wasted both oil and toil; (I iv 62 CWE 31 363) An ox to the wrestling-ring; I iv 63 You are chasing the winds with a net; I iv 64 You are plying windless air; I iv 65 You are flogging a dead body; I iv 66 You are decorating a cooking-pot; I iv 67 You are sticking an egg together; I iv 68 You are beating a wineskin; I iv 69 You are plucking a wineskin; I iv 70 To reopen a closed subject; I iv 71 You are feeding a whetstone; I iv 72 You are calling for Hylas; I iv 73 You are wasting water (time); I iv 75 You are asking for water out of a pumice stone; (I iv 76 CWE 31 370) A naked man cannot be robbed by ten wrestlers; I iv 77 To reap asphodel-stalks; I iv 79 Wool from a donkey; I iv 80 You are shearing a donkey; I iv 83 The sluggard twists the rope; I iv 84 You are talking to the seashore; I iv 85 You are talking to the wind; I iv 86 He addresses the dead; I iv 87 You are singing, or telling a story to the deaf; I iv 88 You sing in vain; I iv 89 You are speaking to a stone; I iv 90 You are talking to the wall; I iv 91 To play the fool; I iv 92 You are shooting at heaven; I iv 93 You are tying a dolphin by the tail; I iv 94 You are holding an eel by the tail; I iv 97 You teach a dolphin to swim; I iv 98 You teach an eagle to fly; I iv 99 You are sticking in the same mud; I v 97 What need was there to play on the long pipes?; I vi 38 You sing to a broken string; I vi 39 You terrify with a wineskin; (I vi 39 CWE 32

31) You terrify with a shadow; I vi 40 You terrify a lion with a mask; I vii 57 To carry wood to the forest; (I vii 57 CWE 32 101) To add water to the sea; I vii 65 To hunt with reluctant hounds; I vii 66 To harness reluctant oxen to the cart; I vii 78 Singing at his post; I viii 59 You join thread with thread; I ix 21 To pursue a flying quarry; I ix 45 The line's caught nothing; I ix 84 I have belaboured the south wind; I x 9 You cut off a hydra's heads; I x 23 To pay by a switching-loan; II i 53 To sow the hollows of Arabia; II i 58 Much hard work, and we're where we were; II i 59 To beat water in a mortar; II ii 40 To make a display of pots; II iii 33 What you ladle out flows back again; II iii 38 Making a round tour; II iv 40 To roll a stone; II v 44 To fight against the gods; II v 72 To belabour a stone; II vi 32 To grind one tooth on another; II vii 28 Attack a man skilled in the art; II vii 91 From empty chaff; II viii 37 You pluck the hair from a bald man's head; II x 16 To turn millet on a lathe; II x 54 To sow hard work; II x 87 You draw water from dry ground; III i 1 The labours of Hercules; III i 42 To plough another man's land; III i 79 To wrestle with Corycus; III i 84 He runs in vain, III ii 9 To strive against the stream; III ii 86 From a wolf-hunt; III iii 39 Do not wash a donkey's head with soap; III iii 44 You look for birds; III iii 64 You trouble me in vain as might a wave; III iv 32 You are trying to sink a bladder full of air; III iv 44 He's looking for onions; III vi 11 Fighting like Phrynichus; III vi 38 To divide the clouds; III vi 66 To achieve nothing (also in v ii 21 CWE 36 614); III vii 60 Keeping off the flies; III vii 98 You're teaching a crab to walk; III vii 99 You are emptying out the sea; III viii 8 Vain effort; III ix 22 You may not fight with the gods; III x 87 You keep on singing; IV i 48 To weave a mantle for Orestes; IV ii 9 You're blowing away the stocks;

IV ii 14 The pig has perished; IV iii 6
A barrel rolls easily; IV iii 30 Gathering fruit from the garden of Tantalus;
IV iv 26 To dig through the Isthmus; IV
iv 50 A bath-keeper's mule; IV iv 52 As
if going to Sutrium; IV iv 56 Putting
the same shoe on every foot; IV v 52
To complain to a stepmother; IV v 58
To burn up the sea; IV v 60 To remove
spring from the year; IV vi 44 He who
had nothing to do, built a wall round
Harmene; IV vi 48 Shadow-boxing, IV
vi 95 To live in an empty house; IV vii
1 To put loaves in a cold oven; IV vii 35
A white crow; IV vii 38 To drill a hole
in a grain of millet; IV viii 16 Don't cultivate barren land; IV x 46 Waste both
toil and net

[71] Difficulty (*Difficultatis*) I iv 1
It is not given to everyone to land at
Corinth; (I iv 1 CWE 31 319) It isn't
everyone who can get near the table; (I
iv 1 CWE 31 319) The sailing's not this
way for prudent mortals; II i 12 Good
things are difficult; II iv 41 To take on
a department. To entrust a department;
II v 3 To walk the tightrope; II vi 9
Azanian ills; III iv 6 Nobody who is
wicked shall know this; (III iv 6 CWE
35 7) Not every pig will get to know
this; III viii 69 With difficulty, but still
we do it; III ix 69 Do not dispute with
a ruler; III x 23 It was difficult, but he
achieved it; III x 39 It is not given to
everyone; IV i 95 To snatch Hercules'
club; IV ii 41 Illegible to anyone but the
Sibyl; IV iii 88 A wagon has a hundred
planks; IV v 32 To escape from every
snare; IV v 34 Capturing a city; IV vii
32 A plank in everything

[72] Natural proclivities (*Proclivitas*)
I i 2 (Pythagoras) CWE 31 36 Stir not the
fire with a sword; I ii 46 To cheer on the
runner (also III viii 32); I ii 47 To spur
on the running horse; I iv 11 Suet for
the weasel; I v 28 A ball runs downhill;

I vi 13 He gave the cart a good shove
downhill; (I vi 13 CWE 32 12) Advice
is nearly as good as a helping hand; I
viii 82 The horse to the plain; II iii 85
Salt fish is baked as soon as it has seen
the fire; II viii 97 A log onto the fire;
II x 65 One whip drives them all; III
iv 76 You are calling a Lydian onto the
plain; III v 70 As easily as a fox eats a
pear; III vi 64 Fire to a torch; III viii 32
Cheering on a willing runner (also I ii
46), IV ii 63 They have the example of
their neighbours; IV iii 82 Ready cash;
IV iv 15 Persuade wolves to go mad;
IV iv 61 As easy as rain can fall; IV iv
78 With one little finger; IV iv 98 As if
from the medicine box; IV v 36 By the
same pole; IV v 82 Merchant, just sail in
and sell; IV vii 11 As soft as a ripe fig;
IV vii 29 The pot has grasped the lentils

**[73] The opposite of natural procliv-
ities (*Proclivitas contra*)** I i 17 Now
my forces are pressed into a narrow
space; I i 42 Against Minerva's will; I
vi 21 Donkey in a ditch; II i 35 Caught
in a well

**[74] Things that can never happen
(*Nunquam*)** I v 83 When the mule
foals; I v 84 At the Greek calends; (I
v 85 CWE 31 458) At full moon; I v 86
When lightning strikes through Harma;
III iii 47 When the cock crows at Nibas;
IV x 15 Since the human race began; IV
x 16 In all human memory

[75] What is always true (*Semper*) III
ix 25 For as long as I live

[76] What is non-existent (*Nusquam*)
II v 71 Where the stags cast their horns;
III ii 80 At Aphannae; IV viii 69 Neither
among men, nor yet upon the sea

**[77] Recompense for a kindness or a
service (*Pensatio beneficii vel officii*)**
I i 33 One hand rubs another; I i 35 To

render like for like (also at IV vi 67 CWE 36 260); I i 36 By the same measure; I vii 95 Lend me your evidence; I vii 98 Old men rub one another; I vii 99 You scratch my back and I'll scratch yours; I vii 100 Iron sharpeneth iron; I viii 78 As you have sown, so also shall you reap; I x 42 With the same yardstick; II iv 14 Work for the money is a fair exchange; III ii 49 Grapes ripen cluster against cluster; III v 83 Reels for good deeds; IV iii 20 Calauria for Delos; V i 48 Make up for failings with noble deeds

[78] Misfortune that is repeated or renewed (*Malum conduplicatum, aut renovatum*) I ii 6 To heal one evil with another; I ii 7 To add sickness to sickness; I ii 8 Do not add fire to fire; I ii 9 To pour oil on the fire; I ii 10 To quench fire with oil; I vi 80 To rub a sore; I viii 99 Quarrel will quarrel breed, and hurt breed hurt; I x 9 You cut off a hydra's heads; I x 67 To purge away mud with mud; II ii 63 One fraud treads on the heels of another; II viii 45 Pylos there is before Pylos; II x 41 One quarrel breeds another; III iii 48 Fire is not quenched by fire; III vii 35 Not blind but eyeless; IV ii 36 It is better to be exposed to one evil than two; (IV iii 12 CWE 36 12) After war there is upheaval; IV iii 13 Another battle follows Marathon; IV iv 55 Suddenly it will be winter; IV vii 40 From the smoke into the fire

[79] Avoiding misfortune as one's cost (*Malum male vitatum*) I v 4 Having escaped Charybdis I fell into Scylla; I v 5 Fleeing from the smoke I fell into the fire; III iii 72 Avoiding the ashes, do not fall into the red-hot coals; III iii 89 To avoid getting wet a man ran through the rain, / Fell into a pit, and was ne'er seen again

[80] Evil to which one is accustomed (*Malum assuetum*) II v 5 Time tempers

grief; II ix 85 An evil thing known is best; III i 35 To grow thick-skinned; III ix 91 Familiarity with misfortune; III x 49 He has grown used to ills; III x 58 For we are no strangers; IV viii 94 You would sooner persuade a dung-beetle; IV ix 25 Habit is a second nature

[81] Retaliation for an evil (*Mali retaliatio*) I i 27 He who says what he would will hear what he would not; I i 89 Termerian evils; I i 90 The revenge of Neoptolemus; I viii 81 To drink of the same cup; II ii 83 I got as bad as I gave; III vi 6 Now we strike, and now expose our shins to arrows

[82] Payment that is inappropriate (*Inaequalis pensatio*) I ii 1 Exchange between Diomede and Glaucus; I vi 38 You sing to a broken string; I viii 73 Bristles for wool; II vi 5 If he asks for wine, give him your fists; II vi 6 Scorpion instead of perch; II vi 16 Flour, not fine words; II x 80 Let each man steal the fire too in his turn; III i 25 A pigeon instead of a dove; III ii 98 Shadow instead of substance; III vi 12 You demand a sow for a sick dog; III x 12 Misfortune compensated with good; IV i 65 Bangles and baubles

[83] Deficiencies compensated by assets (*Alibi diminutum, alibi redditum*) II iii 94 We cannot all do everything; II ix 49 The lame man makes the best lecher; III iii 26 He washed the sea-salt from his ears with words like river-water; III v 2 Deeds of the young, advice of the middle-aged, prayers of the old; (III v 2 CWE 35 68) Advice of the aged; III v 91 To an old man always join a young girl; III viii 70 What is lacking in one way is made up for in another; IV iv 20 All fields do not produce all things

[84] Hope that is disappointed (*Frustrata spes*) I iii 62 Not even in a dream;

I v 33 You are making a bad throw; I vii 15 He's tricked the gaping crow; I ix 13 The gull is about to lay (also II ii 34); I ix 14 The mountains labour, forth will creep a mouse; I ix 30 The treasure consisted of coals; I ix 45 This line's caught nothing; II i 91 He lost his heart to wheaten loaves; II ii 76 The wolf dances round the well; II iii 58 The wolf's jaws are gaping; II iv 5 To buy hope for good money; II v 55 Seeking a dinner, I have lost my coat; II vi 48 Seek not soft things, for fear your lot may prove hard; II vi 69 To lean on a tottering wall; II vi 70 To lean upon a staff of reed; II viii 87 It is a disgrace to stay too long and return empty-handed; II ix 14 Farmers are always rich next year; II ix 75 I've lost the kernel, and he's left the shell in pledge; III i 19 All does not come to pass that you have set your heart on; III i 20 He displayed the mouse instead of the lion; III i 82 Cretans [perform] the sacrifice; III iii 36 He that hunts two hares catches neither; III iv 36 You thought you were going to strike gold; III vi 99 The morsel snatched from one's throat; III viii 7 On disappointed hope; IV iii 5 Burning with empty hopes; IV iii 19 God forestalls the dropping of the anchor; IV iii 57 A river does not always bring axes

[85] **Desperation (*Desperatio*)** I iii 39 All is over; I iii 44; I v 21 It all comes back to the rope; I x 21 Choose your tree and hang yourself; II vii 86 Like a pine-tree; III ii 63 To leap from five rocks into the waves; III v 59 It is the end of good things; III vi 49 Give me a loan of three drachmas to buy a piglet; III vii 45 Slender hope; (III vii 45 CWE 35 243) He hopes some breeze will blow from this direction; III ix 19 Without arms or protection; v i 86 I am nothing

[86] **Good or evil that is unexpected (*Praeter spem bonum, aut malum*)** I i

68 Unexpected appearance of a god; I i 69 Man is a god to man; I i 70 Man is a wolf to man; I i 71 A quail saved Hercules; I ii 87 Aches and pains too give exemption; I iii 6 Hands of the Gods; II v 100 Nisa is Mopsus' bride; II viii 32 Glaucus drank honey and came back to life; II ix 99 Leisure to business turned; II x 56 You would give Pelias a bath; III i 40 All's well: the old man dances; III iv 57 You live a life one could not hope for; III viii 39 Swift relief from danger; III ix 4 An unexpected outcome; IV vii 4 A gift of Mercury; IV viii 61 Much that seems beyond belief

[87] **Misfortune turning out well (*Malum vertens bono*)** II vi 23 War without tears; II ix 78 Now that I've suffered shipwreck, my voyage has gone well; IV ii 31 The snare seems to be a help

[88] **Interventions that occur suddenly (*Subiti interventus*)** II viii 6 If you had even mentioned a wolf; III viii 56 The wolf in the fable (also IV v 50); IV iv 91 Mercury has now arrived

[89] **Promises that are magnificent (*Magnifica promissa*)** I vi 97 Stand surety, and ruin is at hand; I viii 15 You shall be set up at Olympia in gold; I ix 15 To promise mountains of gold; II i 27 To call one to his cap of liberty; II v 9 Cillicon is doing well; II vi 84 Chares and his promises; II vi 100 Hermodorus is an importer of words; II x 7 May I measure by the peck; III i 9 Whole pot-roast oxen; III ii 76 I knead you a white loaf; III iii 54 Theagenes and his shrine of Hecate; (III iii 54 CWE 34 299) Smoke; III v 25 Crystal-gazing; III vi 80 I shall do everything as Nicostratus did; IV i 37 Gifts of an Alybantian host; IV ii 81 Wedding gifts; IV iii 16 The apples of the Hesperides; IV x 14 Mountains of grain; v i 33 Tell out now

[90] What one wishes for (*Votum*) I i
2 (Pythagoras) CWE 31 48 Let those who
intend to worship be seated; I v 98 If
only I had what lies between Corinth
and Sicyon!; I vii 87 What we see in a
dream; (I vii 87 CWE 32 120) Not if you
brought me all false dreams can bring;
(I vii 87 CWE 32 120) Countless as the
sand; II iii 90 Lovers weave their own
dreams; II viii 17 Make for Arbelae
and you'll do great things; II viii 74
Wishes make wealthy; II ix 83 Pray not
against your ox; III iii 66 All my debts
onions and my taxes garlic; III iii 81
He dreams even when he's asleep; III
v 92 Last year's harvest was always the
best; III viii 55 On one whose wish is
fulfilled; III ix 1 Some things are given,
some are denied; III x 60 Not everything
you wish for happens; III x 86 A dog
dreaming of bread

**[91] Hope that is never given up (*Spes
pertinax*)** II iv 12 While there's life
in a sick man, there's hope; III i 92
Hopes are the food of exiles; III vii 45
Slender hope; (III vii 45 CWE 35 243) He
hopes some breeze will blow from this
direction; III ix 42 Thus far some god
has cared for us; IV iv 8 The heavens are
still revolving; IV iv 63 Hope preserves
the afflicted; IV v 90 From the actual
harvest; IV ix 99 In the blade

**[92] Exceptional attributes and dispar-
ities in these (*Excellentia, inaequalitas*)** I i 10 Nothing like Parmeno's pig;
I ii 63 Double diapason; I iii 49 A fawn
against a lion; I iv 21 To lead the way
with white horses; I v 47 Ant or camel;
I v 94 Unworthy to hold out a chamber-
pot to him; I vi 28 This is sovereign;
(I vi 28 CWE 32 22) Victory is with the
better party; (I vi 28 CWE 32 23) The
worse counsel wins; (I vi 28 CWE 32 23)
His choir is larger, but mine sings more
in tune; (I vi 28 CWE 32 23) Might is
right; I vi 42 But second fiddle to a Les-

bian; I viii 72 Jay strives with nightingale, hoopoe with swans; I viii 74 You
match flute against trumpet; I viii 75
You match a cricket against a bee; I viii
76 You match a tortoise against Pegasus; I viii 83 The raven sings sweeter
than the finch; I viii 85 You match crab
against hare; I ix 18 You match eagle
and owl; I ix 20 An eagle in the clouds;
I ix 56 An eagle's old age; I ix 58 Even
a mangy camel bears the load of many
donkeys; I ix 76 You're only a river
striving with the sea; I x 22 Minerva
against a cat; I x 43 To be pointed out; II
i 18 To drag by the feet; II i 41 Whither
away so fast? Not to see the young
man?; II i 99 Alabanda has all the luck;
II ii 45 More scent is made in Campa-
nia than oil elsewhere; II ii 77 A Lydian
chariot; II iii 53 He alone is wise; II iii
61 Slave surpasses slave and master
master; II iii 82 To be many parasangs
ahead; II iii 94 We cannot all do everything; II iv 18 Alpha of those that wear
the cloak; II iv 44 He who is last in Croton is first in the rest of Greece, II iv 79
Roedeer must not fight lions; II vi 41
You match a rose with an anemone; II vi
58 Works worthy of Aceseus and Heli-
con; II x 99 A lion in old age is stronger
than fawns in youth; III i 27 To match a
gnat against an elephant; III i 55 How
much better mules are than asses; III
i 91 To eat hay. He should be fed on
ambrosia; III ii 35 Celmis with sword
in hand; III iv 73 He was the best by
sixteen feet; III iv 96 Among the blind
the cross-eyed man is king; III v 9 Hercules and an ape; III v 23 Many pupils
surpass their teachers; III viii 50 Not
worthy to look me in the eye; III viii
53 One who is equal to many; III viii
62 Exceptional virtue shines out; III ix
13 People excel in different ways; III
x 14 First by far; III x 15 The ancients
should be treated with reverence; III x
85 Other cities are nothing beside Croton; (III x 85 CWE 35 389) Compared

with Croton the rest are wretched little
towns; IV i 53 An Athenian who is honest; IV ii 50 As learned as Prodicus; IV ii
70 Acarnanian horses; IV ii 73 Perseus
approaches the Gorgon; IV iii 8 Crows
are more revered than nightingales; IV
iii 22 A swallow will be miles ahead; IV
iii 29 Yield, since you are a dwarf; (IV
iii 29 CWE 36 22) Two-footers; IV iii 69
If glass is worth that much, what price
pearls?; IV iv 12 The owl sings to the
nightingale; IV iv 18 In no way similar; IV iv 37 Worthy of a Manes; IV iv
68 The steed is in pursuit of the tortoise; IV v 35 I except the gods; IV vi
3 A frog against a tortoise; IV vi 8 To
obstruct someone's light; IV vi 11 The
gods are all powerful; IV ix 9 Water is
indeed the best of things; IV x 48 Add
a penny to Croesus' millions

[93] Differences (*Differentiae*) I ii 63
Double diapason; I iii 79 What a difference between bronze coins and lupins!;
I x 70 Far and away; II iv 50 The bounds
of Mysia and Phrygia are distinct; II
ix 48 Rufillus reeks of lozenges, Gorgonius of he-goat; III iv 37 The waters
of Merrha and Siloam are far apart; III
viii 65 No matter who it might be; IV iii
74 A long distance; IV iv 36 Away with
friend as well as foe; IV iv 85 Not even
a point; IV x 71 A hair in between

[94] Similarity in abilities (*Aequalitas*)
I vi 8 Matched in double harness; III
viii 18 Stubborn quarrelling; III viii 31
Contest between equals; IV vi 67 Half
and half

**[95] Victory and defeat (*Vincere et
vinci*)** I iii 4 To bear the palm; I ix 33
He was the only runner and he won;
I ix 78 To proffer grass; I ix 79 To put
one's hands up; I ix 81 To throw away
one's spear; I ix 82 To leave the arena;
II iv 85 It's my ball; II vi 1 Losers must
expect to suffer; III iv 14 Raise your fin-

ger; III iv 25 Invulnerable like Caeneus;
III v 17 Lay it down on the spot; IV iii
79 The conquered dare not even mut-
ter; IV iv 3 The last one's scab; IV x 74
The life of man is a time of exile

**[96] Victory that is bitter for both sides
(*Victoria utrinque tristis*)** II vi 24 The
loser weeps, the winner's dead; III vii
29 One pot smashed against another;
III ix 2 Not a bloodless victory

**[97] Lack of uniqueness (*Non solus
ille*)** I vi 31 Many good men and true;
II x 24 Many men called Mannius at
Aricia; III iv 17 Brasidas indeed is a
good man

**[98] Freedom from danger and safety
(*Securitatis et tutae rei*)** I i 2 (Pythagoras) CWE 31 33 Do not sit on the grain-
measure; I i 13 Secured by two anchors;
I i 45 In shallow water; I i 46 To navigate in harbour; I ii 81 You have your
feet out of the mire; I iii 40 To consider
a thing done; I iii 93 Out of range; I iii
94 Behind the front rank; I iii 95 Far
from the horse's hooves; I iii 96 Away
from Jove and away from the thunderbolt; I vii 20 A horse to carry me, a king
to feed me; I vii 48 In your kingdom; I
vii 49 It's put in your grove and shrine;
I vii 50 Safe in his own fold; I viii 19
To sleep sound on either ear; I viii 20
On the right ear; I viii 21 To sleep at
full stretch; I viii 62 To live from one
day to the next. To live for the moment;
II ii 6 In calm water; II v 67 Instead of
Hermion; II vi 52 These are halcyon
days in the market; II x 67 The Persians
shall not lie in wait for these; III ii 43
You sing as if you were sailing to Delos; III ii 93 Why judge the Achaeans
from the tower?; (III iii 38 CWE 34 295)
To run risks like tortoises; III vii 31
For those who hold to neither altar nor
oath; III viii 64 Brave when there is no
danger; III ix 58 Relax!; III x 8 Worry

about something else; IV i 43 To sleep on either eye; IV ii 66 A poor man on dry land; IV iii 1 Living on milled fare; IV iii 34 The walls of Semiramis; IV iii 78 A hare's life; IV iv 76 Like a hound's collar; IV v 13 Living on savory; IV v 37 Windproof and watertight; IV v 41 Depending on no ordinary anchor; IV vi 12 A cautious man's mother sheds no tears; IV vii 20 An envoy is not beaten or violated; IV vii 82 Even hares attack a lion when it's dead; IV vii 84 To hold in one's fist; IV viii 6 Away from the smoke and the swell; IV viii 72 Safe riding at two anchors; IV ix 7 First you must drive off the bees; IV ix 29 As if to an altar; IV ix 30 Flee to sanctuary; IV ix 31 Citadel; IV x 79 Not even if to Jove's temple; v i 38 View the shipwreck from the shore

[99] Contempt and worthlessness (Contemptus et vilitatis) (*Adagia* introduction xiii CWE 31 25) Despised as seaweed; I ii 43 Stuff and nonsense; I iii 21 I would not turn a hand. I would not raise a finger; I iii 77 For a crust of bread; I iii 83 Neither here nor there; I v 94 Unworthy to hold out a chamberpot to him; (I v 94 CWE 31 466) Not fit to take off that man's shoes; I vi 41 Sovereignty in Scryos; I vi 77 Lowest of the Mysians; I vii 21 Blue pimpernel too is a vegetable; I vii 31B a burden on the earth; I vii 76 To fart in someone's face, or To fart against the thunder; I vii 79 A slave not worth his salt; I vii 85 Fig-wood; (I vii 85 CWE 32 118) Having a lame and figtree mind; I viii 4 I count it not worth a hair; I viii 5 I care not a mite; I viii 6 I care not a wisp of wool, or, a wisp of wool and no more; I viii 7 I make it not worth a snap of the fingers; I viii 8 I would not buy it for a rotten walnut; (I viii 8 CWE 32 131) I would not swap that for an empty nut; I viii 9 He did not spend a farthing; I viii 10 A three-ha'penny fellow; (I viii 10

CWE 32 132) *triobolares* 'three ha'penny fellows'; I viii 11 A threepenny man; I viii 13 Not worth a one; I viii 37 You're nothing sacred; I viii 38 Rotten to the core; I viii 39 Dion's grunt; I viii 56 Syria is not short of herbs; I viii 79 Carian music; I ix 53 Goods given away will soon decay; I ix 70 The elephant does not catch mice; I ix 71 An eagle confronted with a thrips; I ix 86 He does not know even the shadow of it; I x 4 To drain the dregs; I x 10 Not a splinter. Not even a straw; I x 12 Hippocleides doesn't care; I x 63 The seventh ox; II i 65 The water-jar on the doorstep; II i 79 The Megarians are neither the third nor the fourth; II ii 20 The spoon will grow; II ii 21 Connas' vote; II ii 92 In tuneless company the lark can sing; II iii 23 A mere cypher; II iii 79 Shreds and tatters; II iv 2 A shadow of smoke; II iv 8 To wipe one's nose on one's forearm; II iv 38 A shadow on the wall; II iv 67 To bid one go hang; II iv 68 To show the middle finger; II iv 69 To pull by the beard; II v 10 To cut a man's throat with a leaden sword; II v 79 A tragedy king; II vi 30 More ignorant than Philonides; II vi 45 Do not despise a country speaker; II vi 47 A chickpea Bacchus; II vii 1 Hercules eating apples; II vii 48 A hungry ass does not notice the stick; II vii 90 A flash in the pan; II viii 9 O that I always had such enemies; II viii 27 You owe your blue blood to your purse; II viii 42 To tear in pieces like a shell-fish; II viii 62 A Locrian ox; II viii 63 A figwood sword; II viii 64 A fig to Mercury; II viii 89 A three-letter man; II viii 96 To feed the worms; II viii 98 Laconian spurge; II viii 100 More than a tortoise minds a fly; II ix 2 I wouldn't give four obols for it; II ix 22 Slave city; II ix 28 A party of lazybones; II ix 46 A worn-out brain; II x 5 An abominable dung-beetle; II x 30 Hercules and the apple; II x 89 Greens on the table; III i 29 The heaviest anvil has no fear of noise; III i 67 Bought off the block; III i 76 These things trouble me less than frogs in the marsh; III ii 12 Worth a shell; III ii 45 Shades of a dung-beetle; III ii 52 An ox of the Homolottians; III ii 59 An ass can stand the rain; III ii 65 An eagle does not hunt flies; III ii 94 What use are rotten onions?; III iii 12 Before this, I thought you had horns; III iii 18 The crow irritates the eagle; (III iii 18 CWE 34 288) Nothing to him, either bad or good; III iii 49 He did not help even with earth; III v 22 A threadbare present; III v 26 A buyer of chickpeas; III v 54 Small value even for an obol; (III v 54 CWE 35 99) Two-farthing types; III v 82 A Sicilian soldier; III vi 45 To challenge with the little finger; III vi 73 An earthenware god; III vi 94 Gifts of a Calabrian host; III vi 97 A Carian goat; III vii 52 Not a lead penny; III vii 67 Not even a head of garlic; III vii 75 Not even a drop; III vii 80 Belonging on the lowest bench; III viii 21 For one who is not troubled by mockery; III viii 50 Not worthy to look me in the eye; III viii 54 Of a man who despises his enemy; IV i 5 Woodcock; IV i 23 A dog living on breadcrumb; IV i 51 Snatching a dinner out of the fire; IV i 66 Not worth a tiddler; IV i 72 As useless as a catfish, IV ii 55 You are not exactly shaking everything; IV ii 79 Droopy head; IV iii 23 Haggling brings no money; IV iii 43 I have no interest in asses; IV iii 55 Each is both; IV iii 100 I knew this before Theognis was born; IV iv 29 Cecides and the Buphonia; IV iv 41 Couches of Soterichus; IV iv 75 You be hanged, Papiria; IV iv 99 What you do not need to have is dear at a penny; IV v 42 Worth as little as monkeys; IV vi 18 Not worth harvesting; IV vii 17 Worth not even the snap of a finger; IV vii 95 Barbaric filth; IV viii 3 A tinker's cuss; IV viii 48 Like carriers of mortar; IV viii 55 An itinerant priest of Mithras, no Torchbearer; IV viii 83

Smoke; IV ix 1 To knock down for a penny; IV ix 33 Twopenny fellows (see also III v 54 CWE 35 99); IV x 5 Worth a penny; IV x 22 Gob-hawkers; IV x 98 A rotten mushroom; V i 9 A lead penny; V i 17 An empty acorn; V i 21 No more than a dog; V i 37 He is nothing, or cares for nothing

[100] Rank that is deserved (*Dignitatis*) I iii 42 A pillar of the household; (I viii 13 CWE 32 133) A physician is the equivalent of many other men; I viii 14 He deserves an obelisk; (I viii 15 CWE 32 134) Give him a golden beard; I viii 16 Worth everything (also at I viii 13 CWE 32 133); I viii 17 Worthy of the shield at Argos; I viii 18 Worth breaking bail for; I viii 23 A man with whom you could play morra in the dark; (I viii 23 CWE 32 137) A man you can trust even when he is not on oath; I viii 90 Eighth of the Sages; II i 93 Battus' silphium; II iv 15 He fills both pages; II vi 3 The dog is worthy of his dinner; II vi 4 The bitch is worthy of her basket; II ix 25 A kingly cow; III iv 16 An ox in the city; III viii 48 Life comes before all else; III viii 93 To each according to his status; IV i 22 The prize will be the Thessalian mare; IV i 54 Worthy of cedar; IV i 63 Glaucus has eaten grass and lives in the sea; IV ii 86 Do your job as steward; IV ii 89 Jupiter chose the eagle; IV iii 18 You want a crown of myrtle; IV iii 21 As old as Codrus; IV v 47 The blind and the lame will not enter the temple; IV vii 69 A Roscius; V i 51 Hold first place

[101] One should make use of what one has (*Proximis utendum*) I viii 43 As best we can, since as we would we may not (also at III vi 4 CWE 35 126, IV ii 43 CWE 35 526); II iii 44 Let him be a flute-player who could not play the lyre; II iv 61 After bread barley-cake too is no bad thing; II iv 62 Those who have no meat must make do with salt fish; II viii 4 If you cannot drive an ox, drive an ass; II ix 33 Take your present fortune in good part; III ii 91 Milk the one that's handy, why pursue him that runs away?; III iv 71 The next best way to sail; III x 34 Accept things as they are in good part (also at IV ii 43 CWE 35 526); IV ii 43 What is given . . .; IV v 46 The finishing line; V i 40 What you're given

[102] Unreliability, treachery, deceitfulness (*Inconstantiae, perfidiae, versutiae*) I i 93 Adopt the outlook of the polyp; I i 94 As versatile as a buskin; (I i 94 CWE 31 136) *Cothurnus*; (I i 94 CWE 31 137 and also I vii 2 CWE 32 68) Double-faced or *alloprosallos*; I i 95 As variable as the hydra; I iii 10 A trick of the Thessalians; I v 18 The fox knows many things, but the hedgehog one big thing; I vii 2 To sit on two stools; I vii 3 To whitewash two walls out of the same bucket; (I vii 3 CWE 32 68) To serve two masters; I vii 4 To make two sons-in-law of one daughter; I viii 27 On Greek credit; I viii 28 Punic faith; I viii 30 Out of one mouth to blow hot and cold; (I viii 30 CWE 32 140) Dodonaean spring; (I viii 30 CWE 32 140) To play two notes together low and high (*magadizein*); I ix 62 Man's a Euripus; I x 28 A Thracian stratagem; I x 31 No monkey was ever caught in a trap; II ii 9 From Ceos he, not Chios; II ii 74 As many shapes as Proteus; II iii 62 The works of Daedalus; II iv 66 He shams death like a leopard; II v 33 Locrian loyalty; II v 34 The Cassius knot; II v 41 My tongue did swear it; II v 69 Where the wind lies; II v 70 A field for the wind; II vi 57 The Egyptians have a wonderful gift for weaving webs; II vi 89 The Thracians do not know the rules; (II vii 18 CWE 34 12) Megarian tricks; II vii 54 A devious course; II vii 81 He who knows not the way to the sea, etc.; II viii 79

An invention worthy of Ulysses; II viii 82 He knows by what roads Eucrates escaped; II ix 47 Panagaean Diana; II x 23 You need great knowledge, if you would deceive God with it; III i 11 Up to a dozen tricks; III i 12 Double men; III i 62 Right foot in a sandal, left foot in a basin; III ii 15 A flea in its place; III ii 67 To break treaties like the Parians; III iii 5 One of Pyrrhander's tricks; III iii 56 One thing on his feet and another sitting down; (III iii 56 CWE 34 300) To stand on either foot; III iii 70 As changeable as Metra, Erisichthon's daughter; III iv 1 As changeable as a chameleon; (III iv 1 CWE 35 3) Like Proteus; III iv 3 To drink from a cup with a hole in it; III iv 42 This shoe was stitched by Histiaeus, Aristagoras put it on; III iv 82 A big mover in a little affair; III v 39 To talk Egyptian; III v 56 Phoenicians' bargains; III v 81 If the lion's skin is not enough, a fox's must be added; (III v 81 CWE 35 114) A fox-dog; III v 87 Leucaeus and his writings are not the same; III vi 51 Heart of a woman; III vi 84 Wavering both ways in his opinion; (III vi 84 CWE 35 167) He totters on his feet; III vii 8 An African beast; III vii 9 Africa always produces something evil; III vii 10 Africa always produces something novel; III vii 25 The wiles of Sisyphus; III vii 31 For those who hold to neither altar nor oath; III vii 37 When the polecat flees it makes a dreadful smell; III vii 48 It's useful to have several names; III viii 24 Conflicting loyalties; III x 64 Lies that sound like truth; IV i 34 Lampon swears by a gander; IV ii 77 A fleeting oath; IV iv 43 Spinning tales like a spider; IV iv 74 He carries water in one hand, etc.; IV v 45 From the toga to the pallium; IV vi 29 As temperamental as the sea; IV vi 65 Cork-man; IV viii 9 Now in pallium, now in toga; IV viii 27 Like a whipping-top; IV ix 14 Nothing dries faster than a tear; IV ix 36 A bat; V i

41 A chimaera; v i 43 Abandon one's position

[103] **Change of mind** (*Mutandae sententiae*) I v 55 To take back a move (or counter); I ix 59 To sing a palinode; I ix 60 To turn one's sails about. To pull in the rope; III viii 97 Change your plan for a better one; III ix 5 Censuring what we think; IV i 98 I shall imitate the crab; IV ix 75 Put the counter back

[104] **Change in a way of living** (*Mutati instituti*) I v 35 To leave the nuts behind; II iii 4 He bade a long farewell; II iv 96 From the lime-kiln to the charcoal-burner's fire; II v 93 From Dorian to Phrygian; III iii 32 He has changed rigging and oars for arms; III iv 85 Instead of an elegant physician, a bad poet; III v 11 Since you are a seaman, don't try to become a landsman; III x 32 A different face; IV iv 47 Ulysses has stripped off his rags; IV iv 48 Suddenly another person; IV v 27 To good harvests; IV v 40 He who did great harm as an enemy; IV v 45 From the toga to the pallium; IV ix 43 Circean cup

[105] **Change of fortune** (*Fortunae commutatio*) I i 83 Dionysius in Corinth; I ii 36 The dénouement of the play; I vii 63 All things do change; (I vii 63 CWE 32 105) Man's life (is) a wheel; (I vii 63 CWE 32 105) Turncoat victory; I viii 45 When you are not the man you were, why wish to go on living?; I viii 64 One day's a stepmother and one's a mother; I viii 65 So Jove now rains, now shines in cloudless sky; I ix 5 To his old manger; I ix 6 Change your life and change your style; II i 51 The turning of a potsherd; II iv 29 No mortal man is wise at all times; III i 78 Laughter and tears come by the will of God; III iv 86 From the oar to the bench; III vi 2 There is activity in our market; III vi 20 I am Pitana; III vi 69 Fortune is

like a tidal channel; III ix 72 All things do change; IV i 99 What one cook has seasoned I shall season in another way; IV iv 9 There's many a wheel to turn; IV iv 80 An Osculan battle; IV v 7 Time is good for no one; IV v 28 To pass down from hand to hand; IV v 29 From hand to hand (also II viii 8 CWE 34 52); IV vii 12 A flower is but ash; IV vii 49 Mars is on everyone's side (also I vii 63 CWE 32 104); IV viii 30 Between the hand and the chin; IV x 19 Lady Luck, ruler of the hustings; v i 45 Much in between; v ii 34 Shame it is for those well-born shamefully to live

[106] **Temperance** (*Temperantia*) I x 83 As temperate as Zeno; IV ix 61 Philosophizing

[107] **Intemperance, lust** (*Intemperantia, libido*) I i 4 Gardens of Adonis; I vi 11 Like Bacelus; I vi 12 Batalus; (I vi 12 CWE 32 11) To follow a scandalous and effeminate way of life or *batalizesthai*; I viii 33 Munching mastic; (I viii 33 CWE 32 142) Mastic-munchers or *schoinotrôges*; I viii 34 He scratches his head with a single finger; I viii 35 To scratch one's head with the tip of one's finger; II ii 79 Underarm actions; II iii 34 You live the life of a flute-player; II iv 63 Agathon's tune; II vi 94 A Lydian at noon; II vi 95 A goatherd in the heat; II vi 96 The Lydian is a shopkeeper; II vii 38 Farewell, beloved light; II ix 23 The flowers of Samos; II ix 69 A wooer's life; II x 9 You anoint yourself with honey; II x 18 Here there and everywhere, the randy dog will find his pair; II x 37 In Lydian fashion; II x 43 Fit for Lesbians; III i 94 To go a-horsing; III ii 18 To touch the clitoris; III ii 22 I spy Cleisthenes; III ii 23 Cleocritus; III ii 40 To play the Chalcidian; III ii 41 To 'phicidize'; III ii 99 You behave like Sinope; III iii 9 To try one's wings; III iii 94 To wear a wig; III v 85 To give a Siphnian wave;

III vi 39 A Myconian neighbour; III vi 92 A ram frisking with its horns; III vii 23 A pig among the roses; III vii 27 A Sardanapalus; III vii 70 To behave like a Lesbian; III vii 84 The Laura at Samos; III vii 88 A long-haired Samian; III vii 91 You seem like a Corinthian woman; III x 26 Abominable pleasures; III x 99 You're from Massilia; IV i 77 I think you are a lambda; IV i 81 Watermelons; IV ii 24 Circumcised up to the neck; IV iii 68 To play the Corinthian; IV iv 53 Those who carry their own oil-flask; (IV iv 53 CWE 36 98) Water poured over your hands

[108] Moderation and temperance (*Modestia modusque*) I ii 91 The most delightful sailing is by land, and walking by the sea; I v 3 Run away, but not beyond the house; I v 67 To stretch the rope till it breaks; (I v 67 CWE 31 445) Blow your nose too hard and you'll make it bleed; (I v 67 CWE 31 445) Oft-wounded patience will to madness turn; (I v 67 CWE 31 445) A kind heart wounded makes for deeper rage; I vi 86 To venture down into oneself; I vi 87 Be your own lodger; (I vi 87 CWE 32 58) To live in one's own house; I vi 88 Live up to your own harvest; I vi 92 Keep inside your own skin; I vi 94 Spit into your own bosom; (I vi 94 CWE 32 62) To men with face thrice wiped god gives good luck; I vi 95 Know thyself; I vi 96 Nothing to excess; I vii 32 An Arabian piper; I vii 62 We build the walls we can afford; I vii 64 Variety's the spice of life; I ix 95 The half is more than the whole; II iii 25 Grasp the summit, and halfway will be yours; II iii 26 Ask an unfair share to get a fair share; II v 46 Let not the shoe be too big for the foot; II ix 48 Rufillus reeks of lozenges, Gorgonius of he-goat; III i 52 Sow with the hand and not with the whole sack; III vii 4 Nothing pays less well than really good farming; III x 3 Coming down to

the level of others; IV iii 14 Don't ruin the music; IV iv 22 Neither worst nor first; IV iv 24 Give orders to those you have fed; IV iv 97 Neither Lydian black-puddings; IV v 3 A good home; IV v 77 The bow breaks if strung too tight; IV v 89 The land should be more feeble; V i 32 Take in one's sails

[109] Arrogance and boastfulness (*Arrogantia iactantiaque*) I ii 74 Haughty Maximus; I vi 16 Let the cobbler stick to his last; (I vi 88 CWE 32 58) Beggar-bully; I vi 89 Measure yourself by your own foot; I vi 93 To spread wings greater than the nest; I viii 49 To raise the brows, to relax the brows; I viii 68 To lift one's horns; I viii 69 To raise one's crest; I x 19 An Athenian entering harbour; II i 49 To make many things out of one; II ii 16 To walk on tiptoe; II ii 67 Sybarites in the streets; II iii 30 Sophocleses, Laodiceans; II iv 6 He affrights the sky; II v 12 Not to be my own Suffenus; II v 87 He said himself; II vi 20 Good wine needs no bush; II vi 71 A bumbling man; II vii 76 Jove's sandal; II viii 26 He is as pleased with himself as Peleus with his sword; II viii 41 He gives himself such airs, he might have stolen the shield from Argos; II ix 98 To have a warship look; III ii 69 Wagon-loads; III iii 16 When gold speaks, no words have any force; III iii 28 Here's Rhodes: let's see you jump; III iii 95 Full of grasshoppers; III iv 15 You will seem, when you see me, to see Mars himself; III iv 19 You come straight out of the Academy; III iv 52 The ignorant man who has just put on trousers shows them off to everyone; III v 37 The doors of Phanias; III v 46 To pluck from the lung; III v 62 To have tastes beyond one's wallet; III vi 98 Trifles and bubbles; III x 37 Intolerable arrogance; III x 93 The pride of the giants; IV i 26 Marching in the Iunonium; IV i 31 Calliphanes; IV i 80 Caeneus' spear;

IV iii 67 To touch the heavens with your finger; IV iv 25 A cock has most power on its own dunghill; IV iv 28 To act like Sellus; IV v 30 Wondrous words about a lentil; IV v 35 I except the gods; IV v 94 To make a citadel out of a sewer; IV vi 21 Let the man live; IV vii 10 Sybaritic style; IV viii 14 Campanian arrogance; IV ix 6 A fine thing to have upon one's tomb; IV ix 24 The goddess thought of it; IV ix 54 Every tenth one; IV ix 55 A crowning deed; IV ix 66 Ribaldry; IV ix 87 To look for the sprig of bay in the must-cake; IV x 18 Campanian curtains; IV x 35 Talk Aexonian; IV x 42 Flask-rich; v i 10 Right royal doings; v i 50 Higher than Oromedon

[110] Preoccupation with self (*Philautia*) I i 81 He has hay on his horn; I ii 15 What is one's own is beautiful; I ii 16 The smoke of home, brighter than others' fires; I iii 92 Self-lovers; (I v 62 CWE 31 442) Having a proud and lofty ear; (I v 62 CWE 31 442) To sell oil; I v 63 To carry oil in the ear; I vi 90 We see not what is in the wallet behind; I vi 91 To cast a mote out of another man's eye; (I vi 91 CWE 32 60) Who his friend's pardon for his boils demands, / 'Tis fair that his friend's warts he should forgive; II i 13 Colophonian wantonness; II i 17 To love without a rival; II ii 52 Do not talk big; II iii 13 The springs of silver; II iv 100 That is how they like it; II v 39 To use tragic language; II vii 59 You praise yourself; II ix 91 Not even as far as the porch; II x 26 Many will hate you if you love yourself; III iii 85 He traces his line from the Eteobutadae; III iv 2 Everyone thinks his own fart smells sweet; III v 51 Blow-me-down Myxus!; III vi 90 He's imitating his tragic friends; III vii 34 To fart frank-incense; III ix 46 Boasting is ignoble; III ix 92 Good luck makes people arrogant; III x 2 Everyone rejoices in his own pursuit; IV ii 83 Looking coy in his

armour; IV ii 90 Less ambition or more strength; IV iii 27 Have a good look at yourself; IV iii 64 Lying atraphaxis; IV iv 14 And my mother said I was better than Pollux; IV vii 16 Our wish is for what is holy; IV viii 58 What anyone does himself

[111] Opposite of preoccupation with self (*Contrarium philautiae*) III iii 6 Unenvied wealth; IV v 4 He is not happy who does not know it

[112] Gentleness (*Mansuetudo*) I vii 35 As smooth as oil; I vii 36 As soft as the tip of the ear; I vii 37 As soft, or As ripe, as a pear; I vii 38 As soft as a sponge; (I vii 38 CWE 32 90) As soft as a pumpkin; (I vii 38 CWE 32 90) As mild as mallow; (I vii 38 CWE 32 90) As soft as any fancy-boy; II v 64 Gentler than a tested sacrifice; III ii 33 As pliable as wax; III v 78 A sitting dove; III vi 48 As gentle as a dove

[113] Harshness, captiousness (*Asperitas, morositas*) I vi 46 Weariness loves a wrangle; I vii 44 Hard as iron, Tough as bronze; I vii 45 Heart-strings of horn; II iii 35 Scythian language; II iv 42 Corinth is hilly here and hollow there; II iv 81 Rougher than an urchin; II v 63 Agamemnon's victim; II ix 59 A sea-urchin is rough all over; III i 56 A formidable man; III ii 83 As prickly as a snake's slough; III iii 74 Stir not a twig; III iv 33 Deaf to entreaty; III viii 44; III x 72 Unbending; IV i 9 An Artemon, going the rounds; (IV i 9 CWE 35 446) Shuffler or *peritrimma*; (IV i 9 CWE 35 447) A man carried about, or *periphorêtos*; IV i 49 Pandeletian maxims; IV ii 100 Even the oak dances for Bacchus; IV iii 12 Matioloechus; IV iii 91 Horn-struck; IV iv 49 Unyielding and implacable; IV v 13 Living on savory; IV ix 85 An evil Scythian; v i 81 All-spiny

on quails; III vii 11 An African bird;
III ix 51 On sumptuous displays; IV vii
53 Jove's milk; IV viii 41 Live on hare-
pie; IV x 81 Not from Hymettus; V i 6
A dinner for the people

[119] **Hunger (*Fames*)** I iii 23 The grey
mullet is fasting; II viii 60 Hunger and
waiting fill the nose with bile; III vi 43
Nothing worse than death by starvation; III vii 44 You can think better on a
full stomach; III viii 12 Don't hinder a
hungry man; III x 9 The belly is a trou-
blesome heckler; IV ii 98 You would eat
even the *baetylus*; IV viii 32 Jaws

[120] **Haste, etc. (*Festinationis, etc.*)** I
ii 42 To put wings on one's feet; I iv
17 With sail and horse; I iv 19 With
ships and chariots; I iv 20 With swift
chariots, with the chariots of Jove; I iv
21 To lead the way with white horses; I
vi 35 To put your best foot first; (I vi 35
CWE 32 27) With two helms; I ix 65 Sow
early and be often sorry, sow late and
always lose; I ix 80 Like a dog drinking
out of the Nile; I x 38 But the man who
runs away won't stop to hear the fiddler
play; II ii 12 Whitebait on the fire; II
ii 85 To be at the door; II v 50 It may
be too cunning this way; II vi 92 As
fast as Butes; II vi 98 A drink snatched
from the wolves; II vii 30 A girl has a
baby, even if she consorts badly with
her husband; II viii 83 It's alive, kindle
the fire; II ix 72 No sooner said than
done; (II ix 72 CWE 34 117) With the
shout; II x 71 Before the seventh; II x 82
Fire on the hand; III ii 87 From a ship as
she enters the harbour; III iii 4 A ship
of Salamis; (III iv 71 CWE 35 45) Neither
oars nor winds; III vii 5 As quick as
boiled asparagus; III vii 66 Before the
cock crows twice; III viii 88 As swift as
a hawk; III ix 47 He who acts first wins;
III ix 48 Perform sacred rites promptly;
IV ii 46 As fast as Pegasus; IV vi 22 On
the spot; IV vii 87 To run faster than

Crison of Himera; IV vii 89 As fast as
your feet can carry you; IV viii 95 Wear
someone else's slippers

[121] **Excessive haste (*Festinatio praepropera*)** I vii 55 You triumph before
the victory; I x 100 You wear out your
greatcoat in summer; II i 1 Make haste
slowly; II ii 35 The hasty bitch brings
forth blind whelps; II v 13 A Sicilian
picking unripe grapes; III i 97 To exalt one's dish beyond lentils; III ii 70 To
mow the moss; (III iii 10 CWE 34 285)
Sooner than your beard; (III iii 10 CWE
34 285) A beardless youth teaches a
man older than himself; III iii 86 Erginus' white hairs; (III iii 86 CWE 34 311)
The yearning lover grows old in one
day; III v 60 More haste less speed; IV
i 100 I hate striplings who are precociously wise; (IV i 100 CWE 35 502) A
grown-up child; IV v 55 The end is not
immediately in sight; V i 2 Quicker than
ants move poppy-seed, V i 23 Orange
of Daedalus

[122] **Slowness and taking one's time
(*Tarditatis et cunctationis*)** I iii 60
Between the slaying and the offering;
I v 85 The moon of Acessaeus; (I v 85
CWE 31 458) At full moon; I v 86 When
lightning strikes through Harma; I vi
43 Callipides; I vi 78 The last of the
Mysians on a voyage; I viii 95 To pull
out the mare's tail slowly hair by hair;
I ix 11 Elephants breed faster; (I ix 52
CWE 34 110) You have come too late for
the feast; I x 29 Rome wins by sitting
still; II i 1 Make haste slowly; II i 2 One
step at a time; II i 3 Slowly the ox, II i
4 With silent foot; II v 4 Years ago; II
v 25 Spartan moons; II vi 73 Bunas is
the judge; II vii 74 Amaea has found
Azesia; II ix 52 That's the way to take
part in a battle, when it's all over; II x
61 Hyperberetaean; III i 17 To bring up
the artillery when the war is over; III
i 52 Sow with the hand and not with

the whole sack; III ii 3 A crow in search of water; III iv 8 Nobody is chasing us; III iv 34 Gone to the Apaturia; III iv 55 Time kills hunger and is the best way to overcome it; III iv 80 You can expect grass sometime, ox; III iv 81 Old woman, wait; III vii 63 A Dusk-dinner, and similar expressions; (III vii 63 CWE 35 254) Dinner-chasers; (III vii 63 CWE 35 255) Dinner-devotees; III vii 83 At the altars; III viii 10 Rewards coming late, but generously; III viii 46 Not to be resolved at once; IV i 29 Being a host to Hercules; IV ii 75 Take a long time to think; IV iii 66 To walk on tiptoe; IV iii 97 You have come too late; IV v 38 A sea-lung would have come more quickly; IV v 84 Cuckoo!; IV vi 23 Whoever comes late to a dinner . . .; IV viii 82 Hang about like Nicias; IV x 97 Agones; V i 22 Stilt-walk or tortoise walk

[123] **Healthy living (*Salubritas*)** II iv 43 Healthier than Croton; II viii 86 To be as fit as a pancratiast; III i 77 Healthier than a pumpkin; IV iv 64 The most wholesome three; IV iv 93 You are as healthy as a fish

[124] **Unhealthy living (*Insalubritas*)** I ii 94 Unwilling to die before his time; II iv 26 Hercules' itch; II iv 27 Hercules' disease; II vi 37 Old age is sickness of itself; II x 59 To visit the Isthmian games; III i 93 And children's children; IV ix 42 The Maenian Column

[125] **What is long-lasting (*Diuturnum*)** III i 93 And children's children; IV ix 42 The Maenian Column

[126] **Legacy-seekers (*Haeredipetae*)** I vii 14 If you're a vulture, wait for your carcase; III viii 99 Mouths agape for the same will

[127] **Old age that is premature or death (*Senium praematurum, aut mors*)**

III iii 86 Erginus' white hairs; (III iii 86 CWE 34 311) The yearning lover grows old in one day; III viii 100 Early death; III x 62 Misfortunes hasten age; IV viii 28 Better provoke a dog than an old woman

[128] **Living to a great age (*Longaevitas*)** I ii 59 Be old early; I v 37 To throw the sexagenarians off the bridge; I vi 64 As long-lived as the crows; I vi 65 The old age of Tithonus; I vi 66 As old as Nestor; I vi 67 He outlives his allotted span; I x 77 Accius and Titius take alike; II i 52 To have one foot in Charon's boat; II i 57 Living longer than the phoenix; II iv 3 A living corpse. A living sepulchre; II vi 15 To the old man his jaws are a crutch; II vii 9 Your years are counted in your face; II vii 61 The old age of Hesiod; II viii 67 An old man's skull is as dry as raisins; II ix 16 No mourning for an aged ox; II x 46 The threshold of old age; III i 39 Beyond the thread spun; III ii 100 Length of time wears the marble; III iv 22 The ox is getting old; III v 61 Beyond the count; III vii 96 A copper; III ix 40 His allotted span fulfilled; III ix 43 Death snatches away the best and leaves the worst; III x 22 The weakness of old age; III x 62 Misfortunes hasten age; IV i 50 More long-lived than the Sibyl; IV ii 68 Only in Sparta does it pay to grow old; IV ii 76 Epimenides' skin

[129] **Youth (*Iuventa*)** III viii 66 Youth abounds in physical strength; IV i 83 Behaving like an adolescent

[130] **The wretchedness and brevity of human life (*Vita hominis misera et brevis*)** II i 9 For half their lives there is no difference between the happy and the unhappy; II ii 69 Brief span of life; II ii 70 A point of time; II iii 48 Man is but a bubble; II iii 49 Not to be born is best; II ix 65 An old man is but chaff;

the rancours of the powerful; III x 95 One strong man meets another who is stronger; IV i 10 Placiadae; IV i 28 He's got it!; IV ii 22 A dog getting angry with the stone; IV ii 30 The whole load on your back, Lepargus; IV iii 63 Paying for the weaver's mistake; IV iv 82 The gods' mill grinds slow; IV iv 92 Sweet is the apple that has no guard; IV vii 66 To pay off both principal and interest; V i 39 The first to wound; V i 52 Bite off an ear

[143] **Fear of punishment (***Metus poenae***)** I ii 67 They flee from the reddened cord; I iii 19 Hands off the picture; III iv 61 Never walk without a staff; III ix 31 Fear of disgrace; III ix 64 Beware in good time of the penalty for wrongdoing; (IV i 9 CWE 35 446) Shuffler, or *peritrimma*; IV i 89 You fear the punishments of the Samians; IV i 93 The cautious wolf goes in fear, and so on; IV x 56 Show the sole of one's foot

[144] **Inappropriate to the matter at hand (***Aliena a re***)** I iii 80 When I am dead the earth can burn up; I v 44 It touches neither heaven nor earth; I v 45 Nothing to do with the verse; I v 46 Nothing to do with the lyre; I vi 82 The sowing and reaping there are none of mine; I x 93 To overleap the pit; II ii 10 Beyond the olive-trees; II ii 14 The door is never barred; II ii 49 Sickles I asked for; II iii 22 Fallen from his chariot; II iv 57 What has this to do with Bacchus?; II vi 67 To dance outside the ring; III i 15 Menecles tells one story and the pig another; III ii 92 What's that to Mercury?; III ii 96 I twine my ivy-clusters; III iv 35 I talk to you about garlic, and you answer about onions; III iv 50 You let go the brace and run after the sheet; III vi 31 How does that help with daily bread?; III ix 41 Misfortunes need healing not mourning; III x 33 Nothing to do with the subject; IV iv 86 Ride your horse close to the turning

point; IV v 30 Wondrous words about a lentil; IV viii 89 Politics is not for the man of culture; IV x 17 Dance off; V i 20 Comic characters in a tragedy

[145] **Concern with other people's affairs (***Aliena curantis***)** I vi 69 The things that are above us are nothing to us; I vi 85 The good or ill that's wrought in our own halls; II ii 51 To set foot in other men's dances; II ix 1 As big a fool as Morychus; III iii 11 War shall be Conon's business; III vii 7 Use a cart and you won't have to worry about asses; III viii 75 Don't contend in other people's business

[146] **Germane to the matter at hand (***Ad rem pertinentia***)** I vi 85 The good or ill that's wrought in our own halls; II iv 93 You have touched the issue with a needle-point; II ix 79 Now I've arrived; II x 60 It's his own business; III iii 21 You have touched the very threshold of the door; III vii 42 The tongue is cut out separately; III ix 30 Trifling aside, let's put it to the test; IV v 39 To put foot to foot

[147] **Harassment (***Lacessentis***)** I i 60 To stir up hornets; I iv 29 At close quarters and at long range; I vi 79 To touch on a sore place; II iii 12 He sends out a ram; II vi 90 Spearing tunny-fish; II vii 97 For they have never driven off my cows nor yet my horses; III i 21 Punching and kicking; III vi 83 Let a sleeping drunk lie; III viii 29 Attack with every effort; IV ii 26 I shall not be the first to strike, but I shall repay an insult; IV vii 91 As the wolf loves the sheep

[148] **Setting traps (***Insidiae***)** II v 73 To dangle the bait before men; II viii 88 To cast a spear; III iii 67 Every lark must have one; (III v 78 CWE 35 112) A decoy, or *paleutria*; III viii 3 Of someone wary of hidden treachery; IV ii 1 A wooden

horse; IV ii 4 To lay deep foundations; IV v 22 It's a fine thing to deceive a fox; IV v 70 To lure into the snare; IV v 71 To go after food from a snare; IV vi 92 A dog to food; IV vii 61 To assail with tunnels

[149] Drawing conclusions from partial evidence (*Coniecturae*) I ii 78 From one learn all; I v 57 To mark with stars. To brand with an obelus; I vi 50 As the man is, so it his talk; I vii 94 One swallow does not make a summer; (I vii 94 CWE 32 124) To need many swallows; (I vii 94 CWE 32 124) One man does not make a commonwealth; I ix 34 To know a lion by his claws; I ix 35 The fox is given away by his brush; I ix 36 I judge the fabric from its border; I ix 37 I know by the taste; I ix 38 I judge an Ethiopian by his face; I ix 39 I know the tree by its fruit; I ix 85 To know by sight; I ix 88 At first sight. On the face of it; I x 8 To divine by a sieve; I x 30 To hit the target; I x 41 To judge by the stubble; I x 48 To draw a home-grown conclusion; II iii 78 He who guesses right is the prophet; II iv 4 To see on the face of it; II iv 93 You have touched the issue with a needle-point; II ix 10 Womanish men's language is womanish too; III iii 35 An omen good or else bad; III iv 91 You may say nothing, but it shows from your face; III v 42 To go by the stars; III vi 40 Seeing the dead; III vi 58 To see a lion portends battles with the enemy; III ix 36 Appearance tells you if a man is good; III ix 61 Empty guesses; III ix 62 I foresee it for certain; IV i 18 If you dream that you die, you will be free of your cares; IV ii 3 To guess from the stalk what the grain was like; IV ii 13 Fruitful plants show it straightaway; IV ii 18 To investigate every trace; IV ii 21 The bird can be told by its song; IV ii 47 You will prove it by the sound

[150] Captiousness (*Calumnia*) II ii 13 A penalty for turds; II iii 81 A Syco-

phant; II vi 29 Against a blackmailer's bite there's no known remedy; II vi 35 Hopeless against Hercules; III i 33 A worse blackmailer than Pattaecion; III ii 14 He owes a penalty for abuse; III iv 11 Argive accusation; III vii 18 They use a white net to hunt for other people's goods; IV i 33 A basinful of disputes; IV ii 38 A Chian; IV iii 39 Theocrines, the tragic actor; IV vi 15 Samian ways; IV vi 17 Abydenians; IV ix 23 Some fellow-townsman or a neighbour brought the news; IV ix 82 A sneer without foundation

[151] Disparagement and slander (*Obtrectatio et maledicentia*) I i 5 To flee after planting the dart; I ii 53 To wrestle with ghosts; I ii 54 To cut a dead man's throat; I iv 6 I'll paint you in your own colours; I vii 16 To croak; I vii 74 Cartloads of abuse; I viii 67 Shiploads of abuse; II ii 55 To be gnawed with Theon's tooth; II ii 56 A testimonial in Hipponax' vein; II ii 57 Archilochian edicts; II ii 58 Archilochus' native land; II ii 59 To gnaw with one's cheek-tooth; II ii 84 Sooner criticized than imitated; II iii 56 I will not attack with my tongue; II iv 80 To gnaw dogskin; II v 8 Zoilus and his like; II vi 19 A captious critic; III i 85 The bite of an asp; III i 99 To throw the ball from one to another; III vi 41 Dead men do not bite; III vi 87 Document with teeth; III x 10 Ordinary people are suspicious; III x 69 Do not insult the dead; III x 90 Wearing out Archilochus; IV i 30 Even in the assembly of the gods; IV ii 92 A porcupine's spine

[152] Undefended case (*Causa indefensa*) I v 80 Case undefended; (I v 80 CWE 31 453) To win by default; (I v 80 CWE 31 454) *Erêmodikia* 'judgments by default'; II ii 17 You will not gather the vintage without paying for it; II x 92 A one-sided case; III i 50 Judge not a cause

[153] Self-criticism (*Carpentis seipsum*) I vi 49 To speak ill of one's own good things; I vi 84 To cut down one's own vineyards; III x 1 Where have I transgressed?

[154] Necessity (*Necessitas*) I iii 14 What can't be cured, must be endured; I ix 4 To have Diomede on your track; II iii 32 God will be there whether you summon him or not; II iii 40 Necessity's a mighty weapon; II iii 72 What's done cannot be undone; II viii 92 To drive off course; II ix 57 The besieged find all things edible; III ii 82 An imported, or imposed, oath; III v 65 A hungry man must needs be a thief; III vi 54 To a starving hare even cakes are fig; III viii 16 Put it down to fate; III viii 47 No one may be forced to be a friend; III ix 11 One who falls silent; III ix 12 Death is the common lot; III ix 49 Not even the gods free us from death; III ix 53 Destiny cannot be changed; III ix 86 Destiny is unavoidable; III ix 87 Driven by fate; III x 35 Do not place an obligation on someone who does not want it; IV i 27 Lead a willing ox; IV vii 55 Necessity is a teacher; IV ix 26 Necessity is disagreeable; IV ix 65 Break bail; IV x 37 Compelling reason

[155] Sadness and joy (*Tristitia et laetitia*) I i 2 (Pythagoras) CWE 31 36 Do not wear a tight-fitting ring; I i 2 (Pythagoras) CWE 31 37 Do not eat your heart out; I vii 77 He has consulted the oracle in Trophonius' cave; I viii 48 To smooth the forehead. To wrinkle the forehead; I ix 41 Areopagite; II ii 1 Depressing dispatch; II iv 39 Don't play the wise old uncle to me. As full of wise saws as an uncle; II iv 65 To weep tears of blood; II v 40 To have that tragic look; II v 62 The laughless rock; II vi 22 Admetus' dirge; II vi 88 A titanic glare; II vii 92 The eyes of Atreus; II x 93 The Harmodius song;

III ii 38 To eat, or to sniff, onions; III iii 2 More of an old sailor than Saron; III iv 10 Sing the song of Telamon; III iv 75 You are singing the Lityerses; III v 71 Contracting the brow, inflating the cheeks; III vii 47 To glare like a bull; III vii 73 As happy as someone casting off old age; III ix 73 Lively conversation; IV i 2 You are seeing Argives; IV ii 78 You have been beaten by some gamecock; IV ii 95 A fury from tragedy; IV v 53 The mind lives in the ears; IV v 74 To live on mustard; IV ix 12 Raise hands on high; IV ix 78 To change one's clothes; IV x 79 Not even if to Jove's temple

[156] Anxiousness (*Solicitudo*) I i 2 (Pythagoras) CWE 31 36 Do not wear a tight-fitting ring; I i 2 (Pythagoras) CWE 31 37 Do not eat your heart out; I i 2 (Pythagoras) CWE 31 47 Do not cut up logs on the road; II ii 18 My mind is on hides (also III vii 30); II ii 19 He has hides before his eyes; II ix 7 The Rock of Tantalus; IV ii 8 They look like captives from Pylos

[157] Good News (*Nuntius laetus*) II v 75 You have it from Vulcan's mouth; II viii 5 A bee foretells a stranger and a wasp foretells a friend; II viii 16 What tune has Apollo played for you?; III i 16 Your news is not of war; III vi 8 He kneels to the kites

[158] Threats (*Minantis*) I ii 88 My weapon too has a sharpened point; I x 88 I have heard the sound of many fig-leaves; II ii 30 Raise your spur; II ix 13 You may have a sword, but I too have a spit of my own; III iv 38 False fires; III vi 24 To keep the pot full; III viii 83 Someone ready to resist; IV iii 28 Don't level off what is empty; IV viii 11 Threaten with fire and sword; IV x 13 Sword and flame; IV x 91 Threats worthy of Achilles

blow against filial respect; IV ix 44 His bosom-friend; IV ix 80 Salt and table; V i 26 By use and possession; V ii 50 Carry in one's eyes, etc.

[162] Obsequiousness (*Adulatio*) I viii 58 A deadly honey-brew; I x 54 Fair-spoken; I x 55 Fine words! A likely story!; II i 66 To praise an Athenian in Athens is no problem; II iii 3 It's figs he wants; II iv 26 Hercules' itch; II iv 28 Io Paean; II v 86 He sings his own praises; II vi 61 You've been eating venison; II vii 58 Polycrates looks after my mother; II viii 25 The Phrygian wins; III i 37 To stroke a man's head; III v 89 Pretty monkey; (III v 89 CWE 35 119) To speak sweetly; III vi 95 Good-looking on the doorpost; III viii 2 For one who rejects excessive praise; III viii 43 Speaking with gentler words; IV i 32 Wagging the tail; (IV i 32 CWE 35 461) To fawn; (IV i 32 CWE 35 461) To wheedle; IV i 92 Take care to be what you are said to be; IV ii 25 As kind as a cunning fox; IV iii 76 Bitter enemies are better; IV iv 35 Little stairs; IV v 99 Belly talkers; IV vii 25 Fly-flappers; IV viii 54 Hail, daughters of stallions; IV viii 90 With cookery words; IV ix 16 Gallonius; IV ix 52 Self-interested commendation; IV x 76 The governor's squad; V i 29 A soft-hearted manager of gladiators; V i 31 A music-hall assembly

[163] Pets (*In deliciis*) II iii 59 An Acarnanian sucking-pig; II vii 8 A white mouse; III iii 71 A Maltese lapdog

[164] Hatred (*Odium*) I ii 50 The bitterest quarrels are between brothers; I vii 13 Resentment is the last thing to grow old; (I vii 13 CWE 32 73) Prayers and Mischief; (I vii 13 CWE 32 73) Please a man and he forgets it; hurt him and he remembers; II i 78 Rustic hatred; II ii 46 He will not even walk the same road with him; II ii 94 Hate worthy of

Vatinius; II ii 95 Stepmotherly hatred; II vi 53 A feud worthy of Empedocles; II ix 62 Let them hate, so long as they fear; II ix 63 Hates worse than dog and snake; III iii 29 An Archidamian war; III iii 84 A truceless war; III ix 77 Support from influential people is essential; IV vii 91 As the wolf loves the sheep; IV viii 79 I can't bear Scellius' son either; V i 21 No more than a dog

[165] Anger (*Ira*) I iv 14 To bite on the bit; II x 76 To lie in the leaven; III vii 69 To bite one's lip; III ix 94 Silent vexation; IV vi 40 a soundless wave; IV vi 89 As angry as the Adriatic; IV vi 99 With ears lowered; IV x 77 You could light a lantern

[166] Envy, rivalry (*Invidia, aemulatio*) I ii 25 Potter envies potter and smith envies smith; I ii 85 The doors of the Muses are free from envy; I vi 71 The ox would wear the trappings and the lazy nag would plough; I vi 72 The crop is heavier in another man's field; II ii 22 One bush does not support two robins; II ii 24 One household does not keep two dogs; (II v 8 CWE 31 27) Envious as Zoilus; II vii 4 Shame to be mute; III i 7 The toothless man looks askance at those who have teeth to eat with; III x 52 Envy is the companion of boasting; IV iv 87 Better envied than pitied; IV viii 20 Envious is the neighbour's eye (also III i 22); IV viii 59 Kinship generates resentment; IV x 53 Don't go near a hungry man

[167] Distrust (*Diffidentia*) I i 70 Man is a wolf to man; I iii 35 Gifts of enemies are no gifts; (I iii 35 CWE 31 264) Harm and not good must come from the gifts of an evil man; (I iii 35 CWE 31 264) A poor man's gifts are no gifts; (I v 74 CWE 31 450) That man could not have any faith in faith itself; I viii 31 Hands with eyes in them; I viii 32 A blind day, and

A day with eyes; I x 50 To break one's token; II i 14 Trust no man, unless you have eaten a peck of salt with him first; II iii 31 We have as many enemies as we have slaves; II vi 54 One eye-witness is worth more than ten ear-witnesses; II vi 93 A Lydian shut the door; II vii 56 Even if you persuade me, I'll never believe you; II viii 8 Give and take at the same time; III iii 55 Credulity has cost me money; (III iii 55 CWE 34 300) Uncommon trust; IV iv 17 Walk on your own land; IV v 61 Even if Cato were to say it; IV vii 3 Not even Mercury would be believed

[168] **Deceit by a friend (*Fraus ab amico*)** II ii 25 The prop has let down the vine; IV ii 88 A dog helping a beggar; IV vii 52 To drag round in circles

[169] **Diligence (*Diligentiae*)** I ii 19 Forehead before occiput; I iii 84 To and fro; (I v 6 CWE 31) 390–1 To swerve by a nail's breadth; (I v 6 CWE 31 391) A finger's-breadth; (I v 6 CWE 31 391) A nail's breadth; I v 90 By rule; I v 91 To finger-nail; (I v 91 CWE 31 464) To examine carefully; (I v 92 CWE 31 464) To recook; (I v 92 CWE 31 464) To remake; I v 92 To put back on the anvil; I vii 71 It smells of the lamp; I vii 72 The lamp of Aristophanes and Cleanthes; II i 22 Odds and ends of time; II ii 42 One to one; II ii 43 Night is the mother of counsel; II vi 62 A spring in the field; II viii 38 Be sleep far from your eyes; II viii 68 First the leaves fall, then the trees; II ix 40 They do not sleep as much as nightingales; II ix 42 To gaze fixedly at; III iii 41 He has eyes in the back of his head; III iv 13 Having a Gorgon's eyes; III v 12 Squinting like a tunny fish; III v 86 With a probe; III vi 68 Cranes that swallow a stone; III vi 96 To scratch one's head, and similar phrases; (III vi 96 CWE 35 176) To taste torn nails; III vii 20 You

would have found even a needle; III vii 68 To ruminate the business; (III vii 68 CWE 35 259) To ruminate; III viii 27 Seize control of the affair; III x 4 This business will be my concern; III x 83 These things will be my care, etc.; IV i 16 Ithorus; IV iii 24 You are not sailing at night; IV v 31 Catch with both hands; IV v 48 There is always something for a hard-working man to do; IV v 85 The ploughman is no ploughman unless he is bent; IV v 86 To count up on one's fingers; IV vi 74 With a plumb-line; IV viii 99 Lay the line against the stone; IV ix 22 To owe according to the balance; IV x 57 Done and dealt with; V i 12 He never saw sleep; V i 72 At a quick march; V ii 39 To square up

[170] **Application (*Assiduitas*)** I ii 51 He may bear a bull that hath borne a calf; I iii 2 A tiny rain gives birth to a rainstorm; I iv 24 By night and day; I v 6 Not to stir a nail's breadth; I vi 30 By speaking men learn how to speak; I viii 94 Many strokes fell great oaks; I x 44 Not one foot; II i 40 Without even bending a knee; II ii 53 Practice can do everything; II v 99 A polyp crushed with fourteen blows; III iii 3 Constant dropping wears away a stone; III iv 74 A rolling stone gathers no moss; III vii 51 Following like a shadow

[171] **Negligence (*Indiligentiae*)** I iii 63 Through cloud through darkness as in a dream; I iv 27 With a gentle touch, a light touch; I ix 80 Like a dog drinking out of the Nile; I ix 91 To greet from the threshold; I ix 92 To taste with the tip of one's tongue; I ix 93 With the tip of the lips; I x 64 To smell with the tip of one's nose; II i 23 With folded hands; II vii 70 Phanus' front door; III i 49 To see through a lattice; III x 48 The negligent ruler; IV i 40 Some shield for the town!; IV ii 52 A bad gatekeeper; IV iv 2 With a limp hand; IV iv 83 On the run; IV v

38 A sea-lung would have come more quickly; IV vii 76 A hodge-podge; IV ix 11 One must die before . . .; IV ix 59 Dip the toes

[172] Sleepiness (*Somnolentia*) I vii 81 You sleep on a cargo of salt; I ix 63 You sleep Endymion's sleep; I ix 64 You sleep longer than Epimenides; II vii 95 A ruler should not sleep the whole night through, *or* A captain should not sleep the whole night through

[173] Busyness, leisure (*Occupatio, otium*) II iii 15 He has no leisure even to scratch his ear; II iii 46 Slaves have no leisure; III iv 98 When you can run away, don't look for a quarrel; III x 84 A festival has many; IV ii 73 Tyrrhenian bonds

[174] Justice (*Iustitia*) (I iv 15 CWE 31 396, also at II v 82 CWE 32 277) With equal weight; I v 15 To be weighed on the same scales; I ix 97 Move not the line; II i 67 Justice itself is nothing much; II ii 62 Worthy men always do right; II iii 73 Justice comprises in itself all virtue; II v 36 Gauge your stone against the ruler, not the ruler against the stone; II v 82 As fair as a pair of scales; II vii 65 Bocchyris; II ix 30 The verdict of Rhadamanthys; II x 63 A Law of Zaleucus; III i 28 As long as I my tiller forthright hold; III iii 91 A city-dweller has no righteous thoughts; III iv 27 This is justice; III iv 43 Do not take away what you did not put in place; III v 16 To walk a straight path; III v 27 No one stops anyone from walking on the public road; III v 50 Rhamnusius; III v 73 The laws absolve ravens and harass doves; III vi 9 Prienian justice; III vi 22 Don't choke, share; III ix 33 Don't do yourself what you criticize in others; III ix 45 Do not lay hands on sacred things; IV i 4 Mars is king; IV i 11 A paragon of justice; IV i 12 More just

than justice; IV ii 80 Sharing equally; IV ii 96 Equality never gives rise to war; IV vii 99 An Orphic life; IV viii 5 Virtue is simple; IV x 90 You're on the right track

[175] Injustice (*Iniustitia*) I i 2 (Pythagoras) CWE 31 33 Exceed not the balance; III iii 52 Gain ill-gotten is as bad as loss; IV vi 37 Gnawer of beans

[176] Inflexibility (*Rigor*) I x 25 Extreme right is extreme wrong; II iv 13 To cut to the quick; III iii 34 He shaves close to the skin; (III vii 12 CWE 35 222) I hate the herbalist who pulls out the herb root and all; IV vii 78 To act by the letter of the law; IV viii 26 The Obelus of censure; IV ix 22 To owe according to the balance; IV ix 50 With one's neck in a noose, by the throat

[177] Unjust force (*Vis iniusta*) I vi 28 This is sovereign; (I vi 28 CWE 32 23) Divide by the sword; I vi 61 You move what should not be moved; I vii 89 The lion's share; I x 69 To live like the Cyclops; II i 73 A new neighbour from Athens; II iii 77 Rear not a lion's whelp; II vi 46 City turned country; II vi 85 You dwell in Cescos; II vii 42 The field of Mars; III i 74 A land like Cyrnus; III ii 26 Centaur-like; III iii 60 No admission without a knowledge of geometry (also listed in Greek); III iii 83 To be pitched head foremost; (III iii 83 CWE 34 309) To Panticapaeum; (III iii 83 CWE 34 309) Over the precipice; III iv 90 To push the goad into an unlawful hole; III iv 100 The foreigner drove out the native; III v 18 Shut the door, ye profane; III vi 1 You devour the commons even before you get your share; III x 43 Never do violence to kings; IV i 4 Mars is king; IV vii 50 The law in one's hands; IV viii 10 On with the soldier's cape; IV viii 40 Like the Cyclopes; IV ix 50 With one's neck in a noose, by the throat; IV ix 84

Seize by the hair; IV x 25 Knock my eye out; V i 93 To speak what should be left undisturbed

[178] **Blamelessness** (*Inculpatus*) I v 74 To Satisfy Momus, and the like; II iv 95 As clean as a rudder; III ii 57 Colophon gold; III ii 85 Water poured over what is clean stays clean; IV i 58 Gold tested in the fire; (IV i 58 CWE 35 476) Gold tested by the touchstone; IV ix 19 The accounts are clear enough

[179] **Rashness** (*Temeritas*) I ii 76 The man who has learnt to row should take the oar; I ix 55 With unwashed hands; II ii 82 Each man had best employ what skill he has; II iv 33 Blindfold fighters; III i 4 A self-appointed aedile; III v 49 Teach me to eat; III viii 60 A deal not to be under taken rashly; IV v 54 Ignorance begets overconfidence; IV vi 31 Don't climb a mountain unshod; IV vii 62 Death deprives us of our wits; IV vii 77 Do not rush to swear an oath

[180] **Propriety** (*Pudor*) I ii 64 Where there is fear there is modesty; II i 70 Shame is in the eyes; II vii 2 Bashfulness is useless to a man in want; II viii 99 Sardinian dye; III i 98 They were ashamed to refuse and did not dare accept; III ix 10 Shame and fear; III x 79 Cyzicene dye; V i 7 No one ought to hold back at table

[181] **Shamelessness** (*Impudentia*) I viii 47 To put a bold front on it, Wipe off your blushes; I ix 42 That Attic look; III i 63 Impudence is a goddess; III iv 67 Barefaced; IV vi 38 Crippleman's Pouch; IV vii 83 The tongue is not refuted
[182] **Chastity** (*Pudicitia*) II x 13 As chaste as Melanion; III vi 65 I shall imitate Hippolytus

[183] **Wantonness** (*Impudicitia*) IV iv 81 Speaking Oscan; IV vi 25 Ass-rider

[184] **Origins of things** (*Originis*) I iii 68 Hence those tears; I iii 73 Great rivers have navigable springs; I iii 74 The slip of a noble tree bears fruit at once; I vi 33 Never good son from bad father; I viii 87 Born of oaktrees or rocks; I ix 25 An ill crow lays an ill egg; I ix 26 Wickedness proceedeth from the wicked; I x 61 Ill manners produce good laws; II iii 93 No rose blooms on a squill; II v 65 A small evil and a great good; II vi 66 From your workshop; II viii 47 The plodding donkeys have produced a horse; II x 75 The start of the war; III v 28 This is where the war begins; III viii 23 Greatest things from smallest beginnings; III ix 23 Author and source of everything; IV ii 97 The head of a fish is the first part to smell; V ii 14 Out of a group in the street

[185] **Fame and obscurity** (*Nobilitas, obscuritas*) I viii 86 A son of earth; II viii 33 As nobly born as Codrus; II viii 61 As spirited as Sparta; II x 14 He's called after his mother like a she-goat; III i 45 He could not even tell you his father's name; IV iii 46 You are counterfeit; IV iv 51 Livers-by-lamplight; IV viii 8 More than the heavens can contain; IV viii 23 Before the face, in the sight of; IV viii 65 Bird of a long line of birds; IV viii 71 Virtue begets glory; IV viii 73 From home to home; IV ix 49 A man of standing in his locality; IV ix 79 Smoke-darkened portraits; IV x 12 Shake the bell at; IV x 82 The world's cymbal; IV x 86 Scion of Jove

[186] **Degeneration** (*Degenerantium in peius*) I ii 51 He may bear a bull that hath borne a calf; I ii 58 Things go Mandraboulus' fashion; (I ii 58 CWE 31 198) To conquer oneself; I vi 32 Great men have trouble from their children; I vii 29 From horses to asses; II vi 59 Treated by Acesias; II ix 36 Who shall praise a father except children who are

failures?; II x 94 He does not play the same tune as his father's; III viii 59 That's how men are now; III ix 3 A son going to the bad; IV vi 27 Let us go to Athens; IV vii 65 O house of Antius, what a different master rules you

[187] Beginnings praised (*Initium laudatum***)** II v 61 Aegina bears most noble sons of old; III iii 75 While it is small a thorn seems good; III vi 10 Mars was honoured initially in his sons; IV viii 68 Applaud the first beginnings; IV viii 70 He has his foot in this shoe; IV x 50 To tread on

[188] Improvement (*Proficientium in melius***)** I iv 2 Acorns were good until bread was found; I vii 30 To rise from asses to oxen; II vii 20 To be given better auspices; II viii 36 Rich now, he has ceased to enjoy lentils; II ix 81 No more thorns; III i 2 I have escaped evil, I have found good; III i 81 We're better off than yesterday; III vi 44 Go hunt for a hare, now you have a pheasant; III vi 78 I have been led from one good to another; IV i 68 He has progressed by the cubit; IV i 88 Today a nobody, tomorrow the greatest; IV v 49 Mandro too had a ship made of fig-wood

[189] Concern for one's own advantage (*Proprii commodi studium***)** I iii 89 The tunic is nearer than the cloak; I iii 90 The knee is closer than the calf; I iii 91 Everyone wants things to go better for himself than for others; (I iii 91 CWE 31 311) Each man is a friend to himself; I vi 20 He's wise in vain that's not wise for himself; I x 37 I'll fix my own bath; II i 30 To play privately to oneself *or* A lyre-player from Aspendus; II vii 39 A welcome to any stranger who will be profitable; II vii 85 I will bathe with you; II ix 12 Songs of Simonides; III ii 28 We play cities; III v 6 Wish for something for the neighbour, but more for the pot;

III v 80 Singing your own song (and II i 30); III vi 79 To hunt eels; III vii 19 Each for his own advantage is rightly hard-headed; III ix 81 No matter where from, it's profit they're after; IV i 14 He's a shopkeeper; IV i 42 Each man thinks of his own business; IV ii 10 You should adore yourself; IV iii 15 As crafty as a cuckoo; IV iii 35 To add your hand to

[190] Profit from wickedness (*Lucrum ex scelere***)** II viii 94 Better than tribute; IV ix 60 Bottomry interest

[191] Slaughter (*Internicio***)** I ix 50 We Trojans have ceased to be; I x 26 No one was left even to carry fire; II vii 86 Like a pine-tree; II ix 61 Hands off the holy man; III i 23 Total overthrow; III v 40 Not one bite left; III v 76 To throw away the fare; III x 71 Those who deserved to die; IV iii 26 The leash as well as the dog; IV viii 22 From the foundations, root and all, and similar phrases

[192] Sudden Death (*Subitum exitium***)** II vi 80 For you Pythian and Delian mean the same thing; III i 96 To die the death of a mouse; III ii 34 The wing of slaughter; III v 68 Mouse fashion

[193] Using everything (*Totum ut nihil reliqui***)** II vi 26 Sheaves and all; II viii 85 Dust and all; II ix 51 Every scrap; IV iv 38 Minerals and timber excluded; IV iv 90 Along with temples and altar; IV vii 98 Beginning, middle, and end; IV x 1 Plunder and prize; IV x 58 Meanders; v i 69 Filings and all

[194] Forgetting (*Oblivio***)** I i 2 (Pythagoras) CWE 31 42 Obliterate the trace of the pot in the ashes; I ii 52 One should remember the living; I vii 1 I hate a pot-companion with a good memory; (I vii 1 CWE 32 67, also at II i 94 CWE 33 72) An amnesty; (I vii 1 CWE 32 67) What a woman swears I write in wine; II i 94

Remember no wrongs; II iii 96 To forget one's own name; II ix 55 Oblivion Fields; III iv 46 To cast to the winds; III viii 22 Forgetting wrongs; IV iii 84 To scrape away to the lowest level of wax; IV v 64 To drink mandrake; IV vii 33 Steersmen from a book

[195] **Remembering (*Memoria*)** I vii 40 To pluck by the ear; II ii 44 Where the sore is, there is the hand; II iii 43 Past labour is pleasant; II iv 91 As well as I know my own name, or, my fingers; IV i 57 It is unkind to touch on things that give pain; IV vi 54 To give a firestone; (IV vi 54 CWE 36 250) To nudge the ribs; (IV vi 54 CWE 36 250) To touch the elbow; IV ix 27 The remembrance of past sorrows is pleasurable

[196] **Escaping (*Elabendi*)** III ii 75 To find a chink; III v 21 To fly away; III v 38 To slip through the net (also in Greek); IV v 32 To escape from every snare

[197] **Using one's own resources (*Ex sese*)** I iii 20 Better to buy than to beg; I x 49 He has it at home. It's home-grown; III vi 34 You have not been badly hurt, unless . . .; III ix 65 Private misfortune

[198] **Home is best (*Domi vivere*)** III iii 38 A loved home is the best home; (III iii 38 CWE 34 295) Tortoise safe within its shell; (III iii 38 CWE 34 294) Homekeeping; III ix 44 Better stay at home; III x 38 Home is best

[199] **Women (*Foeminae*)** I iii 12 A Thessalian woman; II ii 48 Fire, sea, and woman, here be evils three; II x 21 Ne'er trust a woman, even when she's dead; II x 22 Women's woes; II x 66 My wife breeds like a woman of Chalcis; III iv 69 A woman's eye; III iv 77 When the lamp is removed there's no difference between women; III ix 39 A modest woman should not be alone

anywhere; III ix 88 Unhappily married; III x 21 Nothing is more noxious than a woman; IV ii 35 If he has no disputes, he's a bachelor; IV iii 45 Bitten by the bug; IV iv 89 Trust neither a woman nor your lap

[200] **Equanimity (*Aequanimitas*)** I i 2 (Pythagoras) CWE 31 40 Do not turn your back when you have come to the final stage; II vii 89 When in office expect both just and unjust criticism; III iv 68 In an evil pass it helps if you face it with courage; III vii 78 To shake the yoke

[201] **Solitude (*Solitudo*)** II i 83 No living creature. What living creature?; II i 84 Not so much as a fly; III v 94 The wilderness of the Scythians

[202] **Ignorance (*Ignoratio*)** I ii 97 In another world; (I ii 97 CWE 31 224) Born under a different sky; I vi 99 I know not whether you are dark or fair; I vi 100 He does not know that they exist; I ix 87 Known by name alone; II ii 90 To plead in a strange court; II x 50 Live in obscurity; III vi 62 In your own arena; III ix 24 Utterly unknown; IV v 65 He has not even seen a picture of it; IV ix 92 No more than the most ignorant of men; IV ix 100 Of no colour

[203] **Unfamiliarity (*Novitas*)** II vii 21 Another sort of oar; II viii 20 Look, what horsemen!; III ix 38 Novelty finds favour; IV ix 37 Proffer in a purse

[204] **Familiarity (*Notus*)** I ix 89 Inwardly and in the buff; I ix 90 Well-known at home; III ix 84 Rulers know each other; IV viii 23 Before the face, in the sight of; IV viii 34 General report not always groundless (also I vi 25); IV viii 50 Even the seers know it now

[205] **Hidden things (*Occulta*)** I iii 47 To speak in the ear; I vii 84 Hidden

music has no listeners; I ix 40 To dance in the dark; II ii 28 Unless some bird saw it; II ii 73 In a ladle; II iv 98 To breed a monster; II v 66 The Athenians and their Eleusinia; II ix 39 The triplets that exist among the dead; III iv 21 You are keeping something hidden in the ground; III v 18 Shut the door, ye profane; III vii 2 Plutus is a coward; IV iii 66 To walk on tiptoe; IV iv 7 You don't need fire to burn someone up; IV iv 65 With head brought near; IV v 67 In a corner

[206] **Doing one's duty** (*Vices officii*)
I iii 61 To complete one's task; II vii 25 To desert one's post; IV i 8 Which day in Ceos?; IV ii 71 When you become a member of the tribe, keep your place

[207] **Loyalty and gravity** (*Fides et gravitas*) I i 100 Better trust eyes than ears; I vi 31 Many good men and true; I vii 24 A gold ring in a pig's snout; I vii 90 Straight from the tripod (with variation To speak like an oracle); I vii 91 A leaf from the Sibyl's book; I viii 23 A man with whom you could play morra in the dark; I viii 25 An Attic witness; I viii 26 Athenian honesty; I ix 23 As true as what happened at the Sagra; II iii 6 Home-grown evidence; II iv 90 Lovers' vows; II v 84 Jupiter's vote; II vi 33 To swear by Jupiter the stone; II ix 31 Rhadamanthys' oath; III iii 43 Cheat men with oaths and children with markers; III iv 53 Minerva's vote; III v 31 An assembly of Amphictyons; III vi 85 Said and done; III viii 5 Of one who promises to stand by what has been promised; (IV iii 54 CWE 36 32) Fine words; IV v 29 From hand to hand; IV vi 9 To give with a long reach and a short reach; IV vi 68 With an upright heart; IV vii 20 An envoy is not beaten or violated; IV ix 28 To the best of one's judgment; IV x 51 Believe the ancients; IV x 78 Ever for some great man . . .

[208] **Treachery** (*Perfidia*) I viii 27 On Greek credit; I viii 28 Punic faith; I viii 29 He bears a stone in one hand and offers a loaf in the other, *or* Scratch a man's head with one hand and box his ears with the other; I viii 30 Out of one mouth to blow hot and cold; (I viii 30 CWE 32 141) To play the magadis; IV iv 74 He carries water in one hand, etc.; IV vi 58 To play the Lydian flute; IV viii 52 To play Thracian; IV ix 95 Better than that Trojan trick; IV x 96 Perjure oneself in set form of words

[209] **Advice** (*Consilium*) II i 47 A counsellor is something sacred; III ix 90 I am advising what I myself would do; IV x 40 Nothing is more miserable than a guilty conscience

[210] **Having help, lacking help** (*Cum auxilio; citra auxilium*) I iii 43 The anchor of the house; I iii 42 A pillar of the household; I v 27 Not without Theseus; I vi 19 By our own prowess; I vii 92 Let a man's brother stand by him; I viii 42 You shall swim without cork; II iii 95 Many hands make light work; II v 51 Woman must never draw sword; III i 51 When two go together; III ii 46 Papyrus seed asks not for a heavy ear; III ii 66 You need artificial fertilization; III iii 82 In place of a string; III viii 25 Fierce with someone else's help; III viii 37 Strong with someone else's help; III ix 7 Help is in the deed, not in words; III ix 54 Without divine help we avail nothing; III ix 89 God willing; III x 56 A self-sufficient man; IV ii 42 An onion would be no good at all; IV vi 2 Money without savings; IV viii 78 Without dogs and nets; IV ix 8 Extend a helping hand; IV x 31 Under my own auspices

[211] **Untimely and useless actions** (*Intempestiva et inepta*) I ii 65 Out you go, slaves, the festival's over; (I ii 65 CWE 31 208) It will not always be

[218] Laughter (*Risus*) I v 69 An Ionian laugh; (I v 69 CWE 31 446) In Ionian fashion; I v 70 A Megarian laugh; I v 71 The laugh of Chios; I vii 46 To laugh like Ajax; II vi 39 Shaking with laughter; III v 1 A Sardonic laugh; IV i 86 To die laughing; IV ii 12 A trifler; IV iv 69 As stupid as Melitides; IV x 60 He kept his laughter within his mouth

[219] Mockery (*Derisio*) I ii 80 You are mocking me from your lofty height; I viii 22 To turn up the nose; (I viii 22 CWE 32 136) Nostril curling; (I viii 22 CWE 32 136) With the nose of a rhinoceros; II x 77 You stand on the very block where the cryer cries his wares; III ii 21 Let the healthy man mock the cripple; III iii 87 To be a target for the finger; IV i 78 A face behind your back; IV viii 97 Well said, all of it

[220] Deceit (*Imposturae*) I v 48 To smear someone's face; I v 49 To give empty words; I v 50 To make sport of someone; I v 51 To cut the hair all round; I v 52 To play a trick; (I v 52 CWE 31 428) Prefers the mask to the face; I vi 59 The first swallow; I x 5 To draw into the net; II vii 40 Parnoetes invented the obol; II viii 49 Ephesian letters; III vi 27 To smother with caresses

[221] Foolishness that turns out well (*Fortunata stultitia*) I v 82 The sleeper's net makes a catch; I viii 44 Thoughtless and headstrong like Athenians; II x 81 In knowing nothing is the sweetest life; IV ii 99 A cheap jar is never broken

[222] Free of toil (*Citra laborem*) I v 79 Without dust; (I v 79 CWE 31 453) Without blood; (I v 79 CWE 31 453) Without sweat; I v 81 Without ploughing; I v 81 Without sowing; I v 82 The sleeper's net makes a catch; (I v 82 CWE 31 454) The gods do this while you're sleep-ing; II viii 77 God gives good things of his own free will; IV vii 37 Picking fruit under someone else's tree

[223] Spur on (*Incitare*) I vii 40 To pluck by the ear; I x 51 To pour cold water; (III v 88 CWE 35 118) To sound the trumpet; III viii 98 By every means he urges; IV iv 66 Why have we stopped?; (IV iv 66 CWE 36 250) To poke in the ribs; (IV iv 66 CWE 36 250) To stick with a goad; IV v 21 Shoot child; IV vi 54 To give a firestone; (IV vi 54 CWE 36 250) To nudge with the elbow; IV vii 71 The lyre incites to war; IV viii 86 To lend wings

[224] Critical situations (*Discriminis*) I i 2 (Pythagoras) CWE 31 43 Turn aside the sharp blade; I i 15 Between the shrine and the stone; I i 16 Between the hammer and the anvil; I i 18 On the razor's edge; I i 19 Things are at a turning-point; I ii 3 Kings have long hands; I iv 10 You have handed the sheep over to the wolf; I v 5 From the smoke into the fire; I vii 93 Not rashly to Abydos; I ix 72 It hangs by a hair (thread); II i 10 You are in the same boat; II i 43 Mind you don't fall in with Blackbottom; II i 80 A hare because of its meat; II ii 87 To dodge with the body; II iii 55 Through sword and fire we needs must break our way; II iv 46 When you double Cape Malea, forget what you left at home; II iv 52 Beware of Thorax; II iv 55 Will not go to Scolon, either alone or with someone else; II v 18 A sword in the hand of a child; II v 85 To go to the bowstring; II vi 36 For fear it break the string; II vii 27 The danger-point is the bench in the prow; II vii 63 From the wolf's mouth; II viii 3 Put the hog under the cudgel; II viii 68 First the leaves fall, then the trees; II viii 75 How I wish I were at home!; II ix 73 To throw lambs to the dogs; II ix 77 May my luck save me now; II x

83 He left me under the knife; II x 85 It's celery he needs; II x 95 No contest here for the wild olive; III i 14 To run through a spear-point; III i 47 He sails the Aegean; III ii 88 By twice seven waves; III iii 62 A fight once started leaves no room for excuses; III iii 77 This then was the thread of the dispute; III iv 60 Run a long way from a bigger man; (III iv 60 CWE 35 37) Avoid the man stronger than you; III iv 94 An abyss in front and wolves behind; III vi 42 Use knowledge in the last resort; III vi 71 It's your concern when next door's wall is burning; III viii 80 It has done harm and will do so again; III viii 81 and III ix 70 An enormous difference; III ix 14 In a dangerous affair you cannot afford to doze; III x 19 Flight is safer; III x 94 You are stepping into fire; IV i 69 Your status is at stake in this meeting; IV ii 20 Out of a dog's bottom; IV ii 65 To shit in the temple of Delphi; IV iv 6 Do not put all your wealth in one ship; (IV iv 19 CWE 36 72) There's need of rue; IV iv 88 To seek food from a fish trap; IV vi 39 In the arms of the waves; IV vi 42 Sheep-wolf; IV vii 6 Although you are bald

[225] At another's risk (*Alieno periculo*) I iv 41 You are reaping another's harvest; (I iv 41 CWE 31 352) A pot cooked by another; II ii 88 You gamble with another man's hide; II ix 71 Unhurt I shall watch another man enduring my trouble; II x 4 This is none of my business; away with it!

[226] Testing or experimenting (*Experientia seu periclitationis*) I i 23 Back to the third line; I i 24 To let go the sheet-anchor; I i 25 I will move the counter from the sacred line; I iv 30 To leave no stone unturned; I iv 31 To move every rope; I iv 32 To cast all the dice; I iv 33 To spread the sails to the wind; I vi 14 Risk it on a Carian; I vi 15 To

learn the potter's art on a big jar; (I vi 15 CWE 32 14) Workmen handle their own tools; I ix 46 Keep your hook in the water; I ix 83 To descend into the arena; II ii 37 Trying got the Greeks to Troy; II iii 66 Either three times six dice, or three; II iii 67 The same as Mus at Pisa; III v 41 A king or an ass; (III v 41 CWE 35 91) The ass sits idle; III viii 96 I trust to God and fortune; IV iii 92 Politics instruct a man; IV iv 62 Even after a bad harvest we must sow; IV v 39 To put foot to foot; IV x 44 I'm a king (and III v 41 CWE 35 92); V ii 8 Throw the first spears; (V ii 8 CWE 36 601) To skirmish

[227] A second attempt (*Secundae experientiae*) I iii 38 Better luck next time; (I iii 38 CWE 31 267) Second thoughts; III x 59 A slip should be pardoned; IV v 79 When the winds desert you, use the oars

[228] Inexperience (*Imperitia*) III v 55 That path has been looked at; IV i 1 War is a treat for those who have not tried it; V ii 11 Hired labourers; (V ii 11 CWE 36 604) Those able to speak

[229] Attempts (*Conatus*) I iii 81 To mingle sea and sky; I iii 82 You will mix sacred and profane; I iii 85 Up and down; I iv 15 With hands and feet; I iv 16 With every sinew; I iv 18 With oars and sails; I iv 25 By land and sea; I iv 26 With the whole heart; I iv 28 To fight with every kind of weapon; I iv 29 At close quarters and at long range; II iii 24 To hoist topsails; II vi 17 To weigh anchor; II viii 55 In great enterprises even to have shown the will is enough; II viii 66 With spear and shield; III i 34 One must put one's best foot forward; III viii 36 A vain attempt; III viii 92 To the utmost of my ability; III x 13 In any sort of contention; III x 67 It is a new thing I begin; IV v 76 In full voice; IV vi 57 To use every kind of tone; IV ix 56 To stir the holy objects; IV x 26 By land or sea

[230] Doggedness, persistence (*Pertinacia*) I iii 76 With a gladiator's spirit; I iv 22 To hold fast with one's teeth; I iv 23 With the whole body, with all one's nails (claws); IV v 83 Unless his legs are broken; IV viii 45 Sticks like a limpet; IV ix 64 He challenges the other tragedians; V i 52 Bite off an ear

[231] Outcome that is uncertain (*Incertus eventus*) I ii 13 If you throw often, you'll throw this way and that; I v 1 There's many a slip 'twixt the cup and the lip; I v 2 Between mouth and morsel; I vii 5 Who know what evening in the end will bring; (I vii 5 CWE 32 69) The sun of all their days had not yet set; II ii 89 To be in the blade; III v 45 Shooting aimlessly; III ix 28 Two possible outcomes; IV vii 49 Mars is on everyone's side

[232] Judgment after the outcome (*Ex eventu iudicium*) I i 29 Once stung, the fisherman will be wiser; I iii 40 To consider a thing done; I v 17 We shall count the entrails when cooked; I x 76 'Tis the place that shows the man; III iv 49 The facts will show; III x 78 Soon we shall know better than the prophet; IV iii 59 Sadder but wiser; IV ix 86 Ill beginning, an ill ending

[234] Large numbers (*Multi*) IV i 61 More than a single ship can carry; IV v 75 Young boys and old men

[235] Fools (*In stupidos*) I ii 70 A Tartessian cat; I iii 1 One ought to be born a king or a fool; I iii 67 Midas has ass's ears; I v 36 Old men are children twice over; (I v 36 CWE 31 415) To become a boy again; I viii 36 It takes blows to mend a Phrygian; I viii 51

Drink hellebore; I viii 53 He has drunk strychnum; I viii 54 Why can't you eat cress?; I viii 55 Sacrifice a pig; I x 6 Boeotian pig; I x 80 Body without soul; II i 19 To lead one by the nose; II i 34 As wise as a tadpole; II i 75 Saturnian rheums; II ii 7 He's seven years old and not yet cut his teeth; II ii 31 You have less sense than the men who write dithyrambs; II iii 7 Boeotian brains; II iii 8 A Boeotian tune; II iii 42 Pluck squills from a grave; II iii 51 There is no saltiness in him; II iii 71 Margites; II v 26 Oilier than a lamp and sleeker than an oil-bottle; (II v 52 CWE 33 265) The donkey who fell over the cliff; II v 68 An Antronian ass; II v 89 The bowels of the earth; II vii 6 He does not know the difference between head and groin; II vii 26 Sheep are no use; II ix 1 As big a fool as Morychus; II ix 11 As stupid as the Adonis of Praxilla; II ix 20 As harshly enslaved as Messene; II ix 64 As foolish as Coroebus; II ix 67 It's folly to believe that Jove exists; II ix 89 There's no difference between you and Chaerephon; II ix 90 There's no difference between you and an elephant; II x 8 Centaurs have no brains; II x 48 A cormorant open-mouthed; III i 91 To eat hay. He should be fed on ambrosia; III i 95 The character of a sheep; III ii 48 A Boeotian ear; III ii 62 Doing as the Arcadians do; III iii 27 A scion of Arcadia; (III iii 27 CWE 34 290) Acorn-eaters; (III iii 27 CWE 34 291) More ancient than Jove, you were there before Cronos and the Titans; III iii 58 Saturn's anus; III iv 40 A head devoid of brains; III iv 51 Moonstruck; III v 5 Don't let a fool have your finger; III v 64 The man looked like a ship beseeching a rock; (III vi 18 CWE 35 134) Fat pig; III vi 21 As blunt as a pestle; (III vi 21 CWE 35 135) An idle pestle; III vi 28 Never anyone more than the Megarians; III vii 39 To be a Corybant; III vii 97 You stood like Bagas; III x 81 I am Embarus; III x 92 It

has no tree; III x 100 The delerium of
flute-players; IV i 38 A mushroom; IV ii
85 Staring at a desert; IV iii 33 As stupid
as a turpentine-tree; IV iii 41 Blind in
ear and mind; IV iv 69 As stupid as
Melitides; (IV iv 69 CWE 36 108) Like
a Mamakuthes; IV vi 28 An Abderan
mentality; IV vi 35 A Dutch ear; IV vi
64 A sacred fish; IV vi 71 A mole who
never stops talking; IV vi 90 A sea-ox;
IV vii 19 A Tanagran monster; IV vii
90 Like a pitcher; IV vii 92 Reared on
ships; IV viii 31 Colophonian footwear;
IV viii 38 The ass prefers straw to gold;
IV x 55 Over eight feet tall; v i 18 A
sheep-brained piece of statuary; v i 35
Letting blood

[236] Extreme size (*Praelongi*) I i 21
The boot of Maximinus; I i 22 The Egyptian clematis; II iii 92 No bad big fish;
III iv 58 Big and foolish; III v 57 Short
as Molon; III vi 18 Fat stomach never
bore fine feeling; (III vi 18 CWE 35 134)
Fat pig

[237] Scoundrels (*Improbi*) I ii 71 To
bear the yoke; I ii 86 To play Eurybatus
(twice); I vii 42 Vilest of two-legged
creatures; I ix 99 Man-eating Memmius
lacerates Largius' limbs; II iii 28 A slave
haircut; II iv 48 The Lerians are a bad
lot; II v 29 A man untried; II v 49 I
know Simon and Simon knows me; II
v 90 A flute-player from Tenedos; II
vi 99 Lupus' gang of ten; II vii 11 You
deserve no praise, even at a feast; II
vii 35 An assembly of Cercopes; II vii
37 Cercopian tricks; II ix 34 He who
in everything and at every season; II
x 28 As impious as Hippomenes; II x
38 Lydians are rascals, and Egyptians
second; II x 62 Ulysses' crew; III ii 6
Of a bad stamp; III ii 97 Rascality takes
shortcuts; III iv 5 Adulterated (also III
ii 6 CWE 34 227); III iv 9 The sea washes
away all mortal ills; III iv 72 Diagoras
of Melos; III vi 81 Double kappa; III vi

82 Nothing worse than three C's; III vii
22 Another Phrenondas; III vii 43 He
gets no sleep if he hasn't done this or
that; III vii 65 An altar-scrounger; III
x 97 Not everyone is mad in the same
way; IV i 73 A mugger; IV i 91 May the
gods give you the mind you deserve;
IV vi 7 To come with a sack; IV vi 25
Ass-rider; IV vii 57 Beast knows beast;
IV viii 1 Ambrones; IV ix 47 Ballio; IV
ix 58 To romance; v ii 48 Aetolians

**[238] Wickedness of character and
forming of character (*Ingenii malitia
& institutio*)** I x 90 The arse beats all
efforts to wash it; II i 68 Rascals have
all they need save opportunity; II iv 11
Once a buffoon never an honest family
man; II iv 19 To acquire a taste; II iv 20
Long will a crock; II vii 14 Though you
cast out nature with a fork, it still returns; II x 42 A twisted branch, never
straight; III iii 19 A wolf may change
his hair, but not his heart; III x 88 The
African cannot become white

**[239] A bad neighbour (*Malus vici-
nus*)** I i 32 Something bad from a bad
neighbour; I vi 37 A brackish neigh-
bourhood; I x 73 If you live next to a
cripple, you will learn to limp; v ii 36
Harming in every way

**[240] Openly and obscurely (*Aperte et
crasse*)** I i 37 With a stupid Minerva, a
crass Minerva; I i 38 Of the more clumsy
Muse; II x 33 Spoonfeeding; III vii 61
You're combing it out thinly; (III vii 61
CWE 35 252) To talk subtleties; (III vii
61 CWE 35 252) To know roughly; (III
vii 61 CWE 35 252) So to speak

[241] Rarity (*Raritas*) I v 86 When
lightning strikes through Harma; I vi
3 milk; II i 21 A rare bird; II i 44 An
owl's egg; II ii 50 A white bird; II vii
10 As rare as the phoenix; IV iii 96 The
cup of friendship

The year; I ii 17 The living word, not the field, produces the yield; I vii 39 How happy he who has a three-months' child; I viii 100 A good leader makes for good following; II vii 7 Excess of generals ruined Caria; III i 86 When the tree is felled, everyone gathers the firewood; III ii 72 Some have a tongue, others have teeth; III x 73 Regaining courage; IV v 10 I would sooner give it to Telegoras

[255] **Driving away** (*Repellentis*) I v 34 Go and shake under the oak-tree; I vii 75 Let someone pull you out who doesn't know you; (I vii 75 CWE 32 112) He finds no innocents; (I vii 75 CWE 32 112) Find a stranger

[256] **Marvellous and strange** (*Mira nova*) I iii 75 To pierce crows' eyes; I x 75 Annus and the oven; II ii 32 A whiplash from Corcyra; II iv 54 A great city, a great solitude; II vi 60 Agamemnon's wells; II vi 75 With slender thread; II viii 30 The art of Glaucus; III i 73 Cyzicene staters; III ii 30 Carcinus' verses; III ii 81 For a necessary purpose; III vii 87 You can drive the ass; IV ii 29 Straight from the bellows

[257] **Proverbs that signify all things** (*Omnia*) II i 24 Grave and gay; IV v 75 Young boys and old men; IV vi 45 Neither animate nor inanimate; IV viii 93 Broad and narrow; IV x 33 Sweet and bitter; v i 15 Of all whom the sun beholds

[258] **Allurement of evil** (*Illecebra mali*) II iv 22 It is risky for a dog to taste guts; II vii 62 He has tasted the lotus

[259] **Practice** (*Exercitatio*) v ii 10 A thing of oil and the wrestling school; (v ii 10 CWE 36 603) Gloss and the wrestling school; (v ii 10 CWE 36 602) Exercise

of the domestic, sheltered training-ground; v ii 12 A sing-song from the schools

[260] **Morals affected by contact with others** (*Contagio morum*) I i 2 (Pythagoras) CWE 31 32 Taste not of anything with a black tail; I x 73 If you live next to a cripple, you will learn to limp; I x 74 Evil communications corrupt good manners; III iv 95 When one yawns another yawns too; IV viii 37 Learn goodness from the good; IV ix 45 Footservants; IV x 27 To out-leaf

[261] **Things bought to great advantage** (*Commodo magno emptum*) II vii 38 Farewell, beloved light

[262] **Turbulent times** (*Tumultus*) IV iv 73 Tyrian seas

[263] **Powerful men** (*Potentes*) IV iv 5 Powerful over all things; IV ix 39 By a nod or a shake of the head; v i 13 To put one's fingers to one's lips; v i 46 Requests backed by force

[264] **Things that are of great importance** (*Magni momenti*) I viii 18 Worth breaking bail for; IV vi 56 To go even to Megara

[265] **Scurrility** (*Scurrilitas*) IV vi 97 I'm coming from the sixtymen; IV ix 34 The horseman should not take to singing

[266] **Weak assistance** (*Auxilium infirmum*) (I vii 85 CWE 32 119) A fig-wood prop; IV vi 49 To take across the river; IV vi 51 A sacred band; IV vii 18 A leather prop; IV vii 73 Moon beams do not ripen grapes

[267] **Fondness for drink** (*Bibacitas*) (III vi 16 CWE 35 132) Drinking like frogs; (IV ii 79 CWE 35 542) Those whose

heads are fuddled with intoxication; IV vi 62 Not even an elephant could empty it; IV vi 63 To be a wine-ladler; IV vi 69 To be in one's cups; IV vii 7 A silver well; IV vii 41 Rowers of wine-cups; IV viii 2 Wine-quinsy; IV ix 74 A booze-up; IV x 21 The more a Parthian drinks

[268] Honour paid to something unworthy of it (*Honos indigno habitus*) (I iii 66 CWE 31 291) Ass in a lion's skin; I vii 10 An ape in purple; I x 63 The seventh ox; IV vi 93 An ox on a silver plate; IV viii 13 Change one's shoes; IV ix 38 Bad accompanist, great chorister; IV x 62 By fate the Metelli; v i 44 Cover a swelling with a purple robe

[269] Invective (*Maledicentia*) IV iii 61 Worse than Hyperbolus; IV vi 85 To iambicize; IV vi 96 To Steniacize; IV vii 47 To sow curses; IV vii 54 Maesonian quips

[270] Trifles (*Nugalia*) IV vi 36 Nonsense-spouter; IV ix 90 Stage nonsense

[271] Combinations (*Mixta*) I vi 2 A horn of plenty; II iv 58 To stuff a patchwork coat; IV vi 76 A cup of five

[272] Parasites (*Parasiti*) (I v 53 CWE 31 403) The pot boils; (II vii 63 CWE 35 255) Dinner devotees; IV iv 53 Those who carry their own oil-flask; (IV iv 53 CWE 36 97) Those who eat other persons'

food; (IV iv 53 CWE 36 98) Water poured over your hands; IV vii 43 Flies; IV viii 24 Like the Myconians; v i 60 Your own slice of pie

[273] Punishment for another's faults (*Puniri pro alio*) III iii 99 The dog offended, the sow paid the penalty; IV vii 46 The flautist gets the beating

[274] Sorcery (*Veneficia*) I iii 12 A Thessalian woman; IV vi 38 Crippleman's pouch

[275] Tolerance (*Tolerantia*) I vii 43 Adamantine; IV vi 59 With guts of bronze; v i 56 Socrates' cockerel or hide

[276] Ferociousness (*Torvitas*) I ix 41 An Areopagite; II vi 88 A titanic glare; III iv 15 You will seem, when you see me, to see Mars himself; (III vii 71 CWE 35 263) Looking daggers; IV vi 60 The look of oregano; IV vii 96 Not from oak or rock

[277] Cosmetics (*Fucus*) IV viii 62 She has the bottle by her chops; IV x 10 Wearers of rush-scent; IV x 92 Shiny as oil

[278] Leisure (*Otium*) III vi 66 To achieve nothing; v ii 20 Gathering seashells; v ii 21 A man is not free unless he sometimes does nothing; (v ii 21 CWE 36 614) To do nothing; (v ii 21 CWE 36 614) Being idle

The topics in English, in alphabetical order

The following is a list for the 278 headings Erasmus used for his topical index, provided on pages 568–621. The T number corresponds to the order followed in Erasmus' Index of Topics.

Laconicism (*Breviloquentia*) T 13
Large *see* Numbers
Late *see* Cures, Repentance
Laughter (*Risus*) T 218
Laziness (*Ignavia et inscitia*) T 24
Legacy-seekers (*Haeredipetae*) T 126
Leisure (*Otium*) T 278
— *see also* Busyness
Lethargy *see* Vigour
Life, The wretchedness and brevity of human (*Vita hominis misera et brevis*) T 130
Likeness *see* Similarity
Living, Healthy (*Salubritas*) T 123; Living, Unhealthy (*Insalubritas*) T 124; Living to a great age (*Longaevitas*) T 128
— *see also* Change, Luxury, Sumptuous
Long-lasting, What is (*Diuturnum*) T 125
Love (*Amor*) T 160
Loyalty and gravity (*Fides et gravitas*) T 207
Lust *see* Intemperance
Luxury and soft living (*Luxus et mollicies*) T 117

Magnificent *see* Promises
Making *see* Errors
Marvellous and strange (*Mira nova*) T 256
Masses *see* Yielding
Matter *see* Germane, Inappropriate
Meanness (*Sordes et parsimonia*) T 43
Mind *see* Change
Misdeed *see* Vengeance
Miserliness (*Tenacitas*) T 39
Misfortune or ruination (*Infortunii sive exitii*) T 49; Misfortune that is repeated or renewed (*Malum conduplicatum, aut renovatum*) T 78; Misfortune turning out well (*Malum vertens bono*) T 87
Mockery (*Derisio*) T 219
Moderation and temperance (*Modestia modusque*) T 108
Morals affected by contact with others (*Contagio morum*) T 260

Natural *see* Proclivities
Necessity (*Necessitas*) T 154
Negligence (*Indiligentiae*) T 171
Neighbour, A bad (*Malus vicinus*) T 239
Never happen, Things that can (*Nunquam*) T 74
Niggardliness *see* Meanness
Noisiness (*Clamosus*) T 14
Non-existent, What is (*Nusquam*) T 76
Numbers, Large (*Multi*) T 234

Obscurely *see* Openly
Obscurity (*Obscuritas*) T 62
Obscurity *see* Fame
Obsequiousness (*Adulatio*) T 162
Obvious and clear, What is (*Perspicuitas*) T 61
Old age that is premature or death (*Senium praematurum, aut mors*) T 127
One should make *see* Use
One's own resources, Using (*Ex sese*) T 197
— *see also* Concern
Openly and obscurely (*Aperte et crasse*) T 240
Opposite *see* Preoccupation, Proclivities
Origins of things (*Originis*) T 184
Others *see* Wise
Outcome *see* Judgment, Uncertain

Parasites (*Parasiti*) T 272
Paying *see* Circumstances
Payment that is inappropriate (*Inaequalis pensatio*) T 82
People *see* Annoying
Perplexed *see* Trapped
Persistence *see* Doggedness
Pets (*In deliciis*) T 163
Pointless action (*Inanis opera*) T 70
— *see also* Worthless
Poverty (*Paupertas*) T 2
Powerful men (*Potentes*) T 263
Practice (*Exercitatio*) T 259
Praised *see* Beginnings, Taciturnity
Premature *see* Old age
Preoccupation with self (*Philautia*) T 110; Preoccupation with self, opposite of (*Contrarium philautiae*) T 111

The topics in Latin, in alphabetical order

Ab initio ad finem (From beginning to end) T 45

Aberrandi (Making errors) T 58

Abominantis *see* Deprecantis

Absolvendi (Finishing) T 44

Absurda, indecora, praepostera (Ridiculousness, improprieties, topsyturviness) T 69

Accersitum *see* Malum

Accessio pusilla aut nimia (Additions that are tiny or excessive) T 246

Ad rem pertinentia (Germane to the matter at hand) T 146

Adulatio (Obsequiousness) T 162

Aemulatio *see* Invidia

Aequalitas (Similarity in abilities) T 94

Aequanimitas (Equanimity) T 200

Alia aliis placent (Difference of taste) T 57

Alibi diminutum, Alibi redditum (Deficiencies compensated by assets) T 83

Aliena a re (Inappropriate to the matter at hand) T 144

Aliena curantis (Concern with other people's affairs) T 145

Alieno periculo (At another's risk) T 225

Aliis sapere (To be wise for others, not for oneself) T 133

Alio *see* Puniri

Amicitia (Friendship) T 161

Amico *see* Fraus

Amor (Love) T 160

Anceps et dubius (What is uncertain and doubtful) T 136

Aperte et crasse (Openly and obscurely) T 240

Approbandi (Approval) T 55

Aptum *see* Munus

Arrogantia iactantiaque (Arrogance and boastfulness) T 109

Asperitas, morositas (Harshness, captiousness) T 113

Assiduitas (Application) T 170

Assuetum *see* Malum

Attentio et contra (Attentiveness and its opposite) T 64

Audacia (Boldness) T 35

Auxilium *see* Cum auxilio

Auxilium infirmum (Weak assistance) T 266

Avaritia (Greed) T 42

Beneficium corruptum (Kindness spoiled) T 217

– *see also* Pensatio

Bibacitas (Fondness for drink) T 267

Bonae *see* Fortunae

Boni *see* Munus

Bonum *see* Malum, Praeter spem

Breviloquentia (Laconicism) T 13

Brevis *see* Vita

Caecutientia (Blindness of vision) T 59

Calumnia (Captiousness) T 150

Carpentis seipsum (Self-criticism) T 153

Causa indefensa (Undefended case) T 152

Cedendum multitudini (Yielding to the masses) T 37

Citra laborem (Free of toil) T 222

Clamosus (Noisy) T 14

Commodi *see* Proprii

Commodo magno emptum (Things bought to great advantage) T 261

Commodum interversum (Profit at another's expense) T 67

Commutatio *see* Fortunae

Conatus (Attempts) T 229

Concordia (Harmony) T 242

Conduplicatum *see* Malum

Congruentiae (Likeness) T 46

Coniecturae (Drawing conclusions from partial evidence) T 149

Coniuncta *see* Prudentia

Conscientia *see* Metus

Consilium (Advice) T 209

Consulendum *see* Munus

Contagio morum (Morals affected by contact with others) T 260

Contemptus et vilitatis (Contempt and worthlessness) T 99

Contra *see* Proclivitas

Contrarium philautiae (Opposite of preoccupation with self) T 111

Copiae *see* Fortunae

Correctio dicti aut facti (Correction of a word or deed) T 66

Corruptela *see* Munerum

Corruptum *see* Beneficium

Crasse *see* Aperte

Crudelitas (Cruelty) T 32

Cum auxilio; citra auxilium (Having help, lacking help) T 210

Cunctationis *see* Tarditatis

Curantis *see* Aliena

Curiositas (Curiosity) T 31

Damnandi (Condemnation) T 54

Decretum (What is immutable) T 138

Deformitas (Ugliness) T 4

Degenerantium in peius (Degeneration) T 186

Deliciis *see* In deliciis

Deprecantis, abominantis (Averting, abhorring) T 214

Deprehensos *see* In deprehensos

Derisio (Mockery) T 219

Desperatio (Desperation) T 85

Dictum *see* Correctio

Differentiae (Differences) T 93

Difficultatis (Difficulty) T 71

Diffidentia (Distrust) T 167

Dignitatis (Rank that is deserved) T 100

Diligentiae (Diligence) T 169

Diminutum *see* Alibi

Discordia (Discord) T 243

Discriminis (Critical situations) T 224

Dissimilitudinis (Dissimilarity) T 47

Dissimulatio (Concealment) T 27

Divitiae (Riches) T 1

Divitum praerogativa (Prerogatives of the rich) T 254

Diuturnum (What is long-lasting) T 125

Docilitas (Teachability) T 253

Domi vivere (Home is best) T 198

Dubius *see* Anceps

Elabendi (Escaping) T 196

Emptum *see* Commodo

Error in initio (Errors made initially) T 11

– *see also* Iteratus

Eventu *see* Ex eventu

Eventus *see* Incertus

Ex eventu iudicium (Judgment after the outcome) T 232

Ex sese (Using one's own resources) T 197

Excellentia, inaequalitas (Exceptional attributes and disparities in these) T 92

Execrandi (Detesting) T 215

Exercitatio (Practice) T 259

Exilium (Exile) T 245

Exitii (Ruination) T 49

Exitium honestum (An honourable death) T 21

– *see also* Subitum

Experientia seu periclitationis (Testing or experimenting) T 226

Experientiae *see* Secundae

Factum *see* Correctio

Facundia (Eloquence) T 19

Fames (Hunger) T 119

Felicitatis *see* Fortunae

Festinatio praepropera (Excessive haste) T 121

Festinationis, etc (Haste, etc) T 120

Fides et gravitas (Loyalty and gravity) T 207

Finis *see* Ab initio

Focus (Hearth) T 247

Foeminae (Women) T 199

Forma (Beauty) T 4

Fortitudo (Bravery) 36

Fortunae, copiae, felicitatis, aut ominis, Bonae (Good fortune, abundance, of good auspices) T 50; – commutatio (Change of fortune) T 105

Iteratio citra taedium (Repetition
without boredom) T 6
– see also Taedium
Iteratus error (Errors repeated) T 10
Iudicandi (Judging) T 56
Iudicium see Ex eventu
Iustitia (Justice) T 174
Iuventa (Youth) T 129

Laborem see Citra laborem
Lacessentis (Harassment) T 147
Laetitia see Tristitia
Laetus see Nuntius
Languor see Vehementia
Laudata see Taciturnitas
Laudatum see Initium
Lautitiae (Sumptuous living) T 118
Libenter (Gladly) T 251
Liberalitas (Generosity) T 38
Libertas (Freedom) T 28
Libido see Intemperantiae libido
Longaevitas (Living to a great age)
T 128
Lucrum ex scelere (Profit from wicked-
ness) T 190
Luxus et mollicies (Luxury and soft
living) T 117

Magni momenti (Things that are of
great importance) T 264
Magnifica promissa (Promises that are
magnificent) T 89
Magno see Commodo
Maledicentia (Invective) T 269
– see also Obtrectatio
Malefacti see Ultio
Mali retaliatio (Retaliation for an evil)
T 81
– see also Illecebra
Malitia see Ingenii
Malum accersitum aut retortum (Evils
brought upon oneself or diverted)
T 51
Malum assuetum (Evil to which one is
accustomed) T 80
Malum conduplicatum, aut renovatum
(Misfortune that is repeated or
renewed) T 78

Malum immedicabile (Evil uncurable)
T 22; – male vitatum (Avoiding
misfortune at one's cost) T 79; –
vertens bono (Misfortune turning
out well) T 87
Malus vicinus (A bad neighbour)
T 239
– see also Praeter spem
Mansuetudo (Gentleness) T 112
Melius see Proficientium
Memoria (Remembering) T 195
Metus et conscientia (Fear and a sense
of guilt) T 140; – poenae (Fear of
punishment) T 143
– see also Inanis
Minantis (Threats) T 158
Mira nova (Marvellous and strange)
T 256
Misera see Vita
Mixta (Combinations) T 271
Modestia modusque (Moderation and
temperance) T 108
Modus see Modestia
Molesti, intolerabiles (Annoying
people, and ailments that are intol-
erable) T 7
Mollicies see Luxus
Momenti see Magni
Morositas see Asperitas
Mors see Senium
Morum see Contagio
Multi (Large numbers) T 234
Multitudo see Cedendum
Munerum corruptela (Bribery with
gifts) T 3
Munus aptum aut ineptum (Suitable
or unsuitable gifts) T 48; – boni
consulendum (Gifts that should be
appreciated) T 250; – non munus
(Gifts that are not gifts) T 20
Mutandae sententiae (Change of mind)
T 103
Mutati instituti (Change in a way of
living) T 104

Necessitas (Necessity) T 154
Nihil see Totum
Nimia see Accessio

Nobilitas, obscuritas (Fame and obscurity) T 185

Non solus ille (Lack of uniqueness) T 97

Non sunt *see* Fuerunt

Notus (Familiarity) T 204

Nova *see* Mira nova

Novitas (Unfamiliarity) T 203

Nugalia (Trifles) T 270

Nunquam (Things that can never happen) T 74

Nuntius laetus (Good news) T 157

Nupera (Recent things) T 9

Nusquam (What is non-existent) T 76

Oblivio (Forgetting) T 194

Obscuritas (Obscurity) T 62

Obscuritas *see* Nobilitas

Obsecundantis (Compliance) T 65

Obtrectatio et maledicentia (Disparagement and slander) T 151

Occasio (Chance) T 114

Occulta (Hidden things) T 205

Occupatio, otium (Busyness, leisure) T 173

Odium (Hatred) T 164

Officii *see* Vices

Officium *see* Pensatio

Ominandi (Prognosticating) T 216

Ominis *see* Fortunae

Omnia (Proverbs that signify all things) T 257

Opera *see* Inanis

Originis (Origins of things) T 184

Otium (Leisure) T 278

– *see also* Occupatio

Parasiti (Parasites) T 272

Parsimonia (Niggardliness) T 43

Paupertas (Poverty) T 2

Peius *see* Degenerantium

Pensatio beneficii vel officii (Recompense for a kindness or a service) T 77

– *see also* Inaequalis

Perficiendi (Completing) T 44

Perfidia (Treachery) T 208

Perfidiae *see* Inconstantiae

Periclitationis *see* Experientia

Periculo *see* Alieno

Perplexus (Trapped and in difficulties) T 137

Perspicacitas (Clear-sightedness) T 60

Perspicuitas (What is obvious and clear) T 61

Pertinacia (Doggedness, persistence) T 230

Pertinax *see* Spes

Pertinentia *see* Ad rem

Philautia (Preoccupation with self) T 110

Philautiae *see* Contrarium

Placeo *see* Alia

Poenae *see* Metus

Poenitentia *see* Sera

Potentes (Powerful men) T 263

Praelongi (Extreme size) T 236

Praematurum *see* Senium

Praepostera *see* Absurda

Praepropera *see* Festinatio

Praerogativa *see* Divitum

Praeter spem bonum, aut malum (Good or evil that is unexpected) T 86

Pro alio *see* Puniri

Probrum, gloria (Disgrace, glory) T 249

Proclivitas (Natural proclivities) T 72

Proclivitas contra (The opposite of natural proclivities) T 73

Proficientium in melius (Improvement) T 188

Profusio (Extravagance) T 41

Promissa *see* Magnifica

Proprii commodi studium (Concern for one's own advantage) T 189

Proximis utendum (One should make use of what one has) T 101

Prudentia (Good sense) T 132

Prudentia coniuncta viribus (Good sense joined with physical strength) T 134

Prudentia senilis (The good sense of the old) T 131

Pudicitia (Chastity) T 182

Pudor (Propriety) T 180

Puniri pro alio (Punishment for another's faults) T 273
Pusilla *see* Accessio

Rapacitas (Rapacity) T 42
Raritas (Rarity) T 241
Re *see* Aliena
Redditum *see* Alibi
Refugium (Refuge) T 252
Reliqui *see* Totum
Rem *see* Ad rem
Remedium *see* Serum
Renovatum *see* Malum
Repellentis (Driving away) T 255
Retaliatio *see* Mali
Retortum *see* Malum
Reus *see* Securitatis
Rigor (Inflexibility) T 176
Risus (Laughter) T 218
Rixosus (Quarrelsomeness) T 15)

Salubritas (Healthy living) T 123
Scelere *see* Lucrum
Scurrilitas (Scurrility) T 265
Secundae experientiae (A second
attempt) T 227
Securitatis et tutae rei (Freedom from
danger and safety) T 98
Seipsum *see* Carpentis
Semper (What is always true) T 75
Senilis *see* Prudentia
Senium praematurum, aut mors (Old
age that is premature or death) T 127
Sententiae *see* Mutandae
Sera poenitentia (Repentance that is
too late) T 52
Servire tempori (Paying strict adher-
ence to circumstances) T 213
Serum remedium aut tempestium
(Cures that are too late or are in
time) T 53
Sese *see* Ex sese
Similitudinis (Similarity) T 46
Simulatio (Pretence) T 27
Solicitudo (Anxiousness) T 156
Solitudo (Solitude) T 201
Solus *see* Non solus
Somnolentia (Sleepiness) T 172

Sordes (Meanness) T 43
Spes pertinax (Hope that is never given
up) T 91
– *see also* Frustrata, Praeter spem
Studium *see* Proprii
Stultitia *see* Fortunata
Stupidos *see* In stupidos
Subiti interventus (Interventions that
occur suddenly) T 88
Subitum exitium (Sudden death) T 192
Sumptuosa (Extravagances) T 115
Sunt *see* Fuerunt
Surditas (Deafness) T 63

Taciturnitas illaudata (Taciturnity cen-
sured) T 16; – laudata (Taciturnity
praised) T 17
Taedium ex iteratione (Boredom from
repetition) T 5
– *see also* Iteratio
Tarditatis et cunctationis (Slowness and
taking one's time) T 122
Temeritas (Rashness) T 179
Temperantia (Temperance) T 106
Tempestiva (Timely things) T 212
Tempestium *see* Serum
Tempori *see* Servire
Tenacitas (Miserliness) T 39
Timiditas (Timidity) T 33
Tolerantia (Tolerance) T 275
Torvitas (Ferociousness) T 276
Totum ut nihil reliqui (Using every-
thing) T 193
Tristis *see* Victoria
Tristitia et laetitia (Sadness and joy)
T 155
Tumultus (Turbulent times) T 262
Tuta *see* Securitatis

Ultio malefacti (Vengeance for a
misdeed) T 142
Usura (Usury) T 248
Ut nihil reliqui *see* Totum
Utendum *see* Proximis
Utrinque *see* Victoria

Vanitas (Things that are worthless or
pointless) T 30

English Index
of Erasmus' Adages

This index covers all the proverbs in the collection, including those that are not the principal subject of an essay, but that are alluded to here and there. It also includes a small number of proverbs in the *Collectanea* that never made it into the longer *Adagia chiliades*. This index leads you in several possible directions: to the main *Adages*, to the *Collectanea*, to Erasmus' Index of Topics, to similar proverbs, and to the listing of Early Modern English proverbs.

Each proverb has only one main entry in this index. Thus, the proverb 'You have handed the sheep over to the wolf' is found under the principal key word 'Sheep.' You can also locate a proverb by its main verb or other nouns as well as many adverbs and adjectives, using cross-references. Thus 'Handed *see* Sheep' and 'Wolf *see* Sheep' in the index will lead you to the main entry:

> Sheep, The character of a III i 95, (II vii 26 CWE 34 15), T 235; Sheep are no use
> II vii 26, T 235; Sheep over to the wolf, You have handed the I iv 10⁺, (IV
> vi 42 CWE 36 242), T 224; cf III vii 36, IV vi 42; Tilley W 602. *See also* Knife,
> Shepherd, Wolf

Here, as in many entries, we have for reasons of space brought together under a key word a number of proverbs ('The character of a sheep,' 'Sheep are no use,' and 'You have handed the sheep over to the wolf'), as well as cross-references to other proverbs in which the word 'sheep' appears. Each entry begins with the key word, and ends when the next key word appears.

( ) For the first of the three proverbs in the example, immediately after the main location, there is a reference in parentheses. Erasmus often quotes or even uses proverbs as part of his other entries, and also introduces proverbs that did not receive a full entry (he often included such proverbs in his own alphabetical and topical indexes). All quoted or additional proverbs are presented in parentheses in the form '(II vii 26 CWE 34 15).' This gives you the proverb essay in which the quoted proverb appears as well as the CWE volume and page number. The parentheses indicate that the proverb is at that location but not as the title of a full entry.

T There is also a reference to T 235. This means that the proverb is listed in Erasmus' Index of Topics (568–621 in this volume) under Topic 235 Fools (*In stupidos*).

Next follows 'Sheep are no use,' with similar information, including the same place (T 235) in the topical index.

Finally we have 'Sheep over to the wolf, You have handed the I iv 10⁺, (IV vi 42 CWE 36 242), T 224; cf III vii 36, IV vi 42; Tilley W 602.' This entry is more complex. The title and location are given as usual. The T number leads you to Topic 224 Critical situations (*Discriminis*).

+ A superscript + after the main proverb location indicates that this proverb is also found in the *Collectanea*. The location in the *Collectanea* is determined by consulting the concordance of the *Adagia* and *Collectanea* (359–66 above). There it is listed as proverb 540 and you will find c 540 printed in this volume among the *Collectanea* (277 above). The small number of *Collectanea* proverbs that did not make it into the full *Adagia* are also indexed as main entries in this index by their c numbers (eg c 716).

cf After the topical reference and a reference to an appearance elsewhere, there is a 'cf' that leads you to two interesting parallels.

Tilley, ODEP A concluding reference to 'Tilley' in this final proverb under 'Sheep' shows you that this proverb also appeared in Early Modern English, and provides you with its number (W 602) in Morris Palmer Tilley's standard *Dictionary of Proverbs in England in the Sixteenth and Seventeenth Centuries*. The proverb is also listed in our Index of Early Modern English proverbs (550–67 above). A proverb not in Tilley but found in the *Oxford Dictionary of English Proverbs* 3rd edition by F.P. Wilson is found by the page reference in the ODEP followed by *sub* indicating the word under which the proverb appears. A 'cf' before Tilley or ODEP indicates that the parallel is only approximate, and may be discussed in the notes to the proverb.

See also refers you to other words in the index where proverbs with the word 'sheep' also appear.

sub Here and there you will also run across a number of cross-references that refer you to parallels or comparisons with other proverbs, and these are indicated by 'cf' followed by the proverb number and then the Latin work '*sub*' that directs you to the key word in this index under which this parallel proverb is given.

If you are looking for a name in the title of a proverb, it will be listed in this index. All other name references are found in the Supplementary Index of Names (767–835 below).

Crabs walk forwards, You'll never make III vii 38, (III viii 98 CWE 35 279), T 68

Cradle, From the I vii 53⁺, T 45

Crafty as Ulysses (*Adagia* introduction xiii CWE 31 26); cf II viii 79. *See also* Cuckoo

Cranes that swallow a stone III vi 68, (III vii 1 n92 CWE 35 194), T 169; cf Tilley C 805. *See also* Ibycus

Crass *see* Minerva

Crassus *see* Croesus

Crawl on the ground, To II x 88⁺

Creature, No living. What living creature? II i 83, T 201; Creature thinks her own fair, Every *see* Own

Creatures *see* Vilest

Credit *see* Greek

Credulity has cost me money III iii 55, T 167

Cress? Why can't you eat I viii 54⁺, (IV vi 60 CWE 36 255), T 235

Crest, To raise one's I viii 69⁺, (III v 89 n3 CWE 35 110), T 109

Cretan and Cretan I ii 26, (II vii 68 CWE 33 34); Cretan and the sea, The I ii 31, T 27; Cretan with a Cretan, To play I ii 29⁺, (*Adagia* introduction xiii CWE 31 28 Mendacious as a Cretan, II viii 79 CWE 34 81, IV i 64 CWE 35 481, IV viii 52 CWE 36 389), T 30, T 46; Tilley C 822; Cretan with a man of Aegina, A I ii 27⁺, T 46

Cretans [perform] the sacrifice III i 82, T 84

Crete, Booty from IV iv 94, T 160

Crew *see* Ulysses'

Cricket, As noisy as a I ix 100, T 12; Cricket against a bee, You match a I viii 75⁺, T 92; cf I viii 72 *sub* Jay and 76 *sub* Tortoise. *See also* Wasp

Cries *see* Block

Crime has an ugly outcome III x 16, T 142

Cripple, Let the healthy man mock the III ii 21⁺, T 219; Cripple, you will learn to limp, If you live next to a I

x 73, (III ii 49 CWE 34 244, IV v 1 n1 CWE 36 128), T 239, T 260; Tilley C 828. *Cf* Lame

Crippleman *see* Pouch

Crisis reveals who is a man, A III viii 84, T 35

Crison of Himera, To run faster than IV vii 87, T 120

Critic, A captious II vi 19⁺, T 151

Criticism, When in office expect both just and unjust II vii 89, (*Adagia* introduction xiii CWE 31 22), T 200; cf Tilley K 58. *Cf* Momus

Criticize in others, Don't do yourself what you III ix 33, T 174; cf Tilley F 107

Criticized than imitated, Sooner II ii 84, T 151

Critics don't make friends IV iii 52, T 161

Croak, To I vii 16, (I vi 26 CWE 32 20), T 12, T 151

Crobylus' yoke II vii 51, T 46

Crock, Long will a II iv 20⁺, T 238; Tilley L 333

Crocodile attacks the man who flees, A C 707; Crocodile tears II iv 60⁺, (*Adagia* introduction iii CWE 31 6), T 27; Tilley C 831

Crocoton, Hercules wearing the (I ii 72 CWE 31 211), T 47

Croesus had, Would I possessed what they say (I v 98 CWE 31 468); Croesus or Crassus, As rich as I vi 74, (*Adagia* introduction xiii CWE 31 27 Rich as Croesus, Wealthy as Crassus, III iii 1 CWE 34 264, V i 57 CWE 36 574), T 1; Tilley C 832. *See also* Arabs

Croesus' millions, Add a penny to IV x 48, T 92, T 256

Cronos *see* Jove

Crop is heavier in another man's field, The I vi 72, T 166; cf Tilley N 115 Our neighbour's ground yields better corn than our own

Cross *see* Aegean

Crossroads of decision, I am at the I ii 48⁺, T 136

Money, Myconos, Planned, Practice, Soul, Water

Everywhere *see* Dog, Everything, Home

Evidence *see* Home-grown, Jove's, Lend

Evil, A necessary I v 26, (II ix 92 CWE 34 126), T 136; cf Tilley W 386, W 703; Evil, Drive out one evil with another (I ii 4 CWE 31 148–9); Evil, Remove the opportunity for III x 41, T 114; Evil, Spit away the v i 25, T 214; Evil, you will yourself hear worse, If you speak (I i 27 CWE 31 75); Evil about one as the north-east wind does clouds, Drawing *see* North-easter; Evil and a great good, A small II v 65⁺, T 184; Evil brought on oneself IV ii 5, T 51; Evil genius, An I i 72⁺, (I vi 53 CWE 32 39, II v 1 CWE 35 242, IV i 1 and n29 CWE 35 407), T 49; Evil grows out of evil v ii 31; cf Tilley M 1012; Evil man, Harm and not good must come from gifts of an (I iii 35 CWE 31 264), T 20; Evil men drink the dregs of their wickedness II x 36, T 142; Evil than two, It is better to be exposed to one IV ii 36, T 78; Evil thing known is best, An II ix 85⁺, T 80; Tilley H 166; Evil thrice over to the evil III iii 98, (II iv 30 CWE 33 205), T 142; Evil with another, To heal one I ii 6, T 78; Tilley P 457. *See also* Africa, Communications, Courage, Disturb, Escaped, Eye, Fountain, Lemnos, Nail, Scythian, Words

Evils come of their own accord IV ii 62, T 49; Evils it is very difficult to stand firm, Against two III viii 78. *See also* Basinful, Iliad, Lerna, Speed, Store, Termerian, Women

Exact *see* Tribute

Exalt *see* Lentils

Examine carefully, To (I v 91 CWE 31 464), T 169

Example, A useful v i 98. *See also* Neighbours

Exceed *see* Balance

Excel in different ways, People III ix 13, T 92

Except *see* Gods

Exceptional *see* Virtue

Exercise of the domestic, sheltered training-ground (v ii 10 CWE 36 602), T 259

Excess *see* Generals

Excessive *see* Nothing, Praise

Exchange *see* Diomede, Work

Excluded *see* Minerals

Excuses *see* Fight

Execestides himself could find, The right way not II vi 49, T 137

Exemption *see* Aches

Exile *see* Life

Exiles *see* Hopes

Exist *see* Know, Triplets

Expect *see* Criticism

Experience (is the mistress of fools) *see* Trouble

Experienced *see* Trouble

Expose *see* Strike

Extend *see* Hand

Extreme *see* Right

Eye, Envious is the neighbour's IV viii 20 repeats III i 22, T 166; Eye, Like a runny IV x 100, T 7; Eye, To avoid the evil IV iv 19; Eye and hand, By IV ix 97; Eye out, Knock my IV x 25, T 177; Eye twitches, My right II iv 37⁺, T 50; cf IV ix 72. *See also* Dust, Justice, Look, Master's, Mote, Neighbour's, Serpent's, Sleep, Warts, Woman's

Eyebrow twitches, My IV ix 72⁺, T 50; cf II iv 37

Eye-witness is worth more than ten ear-witnesses, One II vi 54⁺, T 167; cf I viii 32; Tilley E 274

Eyed *see* Blind

Eyeless *see* Blind

Eyes, As dear as one's v i 62; Eyes, Dear as a man's own (*Adagia* introduction xiii CWE 31 25); Eyes, etc., Carry in one's v ii 50, (I vi 81 CWE 32 54, IV vi 98 CWE 36 278, IV viii 23 CWE 36 369), T 161; Eyes in the back of his head, He has III iii 41, T 169; Tilley E 236; Eyes of all with the same salve,

Five, A cup of IV vi 76, (IV vii 76 CWE 36 334), T 271. *See also* Drink, Knees, Leap

Fix *see* Bath

Fixedly *see* Gaze

Flame *see* Hand, Sword

Flash in the pan, A II vii 90⁺, T 99

Flask-rich IV x 42, T 109

Flatterers *see* Gifts

Flattery wins friends and truth engenders hate II ix 53⁺, T 28; Tilley *T* 562, *T* 569

Flautist gets the beating, The IV vii 46, T 273

Flaw *see* Pot

Flax for the sake of gain, You marry white III ii 77, T 42

Flay *see* Beast

Flea bite, He calls on God for a III iv 4, T 33, T34; Flea in its place, A III ii 15, T 102

Fledgling *see* Mars

Flee *see* Cord, Dart, Sanctuary

Fleeing *see* Smoke

Flees *see* Crocodile, Polecat

Fleeting *see* Oath

Flesh *see* Fish

Flies IV vii 43, T 272; Flies, Keeping off the III vii 60, T 70; cf IV vii 25 Fly-flappers; Flies, The earth I iii 25, T 68; Flies fluttering past, He is afraid of the very I v 66, T 33. *See also* Eagle, Owl, Time

Flight is safer III x 19, T 224

Flock, He is from that III vi 86, (III v 44 CWE 35 94, IV ix 44 CWE 36 450), T 46; Flock as I am, Same (III v 44 CWE 35 94), T 46. *See also* Muses'

Flogging *see* Dead body

Floor *see* Hiding

Flora, Licentious as the carnival of (*Adagia* introduction xiii CWE 31 25)

Flour, not fine words II vi 16, T 82; cf Tilley *W* 791, *W* 786, *T* 97; Flour as we are, Same III v 44⁺, (II viii 55 CWE 34 71, III vii 64 n3 CWE 35 255, IV iii 38 CWE 36 26), T 46. *See also* Wine skins. *Cf* Milled fare

Flourish, Right to the final IV vi 20, (II iii 45 CWE 33 155), T 44

Flow *see* Springs

Flower is but ash, A IV vii 12, T 105. *See also* Fish, Gourd-, Muse, Nectar

Flowers bloom in summer, some in winter grow, Some (IV iv 20 CWE 36 73, I vii 70 CWE 32 108). *See also* Pigs, Samos

Flows back again, What you ladle out II iii 33, T 70

Flushed, but ten times pale, Once III v 90, T 248

Flute against trumpet, You match I viii 74⁺, T 92; Flute player, Like a Latin v ii 38, (v ii 15 n15 CWE 36 609). *See also* Ass, Babys, Lydian

Flute-player, You live the life of a II iii 34, (III x 100 CWE 35 399, IV ii 17 n2 CWE 35 511), T 107; Flute-player who could not play the lyre, Let him be a II iii 44, T 101; cf IV ix 38 *sub* Accompanist

Flute-players *see* Delirium, Tenedos

Fly, Not so much as a II i 84⁺, T 201; Fly, The depravity of the III viii 95, T 7, T 35; Fly an elephant, You make of a I ix 69⁺, (III vii 1 CWE 35 213), T 69; Tilley *F* 398, cf *M* 1216; Fly away, To III v 21, T 196; Fly has a spleen, Even a III v 7, T 142; Fly without feathers, It is not easy to III v 84⁺, T 68; Tilley *F* 407. *See also* Eagle, Hawk, Tortoise. *Cf* Fire-worm

Fly-flappers IV vii 25, (III vii 60n CWE 35 250), T 162

Flying *see* Pursue

Foals *see* Mule

Foe *see* Friend

Fold *see* Safe

Folded *see* Bedclothes, Hands

Folding *see* Hands

Follow *see* Dorian, Effeminate, God, Stream

Following *see* Leader, Shadow, Tide

Follows *see* Fire

Folly it is to strive to no good purpose
v ii 4. *See also* Fools, Jove, Kicking,
Stubbornness

Fond *see* Fish, Gello

Food, Those who eat other persons'
(IV iv 53 CWE 36 97), T 272; Food,
Those who face a long task need III
ix 18; Food as yet unblest out of the
dish, Snatch not I vi 27, (I iii 59 CWE
31 284), T 42; Food from a fish trap,
To seek IV iv 88, (IV vi 50 n3 CWE
36 248), T 224; Food from a snare,
To go after IV v 71⁺, T 148; Food
of the gods I viii 88, T 118. *See also*
Chamber-pot, Dog, Flour, Hopes,
Statues

Fool, To play the I iv 91⁺, T 70; Fool
can see it, When a thing is done a I i
30⁺, (*Adagia* introduction ii CWE 31 5,
IV iii 59 CWE 36 36), T 52; cf I iii 99 *sub*
Sadder; Fool have your finger, Don't
let a III v 5, T 235; Fool who kills
the father and spares the children,
He's a I x 53, (*Adagia* introduction
vii CWE 31 16, III vii 1 CWE 35 209),
T 142; Fool will laugh when 'tis
no laughing matter, The (I vii 46
CWE 31 96). *See also* Gardener, King,
Morychus, Trouble. *Cf* Deceives me
once

Foolish *see* Big, Coroebus, Glaucus,
Wise

Fool's prosperity is hard to bear, A (I
vii 72 CWE 32 72), T 27

Fools in their folly speak I i 98, (I vi 1
CWE 32 4, II ix 10 CWE 34 95), T 46;
Tilley F 459, F 465, F 515

Foot, He has no place to set his I v 7,
(IV x 50 CWE 36 513), T 2; cf IV x 84;
Foot, Not one I x 44, T 170; cf I v
6; Foot, To stand on either (III iii 56
CWE 34 300), T 102; Foot, With silent
II i 4, T 122; Foot first, To put your
best I vi 35, T 120; Tilley F 570; Foot
forward, One must put one's best
III i 34, T 229; cf Tilley F 570; Foot in
a sandal, left foot in a basin, Right
III i 62, T 102; Foot in this shoe, He

has his IV viii 70, T 187; Foot to foot,
To put IV v 39, T 146, T 226; cf v
i 73. *See also* Charon's, Fit, Hand,
Measure, Polypus, Servants, Shoe,
Sole, Swim

Footers *see* Two-footers

Footwear *see* Colophonian. *Cf* Shoes

Force anyone by kindness, Do not III
x 11. *See also* Gold, Requests

Forced *see* Friend

Forces are pressed into a narrow space,
Now my I i 17, T 73, T 137

Forearm *see* Nose

Forebear *see* Bear

Forehead, To smooth (*or* wrinkle) the
I viii 48⁺, T 155; Forehead before
occiput I ii 19, T 169; cf Tilley M 733

Foreigner drove out the native, The III
iv 100, T 177

Foresee it for certain, I III ix 62, T 149

Foresight for others, not for oneself III
viii 73, T 133

Forest *see* Carry

Forestalls *see* God

Foretells *see* Bee

Forever *see* Summer

Forget one's own name, To II iii
96, T 194. *See also* Friends, Malea,
Remember

Forgets *see* Hurt, Please

Forgetting *see* Wrongs

Forgive. *Cf* Who his friend's pardon

Fork *see* Nature

Formidable man, A III i 56, (III vii 1
CWE 35 205), T 113

Forms *see* Gods

Fortunate have many kinsmen, The III
i 88 repeats III v 4, (III v 4 CWE 35
69), T 161;

Fortune, Absolutely hostile III viii
26, T 49; Fortune, Black-listed by I
ii 93, T 249; Fortune, Every man's
character moulds his II iv 30, T 142;
Tilley M 630; Fortune, Seize (I vii
70 CWE 32 109); Fortune favours the
brave I ii 45, (III x 5 CWE 35 359);
Tilley F 601; Fortune has embroiled
me! With what a portent II ix 41,

One I i 33[+], (II iv 14 CWE 33 197, III
ii 49 CWE 34 244, IV iii 20 CWE 36
15, IV iv 100 CWE 36 127), T 77; cf I
vii 99[+] *sub* Scratch; Tilley H 87; ODEP
706 *sub* Scratch my back; Hand to,
To add your IV iii 35, T 23; Hand to,
To put one's IV vi 19; Hand to all
and sundry, Do not hold out your
right I i 2 (Pythagoras) CWE 31 35,
T 161; Tilley H 68; Hand to hand, To
pass down from IV v 28, (v i 7 CWE
36 546), T 105, T 161, T 207. *See also*
Advice, Athenian, Business, Candle,
Celmis, Eye, Lemnian, Mould, Skill,
Sore, Sow, Spring up, Stone, Strike,
Surety, Sword, Torch, Water, Work
Handed *see* Sheep
Handfuls, In II i 16, (I ix 16 CWE 32
190, IV ix 93 CWE 36 480, IV x 61 CWE
36 519), T 38, T 41
Handle, To look for a I iv 4[+], T 114;
cf (IV vi 12 n3 CWE 36 217). *See also*
Strike, Tools
Hands, Pray with veiled v i 74; Hands,
To take with both I ix 16, (I vi 35 CWE
32 27, IV ix 73 CWE 36 467, IV x 61
CWE 36 519), T 38; Hands, With both
(I iv 22 CWE 31 337); Hands, With
folded II i 23, T 171; Hands, With
unwashed I ix 55[+], (II iii 87 CWE 33
182, III iv 86 CWE 35 53), T 179; Tilley
H 125; Hands and feet, With I iv 15[+],
(*Adagia* introduction xiii CWE 31 23,
I ix 12 CWE 32 186, II vii 12 CWE 34
10), T 174, T 229; cf I iv 23 *sub* Nails;
cf Tilley M 923, T 422; Hands are
washed, friends stick closely, Once
(I v 23 CWE 31 403); Hands in one's
pockets, To have one's II x 31, T 159;
Hands make light work, Many II iii
95, T 210; Tilley H 119; Hands on
high, Raise IV ix 12, T 155; Hands to
sleep, A little folding of the (I viii 21
CWE 32 136), T 24; Hands up, To put
one's I ix 79[+], T 95; Hands? What in
the end cannot be done with III vii
28, T 23; Hands with eyes in them
I viii 31[+], T 167; cf Tilley S 212. *See*

also Catch, Cock, Gods, Holy man,
Kings, Law, Picture, Sacred things,
Water
Handsome *see* Nireus
Handy *see* Milk
Hang yourself?, Why not II viii 15,
T 249. *See also* Bid, Choose, Nicias
Hanged *see* Gallows, Papiria
Hangnail *see* Whitlow
Hangs *see* Thread
Happened *see* Sagra
Happening *see* Planned
Happiness, Unhappy (*Adagia* intro-
duction xiii CWE 31 23, II i 1 CWE 33
3). *See also* Friendship, Wisdom
Happy and the unhappy, For half their
lives there is no difference between
the II i 9, T 130; Happy he who has
a three-months' child, How I vii 39,
T 254; Happy is he that owes nothing
II vii 98[+], T 248; Tilley N 254; Happy
who does not know it, He is not
IV v 4, T 111; Tilley K 182. *See also*
Caution, Gods, Man, Old age
Harass *see* Laws
Harbour *see* Athenian, Navigate, Ship,
Shipwrecked, Skill, Torone
Hard life, but a healthy one, A III x 27,
T 116. *See also* Iron, Knot, Opposite
things, Soft things, Suck, Wise, Work
Hard-headed *see* Advantage
Hard-of-hearing *see* Deaf
Hard-working man to do, There is
always something for a IV v 48,
T 169
Hare, He has not eaten II i 15, T 4; cf
Tilley H 159; Hare, now you have a
pheasant, Go hunt for a III vi 44,
T 188; Hare appearing makes your
path unlucky, A II x 45, T 49; Tilley
H 150; Hare asleep, A I x 57[+], (IV iii
78 CWE 36 47), T 27; Tilley H 153;
Hare because of its meat, A II i 80[+],
(*Adagia* introduction xiii CWE 31 26
Timid as a hare), T 224; cf Tilley
B 24; Hare even cakes are figs, To
a starving III vi 54, T 154; Hare
thyself, and goest in quest of game?,

Looked *see* Path, Ship

Looking *see* Armour, Bear, Daggers, Horse, Jupiter, Love, Onions, Ox, Oxen, Wolf's

Look-out, If you're the IV ix 88, T 216

Looks *see* Ass, Health, Polycrates, Toothless

Loose *see* Broom-twigs

Lose one's case on a fault in the formula, To v ii 15; Lose what you have, and get the misfortune you do not now have c 523. *See also* Action, Small, Sow, War

Loser weeps, the winner's dead, The II vi 24, T 96

Losers must expect to suffer II vi 1, (IV iii 79 CWE 36 48), T 95

Loses *see* Hipparchion

Losing heart, Not III ix 96, T 35

Loss *see* Gain, Gift

Lost *see* Belt, Camel, Coat, Kernel, Loaves, Ox, Shipwreck

Lot *see* Chaff, Death, Poverty, Soft things, Wealth

Lots, but few can you find that are prophets, Many the casters of I vii 8, T 27; Lots, drawing (IV 54 CWE 31 431)

Lotus, He has tasted the II vii 62, T 258

Loud words, Don't be put off by III ix 17, T 35. *See also* Stentor

Louder *see* Dogs

Love and be wise, It is impossible to (II ii 80 CWE 33 118); Tilley L 558; Love as in time to come you should hate, and hate as you should in time to come love II i 72, T 161; Tilley T 309; Love blossoming on both sides IV ii 15, T 161; Love comes by looking I ii 79, (III iv 69 CWE 35 43), T 160; Tilley L 501; Love it is a great disgrace not to repay your love, In c 389; Love more readily than love itself, Nothing buys c 388; Love teaches the arts. *Cf* Desire; Love without a rival, To II i 17+, T 110. *See also* Atreus', Cupboard, Hate, Jealousy, Neighbours, Scorn, Sparta's, Tethys. *Cf* Self-love

Loved *see* Beautiful, Home, Phrygius

Lovely *see* Same, Venus

Lover and pursue one who does not love them, They turn away from a (II v 27 CWE 33 255), cf Tilley L 479; Lover grows old in one day, The yearning (III iii 86 CWE 34 311), T 121, T 127

Lovers weave their own dreams II iii 90, T 90. *See also* Falling-out, Self-lovers

Lovers' vows II iv 90+, T 207; cf Tilley J 82

Loves his own age, Everyone I ii 20+, T 46; part of series I ii 20–4; Loves tenderly, Of one who III viii 20, T 160. *See also* Cicada, Earth, Time, Wolf

Lowered *see* Ears

Lowest bench, Belonging on the III vii 80, T 99. *See also* Mysians

Loyalties, Conflicting III viii 24, T 102

Loyalty *see* Locrian

Lozenges *see* Rufillus

Luck (or Troubles) brings men together, Bad II i 71, (I i 11 CWE 31 60–1), T 161; Luck, Here's to good *or* A blessing on it! I vi 53, T 50; Luck, ruler of the hustings, Lady IV x 19, (IV x 62 CWE 36 519), T 105; Luck, Share your (II viii 64 CWE 34 74); Luck, To be in the service of good IV vi 100; Luck, To men with face thrice wiped god gives good (I vi 94 CWE 32 62), T 108; Luck makes people arrogant, Good III ix 92, T 110; Luck next time, Better cf I ii 13; ODEP 54; Luck save me now, May my II ix 77, T 224; Luck than by good management, He does it more by good (I v 82 CWE 31 455, I viii 44 CWE 32 147). *See also* Alabanda, Friends, Fortune

Luckier *see* Strobili

Luckless *see* Homeless

Lucky side, To lean on the I iii 16, T 161. *See also* Outcome, Rascals, Timotheus

Luncheon *see* Ox

T 52; Tilley M 1234; Mouse that did not run into its hole was carrying a gourd, The III iii 79, T 69; Mouse will fasten its teeth in a rascal, Even a I viii 96, T 142. *See also* Mountain, Net, Shrew-mouse

Mouth, An unbridled III iv 47, T 12; Mouth, Whatever came into his I v 72, T 12; cf I v 73; Mouth and morsel, Between I v 2⁺, T 231; cf I v 1⁺, IV viii 30; Mouth is not spoken wholly without cause, What is in every man's I vi 25, T 249; cf IV viii 34; cf Tilley F 43, M 204; Mouth lacking a door, With a (III iv 47 CWE 35 30), T 12; Mouth to blow hot and cold, Out of one I viii 30, (IV vi 58 CWE 36 254), T 102, T 208; Tilley M 1258. *See also* Advice, Drunkard, Heart, Horse, Laughter, Ox, Pap, Vulcan's, Wolf's

Mouthed *see* Cormorant

Mouths agape for the same will III viii 99, T 126

Move not the line I ix 97, (I iv 30 CWE 31 340, III vii 56 CWE 35 249), T 174; Move what should not be moved, You I vi 61, (v i 93 CWE 36 595), T 177; cf Tilley W 260. *See also* Camarina, Counter, Rope, Take

Mover in a little affair, A big III iv 82, T 102

Moving *see* Anagyrus

Mow *see* Moss

Mu, He does not even dare say I viii 2, (IV vi 79 CWE 36 267), T 33

Much in between v i 45, T 105. *See also* Belief, Sense, Work

Muck *see* Pig

Mud, Stick in the (I ii 81 CWE 31 215); Mud, you are sticking in the same I iv 99⁺, T 70; cf I iv 100 and IV iii 70 *sub* Water; Mud and you'll never find any to drink, Foul the clear water with II vi 83, T 51; Mud with mud, To purge away I x 67, T 78. *See also* Dust, Pot

Mugger, A IV i 73, T 237

Mule, A bath-keeper's IV iv 50, T 70; Mule foals, When the I v 83, T 74; Mule scratches another, One I vii 96⁺; Tilley M 1306

Mules are than asses, How much better III i 55, T 92. *See also* Marian

Mullet is fasting, The grey I iii 23, T 119

Munching *see* Mastic

Murder will out. *Cf* Ibycus

Murderer, Well-wishing III ii 7, (v i 29 CWE 36 559), T 27

Mus (*or* Mys) at Pisa, The same as II iii 67, (*Adagia* introduction iii CWE 31 6), T 226

Muscular *see* Milo

Muse, A suitor of the selfsame II i 28, T 46; Muse, Of the more clumsy I i 38⁺, T 240; Muse, The Dorian II v 45⁺, T 3; Muse herself in flower, Now is the III iii 24, T 19. *See also* Attic

Muse-struck IV x 72

Muses, Birds of the IV vi 4 repeats IV x 87, T 12, T 19; Muses, Eloquence of the (I ii 57 CWE 31 197); Muses, Strangers to the II vi 18, (III vii 1 n167 CWE 35 204), T 24; Muses, With the III vi 89, T 216; Muses are free from envy, The doors of the I ii 85, T 166; cf II vii 41; Muses' doors are open, The II vii 41⁺, T 253; Muses' flock, Birds of the IV x 87 repeats IV vi 4, T 19. *See also* Jackdaw

Mushroom, A IV i 38, (IV x 98 CWE 36 541), T 235; Mushroom, A rotten IV x 98, T 98

Music, A life of pure (II iii 34 CWE 33 148, II ix 69 CWE 34 116); Music, Don't ruin the IV iii 14, T 108; Music has no listeners, Hidden I vii 84, T 205; cf (III iii 6 n2 CWE 34 284); Music is cut off, The III iii 100, T 12. *See also* Carian

Music-hall *see* Assembly

Mustard, To live on IV v 74, (IV vi 60 CWE 36 255 The look of mustard), T 155; Tilley M 1333

Wish, Everything; Not fit *see* Shoes;
Not from *see* Hymettus, Oak; Not
if *see* Dreams, Ox; Not losing *see*
Losing; Not my *see* Ox; Not one *see*
Bite, Foot; Not only *see* Atreus'; Not
rashly *see* Abydos; Not so much *see*
Fly; Not to be *see* Born, Resolved,
Slave, Spoken, Suffenus; Not to fret
see Yoke; Not without *see* Theseus;
Not worth *see* Fingers, Harvesting,
Tiddler, Worth; Not worthy *see* Look
me in the eye; Not wrong *see* Reply
Note, To strike the same wrong I v 9⁺,
T 10; cf Tilley S 936; Note, To strike
the wrong (I ii 36 CWE 31 179)
Notes together low and high ('maga-
dizein'), To play two (I viii 30 CWE
32 140), T 102
Nothing, A man is not free unless
he sometimes does v ii 21, T 278;
Nothing, I am I iii 44, v i 86, (v i 70n
CWE 36 581, v i 86 CWE 36 592), T 85;
Nothing, It is better to be idle than
to work for (III vi 66 CWE 35 157)
Tilley N 281; Nothing, or cares for
nothing, He is v i 37, T 99; Nothing,
To achieve III vi 66, (v ii 21 CWE 36
614), T 70, T 278; Nothing, To do (v
ii 21 CWE 36 614), T 278; Nothing
and watch it well, Take IV vii 24;
Nothing can be either added or taken
away IV viii 4, T 44; Nothing except
that I know not, I know (III iii 1 CWE
34 263); Tilley N 276,; Nothing to do
with the lyre I v 46⁺, T 47, T 144;
Nothing to do with the subject III
x 33, T 144; Nothing to do with the
verse I v 45, (III ii 47 CWE 33 98, II iv
57 CWE 33 221, III ii 92 CWE 34 259),
T 47, T 144; Nothing to excess I vi
96⁺, (II ii 38 CWE 33 93, IV iii 1 CWE 36
4, IV iv 99 CWE 36 126), T 108; Tilley
M 793, M 806, T 158; Nothing to him,
either bad or good (III iii 18 CWE 32
288), T 99. *See also* Bed, Conscience,
C's, Farming, Friend, God, Gold,
Happy, Harmene, Justice, Know,
Knowing, Knowledge, Line's, Love,

Parmeno's, Profit, Sacred, Sacrifices,
Salt, Self-deception, Starvation, Tear,
Things, Woman
Nothing's going right today IV viii 46,
T 49
Nothings, Airy (III vii 21 CWE 35 229),
T 30
Notice *see* Elephant
Notion, No firm IV vii 85, T 30
Nought is at all points blest III i 87
Nourishing *see* Serpent
Novel *see* Africa
Novelty finds favour III ix 38, T 203
Now *see* Arrived, Datis', Forces, Gods,
Iron, Men, Muse, Shipwreck, Strike,
Toga, Wisdom
Now's *see* Beans
Nowhere *see* Finger, Mark, Sparta
Noxious *see* Woman
Nudge *see* Elbow, Ribs
Numa, Religious as (*Adagia* introduc-
tion xiii CWE 31 27)
Number *see* Enormous, Sacrifice
Numbers, Yield to III ix 60, T 37
Numenius *see* Attabas
Nurse *see* Dress
Nut, I would not swap that for an
empty (I viii 8 CWE 32 131), T 99. *See
also* Olive. *Cf* Walnut
Nuts behind, To leave the I v 35⁺, (II
viii 11 n1 CWE 34 53), T 104

O *see* Antius, Enemies
Oak, By the darkness around the II i
90, T 49; Oak dances for Bacchus,
Even the IV ii 100, T 113; Oak or
rock, Not from IV vii 96, T 276
Oaks, Many strokes fell great I viii 94,
T 170; Tilley S 941
Oak-tree, Go and shake another I v
34⁺, (IV v 1 CWE 36 133), T 255
Oaktrees or rocks, Born of I viii 87,
T 184
Oar, Another sort of II vii 21, (II viii 20
CWE 34 56), T 203; Oar, The man who
has learnt to row should take the I ii
76, (III iii 4 CWE 34 283), T 179; cf (I
iii 1 CWE 31 232); Oar to the bench,

Owl among crows (I v 41 CWE 31 421),
T 49; Owl flies, The I i 76⁺, (I ii 11
CWE 31 152, II iv 87 CWE 33 233, II
viii 31 CWE 34 60, III i 40 CWE 34 197),
T 50; Tilley O 93; Owl has one cry
and the raven another, The III ii 74,
T 47; Owl sings to the nightingale,
The IV iv 12, T 92. *See also* Eagle

Owl's egg, An II i 44, T 241

Owls to Athens I ii 11⁺, (I vii 57 CWE 32
101), T 70; cf III i 44 *sub* Rivulet; Tilley
O 97 and C 466. *See also* Lauriotic

Own is beautiful, What is one's I ii
15⁺, (I i 21 CWE 31 168, II iv 100 CWE
33 237, II vii 55 CWE 34 27, III iv 2
CWE 35 4, III vii 34 CWE 35 236), T 57,
T 110; Tilley C 812, M 131. *See also*
Samos, Wife

Owned *see* Sisapo

Ox, A Cyprus I x 95⁺, (III vii 1 n150
CWE 35 202, IV i 1 CWE 35 415); Ox,
A sea- IV vi 90, T 235; Ox, drive an
ass, If you cannot drive an II viii 4,
T 102; Ox, Lead a willing IV i 27,
T 154; Ox, Luncheon for a Cyprus I
x 96⁺, (II x 3 CWE 34 130), T 43; Ox,
No mourning for an aged II ix 16,
T 128; Ox, Pray not against your II
ix 83, T 90; Ox, Slowly the II i 3,
(I i 47 CWE 31 98), T 122; Ox, The
seventh I x 63, (II x 71 CWE 34 154,
IV vi 93 CWE 36 275), T 99, T 268;
Ox, You can expect grass sometime,
III iv 80, T 122; Ox, You will keep
watch on the III x 80, T 49, T 245;
Ox and stopped short when he got
to the tail, He ate the whole III iii
68, T 44; Ox at the heap, An III ii 53,
T 50; Ox at the manger, An II i 39,
T 50; Ox in his mouth, He carries an
II iii 10, T 3; Ox in the city, An III iv
16, T 100; Ox in the stable, An IV vi
91, (IV vi 90 CWE 36 274), T 117; Ox
is always looking over the hedge,
A borrowed I x 62, (II v 37 CWE 33
258), T 253; Ox is getting old, The
III iv 22, T 128; Ox? Not my burden:
a saddle on the II ix 84⁺, (*Adagia*

introduction iv CWE 31 8, II vi 74
CWE 33 327), T 48; cf Tilley C 758;
Ox of the Homolottians, An III ii 52,
T 99; Ox on a silver plate, An IV vi
93, T 268; Ox on the tongue, An I vii
18⁺, (*Adagia* introduction iii CWE 31
6, II iv 87 CWE 33 233), T 3; ODEP 604;
Ox putting its head over Taygetus,
An IV ii 59, T 68; Ox raises the dust
to its own harm, The II v 78, T 51;
Ox to the wrestling-ring, An (I iv
62 CWE 31 363), T 70; Ox treads the
more firmly, The tired I i 47⁺, (II i 3
CWE 33 18), T 142; Tilley O 108; Ox
under the yoke, An II vi 74, T 48;
Ox were to speak, Not if an III i 46,
T 30; Ox would be lost, Not even an
IV v 1; Ox would wear the trappings
and the lazy nag would plough, The
I vi 71⁺, T 166. *See also* Fox, Hare,
Locrian, Pyrrhias, She-goat

Ox's hide, Seated on the III iv 99, T 142

Oxen, Whole pot-roast III i 9 repeated
in IV v 19, T 89, T 117; Oxen, Eaters
of CWE 33 327 (ii vi 72); Oxen, To kill
III ii 50, T 41; Oxen looking towards
harvest-time III ii 51, T 50; Oxen to
the cart, To harness reluctant I vii
66, T 70. *See also* Asses. *Cf* Harness

Ox-flaying style, In III ii 47, T 32

Ox-hides, A heart of seven IV i 19, T 35

Pacidianus *see* Esernius

Pactolus, The wealth of I vi 75, T 1

Paean *see* Io

Pages, He fills both II iv 15⁺, T 100

Paid *see* Ram

Pain, It is unkind to touch on things
that give IV i 57, T 195; Pain, more
gain, More C 233; Pain is gain cf (I
i 31 CWE 31 80); ODEP 607. *See also*
Children, Dead, Joy

Pains *see* Aches

Paint you in your own colours, I'll I iv
6⁺, T 151. *See also* Cypress

Painted *see* Monkey

Painters *see* Poets

Pair *see* Scales

Pythia *see* Feast
Pythian and Delian mean the same
thing, For you II vi 80, T 192
Pytho road, Over and again the II x
57, T 5

Quail *see* Hercules, Parrot
Quails, To feed on III ii 24, T 118
Quarrel breeds another, One II x 41,
T 78; Quarrel will quarrel breed, and
hurt breed hurt I viii 99, (II x 41 CWE
34 143), T 78. *See also* Run away
Quarrelling, Stubborn III viii 18, T 94
Quarrels are between brothers, The
bitterest I ii 50, T 164; Tilley H 211
Quarrelsome *see* Dog
Quarries, To the II i 31, (III vii 1 CWE
35 193), T 49
Quarry *see* Pursue
Quarter *see* Wolves
Quarters and at long range, At close I
iv 29, T 147, T 229
Queen her king is fair, To every (I ii
15 CWE 31 160), T 57. *See also* Mind
Quench *see* Oil
Quenched *see* Fire
Quest *see* Hare
Question *see* Reply
Quick, To cut to the II iv 13⁺, (III
iii 34 CWE 34 293), T 176; Tilley Q
13. *See also* Asparagus, Dung-cake,
March
Quicker *see* Ants
Quickly *see* Heraclitus', Sea-lung
Quietly *see* Crow
Quinsy *see* Silver-quinsy, Wine-quinsy
Quips *see* Maesonian
Quiver, A good day out of the II viii
18⁺

Race *see* Fall, Torch
Racing-car *see* Greedy
Radius *see* Centre
Rage *see* Heart
Rags *see* Ulysses
Rain, nor scorched by the sun, Neither
wet with the II v 53, T 24; Rain can
fall, As easy as IV iv 61, T 72; Rain

gives birth to a rainstorm, A tiny I
iii 2, T 170; Tilley D 617. *See also* Ass,
Earth, Wet
Rained *see* House
Raining, get on with the grinding,
When it is (III iv 24 CWE 35 16). *See
also* Sow
Rains *see* Black-puddings, Jove
Rainstorm *see* Rain
Raise *see* Brows, Crest, Finger, Hands,
Spur, Ox
Raisins *see* Old man
Ram, Doing a good turn to a IV vi 87,
T 25; cf II v 92; Ram, He sends out a
II iii 12, T 147; Ram frisking with its
horns, A III vi 92, T 107; Ram paid
for its upbringing, The II v 92, (IV
vi 87 CWE 36 272), T 25
Rampart *see* Ditch
Ran *see* Tale, Wet
Rancours of the powerful, Avoid the
III x 47⁺, T 142;
Range, With a full III i 38, T 45. *See
also* Out, Quarters
Rank, Behind the front I iii 94, T 98.
See also Growth
Rapacious *see* Cats
Rare *see* Bird, Crow, Phoenix
Rascal at the water, A I vi 54, (II i 97
CWE 33 75), T 49. *See also* Mouse
Rascality takes the short cuts III ii 97,
T 237
Rascals are sometimes lucky in the
hunt II v 2, T 50. *See also* Lydians,
Opportunity
Rash *see* Risk
Rashly *see* Abydos, Deal
Rations, Three days' II viii 90, (IV iv
52 CWE 36 96)
Rattle *see* Archytas
Raven sings sweeter than the finch,
The I viii 83, T 92. *See also* Owl
Ravens *see* Laws
Ravine *see* Oenoë
Ravings *see* Old women
Razor against the whetstone, The I i
20, T 49; cf (*Adagia* introduction xiii
CWE 31 25)

78, T 140; Wolf would mate with a sheep, Sooner a III vii 36, T 68; cf I iv 10⁺ *sub* Sheep, IV vi 42 *sub* Sheep-wolf. *See also* Lamb, Man, Sheep, Sheep-wolf, Thief

Wolf's fallen into the trap, The I x 16, T 139; Wolf's jaws are gaping, The II iii 58⁺, T 84; CWE 31 6, (I vii 15 CWE 32 75); cf II ii 76⁺, II iv 24; Wolf's mouth, From the II vii 63⁺, (II vii 80 CWE 34 38), T 224; Wolf's wings, You are looking for the I iv 81⁺, T 69

Wolf-cubs, Keep II i 86, (I iv 71 CWE 31 366), T 25, T 51; cf Tilley W 606

Wolf-hunt, From a III ii 86, T 70

Wolves, A drink snatched from the II vi 98, T 120; Wolves, We shall give them no more quarter than we would to II ii 27, T 32; Wolves have seen him first, The I vii 86⁺, T 3; cf III viii 56 *sub* Wolf, IV v 50 *sub* Wolf, (IV x 77 n2 CWE 36 529); Tilley W 621; Wolves to go mad, Persuade IV iv 15, T 72. *See also* Abyss

Woman, A Thessalian I iii 12, T 199, T 274; Woman, even a good one, There is nothing worse than a (IV ii 35 CWE 35 522); Woman, even when she's dead, Ne'er trust a II x 21, T 199; Woman, here be evils three, Fire, sea, and II ii 48, T 119; cf Tilley H 781; Woman, Nothing is more noxious than a III x 21, T 199; Woman, Silence becomes a IV i 97, (*Adagia* introduction xiii CWE 31 25), T 17; Tilley S 447; Woman, wait, Old III iv 81, T 122; Woman as commander-in-chief and women soldiers, A II v 81⁺, T 33; Woman dancing, An old II viii 11, (III iv 65 CWE 35 41), T 69; cf II viii 12; Woman in the home means a bad time for the man, A (IV ii 35 CWE 35 522); Woman must never draw sword II v 51⁺, T 210; Woman nor your lap, Trust neither a IV iv 89, T 199; Woman should not be alone anywhere, A modest III ix 39, T 199;

Woman swears I write in wine, What a (I vii 1 CWE 32 67), T 194; Woman without words, A (III vi 77 CWE 35 136), T 68; Woman you will have a deep grave, like a horse, As an old II viii 13, T 24. *See also* Chalcis, Corinthian, Dog, Heart, Old. *Cf* Hag

Woman's jealousy sets light to any house, A (IV ii 35 CWE 35 522); Woman's oath is writ in wine (I iv 56 CWE 31 359); Woman's eye, A III iv 69, T 199; Woman's *see also* Rump

Womanish men's language is womanish too II ix 10, T 149

Women marry in May, Bad I iv 9, T 211; ODEP 516 *sub* Marry. *See also* Evil, Lamp, Old, Spartan

Women's woes II x 22, T 199; cf Tilley W 656

Won *see* Gifts, Runner

Wondrous *see* Lentil

Wood *see* Bull, Carry, Fig-wood, Mandro, Mercury, Nephalian, Ship

Woodcock IV i 5, (IV x 18 CWE 36 496), T 99. *Cf* Francolin

Wooden horse, A IV ii 1, (IV ix 95 n2 CWE 36 481, IV x 70 CWE 36 525), T 148. *See also* Sword

Woods *see* Peoples

Wooer's life, A II ix 69, T 107

Wool, I care not a wisp of *or* A wisp of wool and no more I viii 6⁺, T 99; cf Tilley S 917; Wool to a fuller's workshop IV vii 39, T 69. *See also* Bristles, Donkey, Goat's, Gods

Word (or voice), The living I ii 17⁺, T 254; Word, A fat and lardy IV viii 80; Word, A friend in III iii 57, T 161

Words, but knowledgeable, Sparing of III viii 77, T 13; Words, Fine (IV iii 54 CWE 36 32), T 207; Words, In three IV iv 84, (III vii 50 CWE 35 246, IV vi 20 CWE 36 224), T 13; Words, To give empty I v 49⁺, T 220; Words are never rustic, Your III vi 33, T 19; Words are the lightest of things III i 18, (v ii 29 n2 CWE 36 618), T 12; Words can be the source

Supplementary Index of Names in Erasmus' Adages

Proper names that appear in the title of an adage are to be found in the preceding English Index of Erasmus' Adages (635–766). If a name appears anywhere else in Erasmus' text (but not in the notes to the translation) it will be found in this Supplementary Index. Names which occur in both are marked 'see English Index. Also . . .' An asterisk (*) marks names for which a source discussion can be found at 38–83 above. This index is based on a draft prepared by Carolyn MacDonald.

Index of Scriptural References

Proverbs

6:10	II i 23n (CWE 33 348)
9:17	IV iv 92 n3
10:19	I ii 99:6n
11:22	I vii 24n (CWE 32 314)
13:4	II vii 82 n3 (CWE 34 330)
15:1	III i 100 n2 (CWE 34 389)
15:15	IV x 40 n3
16:18	v i 99 n2
17:17	IV v 5 n4
18:21	II ii 39 n3 (CWE 33 371)
26:11	III v 13 n3
26:8	IV vii 4 n2
27:17	I vii 100n (CWE 32 330)
27:20	I x 33 n7 (CWE 32 375)
28:1	I ii 66:7n
30:33	I v 67:16n
31:4	II iii 18 n4 (CWE 33 387)

Ecclesiastes

1:9	IV viii 53 n3
1:18	II x 81 n2 (CWE 34 369), IV vii 51 n3
3:20	IV vii 48 n6
10:19	I iii 87:5n

Song of Solomon

2:4	I iii 91:11n

Isaiah

2:4	II vii 45 n1 (CWE 34 325)
30:22	v i 68 n2
32:6	I i 98:4
42:3	IV i i n151
53:2–3	III iii 1 n16 (CWE 34 406)
64:6	v i 68 n2

Jeremiah

24:3	III iii 88 n5 (CWE 34 423)
31:20	II x 52 n2 (CWE 34 366)
51:7	I viii 81 n3 (CWE 32 345)

Ezekiel

9:4	I v 56:10

Joel

4:10	II vii 45 n1 (CWE 34 325)

Micah

4:3	II vii 45 n1 (CWE 34 325)

1 Esdras

4:14	I vi 10 n4 (CWE 32 286)

Ecclesiasticus

12:10	I iii 35:35n
19:2	II ii 61 n2 (CWE 33 375)
20:32	I vii 84 n2 (CWE 32 326)
22:6	I x 38 n4 (CWE 32 377)
25:23	IV viii 28 n2
27:28–9	I iv 92:8n
27:11	II ii 62 n2 (CWE 33 375)
27:12	I i 93:33n
27:30	I ii 14:58n
33:5	IV viii 27 n2
34:30(25)	IV iii 62 n3

Matthew

3:4	III iii 1 n20 (CWE 34 406)
3:9	v ii 18 n2
4:4	III vi 43 n4
5:3–12	IV i 1 n82
5:3	IV i 1 n125
5:15	I viii 92 n6 (CWE 32 348)
5:17	IV i 1 n78
5:23–4	I i 2:444n
5:39	IV i 1 n83
5:42	IV i 1 n124
5:44	IV i 1 nn78, 121, 124
5:43	I i 2:21n
6:5	IV v 67 n1
6:7	II i 92 n1 (CWE 33 364)
6:10	IV i 1 n87
6:17	IV x 92 n1
6:24	I vii 3n (CWE 32 309), II ii 80 n1 (CWE 33 379)
6:34	III v 62 n2
6:34	IV i 1 n121
7:2	I i 35:15n
7:3–4	I vi 91 n1 (CWE 32 305)
7:3	IV i 1 n150
7:3	IV vii 32 n2
7:6	c 4
7:14	II i 12 n11 (CWE 33 346)
7:26	I iv 57n
9:37	IV i 1 n158

WORKS FREQUENTLY CITED

Allen	Desiderius Erasmus *Opus epistolarum* ed P.S. Allen (H.M. Allen and H.W. Garrod) (Oxford 1906–58) 12 vols
Apostolius	For the collection of proverbs assembled by Michael Apostolius and added to by his son Arsenius see CPG 2 231–744.
ASD	*Opera omnia Desiderii Erasmi Roterodami* (Amsterdam 1969–)
Branca	Ermolao Barbaro *Epistolae, orationes et carmina* ed V. Branca (Florence 1943) 2 vols
Buecheler	*Petronii Saturae et liber Priapeorum: adeictae sunt Varronis et Senecae Saturae similesque reliquiae* ed F. Buecheler (Berlin 1904, 4th ed)
Buechner	See FPL
Bühler 1	*Zenobii Athoi proverbia. Volumen primum. Prolegomena* ed W. Bühler (Göttingen 1987)
Bühler 4	*Zenobii Athoi proverbia. Volumen quartum (libri secundi 1–40 complexum)* ed W. Bühler (Göttingen 1982)
Bühler 5	*Zenobii Athoi proverbia. Volumen quintum (libri secundi 41–108)* ed W. Bühler (Göttingen 1999)
Campanelli	M. Campanelli *Polemiche e filologia ai primordi della stampa. Le 'Observationes' di Domizio Calderini* (Rome 2001)
CCSL	*Corpus Christianorum. Series Latina* (Turnholti 1954–)
CEBR	*Contemporaries of Erasmus. A Biographical Register of the Renaissance and Reformation* ed P.G. Bietenholz and T.B. Deutscher (Toronto 1985–7) 3 vols
Cornucopiae	N. Perotti *Cornucopiae sive linguae latinae commentarii diligentissime recogniti . . .* (Venice 1513). References are to column and line number in this edition. See also the edition of J.-L. Charlet and M. Furno (Sassoferrato 1989–2001), which has cross-references to the 1513 edition.
CPG	*Corpus paroemiographorum Graecorum* ed E.L. Leutsch and F.G. Schneidewin (Göttingen 1839, 1851) 2 vols Reprinted Hildesheim 1965
CRF	*Comicorum Romanorum fragmenta* ed O. Ribbeck (Leipzig 1898, 3rd ed)

CSEL   *Corpus scriptorum ecclesiasticorum Latinorum* (Vienna 1866–)

CWE   *Collected Works of Erasmus* (Toronto 1974–)

Diels-Kranze   *Die Fragmente der Vorsokratiker* edd H. Diels and W. Kranz
                    (Leipzig 1936–42) 3 vols

Diogenianus   For the collection of proverbs ascribed to Diogenianus see
                    CPG 1 177–320.

FGrHist   *Die Fragmente der griechischen Historiker* ed. F. Jacoby (Leiden
                    1957–)

FPL   *Fragmenta poetarum Latinorum epicorum et lyricorum* ed K.
                    Buechner (Leipzig 1982)

Grant   John N. Grant. 'Textual Criticism of Classical Texts in
                    Erasmus' *Adagia*' in *Daimonopylae. Essays in Classics and the
                    Classical Tradition presented to Edmund G. Berry* edd Rory B.
                    Egan, Mark A. Joyal (Winnipeg 2004): 165–81

Green   *The Works of Ausonius* ed R.P.H. Green (Oxford 1991)

Haase   *L. Annaei Senecae opera quae supersunt. Supplementum* ed Fr.
                    Haase (Leipzig 1902)

Heinimann   Felix Heinimann. 'Zu den Anfängen der humanistischen
                    Paroemiologie' in *Catalepton: Festschrift für Bernhard Wyss*
                    (Basel 1985): 158–82

Heinimann (1992)   Felix Heinimann. 'Vergessene Fragmente des Attizisten
                    Pausanias?' *Museum Helveticum* 49 (1992): 74–87, esp 81–2

Holford-Strevens   Leofranc Holford-Strevens *Aulus Gellius* (Chapel Hill, North
                    Carolina 1988)

Husner   F. Husner 'Die Bibliothek des Erasmus' in *Gedenkschrift zum
                    400. Todestage des Erasmus von Rotterdam* (Basel 1936): 228–59

Jordan   *M. Catonis praeter librum de re rustica quae extant* ed H. Jordan
                    (Leipzig 1860)

Körte-Thierfelder   Menander *Reliquiae* ed A. Körte, rev A. Thierfelder (Leipzig
                    1959)

Krenkel   Lucilius *Satiren* ed W Krenkel (Leiden 1970)

Kock   *Comicorum Atticorum fragmenta* ed Th. Kock (Leipzig 1880–8)

Lampas   *Lampas, sive fax artium liberalium …* ed Jan Gruter (1602–23)

7 vols

LB | *Desiderii Erasmi Roterodami opera omnia* ed J. Leclerc (Leiden 1703–6) 10 vols

Maier | A. Politianus *Omnia opera* ed Ida Maier (Turin 1973) 3 vols Facsimile of the Basel edition of 1540

Malcovati | *Oratorum Romanorum fragmenta liberae rei publicae* ed H. Malcovati (Turin 1976–9) 2 vols

Marx | *C. Lucilii carminum reliquiae* ed F. Marx (Leipzig 1904, 1905) 2 vols

Miscellanea | A. Politianus *Miscellaneorum centuria prima* (Florence 1489)

Nauck | *Tragicorum Graecorum fragmenta* ed A. Nauck (Leipzig 1889)

ODEP | *The Oxford Dictionary of English Proverbs* 3rd edition, revised by F.P. Wilson (Oxford 1970)

Otto | A. Otto *Die Sprichwörter und sprichwörtlichen Redensarten der Römer* (Leipzig 1890). Cited by proverb number

Otto *Nachträge* | A. Otto *Die Sprichwörter und sprichwörtlichen Redensarten der Römer. Nachträge* ed R. Haüssler (Darmstadt 1968)

PCG | *Poetae comici Graeci* ed R. Kassel, C. Austin (Berlin and New York 1983–   )

Perry | B.E. Perry *Aesopica* (Urbana 1952)

Phillips | Margaret Mann Phillips *The 'Adages' of Erasmus* (Cambridge 1964)

PL | *Patrologiae cursus completus, series Latina* (Paris 1844–1902)

PMG | *Poetae melici Graeci* ed D.L. Page (Oxford 1962)

Polydore Vergil | *Proverbiorum libellus* Venice 1498. The proverbs are unnumbered. The numbers given in this volume agree with those used in the hypertext edition by Dana Sutton and in ASD II-9.

Pozzi | *Hermolai Barbari 'Castigationes Plinianae et in Pomponium Melam'* ed G. Pozzi (Padua 1973)

Rizzo | S. Rizzo *Il lessico filologico degli umanisti* (Rome 1973)

Roth	*C. Suetonii Tranquilli quae supersunt omnia*, fasc. II ed K.L. Roth (Leipzig 1907)
Suda	*Suidae Lexicon* ed A. Adler (Stuttgart 1971) 5 vols
Suringar	W.H.D. Suringar *Erasmus over Nederlandsche spreekwoorden en spreekwoordlijke uitdrukkingen van zijnen tijd* (Utrecht 1873)
Tilley	M.P. Tilley *A Dictionary of the Proverbs in England in the Sixteenth and Seventeenth Centuries* (Ann Arbor, Michigan 1950)
TLL	*Thesaurus linguae Latinae* (Leipzig 1900–)
Toşi	Renzo Tosi *Dizionario delle sentenze latini e greche* (Milan 1991)
TRF	*Tragicorum Romanorum fragmenta* ed O. Ribbeck (Leipzig 1897, 3rd ed)
TrGF	*Tragicorum Graecorum fragmenta* ed B. Snell, R. Kannicht, and S.L. Radt (Göttingen 1971–85) 4 vols
Vahlen	*Ennianae poesis reliquiae* ed J. Vahlen (Leipzig 1903)
van Gulik	E. van Gulik *The Library of Erasmus* (seen only in manuscript form)
Wesseling	A. Wesseling 'Dutch Proverbs and Ancient Sources in Erasmus's *Praise of Folly' Renaissance Quarterly* 47 (1994) 351–78
West	*Iambi et elegi Graeci ante Alexandrum cantati* ed M.L. West (Oxford 1971–2; 2nd ed 1989, 1992) 2 vols
Zenobius (Aldus)	*Collectio proverbiorum Tarrhaei et Didymi, item eorum quae apud Suidam aliosque habentur* in *Aesopi vita et fabellae cum interpretatione Latina* Venice 1505
Zenobius Athous	See Bühler 4 and Bühler 5

The design of
THE COLLECTED WORKS
OF ERASMUS
was created
by
ALLAN FLEMING
1929–1977
for
the University
of Toronto
Press